Special Edition

USING SGML

Written by Martin Colby and David S. Jackson

with

Steven J. DeRose
Bob DuCharme
David Durand
Elli Mylonas

que®

Special Edition Using SGML

Copyright© 1996 by Que® Corporation.

All rights reserved. Printed in the United States of America. No part of this book may be used or reproduced in any form or by any means, or stored in a database or retrieval system, without prior written permission of the publisher except in the case of brief quotations embodied in critical articles and reviews. Making copies of any part of this book for any purpose other than your own personal use is a violation of United States copyright laws. For information, address Que Corporation, 201 W. 103rd Street, Indianapolis, IN, 46290. You may reach Que's direct sales line by calling 1-800-428-5331.

Library of Congress Catalog No.: 95-72571

ISBN: 0-7897-0414-5

This book is sold *as is*, without warranty of any kind, either express or implied, respecting the contents of this book, including but not limited to implied warranties for the book's quality, performance, merchantability, or fitness for any particular purpose. Neither Que Corporation nor its dealers or distributors shall be liable to the purchaser or any other person or entity with respect to any liability, loss, or damage caused or alleged to have been caused directly or indirectly by this book.

98 97 96   3 2 1

Interpretation of the printing code: the rightmost double-digit number is the year of the book's printing; the rightmost single-digit number, the number of the book's printing. For example, a printing code of 96-1 shows that the first printing of the book occurred in 1996.

All terms mentioned in this book that are known to be trademarks or service marks have been appropriately capitalized. Que cannot attest to the accuracy of this information. Use of a term in this book should not be regarded as affecting the validity of any trademark or service mark.

Screen reproductions in this book were created using Collage Plus from Inner Media, Inc., Hollis, NH.

Macintosh screen reproductions in this book were created using Capture from Mainstay, Camarillo, CA.

Composed in *Stone Serif* and *MCPdigital* by Que Corporation

Credits

President
Roland Elgey

Publisher
Stacy Hiquet

Editorial Services Director
Elizabeth Keaffaber

Managing Editor
Sandy Doell

Director of Marketing
Lynn E. Zingraf

Senior Series Editor
Chris Nelson

Publishing Manager
Jim Minatel

Acquisitions Manager
Cheryl D. Willoughby

Acquisitions Editor
Beverly M. Eppink

Product Director
Benjamin Milstead

Production Editor
Noelle Gasco

Editors
Danielle Bird
Greg Horman
Cara L. Riley

Assistant Product Marketing Manager
Kim Margolius

Technical Editors
David Silverman
Kirsten Robinson
John Bottoms
Brian-Kent Proffitt
Karl Hayes

Acquisitions Coordinator
Ruth Slates

Operations Coordinator
Patricia J. Brooks

Editorial Assistant
Andrea Duvall

Book Designers
Kim Scott
Ruth Harvey

Cover Designer
Dan Armstrong

Production Team
Claudia Bell
Jason Carr
Chad Dressler
Joan Evan
DiMonique Ford
Trey Frank
Damon Jordan
Stephanie Layton
Glenn Larsen
Angel Perez
Julie Quinn
Michael Thomas
Kelly Warner

Indexer
Tim Griffin

Most of all, I owe a sincere thanks to my wife, Kaye, for her tireless support and understanding during the preparation of this book. Any success that it may achieve is largely due to her (the mistakes, omissions, and foibles are all my own).

Martin Colby

To Tish for her endless love, support, and strength. She owns my heart forever.

Dave Jackson

About the Authors

Martin Colby is a computer systems consultant in SGML system development, implementation, and design currently living in San Diego, California. He is particularly enthusiastic about SGML due to its potential as an enabling technology. He expects it to be a key part of the solution to making the knowledge of the Library of Congress available to anyone with a computer and an Internet connection. A perpetual wanderer, he occasionally gets homesick for his hometown of Albuquerque, New Mexico.

David S. Jackson is a freelance writer who lives in San Diego. He writes both fiction and technical manuals, and recently was a contract technical writer and documentation specialist with Solar Turbines where he met Martin Colby. SGML has given him the hope that anyone can become a publisher via the World Wide Web, professional in quality if not in size. He and his wife Tish are expecting their first baby in March of 1996.

Steven J. DeRose earned his Ph.D. in Computational Linguistics from Brown University in 1989. He served as director of the early "FRESS" hypertext system there. He has worked as a technical writer and design consultant for the CDWord hypertext system and a variety of other systems in computational linguistics, hypermedia, and related fields. He has published a variety of papers on markup systems, hypertext, natural language processing, artificial intelligence, and other topics, plus a book with David Durand entitled *Making Hypermedia Work: A User's Guide to HyTime*. He is now Senior System Architect at Electronic Book Technologies, whose DynaText product is the leading SGML-based software for delivering large-scale electronic books on CD-ROM, disk, LAN, and the Internet. He is very active in standards development, serving with groups including the ANSI and ISO SGML and HyTime groups, the Text Encoding Initiative, and several Internet and Web-related groups. He lives, works, and ice-skates in Rhode Island with his wife Laurie and their 2-year-old son Todd.

Bob DuCharme, an SGML developer at the Research Institute of America, is the author of *The Operating Systems Handbook*. He holds a BA in religion from Columbia University and will soon complete a masters degree in computer science at New York University. He lives in Brooklyn with his wife Jennifer and their daughter Madeline.

David Durand is a Senior Analyst with Dynamic Diagrams in Providence, RI. He is co-author, with Steven J. DeRose, of *Making Hypermedia Work: A User's Guide to HyTime*. He worked on the Text Encoding Initiatives Syntax and Metalanguage committee and the Hypertext Committee, defining standards for the use of SGML to encode literary texts of scholarly interest. He is also a Ph.D. candidate in Computer Science at Boston University.

Elli Mylonas is in the Scholarly Technology Group at Brown University where she works with structured text and hypertext. Before this, she was Managing Editor of the Perseus Project at Harvard University, which used SGML for all its texts. She has been working with and publishing on SGML since 1986.

Acknowledgments

I would like to thank my co-author, Dave Jackson, for his enthusiasm and patience as we created this book together.

There are too many other people to thank as well: my friends and co-workers at Solar, Litton, and Syscon who have taught me much with their own unique and helpful perspectives, and the super crew at Que who do so much to include quality in their titles. Lastly, I'd like to thank Ludo for his original, creative, and humorous outlook on the world of SGML. (Ludo, I owe you a Ben & Jerry's the next time you're in town.)

Martin Colby

Thanks to Martin for his patience, goodness, and all that native talent. Last but never least, thanks to all of Que's team, whose skillful hands never left the tiller. Thanks for believing in me.

Dave Jackson

We'd Like To Hear from You!

As part of our continuing effort to produce books of the highest possible quality, Que would like to hear your comments. To stay competitive, we *really* want you, as a computer book reader and user, to let us know what you like or dislike most about this book or other Que products.

You can mail comments, ideas, or suggestions for improving future editions to the address below, or send us a fax at (317) 581-4663. Our staff and authors are available for questions and comments through our Internet site at **http://www.mcp.com/ que**, and Macmillan Computer Publishing also has a forum on CompuServe (type **GO QUEBOOKS** at any prompt).

In addition to exploring our forum, please feel free to contact me personally to discuss your opinions of this book: I'm **bmilstead@que.mcp.com** on the Internet, and **102121,1324** on CompuServe.

Thanks in advance—your comments will help us to continue publishing the best books available on computer topics in today's market.

Benjamin Milstead
Product Director
Que Corporation
201 W. 103rd Street
Indianapolis, Indiana 46290
USA

Contents at a Glance

Introduction 1

SGML Development: Essential Ideas, Terms, and Technology 7

1 Background and Nature of SGML 9

2 SGML View of the World: Structure, Content, and Format 35

3 SGML Terminology 47

4 The Basic Procedure 71

5 Two Scenarios 87

SGML Development

Document Analysis 107

6 Defining the Environment 109

7 Defining the Elements 129

8 Relating Elements to Each Other 143

9 Extending Document Architecture 155

Document Analysis

Content Modeling: Developing the DTD 169

10 Following General SGML Declaration Syntax 171

11 Using DTD Components 189

12 Formatting the DTD for Humans 201

13 Evaluating DTDs and Using Parsers 233

14 Following Good SGML Practice 247

Content Modeling

Markup Strategies 267

15 Automatic versus Manual Tagging 269

16 Markup Challenges and Specialized Content 283

Markup Strategies

SGML and the World Wide Web 293

17 How HTML Relates to SGML 295

18 SGML's Emergence on the World Wide Web 307

19 Should You Upgrade to SGML? 321

20 Practicalities of Working with SGML on the Web 343

21 Integrating SGML and HTML Environments 363

SGML and the WWW

Learning from the Pros 377

22 Developing for the World Wide Web 379

23 Rapid Development and Prototyping 395

24 Understanding and Using Output Specifications 407

25 Handling Specialized Content and Delivery 421

Learning from the Pros

SGML Tools and Their Uses   **431**

26 Tools for the PC: Authoring,
    Viewing, and Utilities   433

27 Tools for the Mac: Authoring,
    Viewing, and Utilities   467

28 Other Tools and Environments 489

**Becoming an Electronic
Publisher**   **497**

29 Understanding the Old
    Paradigm   499

30 Understanding the Information
    Revolution: The New Paradigm   513

31 Object-Orientated Development
    of SGML Applications   527

Appendixes   **555**

A The SGML CD-ROM   557

B Finding Sources for SGML
   Know-How   565

   Index   573

SGML Tools and Their Uses

Electronic Publishing

Appendixes

Contents

Introduction   **1**

SGML: The Mysterious Secret 2
Documents and Their Objects 3
What This Book Is 3
What This Book Is Not 5
Conventions Used in This Book 5
Bombs Away! 6

**I SGML Development: Essential Ideas,
Terms, and Technology   7**

1 Background and Nature of SGML   9

Why Markup Languages Are So Popular 9
SGML and the ISO and CALS Standards for Data 10
   How SGML Relates to ISO 10
   How SGML Relates to CALS 11
   The CALS SGML Standard and the Civilian World 12
How SGML Makes Information Transportable 13
   Hardcopy and Electronic-Specific Markup 14
   Generalized Electronic Markup 15
   Standard Generalized Markup—What SGML Does 17
How SGML Maintains the Integrity of Content and Structure 19
   Individual Document Markup 19
   Document Type Definitions 20
SGML and the Internet 29
   How HTML Is Evolving To Include Larger Numbers of
      SGML Features 29
   The Internet and SGML Browsing and Authoring Tools 29
   SGML Resources on the Internet 30
What the Future May Hold for SGML and Its Applications 32
   Multimedia Extensions and the Internet 32
   From Here… 33

**2 SGML View of the World: Structure, Content,
and Format   35**

Structure, Content, and Format 35
What Is Structure? 36
What Is Content? 37
What Is Format? 37
Why Structure, Content, and Format Are Important in SGML 38
   Indicating Structure Through Visual Cues 38
   Losing Structure in Word Processing Documents 40

An Alternative View 40

Structural Views of Information 40

Defining Structure in SGML 42

Using Structure in SGML 44

From Here… 45

3 SGML Terminology   47

What Are the Components of SGML Documents? 47

Document Declarations 48

Parts of a Tag 51

Elements 53

Attributes 55

Entities 58

Document Content 61

What Are the Components of DTDs? 61

DTDs and Declarations for Elements, Attributes, and
Entities 62

Components of a Declaration in a DTD 62

Connectors and Occurrence Indicators 63

Groups in a Declaration 64

Comparing Declarations in a Document and a DTD 66

Blending Content and Structure in Diagrams 66

From Here… 69

4 The Basic Procedure   71

Document Analysis 72

Defining Your Environment 73

Defining Your Elements 73

Relating Elements to Each Other 76

Extending Document Architecture 76

Developing the DTD (Content Modeling) 77

Making Your DTD Declarations 78

Designing Components for DTDs 79

Evaluating DTDs 81

Formatting the DTD for People (Not Machines) 81

Following Good SGML Practice 81

Defining Output Specifications 81

Incorporating Document Markup 82

Document Parsing 83

Working with Consultants 83

Before the Consultants Come 84

After the Consultants Arrive 85

Combining Your Expertise with Their Expertise 85

From Here… 86

5 Two Scenarios   87

Some Recent History 87

Creating an SGML Environment from Scratch 88

The President's Message 88
What You're Going To Do 89
Defining the Goals 89
Document Analysis 91
Document Modeling 92
Parsing Document Type Definitions (DTDs) 95
Document Maintenance Considerations 95
Converting Existing Documents into SGML (Filtering) 96
Document Analysis 97
Document Modeling and DTD Design 98
Document Conversion 99
Parsing DTDs and Documents 102
Tricks, Traps, and Pitfalls 103
From Here… 105

II Document Analysis   107

6 Defining the Environment   109

Preparation for Defining the Environment 110
Decide How You Are Going To Use Your Documents 110
Decide What Standards and Policies You Must Obey 112
Format Standards 112
Structure Standards 113
Content Standards 115
Types of Policies 116
Identify All Your Document Users and Their Tools 117
External Customers 118
Internal Customers 119
Customer Tools 120
Gather and Inspect All Your Document Types 122
Choose Names for All Your Different Types of Documents 123
Anticipating Document Evolution 123
Mistakes and Redefining Your Environment 125
Assessing Damage Impact 126
Fixing Big Mistakes 126
How to Know When You're Done Defining Your Environment 126
From Here… 127

7 Defining the Elements   129

How Big Should Your Elements Be? 129
Element Content Models 131
Hierarchy and Sequence 132
Occurrence 132
Structure Diagrams 132
Types of Data Content 135
Types of Data for Attributes 136

The Definition Process 137
  Step 1: Pick a Document Type 138
  Step 2: List the Elements 138
  Step 3: Name Each Element and Assign Relationships 138
  Step 4: Keep Listing Elements Until None Are Left 138
  Step 5: Compare the Elements for Relationships
    and Groups 139
  Step 6: Check for Missing Elements 140
  Step 7: Construct a Structure Tree 140
  Step 8: Assemble an Element Dictionary 141
  Step 9: Have Others Check Your Work 142
  Step 10: Revise and Test Your Work as Needed 142
From Here... 142

8 Relating Elements to Each Other   143

Sequencing Elements 144
Element Occurrence 145
Element Hierarchy 146
Element Inclusion and Exclusion 149
Element Groups 150
Structure Diagram Revisited 150
From Here... 153

9 Extending Document Architecture   155

Adding Features to Documents 155
Adding Revision Tracking Information to Documents 158
  Preliminary Steps 158
  Element or Attribute? 159
Adding Hypertext Links to a Document 160
  Local and Remote Links 160
Adding Multimedia Content 161
  Adding a Graphic 162
  Adding a Sound or Video File 163
HyTime 164
  Goals of HyTime 164
  Addressing 164
  Architectural Templates (Forms) 165
  HyTime Requirements 166
Upgrading Your HTML Site to an SGML Site 166
From Here... 167

III Content Modeling: Developing the DTD   169

10 Following General SGML Declaration Syntax   171

Publicly Available DTDs May Be Appropriate 171
  Why Get Involved with DTD Syntax? 172

SGML Declaration Syntax (or, "What Are All Those Angle
    Brackets Anyway?") 172
Regular Expression Syntax 174
Specific Declarations 176
    The SGML Declaration 176
    The DOCTYPE Declaration 177
    The COMMENT Declaration 178
    Elements and the ELEMENT Declaration 179
    Attributes: Their Use and the ATTRIBUTE Declaration 182
    Entities: Their Use and the ENTITY Markup Declaration 184
Tags and Tag Minimization with Omittag 186
Some Practical Examples 187
From Here... 188

11 Using DTD Components   189

When (and Why) To Use DTD Components 190
    Multiple DTDs 190
    Many Developers 191
    A Growing DTD Environment 191
    Change Is Coming 192
    Long Lifetime 193
    Making DTDs Simpler 193
    Making New DTDs Easier To Develop and Maintain 193
    Standardizing Basic Components 194
    Simplifying DTD Maintenance 195
    Making Your DTDs More Consistent 196
How To Make Components 197
    Fragment Assembly 198
    DTD Redefinition 198
    Defining Parameter Entities as Elements 199
From Here... 200

12 Formatting the DTD for Humans   201

Why Formatting DTDs Is Important 201
    Old Documents and New People 201
    The Friendly DTD 205
    The Common DTD 210
Making Comments in DTDs 214
    Full Comment Declarations 215
    Inline Comments 216
Separating the DTD into Logical Groups of Elements 217
Declaring Elements After Their First Content Model 223
Where To Define Attributes 224
Aligning Declarations 224
From Here... 231

13 Evaluating DTDs and Using Parsers   233

Evaluating Your DTD 233
    Document Scope 234
    Document Lifespan 236
    Sanity Checking Your DTD 236
    Standards Enforcement versus Flexibility 238
Maintaining Your DTD 239
Parsing the DTD 241
Parsers...242
    What Validating Parsers Do 242
    What Parsers Don't Do 243
    What To Look for in a Parser 244
    Evaluating Parser Output Messages 244
From Here... 245

14 Following Good SGML Practice   247

Choosing Elements or Attributes 247
    Types of Attributes 248
    Common Mistakes with Attributes 252
Handling Inclusions and Exclusions 255
    Exception Reminders 255
    Common Mistakes 256
Dealing with Mixed-Content Models 258
Dealing with Ambiguous Content Models 259
How Flexible Should DTDs Be? 261
Miscellaneous Reminders 262
    Processing Instructions 262
    User Involvement... 263
    Frequent Validation and Model Testing 263
    Consistent Documentation 264
From Here... 264

IV Markup Strategies   267

15 Automatic versus Manual Tagging   269

Deciding which Markup Method Is for You 269
    Big Installation versus One-Person Hobbyist............................ 270
    Complex versus Simple Hardware and Software 270
    Simple Documents or Complex Document Collection 270
    Short or Long Timeline 271
    Manual Markup 271
    Document Conversion 273
    Structured Authoring 274
Document Conversion and Its Tools 276
    Word Processing Conversion Tools 276
    Conversion Tools for Intermediate File Types 277
    Conversion Between SGML Document Types 279

Structured Authoring and Its Tools 280

From Here… 281

16 Markup Challenges and Specialized Content   283

Using Standard Data in Documents 283

    Using Entity References for Boilerplate 284

Building Conditional Documents 285

    Declaring Marked Sections 286

    Include and Ignore Processing 287

    Using Entities with Marked Sections 287

Including Specialized Content 288

    The NOTATION Declaration 289

Tagging Shorthand 289

    Shortref Usage 290

From Here… 291

V SGML and the World Wide Web   293

17 How HTML Relates to SGML   295

How SGML and HTML Are Related 295

    Why SGML? 295

What SGML Includes That HTML Does Not 297

    What HTML 3.0 Adds 298

    More for SGML To Add to HTML 300

What SGML Can Add to Web Sites 301

    The Case for the Web to Upgrade to SGML 301

    What Is Needed 302

What SGML Flexibility Can Do for Web Sites 303

SGML and HTML Obsolescence 305

From Here… 306

18 SGML's Emergence on the World Wide Web   307

Why the Secret about SGML? 307

    Scholarly and Expert Clientele 308

    The Dearth of Easy-to-Use Books on SGML 309

    Expensive SGML Software 309

    HTML's Many Sister Applications 310

SGML on the Web 311

    SGML Resources That Translate to HTML 311

    Native HTML Documents as SGML Resources 314

    SGML Resources as Non-HTML Document Instances 316

SGML Resources Available on the Web 316

SGML Resources Available on the Web in the Future 318

    Scientific and Technical Data 319

    Stylesheets 319

    Multimedia and Hyper-G 319

From Here… 320

19 Should You Upgrade to SGML?   321

How HTML and SGML Relate 321
What Data Is Already in SGML? 324
From Commercial Publishers 324
From Computer Vendors 325
From Libraries and Universities 326
From Industry 327
From Government and the International Community 328
Why Is This Data in SGML, Not HTML? 328
Five Questions To Ask about My Data 329
What Functionality Do I Need? 329
Do I Need Flexible Data Interchange? 329
How Complex Are my References and Links? 330
What Kind of Maintenance Is Needed? 333
Can I Make Do with HTML? 335
How to Use HTML Safely 336
Challenges of Upgrading 337
Fewer Browsers To Choose from 337
A DTD To Choose or Design 338
More Syntax To Learn 338
Benefits of Upgrading 339
Platform Independence 339
Browser Independence 339
HTML Revision Independence 340
Appropriate Tag Usage 340
Large Document Management 340
Internationalization 341
Better Support for Large Documents.. 342
From Here… 342

20 Practicalities of Working with SGML on the Web   343

Tactics for Using SGML on the Web 343
Tools 345
SGML-aware Viewers (for CD, LAN, and Mostly WAN) 346
Integrated SGML Converters.. 349
Generic Conversion Tools.. 351
Retrieval Engines 353
The Big Document Problem 354
SGML Requires More Thinking Up Front 356
DTD Choice, Design, and Modification 356
Need To Think More Hierarchically 357
SGML Assures More Consistency and Flexibility 357
SGML Helps Make Allowances for HTML 357
Overusing Optional SGML Features Is Dangerous 358
From Here… 361

21 Integrating SGML and HTML Environments   363

Can It Be Done? 363
Novell 364

Text Encoding Initiative (TEI) 364
The Oxford University Text Archive (OTA) 365
University of Virginia 365
Center for Electronic Texts in the Humanities (CETH) 366
Summer Institute of Linguistics (SIL) 366
University of California at Berkeley 366
SGML Open 367
The Online Computer Library Center (OCLC) 367
Compromises To Be Made 368
Conversion Can Be Expensive 368
Non-conversion Can Cost More Later 369
Poor DTD Design Is Very Costly 371
Tools Required and How To Combine Them 371
Getting into SGML 372
Getting Back Out to HTML 373
Getting Back Out to Print 374
Document Management 375
From Here... 376

VI Learning from the Pros

377

22 Developing for the World Wide Web

379

SGML's Future on the Web 379
Batch versus On-Demand Models 381
MIME Issues 383
High-End Search/Retrieval 383
Link Persistence 384
HyTime: SGML and Hypermedia 385
Ultra-Basics of HyTime Links 385
How to Make HyTime Links 386
How To Make Effective SGML Web Pages 389
Support for More Kinds of Documents 390
Support for Big Documents 391
Focus on Your Data 391
Link to Important Related Data 392
Avoid "Only Works in Client X" 392
From Here... 393

23 Rapid Development and Prototyping

395

Scoping/Bounding the Process 396
Defining Your Scope 396
Defining the Document Set 397
Defining Your Goals 397
Defining Your Timeframe 397
Defining Your Environment 398
Assemble Your Team 398
Team Members 399

Team Member Personalities 400
The Dynamics of Participation 401
Data Gathering 402
Document Analysis 403
System Design 405
From Here… 406

24 Understanding and Using Output Specifications   407

The View of a Document from an Output Perspective 408
Formatting Elements Through Their Structural Occurrence 408
Issues Involved with Output Specifications 413
SGML Syntax 413
Group Styles 413
Entity and Attribute Usage 414
Style Inheritance 416
Issues in Specialized Output 417
Handling Hardcopy/Printed Output 417
Handling Electronic Output 418
Handling Dynamic Documents 418
Difficulties with Output Specifications 419
Output Specification Standards 419
FOSI 419
DSSSL 419
From Here… 420

25 Handling Specialized Content and Delivery   421

Handling Tables 421
The Format versus Content Challenge 422
Hybrid Content-Format Table Structure 423
Handling Math and Equations 424
Equations as Graphics 425
External Processing of Equations 425
Equation Structures in the DTD 426
Linking Revisited 427
Footnotes and Endnotes 427
Citations and Bibliographies 428
Multimedia Linking 429
From Here… 429

VII SGML Tools and Their Uses   431

26 Tools for the PC: Authoring, Viewing, and Utilities   433

A New Era in SGML Tools 433
SGML Authoring Tools 434
WordPerfect SGML Edition 434
Near & Far Author 440

SGML Author for Word 445
Other SGML Tools 453
    Panorama Pro 453
    Near & Far 461
From Here… 465

27 Tools for the Mac: Authoring, Viewing, and Utilities   467

Planning an SGML Project on the Mac 467
Authoring and Conversion Tools for the Mac 468
    SoftQuad Author/Editor 3.1 469
    SoftQuad RulesBuilder 3.0 474
    SoftQuad Sculptor 1.0 474
    Stilo 475
    Qued/M, Alpha, and BBEdit 476
    SGMLS 478
Scripting Languages 481
Viewing and Printing Tools 482
    SGML Enabler 483
    FrameMaker+SGML 483
    DynaText 483
Document Conversions 484
    Converting from Plain Text 485
    Converting from an RTF File 485
    Converting from SGML to Another DTD or Data Format 487
From Here… 487

28 Other Tools and Environments   489

Specific Computer Platform Usage 490
SP/NSGMLS Parser 490
The World of Perl 491
    SGML Utilities Using Perl 492
Electronic Book Technologies: DynaText 493
Avalanche/Interleaf: FastTAG 495
From Here… 496

VIII   Becoming an Electronic Publisher   497

29 Understanding the Old Paradigm   499

The Components of Information Delivery 499
The Ways of Organizing Knowledge 500
    Linear Books 501
    Modular Books 502
Implications of the Linear Way of Organizing Information 503
The Role of Format 505
The Role of Structure 508
    The Whole Book or No Book Problem 509
    The Stationary Information Problem 509

The Once and for All Information Problem 510
The Specialist Needed Problem 511
Structure Revisited 511
From Here... 511

30 Understanding the Information Revolution: The New Paradigm   513

How Modular Information Drives the Information Revolution 513
The Reader Is a Collaborator 514
Modular Document Sharing Is Only the Beginning 515
Modular Information and Collaboration 519
Current Collaborative Projects on the Web 519
TEI 520
AAP/EPSIG 521
The Davenport Group 522
SGML Open 522
EWS 523
Collaboration on SGML Standards 523
HyTime 524
SMDL 525
ICADD 525
UTF 525
Fred at OCLC 525
How SGML's Modular Organization Promotes Worldwide
Learning 525
From Here... 526

31 Object-Oriented Development of SGML Applications   527

Object-Oriented Technology: The Basics (and the Confusion) 528
Object-Oriented Development and SGML: Why? 531
Common Vocabulary 532
Class 532
Instance 533
Attribute 533
State 534
Behavior 534
What Can Object-Oriented Development Techniques Do
for DTD Development? 535
What Can a DTD Do for Object-Oriented Development? 537
Booch's Object-Oriented Methodology 538
Rumbaugh's Object-Oriented Methodology 539
Defining Object Relationships in an SGML System 540
Using the DTD To Automate Object-Oriented Development 542
A Sample Smalltalk SGML System 546
Object-Oriented Technology and the Future of SGML
Development 550
Concurrency 550
SGML and Object-Oriented Databases 551

SGML Entity Management 551
The Future of SGML Application Developers 552
From Here... 552

IX Appendixes 555

A The SGML CD-ROM 557

Using the SGML CD 557
Computer Platforms 558
What's Included on the CD-ROM 558
SP/NSGMLS Tools 559
  Software Contents 559
  Installation 559
Perl 559
  Software Contents 560
  Installation 560
perlSGML 560
  Software Contents 561
  Installation 561
Near & Far Lite 561
  Software Contents 562
  Installation 562
  Other Files 562
DynaText 562
  Software Contents 563
  Installation 563
  Other Files 563
Panorama Free 563
  Software Contents 564
  Installation 564

B Finding Sources for SGML Know-How 565

Books on SGML 565
SGML Periodicals 566
SGML User Groups 567
Internet Resources 569
  Internet Mailing Lists 569
  Internet Newsgroups (UseNet) 570
  FTP Archive Sites for SGML 570
  SGML Web Pages 570
Summary 571

Index 573

Introduction

Within the last ten-year period, global superpowers have dissolved, wars have started, ended, and started again, entire national economies have almost disappeared, balances of power have shifted, and earthquakes, famines, and floods have changed the face of the planet. During the same period of time, SGML has been the international standard for document interchange. While the physical and political tumult above cannot rightly be ascribed to SGML, some of the information revolution can be.

SGML, hypertext, and object-oriented technology have all been in the eye of the information hurricane in the last ten years. While you still see the occasional doctor's office whose receptionist still uses a DOS program that doesn't support a mouse, most machines today use the "point and click" type of interface that makes computers friendly and desirable enough to pay $2000 or more for. They play music and movies from CD-ROMs and they even show TV programs and play the radio. But computers are learning to communicate better not only with people, but with themselves.

SGML is now in the eye of the storm because, recently, computers have begun talking together on a wide scale. The explosion of the Internet is the first massive venture into electronic document sharing by people all over the planet. SGML is what enables all these diverse people, with their changing languages, merging cultures, and exploding information revolutions, to communicate via computers that actually understand one another despite all the upheaval. When combined with hypertext and the familiar point and click computer interfaces, SGML allows document sharing on the scale of the World Wide Web, electronic tax return filing for a nation, and perhaps even document sharing between NASA space shuttles and ground control.

Ironically, up until now SGML had remained largely unknown to the public. The public had seen the talking computers and the virtual reality games that take you head-to-head against mortal enemies in a blood-curdling fight for survival, but most people still thought SGML was some sort of medical disease like HIV, or perhaps a rock band. Now that HTML has introduced the idea of document interchange to the world and shown that it's possible and pleasurable, SGML has finally attracted some attention. Finally, the secret life of SGML is being made public.

SGML: The Mysterious Secret

Over the years, SGML has acquired the aura of hidden magic and forbidden mystery; only the "initiated" could participate in its rites. While it's hard to say how this thought got started, it's easy to clear the fog. SGML is not a mystery. It's a *meta-language*. Nothing more.

Note

"Meta" means "later in time" or "having a higher stage of development." In one sense, it means "behind" in the sense of "the force behind the scenes." So a meta-language is a language used to create other languages.

SGML is a meta-language because you use it to create and develop other languages—in this case, other markup languages.

A *markup language* is a tagging system that lets you maintain a document's structure so it can be dismantled and moved electronically, and then reassembled in a new location. Because many documents require far more than letters and numbers to express their content, this is a large task. But that's a job for markup languages.

SGML is a "super" markup language. It's the mother of all markup languages. It's the parent of markup languages like the one the IRS uses and even NASA. It's also the parent of HTML.

Perhaps SGML's popularity among the Department of Defense and among academia has loaned a stiffness and formality to the early writings about the subject. Perhaps there have just been few resources for anyone without a Ph.D and a tolerance for turgid prose to learn SGML. And perhaps, too, the possibilities for using SGML in the real world have been a little remote to imagine until enough people actually went out and *did* something useful with it.

SGML was adopted by the International Standards Organization in 1986 (ISO 8879), and there have been lots of successful projects with it since then. Many of them affect how you live your life today. Ever hear of the World Wide Web? HTML is a chip off the ol' block of SGML. But there are plenty of other real-world successes, too—the Text Encoding Initiative, the Davenport Group, the Oxford Text Initiative, SGML Open, the list goes on and on. But unless you've been reading those scholastic publications, you've probably never heard about these accomplishments.

The fact is that SGML is and has been a silent force *behind* the scenes. It may not be clear *how* electricity works, but that doesn't stop you from reaching for the light switch. SGML has been just as vital to publishing as electricity has been to the lay person. Many thousands of public documents are routinely stored in SGML for instant access or retrieval. Many CD-ROM publishers depend on SGML to organize their content and make it useable. Most of the text you read in newspapers resides electronically in SGML before, and long after, you read it in hard copies. Many of the resources your banker, accountant, or specialist of whatever kind uses to advise you in your daily affairs probably exist, at least partially, in SGML. Just as computers were suddenly "all around us" ten years ago, so SGML is too. Only you don't *see* it, you just see the benefit, sort of like electricity.

Documents and Their Objects

Much of what makes this convenience possible is *structure*, something you might not have thought much about. But as you learn about SGML, rest assured that will change. As you study document analysis, you'll soon never be able to look at a document the same way again. Unconsciously, you'll be asking yourself, "How would I define this phone book as a document type?" and, "What would you call an element for tagging footnotes?" Small features in text that you overlooked before, like superscripts or circumflexes, will suddenly fascinate you. This is because you're finally seeing what SGML people have seen for a long time: structural objects of a document.

There will be a lot of realizations that come with experience, like how much structure is enough in a document, and other realizations that come more quickly, like simpler is probably better for now. Through it all, you'll be dealing with structural components of documents—objects—and distinguishing them from the content of a document. The realization I would like to leave with you in this introduction is that *structure*, *content*, and *format* are actually separate tasks that you'll need to discriminate between.

When you prepare documents to move around the planet with the click of a mouse, you need to be clear about the difference between "the nut and the shell" so to speak. Document content is like the nut and format is like the shell, but without structure you couldn't recognize it as a document at all...or a nut! What lets you recognize a walnut from a cashew is actually the structure of the content within the shell. So it is with an SGML document. The content is what you read, the structure is how it lets itself be recognized, and the format is how it looks while you're reading it. When you pay attention to the structure, the document can get to the other side of the planet *and* be recognizable with the click of a mouse.

What This Book Is

This book is intended to be a comprehensive reference for developing practical and effective SGML applications. Following its instructions, you should be able to build an application as robust and useful as HTML. While this book does not intend to promote Windows-based machines over other machines, you'll see many screen shots of Windows, relatively few Macintosh displays, and no UNIX displays. That's simply a reflection of the marketplace and the prevalence of Windows-based PCs. But that's probably also good for you because, statistically speaking, the odds are good that your machine is a Windows machine, too.

Who should use this book? Anyone with an interest in SGML. The formatting conventions are useful for a veteran SGML user to find handy reference information, and the SGML newbie will appreciate the thorough explanations and familiar tone. There are clear graphics and useful discussions conveniently organized for users of SGML at every level.

The chances are high that you are studying SGML because of your success with HTML. If so, you'll find this book to your liking because it talks about the migration of SGML to the online world. But if you're not coming from the HTML world, that's fine, too, because there are ample discussions from the business and publishing perspectives. SGML was never intended for a single type of enterprise or system. On the contrary, the intention with SGML has always been: have document, will travel.

Here's a brief overview of the book's content with a short description of each part:

- Part I, "SGML Development: Essential Ideas, Terms, and Technology," covers the important background ideas and terminology for studying the development of markup applications.

- Part II, "Document Analysis," introduces the reader to the process of building an SGML application by helping him or her understand document types and their architecture—how they're dismantled and assembled.

- Part III, "Content Modeling: Developing the DTD," takes the SGML student through the process of declarations, design, and validation for the Document Type Declaration (DTD).

- Part IV, "Markup Strategies," covers special concerns with marking up documents, like output specifications, and transforming documents from one SGML document type to another.

- Part V, "SGML and the World Wide Web," helps HTML users appreciate their SGML heritage and consider the larger possibilities it can offer to their Web sites.

- Part VI, "Learning from the Pros," provides special insight into challenging areas of SGML development that you're likely to encounter at some point.

- Part VII, "SGML Tools and Their Uses," addresses the expanding subject of authoring, development, and production tools for SGML; tools for the Mac, the PC, and UNIX are surveyed.

- Part VIII, "Becoming an Electronic Publisher," undertakes the task of analyzing the past of electronic publishing and tracing its destination somewhere in the future.

- Part IX, "Appendixes," Appendix A, "The SGML CD-ROM," covers the contents of the CD-ROM that comes with this book; you'll find lots of handy tools to help you become productive right away.

  Appendix B, "Finding Sources for SGML Know-How," helps you locate further help beyond the scope of this book for your ongoing SGML involvement.

What This Book Is Not

This book does not provide more than the essentials for using SGML in practical day-to-day applications. The intention behind this book is to give someone who needs to develop an SGML application the means to complete that task.

    ▶▶   See "Internet Resources," p. 569

You won't find in-depth discussions of HyTime or multilingual transformations because most people who would buy this book probably wouldn't be interested in that level of depth. This book is intended to be an "everyman's" guide, not a professor's handbook.

Conventions Used in This Book

Certain conventions are used in *Special Edition Using SGML* to help you absorb the ideas easily.

> **Tip**
>
> Tips suggest easier or alternate methods of executing a procedure or approaching a task.

Text that is part of SGML markup in a document's content will look like this: `<TAG>content</TAG>`. This type of text will appear both in the body of the text (like you see here) and in the figures and samples of markup you see throughout the book. These tags, as well as entities and attributes, appear in both upper- and lowercase, since SGML is not case-sensitive.

New terms are introduced in *italic* type and text you type appears in **boldface**. World Wide Web URLS (essentially document addresses) are also presented in **boldface**.

> **Note**
>
> This paragraph format indicates additional information that might help you avoid problems, or that might be considered when using the described features.

> **Caution**
>
> This paragraph format warns you of hazardous procedures.

▶▶ See "Section Title," p. xx

◀◀ See "Section Title," p. xx

Special Edition Using SGML uses cross references so you can quickly find related information in the book. These are listed by section or chapter title and page number for convenience. Right-facing triangles point you to related information in later parts of the book. Left-facing triangles point you to information in previous chapters.

Throughout the book, you'll also see the On the CD icon (shown beside this paragraph) in the margins. Where you see this icon, the text is discussing software or a document that's included on the CD accompanying this book.

Bombs Away!

This book is designed to lead you from an SGML beginner's level to an intermediate level. All you need to have is curiosity about the subject and an open mind. This book will take care of the rest.

As the subject matter progresses, you will most likely be impressed with the enormous possibilities SGML gives to prospective publishers and authors. So as you find yourself daydreaming about what you can do with these powerful techniques and tools, don't be alarmed. I can tell you from experience, no matter how excited you are today, you'll probably be even more excited about it tomorrow!

Part I

SGML Development: Essential Ideas, Terms, and Technology

1 Background and Nature of SGML

2 SGML View of the World: Structure, Content, and Format

3 SGML Terminology

4 The Basic Procedure

5 Two Scenarios

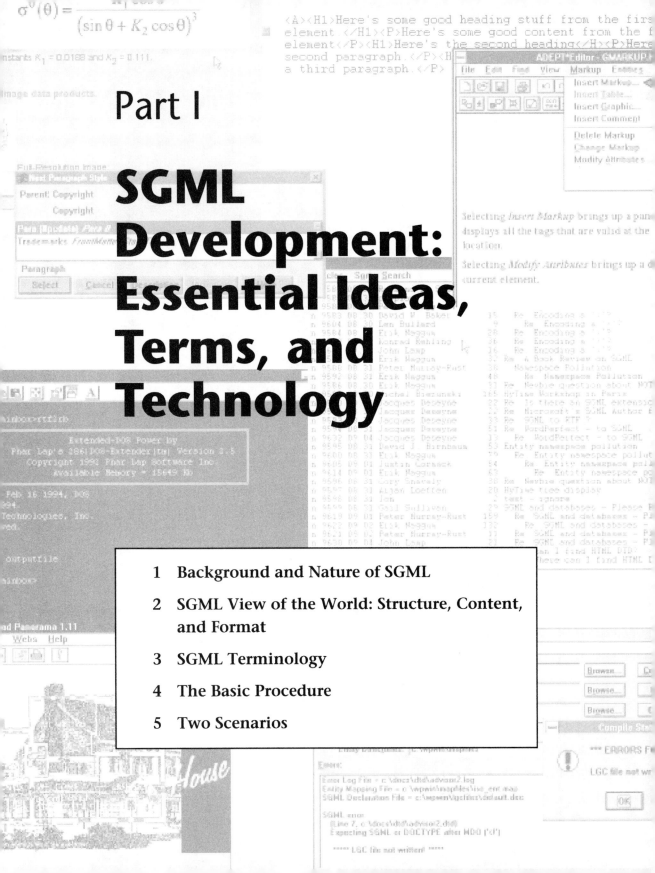

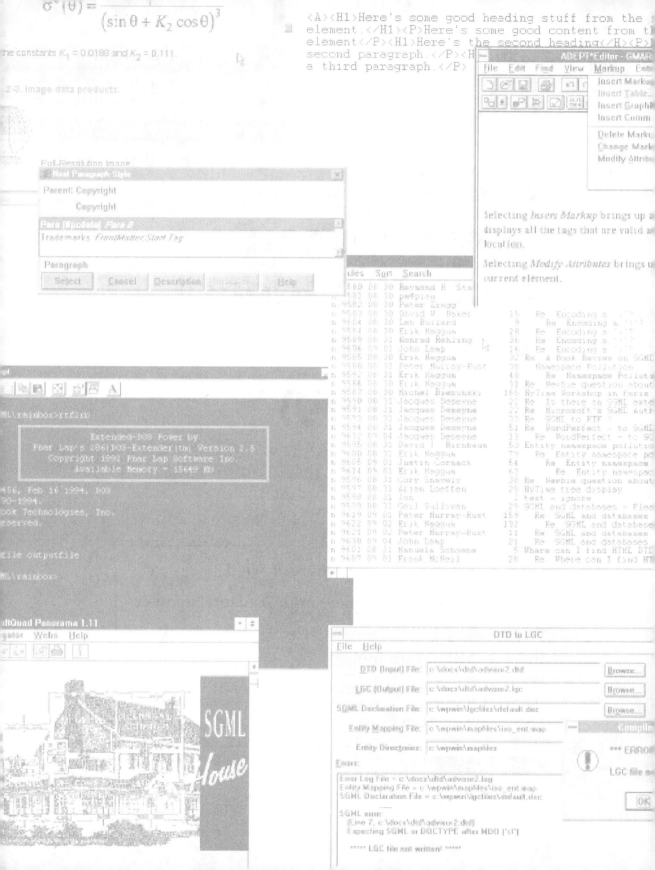

CHAPTER 1

Background and Nature of SGML

SGML and markup languages can make your life easier. In this chapter, you learn:

- Why markup languages are so popular
- What SGML has to do with ISO and CALS
- How SGML makes information transportable
- How SGML protects your formatting and structure
- How SGML is already gaining popularity on the Internet
- What the future holds for SGML

Why Markup Languages Are So Popular

Markup languages, such as SGML and HTML, have changed the nature of information. Thanks to them, you can transport information across the planet and through all kinds of computer platforms and hosts. Your documents always retain their original structure and format.

Presenting information no longer requires a specific machine. It does not matter whether you are writing on a UNIX box, a Macintosh, an IBM mainframe, or a PC. Markup languages—SGML in particular—make your treatise infinitely transportable without changing its original appearance. You can write a zoological treatise, a movie review complete with video and sound clips, or a multimedia presentation, and transport it without losing its structure, content, or format.

SGML also makes your documents modular, interchangeable, and flexible. Hypertext takes advantage of this sort of flexible presentation of information. For example, if you click highlighted text in a help file on your PC, your computer display automatically jumps to information related to that text. For that event to happen, someone had to *mark up* or encode the related information. SGML provides the greatest flexibility possible for this sort of information interchangeability.

When you make documents into SGML documents, you insert tags around document structures, like titles and paragraphs, that an SGML processing system can recognize and reconstruct on demand. The tags provide a blueprint for an SGML processing system to build your document according to your original design, regardless of platform or processing environment.

Tags make your documents look somewhat unrecognizable when not seen through an SGML viewing tool, but tools for dealing with SGML documents are increasingly available.

On the CD

> **Note**
>
> Tools for making and viewing SGML documents are on the SGML CD-ROM included with this book. See Appendix A for information on installing the software.

Because these tools are increasingly available, SGML has become even more popular. Some tools are in the public domain. The CD-ROM included with this book has parsers and editors, and even a copy of Electronic Book Technology's DynaText viewing tool, which includes the 1994 CIA Factbook encoded with SGML tags so you can see firsthand how effective SGML is.

SGML and the ISO and CALS Standards for Data

Individuals are not the only ones who like SGML. In fact, for many years, businesses and government have found that SGML serves their needs for transporting information. The International Standards Organization (ISO), an organization based in Geneva that develops international standards, is responsible for specifying the international SGML standard that businesses have been using for years. The Continuous Acquisition and Lifecycle Support (CALS) standards of the U.S. Department of Defense have also specified that SGML be used.

How SGML Relates to ISO

The document you hear about repeatedly is ISO 8879, which is the SGML standard. It defines the rules that SGML must follow; it is the document that makes SGML a standard. ISO 8879 ensures that everyone follows the same rules when developing a scheme for document markup.

Figure 1.1 illustrates how various types of data and machines can transport documents easily because of these standards. Without these standards, confusion would rule. Companies who don't follow a universal standard have difficulty sharing information because of technicalities like file format conflicts, document incompatibility, document handling inconsistencies, and non-standardized practices. There are so many competing electronic technologies, for example, that if there were no international standard, companies would be forced to choose compatible hardware and software as dictated by their customers. Their inconsistent practices would result in a data flow resembling the messy left side of figure 1.1. With an international standard, companies can choose their hardware and software based on their needs and simply run SGML compliant software to ensure standardized document interchange.

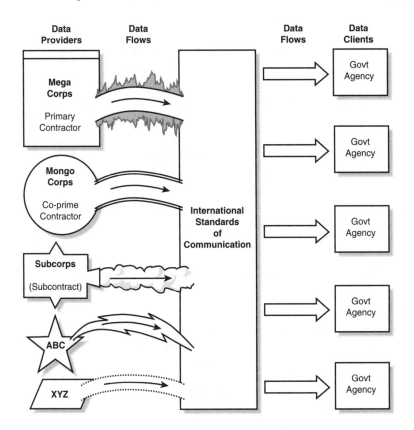

Fig. 1.1

Without international standards, companies cannot understand, let alone interpret, one another's data.

In large-scale sharing of documents, even small inconsistencies can translate into enormous headaches. SGML unifies the different ways of handling data among defense contractors. It helps individuals share documents worldwide, too.

How SGML Relates to CALS

Standards must be very specific. Government contractors must define each type of data that they share. A disinterested third party, however, has to ensure that everyone uses the same definitions. The Defense Department started the CALS initiative to unify data and document exchange among defense contractors. Four standards are part of CALS, one of which is SGML. Table 1.1 summarizes the standards.

Table 1.1 CALS Standards for Documents		
Type of Content	**Standard**	**Description**
Technical documentation	SGML	Text and graphics
3-D CAD drawings	IGES	Layered 3-D models
Bitmapped drawings	CCITT Group 4	BMP files
2-D geometric models	CGM	Computer graphics metafiles

These standards make data flows more uniform and usable by multiple clients and authors. They replace paper flows with electronic documentation and provide for convenient access to information. It costs far less than a hard copy system without standards, and access is instantaneous.

Access can also be remote. When information is paper-based, you and the paper must be in the same location. When information is electronic, however, you can retrieve it from any remote location that has the necessary electronic tools—computers and telecommunications equipment.

> **Note**
>
> The founders of SGML started developing markup languages in the late 1960s and early 1970s. At that time, it was becoming evident that computers and electronic information databases were here to stay.

The goal is to share information databases conveniently and at a reasonable cost. CALS simplifies the document update and distribution process. It extends the life cycle of documents, and lowers the cost of using each document. It provides for inter-changeability of documents and their segments, which lowers the cost of producing future technical manuals. Moreover, CALS promotes collaboration while allowing for competition by not compromising security.

The CALS SGML Standard and the Civilian World

Different agencies of the government have individual information needs, but they can benefit from sharing one another's documents. Individuals are also like that. They benefit from sharing information and suffer when they don't follow the same standards.

For instance, a medical student researching cancer in India could benefit greatly from the latest paper on the subject published by a scholar at Johns Hopkins University. Likewise, a physician at Johns Hopkins might find few case studies of a rare disease in the United States, but a doctor in India might have first-hand experience in assessing the viability of a recommended treatment.

If research is contained in SGML documents on the Internet, for example, relevant information can be tagged, linked, and accessed through hypermedia tools. The HTML standard is beginning to include ever larger sets of SGML features.

> **Note**
>
> The World Wide Web is an SGML application. *Application* in SGML means a particular document type definition (DTD). Each HTML document on the Web is an instance of that document type. Using the rules of SGML, you can create an unlimited number of document types with features like the ones in HTML.
>
> Version 2.0 of HTML is a revision of the HTML DTD. The proposed version 3.0 of HTML is yet another revision. Each revision so far has added more features of the SGML feature set. You can define as many document types as you want in SGML.

Because civilians don't have to worry about defense, they can distribute documents even more liberally than the CALS standard originally had in mind. In this way, they benefit greatly from SGML's ability to make documents easily transportable to someone around the block or around the globe.

How SGML Makes Information Transportable

The challenge of dealing with different types of documents from many types of machines and software is not new. Many types of hardware exist—PCs, Sparc stations, Macintosh and other machines with Motorola processors, dedicated mini and mainframe computers, and niche computers with their own operating systems like Atari and Commodore. Different operating systems run on these systems. When you add differences among software to differences among hardware and operating systems, there are thousands of possible output types.

Originally, markup was what production editors did to manuscripts so that typesetters could apply the correct formatting, according to style conventions. It evolved through several electronic stages, from specific electronic markup that includes low-level formatting to generic markup that is flexible and not specific to any one environment.

Broadly speaking, there are three types of markup. They are described in table 1.2.

Table 1.2 The Three Types of Markup	
Markup Type	**Features**
Hardcopy markup	One-time markup, only for format. Markup is only on paper.
Electronic-specific markup	Contains formatting commands that are specific to a machine or software. Markup is not transportable to other machines. It is good for multiple use as long as the environment does not change.
Generic electronic markup	Contains structural markup that can be used repeatedly on many different types of hardware and software.

Hardcopy and Electronic-Specific Markup

Hardcopy and electronic-specific markup work fine when you don't need to share documents. Each system works because it does what is required:

- It conveys formatting information, such as italics, bold, or uppercase.
- It conveys typesetting layout information, such as margins, justification, and header or footer data.
- It preserves the integrity of textual content.

The problem is that these systems often don't work when you need to share documents. As long as you are working in-house and don't need to communicate with other machines and people who follow different standards, you're fine.

The world has changed, though. Everyone is sharing information. You need something better and less specific to a single environment. You cannot take a hardcopy markup, shown in figure 1.2, and send it along with electronic copy to someone around the planet. It is awkward to mark up someone's Interleaf for Sparc Station document so that it runs on your PC—without SGML, that is.

Note

The disadvantage of these specific systems is that they are machine-dependent. That is, they depend on a single machine or a type of machine. In a way, they are on life-support systems. As soon as you unplug them from their host hardware or software, they die.

Fig. 1.2

Hardcopy markup.

(d) How the CALS SGML Standard Applies to the Civilian World

The government is a microcosm of the world. Different agencies of the government resemble different countries of the world: in that they each have their own information needs and can benefit from sharing other peoples documents. Many examples of this dynamic appear all around us. There are lots of examples.

For example, a medical student researching cancer in India could benefit greatly by the latest paper on the subject published by a Johns Hopkins scholar. Likewise, a medical student at Johns Hopkins might find very few case studies of a rare disease in the United States, but perhaps the Indian student could provide first-hand experience in assessing the viability of a recommended treatment. If their research is contained in SGML documents, on the internet, say, relevant words can be tagged, linked, and accessed through hyper-media tools. The HTML standards of the internet are beginning to include ever larger sets of SGML features. Indeed, the full SGML feature set is already expanding as a percentage of the World Wide Web, with whole sections of documents being solely SGML, and thus becoming more available in the civilian world.

All of the benefits that the government reaps from the CALS Standard extend equally, and perhaps even more so, to the civilian world. Since government defense security is less of an issue, documents can be distributed even more liberally than the CALS standard originally had in mind. In this way, the civilian world benefits greatly from SGML's ability to make documents easily transportable to someone around the block or around the globe.

(c) How SGML Makes Information Transportable

The challenge of dealing with different types of documents from myriad types of machines and software is not new. Many types of hardware exist: PC's, Sparc stations, Macintosh and other Motorola machines, dedicated mini and mainframe computers, niche computers with their own operating systems, not to mention different operating systems that can run on each of the systems above. When you add software differences to hardware and operating system differences, there are more permutations of output types than you can shake a stick at.

Generalized Electronic Markup

Generalized markup tries to make machine- and software-specific markup transportable. Originally, typesetters used it to prepare documents to be typeset on different brands of typesetting machines. Documents typeset on one model of a manufacturer's typesetter often could not be printed from another model of the same typesetter. Compatibility is a relatively recent phenomenon.

This type of markup tried to pick up where specific markup left off. A common language was needed to enable documents to be moved from one typesetting/publishing system to another. In the late 1960s, Charles F. Goldfarb led a team, in conjunction with the CGA (Computer Graphics Association) in creating GML (Generalized Markup Language), which is the distant predecessor to SGML. Dr. Goldfarb's work with generalized markup is foundational in the development of SGML.

> **Note**
>
> Dr. Goldfarb is still active today. His well-known *The SGML Handbook* is a must for your SGML reference library. Several other books and numerous papers are available in bookstores and on the Internet. See Appendix B, "Finding Sources for SGML Know-How."

Generalized markup provides machine-readable style and format markup that is not specific to any one machine. It separates content, format, and structure without violating their integrity. It imposes a general structure on documents, and it handles all documents according to that structure.

There are many kinds of generalized markup language. Some have been around for a long time, whereas others are experimental. LaTeX, for example, depends on a generic macro system based on TeX, yet another document preparation system (see fig. 1.3). These forms of markup work as long as the formatting mechanism recognizes the formatting codes and understands the document structures that it encounters.

Fig. 1.3

This example of the TeX generalized markup language shows some features it has in common with SGML.

```
%
\noindent
MEMORANDUM
\noindent


\noindent
settabs8 \columns
\+TO:&Mr. Jones\cr
\+\cr
\+FROM:&Mrs. Smith\cr
\noindent

The office supplies are running very low.
I recommend we replace them right away.  My department
manager said, {it"...I'll have to take Mr. Bigs out
to the office warehouse myself to get this job done!"}
I think that stresses the urgency of these supplies,
Sir.  Please see what you can do.

\noindent
Yours Very Truly,

\noindent
\+&&&Mrs. Smith\cr

\end
```

> **Tip**
>
> Generalized markup is not portable unless it adheres to a standard set of rules. If it is not standard, the recipients of a document will not know what to do with it.

Standard Generalized Markup—What SGML Does

SGML goes beyond generalized markup by standardizing it. SGML is a standard set of rules for defining document types by their structures and for marking them up so machines can recognize and process documents by those structures. For example, when you define a book chapter like this by its standard structures—such as titles, headings, notes, and so on—a machine can recognize those structures by standardized tagging schemes and build the chapter from them.

> **Note**
>
> SGML is the mother of all markup languages. Using its rules, you can create an infinite set of smaller markup languages according to your individual document needs. HTML is one of the language offspring of SGML and is, therefore, an SGML "application." That is because HTML is actually a single DTD.

Each markup language that SGML engenders must be consistent within itself. It must also be consistent with all the other documents that have ever been marked up in SGML. It must be consistent with ISO 8879, the international standard for SGML.

Figure 1.4 shows an SGML document instance. It has the following components:

- The overall card
- Address
- Return address
- Graphic image
- Salutation
- Body of message with paragraphs
- Signature

▶▶ See Chapter 24, "Understanding and Using Output Specifications," p. 407

> **Note**
>
> In SGML, you are not greatly concerned with how a document looks. If you captured the structure of a document, you can represent it with many different appearances. SGML uses *output specifications* to make it look like you want.
>
> Further, you'll notice an encoding scheme for the graphic consisting of encrypted characters. SGML also allows you to call upon external processing systems that can translate these characters into the intended image.

Fig. 1.4

This SGML document instance appears complex, but its structure is simple.

```
<!DOCTYPE postcard SYSTEM
"sgml/dtds/postcard.dtd">

<CARD>
<ADDRESS>
Joe A. Guy
1234 AnyStreet
Anytown, CA 91211-1000
</ADDRESS>

<RETADDR>
Sue A. Gal
5678 NutherStreet
Nuther Town, CA 92111-0001
</RETADDR>

<IMAGE>(image file) begin 421M'0(!'0$"'@("'P4#'P("'P8$!',%!P8P
'!P8('P8<"('@'''@'8'"''8''@T*"'@L,M#'T,!PD.#@'PP,T#'P!''@''''P8(
0P0(!P8P(!!P,#'P,#'P,#'P,#'P,#'M#'P,#'P,#'P,#'P,#'P,#'P
#'P,#'P,#'P,#'P,#'/_"!$'$"+',!,!M$'"!M00'"''$0'$0'B'!!0$!'0$!'0$!'0
'0(#!'4&!!P@)"!M'P,"!'',%!!O0$'!?0$"'P'$$042(3%!!A-180<B
<10Rend 421</IMAGE>

<SALUTATION>Hi Joe!</SALUTATION>

<BODY><PARA>Well, Joe, it's been too long since we spoke!
I've just got to tell you all that's been happening!</PARA>

<PARA>First, yadayadayada.  And then bla bla bla.  But most
of all, I've blada yada blada yada!  Isn't that just the
living end!</PARA>

<PARA>I'm afraid I have to run now.  Sorry I couldn't say more!
</PARA></BODY>

<SIGNATURE>Sue</SIGNATURE>
</CARD>
```

You could have just as easily structured the postcard in figure 1.4 into another configuration. For example:

- Side 1
- Side 2

Or this:

- Image on side 1
- Line 1 on side 2
- Line 2 on side 2
- Line 3 on side 2
- Line 4 on side 2

Neither approach is recommended, for reasons you will learn later. SGML, however, supports many approaches for structuring your documents. Some are better than others.

SGML enables you to define document types by their common structures. Each new document type definition will require its own markup language. These markup languages become the collection of tags that tell any SGML processing system how to structurally build the document type for which the markup language was designed. Documents must be marked up consistently according to that markup language or else the SGML processing system will not be able to build them correctly.

How SGML Maintains the Integrity of Content and Structure

SGML maintains the integrity of document content and structure by defining all the document types and their structural elements and by defining their relationships among one another. It accomplishes this through document type definitions (DTDs) and by marking up specific document instances according to the rules in that DTD.

If you have browsed the World Wide Web, you have seen how HTML—itself a markup language with its own DTD—preserves the integrity of document content and structure. SGML enables you to develop your own DTD, like the HTML DTD or even better, to include the document structures you want.

Individual Document Markup

Each SGML document is marked up according to SGML standards. Among the types of markup that you find in SGML documents are the SGML declaration and a reference to the document's DTD. The DTD contains all the information needed to tell an SGML processing system how to build that type of document. The document must be identified as a particular document type. Therefore, it must be associated with its applicable DTD. The basic parts of an SGML document are:

- The SGML declaration
- The reference to its DTD
- The data content of the document
- The individual tag markup

Figure 1.5 shows a marked-up document.

Fig. 1.5

An individual instance of an SGML document contains an SGML declaration, a reference to its DTD, data, and a markup tag.

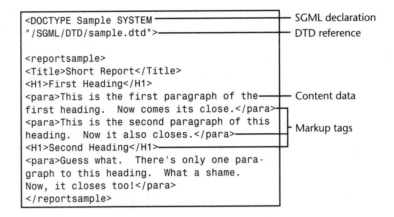

```
<DOCTYPE Sample SYSTEM
"/SGML/DTD/sample.dtd">

<reportsample>
<Title>Short Report</Title>
<H1>First Heading</H1>
<para>This is the first paragraph of the
first heading.  Now comes its close.</para>
<para>This is the second paragraph of this
heading.  Now it also closes.</para>
<H1>Second Heading</H1>
<para>Guess what.  There's only one para-
graph to this heading.  What a shame.
Now, it closes too!</para>
</reportsample>
```

SGML declaration
DTD reference

Content data

Markup tags

Document Type Definitions

Every SGML document must refer to the DTD for its document type. DTDs can appear very different from one another; you can structure and build them in many ways. DTDs are also very flexible.

> **Note**
>
> *Elements* are structural components of a document that are surrounded by tags to tell an SGML system where those components begin and end and where to place them in the document. *Attributes* are further definitions for elements.

Listing 1.1 is the official Boeing DTD used by aircraft manufacturers for service bulletins. It's large, but you can learn a lot from it. It has the following components:

- Introductory comments and description (optional, but recommended)
- Revision history (optional)
- Opening delimiter for all declarations
- Comment on how to refer to this public DTD
- Notation callouts
- Entity declarations
- Revision tracking
- Transmittal information
- Front matter elements
- Body sections and subsections
- Appendix elements
- Table elements
- Graphics elements

- List elements
- Warning, caution, and note elements
- Paragraph and reference elements
- Elements for miscellaneous structures
- Elements for effectivity coding
- Close delimiter as a comment

Listing 1.1   The Boeing ATA Service Bulletin DTD

```
<!-- ==================================================== -->
<!--                    DTD Header                        -->
<!-- ==================================================== -->
<!--                                                      -->
<!-- This is the BOEING Service Bulletin DTD              -->  ———— Introduction and description
<!--                                                      -->
<!-- DTD Reference : SBBOE.02                             -->  ┐
<!-- Revision Date : 1993-11-05                           -->  ┞— Revision history
<!--                                                      -->
<!-- ATA Reference : SBREV31.DTD  sb31-2.01a              -->
<!-- DECL Reference: DECL31-2.01                          -->
<!--                                                      -->
<!-- Highlights                                           -->  ┐
<!-- (1)           : Commented out the DOCTYPE and        -->  │
<!--                 close parameter for the GEF          -->  │
<!-- (2)           : Added EFFXREF as an inclusion        -->  │
<!--                 to PLANSECT                          -->  ┞— Revision comments
<!-- (3)           : Added MDNBR and OLDPNR to PARA       -->  │
<!--                                                      -->  │
<!-- DTD Level     : 3                                    -->  ┘
<!--                                                      -->
<!--DOCTYPE sb [                                          -->  ———— Opening delimiter
                                                                    for declarations
<!-- The following set of declarations may be referred    ┐
 to using a public entity as follows:                     │  This is a public DTD, so
   <!DOCTYPE sb    PUBLIC                                  ┞— you can refer to it in your
"-//ATA-BOEING//DTD SB-BOEING-VER2-LEVEL3//EN"         -->  ┘  document instances


<!-- ==================================================== -->

<!-- ==================================================== -->
<!--       NOTATIONS                                      -->
<!-- ==================================================== -->
<!NOTATION     cgm  PUBLIC                                    ┐
   "-//USA-DOD//NOTATION Computer Graphics Metafile//EN">    │
<!NOTATION     ccitt4     PUBLIC                              ┞— Notation callouts
   "-//USA-DOD//NOTATION CCITT Group 4 Facsimile//EN"  >     ┘


<!-- ==================================================== -->
<!--       ENTITIES                                       -->
<!-- ==================================================== -->
<!ENTITY  % wcn   "(warning* ¦ caution* ¦ note*)"        >   ┐
<!ENTITY  % text  "(para ¦ table ¦ unlist ¦ numlist          │
                   ¦ %wcn; ¦ list1)+"                    >   ┞— Entity declarations
```

(continues)

Listing 1.1   Continued

```
<!ENTITY  % yesorno        "NUMBER"                          >

<!ENTITY  % revatt
      "chg      (N¦R¦U¦D)  #REQUIRED
       key      ID         #REQUIRED
       poschg   (A¦I)      #IMPLIED
       poskey   CDATA      #IMPLIED
       revdate  NUMBER     #IMPLIED"                          >

<!ENTITY  % ISOtech PUBLIC
      "ISO 8879-1986//ENTITIES General Technical//EN" >
<!ENTITY  % ISOpub  PUBLIC
      "ISO 8879-1986//ENTITIES Publishing//EN" >
<!ENTITY  % ISOnum PUBLIC
      "ISO 8879-1986//ENTITIES Numeric and Special Graphic//EN" >
<!ENTITY  % ISOgrk1 PUBLIC
      "ISO 8879-1986//ENTITIES Greek Letters//EN" >
%ISOtech; %ISOpub; %ISOnum; %ISOgrk1;

<!-- ================================================= -->
<!--        Service Bulletin HIGH LEVEL STRUCTURE         -->
<!-- ================================================= -->
<!ELEMENT sb    - -  ((title, ts?, sbfmatr?, body, append*)
                      ¦ increv)
                     +(revst ¦ revend ¦ hotlink ¦ effect) >

<!ATTLIST sb
          model     CDATA      #REQUIRED
          docnbr    CDATA      #IMPLIED
          spl       CDATA      #REQUIRED
          tsn       CDATA      #REQUIRED
          oidate    NUMBER     #REQUIRED
          revdate   NUMBER     #REQUIRED
          chapsect  NUMBERS    #IMPLIED
          chapnbr   NUMBER     #REQUIRED
          seqnbr    NUMBER     #REQUIRED
          sbtype    (Alert ¦ Standard)  'Standard'
          chg       (N ¦ R ¦ U) #REQUIRED
          lang      CDATA      #REQUIRED
          regact    (Yes ¦ No ¦ See-Compliance)    'No'
          appcode   CDATA      #IMPLIED               >

<!-- ================================================= -->
<!--        INCREMENTAL REVISION                          -->
<!-- ================================================= -->
<!ELEMENT increv     - -  (ts ¦ tssect ¦ sbfmatr ¦ sbfmsect
                           ¦ body ¦ plan ¦ matinfo ¦ instr
                           ¦ plansect ¦ matsect ¦ instsect
                           ¦ append ¦ graphic ¦ sheet)+   >

<!-- ================================================= -->
<!--        TRANSMITTAL SECTION                           -->
<!-- ================================================= -->
<!ELEMENT ts         - -  ((effect?, title, para*, tssect+)
                           ¦ deleted)                   >
```

The overall name for service bulletins (sb) and attributes that you can use with your individual service bulletins

This helps with revision-level tracking on your service bulletins

This tells you how to include transmittal data in your service bulletin

```
<!ATTLIST ts
        %revatt;                                        >

<!ELEMENT tssect    - -  ((title, %text;) ¦ deleted)    >
<!ATTLIST tssect
        %revatt;                                        >

<!-- ================================================ -->
<!--     SB FRONT MATTER                              -->
<!-- ================================================ -->
<!ELEMENT sbfmatr   - -  ((effect?, chgdesc*, title, para?,
                         sbfmsect+, graphic*, effxref?) ¦
                         deleted)                       >
<!ATTLIST sbfmatr
        %revatt;                                        >

<!ELEMENT effxref   - -  (effdata+)                     >
<!ELEMENT effdata   - -  (set?, (sunit ¦ munit)+)       >
<!ELEMENT set       - -  (#PCDATA)                      >
<!ELEMENT sunit     - -  (#PCDATA)                      >
<!ATTLIST sunit
        unittype  CDATA      #IMPLIED                   >
<!ELEMENT munit     - -  (stunit, endunit)              >
<!ATTLIST munit
        unittype  CDATA      #IMPLIED                   >
<!ELEMENT stunit    - -  (#PCDATA)                      >
<!ELEMENT endunit   - -  (#PCDATA)                      >

<!ELEMENT sbfmsect  - -  ((chgdesc*, title, %text;) ¦ deleted)>
<!ATTLIST sbfmsect
        %revatt;                                        >

<!-- ================================================ -->
<!--     SB BODY                                      -->
<!-- ================================================ -->
<!ELEMENT body      - -  ((para?, plan, matinfo, instr )
                        ¦ deleted)                      >
<!ATTLIST body
        %revatt;                                        >

<!-- ================================================ -->
<!--     SB BODY SECTIONS                             -->
<!-- ================================================ -->
<!ELEMENT plan      - -  ((effect?, title, plansect+,
                         graphic*) ¦ deleted)           >
<!ATTLIST plan
        %revatt;                                        >

<!ELEMENT matinfo   - -  ((effect?, title, (para ¦ matsect+))
                        ¦ deleted)                      >
<!ATTLIST matinfo
        %revatt;                                        >

<!ELEMENT instr     - -  ((effect?, title, instsect+,
                         graphic*) ¦ deleted)           >
<!ATTLIST instr
        %revatt;                                        >
```

————— Tags for front matter

————— Body element

————— Body sections

You can consider structure in many different ways

(continues)

Listing 1.1 Continued

```
<!-- ==================================================== -->
<!--     SB BODY SUBSECTIONS                              -->————— More markup
<!-- ==================================================== -->
<!ELEMENT plansect  - -  ((effect?, chgdesc*, title, %text;)
                         ¦ deleted) +(effxref)   >
<!ATTLIST plansect
        sectname  (EFF ¦ CON ¦ RES ¦ DES ¦ COM ¦ APP ¦
                   MAN ¦ WAB ¦ ELD ¦ SAS ¦ REF ¦ PUB ¦
                   FTC ¦ OTH)  #REQUIRED
        %revatt;                                        >

<!ELEMENT matsect   - -  ((effect?, chgdesc*, title, %text;)
                         ¦ deleted)                     >
<!ATTLIST matsect
        sectname  (MCA ¦ ISI ¦ MNU ¦ MNS ¦ RIP ¦ TPA ¦
                   OTH)          #REQUIRED
        %revatt;                                        >

<!ELEMENT instsect  - -  ((effect?, chgdesc*, title?, (%text;
                         ¦ graphic)+) ¦ deleted)     >

<!ATTLIST instsect
        %revatt;                                        >

<!-- ==================================================== -->
<!--     APPENDIX                                         -->————— Tags for appendixes
<!-- ==================================================== -->
<!ELEMENT append    - -  ((effect?, chgdesc*, title, (%text;
                         ¦ graphic)+) ¦ deleted)      >
<!ATTLIST append
        %revatt;                                        >

<!-- ==================================================== -->
<!--     TABLE (CALS)                                     -->————— Tags for tables
<!-- ==================================================== -->
<!ELEMENT table     - -  ((title?, tgroup+) ¦ graphic+)
                         -(table)                     >
<!ATTLIST table
        frame     (top¦bottom¦topbot
                   ¦all¦sides¦none)  #IMPLIED
        colsep    %yesorno;          #IMPLIED
        rowsep    %yesorno;          #IMPLIED
        orient    (port¦land)        #IMPLIED
        pgwide    %yesorno;          #IMPLIED
        id        ID                 #IMPLIED        >

<!ELEMENT tgroup    - o  (colspec*, spanspec*, thead?,
                         tfoot?, tbody)              >
<!ATTLIST tgroup
        cols      NUMBER             #REQUIRED
        colsep    %yesorno;          #IMPLIED
        rowsep    %yesorno;          #IMPLIED
        align     (left¦right¦center
                   ¦justify¦char)    "left"
```

```
             charoff    NUTOKEN                 "50"
             char       CDATA                   " "              >

<!ELEMENT colspec   - o  EMPTY                                   >
<!ATTLIST colspec
             colnum     NUMBER                  #IMPLIED
             colname    NMTOKEN                 #IMPLIED
             align      (left¦right¦center
                        ¦justify¦char)          #IMPLIED
             charoff    NUTOKEN                 #IMPLIED
             char       CDATA                   #IMPLIED
             colwidth   CDATA                   #IMPLIED
             colsep     %yesorno;               #IMPLIED
             rowsep     %yesorno;               #IMPLIED         >

<!ELEMENT spanspec  - o  EMPTY                                   >
<!ATTLIST spanspec
             namest     NMTOKEN                 #REQUIRED
             nameend    NMTOKEN                 #REQUIRED
             spanname   NMTOKEN                 #REQUIRED

             align      (left¦right¦center
                        ¦justify¦char)          "center"
             charoff    NUTOKEN                 #IMPLIED
             char       CDATA                   #IMPLIED
             colsep     %yesorno;               #IMPLIED
             rowsep     %yesorno;               #IMPLIED         >

<!ELEMENT thead     - o  (colspec*, row+)                       >
<!ATTLIST thead
             valign     (top¦middle¦bottom)        "bottom"     >

<!ELEMENT tfoot     - o  (colspec*, row+)                       >
<!ATTLIST tfoot
             valign     (top¦middle¦bottom)        "top"        >

<!ELEMENT tbody     - o  (row+)                                  >
<!ATTLIST tbody
             valign     (top¦middle¦bottom)        "top"        >

<!ELEMENT row       - o  (entry+)                               >
<!ATTLIST row
             rowsep     %yesorno;               #IMPLIED         >

<!--ELEMENT entry   - -  ((para ¦ unlist)+ ¦ graphic)   -->
<!--ELEMENT entry   - -  ((#PCDATA ¦ para ¦ caution ¦ note ¦ unlist)+ ¦
graphic)   -->
<!ELEMENT entry     - -  ((#PCDATA ¦ para ¦ unlist)+ ¦ graphic)     >
<!ATTLIST entry
             colname    NMTOKEN                 #IMPLIED
             namest     NMTOKEN                 #IMPLIED
             nameend    NMTOKEN                 #IMPLIED
             spanname   NMTOKEN                 #IMPLIED
             morerows   NUMBER                  "0"
             colsep     %yesorno;               #IMPLIED
             rowsep     %yesorno;               #IMPLIED
```

(continues)

Listing 1.1   Continued

```
        rotate      %yesorno;               "0"
        valign      (top¦middle¦bottom)         "top"
        align       (left¦right¦center
                    ¦justify¦char)          #IMPLIED
        charoff     NUTOKEN                 #IMPLIED
        char        CDATA                   #IMPLIED        >

<!-- =================================================== -->
<!--     GRAPHIC                                          -->———— Tags for graphics
<!-- =================================================== -->
<!ELEMENT grphcref  - -  (#PCDATA)                        >
<!ATTLIST grphcref
        refid       IDREF       #IMPLIED
        sheetnbr    CDATA       #IMPLIED
        objid       CDATA       #IMPLIED
        shownow     %yesorno; "0"                          >

<!ELEMENT graphic   - -  ((effect?, chgdesc*, title?,
                         sheet+) ¦ deleted)               >
<!ATTLIST graphic
        %revatt;                                          >
<!ELEMENT sheet     - -  ((effect?, chgdesc*, title?,
                         gdesc?) ¦ deleted)               >
<!ATTLIST sheet
        sheetnbr    CDATA       #REQUIRED
        gnbr        ENTITY      #REQUIRED
        %revatt;                                          >

<!ELEMENT gdesc     - -  (%text;)                         >

<!-- =================================================== -->
<!--     LISTS                                            -->—┐
<!-- =================================================== -->
<!ELEMENT list1     - -  (title?, l1item+)  -(list1)      >
<!ELEMENT list2     - -  (title?, l2item+)               >
<!ELEMENT list3     - -  (title?, l3item+)               >
<!ELEMENT list4     - -  (title?, l4item+)               >
<!ELEMENT list5     - -  (title?, l5item+)               >
<!ELEMENT list6     - -  (title?, l6item+)               >
<!ELEMENT list7     - -  (title?, l7item+)               >

<!-- =================================================== -->
<!--     LIST ITEMS                                       -->—— Tags for lists
<!-- =================================================== -->
<!ELEMENT l1item    - -  (effect?, %text;, list2?)        >
<!ELEMENT l2item    - -  (%text;, list3?)                >
<!ELEMENT l3item    - -  (%text;, list4?)                >
<!ELEMENT l4item    - -  (%text;, list5?)                >
<!ELEMENT l5item    - -  (%text;, list6?)                >
<!ELEMENT l6item    - -  (%text;, list7?)                >
<!ELEMENT l7item    - -  (%text;)                        >

<!-- =================================================== -->
<!--     NUMBERED & UN-NUMBERED LIST                      -->—┘
<!-- =================================================== -->
```

```
<!ELEMENT numlist      - -  (numlitem+)                    >
<!ATTLIST numlist
          numtype   CDATA     #IMPLIED                     >
<!ELEMENT numlitem     - -  (para+)                        >

<!ELEMENT unlist       - -  (unlitem+)                     >
<!ATTLIST unlist
          bulltype  CDATA     #IMPLIED                     >
<!ELEMENT unlitem      - -  (%text;)                       >

<!-- ================================================ -->
<!--      WARNING, CAUTION, NOTE                      -->
<!-- ================================================ -->
<!ELEMENT warning      - -  (%text;)   -(warning | caution |
                            note)                          >
<!ELEMENT note         - -  (%text;)   -(warning | caution |
                            note)                          >
<!ELEMENT caution      - -  (%text;)   -(warning | caution |
                            note)                          >

<!-- ================================================ -->
<!--      PARAGRAPH                                   -->
<!-- ================================================ -->
<!ELEMENT para         - -  (#PCDATA | cb | con | csn | ein |
                            equ | ncon | pan | refext | refint
                            | std | ted | toolnbr | toolname |
                            price | zone | sbnbr | manhour |
                            elaphour | pnr | kitnbr | weight |
                            moment | custname | set | kwd |
                            dwg | cus | msnbr | grphcref |
                            oldpnr | mdnbr)+  >

<!-- ================================================ -->
<!--      PARAGRAPH and REFERENCE ELEMENTS CONTENTS   -->
<!-- ================================================ -->
<!ELEMENT cb           - -  (#PCDATA)                      >
<!ELEMENT con          - -  (connbr,conname)               >
<!ELEMENT connbr       - -  (#PCDATA)                      >
<!ELEMENT conname      - -  (#PCDATA)                      >
<!ELEMENT csn          - -  (#PCDATA)                      >
<!ELEMENT ein          - -  (#PCDATA)                      >
<!ELEMENT equ          - -  (#PCDATA)                      >
<!ELEMENT ncon         - -  (#PCDATA)                      >
<!ELEMENT pan          - -  (#PCDATA)                      >
<!ELEMENT refext       - -  (#PCDATA)                      >
<!ATTLIST refext
          refman    CDATA     #IMPLIED
          refloc    CDATA     #IMPLIED
          refmodel  CDATA     #IMPLIED
          refspl    CDATA     #IMPLIED                     >
<!ELEMENT refint       - -  (#PCDATA)                      >
<!ATTLIST refint
          reftype   CDATA     #IMPLIED
          refloc    IDREF     #REQUIRED                    >
<!ELEMENT std          - -  (#PCDATA)                      >
<!ELEMENT ted          - -  (toolnbr,toolname)             >
```

For warnings, cautions, and notes

Simple paragraphs and their sub-components

(continues)

Listing 1.1 Continued

```
<!ELEMENT toolnbr    - -  (#PCDATA)                              >
<!ELEMENT toolname   - -  (#PCDATA)                              >
<!ELEMENT zone       - -  (#PCDATA)                              >
<!ELEMENT price      - -  (#PCDATA)                              >
<!ATTLIST price
          currency   CDATA      #IMPLIED                         >
<!ELEMENT sbnbr      - -  (#PCDATA)                              >
<!ELEMENT manhour    - -  (#PCDATA)                              >
<!ELEMENT elaphour   - -  (#PCDATA)                              >
<!ELEMENT pnr        - -  (#PCDATA)                              >
<!ELEMENT kitnbr     - -  (#PCDATA)                              >
<!ELEMENT weight     - -  (#PCDATA)                              >
<!ELEMENT moment     - -  (#PCDATA)                              >
<!ELEMENT kwd        - -  (#PCDATA)                              >
<!ELEMENT dwg        - -  (#PCDATA)                              >
<!ELEMENT custname   - -  (#PCDATA)                              >
<!ELEMENT cus        - -  (#PCDATA)                              >
<!ELEMENT msnbr      - -  (#PCDATA)                              >
<!ELEMENT mdnbr      - -  (#PCDATA)                              >
<!ELEMENT oldpnr     - -  (#PCDATA)                              >


<!-- ================================================= -->   Tags for
<!--      MISCELLANEOUS CONSTRUCTIONS:                 -->   miscellaneous
<!--      REVISION MARKERS, HOTLINK,                   -->── elements; most
<!--      TITLE and CHANGE DESCRIPTION                 -->   DTDs have
<!-- ================================================= -->   these tags
<!ELEMENT revst      - O  EMPTY                                  >

<!ELEMENT revend     - O  EMPTY                                  >

<!ELEMENT hotlink    - O  EMPTY                                  >
<!ATTLIST hotlink
          targetid        CDATA      #IMPLIED
          targetrefid     CDATA      #IMPLIED                    >

<!ELEMENT title      - -  (#PCDATA)                              >

<!ELEMENT chgdesc    - -  (#PCDATA)                              >


<!-- ================================================= -->   This is a must
<!--      EFFECTIVITY CODING ELEMENT                   -->── in the aircraft
<!-- ================================================= -->   industry
<!ELEMENT effect     - -  (effsb*)                              >
<!ELEMENT effsb      - O  EMPTY                                  >
<!ATTLIST (effect ¦ effsb)
          effrg       CDATA      #IMPLIED
          efftext     CDATA      #IMPLIED                        >


<!-- ================================================= -->
<!--      DELETE ELEMENT                               -->
<!-- ================================================= -->
<!ELEMENT deleted    - O  EMPTY                                  >   Close delimiter
<!-- ]-->                                                           as a comment
```

This DTD is well documented with many comments to help you follow its logic.

> **Note**
>
> For now, think of SGML as an enormous cookbook. The document content is the list of ingredients for a recipe. The DTD is the instructions for making the recipe. The SGML markup in the document combines the ingredients with the directions for a complete recipe of how to make a document.

SGML and the Internet

The DTD is how SGML maintains the integrity of the content and structure of a document. Its ability to do this explains, in part, why SGML is becoming so popular on the Internet.

The World Wide Web is written largely in HTML, which is one application of SGML. The explosive growth on the World Wide Web demands richer and larger sets of markup features in HTML. Newer revisions of HTML include greater numbers of SGML features. As the Web continues to grow, SGML will likely become the standard for more markup languages on the Internet.

How HTML Is Evolving To Include Larger Numbers of SGML Features

Each version of HTML is made from an SGML DTD in which all the HTML document features are defined. HTML tries to remain simpler than SGML, but as it evolves, it includes more SGML features.

You don't create DTDs for HTML documents, because HTML is itself a DTD. Each version of HTML has its own DTD. HTML versions 1.0, 2.0, or 3.0 are actually three different DTDs, all of which are SGML applications.

HTML version 1.0 is a simple subset of SGML. It lacks flexibility and cannot handle tables, equations, and forms used to fill in information. Version 2.0 adds elegance and stability, but it still has difficulties. Version 3.0 is a proposed improvement upon version 2.0. Features that version 3.0 adds to HTML include:

- Overriding stylesheets
- Object linking and embedding
- Multimedia and metafile extensions
- Enhanced math and equation capabilities

The Internet and SGML Browsing and Authoring Tools

SGML fans are fond of the Internet. Although HTML is currently the favorite markup language on the World Wide Web, it is moving toward the larger feature set of SGML. Consequently, more SGML tools are starting to appear for the average user.

SoftQuad has introduced Panorama, an SGML browsing tool designed to work in conjunction with Netscape or Mosaic. It works alongside your HTML browser. When you encounter an SGML Web page, Panorama enables you to browse it as easily as an HTML page.

▶▶ See "Panorama Pro," p. 453

Panorama is the first SGML Web browser that works alongside an HTML browser. A free version of it is available on the Web and from FTP sites, and is also included on the CD-ROM included with this book. A full-featured version, called Panorama Pro, is available commercially from SoftQuad. These browsers are discussed in Chapter 25. The SGML home page in figure 1.6 lists links to other SGML-related Internet resources.

Fig. 1.6

Panorama, by SoftQuad, activates whenever your browser encounters an SGML Web page.

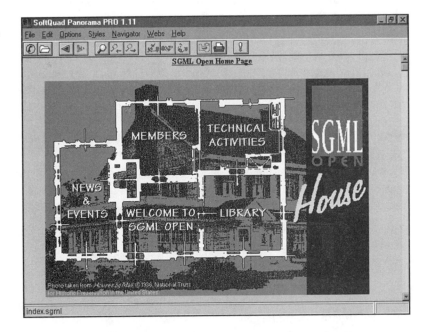

SGML Resources on the Internet

Resources for SGML abound on the Internet, including Gopher sites, FTP sites, Web sites, and chat channels. You can Telnet to SGML BBSes and talk with SGML gurus by using Internet Phone.

Figure 1.7 shows an Archie search on SGML. It turned up 37 hits on one Gopher server in the United Kingdom. Each hit might lead to even more information on SGML documents.

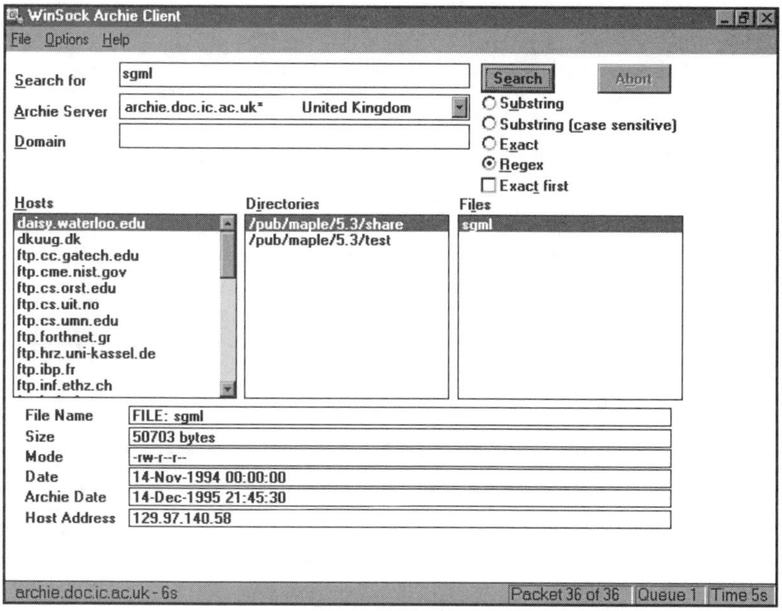

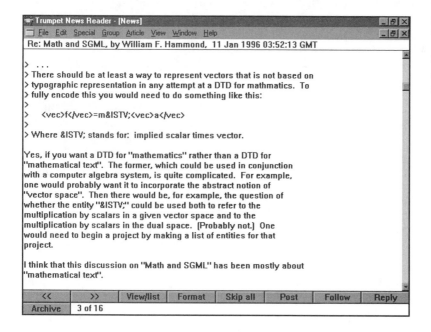

Fig. 1.7

A sample Archie search on SGML shows 37 hits from just one server. Numerous SGML archives exist.

One newsgroup where gurus hang out is COMP.TEXT.SGML on UseNet. Figure 1.8 shows the range of topics covered on a normal day in this newsgroup.

Fig. 1.8

The COMP.TEXT.SGML newsgroup is a popular source for detailed information about SGML.

> **Tip**
>
> There are enough SGML resources on the Internet to bury you. If you want to stay busy for the next few months, check out one of the SGML home pages and trace the links. A popular one is **http://www.sil.org/sgml/sgml.html**.

This is just a small sample of what is available on the Internet. You can start at any one of these places and quickly find related sources too numerous to count.

What the Future May Hold for SGML and Its Applications

The World Wide Web is just starting out. The first browsers became available only a few years ago. HTML is in its infancy, and already the Web has exploded with growth. Businesses connect to the Web every day. It is hard to underestimate all the changes that will occur over the coming years.

HTML enables the Internet to present information graphically as well as textually. Sound and video clips are also easily available over the Web. The biggest problem with these types of files is they are difficult to transfer over the Internet because of their immense size and bandwidth requirements. Compression technology will enable them to take up no more space than text or small graphics. These types of files are just the beginning.

Multimedia Extensions and the Internet

Interactive gaming shows how popular enhanced multimedia extensions can be on the Internet.

Imagine sitting in your den, running a flight simulator program on your PC, engaging in a dogfight with someone around the world in front of his PC (see fig. 1.9). You are flying against each other in real time. The sounds are cracking, screeching, and whooshing from your stereo speakers, and the three-dimensional graphics draw you right into the action with a display as vivid and real as in any movie—and more interactive, too. Does that sound far out?

You can do this today by running game software over Internet Relay Chat (IRC) lines on the Internet. The technology is still rather crude, though. A better bet is to play on local bulletin board systems (BBSes) that have special software. Enthusiasm for easier tools is high.

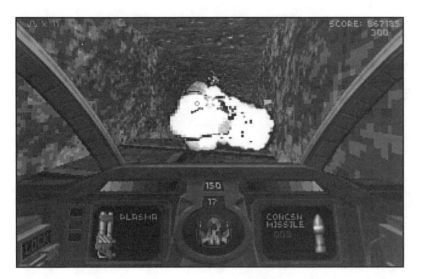

Fig. 1.9

Descent, a popular interactive virtual reality game, might eventually be played over the World Wide Web using SGML markup on Web pages with expanded multimedia extensions.

The multimedia extensions that are so popular from the gaming world can be added to all the types of information currently found on the Internet. Applications available through a multimedia SGML Web browser might include:

- A talking Gopher client that encourages you to keep looking for what you cannot find
- An e-mail client that sings "Happy Birthday" to a loved one
- A movie viewer that plays movie clips from within the Web browser in real time
- A full-screen game window that plays all current virtual reality games and simulations interactively with opponents from anywhere on the Web

The sky is the limit. If it can be represented digitally, it can be typed, structured, and distributed through SGML over the World Wide Web—perhaps not right away, but eventually. What everyone is waiting for is compression technology that enables extremely large files to be moved at a reasonable speed. There are many technical hurdles to be jumped, but the SGML groundwork is in place.

From Here...

The SGML standard enables you to define a markup scheme to transport documents between processing systems regardless of distance, hardware, and software. Government and civilian use of the standard has proven its value for individual users. HTML on the Internet is one small example of how valuable and important a single SGML implementation can be. The future prospects for SGML are staggering.

For more information, refer to the following:

- Chapter 2, "SGML View of the World: Structure, Content, and Format," discusses the structure of documents.

- Chapter 3, "SGML Terminology," defines the terms you need to know to use SGML effectively.

- Part V, "SGML and the World Wide Web," tells you how to upgrade an HTML Web site to an SGML Web site.

 On the CD

- Part VII, "SGML Tools and Their Uses," discusses how to use SGML tools to produce documents and DTDs. Some of these tools are included on the CD-ROM that comes with this book.

CHAPTER 2

SGML View of the World: Structure, Content, and Format

SGML is a language for relating structured information. If you want to create documents and transmit them in hard copy, electronically, or even in Braille, SGML is worth considering. If you are creating or packaging data that you expect to use for 20 years, SGML offers the capability to take your information with you, no matter what software package you will be using 10 years from now.

By design, SGML is suited to complex, technical information traditionally packaged in documents. Through its ways of identifying and defining document components, SGML provides a rich environment for transmitting structured information sets—or documents—in many ways through a variety of media. SGML is not really too complex, although it provides a structure for defining and exchanging complex information. In other words, it can be as complicated or as simple as the documents that use it.

Because most people are familiar with creating and editing documents with word processors, the examples throughout this chapter contrast the concepts common to word processing programs with SGML concepts. Understanding the three central concepts of SGML document structure is essential. Some people say that when you understand them, the rest is easy.

In this chapter, you learn some of the key components of SGML, including:

- How SGML views documents (structure, content, and format)
- Why this view is important
- How SGML works with this view

Structure, Content, and Format

To understand SGML, you must understand some basic ideas about document structure. Central to SGML is the concept that documents have *structure, content,* and *format* (see fig. 2.1). These three ingredients combine to form a document. They interrelate in subtle ways, and you can easily confuse them as you work with documents.

Fig. 2.1

Structure, content, and format play important roles in the construction of an SGML document.

"The SGML View of a Document"

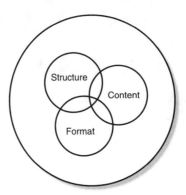

How you approach a document when you create one on a word processor usually adds to the confusion in understanding the distinctions among these three concepts. For example, when you write a technical memorandum, you might use special formatting, such as a bold typeface, to indicate elements of the document structure.

Later in this chapter, you look at a document created with a word processor. As you examine it, you can contrast a word processing program's view of structure, content, and format with the SGML approach.

What Is Structure?

Structure is the blueprint or plans of a document. It consists of the document's logical organization. The structure defines how the document is laid out and in what order the elements are assembled. In the SGML world, it also defines relationships, indicating how individual information objects relate to one another. For example, a bicycle assembly manual might consist of the following sections in this order: an introduction that describes the document and lists the manufacturer's address, assembly instructions, a parts list, instructions for order replacement parts, troubleshooting advice, and an index.

Within a word processing program, for example, structure is generally left up to the author. Styles and stylesheets help, but structure is usually not explicitly supported. SGML departs from this philosophy in that it requires the author to define a document structure explicitly ahead of time. The author, however, can decide how strict—or lenient—the structure will be.

For example, the document structure for an office memorandum might contain a title, an addressee block, a sender block, the date, a salutation, and the body of the memo. When you create this memo with a word processor, the structure is implied. In SGML, the structure must be defined.

What Is Content?

Content is the actual data within a document. The words and illustrations that make up a bicycle assembly manual are its contents, just as the text and figures in this chapter are its content. Different word processors handle textual content similarly, but they vary in how they support illustrations and graphics.

Note

SGML does not directly address the issues involved in supporting graphics. It is a structured text markup language, but provides the capability to support non-text objects, such as graphics. With the widespread adoption of electronic documents, the importance of supporting multimedia objects, such as video and sound clips, is increasing.

Underlying most word processors, the textual data is stored in a specific way—in a binary format or in a version of ASCII text. In most instances, it is stored sequentially—word after word, just as the author intended. Only in the case of specialized formatting does it appear different from what the author had in mind as he entered the information.

What Is Format?

Format consists of how the words, sentences, and paragraphs are visually presented and distinguished from one another within a document. Boldface for titles, italics for special terms, and blank lines between sections are examples of document formats. Specific formatting serves a variety of uses—emphasis, hints on structure, and the overall aesthetics of the document.

People often confuse format with structure. This is because structure is commonly implied within word processing programs through the use of specialized, tailored formatting called *styles*. By using defined styles, an author can specify that a style name should be associated with a block of content and special formatting.

People sometimes forget what they are using specific formats for, and then use the same type of formatting to indicate multiple things. Novice users of word processors often use a wide variety of fonts, font sizes, and other formatting attributes in their documents. While visually interesting, their documents can be hard to read and difficult to understand.

Different word processors handle formatting issues in widely different ways. As a result, translating from one format to another can be an adventure in large, complex documents.

Caution

Using formatting to indicate structure is both commonplace and dangerous. Because people tend to make assumptions as they read, they can easily misinterpret a document's content. This is particularly true with documents that have been translated from one format to another, such as from one word processor format to another. It is also a source of agony when you attempt to translate a document from one proprietary format to another.

Why Structure, Content, and Format Are Important in SGML

SGML provides a mechanism for delivering documents or structured information in a number of ways, including a mechanism for delivering the same content and structure through different programs, formats, and delivery media. To do this efficiently, SGML must define the structure and separate the content from the delivery-specific format.

Through this approach, the actual document—its content and structure—becomes mobile. That is, it can be used with different programs, on different computers, and in different formats across time. With a document repository stored in SGML, your organization can switch to a new word processor with a minimum of pain. The documents that you created years ago can be reused with a minimum of effort even though you might have switched word processors twice since then.

For example, imagine a company that prepares a series of product advisory bulletins. It distributes the bulletins as printed hard copy and in electronic form. To support this, it applies formatting differently, depending on the delivery approach.

Now examine these advisories in the two worlds—hard copy and electronic delivery. You should begin to understand the benefits of SGML.

The printed version of the advisory is shown in figure 2.2. It is a typical document with a standard logical organization designed to communicate specific information.

Indicating Structure Through Visual Cues

Printed documents typically indicate structure through visual hints, or cues. By using various formatting techniques, documents can "suggest" their structure.

As you view the product advisory, your mind divides the document into pieces. The title tells you what the document is. Identification data in the upper-left corner identifies specific values associated with the document. The body of the document consists of two separate sections, each of which is identified by a section title.

You can distinguish the sections from their visual cues. For example:

■ The larger typeface for the document title

- Captions—Number, Type, Date, Revised, and Subject—and boldface type for the identification data
- Space separating the body of the document from the identification data

PRODUCT ADVISORY

Number: 146
Type: Parts
Date: 8/15/95
Revised:

Subject: Revised Replacement Parts List (AnyCorp Model 501)

Model 501 User-Replaceable Parts

The parts list identified in the AnyCorp Model 501 User's Maintenance Guide has been superseded, effective immediately. User-replaceable parts are identified in the revised parts list below. Parts orders which reference items on the previous list (dated 2/5/94) will be honored up to 3/14/96.

Customers are advised to order from this revised list in order that they may achieve higher reliability at a lower unit cost. Questions on this subject should be directed to the Central Spares Organization.

New Parts List

1. 345-234 (Filter, cooling fan)
2. 148-745 (Fuse, power:1.5amp)
3. 345-712 (Lamp, indicator)
4. 2346-92 (Disk, cleaning)
5. 347-622 (Swabs, cleaning)

Fig. 2.2

This printed version of a product advisory bulletin is an example of a typical hardcopy document.

Unfortunately, this structure is apparent only when the formatting is available. If you translate this document into simple text without the formatting, the structure becomes more difficult to identify. Figure 2.3 shows how the document looks without formatting.

```
PRODUCT ADVISORY
Number:146
Type:Parts
Date:8/15/95
Revised:
Subject:Revised Replacement Parts List (AnyCorp Model 501)
Model 501 User-Replaceable Parts
The parts list identified in the AnyCorp Model 501 User's
Maintenance Guide has been superseded, effective immediately.
User-replaceable parts are identified in the revised parts
list below. Parts orders which reference items on the previous
list (dated 2/5/94) will be honored up to 3/14/96.
Customers are advised to order from this revised list in order
that they may achieve higher reliability at a lower unit cost.
Questions on this subject should be directed to the Central
Spares Organization.
New Parts List
1.345-234 (Filter, cooling fan)
2.148-745 (Fuse, power:1.5amp)
3.345-712 (Lamp, indicator)
4.2346-92 (Disk, cleaning)
5.347-622 (Swabs, cleaning)
```

Fig. 2.3

Here is the same product advisory bulletin viewed as unformatted text.

In the unformatted version, the document structure is not as obvious as it was in the document with formatting. Because document structure in word processing documents is often only "hinted" at through formatting, you can be highly dependent upon such formatting to understand the structure.

Losing Structure in Word Processing Documents

Figure 2.4 shows a word processor's view of the fully formatted document from figure 2.2. In this example, the formatted version is stored in rich text format (RTF), a word processing interchange format.

The RTF formatted version of the document uses codes to indicate formatting. These codes are often specific to a software package or vendor. Even with RTF, how the codes are interpreted varies among software packages.

By specifying document structure through formatting hints, you become dependent on format. What happens if you lose this format? That might occur when you translate a highly structured document from one word-processing format to another. The text will likely translate correctly, but the formatting might translate less accurately. If this translation process is particularly troublesome, the formatting might end up in a jumble, making the document extremely difficult to read. Important parts of the structure could be lost.

Likewise, suppose that you want to view the document in a different medium. To display electronically—for example, on the World Wide Web—a document that you created in a word processor, you must convert its format. See Chapter 26, "Tools for the PC: Authoring, Viewing, and Utilities," for a look at some powerful new SGML authoring tools.

An Alternative View

Figure 2.5 shows the product advisory bulletin presented in electronic format. The content is the same, but the formatting has been altered to suit the electronic environment in which it is presented.

Structural Views of Information

Now consider the product advisory bulletin from a structural perspective. You can break it into its parts. One way to do this is to lay out what it contains in the format of an indented, or structured, list. For example:

```
{\rtf1\ansi \deff0\deflang1024{\fonttbl{\f0\froman Times New Roman;}
{\f1\froman Symbol;}}{\f2\fswiss
Arial;}}{\colortbl;\red0\green0\blue0;\red0\green0\blue255;
\red0\green255\blue255;\red0\green255\blue0;
\red255\green0\blue255;\red255\green0\blue0;\red255
\green255\blue0;\red255\green255\blue255;\red0\green0
\blue127;\red0\green127\blue127;\red0\green127\blue0;
\red127\green0\blue127;\red127\green0\blue0;\red127
\green127\blue0;\red127\green127\blue127;
\red192\green192\blue192;}{\stylesheet{\fs20\lang1033 \snext0
Normal;}}{\info{\title Sample Advisory}{\author mc}{\operator
mc}{\creatim\yr1995\mo9\dy4\hr16\min13}{\revtim\
yr1995\mo9\dy6\hr23\min18}{\printim\yr1995\mo9\dy4
\hr16\min49}{\version5}
{\edmins70}{\nofpages1}{\nofwords119}{\nofchars806}
{\vern16433}}\paperw12240\paperh15840\margl1800
\margr1800\margt1440\margb1440\gutter0 \widowctrl
\ftnbj \sectd \linex0\endnhere \pard\plain \fs20\lang1033
\par
\par \pard \qc {\b\fs28 PRODUCT ADVISORY
\par }\pard
\par \pard {\plain \b\lang1033 Number:\tab }{\plain \lang1033 146}
{\plain \b\lang1033
\par }{\plain \b\lang1033 Type:}{\plain \lang1033 \tab \tab Parts}
{\plain \b\lang1033
\par }{\plain \b\lang1033 Date:}{\plain \lang1033 \tab
\tab 8/15/95}{\plain \b\lang1033
\par }\pard {\plain \b\lang1033 Revised:}{\plain \lang1033
\par }{\plain \lang1033
\par }\pard {\plain \b\lang1033 Subject:}{\plain \lang1033
\tab Revised Replacement Parts List (AnyCorp }{\plain
\lang1033 Model 501)
\par }\pard {\plain \lang1033
\par }{\plain \lang1033
\par }{\plain \lang1033
\par }{\plain \b\lang1033 Model 501 User-Replaceable Parts
\par }{\plain \lang1033
\par }\pard {\plain \lang1033
The parts list identified in the AnyCorp Model 501 User's
Maintenance Guide has been superseded, effective immediately.
User-replaceable parts are identified in the revised parts
list below. Parts orders which reference items on the previous
list (dated
}{\plain \lang1033 2/5/94) will be honored up to 3/14/96.
\par }\pard {\plain \lang1033
\par }\pard {\plain \lang1033 Customers are advised to order
from this revised list in order that they may achieve higher
reliability at a lower unit cost. Questions on this subject
should be}{\plain \lang1033  directed to the Central Spares
Organization.
\par }\pard {\plain \lang1033
\par }{\plain \b\lang1033 New Parts List}{\plain \lang1033
\par }{\plain \lang1033
\par }\pard \fi-360\li360\tx0\tx90\tx3060 {\plain \lang1033 1.
\tab 345-234 (Filter, cooling fan)
\par }{\plain \lang1033 2.\tab 148-745 (Fuse, power:1.5amp)
\par }{\plain \lang1033 3.\tab 345-712 (Lamp, indicator)
\par }{\plain \lang1033 4.\tab 2346-92 (Disk, cleaning)
\par }{\plain \lang1033 5.\tab 347-622 (Swabs, cleaning)
\par }{\plain \lang1033
\par }{\plain \lang1033
\par }}
```

Fig. 2.4

Here the product advisory bulletin is viewed in Rich Text Format (RTF), a document interchange format. Notice that many formatting instructions are embedded within the textual content of the document.

SGML Development

```
Product advisory
   Identification number
   Advisory type
   Date
   Revision date
   Subject
   Body
      Subsection
         Title
         List
      Subsection
         Title
         List
```

This is how SGML looks at documents. One of the advantages of requiring a structured view of data is that SGML makes it easier to use data in a wide variety of environments.

Fig. 2.5

Here is the product advisory bulletin presented electronically, with the format altered to suit the electronic environment.

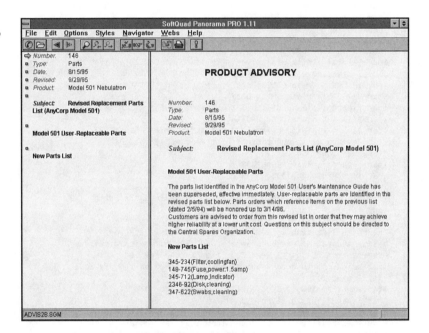

Defining Structure in SGML

The structure of a document—its *type*—is defined by a *document type definition,* or DTD. The DTD is a blueprint of the document; it can be simple or complex. It specifies what elements are allowed, whether they are required or optional, and the order in which they can occur.

The DTD lays out the rules for a document through the use of elements, attributes, and entities (see Chapter 3, "SGML Terminology"). To get an idea of how SGML handles structure, consider figure 2.6, which shows a simple DTD.

```
<!-- *********************************************** -->
<!-- AnyCorp, USA                                    -->
<!--                                                 -->
<!-- Product Advisory DTD version 1.1, 21 Jul 95     -->
<!-- *********************************************** -->
<!DOCTYPE advisory [
<!--   Entity Definitions    -->
<!ENTITY % parael "para¦blist¦nlist¦graphic">
<!ELEMENT advisory - - (idinfo,subject,subsec+)>
<!ELEMENT idinfo   - - (advnbr,type,dateiss,daterev,product)>
<!ELEMENT subject  - - (#PCDATA)>
<!ATTLIST subject      safety (y¦n) "n">
<!ELEMENT subsec   - - (title,(%parael;?))>
<!ELEMENT advnbr   - - (#PCDATA)>
<!ELEMENT type     - - (#PCDATA)>
<!ELEMENT dateiss  - - (#PCDATA)>
<!ELEMENT daterev  - - (#PCDATA)>
<!ELEMENT product  - - (#PCDATA)>
<!ELEMENT title    - - (#PCDATA)>
<!ELEMENT para     - - (#PCDATA)>
<!ELEMENT blist    - - (item+) -(nlist)>
<!ELEMENT nlist    - - (item+)>
<!ELEMENT item     - - (para¦blist¦nlist¦graphic¦#PCDATA)+>
<!ELEMENT graphic  - o EMPTY>
<!ATTLIST graphic      filename CDATA #REQUIRED
                       artno    CDATA #IMPLIED>
                 ]>
```

Fig. 2.6

This document type definition defines the document structure of the product advisory bulletin.

I

SGML Development

The DTD defines the product advisory document. Even though its structure is simple, it still has rules. Within the DTD, elements are the building blocks of the document structure. The DTD defines the rules for what an element can contain—specific characters, values, or collections of other elements.

In the DTD, the element advisory contains child elements, or *subelements,* that make up the bulletin. Table 2.1 describes the subelements that represent the major components of the document.

Table 2.1   Subelements in the Product Advisory Bulletin

Element Name	Description
advnbr	Advisory number
type	Advisory type
dateiss	Date issued
daterev	Date revised
subject	Advisory subject
subsec	Subsection

▶▶ See "What Are the Components of SGML Documents?" p. 47

▶▶ See "Entities," p. 58

Note

The element subsec contains additional elements, some of which are referenced via entities.

Using Structure in SGML

The DTD also defines the tag set that corresponds to the structural notation of the document. Combined with the text of the document, these tags fit the text into the structure that's defined in the DTD. If this sounds confusing, take a look at a tagged document. Figure 2.7 shows the SGML tagged text—or *markup*—of the product advisory bulletin.

Fig. 2.7

This is a view of the product advisory bulletin as an SGML document "instance."

```
<advisory>
<advnbr>146</advnbr>
<type>Parts</type>
<dateiss>8/15/95</dateiss>
<daterev></daterev>
<subject>Revised Replacement Parts List (AnyCorp Model 501)</
subject>
<subsec>
<title>Model 501 User-Replaceable Parts</title>
<para>The parts list identified in the AnyCorp Model 501 User's
Maintenance Guide has been superseded, effective immediately.
User-replaceable parts are identified in the revised parts list
below. Parts orders which reference items on the previous list
(dated 2/5/94) will be honored up to 3/14/96.</para>
<para>Customers are advised to order from this revised list in
order that they may achieve higher reliability at a lower unit
cost. Questions on this subject should be directed to the
Central Spares Organization.</para>
</subsec>
<subsec>
<title>New Parts List</title>
<nlist>
<item>345-234 (Filter, cooling fan)</item>
<item>148-745 (Fuse, power:1.5amp)</item>
<item>345-712 (Lamp, indicator)</item>
<item>2346-92 (Disk, cleaning)</item>
<item>347-622 (Swabs, cleaning)</item>
</nlist>
</subsec>
</advisory>
```

From Here...

You now have completed an initial tour of the SGML view of documents. You have examined the key concepts of structure, content, and format. You saw how SGML uses these components to create modular and transportable documents.

For more information, see the following:

- Chapter 3, "SGML Terminology," gives you the specifics of SGML terminology and structure.
- Chapter 4, "The Basic Procedure," takes you through the process of creating an SGML document environment.
- Chapter 5, "Two Scenarios," discusses the two common approaches for getting your documents into SGML.
- Part II, "Document Analysis," takes you through the process of analyzing the structure of your document collection.
- Part III, "Content Modeling: Developing the DTD," discusses the process of creating DTDs that accurately reflect your documents.
- Part VII, "SGML Tools and Their Uses," examines some of the powerful SGML software tools that are just now becoming available.

CHAPTER 3

SGML Terminology

This chapter covers the basics of SGML documents. The terminology found in this chapter applies to just about every SGML document known to man; if you have much experience with SGML, these terms will probably be familiar. If you're new to the "language," knowing these terms will serve you well.

This chapter covers documents, elements, attributes, entities, and their tags. You need to know these building blocks of SGML backward and forward. You must know what these terms mean, as well as how to make declarations for them in documents and in DTDs in order to build an SGML application. Because you must also understand how the structural components of your documents differ from content, this chapter makes some suggestions in that vein.

In this chapter, you learn:

- What the document components, elements, attributes, entities, and content are and how to use them
- What the components of a DTD and its markup are
- What tags are
- What declarations you find in documents and DTDs
- What the difference is between declarations in DTDs and documents
- Tips on keeping your content and structure straight with structural diagrams

What Are the Components of SGML Documents?

SGML documents consist of *content* and *markup*. Note that format is not necessarily considered an integral part of an SGML document since a single document's content can appear in many different formats. The content is what you want to say and the markup is the SGML that keeps the document's integrity as it moves through different environments. Your document's markup consists of two things: *tags* and *declarations*.

Tags are the marks that tell your SGML system—and all SGML systems—what structural role the content within the tags plays. SGML systems process all documents by interpreting SGML markup and portraying documents with their intended structure and content. Tags make for easy dismantling and reassembly of documents, just like professional movers who tag and box your belongings when they move you to a new house. For example, if your SGML processing system encounters `<TITLE>This is the title </TITLE>` in a document, it will treat the content appropriately and not lose track of it or its properties.

Document Declarations

Declarations are markup that makes special statements directly to your SGML processing system about how to process your document. They don't describe the structural role of particular content like tags do, but they tell the processing system standardized information, like what type of document is being processed and where its DTD is located. You normally make most declarations in DTDs, where tags are defined for document types, but individual documents must have declarations too.

Each SGML document is called a document *instance*. But you need to distinguish the document *type* from the *instance* of that type. For example, think of two document instances: a memo from the boss and a service bulletin on widget replacement. SGML systems need to be told that the memo from the boss is a "memo" document type and that the service bulletin on widget replacement is a "service bulletin" document type. (Though some SGML systems can nearly figure this out for themselves, they are the exception.) In SGML parlance, the memo from the boss is an *instance* of the memo document *type,* and the service bulletin on widget replacement is an *instance* of the service bulletin document *type.* The SGML processing system learns what type of document it is from special declarations at the beginning of each document.

The SGML Declaration and the DOCTYPE Declaration. Document instances in SGML require two types of declarations: the *SGML declaration* and the *DOCTYPE (document type) declaration.* (The word DOCTYPE actually appears in the declaration itself.) The SGML declaration tells the system that the document is an SGML document so that the system knows it should follow SGML rules while handling this document instance.

▶▶ See "The DOCTYPE Declaration," p. 177

But the system must also know the type of SGML document. The document type declaration tells the SGML system what type of document the instance is and says where the DTD for that document type resides.

These two declarations can exist in the same document together with the content and the rest of the SGML markup for that content, or they can reside in a separate document by themselves. Some SGML processing systems prefer these declarations in a separate document. The system then asks the user to identify the declaration file during processing. For example, when you use Microsoft's SGML Author for Word to create an SGML document instance, the program will want to know where the separate declaration file is. Other SGML document instances might have the declarations right at the beginning of the document itself, first the SGML declaration and then the DOCTYPE declaration.

The SGML declaration is not always necessary. If there isn't an SGML declaration for a document, the processing system will choose default values for certain processing variables like character set (English or Hebrew, for example). Figure 3.1 shows a document example with the SGML declaration followed by a DOCTYPE statement.

```
  <!SGML     "ISO 8879:1986"
  -- Default SGML declaration using the core concrete syntax --
  -- CHARSET Default SGML declaration using the core --
  -- concrete syntax --
  CHARSET
  BASESET    "ISO 646-1983//CHARSET International Reference Version
  (IRV)//ESC 2/5 4/0"
  DESCSET  0    9  UNUSED
          9     2  9
         11     2  UNUSED
         13     1  13
         14    18  UNUSED
         32    95 32
        127     1 UNUSED
  — CAPACITY   PUBLIC "ISO 8879-1986//CAPACITY Reference//EN" --
  CAPACITY   SGMLREF TOTALCAP 50000
  SCOPE      DOCUMENT
  SYNTAX
  SHUNCHAR   CONTROLS 0 1 2 3 4 5 6 7 8 9 10 11 12 13 14 15 16 17
             18 19 20 21 22 23 24 25 26 27 28 29 30 31 127 255
  BASESET    "ISO 646-1983//CHARSET International Reference Version
  (IRV)//ESC 2/5 4/0"
  DESCSET  0  128  0
  FUNCTION   RE          13
             RS          10
             SPACE       32
             TAB   SEPCHAR 9
  NAMING     LCNMSTRT ""
             UCNMSTRT ""
             LCNMCHAR "-._"
             UCNMCHAR "-._"
             NAMECASE GENERAL YES
         ENTITY   NO
  DELIM      GENERAL   SGMLREF
             SHORTREF SGMLREF
  NAMES      SGMLREF
  QUANTITY   SGMLREF
             LITLEN 650
             NAMELEN 32
          TAGLVL 60
  FEATURES
  MINIMIZE DATATAG NO OMITTAG   YES    RANK    NO    SHORTTAG YES
  LINK     SIMPLE  NO IMPLICIT  NO     EXPLICIT NO
  OTHER    CONCUR  NO SUBDOC    NO     FORMAL   YES
  APPINFO   NONE>
  <!DOCTYPE SB PUBLIC "-//ATA-BOEING//DTD SB-BOEING-VER2-LEVEL3//EN">
```

Fig. 3.1

ATA's SGML declaration and DOCTYPE statement for a Service Bulletin.

You'll notice the SGML declaration seems long and complex. At the early stage of learning SGML, you don't need to understand each facet of this declaration. You just need to know that it exists and that it precedes the DOCTYPE declaration that locates the DTD for the processing system. Often, the SGML declaration is omitted simply because a default set of values is used. For now, just pay close attention to the last line, which is the DOCTYPE statement.

System and Public Identifiers. In figure 3.1, the SGML processing system will look for the DTD in the DOCTYPE statement under `-//ATA-BOEING//DTD SB-BOEING-VER2-LEVEL3//EN`. The system must find this DTD in order to complete processing. There are other possible formats for a DOCTYPE statement; you'll see some of them in future examples in this chapter and other chapters. A brief explanation of them will help you.

Identifiers are the part of the declarations that locate resources for the SGML processing system. Identifiers are like addresses with zip codes. When you have identifiers, the processing system can jump right to the correct resource's location whether it's on your personal computer's hard drive or on some enormous main frame's CD-ROM jukebox on the Internet in Fiji. There are basically two types of identifiers: system and public.

System identifiers point to resources on your local system while *public* identifiers point to remote resources somewhere in the public domain. The syntax for each is easy to recognize:

```
<!DOCTYPE manual SYSTEM "c:\SGML\DTD\manual.dtd">
```

This sample illustrates what the SYSTEM identifier looks like; you don't have to look very far for the `manual.dtd`. If you were storing the DTD in the same directory, the statement might read:

```
<!DOCTYPE manual SYSTEM "manual.dtd">
```

In either case, the word SYSTEM is used to locate the DTD on the local system.

Public identifiers point to resources that are publicly available. The word PUBLIC says that the resource is a shared resource. Here's a sample:

```
<!DOCTYPE sampledoc PUBLIC "-//AnyCorp//DTD sampledoc/EN">
```

This says that the `sampledoc` DTD is owned by AnyCorp Ltd. The EN means that the resource is in English. The `-//` means the resource is unregistered by AnyCorp.

Formal public identifiers are either defined by the International Standards Organization (ISO)—and are publicly accessible or registered by somebody other than the ISO—or they are unregistered. Samples of each follow.

First, the ISO sample:

```
<!DOCTYPE docname [
<!ENTITY % ISOpub PUBLIC "ISO 8879-1986//ENTITIES Publishing//EN"
--other declarations could go here--
%ISOpub;]>
```

You recognize the DOCTYPE statement, but the word ENTITY probably looks new. Suffice it to say that it's a structural component of a document that's discussed later in this chapter. But the nice thing about an international standard like SGML is that you can reuse many of the same resources, like this entity, at the same time all over the world. That's the purpose behind the ISOpub entity. It consists of a host of declarations and definitions that can be recognized by any SGML processing system. It's like a contract boilerplate that all lawyers recognize when they see it. When the system sees this ISOpub statement, it recognizes a familiar contract boilerplate, so to speak. It knows just what's expected of it during the processing of the document markup.

Next, here's a sample of a public resource that someone other than the ISO has registered:

```
<!DOCTYPE docname [
<!ENTITY % IBMchars PUBLIC "+//IBM//ENTITIES IBM PC Character Set//EN"
--other declarations would go here--
%IBMchars;]>
```

Notice the +// after PUBLIC. That means it's a registered public entity or resource. International Business Machines made their character set public for personal computers. Since they made it public, the information is like that contract boilerplate that everyone can use. This idea saves the lawyers the necessity of having to reinvent the wheel for every contract. The same idea saves SGML processing systems from having to reinvent the same public information over and over again for every document they have to process.

Last, here's a sample of a public resource that is unregistered:

```
<!DOCTYPE sampledoc PUBLIC "-//AnyCorp//DTD sampledoc/EN">
```

Notice the -//. The minus sign tells the system this resource is unregistered. That means that the sampledoc DTD had better be handy so the processing system can use it. This is the same example used a few paragraphs above. But does it make a little more sense now? When put in context with the other PUBLIC identifiers, it's a little easier to understand.

Parts of a Tag

One thing you haven't learned about yet are the individual tags themselves. They are the actual characters that the processing system must recognize as markup and not confuse with the document's content. The SGML system's ability to make this distinction is what enables SGML to work. For the system to work, it must rely on very special characters in very consistent locations in a very standard order. If these characters are out of order or are missing from the expected order, the SGML processing system will not be able to process the document.

SGML documents come to the processing system as if they were on a conveyor belt in an assembly line. To be automated, the assembly line must have the right part at the right place at the right time. If a bumper is supposed to be put on a car on the assembly line, the object on the conveyor belt had better not be a raw engine block. The body has to be on the conveyor belt with the holes drilled for the fastening of the bumper. Tags are on a similar SGML conveyor belt, and the right tags have to show up at the right time, or else the conveyor belt might stop or, worse yet, build something wrong that has to be fixed at your expense. Therefore, tags must follow a certain *syntax*, or precise method of expression, so that any SGML processing system will recognize and interpret them properly. Consider the following sample:

```
<TITLE>Here's A Whiz Bang Title</TITLE>
```

Notice that there are six basic components as you read from left to right:

Component	Description
<	Start tag open delimiter
TITLE	Tag's generic identifier
>	Start tag close delimiter
</	End tag open delimiter
TITLE	Tag's generic identifier
>	End tag close delimiter

Each of these tag components has what is called an *abstract name*. Abstract names are frequently used in SGML as a quick way of referring to parts of declarations by their position. Because it's critical for a document processing system to interpret every mark correctly, every character has a special name and abbreviation. If the correct syntax for these tags is not followed and misses by only a character, it could cause a big problem. That's why every single character in a tag must be accounted for. To help account for each character in a tag, abstract names and their abbreviations have been useful. You'll learn more about this in Chapter 10, "Following General SGML Declaration Syntax." Here are some examples:

Example	Abstract Name
<	STAGO (Start Tag Open)
>	STAGC (Start Tag Close)
</	ETAGO (End Tag Open)
>	ETAGC (End Tag Close)
TITLE	GI (Generic Identifier)

You now have a framework for learning about elements, attributes, and entities. These are the larger SGML boxes into which your document's belongings will be loaded for professional moving to another system. What you've learned about until now has had more to do with the immediate and rudimentary tasks an SGML processing system must complete before it starts seeing any document content. When it sees its first element tag, it's ready to begin working on the content of the document. This is where SGML gets interesting because these are the tags that determine how well your document weathers its electronic voyage.

Elements

Elements are the major structural components of your documents. If you were to box up your house and have professional movers move you to another city, they would probably label boxes for each room in the house and attach the appropriate labels to those boxes so you would know what room each box belongs in when it arrives at the new house.

Likewise, when SGML documents make an electronic journey, they need boxes in which to make the trip. Elements are the labeled boxes that make your document's electronic trip happen in an organized way. There are large elements that cover large segments of your documents and small elements that cover very small segments of your document. Big elements often include smaller elements.

You'll notice in the following memo example that there are several *elements* (see fig. 3.2). They have names like <MEMO>, <TO>, <FROM>, and <BODY>.

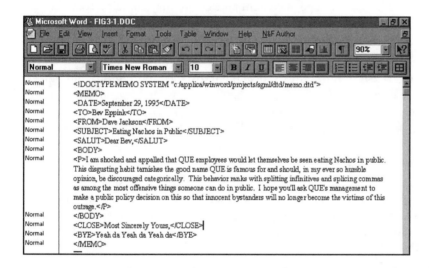

Fig. 3.2

This memo with SGML markup shows the SGML declaration and the elements that comprise it.

You'll notice, too, that all of the elements in figure 3.2 appear in a particular order. <DATE> comes before <TO>, <TO> comes before <FROM>, and so on. You're back to the SGML conveyor belt and assembly line idea. Your SGML system checks the DTD and then expects to see these elements in their correct positions on the conveyor belt so the document can be properly assembled. <DATE> must come before <TO> or the assembly line will stop or make a mistake with your document.

Also, notice that some elements can include other elements. For example, <P> occurs inside of the <BODY> element, and the <BODY> element occurs inside of the <MEMO> element. The <BODY> element is said to *contain* the <P> element and the <MEMO> element is said to contain the <BODY> element.

SGML Development

Hierarchy in SGML is a word that describes which elements fit within which other elements. Just as big moving boxes have little boxes inside, so it is that big elements have little elements within them. If the <MEMO> element contains the <BODY> element, the <MEMO> element has a higher hierarchy.

The order and hierarchy of a document's elements are part of the structural definition for that document type. The DTD for the memo in figure 3.2 must define the relationships between elements. Relating elements in a document type is covered in Chapter 8, "Relating Elements to Each Other." Like characters in a play, elements must come on stage "on cue," not before or after the DTD says for them to.

Also, elements must contain only the type of document content that the DTD says they can contain. They must have no "unauthorized" content. For the <P> element to occur outside of the <BODY> element would be like the families of Romeo and Juliet reconciling in the first act. They would not be true to the characters and would undermine the dramatic tension of the entire production. <P> content occurring outside of <BODY> content would invalidate this SGML instance as a type of MEMO document.

Speaking of content, you'll often hear the term *content model*. A content model is the statement in the DTD of what type of content an element may contain. In the example <P> and <BODY>, you could say that <P> must be part of the content model for <BODY>.

Look at figure 3.2 again. The SGML system must know when the document instance starts and stops, so <MEMO> must start the document instance and </MEMO> must appear at the end of the document. This is like a dramatic script, where stage directions come first and THE END occurs last. Otherwise, just like an SGML processing system, if you got to the last page, but there was no THE END, you might think you were missing something.

Elements can have *attributes*. Attributes are markup of an element's tags that further defines aspects of the element and helps them tell the SGML processing system more information than elements can tell by themselves. Elements can have many attributes or no attributes. Extending the script for a dramatic production analogy, the character of Romeo could be a single element with attributes. The attributes for <ROMEO> could be similar to the following:

Attribute	Value
Age	16
How Many Scenes	17
Number of Lines	297
Gender	Male
Survives	No

> **Note**
>
> Please don't take the time to check the values in this example. The values in the right-hand column are mostly fictitious.

Attributes come in handy when talking about elements. Attributes save you from inventing lots of redundant elements. They let you create different strains of a single element. By doing so, they simplify the markup in your document. They make life much easier. You'll learn more about them in the next section of this chapter, which discusses the syntax and looks at examples of attributes.

In summary, here are some characteristics of elements:

Characteristic of Elements	Purpose of Characteristic
Labeled "boxes" of document content	Marks beginning and end to content of element
<ELEMENTNAME> begins element tag	Shows where elements start in a document
</ELEMENTNAME> ends element tag	Shows where elements end in a document
Elements may appear only in the order and hierarchy the DTD says they can	Further defines document structure
Elements include other elements	Elements with smaller scope can be freely used inside elements with broader scope
Can have attributes	Enables you to use one element in a variety of contexts without having to create many similar elements that resemble each other
Used in every SGML document	These are the basic building blocks of SGML documents

Attributes

Attributes are like the different flavors of an element. If ice cream were an element, "flavor" could be equal to "strawberry," "vanilla," or "chocolate." As mentioned above, attributes are the different aspects of the element that must be defined for the SGML system to process an element in a document. For example, if your document has a graphic image that is embedded in its content but that must be loaded into the document during processing, there had better be some attribute to the <GRAPHIC> element that tells the system where to find the image. So, <GRAPHIC> could have a location attribute whose value could be either "remote" or "local."

In an SGML document, attributes appear as part of the opening tag for an element. For example, the graphic with the location attribute just mentioned would look like this:

```
Here's sample text for a document.
Now see a reference to this sample figure. See Figure 1.
```

```
If you wanted to insert the figure here <GRAPHIC location="local">
then the rest of the text could come later.
```

The syntax for the attribute is as follows:

```
<GRAPHIC location="local">
```

An element can have as many of these attributes as it needs. Take the example of a memo—again, similar to the one in figure 3.2. But this time, suppose that the memo contains sensitive information and must have a restricted distribution. Also suppose that the memo is secret and requires a security clearance. You have two conditions that you want to keep track of in all your memo type documents, so you want to add two attributes to the <MEMO> element; call them *distribution* and *clearance*. Give each of these attributes two possible values, although they each could have more. Suppose that distribution can be either "full" or "limited" and that security clearance can be either "required" or "none." How would a memo like that look? Here's one possible example:

```
<MEMO distribution="limited" clearance="required">
<TO>Joe Mainman</TO>
<FROM>Cloak N. Dagger</FROM>
<BODY><P>The bird has flown South for the winter.</P></BODY></MEMO>
```

So, attributes can apply to any element at any level in the document. Big elements can have them and even very small elements can have them. Elements with any type of content model can have them. Figure 3.3 shows another example of how the memo from figure 3.2 might look with attributes added.

Fig. 3.3

The <DATE>, <SALUT>, and <P> elements have been modified. For example, "format" and "abbrev" further modify <DATE>, so different presentations for this element can exist in the same document.

Modified elements

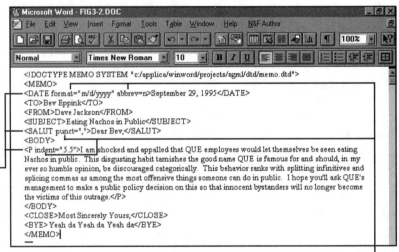

Attributes

Two Styles of Attributes. As you've seen, attributes in a document instance must be set to a value if such a value applies. There are two basic styles (or forms) for setting an attribute's value. One style includes the equal sign (=) and one does not. One is a sort of shorthand, while the other style "spells it out," so to speak. The style with the equal sign is the more common form, while the other form allows attribute values to appear by themselves. Both styles are acceptable. Both accomplish the same function, to tell the SGML system that is processing your document the current value of the attribute in question. Here are examples of each:

```
<GRAPHIC location=local>
```

or

```
<GRAPHIC local>
```

Which method should you use? You'll be safest if you always use the equal sign. Just stating the value of the attribute without the equal sign is the shorter way, but it's not as explicit. Adding the equal sign won't add that much more work. See table 3.1 for a summary of these two styles of attributes.

Table 3.1   Styles or Forms of Attributes

Style	Example
Common (with =)	`<SALUT punct=",">`
Shorter form (without =)	`<SALUT ",">`
Without quotes	`<SALUT comma>` or `<SALUT punct=comma>`

When To Use Quotation Marks with Attributes. You probably noticed that sometimes attributes use quotes and sometimes they don't. Basically, if an attribute's value contains anything other than numbers or letters, the value must be set off with quotes. That means that if there are spaces, punctuation, symbols, or any non-letter or non-number, you must use quotes around the value. It can be confusing at first, but the rules are pretty simple. Table 3.2 gives you the basic idea.

Table 3.2   Determining When To Use Quotations with Attributes

Description	Example
Attribute value includes only alpha or numbers	`<SALUT punct=comma>` no quotes required
Attribute value includes non-alphanumeric characters	`<SALUT punct=",">` quotes required
Attribute doesn't include "="	`<SALUT ",">` or `<SALUT comma>` quotes are optional

The thing to remember is whether or not your attribute value has any character other than letters or numbers. If you have so much as a blank space between two words, use quotation marks. Your safest bet is to just use quotation marks. You can't go wrong that way.

When Attributes Aren't Enough. Some types of content can't be described by elements and attributes alone. There are a number of times when you want to introduce something that is unique—say a special character, like a circumflex (^), for example—and you don't want to associate it with either an element or an attribute. That's when you want to use what's called an *entity*.

An entity is a markup component of a document, something like an element. But entities are more like superelements because you can do more with them than you can with elements. Entities are multipurpose moving boxes that not only can move your document's content, but can also provide for transport shortcuts along the way. They help the SGML processing system do its job smarter. If elements and entities were chess pieces, elements would be like bishops or castles that move many spaces either at right angles or diagonally, but not both. Entities would be like the queen who can move in any direction, except you can use as many of them as you need. Entities are no less valuable to your document than the queen is to a chess player. They are extremely flexible and will save the day when nothing else can.

Entities

There are at least five cases when you need to use entities in your SGML document. For each of these five cases, elements and attributes are not enough:

- You need to use some special character, like a dollar sign ($), that isn't in your character set. (Since SGML was developed long ago on ASCII terminals when only alpha-numeric ASCII characters could support document interchangeability, any other characters are considered "special characters.")
- You need to include information from some external file in an SGML document, such as a spreadsheet that's updated everyday.
- You want to use a shorthand notation in the authoring process without the shorthand being visible to the document user. For example, if you want to author SGML legal documents, you can substitute "POFP" for "party of the first part," and whenever you type the abbreviation, the entire text appears in the SGML document.
- You want to use *parameter entities*—meaning a "variable" within your DTD. You learn more about these in the next section.

Two Types of Entities: General (&) and Parameter (%). When entities appear in documents, they look like these examples: &CALS;, %ememo;, %ISOpub;. Entities either use & or % in front to identify themselves. *General entities* always use & and *parameter entities* always use % in documents. Furthermore, there are internal and external entities for both general and parameter entities. Both entities require a *close delimiter*, or something that turns it off. The close delimiter is a semicolon.

General entities are substitutes for characters or strings. Use them when you want to denote a special symbol or string of characters. For example:

&CALS;   Computer Aided Logistics Support

}   ASCII value for character 125 of the set: "}"

Parameter entities are substitutes for larger objects like document types or character sets in DTDs. Use them when you want to refer to public entities or make model group references. For example:

%ememo;   Special model of document good for this one instance only

%ISO123;   ASCII character numbered 123 in the current character set

There are two types of both general and parameter entities. Both types of entities can be grouped further by *internal* and *external entities*. See figure 3.4 for an illustration of these groupings.

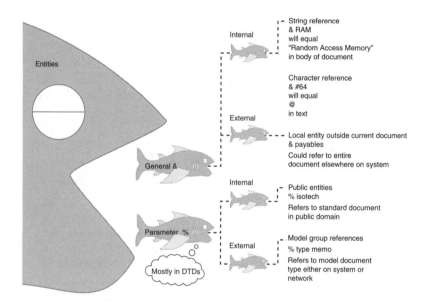

Fig. 3.4

Entities fall into two broad categories, general and parameter entities.

Each of the two categories in figure 3.4 falls into internal and external entities. There are internal and external parameter entities, as well as internal and external general entities. Parameter entities usually show up in DTDs, while general entities can show up in documents or in DTDs.

General entities deal with string and character substitutions of one kind or another for document content. Parameter entities contain system processing information.

Internal and External General Entities. Think of internal general entities in terms of character references and string references. These characters or strings could be like small sections of contract boilerplate or special foreign characters for which you need a convenient way of referring to in text. Or, suppose you want to tell the SGML system that CALS always means *Continuous Acquisition and Lifecycle Support* rather than the now-obsolete *Computer-Aided Logistics Support*. You could use an internal general entity, &CALS, for example. You could also use these characters or strings with equations or special features of text, such as superscripts and subscripts. See the following example of the De Broglie relation, which is an important physics equation, developed in 1927, that expresses the wave-like properties of the electron.

SGML Development

I

Here's what it would look like before it became tagged with SGML:

```
Now we turn our attention to the De Broglie relation: Λ=h/p
```

Here's what it might look like in an SGML document instance:

```
<para>Now we turn our attention to the De Broglie relation:
<equation id=broglie>&wavelen;=&hvalue;<over>&momentum;</equation><para>
```

Somewhere, the symbols for Λ and h and p would have to be defined; in this case as &wavelen;, &hval;, and &momentum; respectively. And the division symbol would have to be defined as <over> in this case.

External references are references to bigger objects, like a chapter or block of text. These could be whole modules of your document content, or even documents within documents. The external general entity could be a file that gets loaded into your document from some external resource. If you were processing an entire book at one time, you could make each chapter an external general entity—&chp1;, &chp2;, and so on—so your processing system wouldn't have to load the entire book at one time. It could process your book dynamically as necessary.

> **Note**
>
> During processing, the SGML system must be able to locate all external and internal entities and resolve their values. If they are not available locally, they must be made available or you will get a parsing error.
>
> A *parsing error* is an SGML system error during document processing. It means the SGML processing system, like a conveyor belt in an assembly line, is experiencing a technical difficulty and might even have to stop. At the very least, you will have to address the technical difficulty.

 ▶▶ See "Evaluating Parser Output Messages," p. 244

Internal and External Parameter Entities. *Parameter entities* deal with document substitutions or references that are usually outside the scope of the document itself. On the document level, you would normally see parameter entities in the SGML declaration, particularly if you're calling on external character sets for special symbols, or on PUBLIC information like that mentioned in the discussion on declarations earlier in this chapter.

Parameter entities always start with the opening delimiter, which is a % sign, followed by the name of the entity and the closing delimiter, which is a semicolon (;).

You'll run into parameter entities in documents when there's some section of text that must be treated specially. For example, sometimes you want to tell the SGML system to ignore a section of text, but because IGNORE is a reserved word that can only be used under special circumstances in SGML markup, you would probably want to use a parameter entity for it. Suppose you tell the SGML system in your DTD for a document that the entity `%ign` means "IGNORE" in your markup and elicits the proper behavior from the SGML system without alarming it with a reserved word. Your document instance might have markup like this:

```
There are two sentences of text that might apply here.
This phrase does apply, it so happens.
<![ %ign; [But this text does not apply, so we must ignore it now.]]>
Here's where the normal text continues after the ignored text.
Just like nothing happened. And all we'd have to do is change the value
of %ign to "INCLUDE" in the DTD and the section would not be ignored in
any of the instances for that DTD.
```

This example is for an *internal* parameter entity because the entity applies just to this document. The processing system is not going beyond the local scope of this system to resolve the value of this entity.

External parameter entities become important when you refer to public DTDs or fragments of data that you need to borrow for the processing of your document. Public DTD fragments frequently are referenced by using external parameter entities. Basically, if there's some DTD in the public domain to which you want to refer or if there's some document type that you want to use as a model, you can do so using a parameter entity in your DTD. The machine that processes your DTD has to be able to find it on your system or network, however.

Document Content

The most important part of your SGML document is the content itself. Content isn't just the alpha and numeric characters strung together to form words and sentences, it's also the meaning you want to convey with them. The characters all strung together are just the medium through which that meaning gets conveyed. So *content* can loosely refer to both the vast character string, as well as the meaning you want them to convey when they're assembled properly.

What Are the Components of DTDs?

The building blocks of DTDs are much the same as those of SGML documents. It's just that they're more involved and thorough in DTDs. Just as documents have elements, attributes, and entities, so do DTDs, but they look different and are more specific. That's because every element, attribute, and entity that is mentioned in a document must be *defined* in a DTD for that document type. How those definitions appear in the DTD is called *DTD syntax*.

> **Note**
>
> Because the DTD must *define* all the elements, attributes, and entities found in all documents of its document type, it must follow a specific format for doing so. While there is a fair amount of flexibility one can have with DTDs, *syntax* is not negotiable. If you fail to follow DTD syntax, your documents will not parse.

▶▶ See "SGML Declaration Syntax (or "What Are All Those Angle Brackets Anyway?")," p. 172

DTDs and Declarations for Elements, Attributes, and Entities

DTDs have a lot to do. When it comes to declarations, DTDs must define all the elements, attributes, and entities of the document type and describe everything possible about that definition. And it must all happen within a very short space. Specifically, here's the minimum of what a DTD must accomplish in its declarations:

- Provide the names of all elements used in a document type.
- Specify the type of content of each element, including which other elements may compose each element.
- Specify which order each element must appear in.
- Define how often an element may appear in a document.
- Decide whether shorthand can be used with the tag delimiters (this is called *minimization* and mainly applies to the manual tagging process, which may not be applicable to your situation).

 ▶▶ See "Tag Minimization," p. 186

- Specify whether *short references* (shorthand references to an entity within the text content of a document) can be used. (This is primarily for the manual tagging process and may not apply to your situation).

 ▶▶ See "Tagging Shorthand," p. 289

- Define which attributes for each element exist.
- Define the default values for each attribute.
- Define any entities that may exist in the document type.
- Declare the document type.
- Declare any comments regarding any of the above or any general comments about the document type of which anyone else reading the DTD should be made aware.

Components of a Declaration in a DTD

Declarations contain groups, connectors and/or tokens, and names. An example of an element declaration with its attribute declaration appears below:

```
<!ELEMENT table  - - (title, ((tgroup+, tnote?)¦graphic))>
<!ATTLIST table      %stdatt;
                     label CDATA #IMPLIED>
```

This declaration declares `table` as an element and says it must be composed of `title`, followed by either one or more instances of `tgroup` and possibly `tnote`, or one instance of `graphic`. That is, you get `title` followed by `tgroup` possibly followed by `tnote`; or you get `title` followed by `graphic`. The declaration further lists two attributes of `table`: one is the entity `stdatt` and the other is the element `label`. `Label` is composed of CDATA (character data), and the attribute default is determined by the processing system.

SGML knows what to expect after it sees certain keywords and symbols. Everything means something in a DTD. Let's just start with the `table` element declaration (see table 3.3).

Table 3.3 Parts of the Element Declaration

Component	What It Means
`<!ELEMENT`	Tells SGML you're declaring an element
`table`	The name of the element
`- -`	Says no minimization of either start tag or end tag delimiter
`(title,` `((tgroup+, tnote?)¦graphic))`	This is the whole name group
`(title,`	First component of `table`
`((tgroup+, tnote?)¦graphic))`	Second component of `table` (this component uses one of two possible subcomponents)
`(tgroup+, tnote?)`	First possible subcomponent
`graphic`	Second possible subcomponent
`>`	End declaration delimiter

The `,`, `(`, `+`, `¦`, and `?` are called *connectors* and *occurrence indicators*. They tell the parser when and how often to expect components specified in a declaration. These occurrence indicators are used in the groups of a DTD.

Connectors and Occurrence Indicators

Connectors and occurrence indicators are the symbols that tell the parser how many and in what order elements must appear in a document. For more information, please refer to Chapter 10, "Following General SGML Declaration Syntax." Table 3.4 summarizes each symbol and its meaning.

Table 3.4 Connectors and Occurrence Indicators	
Symbol (Connectors)	**Meaning**
,	Sequence (means "followed by")
&	and (all items must occur but they can be in any order)
¦	or (only one of the alternatives may be used)
Symbol (Occurrence Indicators)	**Meaning**
?	Optional (only zero or one may appear)
*	Optional and repeatable (zero or more may appear)
+	Required and repeatable (one or more *must* appear)

You'll see these connectors and occurrence indicators again and again. DTDs are full of them. Of course, if you're lucky enough to be working with an installation where the DTDs are already developed, you won't need to learn these. But in that case, you probably won't have to worry much about learning SGML either.

Occurrence indicators are handy because you want to enforce the right amount of structure in your document types. This golden means of flexibility is tricky to build into a DTD unless you can tell a processing system to make a "roll call" for each type of element in every type of model group. Some document structures require great flexibility and will have occurrence indicators with the zero or repeatable indicator (*). Paragraphs within a <BODY> structure would probably be required and repeatable (+) because you'll need at least one paragraph, but you will want to allow for as many as needed, and no fewer. You would need a lot of flexibility for that <PARA> element. But other elements might be required once or not at all. For example, a memo would require only one date, if any were necessary at all. So, you might want to give the <DATE> element an occurrence indicator of optional (?). In an SGML "roll call," not only must every document structure be present and accounted for, any present but unaccounted for structures get "thrown out!"

Groups in a Declaration

Declarations usually fall into groups in a DTD. Especially with large SGML installations, DTDs can become rather lengthy. This length calls for some sort of order in which to place the declarations in the DTD.

Comments will usually set off different groups of declarations of the DTD. See Chapter 12, "Formatting the DTD for Humans," for more about this. The basic idea is that whenever someone else has to go in and try to read the DTD, it would be nice if it all made sense to that person. These groups of declarations are different from groups in a single declaration. Within a single declaration, you normally group names with the connectors mentioned above. This keeps the naming easier to understand in a DTD.

> **Note**
>
> You should keep in mind the different uses of the word *group* in DTDs. One type of group refers to the three types of groups in declarations: model groups, name groups, and name token groups.
>
> The other use of the word group refers to the formatting of the overall DTD. It's good practice to separate declarations together into various groups. This improves clarity and makes the DTD easier for newcomers to read.

Using groups in a declaration improves the clarity of that declaration. Excluding Data Tag and Data Tag Template groups (you probably don't have to worry about those), there are three types of groups in DTD declarations:

- Model groups
- Name groups
- Name token groups

Model Groups. Model groups are those collections of elements in parentheses that you've seen earlier. They look like this:

```
<!ELEMENT table - - (title,(tgroup+, tnote?)|graphic))>
```

They are simply groups of *models* used in the declaration. So tgroup would be one model, tnote would be another, graphic would be another, and title would be still another. Their purpose is to define the contents of whatever is being declared.

Name Groups. A *name group* is actually part of a model group. The name group is the list of names within the parentheses. For example:

```
((tgroup+, tnote?)|graphic))
```

consists of the name group tgroup, tnote and the name group graphic. Each grouping within a pair of parentheses is one name group. Name groups have to have the same connector type. They can consist of one or more name token groups.

Name Token Groups. The individual names themselves are called *tokens*. The key here is that only one type of connector appears within a name token group. The example above shows tgroup and tnote in the same name token group. graphic is not in the same name token group. Here's another example:

```
<!ELEMENT strentry oo (para|nlist|blist|note|caut|warn|txteqn)+)>
```

The *name token group* consists of all the names from the left parenthesis and para to txteqn and the closed parenthesis, because they are all within the same parentheses and are all joined by the same connector.

Comparing Declarations in a Document and a DTD

The DTD is where the heavy-duty declaration happens. Any declarations in the SGML document are usually only echoes of the DTD. In fact, the primary declaration found within document instances is simply the SGML declaration. The following tables summarize the two sets of declarations, one for SGML documents and one for DTDs.

Table 3.5 Declarations Found in an SGML Document	
Declaration	**Purpose and How Different**
Doctype declaration	Says which DTD is applicable. This is also used to include various entity inclusions for the document.
SGML declaration	Contains specific information for SGML processing system that says which features are supported and which are not.

Table 3.6 Declarations Found in a DTD	
Declaration	**Purpose and How different**
Markup declaration	Purpose covered earlier. These are not covered in document instance.
	Includes keywords like ATTLIST, ELEMENT, and ENTITY. These are not found in documents.
Element declaration	Sets up each element so it can be used in individual documents.
Attribute declaration	Sets up all attributes for each element so they can be used in individual documents.
Entity declaration	"Initializes" entities so they can be used in documents. (Some entities can be set up in individual documents first, however, without having been set up in a DTD.)

As you can see, declaration happens a lot in DTDs, while only once in document instances. For further details on declarations and how to handle the details of DTD declarations and declarations in document instances, see Chapter 10, "Following General SGML Declaration Syntax."

Blending Content and Structure in Diagrams

As discussed in Chapter 2, blending content and structure in diagrams represents one of the most difficult challenges in SGML. But there are tools that you can use to help. *Structure diagrams* are one such tool.

Structure diagrams are much like tree diagrams that you read downward and to the right. The "blocks" on the left are structural blocks, while on the far right they become content blocks. The structure represents containers that the content fits into. When you take the content out of the structural containers, what you see is something like a structural diagram. It's possible to look at structure in different ways. It's also possible to structure a single document in different ways. Figure 3.5 shows the memo you examined earlier in figure 3.2.

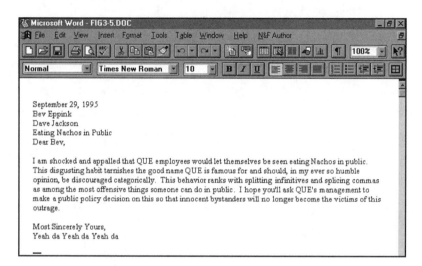

Fig. 3.5

The structure of this memo could actually be looked at in different ways.

SGML Development

For example, the memo could be structured as any one of the structure diagrams shown in figure 3.6.

As you can see, there are several ways to look at the memo example. Basically, you can gauge a document's structure by how much of a hierarchy is involved. If elements are nested 15 levels deep within each other, you either have a very complex document, or you should restructure it. The rule of thumb is to structure it as simply as your collection of documents will allow. You don't want to build in any more complexity than what already exists. If anything, you want to simplify your documents by making their structures accessible.

Example 1 is pretty good, except for the <INTRO> element. It doesn't really need to be there, and it introduces complexity that could be avoided. This means that for every collection of <DATE>, <SUBJECT>, <TO>, <FROM>, and <SALUTATION> tags, you have to add an extra set of <INTRO> tags. Why do that here? It doesn't really buy you anything.

Example 2 has a different problem. It's too flat. There's not enough hierarchy there. What that means is the paragraph can only appear after the salutation and before the closing. What if you wanted two or more paragraphs? It would be easier if you had a <BODY> element that included one or more <PARA> elements.

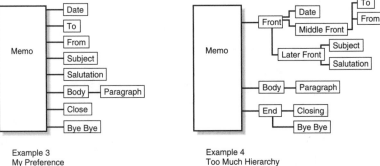

Fig. 3.6

This figure shows four different ways the same memo could be structured.

Example 1
Superfluous Element "Intro"

Example 2
Too Little Hierarchy of Elements

Example 3
My Preference

Example 4
Too Much Hierarchy

Example 3 is my personal preference. You don't have any more hierarchy than you need. Everything that needs to be there is there, and the structure doesn't add any more complexity to the document.

Example 4 has way too much complexity for the document. Even a two line memo would have to have <OPEN> and <CLOSE> tags for <FRONT>, <BODY>, and <END>, and the <FRONT> element would have to include <DATE>, <MIDDLE FRONT>, and <LATER FRONT>. The <TO> and <FROM> elements would have to be contained in the <MIDDLE FRONT> element, and <LATER FRONT> would have to include <SUBJ> and <SALUTATION>. That's very complex, and you're not even out of the first part of the two line document.

You want to find the golden mean when it comes to designing document structure. You don't want any more than is necessary, but you want enough for your needs. If you have too many structural elements, they complicate your markup and cost you more time with no added benefit. If you have too few structural elements, it's like trying to move your household without enough boxes in which to pack everything. With SGML, you want to be able to move your document's content smoothly, just like when the best professional movers pack up your household belongings and move them across the country for systematic unpacking in your new home. Moving documents is easier than moving people any day!

From Here...

In this chapter, you've covered what components go into SGML documents and DTDs. You've seen a little about how they look and what they do. You've seen what components make up the tags for all the tags used in SGML. You've briefly been exposed to how the tags between documents and DTDs are different in appearance and function. Declarations appear very differently in SGML documents and in DTDs. The syntax is completely different. Finally, you've seen how structure diagrams can help you keep structure and content straight.

- If you're ready for more in-depth coverage of writing DTDs, jump to Part III, "Content Modeling: Developing the DTD."

- If you specifically want more detail about elements, attributes, and entities, visit Chapter 10, "Following General SGML Declaration Syntax."

- If you want more details about DTDs, see Chapter 16, "Markup Challenges and Specialized Content."

- If you're ready for the next step in the overall process of doing SGML, see the next chapter, Chapter 4, "The Basic Procedure."

SGML Development

The Basic Procedure

Chapter 3 introduced you to many of the basic terms you'll encounter again and again; this chapter shows you the overall process that makes use of those terms. By following a consistent procedure for publishing SGML documents, you can take advantage of the experience of other publishers before you. This procedure has worked for many, and it can work for you.

There are two basic categories of tasks you must complete to become an SGML publisher: design tasks and production tasks. Just as you need plans to build a skyscraper or a home, you need to design your SGML endeavor before you actually go into the production of SGML documents. Once you have the design plans, you need an orderly way of producing what you designed. The basic SGML procedure includes five tasks all together, three design tasks and two production tasks. This chapter introduces these five tasks and talks about working with consultants.

In this chapter, you learn about how to:

- Conduct document analysis
- Develop content models
- Understand output specifications
- Understand native authoring and document conversion
- Parse your documents and your DTDs
- Work with consultants

This chapter gives you the conceptual foundation for the rest of the book. For example, Part II of this book expands on the first task discussed in this chapter, document analysis. Parts III and IV deal with content modeling and markup strategies. Before you are bombarded with the details of document analysis in chapters 6 through 9, for example, you'll need some framework to know where the process of document analysis fits.

Design tasks in this book receive more emphasis, largely because production tasks are becoming more and more automated with the introduction of "smarter" tools. Also, design tasks represent more of a mine field than production tasks because a mistake in design could cause you more problems, generally speaking, than a production problem. If you were building a house and your plans for the basement were wrong, the fact that the cement truck was an hour late would be less important. It's more important that the house you build fits on top of the foundation than that you build the house quickly. Preparing to build an SGML publishing enterprise is much the same way—your planning needs to be right if your production is to be effective.

Document Analysis

To build an SGML publishing enterprise, you must analyze the types of documents you will publish. SGML is very concerned with document structure; it requires you to understand the structural design for each of your document types. To understand this design, you must individually look at each different type of document you deal with: memos, service bulletins, technical manuals, technical papers, parts lists, customer literature—all your document types. Document analysis is the process of understanding each different document type, such as how your memos are structurally different from your service bulletins, for example. It's the process of understanding each type of document like a surgeon understands the human skeleton.

But just as the human skeleton is affected by the environment and other external factors over time, so SGML documents are affected by external factors. For this reason, documents must be examined first, not for their structure, but for their relationship with external policies and procedures. Only when you know what external requirements your documents must accommodate can you be certain which internal structure best suits each type of document. First you define the environment, and then you pick a document type and define it in detail. You repeat the definition process for each document type.

A surgeon must know more than the names of each part of the body; he must understand how each part relates to the rest of the body. In document analysis, you likewise must understand how each element of a document type relates to every other element in that document type; this is called defining your element relationships.

Since you're designing the types of documents you'll be using, you are taking a step beyond what a surgeon must know. You actually can improve upon your creation. In document analysis, this is called extending the architecture of your documents.

Whether you have a large publishing company and will deal with many document types, or whether you will publish a single type of document for the World Wide Web site, your steps in document analysis are the same. Here are the summarized steps:

1. Define your environment.
2. Define your elements.
3. Relate your elements to each other.
4. Extend your document architecture.

Defining Your Environment

This is the process of understanding what document types you have and how you use those documents. This includes considering the policies and guidelines (including any industry or company standards you must follow) and deciding if and how they will change your documents.

▶▶   See "Decide What Standards and Policies You Must Obey," p. 112

Defining your environment is like designing your dream house. You have to plan it before you build it. You have to make sure everything fits together on paper before you try to make it fit with physical building materials. If it doesn't fit (it's never perfect at first), the fix is easier to make while it's still on paper than it is to make once your dream house is under construction.

Caution

Don't be too quick to breathe a sigh of relief because you think you're a small one-person installation. You can still have complex policies and external considerations that will slow down your progress. Defining your environment is crucial for discovering and resolving these conflicts.

For example, your Internet provider can have space restrictions or equipment maintenance schedules that dictate how and where you link structural components of your online documents together. This type of conflict should become evident during the process of defining the environment.

When you've completed the process of defining your environment, you should know all your different types of documents and what you intend to do with them. If there are any "land mines" that will affect the path you chose, this is the time to map them out. In fact, following the dream house analogy, this is where you identify not only what type of house it is (i.e., Tudor, French Country, Colonial, and so on), but also the potential environmental hazards (frequent flooding, forest fires, mosquitoes, and so on).

For example, what if you're doing a government contract and you forget that security status, configuration management, and usable on codes (applicable to Illustrated Parts Manuals for the government) all have to be maintained in your documents? You must know these requirements before you start the SGML publishing process. After you define your environment, including defining which military specifications you must follow in your contract, you know the requirements you must build into your documents.

Defining Your Elements

Once you have established which environmental considerations you must accommodate and which document types you will design, you're ready to begin studying your first document type. A simple one is best to start, like the magazine article sample shown in figure 4.1.

You cut into the first document, pick out the structural components, and lay them to the side, much like a physiology student dissects a lab specimen. But in this case, your document is the first-ever lab specimen, so it's up to you to define each structural component as you go.

> ▶▶ See "The Definition Process," p. 137

During this step, you'll take each document type and list all its building blocks—its elements, attributes, and entities, only they won't look like `<para>tagged stuff</para>` yet. They'll be a little friendlier looking. See figure 4.1 for an idea of what this process looks like with a sample magazine article.

Fig. 4.1

Defining your elements is dismantling your document into its building blocks.

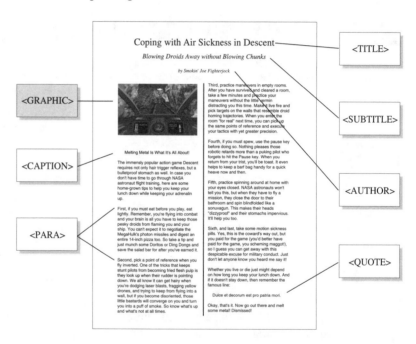

After dismantling your document, you'll have a summary of its building blocks. A magazine article could contain the building blocks listed in table 4.1.

Table 4.1 A Document Requires a Simplified Summary of Its Elements	
Element	**Description**
`<TITLE>`	Title of article for beginning of document
`<SUBTITLE>`	Optional subtitle for explanatory info about story

Element	Description
<AUTHOR>	Element used as byline
<PARA>	Paragraphs within article
<GRAPHIC>	Photos, cartoons, drawings, images
<CAPTION>	For use with <GRAPHIC> element
<QUOTE>	For indented text within paragraphs

Elements for other document types can be collected and listed, as shown in figure 4.2.

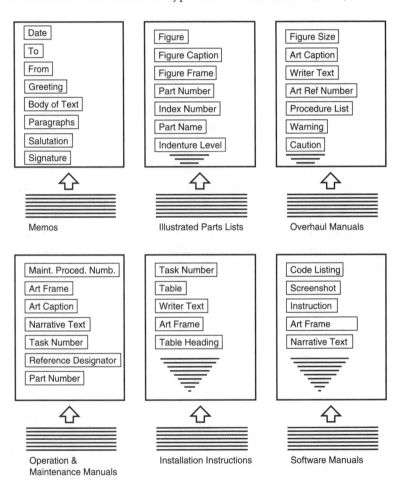

Fig. 4.2

Defining your elements is breaking your document types into their respective building blocks.

Memos

Illustrated Parts Lists

Overhaul Manuals

Operation & Maintenance Manuals

Installation Instructions

Software Manuals

SCML Development

Note

Don't worry about SGML syntax at this stage. Don't even worry about making it "look" like an SGML element.

At this stage, you can make notes on elements and attributes for DTDs, but you'll actually create those later (in content modeling).

Just have a clear idea of what you're going to put in those DTDs later.

Relating Elements to Each Other

The next step is determining sequence, hierarchy, and occurrence for each element of your selected document type. The elements in the magazine article example must appear in a certain sequence. For example, the title comes before the subtitle and the byline, and so forth. Also, certain elements may not occur outside of other elements, so they have a hierarchy. (For example, a graphic image could not be found outside of a paragraph. A quote could not be found inside a subtitle.) Some elements might occur only once, like the <TITLE> and <AUTHOR> elements, but there may be many <PARA> and <GRAPHIC> elements. However, for each <GRAPHIC> element, you must have a single <CAPTION> element. These are all examples of relating elements by sequence, hierarchy, and occurrence.

In addition to determining sequence, hierarchy, and occurrence, you can also group common elements together in this step. The magazine article example above is quite simple, but if you have to deal with complicated articles that have tables and math equations, you would need to define many more elements. In such a case, you could collect all table elements together in one group and all math equation elements together in another group. These groups of elements, and any others of your choice, would be very convenient when you design your DTD.

Extending Document Architecture

You extend a document's architecture when you add features to its design. Suppose you want to show equations in your magazine article documents. How do you get superscripts and subscripts? How would you get all the special symbols so commonly used in mathematics? You have to add them to your document design. That's an example of *extending* document architecture.

Sometimes in the middle or even after the design process is completed, you'll find capabilities you need to add. Fortunately, SGML allows you to do this. To make these changes easier to add in the future, you should count on allowing room to grow while you extend your document architecture. Just because you extend the architecture of documents by adding elements and attributes does not mean you have to use all those structures right away. You could even add elements like `<future1>` and `<future2>` that you'll rename at some point in the future when their use becomes expedient. Figure 4.3 shows an example of how you might add functionality to a memo document type.

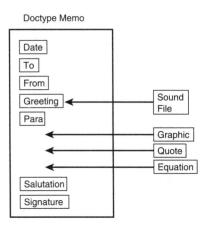

Fig. 4.3

Extending a document's architecture means adding functionality to it.

Note

The word "feature" has special meaning in SGML. The ISO 8879 standard specifies many different *features* that legally may be used within an SGML application. These features are commonly specified in the SGML Declaration and would explain whether, for example, features like short references are used and templates are permissible. I'm using "feature" here in the more familiar sense of the word rather than in the SGML sense of the word.

Developing the DTD (Content Modeling)

The second task of the design phase is to develop the DTD. This is where you state the results of your document analysis according to SGML syntax. Up until now, you've been doing the real work (believe it or not!). Once you understand SGML syntax, developing your DTD is primarily just a necessary detail. Completing your document analysis requires far more scrutiny than developing the DTD. Now you just have to express your document analysis in SGML form.

Developing the DTD involves four basic tasks:

- Make your SGML DTD declarations
- Express all your content models and element groups (DTD components) and their relationships
- Parse your DTDs
- Follow good SGML design practice

As usual, the scope of your SGML endeavor determines the length of this overall process. This step can be either very extensive or completed in an afternoon. Two different operations can look very different in terms of the complexity of their DTD development process. Part III of this book is devoted to developing the DTD for both large and small installations.

 ▶▶ See "Creating an SGML Environment from Scratch," and "Converting Existing Documents into SGML (Filtering)," pp. 88, 96

Note

Large SGML publishers differ from small publishers, not only in their document complexity but in the amount of historical or legacy data they must convert into SGML documents. Conversion of existing documents can be a major undertaking and can require extra DTD development above and beyond what is required for SGML authoring.

Making Your DTD Declarations

After you've decided what elements go into your DTD, you need to formally declare your document structures.

There are five structures you have to know how to declare:

- Document types
- Elements
- Attributes
- Entities
- Comments

When you've learned how to declare these document structures, you're well on your way to knowing SGML. The purpose of having an international standard like SGML is to specify a common universal way of expressing document structures so that any machine anywhere can recognize and reconstruct any type of document. In order for a machine to recognize something so abstract as a document structure—say, a quotation or a title—there must be highly standardized ways of identifying these structures. When you make the five declarations identified above in your DTD, you're giving the machine, as well as any human operator, a blueprint by which to assemble and disassemble any document instance of the type defined in that DTD.

Tip

It's best to start the DTD simply, with just a few elements, and then parse it. That way you can make sure it's working with just a few elements. Then add more elements and parse it again. Do this, and you'll identify problem areas easily and save time. You won't spend hours trying to find the bad declaration. Also, you'll get extra practice parsing!

Designing Components for DTDs

Often you'll have several DTDs you deal with on a regular basis. You'll increase your overall efficiency if you design modular components or groups of structures that can be used by several DTDs. When there are many different types of documents with similar structures, these modular components make maintaining your DTDs a lot easier (see fig. 4.4).

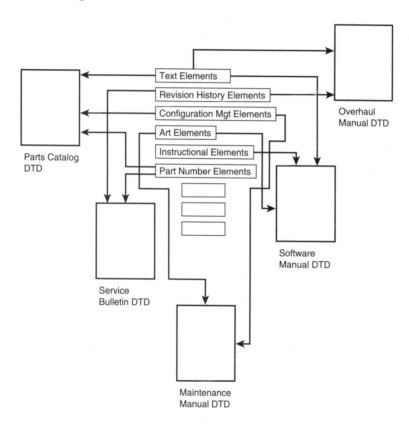

Fig. 4.4

DTD components help you reuse parts of your DTDs. They also make maintaining your DTDs much easier.

Many times, especially in big companies, there's more than one developer of DTDs. Usually, there is a team that develops the DTDs. Often, other people have to maintain the DTDs after the original developers are gone. The people who maintain the DTDs will change over time also. Making modular DTD components makes maintaining them far easier for everybody over the life of your documents and DTDs.

▶▶ See "When (and Why) To Use DTD Components" and "How To Make Components," pp. 190, 197

▶▶ See "Maintaining Your DTD," p. 239

> **Note**
>
> SGML's tremendous flexibility allows you to handle groups of document structures in many different ways to suit your own objectives. For example, if you observe that your magazine articles and your service bulletins both require math equation structures, you might find it helpful to build a *common DTD* that contains these structures so both your service bulletins and magazine article DTDs can take advantage of the same common structures. Common DTDs contain groups of structures that can be used by multiple DTDs. This makes maintenance much more convenient and orderly than having duplicate structures in several DTDs.

DTDs are like computer programs. They grow and evolve as people's needs evolve. Even if you have a single DTD to manage, you're still going to have to "tweak" it in time.

There are basically three ways to make modular components for DTDs, and they all depend on using parameter entities in DTDs:

- Make DTD components by *fragment assembly*. These are sometimes called DTD fragments. They are collections of common DTD structures that you reuse as much as you can between like DTDs. Keep a collection of these element subassemblies and use them to make whole DTDs. The earlier note about the common DTD for equations and tables is an example of this.

- Make DTD components with parameter entities. Sometimes you don't want to build entire DTDs with common elements, but you can still make parameter entities that perform "extra duty" so they can be used in multiple contexts and document types. Then, when you want to maintain the DTD component, just fix the one entity and you've fixed all DTDs that refer to that parameter entity. If you just want to use a small part of a table structure—a table caption definition, for instance—you can put the caption structure into a parameter entity and then define that entity as an element in your DTD.

- Make DTD components by redefining entities. You can redefine an entity within a DTD and then call another DTD or subassembly that defines the same entity. Thus, you're getting double duty out of that entity. For example, perhaps you want to use an existing table entity structure from the public domain but want to modify its caption element for your own needs. You could refer to the public entity, redefine the caption element in another one of your DTDs, and then refer to that DTD's redefinition. This way you can have the public table definition customized with your own caption definition.

▶▶ See "Fragment Assembly," p. 198
▶▶ See "DTD Redefinition," p. 198
▶▶ See "Defining Parameter Entities as Elements," p. 199

SGML Development

I

Evaluating DTDs

You evaluate DTDs by parsing them. The parser checks the DTD for compliance with the SGML standard and reports errors. Not only must your DTD specify your document design, it must do so within the rules of the SGML standard.

 ▶▶ See "Evaluating Your DTD," p. 233

Parsing a DTD is different from parsing an SGML document. The parser ensures that a document instance conforms to the definition specified in its DTD. The same parser ensures that the DTD follows the logic and syntax rules specified in the SGML standard. The DTD must strictly follow the international SGML standard so that when document instances are compared to it, the parser's analysis will be accurate.

Formatting the DTD for People (Not Machines)

If you don't want to be the cause of someone else's misery, you'll format your DTDs for people, not just the parser. Structure your declarations into groups so they can be easily located in the DTD. Add comments and notes throughout, just as you would in a computer program, so the next person can pick up the threads that you leave behind. Remember, there might be four or five different people—or more—who will maintain a DTD over its lifetime.

 ▶▶ See "Why Formatting DTDs Is Important," p. 201

Following Good SGML Practice

Because SGML is designed to be flexible, its conventions can tempt you to be too flexible and make unwise design decisions in your DTDs. Here are some common examples of poor decisions that you could make:

- You decide to use an element when you should have used an attribute
- You fail to handle content models properly, so you have ambiguous content that parses but causes your users a lot of problems
- Your DTDs parse, but you didn't test them under the same circumstances under which they will be used in production, so the DTDs don't actually work as promised

Defining Output Specifications

An *output spec* defines how your document looks and through what medium it's presented.

For example, suppose you have a database or archive of product information files. You'd like it to be downloadable by people from your company's electronic bulletin board system, as well as viewable by people who visit your Web site. You'd also like to be able to print copies of the product information files from your network printers by using an SGML browser application. And, you'd like people on your network to be able to load the files into their word processing documents as embedded objects. How those files look in each context is determined by your output specification.

Unfortunately, output specifications are a difficult and very specialized topic in SGML. The problem is that with output specifications, you move away from dealing with document structure and toward document format. Format and appearance controls will vary from machine to machine, so it's very difficult to provide a single specification that is usable on any type of processing system. There has been a project underway for several years to provide a *Document Style Semantics Specification Language* (DSSSL), but as of today it is still not complete.

▶▶ See "The View of a Document from an Output Perspective," p. 408

▶▶ See "Difficulties with Output Specifications," p. 419

▶▶ See "Output Specification Standards," p. 419

Just as application programmers must provide drivers (special hardware-specific programs for controlling hardware devices) for many popular printers so character fonts will print the same way on all printers, so must output specification designers make their formatting instructions comprehensible to all types of processing systems. It's tougher for output spec designers, however. When you buy WordPerfect in English, for example, the odds are that you have one of the popular American printers. But when you design an output spec for a document, that specification may need to be processed anywhere in the world on any type of machine, not just one that's popular in English-speaking countries. The DSSSL needs to be a universal language.

There is something called *DSSSL Lite* that is a subset of a universal language for output specifications. This is more of a draft specification, and it is not intended to meet the needs of all designers or processing systems, but it does provide a starting point for developing usable output specifications. For more information about the latest changes proposed to the DSSSL Lite, point your Web browser to:

http://www.sil.org/sgml/related.html#dsssl

You may be able to use an existing output specification. There are plenty in the public domain. You may be able to modify one for your purposes and make it conform to your standards.

Incorporating Document Markup

When you mark up a document, you are moving from the design phase to the production phase of the basic SGML procedure. Incorporating document markup involves putting tags into the individual document instances. How you do this depends on your situation. Do you have a lot of documents that have already been authored and now need to be tagged, or do you have a host of new documents that you want to author in SGML?

If your documents are already created, you have to convert them into SGML documents, using a conversion utility, such as Earl Hood's SGML extension to Perl. If the documents aren't created yet, you have the option of choosing an SGML author/ editing tool to create them. This is called *structured authoring*.

▶▶ See "The World of Perl," p. 491

▶▶ See Chapter 5, "Two Scenarios," p. 87

There are basically four types of tag insertion tools to use with SGML:

- Autotaggers (automated tagging tools)
- Transformers (conversion tools)
- Text editors (authoring and editing tools)
- Hybrid tools (combination of some of the above tools)

Document Parsing

Parsing document instances is easier than parsing DTDs. The main challenge of parsing document instances is handling documents that have specialized content. Even though parsing documents is usually a routine production task, specialized content can turn your documents into small nightmares.

Two of the more difficult examples of specialized content are tables and equations. Since tables are a delicate mix between format and structure in SGML, it is often best to parse them separately from the rest of your documents. Likewise, you may wish to parse equation-laden documents separately from simpler document instances. Since documents with specialized content can cause challenging parsing errors, it's probably best to not let them slow down parsing for the rest of your documents.

▶▶ See "Handling Tables" and "Handling Math and Equations," pp. 421, 424

Working with Consultants

To optimize your time with consultants, consider your work in two parts—the preparation work before they arrive and the actual consulting work while they're with you.

Before the Consultants Come

The more prepared you are for the consultant, the more value you'll get for your dollar per hour after he arrives. Most of what the consultant does depends on understanding your operation. If you can clearly communicate to the consultant what he needs to know, you'll make his job very easy, and your checkbook will reward you (it won't deflate as quickly). You should try to do three things before the consultant arrives: define your project, understand your essential document structure, and examine your legacy data issues.

Defining Your Project. You've chosen SGML because of the value it can add to your documents. You need to know which benefits you are most interested in. Which benefits are necessary and which are simply beneficial? For example, do you need to electronically deliver documents to your customers over a network? Must you publish books on CD-ROM? Will you need to query a database of SGML documents? You need to be able to list all the uses for your SGML documents so the consultant doesn't overlook any design features that must be built into your operation.

Understand Your Essential Document Structure. The difficulty here is that if you're hiring consultants in the first place, you're probably a fairly large operation, and you may be a manager who is not intimate with the documents you need to deal with. If you are very familiar with the documents, that's great. But if you aren't, you either need an in-house expert who is, or you need to become familiar with them yourself.

You're probably safest by both becoming as familiar as you can with the documents, but also involving your in-house expert(s) as early in the SGML process as you can. When the consultant asks questions like, "Do your service bulletins ever omit effectivity coding?" you must have the right answer. If you don't, you'll be wasting valuable time. And if you try to guess your way through and give a less than accurate answer, you could cause a bigger problem that you'll have to pay to resolve later.

Tip

If you must depend on one or more in-house experts, make sure they will be available to the consultants at any time. This may require you to reschedule their other responsibilities to allow them the flexibility they'll need in their schedule. Try to keep several people "up to speed" with your SGML project to prevent delays due to sickness, vacations, and so on.

Understand Your Legacy Data Issues. One thing your consultants will want to know is how much of your old data (*legacy data*) needs to be converted to SGML documents.

 ▶▶ See "Tricks, Traps, and Pitfalls," p. 103

Legacy data can be challenging because of gross inconsistencies between older documents and newer documents. For example, a service bulletin could appear nice and orderly if it's a current vintage. But if you intend to scan in service bulletins from 15 years ago, you'll run into instances where they don't even look like the same type of document. They could have been typed on manual typewriters, and there might not have been any authority for style and structure. So, heaven only knows how many variations you'll have to account for in your DTD if you insist on dealing with very old document types. Your consultant will want to know how intent you are about converting old data. It will make life much easier if you are able to omit converting very old documents.

After the Consultants Arrive

By doing the preparatory work above, your time with the consultants will be very productive. Your initial meetings will be smoother because you have a specific project definition. When the consultant asks detailed questions about the documents and their structure, you're ready to give accurate answers. And when the question of legacy data comes up, you're clear about what document conversion you need and what would be merely convenient.

Consultants need some specific guidelines for their relationship with you during your project together. You'll need to agree on specific performance objectives and when they'll be completed. The following are common points to agree on:

- Develop mutually agreeable milestones
- Agree on test and acceptance criteria
- When converting existing documents, agree on how you'll handle data that does not conform to your normal document structure
- When starting an SGML authoring process, expect to establish a long-term relationship with consultants; you'll need one, because it takes time to become confident in SGML

Note

One of the first things the consultants want to see is your document samples. Try to take them into your library so they can examine a range of samples of each document type. Be sure to include a lot of old documents if you plan on converting them. Show them the ugly old type-written service bulletins as well as the brand new service bulletins with the fancy tables. The only way to ensure an adequate design is to have a large document sample for each document type.

Combining Your Expertise with Their Expertise

Let's face it. You each have your areas of expertise. Consultants know SGML and you know your installation's goals and requirements. So how can you best combine your respective talents without stumbling over your respective weaknesses?

One approach is for each of you to remember what you need as well as what you can give. Focus on the process of exchange. To optimize your time together with consultants, be aware of what expertise you each bring and don't bring to your discussions, as shown in the following table.

Consultant's Expertise	Your Expertise
SGML design and syntax	Knowledge of purpose of project
Experience with similar projects and the time required for implementation systems	Knowledge of internal document handling procedures and processing
Knowledge of existing SGML compatible processing systems and their cost	Knowledge of current network infrastructure
Knowledge of what issues are relevant to overall SGML design	Knowledge of your customer's needs from documents

Tip

If you use a local area network, invite your systems administration personnel to meet your consultants. They'll need to communicate during the project. Also, ask your consultants how easy it will be to make changes to your structure in the future. That will determine whether they incorporate changes now or add features later.

For example, if you want to add multimedia extensions to your documents, ask them how easy it is to add later versus now, when you don't really have an application for it yet. It might be easier for them to set it up now for you to use later.

From Here...

This chapter has provided an overview of the basic procedure for becoming an SGML publisher. The design and production tasks described here are common to nearly every SGML publishing enterprise in existence. The cross references provided above will also direct you to the details on how to conduct each of the tasks associated with the basic SGML procedure.

For more information, refer to the following:

- Part II, "Document Analysis," covers document analysis.
- Part III, "Content Modeling: Developing the DTD," deals entirely with content modeling and DTD development.
- Chapter 24, "Understanding and Using Output Specifications," discusses specification design and practicalities.
- Part IV, "Markup Strategies," covers document markup and tagging.
- If you're considering SGML as an upgrade to HTML, look at Part V, "SGML and the World Wide Web."

CHAPTER 5

Two Scenarios

You have explored the basics of SGML—what it is, what the rules are, and how it all goes together. Before you can start producing SGML, you might want to consider a few more issues. Foremost among these are whether to generate your documents in a native SGML format or convert your documents into SGML. If you already have SGML authoring tools and you want to quickly generate some simple documents in SGML, you should skip to Part VII, "SGML Tools and Their Uses." If you want to set up a full-blown SGML authoring environment or if you have a collection of documents that you want to convert to SGML, this chapter is for you.

In this chapter, you learn about:

- Considerations when building an SGML authoring environment from scratch
- What issues to consider when converting existing documents into SGML
- The use of SGML parsers in validating documents

Some Recent History

Until recently, the process of getting documents into an SGML format was often a painful one. Getting authors to understand the SGML approach was difficult. Finding the right tools to produce SGML was even harder.

In the past, your options for producing SGML were restricted to either:

- Buying a high-end publishing system for a lot of money, installing it on an expensive computer system, and learning SGML; (You get the chance to do this while also learning the system and putting out SGML documents)
- Continuing to produce your documents with a standard word processor and then translating them into SGML

Today, there are many tools available, some better than others. New tools are appearing all the time, most of which add interesting improvements and approaches and provide a wealth of choice for authoring, viewing, and other supporting areas related to SGML.

As a budding SGML writer/publisher, you have some choices to make. Many of the choices depend on your situation, taking factors such as these into consideration:

- Will you be creating new documents or do they already exist?
- How many people are/will be authoring the documents?
- Are your authors the types who can readily accept the requirements of SGML authoring?
- What is your authoring environment (Microsoft Word, WordPerfect, Interleaf, Frame, etc.)?
- How are your documents structured?
- How do you expect the structure of your documents to change?

This chapter examines these issues and more. To help you figure out the best approach, you'll examine two ways of producing SGML: starting from scratch and converting existing documents into SGML.

Creating an SGML Environment from Scratch

Imagine you work for a company called AnyCorp. You have been directed to build an SGML authoring environment from scratch.

AnyCorp is a new, high-tech manufacturing company that produces widgets for consumer use. Naturally, AnyCorp's widgets are radically different from the competition's widgets. Its widgets are eagerly embraced by the buying public and acclaimed in a number of magazines as "the widget of the future."

In the glow of success, the president of AnyCorp calls you into his office. Although you feel good about AnyCorp's success (and your pivotal part in it), the president looks concerned. After a few pleasantries, the president begins, "It may look good for AnyCorp, but I'm concerned…"

The President's Message

"Although our widgets are revolutionary, that's not enough. Consumers are on waiting lists, buying them as fast as they can," the president intones. "Although it sounds good, there may be trouble brewing, just as it did with our competitors, Pterodactyl Corp. They came out of nowhere, just like us, ahead of the competition. They were very successful for a few years, and then trouble set in. First product problems arose, then sales plummeted, and then bankruptcy."

"Our sales are great, but they create problems of their own. Demand is so high, we can't get product information out to potential customers around the world. We've sold so much, we aren't even sure where the distributors are. When we don't know where they are, we can't get parts, repair and service instructions, or support information to them. Our products are improving so fast, we can't revise our manuals quickly enough." With a glum look, the president concludes, "If we don't do something different, we'll become another Pterodactyl."

What You're Going To Do

Turning to the president, you say, "I think SGML might be the answer. Using SGML, we can get product information out to the customer as soon as it's complete, we can support distributors and find out where they're located, and we can revise the manuals much more efficiently."

With a sigh, the president says, "Okay, I'll give SGML a try. You work out a plan and give me the results on Monday."

How are you going to save AnyCorp? With your knowledge of AnyCorp's documents, you're ready to build your SGML environment. This involves a number of steps, including the following.

- **Define your goals**. List what you want to accomplish by using SGML in this situation.

- **Document analysis**. Examine the documents to be included in your SGML library, analyzing their content to discern significant structural elements.

- **Document modeling**. Construct SGML models of the documents in your library in the form of Document Type Definitions (DTDs).

- **Parse your DTDs**. Confirm that the document models you have constructed are both structurally sound and legal according to the SGML standard (ISO standard 8879).

Defining the Goals

As you recall your conversation with AnyCorp's president, you come up with the following list of goals:

- Get product information to prospective customers
- Identify distributors
- Get parts information to distributors
- Get repair and service instructions to distributors
- Get support information to distributors

▶▶ To examine document component reuse, see "Using Standard Data in Documents," p. 283

▶▶ For information on linking to related objects, see Chapter 25, "Handling Specialized Content and Delivery," p. 421

As you look at your goals, you start brainstorming. You know that your customers and distributors are computer types; in fact, they probably have the latest, biggest, and fastest machines available that include multimedia set ups with CD-ROM drives and ISDN Internet connections. After pondering this, you add the following information to your list of goals:

- Get product information to prospective customers

  CD-ROM marketing disc with product information
- Identify distributors

  World Wide Web home page special area for registered distributors
- Get parts information to distributors

  Parts lists on diskette
- Get repair and service instructions to distributors

  Electronic service advisories on CD-ROM
- Get support information to distributors

  Support bulletins on World Wide Web home page

This is a pretty good approach for dealing with the trials and tribulations facing AnyCorp. Although some of the information relating to the World Wide Web is discussed in Part V, "SGML and the World Wide Web," you certainly have enough information to proceed to the next step in the process.

In working through this process, you identify your issues and a solution that addresses them. In the scenario above, you dealt with the problems faced by a rapidly growing company. Its success caused problems of its own, relating to supporting current and potential customers, along with the distributors that helped the company become successful.

Although it may sound simplistic, this is a key step in the process of successfully creating your SGML environment. If you skip it or rush through the process, you risk creating an environment that does not meet your needs. Table 5.1 lists some of the key issues in goal definition for an SGML project.

Table 5.1 Defining Your Goals	
Issue	**Description**
Environment	What environment are you working in? What do you want to accomplish? What kind of resources do you have to address the tasks at hand?
Constraints and Challenges	Do you have any special constraints, standards, or challenges to deal with? Do they raise additional issues that must be addressed? What are the most important? The least important?
Facilitators	Are there some special issues that might make it easier to address the constraints or challenges that you're facing?

Issue	Description
Current Issues	What are the most pressing issues surrounding the task at hand? Which issues must be addressed, which should be addressed, and which might be addressed? How much time do you have to address each of them?
Future Issues and Trends	What issues are likely to be important in 3 years? In 5 years? In 7 years? How much (and how often) do you expect your environment to change between now and then?

Document Analysis

Document analysis is simply the art of mapping out the logical components of your document. It is an "art" because there is no right way or wrong way to lay out the map. (In fact, there may be no "perfect" map.) As with goals definition, it is best performed in an informal group setting.

As with many of the brainstorming sessions that I've participated in, successful document analysis sessions are full of give-and-take. In the process of defining the structure of your documents, the group may wander down a particular path only to run into a dead end and have to start over.

By taking this wandering path, the group is performing other tasks, such as:

- Reaching consensus as to the layout of the document architecture
- Incorporating individual perspectives on the document into the global view
- Achieving group ownership of the document architecture and components
- Developing acceptance by individual participants of the group/consensus approach

Part II examines document analysis in much greater detail. In the meantime, let's look at some of the issues you face as you perform document analysis in a new environment.

First of all, you are lucky. Because you don't have to design a DTD that matches an existing collection of documents, you have a bit more leeway as to how to proceed. I have participated in document analysis sessions where our group was working with a large quantity of existing documents and document components. The structure and organization of these documents was based on their visual appearance on the printed page. (In the pre-SGML world, appearance was all that mattered; how you achieved that appearance just wasn't important.) Tables that looked similar on a page were actually done six or seven different ways depending on which author created them.

Running across such situations is all too common in a pre-existing document environment. It's also quite understandable. As the specialist, you must deal with all the combinations, permutations, and assorted headaches in translating the documents into structured SGML.

With the "new document" approach, you're creating documents in accordance to an existing DTD. In fact, if you perform structured authoring with an appropriate authoring tool, you must author according to the rules defined by the DTD. If you're authoring in a looser environment, you still have the document structure defined and in mind when you create your document.

Going back to the AnyCorp example, suppose you want to address the issue of getting repair and service information to your distributors. Because your product line is evolving so quickly, you're having trouble keeping the distributors informed of all the changes.

You have a great idea on a type of document to cover these changes: a "Product Advisory." Created in the form of a bulletin, it can cover a variety of subjects, including parts, repairs, maintenance, safety, or general information.

But what should be in this document? The identification information and the body of the advisory. With the basic parts determined (identification information and advisory body), it's time to work on the details.

For ID information, you can include advisory numbers to tell individual advisories apart and dates to show when they are created and revised. There should also be a subject line to tell what the bulletin is about.

The body of the advisory proves to be a little trickier. Because you have envisioned the advisory to be a multipurpose document, you just aren't sure what may be included in individual advisories. Maybe just a few paragraphs describing a safety issue. Perhaps a numbered list of replacement parts for a new model. Or how about an illustration of a repair procedure? What about several of the above? After debating the issues awhile, you finally come up with your DTD.

Document Modeling

Figure 5.1 illustrates the DTD that was developed for AnyCorp's product advisories.

As you look at the DTD, notice that it begins with a header containing descriptive text:

```
<!-- ********************************************** -->
<!-- AnyCorp, USA                                   -->
<!--                                                -->
<!-- Product Advisory DTD version 1,0 20 Jul 95     -->
<!-- ********************************************** -->
```

This header contains easily readable identification information that shows:

- The name of your company (AnyCorp, USA)
- The name of your DTD (Product Advisory)
- The version of your DTD (1.0)
- The date that you created or revised it (20 Jul 95)

```
<!-- ********************************************* -->
<!-- AnyCorp, USA                                 -->
<!--                                              -->
<!-- Product Advisory DTD version 1, 20 Jul 95    -->
<!-- ********************************************* -->

<!DOCTYPE advisory [

<!-- Entity Definitions   -->

<!ENTITY % parael "para|blist|nlist|graphic">


<!ELEMENT advisory - - (idinfo,subject,subsec+)>
<!ELEMENT idinfo   - - (advnbr,type,dateiss,daterev,product)>
<!ELEMENT subject  - - (#PCDATA)>
<!ATTLIST subject      safety (y|n) "n">
<!ELEMENT subsec   - - (title,(%parael;)?)>

<!ELEMENT advnbr   - - (#PCDATA)>
<!ELEMENT type     - - (#PCDATA)>
<!ELEMENT dateiss  - - (#PCDATA)>
<!ELEMENT daterev  - - (#PCDATA)>
<!ELEMENT product  - - (#PCDATA)>

<!ELEMENT title    - - (#PCDATA)>

<!ELEMENT para     - - (#PCDATA)>
<!ELEMENT blist    - - (item+) -(nlist)>
<!ELEMENT nlist    - - (item+)>
<!ELEMENT item     - - (para|blist|nlist|graphic)+>
<!ELEMENT graphic  - o EMPTY>
<!ATTLIST graphic      filename CDATA #REQUIRED
                       artno    CDATA #IMPLIED>

                   ]>
```

Fig. 5.1

This Document Type Definition (DTD) defines the document structure of the AnyCorp product advisory.

SGML Development

Look at the first element in the DTD, advisory. This is the top level element. It defines the major sub-sections (or subelements) of the document: idinfo, subject, and subsec.

```
<!ELEMENT advisory - - (idinfo,subject,subsec+)>
```

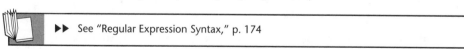

▶▶ See "Regular Expression Syntax," p. 174

The plus sign (+) following subsec is shorthand notation for describing an element's occurrence.

Following the top level element are the element definitions for the primary subelements contained within the top-level element (advisory): identification information (idinfo), subject, and subsection (subsec):

```
<!ELEMENT idinfo    - - (advnbr,type,dateiss,daterev,product)>
<!ELEMENT subject   - - (#PCDATA)>
<!ELEMENT subsec    - - (title,(%parael;)?)>
```

▶▶ See "Attributes: Their Use and the ATTRIBUTE Declaration," p. 182

The ATTLIST declaration is a way of declaring element attributes (or values associated with the element).

The elements listed below are those that are included in the idinfo element. In other words, they are subelements of the idinfo element.

```
<!ELEMENT advnbr    - - (#PCDATA)>
<!ELEMENT type      - - (#PCDATA)>
<!ELEMENT dateiss   - - (#PCDATA)>
<!ELEMENT daterev   - - (#PCDATA)>
<!ELEMENT product   - - (#PCDATA)>
```

The subsec element is defined as containing a number of objects: the subelement title and the entity parael:

```
<!ELEMENT title     - - (#PCDATA)>

<!ENTITY % parael "para¦blist¦nlist¦graphic">
```

The entity parael, or paragraph element is used as a mechanism to define multiple elements.

The definitions for the element parael could also be done in the following manner:

```
<!ELEMENT parael - - (para¦blist¦nlist¦illus)>
```

◀◀ See "Entities," p. 58

For this example, you use an entity to define the paragraph element parael instead. Recall from Chapter 3, "SGML Terminology," that an entity is a mechanism for referencing symbolic names. In this case, you use an entity rather than an element to define parael:

```
<!ENTITY % parael "para¦blist¦nlist¦illus">
```

▶▶ See "Entities: Their Use and the ENTITY Markup Declaration," p. 184

You do this for a number of reasons. In this case, it serves as a shorthand method of using a long string. This method can also be used to include document components that are external to this DTD (you learn more about this in Chapter 11, "Using DTD Components"). It's also useful for including special characters such as scientific symbols, foreign language characters, and other symbols that aren't readily accessible from a standard keyboard.

You don't have to structure the document this way. The document definition is there to define the document according to what makes sense to you, the document architect. How you define a DTD to meet the needs of your situation may be quite different from the way I do. The true test of the DTD is how well it meets your needs, not how it compares to someone else's.

Parsing Document Type Definitions (DTDs)

Before you can start using your new DTD, you must run it by a review committee of sorts, a validating parser. As you learned in Chapter 4, the validating parser is used in the SGML environment to confirm that an SGML document conforms to its corresponding DTD.

However, before you can validate SGML documents against a DTD, you must confirm that the DTD itself is legitimate. This means that the DTD must be checked for internal consistency in its document definition scheme. The syntax of the DTD must be checked and confirmed to be in accordance to the rules. It must also be confirmed that it is not ambiguous; it must be explicitly clear where tagged elements may occur. (SGML does not allow ambiguous content models!)

▶▶   See "Tags and Tag Minimization with Omittag," p. 186

> **Note**
>
> An ambiguous content model is evident when an element or character string can fit into several possible locations within the current content model. (It is unclear as to which possible location in the content model it belongs.)

> **Note**
>
> The SGML prohibition against ambiguous content models is for your own protection. By outlawing ambiguous content models, SGML ensures that your document is organized as you intended it, not as some unforeseen variation of what you were intending.

DTDs must be parsed when they are created and each time they are modified to confirm their conformance to the SGML standard.

Document Maintenance Considerations

When you create an SGML environment from scratch, there are a few issues that need special attention. If you are starting out in the SGML world, expect a few bumps in the road. Your first DTDs will likely be a little "off," especially if you're modeling complex documents. As a result, you'll probably have to tinker with them a few times to get them right.

If your organization is composed of a number of writers who will be using your DTDs, you'll want to spend a fair amount of effort confirming that they're right. After all, you'll probably be educating your writers about SGML, structured authoring, DTDs, and a host of other topics simultaneously. Constantly changing the "rules" (as defined in your DTDs) while your writers are getting comfortable in an SGML authoring environment will probably not help the learning process!

Constant changes in your document architecture (as defined in the DTDs) can also play havoc with your existing SGML document collections. After all, these existing documents will also have to fit the modified DTD.

The readers of your SGML document library also play into this scenario. Significant changes to your DTD will also have to reach your readers, wherever they may be. If the content model changes significantly, it will affect the readers using all of the previous versions of your documents! After all, they might be rather unhappy if their existing library of documents suddenly becomes unreadable.

Tip

Whenever possible, consider making any necessary changes to your DTD in ways that make it broader in scope than its predecessor. When this can be done, problems with existing legacy data compatibility can be minimized.

For example, if an element named `catalog` currently contained the following:

```
catalog (id,subject,location)
```

and it was modified so that subject was replaced by topic:

```
catalog (id,topic,location)
```

the following definition would ensure that both versions were still legal, thus accommodating old and new documents.

```
catalog (id,(topic|subject),location)
```

Converting Existing Documents into SGML (Filtering)

Creating your SGML environment by converting existing documents has some similarities to creating an SGML environment from scratch. Yet it differs in that you have a few more issues to consider. The nature of your existing documents, including their structure, variability, and complexity, all factor into your conversion strategy.

The native format of your source documents can be a significant issue. Is this format easy to work with? Can your conversion tools easily handle the format? (If not, are there any intermediate formats that you can readily convert that are easier to deal with?)

In some situations, the conversion process may involve a number of conversion steps requiring specialized expertise (such as in the conversion from paper or microfilm-based source documents). For complex conversions (or if you lack the resources in your own organization), a document conversion company qualified to do SGML conversions may be your best alternative.

The tools that are at your disposal for the conversion process are also important. Are they easy to use? Can they be adjusted and modified to support your changing needs? Do they support the file formats from which you will be converting? Will they support other formats that you might be using later? These and other issues figure into the selection process as you build your toolkit.

> **Note**
>
> For programmers, one of the handiest and most flexible conversion tools is available for free! Perl, a pattern recognition and text manipulation language, is widely available for a variety of computer platforms. PerlSGML is a publicly available enhancement package that adds specific SGML features to the basic Perl package.

On the CD

    ▶▶   See "The World of Perl," p. 491

Document Analysis

The issues faced in document analysis when converting documents are somewhat different than those related to documents created in a structured SGML authoring environment. The latter documents have the benefit of having structure included (and hopefully, verified) during the authoring process.

When converting documents, you must take into careful consideration the nature of your source data (which you'll be converting into SGML). Its nature and characteristics can have a great influence on how you develop your DTDs.

Table 5.2 describes some of the issues you'll need to examine in your existing documents, and with the people and programs that create them.

Table 5.2 Source Document Considerations When Filtering into SGML	
Issue	**Considerations**
File Format	Do your tools directly support this format? Are there any parts of this format that cause problems (such as table definitions, equation support, or embedded graphics)? How much structure is embedded in the file format?

(continues)

Table 5.2 Continued	
Issue	**Considerations**
Authoring Package	How sophisticated is the authoring package/program? Does it support structure in a document? If so, how? How does it handle text formatting? Can it export formatted documents in a non-binary ASCII interchange format, such as Rich Text Format (RTF)?
Document Structure	How consistently are your documents structured? Is the structure "tight" or "loose"? (That is, is a highly rigid and defined structure tightly enforced?) Is the structure simple or complex? Do the authors use a number of approaches to achieve the same look (or visual structure)? Are the authors consistent within a document in presenting the same data structures in different places?
Document Authors	How flexible are they? (Can they modify their authoring approach if necessary?) Do they write in a structure that is logically consistent? Do they understand the concepts of SGML? If not, are they willing to learn? What is their attitude toward SGML? (Do they feel threatened by the use of SGML?)

Once you understand the nature of your legacy (or source) data, you can focus on defining your goals. This process is much the same as when you are starting from scratch. The process that you went through earlier for AnyCorp could just as well apply to the conversion approach.

Document Modeling and DTD Design

Developing a document model with a corresponding DTD design can be straightforward in the conversion approach. After all, you have a source document from which to work. Usually, you can visually analyze a document and rather easily define the model.

Once you have defined the document model for your source document, you should look it over, study it, and decide if this model meets your needs for your output SGML document. In other words, is the existing model sufficient to meet your goals? If it is, then it's a rather simple process to define it according to SGML syntax in its own Document Type Definition.

If the document model doesn't meet your needs, you need to figure out why. Common issues to address might include:

- Changes in the presentation medium of the document, such as going from printed documents to electronic delivery
- The desire for document enhancements, such as adding hypertext links to other document sections (and other documents)
- Changes to the document usage or audience
- The desire to support the use of modular document components (both within this document and across a range of documents)

Quite often, you see organizations moving to SGML in order to make their documents more transportable. This can be as simple as moving between word processing systems or as complex as gaining the ability to present data in both printed and electronic environments.

When moving to the electronic environment, it is useful to consider several generations of your (future) SGML documents when developing your DTD. For example, your first version may be a simple electronic equivalent of your original paper-based document. The second version may include hypertext links between sections of your documents. Version three may have links between documents in your collection, as well as multimedia objects (like sound and video clips).

If you can anticipate the progression in the beginning (to some degree, at least), you can build many of the structural links to support these enhancements into your DTD in the beginning.

Document Conversion

Due to the wide range of possibilities involved with converting documents into SGML, a thorough discussion of this subject is beyond the scope of this book. Software packages available to perform these conversions range in price from free (in the case of Perl) to many thousands of dollars.

Quite often, your best bet may be to contract the conversion of a large amount of legacy data to a document conversion company that is experienced in SGML conversions.

Converting AnyCorp's Documents. Going back to AnyCorp for a moment, imagine a slight change to the situation. You have been asked to put the information into SGML, but there is a catch: You also have to convert the legacy documents that have been produced in the past 20 years into the new format as well.

"No big deal," you think. You'll just dig up the disks containing the data, read them into your SGML authoring package, and add the necessary tags. In going about locating the data, however, you discover that the format of these documents has changed several times during the last 20 years:

- For the first 5 years or so, the documents were created by a typist (no electronic data is available, only hardcopy documents).
- For the next 7 years, they were prepared on proprietary word processing hardware. (This hardware was replaced years ago and your computer doesn't read the disks for these files.) You have hardcopy versions of these documents as well.
- Documents produced since then generally can be read by some version of word processing program that you have.

In this situation, you realize that some of the documents must be scanned with a document scanner to bring them into your computer. As you look at some of the older documents, you realize that their quality is sometimes poor (see fig. 5.2).

Fig. 5.2

Legacy data conversions of hardcopy documents are sometimes dependent on poor-quality originals.

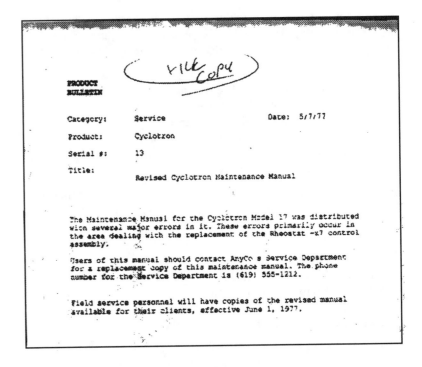

Your earlier approach in working out a plan for creating new documents will work in converting existing legacy data, with one addition: You need to work out a plan to convert the legacy data.

 ◄◄ See "What You're Going To Do," earlier in this chapter, p. 89

This includes a number of steps:

- Convert legacy data into a common electronic format
- Convert legacy data into a common structural format
- Convert legacy data into a tagged SGML document instance

To get your documents into a common electronic format, you must first decide what that format will be. (For many situations, plain ASCII text works best.) From there, you can choose to scan the hardcopy originals into raster image files, and then convert them to text via an optical character recognition program. For some document originals, actually retyping them may be easier.

You might be able to convert documents that you have electronic copies of via a format conversion program.

> **Tip**
>
> When performing data conversions, be sure to visually confirm the quality of the conversion! Optical character recognition and data format conversions will not provide 100 percent accuracy.

Once you have your documents converted into a common electronic format, you will need to convert them into a common structural format. Often, legacy data that spans a number of years also spans a number of structural formats. (People change the look and structure of a document over the years.)

In the case of your product advisory, take a moment to examine its current structure (see fig. 5.3).

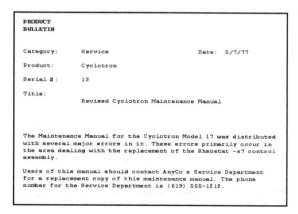

PRODUCT ADVISORY

Number:	146
Type:	Parts
Date:	8/15/95
Revised:	
Subject:	**Revised Replacement Parts List (AnyCorp Model 501)**

Model 501 User-Replaceable Parts

The parts list identified in the AnyCorp Model 501 User's Maintenance Guide has been superseded, effective immediately. User-replaceable parts are identified in the revised parts list below. Parts orders which reference items on the previous list (dated 2/5/94) will be honored up to 3/14/96.

Customers are advised to order from this revised list in order that they may achieve higher reliability at a lower unit cost. Questions on this subject should be directed to the Central Spares Organization.

New Parts List

345-234 (Filter, cooling fan)
148-745 (Fuse, power:1.5amp)

Fig. 5.3

The current version of your document has a specific collection of data objects in a specific order.

Notice that specific data objects (or elements) occur in a specific order in this document. For example, there is an advisory number, followed by an advisory type, a date, a revision date, and a subject.

Now take a look at a sample of this document as it looked some 18 years earlier (see fig. 5.4).

PRODUCT BULLETIN

Category:	Service
Product:	Cyclotron
Serial #:	13
Title:	

Date: 5/7/77

Revised Cyclotron Maintenance Manual

The Maintenance Manual for the Cyclotron Model 17 was distributed with several major errors in it. These errors primarily occur in the area dealing with the replacement of the Rheostat -x7 control assembly.

Users of this manual should contact AnyCo s Service Department for a replacement copy of this maintenance manual. The phone number for the Service Department is (619) 555-1212.

Fig. 5.4

Earlier versions of documents often have different document structures and content.

Notice that this earlier version of the document looks different. The identifying data at the top (category, date, product, serial #, and title) is not the same as the current version. In the process of converting your documents into a common structural format, you'll have to decide how to map these earlier data objects into your current element structure.

In addition to developing a mapping approach and converting your documents into a common structural format, you'll also have to convert them into SGML, ensuring that the final converted document is properly tagged as a valid SGML document instance.

Note

The actual order of the conversion steps can depend on the nature of your legacy data. In some cases, the common structural format conversion and the conversion into SGML may be performed in the same processing step.

Selecting appropriate tools to perform your conversions can be easy or extremely complex, depending on many interrelated factors. The quantity of legacy data, your ongoing document volume and complexity, the data formats, and many other issues can factor into your choices.

Tip

In many cases, you might want to have legacy data conversions performed by a data conversion company familiar with SGML conversions.

As you have seen, the conversion of legacy data into SGML can get complicated. Before performing any conversions of a large number of documents, it can be very helpful to map out the steps in the process in some detail.

Parsing DTDs and Documents

When filtering documents from other formats into SGML, parsing takes on a much greater importance. Parsing your DTDs is the same as in the ground-up approach; you must parse them after each modification you make.

Converted documents are different beasts entirely. Because no conversions of complex documents are perfect, errors in the conversion process creep in. As a result, it's wise to parse all converted documents (*document instances*) with a validating parser.

Generally, early conversions can have many parsing errors. As your heart sinks when you see all of these errors, don't feel too bad. As you tweak both your input documents and conversion programs, the number, variety, and frequency of errors can be greatly reduced.

On occasion, you may hear people say that they don't parse all of their converted documents, it's not necessary, and so on. Don't believe it! The scope of possible combinations of tags within even a simple DTD is tremendous. For very similar documents, a regular parsing step may show few and minor errors for a long time. However, just when you think that the parsing step is unnecessary, some major parsing errors surface. Think of parsing as cheap insurance for ensuring solid, reliable SGML documents.

> **Tip**
>
> Parsing can be a strange, mysterious, and complex experience. If you encounter parsing errors that you can't track back to identifiable SGML errors, consider cross-checking with another parser. No parser is perfect, and the parsing function is an extremely difficult task to perform!

Tricks, Traps, and Pitfalls

Earlier in this chapter, you explored two approaches to setting up an SGML environment: authoring in SGML from the beginning, and filtering existing documents into SGML. Each approach has its pros and cons.

If you're undecided on which approach to take (structured authoring versus conversion), you might want to think of it as a "You can pay me now, or you can pay me later" issue.

With structured authoring, you must contend with all the restrictions that are imposed by the document structure defined in the DTD. You might find it slow going at first, as you figure out what you can do at any spot in the document. The learning curve can be steep in the beginning. You might discover you don't like operating within the confines of a set of rules policed by a machine.

On the plus side, those rules ensure that your documents fit the architecture that you have defined for them. A consistent set of documents is much more manageable across different software packages and delivery environments.

The document conversion approach permits you to put off some of the difficulties in arriving at consistently structured documents until later, at the conversion step. Rest assured that if you have wildly varying documents (by wildly varying authors), the conversion process will be an adventure.

The document conversion process can be tedious and frustrating at times. It requires an eye for detail, particularly on large, complex conversions. Getting good at it may take some time.

> **Tip**
>
> If you're going the conversion route and the people doing the conversion are not the document authors, make sure that you implement "feedback loops." Through this approach, the conversion people can let the authors know of ongoing problems with input documents (such as writing styles and techniques) that commonly cause conversion errors. If the document converters are constantly fixing the same types of errors, they may become morose, moody, or withdrawn! If they have the chance to improve the process, their outlook may remain bright.

When parsing document instances on an ongoing basis, note the types and frequency of errors that you encounter. Do a little analysis on them. Does one particular author generate a large percentage of the errors? If so, can you figure out why? I once worked in an environment where one author producing five percent of the documents also produced 80 percent of the parsing errors. After I noticed this, I did a little checking. I found out that he had been away for a three-week period during which everyone else was instructed on the issues involved with authoring for SGML. After some quick refreshers on the topics he had missed, the error rate on his documents was similar to those of his fellow writers.

You're fortunate to have a choice today. Until recently, the options available to turn your words into SGML documents were much more limited. With the advent of ever more tools, you can pick and choose the tool that bests fits your needs.

If you choose to create SGML via the route of structured authoring tools that only allow valid SGML components in your document (as defined by your DTD), the need for parsing each document instance can be reduced (or possibly eliminated). But beware! Some structured authoring tools have a feature that allows you to "turn off" the validating feature that ensures your compliance with your DTD. If your authoring package is one of these (and you avail yourself to this "feature"), you must treat your documents as if they were filtered into SGML. That means you need to parse them against your DTD! If, for any other reason, you have doubts about the validity of your document instances, parse them.

Even if your DTD modification is incredibly minor, parse it after the change. After all, sometimes the smallest errors are the hardest to spot, particularly among all of those tags.

Re-examine your goals, content models, and DTDs from time to time. Although you don't want to be constantly changing your DTDs, it is an evolutionary learning process. Sooner or later, you'll want to make a few enhancements. When you do, make sure that you have a system for tracking versions! As with software, there's nothing worse that having three or four versions of the same DTD and not being sure which version applies to which documents.

Most of all, involve people in the process! All too often, SGML is introduced into an organization without a reasonable amount of discussion and explanation. More than once, I've been in departments where people have felt that it was being introduced in order to "get rid of the people and replace them with computers." That may occasionally be the motive, but I've yet to experience it. More commonly, the intent is to use the information more flexibly while automating the more mundane and tedious parts of the process.

From Here...

This chapter explored the issues involved with implementing an SGML system in two different ways: from the ground up with all new documents produced directly into SGML and through the process of converting existing documents into SGML. With these two situations, you have some issues that are the same, and others that differ.

This examination of SGML parsers looked at how the parsing step ensures the consistency of both Document Type Definitions and individual SGML document instances.

For more information, refer to the following:

- Part II, "Document Analysis," looks at the issues involved with mapping your documents in SGML in more detail.
- Chapter 10, "Following General SGML Declaration Syntax," tells you more about the SGML syntax.
- Chapter 23, "Rapid Development and Prototyping," examines the issues involved with rapidly developing an initial SGML system in your organization.

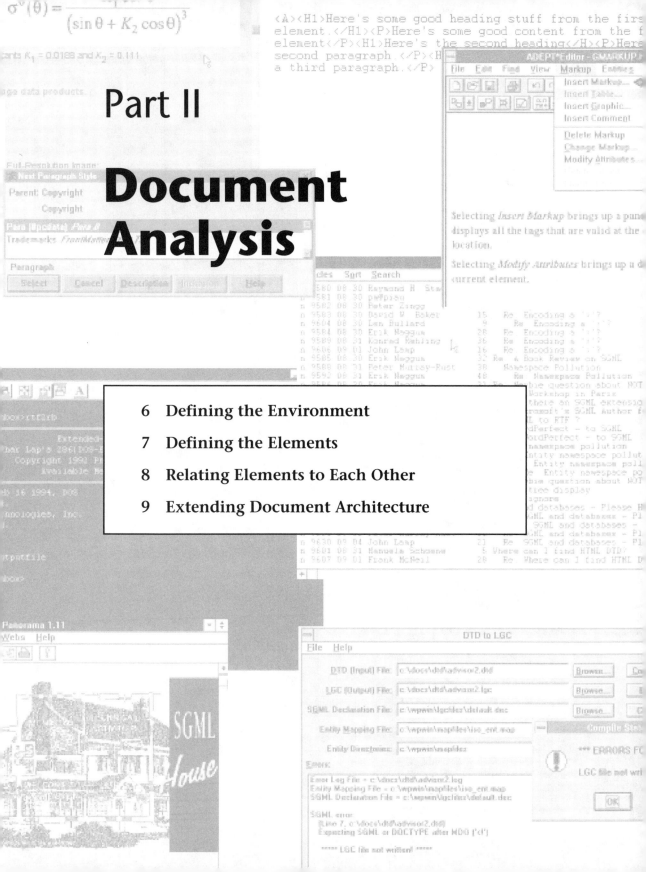

Part II

Document Analysis

6   Defining the Environment

7   Defining the Elements

8   Relating Elements to Each Other

9   Extending Document Architecture

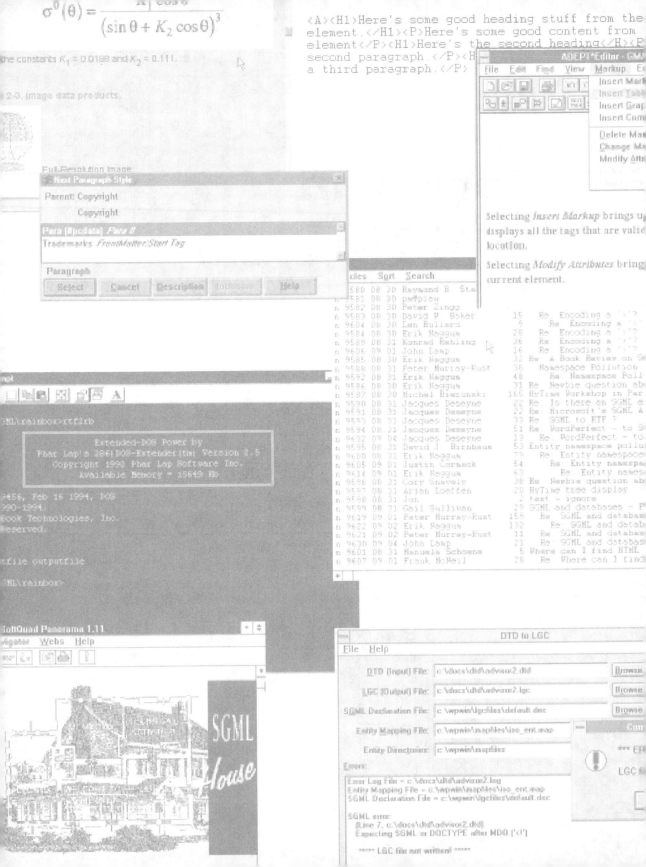

CHAPTER 6

Defining the Environment

When you're building your dream home, you don't just start building the first house that drifts into your mind. You have to ask a lot of questions about what it is you really want. Imagine, you won the lottery, you're out on some bluff that overlooks a picturesque valley on one side and a country lake on the other side. This is the site where you'll build your new home. You're visualizing your house among all the natural surroundings—how it will look, where your driveway will be, and what shape your swimming pool will be. That's what the first step of document analysis is about: designing your SGML dream house.

Your natural surroundings for your SGML "site" are the myriad documents you have. Your surroundings also include your customers, or the people you're preparing documents for. Your business or enterprise probably has standards or guidelines you must follow; those too are part of your surroundings. To be realistic, you can't ignore how your documents will probably change in the future. All of these considerations, and more, make up your environment. To build an SGML "house" you can live with, you have to pay attention to all of these issues.

This chapter guides you through the process of defining your environment. Much of what is presented in this chapter is common sense, but still the process seems much clearer after you've done it once.

In this chapter, you learn:

- How to prepare for defining the environment
- How to decide the use of your SGML documents
- How to define what standards and guidelines you have to obey as you conduct your business
- How to come up with names for all your different types of documents
- How to gather and examine examples of all the different types of documents you're going to be using
- How to determine how people use your SGML documents
- How to anticipate how documents will have to change in the future

Preparation for Defining the Environment

As you work through these steps, be sure you have your group together. This is a brainstorming process. Your group should consist of everyone who shares responsibility for your enterprise. If you run a small Web site, then gather some of your faithful users around, or perhaps some of your fellow Web site entrepreneurs.

> **Note**
>
> This chapter is primarily written for the big enterprise (say, a 30+ person publications department or a commercial publisher). If you're a small enterprise, you can follow the same basic steps with no problem, except that you'll probably get done a whole lot quicker!

Bear in mind, some enterprises have to deal with thousands of documents of many different types and users and customers of every description. No matter how big your enterprise is, these six steps will be your milestones:

- Decide how you're going to use all the documents.
- Decide what standards and guidelines you have to obey as you conduct your business.
- Come up with names for all your different types of documents.
- Gather examples of all the different types of documents you're going to be using and examine them closely.
- Pick out all the different types of people who will be using your documents and determine how they will be using them.
- Anticipate how your documents will have to change in the future.

You're sketching plans to build that dream house. If you don't plan correctly now, you may have to rebuild it later. You don't want to go through that with all your documents after they've been converted into instances of SGML DTDs.

Preparing to define your environment involves just thinking about the steps and rehearsing the scenarios of how this process could look in practice. You should be thinking about who your key people will be and what resources they'll need to help you.

Decide How You Are Going To Use Your Documents

This step forces you to define your goals for starting an SGML publishing enterprise. There are a lot of different ways you can use documents, and more arise every few months as technology introduces new applications. Here are some ideas on how you might want to use the documents in your environment:

- Database storage, access, and retrieval for research and reports
- Hardcopy publishing for customer books
- Commercial journal or magazine publishing
- CD-ROM publishing
- World Wide Web navigation with graphical browsers
- Multimedia documents for training co-workers
- Electronic co-authoring and editing of documents that are shared across networks
- Interactive entertainment documents that get modified as users work with them
- Standards documents that get compared with other documents for validation of content and structure

See figure 6.1 for an illustration of how this goal definition step could look.

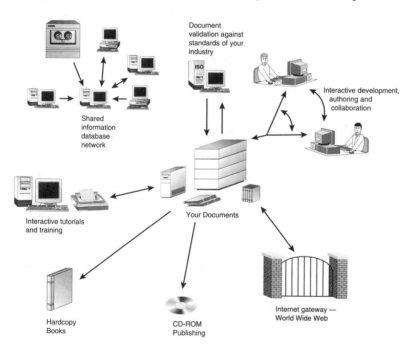

Fig. 6.1

Decide how you intend to use your documents; consider all possible uses and tools.

Document validation against standards of your industry

ISO

Interactive development, authoring and collaboration

Shared information database network

Interactive tutorials and training

Your Documents

Hardcopy Books

CD-ROM Publishing

Internet gateway — World Wide Web

Document Analysis

This is by no means a complete list. It's just a start. There's really no limit to the ideas you and your group can have. Spend some time expanding this list of uses and mediums. If yours is a big enterprise, this step can take months.

Even with the many deadlines you currently may observe, everyone must follow standards if you are going to use SGML. Some publication departments deliver several dozen books each month. Commercial publishers often produce several monthly periodicals each month. You have to meet your deadlines *and* abide by SGML's rules. So, don't rush this step, and don't be afraid to redefine your goals at some point in time if it becomes necessary.

Tip

Don't plan your existing deadlines for SGML resources that are not yet operational. Wait until your SGML system has a proven track record with many real document samples before you depend on it for meeting time-sensitive deliveries. And then give yourself much more time than you would using existing resources.

Decide What Standards and Policies You Must Obey

Many standards and policies exist that you already must follow. Each of these standards or policies that you obey is part of your overall environment. These standards are sort of like lakes or streams on the lot where your dream house stands. You have to adjust to them. They become a part of your daily life.

There are three types of standards that influence your documents: format, structure, and content. If you break all your standards down into these three categories, you'll simplify your task of defining your environment, as well as prepare yourself for designing your environment later.

Format Standards

SGML does not specifically concern itself with format since its goal is to define and maintain the structural integrity of your documents. Format considerations depend on your SGML processing system, and the international standard is flexible enough to accommodate many approaches to format. Many SGML enterprises allow for several different formats of a document, such as spreadsheets that appear in service bulletins or in maintenance instruction manuals, each time with a different format. Commercial publishers have extensive format guidelines and policies, and SGML systems must be capable of rapid implementation of format changes. Fortunately, since SGML focuses on document structure, many of the format details are left to those who define the SGML processing systems involved.

 ◀◀ See "Structure, Content, and Format," p. 35

Tip

If you are a commercial publisher or produce unusually formatted documents, or if you must use unusual hardware in your SGML processing system, consult an SGML specialist who deals with enterprises like yours. He or she may be able to advise you on compatibility issues between your processing system and your related format issues.

Anything that describes a document appearance is a *format standard*. Format is like the make-up and costume of an actor. It's not who the actor is or what role he's playing. Format is decoration. It's not the action or plot of your production.

If your standard deals with any of the following, it's most likely a format standard:

- Paper size
- Character font or typeface
- Orientation of graphics on the page
- Page layout
- Anything that governs how lines of text or graphics appear on the page

Format standards aren't always easy to identify. For example, style guides govern appearance, but they often deal with content and structure as well. Your style guide might specify titles that must appear in certain locations of a document, and might further specify that those titles appear in a 16-point Bookman bold typeface. The fact that the title must exist in only certain document locations would be a structural consideration. The details of font and point size are format considerations. You have to separate format from structure. Since SGML DTDs define document structures to a machine that processes them, it first must build the document correctly before it applies stylistic formats. If a machine incorrectly builds a document and places the document title at the end of a magazine article, it doesn't really matter if the title appears in the correct size and font.

The trick is to always think of only three standards: format, structure, and content. For example, if asked what your format standard is, your answer is *The Chicago Manual of Style*. If asked what your structure standard is—*The Chicago Manual of Style*. And your content standard? *The Chicago Manual of Style*. You have to think of *The Chicago Manual of Style* as three different style guides. You have to think of one standard at a time.

> **Note**
>
> Many standards can serve multiple purposes. A style guide might pass as the format standard as well as the structure standard. But ultimately, your format standard is that collection of sources that tell you what your documents look like. You might even keep exhibits of format examples as a sort of standard themselves.

Structure Standards

The most crucial standard, document structure, is tricky because it's abstract and hard to differentiate between it and content and format. *Structure* gets into the heart of what the document is. Your DTDs will define the structure of each of your document types. They will be a blueprint for your processing systems to disassemble and reassemble any type of document in your organization as it moves from one machine to another. For example, your authors may create documents on PCs, but your editors may edit documents on Macintoshes, and your production staff may use Sparc stations to produce your publications. Your document structures must be thoroughly defined so that transfers between these machines lose nothing of your documents.

Once you've defined a document's structure, you've established pigeonholes in which to place content. Once a machine knows there's a title at the beginning of a document, it expects to see a string of characters designated as title content, and it must be at the document's beginning. Now that the machine knows where the title is and what character string goes in that title as content, it can apply a format to that character string. But the machine must think of structure first, then the content of that document structure, and then it can think about what format that structure can appear in.

As Chapter 2, "SGML View of the World: Structure, Content, and Format," points out, you have to re-think all documents in terms of the information building blocks they're composed of. Your structure standards, if you have any, probably don't do this. You might have something that tells you that all interoffice memos will have a greeting, a body, a salutation, and an electronic signature. However, the person who wrote the "standard" that contains that information probably didn't have SGML in mind when he or she wrote it. Your standards for structure will largely be what you decide is both necessary and practical in your documents.

◀◀ See "Defining Structure in SGML," p. 42

◀◀ See "What Are the Components of SGML Documents?" p. 47

◀◀ See "What Are the Components of DTDs?" p. 61

Note

You'll probably have to develop your own structure standard out of a collection of sources. These structure standards will become your DTDs.

It will help you immensely if you use some specific forms to define your structural standards. Because they are composed of different documents and don't look at your collection of document types the way you are looking at them now, some forms, such as the one shown in figure 6.2, can help make the difference between clarity and confusion your first time through this process.

The names you choose aren't carved in stone. You'll get a chance later to change whatever names you put on the forms. You can consider these nicknames for now.

Office Memo	
Document nickname	
Document name (TBD)	
Address	Mail address of recipient
Structural component	Description of component
Time stamp	When memo was authored
Structural component	Description of component
Author	Who wrote it
Structural component	Description of component
Greeting	Body of text
Structural component	Description of component
Body text	Author addresses recipient
Structural component	Description of component
Salutation	Sign off to recipient
Structural component	Description of component
PS	Only if necessary, last note
Structural component	Description of component

Fig. 6.2

The form you use should identify the type of document and provide room to list all its structural parts.

Document Analysis

Content Standards

Content standards usually tell you what you can say and what to cover. You might have standards that forbid you to put obscenity into your documents. This has to do with content, and content only. Perhaps you have standards that encourage you to use only black and white photography in your documents; this is also a content standard.

Particularly important are documents that tell you what to put *in* your documents. For example, for field repair manuals or overhaul manuals, how do you know how deep your level of breakdown should go? What document tells you when to use a warning in your manuals? How do you know what manuals to talk about software installation in? What standards describe the editorial slant in your newspaper or magazine?

What content standards determine and follow:

- Which publications cover which subjects
- How deeply to cover each subject in the specified publication
- Which specific details are not appropriate for various publications

- What components of publications should contain (for example, what tells you what a warning or a sidebar should contain)
- Directions to exhibits of publications or examples of common practices
- Industry standards, if any, that apply to your collection of documents
- How graphics and non-textual information are composed

These questions get you started in the right direction. Keep your Standards and Policies sheet handy so you can write down ideas as they pop up (see fig. 6.3).

A scholastic journal might consider color graphics inappropriate for their audience while a magazine publisher might consider black and white photos undesirable. A literary magazine might publish only fiction with an occasional piece of literary criticism, while a software manual publisher might not permit actual software code to appear in his manuals. The documents that specify these types of policies are what should interest you at this point.

Types of Policies

Your purpose in identifying policies is finding any requirement not already covered in your standards. Policies can influence the structure, content, and format of your documents. Sometimes policies are not so clearly expressed as standards, but they can still have an impact on your SGML enterprise. Hopefully, every document requirement you identify in your policies you will already have identified in your standards.

Policies fall into two main categories: internal and external, both of which can affect your documents. Internal policies are like domestic affairs. They tell you how to conduct business inside your organization. External policies are like foreign affairs. They tell you how to conduct business outside your organization. Thinking of policies in this way can help you identify all the policies that affect your documents.

 ▶▶ See "Adding Features to Documents," p. 155

Be aware of unexpected policies that might influence your document structure, content, or format. Some examples of "surprise" policy standards that can affect your document are:

- Policies that forbid certain people to see certain documents. This causes you to add a security clearance tag to your documents.
- Policies that tell you to include or exclude information based on content. For example, obscenity policies might cause you to filter your documents for certain words and phrases.
- Policies that tell you how long information is to be considered valid. If your documents are to be considered obsolete after a certain period of time, a date should be attached to each of your documents, or perhaps even to your structural elements.

- Policies that specify an order of people who will view documents. For example, if a document must first be submitted to an editor or a quality checker before it's returned to a customer, some feature to indicate this will have to be added to the SGML structure eventually.

- Policies that dictate where physical copies of books will be stored and distributed might require you to tag your documents. This involves adding a storage location field to your documents, or perhaps some field that says whether the document exists physically or only electronically.

These policies might already be reflected in your structural standards—hopefully they are. But if not, by examining your policies you have uncovered yet more structures and capabilities to build into your documents beyond what your standards told you.

Because summarizing all your standards is a pretty big chore, you can use another form to help you. When you've identified relevant standards and policies for your publishing enterprise, try completing a form like the one shown in figure 6.3.

Standards & Policies

Format standards

Chicago Manual of Style, GPO, Mil-M-38387...

Structure standards

Vaguely defined...to be determined at length. Use existing practices to develop standard...

Content standards

Company policy statement ABC on improper speech. Ten Commandments, Presidential memo of last week...

Policy standards

Correspondence specifying delivery timeline of manuals. Contractual boilerplate, project management memos of 01/01/01...

Fig. 6.3

A simple form like this that summarizes your standards and policies will help you later when you have to talk intelligently about them.

II

Document Analysis

Identify All Your Document Users and Their Tools

How your customers use the documents you create often suggests structural capabilities that should be built-in to your DTDs. Your documents have internal or external users, too. Internal users are people in your own operation, people who work for you. External users are customers outside your organization. They're people who pay you. Payments can also help you to focus on the best ways to look at your documents. A document's worth lies in its use.

External Customers

First stop and ask yourself what it is about your documents that your customers want and need. Then ask yourself how you can better present it to them. Identify aspects of your documents that keep the customers happy, and perhaps aspects that they never liked that you just haven't gotten rid of yet. If you don't think about your documents from your customers' point of view, you'll miss the opportunity to see your document structures and functions in a new light.

Note

You may not be used to looking at your documents through your customers' eyes, but doing so can help you break out of your own mold and focus on what keeps your customers happy.

External customers have priorities as far as what they want to get from your documents. Use a form to focus your attention on the aspects of your documents that your customers are willing to pay for (see fig. 6.4).

Your group discussion about your external customer needs should still involve brainstorming. But your customers are the best authorities on what they like. So please take advantage of some of the following when answering the question of who your external customers are and what they like:

- Written customer surveys
- Phone surveys
- Relationships you already have with long-term customers who will give you honest feedback
- Talk with different internal departments to see if there are any "sagas" of customer dissatisfaction that relate to your documents in any way
- Talk with partner companies or publishers to see if they have heard of any complaints your customers have with your documents
- Practice being a customer for your company's documents; try to use your documents as if you were an external customer or subscriber

---

Tip

You can structure this form however you like. If you have many customers, as most large companies do, it helps to replace the Customer field with Categories of Customer or reader instead (for example, home reader, business reader, recreational reader, and so on).

Parts Catalog (illustrated)
Document nickname

Part numbers
Information

Exploded breakdown in art
Information

Recommended spares
Information

Mechanics at XYZ order from field
Customer use

ABC keeps maintenance inventory
Customer use

QRT company tracks failure rates of pumps
Customer use

Qwik Buk Inc. repairs major subassemblies
Customer use

Oldtimers Co. uses art to train field mechanics
Customer use

Ace Co. said they hate this info – delete it!
Customer use

Five company's complain of bogus part numbers
Customer use

7 out of 10 surveys complain of bad accuracy
Customer use

Fig. 6.4

Forms like this can help you identify what information in your documents is critical to your external customers. Notice, it focuses on the customer's product.

Document Analysis

Internal Customers

Internal customers can tell you a lot about what's important in your documents too. Everyone who sends documents from one part of a company to another has customers. Anyone who uses your document within your organization is your *internal customer.*

If you're in a management position in your company, and you're involved in setting up your SGML environment, this is a great excuse to ask questions within your department! This is one time when asking for complaints from the troops will pay great dividends!

There are a lot of strategies for getting feedback from "the troops" on how to make your documents better. You can:

- Call everyone together in a room and talk it out. Everyone might feel free to speak his peace if it's not in writing and if everyone else is in the room together. There's some security in numbers, and you might get some candid input.

- Have everyone respond in writing or e-mail to a survey. This has the advantage of being written down, but the major disadvantage is that it has everyone's name right on the paper. Some people might hold back their remarks because they think they'll be approached about them at a later time.

- Have everyone gather in a conference room and respond to an anonymous written survey. This has the advantage of "safety in numbers" for the people, and it also has the advantage of getting suggestions in writing. If you precede the survey with some brainstorming, you can also benefit from the group dynamics!

Since many managers wind up putting out fires in the department, they sometimes don't get to stand back and look at their department objectively. Combining the opinions of internal and external customers are a chance to get this objectivity. When both internal and external customers identify the same issues over and over again, you know those issues will likely influence your SGML enterprise.

Customer Tools

Your customers use hardware and software as tools to access your documents, and those platforms have their own requirements and limitations. The point here is to consider how both your internal and external customers access your documents. If you're a commercial publisher of computer books, you might be interested in whether your readers would enjoy reading your book on a CD-ROM. Or, would they prefer both the hardcopy book and the CD-ROM. Obviously, if all your customers can only access your documents in paper form, SGML won't do them a whole lot of good! If their tool is primarily shelf space for hardcopy books, SGML will be primarily for you.

Realistically, however, if your customers are currently committed to hard copy alone, that will have to change. It's only a matter of time before electronic resources will be everyday tools for them. Your SGML work will pay off for them eventually. It will pay off for you quickly after you get everything up and running.

> **Tip**
>
> Try looking at access tools by internal and external customer, and also by local and remote access.

 ▶▶ For more on content-sensitive tables, see "Handling Tables," p. 421

Your first task is to classify the tools your customers use so you can decide whether they present any challenges or additional considerations for defining your environment. Do you have people who access your documents remotely as well as locally? For example, if you have customers who access your documents over a networked database, you might need to build more intelligent document structures into your DTDs to facilitate the various uses they will serve in that database. This is particularly important with table structures, for example. If people will sort your tables, then you must build content-sensitive tables into your DTDs. As usual, a form helps you focus your efforts where it counts (see fig. 6.5).

Tool Summary	
Internal customers	**Most popular tools**
Cost accounting	CICS system
Field service	IPX LAN
Customer service	UNIX LAN with spare stations
Project mgt.	PC stand alones
Provisioning	
	Problem (unusual) tools
External customers	Wang — some people still rely on
ABC Co.	CICS — very inflexible, hard to support
XYZ Co.	
Household users	**Most popular tools**
College student users	PC clones and compatibles
Big Time Inc.	Macintosh based networks
	Internet connected LANs
	Least popular tools
	WiCAT minicomputers
	Unusual tools
	WiCAT minicomputers — still ABC Co. committed to big outlay — we have to find way to support!

Fig. 6.5

This sample tool sheet helps you figure out what tools all your internal and external customers are using, and whether they are using local or remote tools.

II

Document Analysis

You'll notice that each tool has the potential to present challenges. For example, if someone is using an old Wang word processing system, and he needs to access your SGML documents through it, that means you have to check for an SGML viewer for Wang! Or, at least, you need to be alerted to that prospective problem. (Whose problem it ultimately is you'll have to figure out!)

> **Note**
>
> Keep an eye out for big, obscure tools that your customers have a big commitment to. For example, old mainframes running old operating systems may not support the more recent SGML tools.
>
> Also, look for niche products for which there might be a smaller range of available SGML tools available. This situation is a little more common. There are some excellent computers out there that don't have a wide following of software developers. The Apple Macintosh, for example, is an exquisite machine that doesn't have a lot of support, compared to the PC, its big competitor. There are plenty of tools for the Macintosh, but not nearly as many as there are for the PC.

▶▶ See "Authoring and Conversion Tools for the Mac," p. 468

Decide whether any of these tools will cause you any problems. If you don't know whether your customer's tools are unusual or not, simply ask. As long as they use mainstream computers, there should be no major problem.

Gather and Inspect All Your Document Types

What you'll need to look for is whatever document requirements you have missed before. Ask yourself, "What am I missing?" Particularly, are there any documents that you haven't thought of? Are there any standards or customers or their computers that you haven't thought of?

Up until now, you've looked at your documents casually. Now it's time to get serious. Where you've generalized before, now you'll want to be specific.

The following steps can help you to analyze your documents:

1. Put all your sample documents on a table. Your table will be full of binders, folders, periodicals, loose sheets of paper, and perhaps CD-ROMs and floppy disks—all your publications. You might even set up a CRT on your table to display documents through a Web browser. If you want to represent an electronic document, you might just print out a page from one.

2. Spread all your document identification forms out on a large table (your document identification forms may look like figure 6.2). Tape them to the documents on the table like a nametag so they are both plainly visible.

3. Review your standards, customer, and tools forms. Lay them out where you can see them, either on the table or on the floor.

4. Have everybody walk around the table with a large pad of Post-It notes. When anyone sees a form that doesn't seem right, he or she writes up a note on a Post-It note and puts it on that form. You might want to repeat this process as often as needed to get a good collection of Post-It notes on everything.

5. Have everybody talk about the Post-It notes afterward. Put more Post-It notes on forms or documents if they require further discussion or a solution to a problem must be postponed. After everyone is satisfied that each note has been discussed, put a check mark on it and remove it. You should have no remaining notes visible when this step is completed.

Tip

If someone needs to use the conference room before you get done with this whole project, use a camera to take pictures of how everything was spread out.

Choose Names for All Your Different Types of Documents

So far, you've been operating with names you may have been less than satisfied with. You improvised names on all your document type forms (refer to fig. 6.2). Now it's time to decide what to call your documents.

From the last step, you should still have examples of each of your documents in the room with you. And each of those documents should have a document identification form stuck to it. Hopefully, you have worked through all of your Post-It notes (it's okay if you haven't, but you really should before you move too much farther).

If you have room, have everyone sit down, pick up a document form, and discuss it as a group. Decide if the name you have come up with works for everyone. As you change any names, simply make that change on the forms themselves.

> **Note**
>
> This doesn't need to be a long step. Just change any names that don't seem to fit and move on. You just want to make sure that all the names you've chosen are something you're willing to live with. They have to make sense and be unique.
>
> For example, if you have two types of service bulletins, one for field service personnel and another for customer service personnel, you don't want to use the same name for each.

Anticipating Document Evolution

Imagine your dream house in five to ten years. Will you add a Jacuzzi or some tennis courts? How about some horse stables? Sure you may want to build them right from the start, but you have to draw the line somewhere. You can't fit it all in at once. The same is true of your SGML environment. Fortunately, SGML is flexible, so you have room to grow later.

Some of the following questions can help you predict changes in your document environment:

- Are there any types of documents you have left out or any types you should delete because of duplication, or some other reason?
- Are there any types of documents that will become obsolete in the near future?
- Are there any new types of documents on the horizon that you will need to incorporate in your collection?

- Will your industry make any changes that will affect the type of data your documents must cover? For example, will you need to incorporate configuration management into your database? Will you need to change the way you identify security classification? Will old documents be converted to hypertext documents?

- How will changes in technology over the next few years affect the scope of data your documents cover? For example, will new technologies force you to add new sort fields to your databases?

- Will any standards or policies you currently use become obsolete or revised? What changes might these make to your documents?

- What aspects of your documents would you like to leave open because you can't fully anticipate all the relevant changes?

- Will your customers' change of tools affect how you make your documents? What new tools could cause you to change the way you currently structure your documents, thereby changing your environment?

- Do you anticipate the character of your customer base to change over the next few years? That is, will your "typical customer" change in any way that will affect how he uses your information or how you must prepare it for him?

- After considering all of the above questions, are there any other issues that will affect how any of your documents are structured? Will the building blocks that make up each of your documents change to fit any of the issues raised up until now?

- What areas do you not feel confident in that you have fully defined?

If you're sure you've remembered or discovered all relevant aspects to your environment, here are some possibilities you may have overlooked:

- Maybe some technical problem will arise that makes a vital database field inaccessible.

- Perhaps there's going to be some procedural change that will upset what you have done.

- There might be some restructuring in your company that will reallocate 50 percent of all your customer base to some other department.

- Maybe your legal department will say your documents can no longer contain any hardware dimensions because of some liability issue that makes it too costly.

- Maybe the current administration will come out with some executive order that will eliminate (by embargo, say) your most profitable middle eastern clients and skew your entire document base.

Spend some time dreaming up doomsday scenarios. Pretend you're in some Pentagon war room, deep beneath the ground surface, plotting your contingency plans and inventing your counter reactions. The more flexibility you can build into your definition, the better you will be.

Mistakes and Redefining Your Environment

Even after all this, you'll probably still make some mistakes. But, if you've done all the work described above, the damage is likely to be repairable. If you've taken shortcuts, your risk of having problems is higher; so is the risk that your problem is farther reaching.

Note

The way you decide whether your oversight is big or small is by how much it changes what you've done to date.

Some examples of major problems that can occur are:

- Major types of documents have been overlooked
- Fundamental types of information—critical to just a few customers at certain times of the year—have not been accounted for
- Several types of documents are actually the same, but somehow have been confused as being different
- Some commonplace tool that affects all employees and all documents has not been accounted for (like a peculiar network server or archaic mainframe that produces data in rigid and strange formats, but that everybody must use anyway)
- Your company is being acquired by another company
- Your department is being merged with another department
- A new industry-wide standard is being adopted that will affect every piece of information your department distributes
- You forget to indicate which documents might get translated to foreign languages (and which foreign languages)
- Some catastrophe happens, and you must restore all your data from tape (or other) backups—and you forgot that your data is backed up before it is tagged with SGML
- Your company must move to a different state, and you have no provision for how the data will be transported
- You forgot to talk with some group of people in your department who were responsible for a realm of documents you overlooked.

The list could go on. But when something does go wrong, decide whether it's a major or minor problem.

Assessing Damage Impact

You know the damage is big when someone asks, "Did I forget to mention that Mr. Shmagmotz, the president of the corporation, wants every field of the company database to be translated into New Swedish?" and everyone in the room just stares at the person asking the question. Something like this could possibly cause you to start all over again.

Translating your documents into another language was already covered immediately above. So if you asked these questions, you would not have been surprised by Mr. Shmagmotz's predilection for New Swedish.

Usually, big problems mean you have to start over considering a new group of document types that you didn't know existed. Then you have to hold up your progress on the rest of your older documents while you go through all the steps with those newer documents. If you run into something that changes the way you look at all your types of documents, that is a mistake that causes a big impact.

Fixing Big Mistakes

Suppose somebody makes a mistake, and it looks as though you have to start the whole process over from scratch. You have a choice:

- Take a recess and let your coworkers collect themselves—talk about it again after coffee today. Maybe it's not a problem after all.
- Finish up what little business you have for the day. Withhold further discussion on the problem until tomorrow. Perhaps a day later the problem won't appear so nasty.
- Assign people to research the problem to see if there are related facts that could lead to a solution. Get the facts.
- Ignore the problem for now; maybe you'll find a way around it. (Give yourself a time limit or dollar limit on this.)
- Just start over. Salvage what you can from what you've done. Discard the rest. Chalk it up as a learning experience.

How to Know When You're Done Defining Your Environment

You may never know if you're done defining your environment. But the proof, at least for now, is: does everything work? You won't know this until you're in production mode and have been for at least six months. Larger operations require a longer testing period. If your department has 40 people, and you publish 20 books per month, you might easily need two years of testing. It might take you that long to get the bugs worked out of all your different types of tools and customer connections and relationships.

If you went through all the steps described above, you did about as much as anyone can do. When you do find that you need to make a change in how you've defined your whole "universe" of documents, go and make the change. But make it *carefully*. You could easily confuse everything you have done so far if you change something haphazardly. *Be careful!*

Two years later, if you've had basically painless production and your employees and customers are happy about your endeavor, *then* you are done...for now.

From Here...

Defining your environment takes you through the process of matching your aspirations for an SGML enterprise with the realities of your current ways of doing business. This process forces you to isolate inconsistencies and resolve them. It's the first step of document analysis because there's no point of defining your document elements if you have serious conflicts between your policies and your aspirations. You have to take care of first things first.

Besides defining your environment, other chapters round out the document analysis task:

- Chapter 7, "Defining the Elements," takes you a step further in dismantling your documents to their basic components. You'll understand the bones of their structure at the end of this chapter.

- Chapter 8, "Relating Elements to Each Other," teaches you how to make the elements you identified in Chapter 7 all work together harmoniously.

- Chapter 9, "Extending Document Architecture," teaches you how to make your collection of elements richer and fuller.

- Part III, "Content Modeling: Developing the DTD," takes you into preparing the DTDs for all your document types.

- Chapter 23, "Rapid Development and Prototyping," takes you into an advanced situation applying the basic principles learned in this chapter to a real world professional example.

II

Document Analysis

CHAPTER 7

Defining the Elements

You now know how document analysis fits into the overall SGML procedure, and you understand how important defining elements is to document analysis. This chapter discusses some points that you should keep in mind as you define elements. It is not about declaration syntax, which is covered in Chapter 10. There is a big difference between *defining* elements and *declaring* them.

In this chapter, you learn:

- How big your elements should be
- What element content models are
- How to make an element dictionary
- How to use structure diagrams
- What types of content elements have
- What the ten steps to defining elements are

How Big Should Your Elements Be?

You determine the optimal size of an element. It is mostly a matter of taste and utility. You are the one who has to use them.

It is sort of like nuclear physics. First came molecules. Then there were atoms inside the molecules—surely nothing could be smaller than an atom. Then somebody split one, and people are still finding particles that they have to name. Aristotle would be pretty frustrated if he came back today and saw how much more complicated atoms are than he thought.

Take an element of a document with which are you are familiar—a single listing in a residential telephone book (see fig. 7.1).

Fig. 7.1

This telephone listing looks very simple, but it's probably not detailed enough.

In general, your elements should be just small enough to be useful—and not larger. Break your documents down into the smallest meaningful elements, or building blocks. The example in figure 7.1 is not broken down enough. There are still meaningful structural elements within smaller elements. That is the key.

In deciding whether you have broken down your elements enough, you should ask these questions:

■ Will I need to access the information nested in the element?

■ Are there any formatting peculiarities that indicate a structural and logical element that I should identify?

■ Would the nested information be useful during a database search?

■ Have I gone too far by identifying more structure than I need?

It might be useful to search by subelements within the individual item listing—for example, Mrs and 555-1234. Figure 7.2 shows you how to specify more elements.

Fig. 7.2

This example contains more detail than the previous example, but now there's a superfluous element—the type of street.

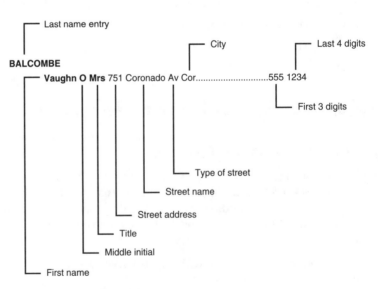

Conceivably, each of the elements suggested in figure 7.2 could be useful, depending on the application. If your database is huge, it could be helpful. If you are making an SGML telephone book for your home use, it is probably too detailed.

You need to sort by first name, street address, and telephone number. You can see that the formatting of the street address is different from the formatting of the name. Whether you need to search by telephone number prefix probably depends on how big your database is. In this case, it is the San Diego area telephone book, so it is enormous.

You might have gone too far in specifying Mrs as a title, but maybe not. You might want to search for physicians, for example. It would be handy to have a title element into which you could put Dr. You should make the title element not required, so that you don't have to put in Mr, Ms, or Mrs in every listing.

The big issue to consider is whether you will need information about an element in the future. Talk with the people in the trenches—the ones who use your documents—to get an idea.

> **Note**
>
> Not every element must be visible. Elements often do not print. For example, if Mrs. Balcombe resided in San Diego, the telephone book would have printed only her street address and not indicated that she lives in Coronado. You can then customize your processing system to hide or print elements as you deem appropriate.
>
> If you are not sure what sort of data you will need in the future, allow for expansion. Maybe Mrs. Balcombe could use an AT&T subscriber element, or a bill overdue element later on.

There is no right answer to how big your elements should be. It's up to you to figure out whether you have too many elements. What matters is that they are useful to you.

Element Content Models

In the previous example, some elements live inside other elements. When you find subelements living inside an element, you must decide what their relationships are to one other.

 ◀◀ See "Model Groups," p. 65

II

Document Analysis

Hierarchy and Sequence

When you find elements nested within other elements, you need to establish the relationships among them. The two questions to ask are:

- What is the hierarchy of elements?
- What is the sequence of elements?

Consider Mrs. Balcombe. You might be better off if you added hierarchy to the listing. For example, does the prefix element live inside the last name entry?

Likewise, the sequence of elements might be important. Does it matter whether the first name entry comes before the street address entry? Sequence is important in a telephone book. A listing makes no sense if its elements do not appear in a distinct order.

Occurrence

It's important to consider how many times an element shows up inside its parent. For example, the middle initial element probably does not apply to every other listing in the telephone book. Therefore, its occurrence is different from the actual telephone number, which must appear in every listing. The four possibilities are:

- *Required*: Occurs once and only once
- *Optional*: Occurs once or not at all
- *Optional repeatable*: Occurs more than once or not at all
- *Required repeatable*: Occurs more than once

Structure Diagrams

If you like drawing pictures, you will love structure diagrams. They help you understand the structure of documents because they are concrete and visual. Drawing them engages the creative side of your brain. Just remembering what elements come out of other elements can get abstract. Structure diagrams tell you in an instant where elements fit in terms of hierarchy, order, and occurrence, and they make it much easier to construct the DTD for a document. Figure 7.3 gives you an idea of what a structure diagram can tell you.

Figure 7.3 does not indicate how many times a middle initial can occur in each listing or whether the city must appear. You add that information later with occurrence symbols.

Grouping elements is a good habit to get into. Two large content models that include smaller elements have been added in figure 7.3—the address and the telephone number.

 ▶▶ See "Standardizing Basic Components," p. 194

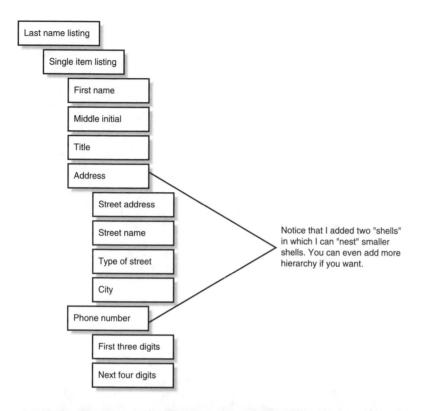

Fig. 7.3

This is one representation of a structure diagram.

Notice that I added two "shells" in which I can "nest" smaller shells. You can even add more hierarchy if you want.

Tip

Grouping under large shells often makes the small shells easier to manage. It also helps in developing a common DTD.

The structure diagram in figure 7.3 does not indicate how many of each element may appear or whether any elements must appear. You can add occurrence symbols to the structure diagram to show how often each element occurs. Table 7.1 describes the occurrence symbols.

Table 7.1   Occurrence Symbols

Occurrence	Symbol
Once and only once (required)	(none)
Optional	?
Optional repeatable	*
Required repeatable	+

Whenever subelements live inside one of your elements, draw a structure diagram and use the occurrence symbols, as in figure 7.4.

Fig. 7.4

Adding occurrence symbols to structure diagrams makes them more meaningful.

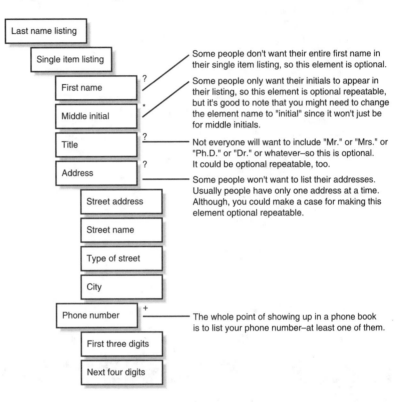

You can look at documents in many ways. SGML beginners often confuse structure with content. For now, you should concentrate on logical structure, not content. Take the following table, for example. You can think of this table either by logical structure or type of content. The safest way is to think of logical structure (see fig. 7.5).

Part Number	Part Description
157923C1	Nut, wing, 0.75
923872C3	Washer, 0.75
923579C2	Stud, SS, 1 1/2×0.75
47623-100	Lockwasher, 0.75

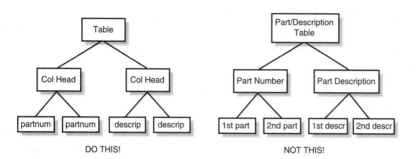

Fig. 7.5

Keep structure and content straight as you define your elements. This is one of the biggest stumbling blocks for new SGML users.

Types of Data Content

You have learned that elements can contain other elements. What happens when no more elements are left? What do the final elements contain? The answer is data. Table 7.2 describes the types of data that elements can contain.

Table 7.2   Types of Data That Go into SGML Elements

Data Type	Meaning
CDATA	Character data
RCDATA	Replaceable character data
#PCDATA	Parsed character data
SDATA	Specific character data
NDATA	Non-SGML data
EMPTY	No data—empty element
ANY	Any type of data

Note

#PCDATA is element content that contains data that should be parsed. It contains no other elements. These characters are recognized as data content rather than as markup.

CDATA consists of valid SGML characters that will *not* be parsed. This should be used for data that is specific to a unique processing system, like data content for a specific external application.

RCDATA is treated just like CDATA, except entity references are replaced.

II

Document Analysis

> **Note**
>
> Most straight text is #PCDATA.

In the following element declaration, for example, all the para elements contain parsed character data. The # is known as the SGML *reserved name indicator,* or RNI.

```
<!ELEMENT para (#PCDATA)>
```

Empty data is useful for elements that you expect to use at a later time. Suppose, for example, that you want to add revision tracking to numbered list elements, but your boss does not want to do it yet. You know that he will want to add it later on, so you create an element and fill it with empty data. SGML holds a place for it. The data must remain empty, though. You cannot put anything in it. The declaration looks like this:

```
<!ELEMENT numlist ((text¦graphic), revtrack)
<!ELEMENT text #PCDATA>
<!ELEMENT graphic EMPTY>
<!ELEMENT revtrack EMPTY>
```

Whenever the parser runs into <revtrack>, it considers it empty. The <graphic> element consists of an EMPTY content marker. That is because photographs are represented by encoded binary steams, which the parser does not know how to handle. You mark the element EMPTY, so that the parser treats it as though it is not there.

Types of Data for Attributes

▶▶ See "Attributes: Their Use and the ATTRIBUTE Declaration," p. 182
▶▶ See "Where To Define Attributes," p. 224

Other content types also show up in attributes. Attributes often are declared immediately after the element. (Attributes can be declared in their own section of a DTD, but it's clearer if you declare them together with the element they modify.) They are practically part of the element declaration. For example:

```
<!ELEMENT graphic    - -  EMPTY     >
<!ATTLIST graphic
            file      CDATA         #REQUIRED
            frame     CDATA         #REQUIRED
            units     (in¦cm¦pt)    "in"
            size      NUTOKEN       #IMPLIED  >
```

Table 7.3 summarizes the 15 types of declared value content that can be used in attributes.

Table 7.3 Types of Content That Appear in Attribute Declarations	
Keyword	**Attributive Value**
CDATA	Character data
ENTITY	General entity name
ENTITIES	General entity name list
ID	Unique identifier
IDREF	Identifier reference value
IDREFS	Unique ID reference value list
NAME	Name
NAMES	Name list
NMTOKEN	Name token
NMTOKENS	Name token list
NOTATION	Notation name
NUMBER	Number
NUMBERS	Number list
NUTOKEN	Number token
NUTOKENS	Number token list

> **Note**
>
> Don't confuse the keywords used in the attribute content types with the keywords used in element content types. Table 7.2 applies to element content, while table 7.3 applies to attribute content.

SGML looks at characters that stream through it in various ways. It classifies characters by function and as names, SGML characters, non-SGML characters, and data.

Tokens are a way in which SGML recognizes content with a type of shorthand. Names and numbers can have tokens, which make dealing with them easier when you have to follow SGML syntax rules.

The Definition Process

The definition process consists of ten steps. You should go through them systematically. You'll write a better DTD that will be easier for others to understand. You'll probably have the greatest success if you follow a workshop approach similar to the

II

Document Analysis

one that you followed in the last chapter when defining your environment. This process should emphasize the cooperation of everyone involved, because no matter how confident you are that *you* understand what should be defined, this process will improve even *your* best efforts at defining the elements.

Step 1: Pick a Document Type

You are probably dealing with several types of documents. Gather ten to twenty samples of your chosen document type. If you choose service bulletins, have many samples on hand. Also bring in some departmental experts (or your in-house experts) on service bulletins. Ensure that everyone in the room has a copy of all the samples and gets a chance to voice ideas and concerns about special features of that document type. SGML consultants can help you with syntax, but they do not know how you create your documents or how you use them. So count on your in-house experts.

Step 2: List the Elements

The first general element should be the most inclusive element. It's probably something like `<SERVBULL>service bulletin document content<\SERVBULL>`. Now write down the names of the other elements on a chalkboard, overhead projector, or some place where everyone in the room can see and approve them. These elements have relationships with one another, so use a structure diagram to keep track of the relationships. Keep listing elements until you have them all accounted for.

Step 3: Name Each Element and Assign Relationships

There are many ways to keep track of the relationships among elements. The GLA Consortium sells a jigsaw puzzle kit that lets you write the names of elements on puzzle pieces and connect them to show relationships between elements. You can move the puzzle pieces around to show different relationships and add attributes and entities to elements.

You can also label empty wastebaskets with the names of the large elements. In the case of service bulletins, you can label wastebaskets with major elements for that document type—`servbull`, `action`, `effectivity`, `material information`, and so on. Drop each subelement into the appropriate wastebasket.

You can accomplish much the same thing with a piece of paper and a structure diagram for each element and its subelements. Include a brief description of what the element is and what it does. Put into words what its relationship is to the rest of the elements. This is only a draft, so don't worry about making the definition perfect yet. Each element can have a written description, as well as a graphic structure tree of what it contains. You'll need these descriptions for step 8, so don't skip over this description step.

Step 4: Keep Listing Elements Until None Are Left

This step doesn't take long with simple document types. As you proceed, keep in mind the difference between content and structure. *Structure* is the logical place for the data, whereas *content* is the description of the data itself.

Suppose, for example, that the service bulletin's paragraphs can have a parts description table. One column contains the part number, and the other column contains the description. You obviously need a table element. The column headings need tags because they are a subelement of the table element.

Structurally, the column heads have tags such as `<COLHEAD1>Part Number<\COLHEAD1>` and `<COLHEAD2>Part Description<\COLHEAD2>`. You also could use just `<COLHEAD>`. As for content, the tags might look like `<PARTNUM>Part Number<\PARTNUM>` and `<PARTDESC>Part Description<\PARTDESC>`. For now, though, think only of structure.

 ▶▶ See "Handling Tables," p. 421

> ### Note
>
> Tables are a complex issue in SGML. The `<COLHEAD>` example above is just to illustrate the importance of focusing on structural elements at this point. If your table needed to be part of a searchable database, `<COLHEAD>` would probably not suffice as an element name. For more discussion about the implications of format and content in tables, see Chapter 25, "Handling Specialized Content and Delivery." If you want tables in your service bulletins, flag this fact and be sure you enlist the help of experienced SGML practitioners in your document analysis.

Step 5: Compare the Elements for Relationships and Groups

Now that you have identified all the structural elements in your service bulletin, try to assemble an experimental service bulletin using these elements. But as you do, pay close attention to the relationships that they have to each other. You're looking for occurrence, hierarchy, and sequence. Three questions can guide you:

- What is the sequence of the elements?
- What elements are included by other elements?
- What elements can pop up anywhere?

 ▶▶ See "Sequencing Elements," "Element Occurrence," "Element Hierarchy," and "Element Groups," pp. 144-146, 150

Elements that can pop up anywhere sometimes include footnotes, warnings and cautions, notes, and special text.

Look through the copies of your sample service bulletins. Your documents are the final proof of the quality and accuracy of your analysis. If you analyzed correctly, the experimental service bulletin you try to create now will match the real-world documents in their structure. Otherwise, you might need another element or element

II

Document Analysis

group, or you might need to modify your elements' content models. In any case, review the elements and their relationships. Check whether you should create new elements or consolidate elements you identified.

For example, in your service bulletin, you might like to add a <FrontMatter> element to group your <background>, <action>, and <effectivity> elements into. You might also add <Planning> and <Material> elements to group other elements into. This would be an example of adding elements to your structural definition, which you do in the next step.

Step 6: Check for Missing Elements

If you decide that you need more elements, create them now. You should check them to make sure that they are not already covered in another element description or content model. If they are, rename elements to avoid confusion. For example, if you discover a <material> element inside the <FrontMatter> element and another <material> element that is at the same level of hierarchy as the <FrontMatter> element, you should rename them to avoid confusion. In a service bulletin, you could easily expect to see a brief section about affected materials in the front matter, and another fully-detailed section about materials deeper in the document. These elements are structurally different, so they require different element names.

Some things you should look for are:

- Extra formatted items (such as a bulleted list)
- Included elements (such as a bullet graphic)
- Subtle changes in structure or appearance (like extra spacing after certain paragraphs)

Step 7: Construct a Structure Tree

Create a diagram like the one in figure 7.3. Add occurrence symbols like the ones shown in figure 7.4 to help you keep track of elements. Go through the whole document, and account for its entire structure.

You should test whether anything in your document type samples can be accounted for by more than one element. In other words, is there any ambiguity in your element definitions?

Some SGML software can help you to create a structure tree. Figure 7.6 shows a structure tree of the ATA service bulletin model.

▶▶ See "Near & Far Author" and "Near & Far," pp. 440, 461

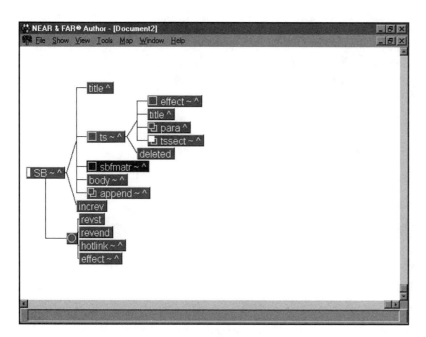

Fig. 7.6

Software like Microstar's Near & Far Author can help you create structure diagrams.

Step 8: Assemble an Element Dictionary

Collect the element descriptions from step 3. These should have been modified throughout this process as you modified your elements. The purpose behind a dictionary of elements is to help people who will use your model later. Unless you work with it every day, it's easy to forget all the details of a model. You need to have a way of recording what your elements mean.

A dictionary of the elements for each document type is useful not only for you but also for anybody else who maintains your DTDs, such as SGML consultants or even ambitious authors. The only time you can have too much documentation is when several people keep documentation that is not consistent. Therefore, make sure that revisions to your dictionary are consistent.

As element definitions and content models are modified with use over time, DTDs must be modified. DTDs and element definitions should track each other exactly. If Revision A of the Service Bulletin DTD affects the <material> element's content model, there should be a Revisions A in the element dictionary that tracks with that change. Don't let revisions to the element dictionary and the DTD get out of sync. You should maintain a controlled copy of this dictionary. You will probably want to set up a procedure for updating the dictionary that involves input from the people who use it.

Step 9: Have Others Check Your Work

Just when you think you're done, you're in for a surprise. Someone who works with service bulletins daily might say, "That definition sounds great, but the effectivity paragraph hasn't been part of the front matter for three months now!" Change happens all the time.

Managers do not want to involve their troops in decisions and, consequently, often have no idea of how documents are used and how work really gets done. This is why it is so important to get the advice of the document users early on.

Once you fix the problems that others find, you're ready for the final step.

Step 10: Revise and Test Your Work as Needed

This process is not complete until there are no more hang ups. All problems must be accounted for, or else you must continue revising and testing your work.

 ▶▶ See "Dealing with Mixed-Content Models" and "Dealing with Ambiguous Content Models," pp. 258-259

Consultants are a big help in this area. They can point out ambiguous definitions and mixed content. They might tell you to start all over again. That is not likely, but they will let you know whether you have stumbled into a hornet's nest of problems. Their advice can save you time in the long run.

From Here...

Defining elements is only part of the adventure of SGML. You must also declare them, add attributes, add entities, and refine your document analysis. The process eventually flows together. While you learn SGML, though, you have to take it step by step.

For more information, refer to the following:

- Chapter 8, "Relating Elements to Each Other," covers hierarchy, order, and occurrence.
- Chapter 9, "Extending Document Architecture," discusses how to add different capabilities to your documents.
- Chapter 10, "Following General SGML Declaration Syntax," includes detailed information on declaring elements, attributes, and entities.
- Chapter 11, "Using DTD Components," discusses element groups and their design implications.
- Chapter 16, "Markup Challenges and Specialized Content," covers document design for standard data and conditional documents.
- Chapter 25, "Handling Specialized Content and Delivery," shows you how to deal with tables, math, and other specialized content.

CHAPTER 8

Relating Elements to Each Other

One of the most powerful features of SGML is its ability to define detailed relationships among elements. Through its precise syntax, you can define a document model that might be simple or quite complex, depending upon your needs. You briefly saw this syntax in Chapter 7, "Defining the Elements." Now you will examine it in more detail. The mechanisms provided in SGML enable you to define all the possible relationships among elements. In this chapter, you learn how to use the constructs of the SGML syntax to define these relationships in terms of:

- Sequence
- Occurrence
- Hierarchy
- Groups
- Inclusion

Consider, for example, this book. It has different data elements, including:

- Table of contents
- Introduction
- Chapters and related items (title, reference, and sections)
- Figures and related items (title and reference)
- Tables and related items (rows, cells, and so on)
- Bulleted lists
- Numbered lists
- Appendixes
- Notes
- Index
- Paragraphs
- Sentences
- Words

Consider all the relationships possible among these elements. Some of these elements occur only once. Some occur many times and in a specific order. Some pop up at unforeseen times. Many are closely related to one other, like a family. Others are more distantly related, like a tribe or clan. Specific pairs of elements even feud with each other, like Hatfields and McCoys; only one can be present at a time. You can define all the relationships among these elements in SGML.

Sequencing Elements

Sequencing elements is just a way of saying that a certain set of elements will occur, possibly in a specific order. Suppose, for example, you are driving from San Diego to Albuquerque. You want to mark the progress of your trip, so you pick out particular milestones:

- Leave San Diego
- Complete one quarter of journey
- Complete half of journey
- Complete three quarters of journey
- Arrive in Albuquerque

You define the elements of the group—your trip to Albuquerque—in an ordered sequence. For example:

```
Trip = (Leave San Diego,1/4 journey complete,1/2 journey complete,3/4
journey complete,Arrive in Albuquerque)
```

Here you specify that the trip includes all those specific milestones in that particular order. This is similar to a book, whose table of contents you can specify to come after the title page.

If the contents change, however, your ability to specify the order might change. Imagine that your Albuquerque trip is a vacation and you want to see a number of sights along the way. You are not going to plan a specific itinerary. Instead, you have merely compiled a list of places along the way that you will see. On your trip, you want to visit:

- The Grand Canyon
- Flagstaff
- Meteor Crater
- Phoenix
- Window Rock
- Gallup
- Albuquerque

Because of the limited time available, you can't go to all these places. You figure that you can squeeze all the places on the list into your trip except that you can go only to either Phoenix or Window Rock, but not both. You also know that you are leaving from San Diego and ending up in Albuquerque.

With this in mind, you can define the trip in the following way:

```
Trip = (Leave San Diego,(Grand Canyon&Flagstaff&Meteor
Crater&Gallup&(Phoenix¦Window Rock)),Arrive Albuquerque)
```

The notation now indicates that you depart from San Diego; the comma indicates what follows after that. You visit the Grand Canyon, Flagstaff, Meteor Crater, Gallup, and either Phoenix or Window Rock. The ampersand (&) indicates all the items in no specific order. The vertical bar (¦) indicates one or the other, but not both.

Note

Although it provides a great deal of flexibility, the ampersand, or AND connector, tends to strain SGML parsers because of its ambiguity. Therefore, you should minimize its use in actual document models.

In defining document content models, you rarely need the ultimate flexibility of the AND connector. In most cases, you can construct an alternate model that fits your needs while minimizing its use.

You have seen how many symbols are used. They are defined in table 8.1.

Table 8.1 **Data Model Sequencing Symbols**			
Notation	**Usage**	**SGML Term**	**Description**
,	X,Y	SEQ	X followed by Y
&	X&Y	AND	X and Y in any order
¦	X¦Y	OR	X or Y

Element Occurrence

As you examine the occurrence of elements in a document, you know that certain elements are present more than once. In this book, for example, the chapter element occurs many times. Other elements occur only once, as in the case of a title page. Still other elements, such as a section reference, might or might not occur within a chapter.

Consider this in terms of your trip to Albuquerque. You are planning the trip. You want to sketch out the tasks along the way. You know that you must fill the gas tank several times, but you are not sure how many fill-ups will be needed. You are not sure whether you will need to change the oil on the trip. If you do, you will get it done when you get to Albuquerque. After you arrive in Albuquerque, you might have a few big dinners. Now you can diagram your trip in this way:

```
Trip = (Fill Tank,Leave San Diego,Fill Tank+,Arrive Albuquerque,(Oil
Change?&Big Dinners*)
```

This notation indicates that you will fill the gas tank, leave San Diego, fill the gas tank at least once more, and arrive in Albuquerque. After arriving, you might change the oil once, or you might not. You also might go out for one or more big dinners.

Table 8.2 describes the structure notation for occurrence that you have just used in modeling this trip.

Table 8.2 Data Model Occurrence Symbols			
Notation	**Usage**	**SGML Term**	**Description**
(none)	X	(none)	X occurs once.
+	X+	PLUS	X is required. It occurs at least once.
?	X?	OPT	X is optional. It occurs never or only once.
*	X*	REP	X is optional and repeatable. It occurs never, once, or more than once.

This notation is also useful in describing the contents of this book. For example, you would define the chapters as chapter+ because you know that there is at least one of them. You would define the title page as title page, with no symbolic notation, because there is only one title page. You would define the section references as section reference* because each section might or might not have one or more of them.

You now have a way to specify both the sequence and the frequency of elements. Now take a look at how you can specify the hierarchy of elements.

Element Hierarchy

As you have seen, you can define your trip to Albuquerque in several different ways. You first looked at it in terms of the legs of the trip. You next defined it in terms of the places you will visit along the way. Finally, you considered the trip in terms of servicing—for your car and yourself.

In all these examples, the trip consists of various elements that make up the whole journey. When you looked at it in terms of servicing, you defined it as:

```
Trip = (Fill Tank,Leave San Diego,Fill Tank+,Arrive Albuquerque,(Oil
Change?&Big Dinners*)
```

You specified some items, but you did not specify any details about what each item entails. For example, you perform the task `Fill Tank` several times during the course of the trip, but you never specify what filling the tank really involves. Through the process of specifying element *hierarchy*, you can define each element in the process.

Suppose that you define `Fill Tank` as follows:

```
Fill Tank = (Find Gas Station,Pull Into Station,((Pull Up To Pump,Pay For
Gas,Pump Gas,Get Change)&Stretch Legs&Use Restroom?),Leave Station)
```

This definition describes the task in more detail. It specifies all the steps and the order in which they are performed.

You have now defined the elements of your trip down two levels: the steps of the trip itself and the individual steps of one of the steps contained within the trip (`Fill Tank`).

In the same way, SGML documents can be composed of many elements, ranging from very large ones that consist of numerous subelements to others that might contain only a bit of text.

Earlier in this chapter, you saw some of the elements that this book contains. The list includes large elements, such as chapters, and small elements, such as chapter titles. When you think of all the elements that make up this book, you realize that you need a mechanism for defining the hierarchy.

Just as with your road trip, you can use the concept of hierarchy to define all the elements that make up this book. Through this hierarchy, the list of elements becomes more meaningful. This is because you can use the hierarchical approach to go recursively down through layer after layer, as deep as necessary, to define the data model thoroughly.

Take a look at figure 8.1. It shows a structural diagram of a book.

This diagram adds to your understanding of the book. Looking at it tells you much about how the elements within the book relate to one another and to the book overall.

You can now tell, for example, that a chapter includes a title, body, and one or more sections. One level below, sections contain a title and a body. This hierarchical structuring, or nesting, explains the relationships among the elements of this book. It is useful in content models, for it enables you to go as deep as you need to in defining structural relationships.

Take another look at the structure chart in figure 8.1. You could define this book by recursively defining each subsequent level in the structural tree. For example:

```
Book=(TitlePg,TableContents,Foreword,Chapter+,(Bibliography&Appendix+),Index)
TableContents=(TOCentry+)
Foreword=(ForewordTitle,ForewordText)
Chapter=(ChapTitle,ChapterBody,ChaptSect+)
Bibliography=(ItemDesc,ItemPgNum)+
```

II

Document Analysis

```
Appendix=(ItemDesc,ItemPgNum)+
Index=(IndexItem)+
```

Fig. 8.1

This is a structural view of a book, illustrating the major components.

This is very close to how a DTD representation of the book's content model looks. A DTD for it appears at the end of this chapter.

Now that you have seen how to define structural hierarchies among nested elements, you can find out how to handle odd elements that might occur anywhere in the structure.

▶▶ See Chapter 10, "Following General SGML Declaration Syntax," p. 171, for a discussion of SGML declaration syntax

Element Inclusion and Exclusion

As you think of this book, you can picture a document model containing a foreword, a number of chapters, an index, and so on. In examining the structure of our content model, you can visualize an ordered relationship with each element having a place.

In some cases, however, elements float about freely and occur in a number of places. To understand this better, consider your road trip to Albuquerque.

You could define the journey in the following way:

```
Trip = (Leave San Diego,First 1/4 journey,Second 1/4 journey,Third 1/4
journey, Fourth 1/4 journey,Arrive Albuquerque)
```

You can modify this definition to include meals. However, there is a complication. When you travel, you don't always eat at predictable times. You might skip meals to cover more miles, or you might stop a few times, walk around and take in the sights, and work up a hearty appetite. In short, you just don't know how often and when you will stop to eat.

In this situation, you can use *inclusion* to specify meals along the way. Inclusion is a method of specifying elements or other data that can occur anywhere within another element. It is particularly useful for items that float throughout a structure.

In the case of the trip, you can modify the definition:

```
Trip = (Leave San Diego,First 1/4 journey,Second 1/4 journey,Third 1/4
journey, Fourth 1/4 journey, Arrive Albuquerque) +(Meals+)
```

The trip now consists of the following parts in this order:

- Depart San Diego
- Complete the first quarter of the trip, the second quarter, the third quarter, and the fourth quarter
- Arrive in Albuquerque
- Along the way, eat one or more meals; they can occur anywhere within any of the elements specified—leave San Diego, second 1/4 journey, and so on

The notation +(*item*) is a mechanism for indicating that *item* can occur within any of the elements in the model group—that is, within any of the elements within the parentheses. In this case, the inclusion element is specified as Meals+, or one or more meals.

You might say, "This is fine for meals on the road, but what does it have to do with document structures?" After all, you don't want to have title pages or indexes floating about in a document. On the other hand, elements such as figure references, footnotes, and hypertext links in electronic documents can float throughout a document, popping up legitimately in many places.

> **Note**
>
> Inclusion implies floating objects that can occur anywhere, while structure is generally a bit more rigid, implying order as well as content. Therefore, inclusion generally should not be used for structural elements or for elements that are tied to the ordered sequence of a document structure.

Exclusion works much like inclusion, except in reverse. For example, if you want to exclude getting speeding tickets from the trip, you can do this:

```
Trip = (Leave San Diego,First 1/4 journey,Second 1/4 journey,Third 1/4
journey, Fourth 1/4 journey, Arrive Albuquerque) -(Speeding Tickets)
```

> **Note**
>
> Inclusions and exclusions can occur in the same element definition. If they cover the same element, exclusion wins (as defined in the SGML standard, ISO 8879).

Element Groups

Inclusion and exclusion are often used in conjunction with specific model groups—groups of elements. In the definition of this book, for example, you can enable specific elements to float. That is, they are permitted to occur within other elements.

Suppose that you want to permit a paragraph to contain a number of elements. They might include tables and figures; references to tables, figures, chapters, and appendixes; and special typefaces, such as bold or italic. In a similar way, you might want to exclude specific elements from other structures. For example, you can exclude bulleted lists from footnotes.

Structure Diagram Revisited

Take a look at figure 8.2. It shows a revised structure diagram of a book. Inclusion has been added for references that can occur anywhere within the ChapterBody and SectionBody element definitions.

Figure 8.3 is a DTD that models this structure. It shows how you can define the element relationships discussed in this chapter.

If some of the DTD syntax is unfamiliar, don't worry. You will explore DTDs in much more detail in Part III, "Content Modeling: Developing the DTD." See Chapter 10, "Following General SGML Declaration Syntax," for a discussion of the syntax in DTDs. Chapter 11 discusses how to make DTD components. Chapter 13 examines the evaluation of DTDs and the use of parsers.

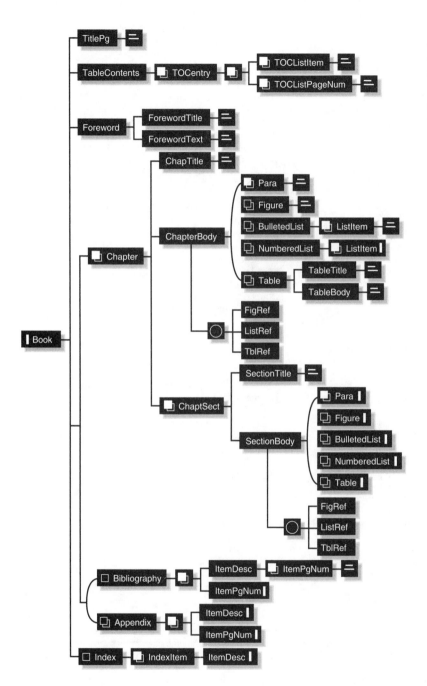

Fig. 8.2

Here is a revised look at a book structure, using inclusions for references to figures, lists, and tables.

Fig. 8.3

This is an example of a document type definition (DTD) for a book.

```
<!DOCTYPE Book [
<!--Book Structure Model -- >
<!ELEMENT Book          - - (TitlePg,TableContents,Foreword,(Chapter+,
                            (Bibliography?&Appendix*)),Index?) >
<!--Major Sub Elements -- >
<!ELEMENT TitlePg       - - (#PCDATA)  >
<!ELEMENT TableContents - - (TOCentry+)  >
<!ELEMENT Foreword      - - (ForewordTitle,ForewordText)  >
<!ELEMENT Chapter       - - (ChapTitle,ChapterBody,ChaptSect+)  >
<!ELEMENT Bibliography  - - (ItemDesc,ItemPgNum)+  >
<!ELEMENT Appendix      - - (ItemDesc,ItemPgNum)+  >
<!ELEMENT Index         - - (IndexItem+)  >
<!--TOC elements -- >
<!ELEMENT TOCentry      - - (TOCListItem+,TOCListPageNum+)+>
<!ELEMENT TOCListItem   - - (#PCDATA)  >
<!ELEMENT TOCListPageNum - - (#PCDATA)  >
<!--Content elements -- >
<!ELEMENT ForewordTitle - - (#PCDATA)  >
<!ELEMENT ForewordText  - - (#PCDATA)  >
<!ELEMENT ChapTitle     - - (#PCDATA)  >
<!ELEMENT ChapterBody   - - (Para+&Figure*&BulletedList*&
                            NumberedList*&Table*)
                                    +(FigRef,ListRef,TblRef)  >
<!ELEMENT SectionTitle  - - (#PCDATA)  >
<!ELEMENT ChaptSect     - - (SectionTitle,SectionBody)  >
<!ELEMENT SectionBody   - - (Para+&Figure*&BulletedList*&
                            NumberedList*&Table*)
                                    +(FigRef,ListRef,TblRef)  >
<!ELEMENT Para          - - (#PCDATA)  >
<!ELEMENT Figure        - - (#PCDATA)  >
<!ELEMENT Table         - - (TableTitle,TableBody)  >
<!ELEMENT TableTitle    - - (#PCDATA)  >
<!ELEMENT TableBody     - - (#PCDATA)  >
<!--Index elements -- >
<!ELEMENT IndexItem     - - (ItemDesc)  >
<!ELEMENT ItemDesc      - - (ItemPgNum+)  >
<!ELEMENT ItemPgNum     - - (#PCDATA)  >
<!--List elements -- >
<!ELEMENT NumberedList  - - (ListItem+)  >
<!ELEMENT BulletedList  - - (ListItem+)  >
<!ELEMENT ListItem      - - (#PCDATA)  >
<!--Reference elements -- >
<!ELEMENT ListRef       - - (#PCDATA)  >
<!ELEMENT TblRef        - - (#PCDATA)  >
<!ELEMENT FigRef        - - (#PCDATA)  >
]>
```

Note

#PCDATA is the SGML terminology for character data that can be evaluated by an SGML parser. See Chapter 10, "Following General SGML Declaration Syntax," for a description of #PCDATA.

From Here...

In this chapter, you've seen how elements can relate to each other through the use of hierarchy, sequence, inclusion/exclusion, and occurrence. You also examined the notation for defining the relationships among elements. From here, you will examine the details involved in developing a DTD.

For more information, see the following chapters:

- Chapter 9, "Extending Document Architecture," discusses the use of links in SGML documents.
- Chapter 10, "Following General SGML Declaration Syntax," explores the specifics of SGML terminology.
- Chapter 11, "Using DTD Components," shows how to make modular components for use in DTDs.

II

Document Analysis

Extending Document Architecture

You have accomplished all the tasks related to document analysis. You now can add bells and whistles—extended features—to your documents. The bells and whistles show up as more elements. This chapter shows you how to handle nonprinting (control) information. It's still basic SGML; it does not even push the envelope of SGML's capabilities.

In this chapter, you learn:

- How to add more features to a document
- How to add revision tracking information to a document
- How to add hypertext links to a document
- How to add multimedia capability to a document
- What HyTime is
- How to upgrade an HTML Web site to an SGML Web site

Adding Features to Documents

When you add features to your documents, you add features to your document types. You must first decide which document types get which nonprinting (control) features. You take one document type at a time and decide all the features that it should have.

When you add features to a document type, you modify the document instance. You also must modify the DTD because you are dealing with all the document instances of that type. The DTD must conform to SGML and parse completely.

> **Note**
>
> Be careful that the features you add to one type of document apply to *all* the instances of that document type. In the case of the HTML DTD, that could involve all the documents on the World Wide Web.
>
> If you modify document instances without modifying the agreed-upon DTD—in this case, HTML version 2.0—you run the risk of creating documents that cannot be viewed using standard HTML compliant browsers. This sort of problem is the seed of a current controversy on the Net: the conflict between innovation and standardization. The result is the rise of mutations of standard HTML documents that can only be viewed through proprietary browsers like Netscape.

▶▶ See "Standardization versus Innovation," p. 315
▶▶ See "Handling Tables" and "Handling Math and Equations," pp. 421, 424

Extending document architecture, therefore, involves modifying a DTD. You can add attributes to elements and add elements to the DTD. You can also add entities. This procedure might look like the following:

1. Decide which document types get which features.
2. Add the appropriate document structures (elements, attributes, and entities) to the first document type.
3. Add the appropriate structures to the subsequent document types.
4. Add the appropriate attributes to the first new element of the first document type.
5. Add the appropriate attributes to the subsequent elements of the subsequent document types.
6. Modify the DTDs for each document type that was modified.
7. Parse the modified DTDs to ensure that they conform to SGML standards.

Using the HTML DTD as an example, suppose you wanted to add the ability to express complicated math equations to the HTML standard. (The proposed version 3.0 of the HTML DTD does this.) Since you have just one document type, this simplifies the process. But you first add a group of entities with which to express special math symbols. Then you must add elements that utilize these symbols in the required mathematical ways—you must add superscript and subscript elements, for example. In the case of HTML 3.0, there are structures to incorporate LaTex-like arrays for storing formatting macros to display complicated formulas. This whole architectural extension relies on a systematic modification of the DTD, as described earlier.

Figure 9.1 shows a graphical representation of how to extend document architecture.

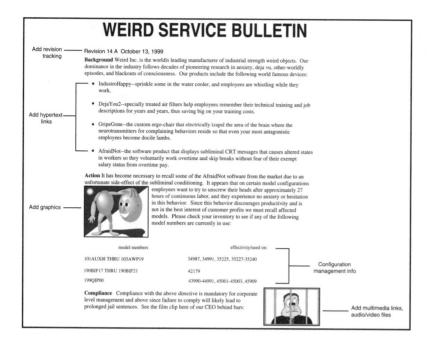

Fig. 9.1

Extending document architecture involves adding features to the structure of a document type.

Before you add a feature to your document types, ask yourself these questions:

- Will the feature affect other document types?
- Will the feature change any DTDs that I do not control?
- Will the feature require any temporary tags?
- Does the feature require format-related extensions that I should think about?
- Do I have input from all the people who will use the feature?
- What notes should I make so that others can understand how all the features work together?

◄◄ See "The Definition Process," p. 137

►► See "Choosing Elements or Attributes," "Dealing with Mixed-Content Models," "Dealing with Ambiguous Content Models," and "How Flexible Should DTDs Be?" pp. 247, 258, 259, 261

Tip

When you design features, always keep in mind the people who will use them. Add the new features to your element dictionary, which records and explains all the elements that you have created for your documents and DTDs. Don't shortcut this task. The people who follow you in the project will need the information.

Adding Revision Tracking Information to Documents

Documents often exist at several revision levels. The revision level can be critical, especially in engineering documents. People often deal with similar documents at different revision levels, and the revision level affects how a document must be processed.

> **Note**
>
> Although many environments require revision tracking, engineering and manufacturing environments especially need the feature. If you expect to work on SGML documents in this type of environment, you should become an expert at adding features such as revision tracking to documents and DTDs.
>
> Any environment where different configurations of a product or of information can possibly be confused or mixed together incorrectly should probably include revision tracking. For example, if you are building one configuration of a software or hardware product for one customer, but a slightly different configuration for a different customer, you want to ensure each customer gets the correct documentation for his or her configuration. Revision tracking helps maintain compatibility.

Preliminary Steps

When you add a feature such as revision tracking to a document, you must decide where and how to add it. Ask yourself these questions:

- Can I add the feature as an element tag, attribute, or entity?
- Can I avoid adding an element or entity and add an attribute instead?
- Will the feature be printed on the document, or is it nonprintable information?
- What information is in the feature?
- Whether the feature is printed or not, how is the information in the feature updated?
- Where in the document should the information be stored?

When you add a feature to the document, you need to be specific. Your intentions should be clear.

Figure 9.2 shows a technical document with a printed revision tracking feature that shows the revision level of the document. You can also show the revision level of each page, paragraph, or section in the document.

Section IV: Downloading the Stock Data from Dial Data

(REVISION: 08/19/95)

Several options exist updating your data from Dial Data, and they all start from the PeerComm menuing The PeerComm menu structure is an alternative to the Tiger pull-down menus. The pull-down menus allow you t manipulate charts and display technical indicators, but they also allow access to data file editing utilities as well as updating features. Since these other features can become quite busy, the PeerComm menuing structure focuses just maintenance and updating features necessary for day-to-day program performance.

Dial data is the premier stock data service, so the program is custom tuned to access and process their sto They give a special data discount to PeerComm users.

Downloading Options in PeerComm

There are four types data options available from the PeerComm subsystem. Dial data is responsible for all the nur you receive through any of the following sources. Each of these options launches by clicking the appropriate butto first page of the PeerComm "launch pad."

Tiger BBS

The Tiger BBS is updated at the close of each market day and provides you weekly, monthly, and 10 day of your regular stock lists so you don't have to retrieve them each day. The BBS remembers your default preferences and prepares files for you automatically. Your custom news and stock data transfers to your directories automatically when you push the BBS Button on the PeerComm menu.

Index Data

Index data is updated directly from Dial data when you click the "Index Button" object. These files autor update to the latest market date for which data exists. If you dial in during market hours, yesterday's clos date. Your system automatically tells Dial what the last index close is for which you have data, and it ret

---

Fig. 9.2

The revision level date of this document appears on-screen.

II

Document Analysis

Element or Attribute?

> **Tip**
>
> Attributes can certainly be printed values, but this example lends itself to a distinction between a printed and a nonprinted revision tracking.

If a feature will be printed, the section in which it appears could contain its own revision element. If the feature is nonprintable, you could make it an attribute of the section element. Simply place revision tags around the revision information.

For example, you can place the feature anywhere in the section, so long as the structure tree permits it within the section content model. This method works well when you are dealing with a particular date because the date can change to any date. Sometimes you have many revision levels, however, and the revision information can be expressed as only one of several alternatives—A, B, C, or D.

When there are only a few revision levels to worry about, you can add the feature with just an attribute. For example:

```
<SECTION Revision="b">Section IV. Turbine Removal
<H3>Orienting the Lifting Device</H3>
<P>Here's the first paragraph</P>
<P>Here's the last paragraph</P>
<H3>Disconnecting the Turbine from the Skid</H3>
<P>Here's the first paragraph</P>
<P>Here's the last paragraph</P>
<H3>Lifting the Puppy Out<H3>
```

```
<P>Here's the first paragraph<P>
<P>Here's the last paragraph<P>
<H3>Taking a Bow<H3>
</SECTION>
```

The attribute is set up in the DTD. Therefore, you must provide a content model for the attribute that contains all the revision levels in the DTD under the `<SECTION>` element.

Note

SGML offers many ways to add revision level tracking. For instance, you can use entities that contain other elements as content models. However, you should use the simplest method possible because it will probably be the easiest in the long run.

Adding Hypertext Links to a Document

The most common examples of adding hypertext links to a document are for HTML documents. You can easily create your own hypertext help file and work from the HTML DTD, using Netscape or another browser as your help file viewer.

Local and Remote Links

You need to distinguish between local and remote links. It's easy to forget where files are coming from when you click a Web browser. You forget whether the document that you are accessing is on your own hard drive or local network, or whether it's from a server on the other side of the planet. Local and remote links are an important distinction in SGML, however, because you must mark them differently.

In HTML, a local reference in a Web document is usually indicated by:

```
<A HREF="home.htm">Jump to My Home Page</A>
```

and a remote reference is usually indicated by:

```
<A HREF="http://www.someplace.com">Jump to my page</A>
```

There are variations, but these follow the basic DTD. In figure 9.3, you can see the delimiters and attribute format that surrounds the tagged text.

Sometimes you want to link to a local graphics image, which is another type of link. In the HTML DTD, a call to the graphic looks like:

```
<IMG SRC = "graphic.gif"><PARA>Bla bla bla bla</PARA>
```

All the elements are defined in the appropriate definition for the document type for the DTD. In the HTML 2.0 DTD, the line markup section calls the `<A>` element—short for *anchor*—with attributes:

```
<!ELEMENT A      - - %A.content -(A)>
<!ATTLIST A
```

```
HREF    %URI #IMPLIED
NAME    %linkName #IMPLIED
%linkExtraAttributes;
%SDAPREF; "<Anchor: #AttList>"
>
```

Notice the HREF attribute with the %URI content model. This is just one example of how a DTD makes a link.

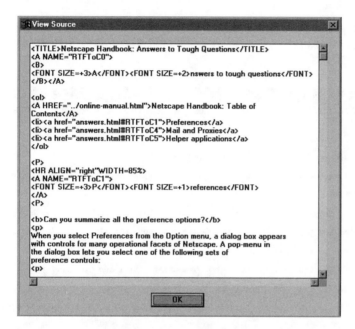

Fig. 9.3

Netscape's online handbook contains references to hypertext links that include special Netscape extensions.

II

Document Analysis

> **Note**
>
> The HTML DTD is somewhat limited in its linking capability. More robust links can be created in SGML using ID and IDREF attributes described in "Identifying Internal and External Objects (ID & IDREF)" in Chapter 14.
>
> Also note that URI (universal resource indicator) is a more generic term than URL (universal resource link). A URL is only one kind of URI.

Adding Multimedia Content

Adding multimedia capability to documents essentially involves linking them to other types of files. Your documents are primarily text documents. You are pointing to binary files or executable programs. SGML handles this well, but it must turn over control of this type of file to a specialized viewer.

Suppose, for example, that you want to put a button that starts an audio-visual film clip on one of your document instances. When you point to the clip file, the SGML processing system gives control over the binary media file to the appropriate viewer. When the clip finishes, the control returns to the SGML tool. Much of this depends on the characteristics of the browsing tool that you use to look at the SGML file. With Web documents, the job of SGML is to point to the target file and to keep the link clear.

Adding a Graphic

Figure 9.4 shows a call to a JPEG graphic called IDUNNO.JPG from an HTML document.

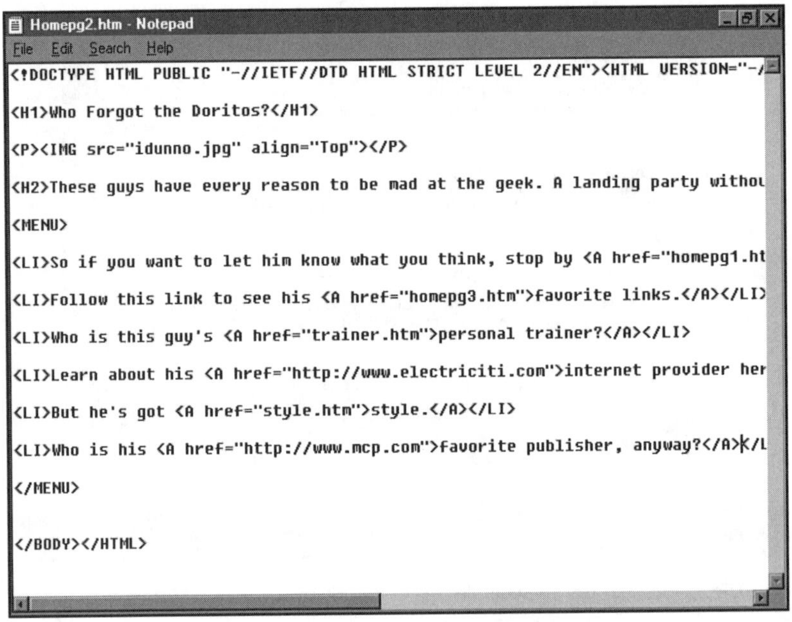

Fig. 9.4

The call to IDUNNO.JPG is made with the SRC *attribute inside the* <IMG> *element.*

```
Homepg2.htm - Notepad
File  Edit  Search  Help
<!DOCTYPE HTML PUBLIC "-//IETF//DTD HTML STRICT LEVEL 2//EN"><HTML VERSION="-/
<H1>Who Forgot the Doritos?</H1>
<P><IMG src="idunno.jpg" align="Top"></P>
<H2>These guys have every reason to be mad at the geek. A landing party withou
<MENU>
<LI>So if you want to let him know what you think, stop by <A href="homepg1.ht
<LI>Follow this link to see his <A href="homepg3.htm">favorite links.</A></LI>
<LI>Who is this guy's <A href="trainer.htm">personal trainer?</A></LI>
<LI>Learn about his <A href="http://www.electriciti.com">internet provider her
<LI>But he's got <A href="style.htm">style.</A></LI>
<LI>Who is his <A href="http://www.mcp.com">favorite publisher, anyway?</A></L
</MENU>


</BODY></HTML>
```

The basic syntax is:

```
<P><IMG src "idunno.jpg" align="top"></P>
```

The <P> element is a paragraph tag. The <IMG> element stands for image. Their corresponding definitions in the HTML 2.0 DTD are:

```
<!--==============Images==========================-->
<!ELEMENT  IMG     - O  EMPTY
<!ATTLIST  IMG
           SRC   %URI;        #REQUIRED
           ALT   CDATA        #IMPLIED
           ALIGN (top¦middle¦bottom)   #IMPLIED
           ISMAP (ISMAP)   #IMPLIED
           %SDAPREF;   "<Fig><?SDATrans Img: AttList>#AttVal(Alt)</Fig>"
             >
```

```
<!-- <IMG>              Image; icon, glyph or illustration -->
<!-- <IMG SRC="...">    Address of image object           -->
<!-- IMG ALT="...">     Textual alternative               -->
<!-- IMG ALIGN=...>     Position relative to text          -->
<!-- IMG ISMAP>         Each pixel can be a link           -->
```

The documentation in this DTD excerpt clearly tells what each element means and gives an example of its use. The comment lines are valuable.

The DTD calls an element that is used only for loading images, and the document instance deploys it with the address of the desired image file. The DTD and the document instance must work together.

The process is simple. You tag the document feature with the appropriate tag and use attributes to locate the binary file. The ALIGN attribute locates the file. You can set it up differently in another SGML application, of course. The steps are:

1. Tag the object with the correct element.
2. Reference the file with an attribute.
3. Locate the file on your system or network with the value of the attribute.

Tip

If you can do this three-step approach, you can keep many applications running correctly. Other applications of SGML get even more involved. For example, check out how the TEI p3 DTD handles image and similar files; see **http://www.sil.org/sgml/acadapps.html#tei**.

Adding a Sound or Video File

Take a look at figure 9.5. It's from the Web home page for the TV Themes Home Page.

Fig. 9.5

The TV Themes Home Page makes calls to different kinds of multimedia files.

The sound files include alenat.au, amaze.au, and automan.au. Notice the anchor element <A> and the attribute HREF. The pattern is the same as with hypertext links. How the file gets viewed or played depends on the viewing tool. Web browsers enable you to configure external viewing software to handle it. You can configure your own DTD with macros to launch specific applications, but that makes your SGML documents less portable.

HyTime

HyTime stands for Hypermedia/Time-based Structuring Language and is a whole book in its own right. It's a structured method for expressing relationships among multimedia objects in a document. The internal coding and processing semantics of these objects are ignored by SGML, just as graphics formats that are not standardized are ignored. HyTime, like SGML, does not define a language or even a single application. Instead, it is the seed from which many applications can grow while remaining compatible with SGML standards. You can think of HyTime as the SGML Hypermedia standard. Developers use it to design multimedia environments for SGML applications.

> ▶▶ See "HyTime: SGML and Hypermedia," p. 385
> ▶▶ See "HyTime," p. 524

Goals of HyTime

The goals of HyTime and hypermedia in SGML include:

- To link different document and DTD structures without changing the structures themselves or their content.
- To link hypertext and hypermedia documents and files as objects.
- To provide guidelines for the modular structuring of hypermedia links so that applications can support many kinds of external applications.
- To link documents and files as objects irrespective of time sequencing, platform, and native software.
- To link to any structural levels of any file, not just logical components or elements.
- To enable anyone affected by a link to maintain it without altering the work of others.

Addressing

Some of the magic of HyTime comes from how it addresses multimedia objects. You can reference an object in real life in many ways:

- By a unique name; for example, "Bring me the Craftsman three-quarter-inch drive socket, serial number 34n368c."

- By its position in Cartesian space; for example, "Bring me the object that is located 10 feet due southwest of my position, at an altitude of 36 inches."

- By its location relative to some other object; for example, "Bring me the wrench on the table next to the paint can."

Normal SGML hyperlinks often require a unique name, as in the first example of addressing above. ID and IDREF, which you learn about in Chapter 14, are normal ways of referring to a document or a file with SGML. You can locate and reference individual entities and elements with their IDs, thereby creating a link. HyTime adds even more flexibility and robustness in addressing objects of many kinds.

▶▶ See "Identifying Internal and External Objects (ID & IDREF)," p. 251

Architectural Templates (Forms)

HyTime uses templates (or forms) that attach extra information to elements. You use these forms to attach attributes to an element without changing the DTD or the parsing for the document instance. This way, you can swap documents and data even with different DTDs and different tags. If you can use forms, you can attach many types of attributes at different times. The forms and their targeted elements can have a dynamic relationship, which greatly expands your ability to make hypermedia links.

The basic types of architectural templates or forms include:

- *Attribute list forms.* These forms look like regular SGML attribute lists, but they are added to a DTD's attribute lists. One attribute identifies the architectural form; the other attributes identify values.

- *Element type forms.* These forms require an element declaration and an attribute list.

- *Location address forms.* These forms identify a specific location by path, name, coordinate, and so on.

- *Object forms.* These forms are used for anything in a HyTime event. A HyTime *event* is a specialized term; it signals the occurrence of an object.

- *Resource forms.* These forms specify what is permitted in a HyTime event.

There are more types of forms. They all, however, add linking capability to DTDs and documents and make it easier to launch links.

> **Note**
>
> Generic SGML linking has some drawbacks. You can only link to and from whole documents—unless you use a unique ID to each linkpoint.
>
> (continues)

Document Analysis

II

(continued)

HyTime extends SGML's ability to make links to places that do not have an ID to each linkpoint. It uses the pointer or address forms mentioned above. The forms add the ID information or provide enough data to locate the desired object. HyTime creates a local ID, or it uses the link itself to find the object. For example, when you say, "I want the wrench on the bench," HyTime can determine which bench you mean and find the wrench on it.

HyTime Requirements

To work in your environment, HyTime requires three component pieces:

- *A HyTime application.* This provides the user interface and controls external programs and how multimedia events are displayed.
- *A HyTime engine.* This helps the application talk with the parser. It builds links and controls synchronization between external programs and the application.
- *An SGML parser.* This validates DTDs and document instances and updates the HyTime engine with that information.

HyTime is an extension of SGML. Therefore, you handle declarations, comments, and the like in HyTime just as you do in SGML. For example, you use standard SGML declarations to specify HyTime architectural forms and element types. The HyTime declaration looks slightly different, however. It shows up as an SGML processing instruction, as in:

```
<?HyTime DECLARATION PARAMETERS>
```

A DTD can contain both HyTime and other elements, and the architectural forms say where each one can occur. The only constraint in HyTime is in how you put together document instances—not DTDs.

Note

You can read about the HyTime specification at **http://www.sil.org/sgml/ gen-apps.html#hytime**. There are more links, but the **sil.org** site is a good one. You can do a Web search for HyTime resources. There are plenty. A copy of the HyTime specification costs approximately $100.

Upgrading Your HTML Site to an SGML Site

You should consider upgrading your Web site from HTML to full-blown SGML, which offers more functionality. With SGML Web browsers such as SoftQuad's Panorama arriving on the scene, you can provide your Net guests with more than you can with just HTML. The main advantage is the diversity of document types that you can make available. HTML is just one application of SGML; many other document types have been written.

For example, it would be difficult to put an entire set of software manuals in HTML for your clients. Many companies put their software manuals on CD-ROM instead of hard copy. If you write your software manuals in SGML, you can place them online. Your customers then can access the most recent versions as if the files were on their own local CD-ROM.

▶▶ See "What SGML Can Add to Web Sites," p. 301

▶▶ See "SGML on the Web," p. 311

▶▶ See "Challenges of Upgrading" and "Benefits of Upgrading," pp. 337, 339

▶▶ See "How To Make Effective SGML Web Pages," p. 389

▶▶ See "Current Collaborative Projects on the Web," p. 519

If you are committed to writing only simple HTML documents, don't worry about upgrading. The world of SGML has an enormous number of documents, however. The advantages include:

- HyTime multimedia links
- More DTDs, which add functionality to your links, such as TEI (P3), Euromath, DocBook, AAP, and even ICAD
- More ways of handling special situations or circumstances
- More powerful features for your Web site, such as the ones that big businesses and governments use in their documents

From Here...

You have finished learning about document analysis. You have been introduced to DTDs, which you'll learn even more about in the following chapters on DTDs and content modeling.

Document architecture is a simple idea, but it is often a complicated practice. Extending architecture can be even more complicated. It boils down to adding features to your documents. You now know the basic way to add features. You will learn the syntax for those features later.

For more information, refer to the following:

- Part III, "Content Modeling: Developing the DTD," discusses DTDs in detail.
- Part IV, "Markup Strategies," deals with special situations. You'll learn how to avoid having to mark up existing documents manually.
- Part V, "SGML and the World Wide Web," is a must if you're interested in the World Wide Web.
- Chapter 25, "Handling Specialized Content and Delivery," discusses much of the material in this chapter in greater detail.

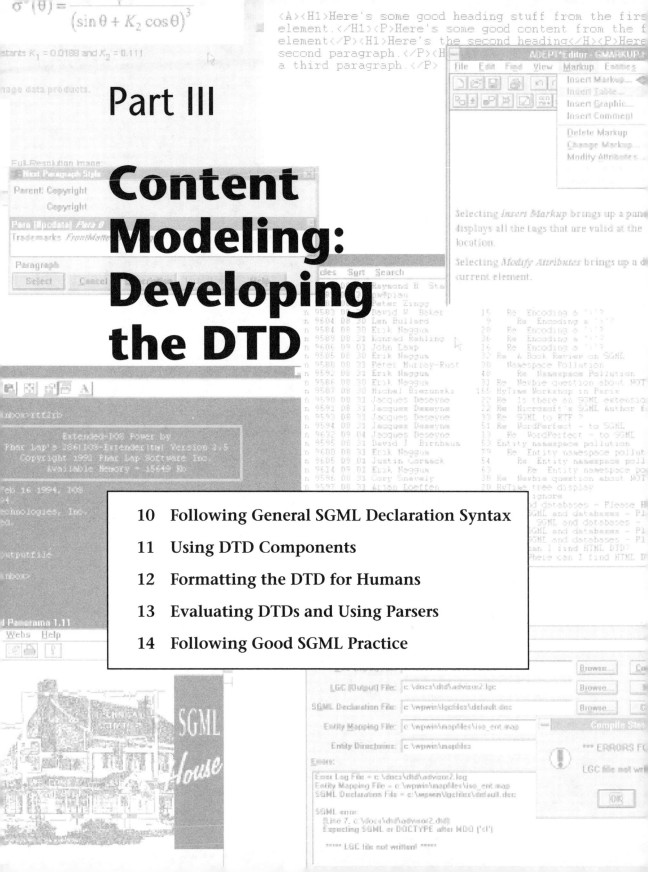

Part III

Content Modeling: Developing the DTD

10   Following General SGML Declaration Syntax

11   Using DTD Components

12   Formatting the DTD for Humans

13   Evaluating DTDs and Using Parsers

14   Following Good SGML Practice

CHAPTER 10

Following General SGML Declaration Syntax

This chapter explores some of the basics of SGML and DTD structure (or architecture). Initially, you'll explore the general syntax of the language (remember, SGML = Standard Generalized Markup Language).

Specific sections explore the use of the key components of SGML in the DTD:

- General SGML declaration syntax
- The DOCTYPE declaration
- Use of comments
- ELEMENTS: declaration and usage
- ATTRIBUTES: declaration and usage
- ENTITIES: declaration and usage

By the time you finish this chapter, you will have gained a perspective on DTDs that will enable you to read and understand them. Those of you from the HTML world may find yourselves gaining a new knowledge and perspective of the underlying architecture that you have already been using for some time.

Publicly Available DTDs May Be Appropriate

Most authors writing in SGML have little need to delve into the myriad of details involved in creating Document Type Definitions (DTDs). In many cases, you are presented with DTDs to use in writing tasks, much as you might receive a combination of writing style guides, outlines, and word processor stylesheets when writing in a traditional word processor-based environment.

In the structured authoring environment of SGML, you are presented with similar guides. These, most likely, include a DTD containing the structural rules of the document type that you're authoring, instructions on using the DTD, and perhaps an output specification that corresponds to the output formatting of the document. If the document has multiple forms of delivery (such as hardcopy and electronic), you might receive several output specifications.

The DTD that you receive can be specifically designed for a delivery medium, such as the HTML 2.0 DTD designed to be used for delivery on the World Wide Web. It can be industry specific, such as a CALS DTD (defined according to the MIL-M-28001 standard) for the defense industry, or it can be a company-specific DTD designed for a specific class of corporate documents. Table 10.1 illustrates some current standard DTDs that are available.

Table 10.1 Industry-Specific Document Type Definitions	
Industry	**DTD Type**
Airline/Aviation	ATA 100
Defense	CALS (MIL-M-28001)
Publishing	AAP (ISO 12083-1994)
Historical and New Scholarly Materials	TEI (Text Encoding Initiative)
Internet/World Wide Web	HTML
Electronics/Semiconductors	Pinnacles and SEED

Why Get Involved with DTD Syntax?

Since standard DTDs are publicly available, you might find yourself asking, "Why should I get involved with all the details of DTDs and DTD syntax?" After all, with today's tools and the range of existing DTDs, you may not ever have to write one. Most people writing documents in HTML for use on the World Wide Web haven't the foggiest notion of what DTD they are using when they create documents, home pages, and so on.

Yet even if you never anticipate writing your own DTD, knowing the rules and syntax of how they are constructed can prove to be very useful later. Just as a homeowner might take a building construction course to understand the basics of home construction, you might want to understand some of the mechanics of DTDs.

SGML Declaration Syntax (or, "What Are All Those Angle Brackets Anyway?")

The syntax for SGML is fairly straightforward, much as with many computing languages. It is also fairly rigid in its requirements for specific things in a specific order. This rigidity aids tremendously in allowing the automated processing of SGML encoded documents. Because computers are abysmal at handling ambiguity, the rules of SGML syntax permit ambiguity only in specific, predefined ways in specific, predefined places.

The rules for SGML declaration syntax are fairly simple (although they may seem a little arcane at first glance). The following illustrates the basic components of an SGML declaration:

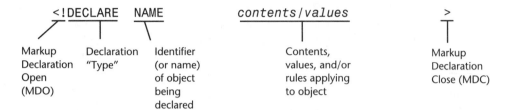

`<!DECLARE`	`NAME`	`contents/values`	`>`
Markup Declaration Open (MDO)	Declaration "Type"	Identifier (or name) of object being declared	Contents, values, and/or rules applying to object	Markup Declaration Close (MDC)

As you examine the above declaration, note that there is a way to define the beginning and end of a markup declaration. The Markup Declaration Open (MDO) specifies the beginning of the declaration. Because a declaration can span more than one line, you need to specify the end of the declaration, hence the Markup Declaration Close (MDC).

◄◄ See "The SGML Declaration and the DOCTYPE Declaration," p. 48

Now that you've specified the bounds of the declaration (using the MDO and MDC), let's examine the actual contents. The region identified by DECLARE is where you put the term that identifies the type of object that you are declaring. (Although you can declare a number of objects, the ones that you will declare most often are elements, attributes, and entities.)

NAME is the area where you assign a name to the object that you are declaring. From the time you declare an object, the properties defined in the declaration will be applied to the named object when it is referenced.

The specific content or value of the named object is then defined in the area indicated by *contents/values*. Note that this area varies considerably depending upon which type of object you are declaring.

Last (and maybe least) is the Markup Declaration Close (MDC). This specifies the end of the declaration.

Tip

Errors in DTD parsing are often related to a missing MDC. When debugging DTD parsing errors, keep on the lookout for that missing angle bracket!

If this sounds pretty abstract and obscure, don't worry. It will start to make more sense as you delve into the specifics of various declarations.

III

Content Modeling

Regular Expression Syntax

> **Note**
>
> For those readers who have experience in the computer programming world, the use of regular expression syntax to define content models may seem like old hat (or Programming 101). If you fit into this category, you might want to skip ahead to the section "Specific Declarations."

Regular expressions provide a mechanism to sketch out the ingredients of SGML content models. They provide a shorthand way to indicate order, occurrence, exclusion, and logical grouping.

The specific notation for the use of regular expressions within SGML is illustrated in table 10.2.

Table 10.2   SGML Regular Expression Notation

Item	Type	Usage
,	Sequencing	in order or followed by
|	Sequencing	logical OR
&	Sequencing	logical AND (in any order)
*	Occurrence	occurs 0 or more times (Optional)
?	Occurrence	occurs 0 or 1 time (Optional)
+	Occurrence	occurs 1 or more times (Required)

So how do you use regular expressions? It's quite simple, really. When used in combination with named objects and parentheses, you can define quite complex groupings of objects in specific orders or combinations.

For example, suppose you want to define a product announcement that contains the following: a title, the date, an announcement number, and additional information. This additional information will include a number of paragraphs and perhaps an illustration.

Using regular expressions, you can define the announcement in the following way:

```
announcement = (title,date,number,((paragraph+)&(illustration?)))
```

The preceding definition of announcement specifies that it consists of the following objects in the following order: one title, one date, one number, followed by some additional data. The additional data will include one or more paragraphs and may include one illustration. This additional data may begin with either an illustration or the paragraph(s).

Note

Because the ampersand (&) is used to join "one or more paragraphs" and "0 or 1 illustrations," these two collections can occur in either order. However, this definition does not permit an illustration to be in the middle of multiple paragraphs.

Suppose that you want to define your product announcement a little differently. You want to avoid the use of the ampersand (&) and allow for any combination of the following items in the additional data area: paragraphs, illustrations, and numbered lists. You can then redefine your announcement in the following way:

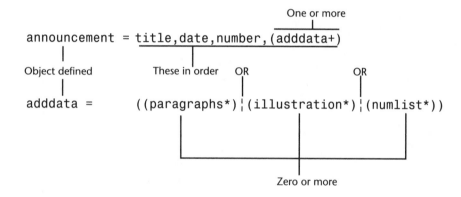

Through this approach, you have specified that the standard data that always occurs in order (`title,date,number`) will be followed by additional data (`adddata`). Defined separately, you specify that `adddata` can consist of any combination of paragraphs, illustrations, and numbered lists occurring in any order.

Caution

Even though it is allowed, it's good practice to avoid the use of the ampersand (&) connector whenever possible in SGML. As you have seen, it's rarely needed. Its usage tends to strain validating parsers (and occasionally generate parsing logic errors) because of the potential complexity possible to document models.

Additional examples of data structures defined via regular expressions are as follows:

```
book = (titlepg,tblcontent,chapter+,bibliogr?,appendix*,index?)
chapter = (chapt-title,((sect-title?),section-body)+)
catalog = ((section)|(section+,index))
```

The previous examples of syntax can be described (defined) as follows:

■ A book consists of (in order) a title page, followed by a table of contents, followed by one or more chapters; following the chapters may be a single bibliography (optional), zero or more appendixes, and a single index (optional)

■ Chapters consist of (in order) a chapter title and one (or more) sections; sections may include a title, and always include a section body

■ Catalogs may consist of one section only, or, one or more sections and an index

As you have seen, the use of regular expression syntax gives you the opportunity to define data structures in a compact way. As you start to examine the details of specific declaration statements, you'll see how they are used in SGML.

Specific Declarations

The syntax for the DOCTYPE, COMMENT, ELEMENT, ATTRIBUTE list, and ENTITY declarations follow the same general syntax. Specific variations occur in the specific characteristics defined by each declaration type.

The SGML Declaration

This declaration tells the processing system about character sets and control information, and also about any limitations of processing power. The originators of SGML wanted any machine, even those with limited processing power, to be able to run SGML applications. This declaration can tell the processing system the parameters it must assume to do its job.

Since most current generation computers have sufficient processing power to run SGML applications, it will probably not be necessary for you to deviate from what is called the Reference Concrete Syntax. This is the most commonly used set of parameters for SGML processing systems. You can find a copy at:

ftp://ftp.ifi.uio.no/pub/SGML/declaration

Many systems assume the reference concrete syntax when you don't specify another, and some systems even prohibit you altogether from specifying another syntax. Thus, you may avoid ever having to define parameters outside this widely used default, but in case you must, the basics are given in table 10.3.

Table 10.3 The SGML Declaration	
Part of Declaration	**Description**
<!SGML "ISO 8879:1986"	Tells parser markup to conform to the ISO standard version of SGML.
CHARSET	Includes base character set (BASESET)—usually standard ASCII—and described character set (DESCSET)—those character numbers parser is instructed to recognize.

Part of Declaration	Description
CAPACITY	Defines amount of memory needed to parse the documents. This portion is ignored by most parsers today because of sufficient computing power.
SCOPE	Scope of concrete syntax: can be either DOCUMENT or INSTANCE. The latter means concrete syntax used in prologue to document and another declared concrete syntax applies to the document instance.
SYNTAX	This is where reference concrete syntax starts and ends—this portion defines eight values: SHUNCHAR CONTROLS (unsupported characters), BASESET and DESCSET (base character set and described character set), FUNCTION NAMECASE (specifies function characters), NAMING (rules for naming tags), NAMECASE (specifies whether uppercase and lowercase names are equivalent in elements and entities), DELIM (makes it possible to change values of standard delimiters in SGML), and QUANTITY (tells parser to watch certain quantities like length of tag names).
FEATURES	Defines markup minimization for processing system.
APPINFO	Specifies information about processing application system, such as HyTime.
>	Closing delimiter for SGML declaration.

Tip

The likeliest items that you may wish to modify in the SGML declaration are specific values such as the length of attribute values (literals), the length of tags, and the nesting level of open tags that is allowed. Desired optional features are sometimes also useful.

It should be very rare that you ever need to modify your processing system's SGML environment in the SGML declaration. Before you consider doing so, check the public domain for existing SGML declaration alternatives that you might use. CALS, for example, modifies the reference concrete syntax to support long file names. Other alternatives are freely available. Check out the SGML archives listed at the following URL:

http://www.sgml.com/sgmlig/Appendix6.html

The DOCTYPE Declaration

The DOCTYPE (or Document Type) declaration serves to associate an SGML document (or document instance) with its corresponding DTD. Although a document instance can include its corresponding DTD, it's often more practical to simply reference it through the DOCTYPE declaration.

The following illustrates the components of the DOCTYPE declaration:

III

Content Modeling

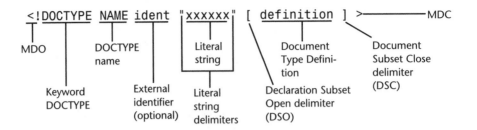

The COMMENT Declaration

Comments can be included within a DTD or a document instance by the use of a COMMENT declaration. It's a simple declaration. By including it, you're able to include comments that you want any and all SGML processing systems to ignore (or not process).

You may ask, "Why include comments if they're not processed?" Good question. Their primary purpose is to make SGML objects (such as DTDs and document instances) intelligible to you and I rather than the machine processing them.

For example, you can use comments to separate the various sections of a DTD so it's easier to read and understand. After all, what's crystal clear to you when you develop a DTD might seem a little cryptic when you go back to modify it in a few years. The syntax of the COMMENT declaration follows:

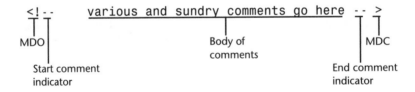

> **Note**
>
> Because you have start and stop indicators for comments, you can span multiple lines with comments.

Comments are also useful in building descriptive headers that can be used to describe a DTD, explain its revision history (with dates and authors), and include other useful information for describing its role and purpose. If the DTD is a fragment called by other DTDs, this can be described as well, along with a list of the DTDs that call it.

You can also include comments nested within other SGML declarations. For example, if you want to note that an element had been modified on a certain date, you can include a comment within the element declaration. In this case, you do not include separate MDO and MDC notation for the comment itself; rather you indicate the start and end of the comment through double hyphens alone:

```
<!ELEMENT  section   - o    (title,(para+),epilog?)
                            -- modified by BH 9/24/94 -- >
```

Elements and the ELEMENT Declaration

Many people consider elements to be the fundamental building blocks of the SGML world. As you consider all of the components of a document (such as the title, section, paragraph, illustration, etc.), remember that they usually have one thing in common; they are normally defined as elements. (In some cases—such as tables of content—they are derived from other elements.)

If you have been skimming this section up to now, pay special attention to this examination of elements. Because they are the basic building blocks of SGML, you will encounter elements within your SGML tagged documents often. Because elements are so fundamental to the concept of SGML, it pays to have an in-depth knowledge of what they are and how they are tagged within a document instance.

Does this seem a little vague? If it does, don't worry. At the end of this chapter (in the section "Some Practical Examples"), you'll examine a sample DTD and a document instance that corresponds to it. As you examine them, the theoretical should come to life.

The ELEMENT declaration has a few interesting items in it:

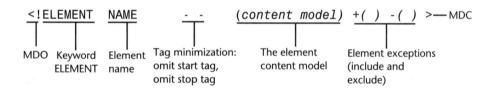

As with the other declarations, note that the ELEMENT declaration starts with the familiar Markup Declaration Open (MDO) and ends with the Markup Declaration Close (MDC). You can tell that it's a declaration for an element because it has ELEMENT as the keyword. The name of the element follows the keyword.

Tag Minimization. The two dashes that follow the element name specify the rules for *tag minimization* in the SGML document instance. Minimization allows you to omit tags in SGML markup that are unnecessary to the element usage. You'll learn more about minimization a bit later in this chapter (in the section "Tags and Tag Minimization with Omittag"). For now, know that the two dashes indicate that an element start tag (indicated by the first dash) and stop tag (indicated by the second dash) are required.

An element in which a stop tag is omitted can be defined as follows. Note that to indicate omit, the lowercase letter "o" is used (not zero):

```
<!ELEMENT  graphic   - o    EMPTY >
```

In this case, you have defined the element graphic. The end tag is omitted, and the element has no content. If you're wondering why you might define an element with no content and no end tag, hang on. You'll analyze this example further when you examine the use of attributes in "Attributes: Their Use and the ATTRIBUTE Declaration."

Caution

You should rarely even consider omitting the start tag in an element. You should never omit both the start and stop tags; your parser will have a difficult time recognizing such an element.

You might want to consider tag minimization in the following circumstances:

- You are entering the tags manually (heaven forbid!)
- People need to regularly read the tagged document instance
- A tag is being used as a placeholder

Defining the Element Content Model. To define the content model of an element, you can proceed in a number of directions. In some cases, your element model might be composed of a number of subelements, perhaps in a particular order.

In other instances, the element might contain only the basic text of the document and no subelements. In this case, the content model definition can contain #PCDATA, which signifies parseable character data. The pound sign (#) signifies a reserved name, which in this case is PCDATA. PCDATA stands for character data, which can be interpreted by the parser to resolve. It is useful to allow the parser to resolve the character data in case you reference other objects, such as *entities,* within your data. (Entities are discussed in more detail in "Entities: Their Use and the ENTITY Markup Declaration.")

Sometimes, you might want to have textual content receive special treatment from the parser. In this case, you will use other special data types (indicated by reserved names). Examples of these are shown in table 10.4.

Table 10.4 Special Declared Content (Reserved Names)

Reserved Word	Name	Typical Usage Identifier
EMPTY	Empty element (without content)	Place holder or processing instruction
CDATA	Character Data	Include valid SGML instructions as a text which will be ignored by a parser and SGML applications
#PCDATA	Parseable Character Data	Textual content data that is evaluated by SGML parsers

Reserved Word	Name	Typical Usage Identifier
RCDATA	Replaceable Character Data	Same as CDATA, except entity and character references are recognized; useful for special notation like equations
ANY	Any content valid	States that any element in DTD (or #PCDATA) is allowed (avoid using this type of declared content!)

Note

The declared content type #PCDATA includes the pound sign to indicate to the parser that markup within it should be evaluated.

Caution

The declared content type ANY essentially bypasses document parsers by allowing any type of data content. Because its use bypasses the structure of SGML, it should be avoided. It is sometimes used in the early stages of DTD development.

Element Exceptions (Include and Exclude). The use of *element exceptions* within your element definition can be thought of as a type of "Yes, but..." statement. Put simply, they allow you to override your (just completed) definition of the element by specifically permitting or forbidding the occurrence of an exception element.

To illustrate inclusion, for example, the element declaration for catalog (shown below) allows the element note to occur anywhere within the catalog element, any number of times, and in any of the subelements:

```
<!ELEMENT catalog  - -    ((section)¦(section+,index)) +(note) >
```

Note that you can include multiple elements in your inclusion notation but that only one type of regular expression sequencing (followed by OR, AND) is allowed within the inclusion.

Caution

Don't use inclusions for elements that you forgot to include! They shouldn't be used for subelements that are key structural components, but rather for those that float in document content (such as notes, keywords, and so on).

III

Content Modeling

Exclusions are similar to inclusions in many ways, although your usage of them is somewhat different. Indicated in the markup declaration by a minus (–) rather than the plus sign (+) of inclusion, you commonly use them to prevent recursive nesting of an element within itself. For example, you might want to prevent the element note from occurring directly within another note, but might want to allow it to occur in a paragraph within a note.

Inclusions and exclusions can occur within the same element definition. However, according to the SGML standard, if you include and exclude the same content, the exclusion takes precedence.

Element Summary. In this chapter's examination of elements within SGML, you looked at how they are declared and how you can define omitted tags in the element declaration. You took a brief look at your options for defining the content model of an element, showing that an element can contain other subelements or character data (or a combination of the two). You also took a look at the method for handling exceptions to the content model via inclusions and exclusions. But before you can really examine elements in their common setting (a document instance), you need to examine two additional SGML objects: attributes and entities.

Attributes: Their Use and the ATTRIBUTE Declaration

In the SGML world, you are able to use *attributes* when you need to specify some additional descriptive information or values that pertain to a specific element. They are particularly useful in describing values (or qualities) that apply to an element.

Attributes can be either optional or mandatory. In cases where they are omitted, the attribute declaration can specify a default value.

Attributes are particularly useful for including information that relates to external objects (such as illustrations, videos, or sound clips), indicating the security level of a document, including cross reference information to tie one element to another (for hypertext linking), and other element descriptive data.

Though they are defined separately from elements, the attribute values occur within the element tags in an SGML document instance. (You will see this when you examine an example of an SGML document instance and its corresponding DTD.)

To define attributes that correspond to one of your elements, use the Attribute List declaration. Here's how the syntax works:

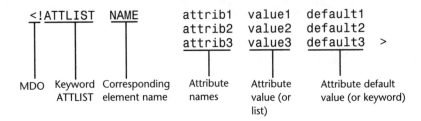

The Attribute List declaration opens with the MDO, followed by the keyword ATTLIST, or attribute list. The value indicated by NAME corresponds to the named element to which the attribute(s) apply. Following the element name is the name of the attribute, its value (or list of possible values), and either a default attribute value or a keyword. Note that in the case of the sample declaration above, you define three attributes that relate to the same element. This indicates that you can use a single attribute list declaration to define all attributes that apply to an element.

Here are some sample attribute list declarations with their corresponding element declarations:

```
<!ELEMENT subject   - - (#PCDATA)>
<!ATTLIST subject       safety (y|n) "n">
```

In this example, you have the element subject. It has a corresponding attribute list defined that contains one attribute, called safety. Its value can consist of either the letter y or the letter n. If no value is specified for the safety attribute, the default value is n.

```
<!ELEMENT table   - - (title,((tgroup+,tnote?)|graphic))>
<!ATTLIST table       label CDATA #IMPLIED>
```

Here you have the element table, with its corresponding attribute of label. label consists of character data (CDATA); as you probably recall, CDATA is a reserved word identifier that can contain any type of characters, including those that are normally interpreted as SGML instructions.

The keyword IMPLIED (indicated by the pound sign preceding it) tells you that the attribute is not required. If it is not present, the application processing the SGML document instance will select a default value.

The range of allowable attribute keyword default types (and their meanings) are shown in table 10.5.

Table 10.5 Attribute Keyword Defaults

Keyword	Meaning
#REQUIRED	Attribute value is required. Default value is not allowed.
#IMPLIED	Attribute value is optional. If not present, value is supplied by processing application.
#CURRENT	The last supplied value for this attribute becomes the default value.
#CONREF	Stands for content reference. The processing application can use the value of the attribute to generate the content value.

Tip

#CONREF is useful in situations where you might refer to elements that may or may not be present, such as in large documents that are not always processed in their entirety. In such situations, the use of #CONREF avoids problems with unresolved references.

Content Modeling

In the previous examination of elements and element tag minimization, you looked at a declaration for the element graphic. If you take another look at it with its corresponding attribute list declaration, it might make a little more sense:

```
<!ELEMENT  graphic    - o    EMPTY >
<!ATTLIST  graphic           filename CDATA #REQUIRED
                             artno    CDATA #IMPLIED>
```

In this example, you have the element graphic, with no content or end tag. You now have a corresponding attribute list that defines the attributes filename and artno, both of which consist of character data.

Notice that the attribute filename is required. Through this use of SGML declarations, you are able to put in a place holder in the document instance that points to a related illustration. The element graphic has no content, but it must contain an attribute value for filename that points to the file containing the illustration.

On occasion, it might be useful to navigate between specific occurrences of elements in the document instance. When this situation occurs, you can use the attribute types of ID and IDREF.

To do this, define an attribute using the keyword ID. You must ensure that this keyword value is unique. (This attribute can be either #REQUIRED or #IMPLIED. If it's #IMPLIED, the processing program must supply a unique value.)

```
<!ELEMENT sect    - - (para)+>
<!ATTLIST sect         id    ID #REQUIRED>
```

Now that you have a specific address within your SGML document instance (consisting of an element with a unique ID), it's relatively simple to cross-reference (or hyperlink) to it. Through the use of the IDREF (or ID reference), you can refer back to your original element.

```
<!ELEMENT xref    - - (misc)+>
<!ATTLIST xref         findit  IDREF #REQUIRED>
```

Note

Refer to Chapter 25 for more detailed information on document links.

Entities: Their Use and the ENTITY Markup Declaration

Within SGML, *entities* provide a powerful and compact shorthand mechanism for using symbolic notation. With them, you can point to a specific character string that may be difficult or laborious to include otherwise. They perform their work via the parser, as it resolves the symbolic references during the parsing process by performing string replacement.

To use entities, two things must be done. First, you must define the entity with an ENTITY declaration, and then you must call the entity via an entity *reference*.

Entity references can be particularly useful for the following purposes:

- Indicating special characters not easily accessible from a keyboard (such as scientific symbols or foreign language characters)
- Substitution of long character strings via a shorthand notation
- Inclusion of a reusable document content model fragment (throughout a DTD and across DTDs)
- Machine-specific processing commands
- As a pointer to a specific file on your computer system

There are two basic types of entities: general entities and parameter entities. *General entities* can be used in a number of circumstances, while *parameter entities* can only be used within specific markup declarations (in DTDs).

Either type of entity can be internal or external. *Internal entities* reference objects defined within the DTD, while *external entities* point to an object beyond the boundaries of the DTD.

 ◀◀ See "Two types of Entities: General (&) and Parameter (%)," and "Internal and External General Entities," pp. 58-59

The ENTITY Declaration. The ENTITY declaration is a relatively simple one. (By now, you're probably rather familiar with the general syntax of SGML declarations.) The following illustrates the components and layout of an entity declaration:

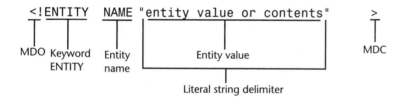

Notice that the entity declaration has the usual markup delimiter open and close (MDO and MDC) and the keyword that identifies it as an entity. The content between the literal string delimiters is the actual entity value.

General Entities. Through the use of *general entities*, you can define special characters and symbols not easily typed on a standard keyboard and call them up via entity references.

Parameter Entities. Within a DTD, parameter entities can be used to access content model fragments from a single location. Through this mechanism, you can ensure that you're using a common, consistent set of content model "chunks." Parameter entities can reference fragments that are internal or external to the DTD.

Externally referenced entities can be either *local* to a specific installation, or they can be *public* (or *published*) standard reference entities.

III

Content Modeling

The declaration for a parameter entity varies slightly from the general entity declaration noted previously:

```
<!ENTITY %       NAME    entity-value    >
```

Notice the percent sign (%), which indicates a parameter entity. Also note that the entity value may contain a literal (or textual) content, a reference to an external entity specification, or a specialized processing instruction.

Tags and Tag Minimization with Omittag

The Omittag feature of SGML is an optional function that allows you to leave out start and stop tags that have been designated as optional in your DTD. This can be useful in systems where the SGML markup is manually inserted in a document.

To use Omittag, this feature must be designated in the SGML declaration as a permitted feature *and* it must be specifically allowed in the element declaration where you want to use it.

In the element declaration that follows, no tags can be omitted.

```
<!ELEMENT subject  - - (#PCDATA)>
```

If you want to allow the omission of the end tag on this element, you would define the element a little differently:

```
<!ELEMENT subject  - O (#PCDATA)>
```

Note that the second hyphen (-), has been replaced with an uppercase letter "O." This indicates that the end tag can be omitted. (Similarly, if you want to allow omission of the start tag, you would replace the first "-" with an "O.")

In general, tags can be omitted only when their omission does not create ambiguity in the document instance. For example, take a look at the following DTD fragment:

```
<!ELEMENT document  - - ((section),para?)  >
<!ELEMENT section   - O (para+)            >
<!ELEMENT para      - - (#PCDATA)          >
```

This example is illegal. You cannot allow the omission of the end tag for the element section. This is because you would not be able to tell whether the last occurrence of the element para occurred within the section element or just after it. (It is ambiguous.)

Tip

There are several other instances where start tags cannot be omitted: the element has a required attribute, the element begins with a SHORT REF delimiter, the element has declared content (CDATA, RCDATA, EMPTY).

In the first scenario, omitting the tag would leave no place for the attribute. In the second, the short reference mapping would probably become misleading. In the third, the parser would be unable to understand when to stop parsing content.

Not all SGML processing systems support tag minimization. As a result, all markup tags should be restored if you are going to send your SGML to a recipient who might not be able to support it.

Some Practical Examples

To follow up on the subjects covered in this chapter, let's take a look at a DTD. Let's look again at the DTD that was introduced in Chapter 5, "Two Scenarios" (see fig. 10.1).

```
<!-- ******************************************* -->
<!-- AnyCorp, USA                                -->
<!--                                             -->
<!-- Product Advisory DTD version 1.1a, 23 Jul 95  -->
<!-- ******************************************* -->

<!DOCTYPE advisory [

<!-- Entity Definitions    -->

<!ENTITY % parael "para¦blist¦nlist¦graphic">


<!-- Document High Level Elements    -->

<!ELEMENT advisory  - - (idinfo,subject,subsec+)>
<!ELEMENT idinfo    - - advnbr,type,dateiss,daterev,product)>
<!ELEMENT subject   - - (#PCDATA)>
<!ATTLIST subject       safety (y¦n) "n">
<!ELEMENT subsec    - - (title,(%parael;)?)>

<!-- Document Sub-Elements    -->

<!ELEMENT advnbr    - - (#PCDATA)>
<!ELEMENT type      - - (#PCDATA)>
<!ELEMENT dateiss   - - (#PCDATA)>
<!ELEMENT daterev   - - (#PCDATA)>
<!ELEMENT product   - - (#PCDATA)>

<!ELEMENT title     - - (#PCDATA)>

<!ELEMENT para      - - (#PCDATA)>
<!ELEMENT blist     - - (item+) -(nlist)>
<!ELEMENT nlist     - - (item+)>
<!ELEMENT item      - - (para¦blist¦nlist¦graphic)+>
<!ELEMENT graphic   - o EMPTY>
<!ATTLIST graphic       filename CDATA #REQUIRED
                        artno    CDATA #IMPLIED>

            ]>
```

Fig. 10.1

This sample DTD contains a number of declarations including those for doctype, elements, comments, attribute lists, and entities.

As you look at this DTD, notice how the various components that you have examined in this chapter are used. For example, the entity `parael` (or paragraph element) is defined early in the DTD, before it is referenced.

The declaration for the element `blist` specifically excludes the element `nlist` (indicating that a bulleted list cannot include a numbered list within it).

Look at the element `graphic`. Notice that it is empty, and that its end tag can be omitted. In this situation, the element is used solely as a placeholder for an external graphics file.

Finally, take a look at the regular expressions used in this DTD. (For example, you'll notice that the element `item` can contain one or more of any of the following elements: `para`, `blist`, `nlist`, or `graphic`.)

From Here...

This chapter examined SGML declarations and syntax, paying particular attention to the usage of comments, elements, attributes, and entities. This examination also included a look at the regular expression notation and the types of declared content used in SGML.

For more information, refer to the following chapters:

- Chapter 11, "Using DTD Components," illustrates how to make reusable DTD document structures.
- Chapter 12, "Formatting the DTD for Humans," discusses how to organize your DTDs to make them readable and understandable.
- Chapter 13, "Evaluating DTDs and Using Parsers," looks at how to ensure that a DTD meets your needs and the use of parsers.
- Chapter 14, "Following Good SGML Practice," provides a framework to follow for optimal SGML usage.

CHAPTER 11

Using DTD Components

As you saw in the previous chapter, defining a DTD can get rather involved because of all the elements, attributes, and entities that can be included in a complex document. If your head is spinning as you consider the possibilities involved in defining every object—chapters, sections, paragraphs, bulleted lists, and so on—don't worry.

Although SGML requires that the objects in a DTD be defined, it provides much flexibility in how to do it. It is usually possible to define the objects in a document only once and to reference them later as they are needed. This approach reduces the effort required to modify document models. It ensures a common approach to standard document components and provides for a common "look" across your document library.

This chapter examines reusable document components. You learn how to:

- Use reusable document components
- Use fragment DTDs
- Use DTD redefinition
- Create elements by means of parameter entities

You will examine the various methods of using modular DTD components and look at a few examples. When you complete this chapter, you will be able to modularize your document type definitions so that you can reuse the portions that are common across various document types.

Tip

If you intend to use standard DTDs off the shelf with only minor modifications, modular techniques can greatly simplify your efforts.

When (and Why) To Use DTD Components

You might find that using DTD components often helps in reducing clutter—for example, when you start with a few simple DTDs but expect that you will need to add additional definitions of new document types over time.

It might be helpful to think of DTD components as types of tools, such as those you might use in a home shop. If you were going to build window frames, you would probably construct a few tools to make common parts of the window production process easier.

Similarly, the construction and maintenance of DTDs usually involves shared document elements. When you expect this to be the case, why not spend a little time up front constructing a DTD module that you can use repeatedly? To get an idea whether you should use modular DTDs, refer to the checklist in table 11.1. In general, if any of these issues apply to your DTDs, you should consider using modular DTD components.

Table 11.1 Modular DTD Checklist	
Issue	**Question**
Multiple DTDs	Will you build and use multiple DTDs that share many elements?
Many developers	Are many people involved in DTD development for this project?
Complex documents	Are the documents and DTDs complex?
Common look	Does it matter whether the document types share a common look and feel?
DTD changes	Do you expect many changes to the DTDs?
Document lifespan	Will your documents and DTDs be around longer than the staff that maintains them?

Multiple DTDs

As you begin developing your SGML document environment, ask yourself, "Will this be something that grows? Will I have many document types before I am done?" If the answer is Yes—or even if multiple, related document types are a possibility—dividing your DTDs into modules could pay great dividends in the long term.

It might take a little extra time in the beginning, but you will save time and effort over the lifetime of your SGML document library if you can reuse modules that your documents share. Those modules can be, for example, section or chapter definitions, or more specialized objects such as product descriptions. In any case, modular DTDs enable you to reuse both document definitions and the actual contents of SGML documents.

Many Developers

Many people are often involved in developing an SGML document system. Projects often depend on the help of outside consultants, who guide the initial document development. These consultants help educate the participants of a project in the basics of SGML development, and they facilitate the process of designing and constructing SGML DTDs.

After the initial efforts are under way, additional document types might be added to the SGML collection. New developers might join the team to help construct other documents, which will be added as the SGML project progresses.

When new developers come in, they must come up to speed on the existing document environment. If they are fairly new to SGML, they must cope with the intricacies of the language while they become familiar with the existing document types. A modular DTD environment can help. Developers can learn the SGML syntax by examining a shared document structure defined in reusable DTD components.

A Growing DTD Environment

As you go through the DTD process, you might find yourself adding more document types to your SGML collection. Each new type of document, of course, requires the development of its own DTD.

Developing DTDs can be a slow process at first, as you painstakingly examine all the detail involved in the document that you are modeling. In the early stages of SGML implementation, you might find it painful to examine all the objects that a document can contain—chapters, sections, paragraphs, tables, lists, graphics, and so on. As you develop more DTDs, however, the process gets easier.

When you are using DTD modules, you might find yourself looking at a new document type with a form of mental shorthand. That is, you visualize the new document model in your head and say, "How does the bulk of this one differ from what has come before? How much of it is the same?"

In many situations, the answer is that much of it is the same. Although documents can be rich in their complexity, the basic building blocks are often repeated. Many companies have documents that share key aspects of how they are put together. The same group of people are often involved in creating or writing several types of documents. Therefore, they bring the same perspective to all the documents that they create. From this type of situation, a range of documents that have a similar style may evolve. With a modular document component structure, an organization can make a more conscious effort to encourage a common look across collections of documents.

In short, with reusable document components, you can manage the growth phase as you add new document types to your SGML document universe.

III

Content Modeling

Change Is Coming

In today's world, change is everywhere. The scope of change can be dizzying. What your parents took for granted—lifetime employment with the same company, or the value of a dollar—are now subject to constant change.

In many organizations, documents are subject to change as well. Whether the cause is a company reorganization, a change in the standard document processing software, or a desire to get information on the Internet, standard documents can change over time.

If you use SGML, though, you can be protected from some of this change. For example, you are insulated from changes in document processing software. Without SGML, your collection of documents might become unusable because they rely on obsolete software.

> **Note**
>
> Recall the multitude of word processors that were all the rage in the late 1970s and early 1980s. Generally consisting of a typewriter-like device, a disk drive, and maybe a video display, they stored documents in a proprietary format that could not be understood by other word processors. In those days, the common format was often the printed page.

Yet some changes will be inevitable. In fact, as you build your SGML document universe, you will probably need to make a few changes of your own. In your initial efforts in building document models, you will probably make mistakes, omissions, and faulty assumptions. The standard pieces of your modular document set will often grow as you find more shared objects.

By using modular components, you can simplify the process of making changes to your DTDs. For example, if you find that you need to add a new element to your standard chapter DTD module, you can make the change in one place—the common DTD module. Because the DTDs for each document type reference this common DTD module, you have to make only one update; all the DTDs that reference this common module require no additional changes. Had you not used a common DTD module, you might have had to make the same change across many DTDs.

▶▶ See "What Can Object-Oriented Development Techniques Do for DTD Development?" p. 535

In other words, although changes to your document structures may be inevitable, the judicious use of modular components can make those changes simpler and more manageable.

Long Lifetime

In this digital age, products often last only as long as the computers that you use. The first personal computer included a 360K floppy drive, a monochrome display, and—if you were lucky—a whopping 10M hard drive. It seems so quaint now, such a simple machine.

Although computers evolve with blinding speed, many other products do not. For example, the washing machine in your house might not be all that different from the one that many people used in the 1950s, and the lifespan of a household refrigerator runs 25 or 30 years.

It is easy to forget that products can last so long. Many of these products that last decades have documents associated with them. These documents include such things as parts lists, repair manuals, overhaul guides, and owner's manuals.

Similarly, other documents in a company or organization have a long lifespan. Policy manuals, purchasing instructions, and employee benefit guides might evolve over the course of many years. In some cases, documentation changes only gradually in content. Other times, contents must be redone when the word processor program in use changes. Using SGML with a modular document definition can facilitate the process of maintaining documents over their lifetimes.

Note
The longevity of your documents might be longer than you first think.

Making DTDs Simpler

Real world DTDs are often long and complex documents that include a highly detailed model of the document architecture. Any method that simplifies DTDs and the document instances that they model can pay great dividends by making the whole process more manageable. When you use common document objects through references to shared DTD fragments, you remove the need to retype detailed document object definitions. An additional benefit is the appearance of the referencing DTD itself. Because it does not have to include all the details of common building blocks— such as paragraphs, tables, and lists—it becomes much easier to read and understand.

Making New DTDs Easier To Develop and Maintain

As you develop more DTDs, you will find more common data objects. By adding them to your reusable document modules, you can create a standard library of reusable data. Over time, this standard library can provide most of the detail that you need as you model new documents by means of DTDs. In many cases, creating new documents involves a small amount of document analysis, a quick review (and maybe revision) of the common modules, and creation of a short DTD that models the new high-level elements.

III

Content Modeling

Standardizing Basic Components

Figure 11.1 shows the DTD that you developed in Chapter 5, "Two Scenarios," for product advisories at AnyCorp. As you look at this DTD, think of the document components that are likely to occur in other documents.

Fig. 11.1

This DTD contains objects that may be shared with other DTDs.

```
<!-- ************************************************ -->
<!-- AnyCorp, USA                                     -->
<!--                                                  -->
<!-- Product Advisory DTD version 1.1, 21 Jul 95     -->
<!-- ************************************************ -->
<!DOCTYPE advisory [
<!-- Entity Definitions    -->
<!ENTITY % parael "para¦blist¦nlist¦graphic">
<!ELEMENT advisory - - (idinfo,subject,subsec+)>
<!ELEMENT idinfo   - - advnbr,type,dateiss,daterev,product)>
<!ELEMENT subject  - - (#PCDATA)>
<!ATTLIST subject      safety (y¦n) "n">
<!ELEMENT subsec   - - (title,(%parael;)?)>
<!ELEMENT advnbr   - - (#PCDATA)>
<!ELEMENT type     - - (#PCDATA)>
<!ELEMENT dateiss  - - (#PCDATA)>
<!ELEMENT daterev  - - (#PCDATA)>
<!ELEMENT product  - - (#PCDATA)>
<!ELEMENT title    - - (#PCDATA)>
<!ELEMENT para     - - (#PCDATA)>
<!ELEMENT blist    - - (item+) -(nlist)>
<!ELEMENT nlist    - - (item+)>
<!ELEMENT item     - - (%parael;)+>
<!ELEMENT graphic  - o EMPTY>
<!ATTLIST graphic      filename CDATA #REQUIRED
                       artno    CDATA #IMPLIED>
                   ]>
```

Some of the elements in this DTD are specific to the document that it models, a product advisory. These elements might include high-level structures (such as the advisory itself) and most top-level subelements (such as `advisory`, `idinfo`, and `subject`). These are not the best components to include in a common reusable data set—although in some cases, particular ones might be. A few objects should be included, such as the entity definition for a paragraph element (`parael`) and the definition for the subsection element (`subsec`).

Various lower-level components also apply specifically to the product advisory: advisory number (`advnbr`), type of advisory (`type`), advisory issue date (`dateiss`), advisory revision date (`daterev`), and product line (`product`). They are not good candidates for reuse.

The final portion of the DTD includes generic object definitions for things such as paragraphs (`para`), bulleted lists (`blist`), numbered lists (`nlist`), group items (`item`), and illustrations (`graphic`). Because they are generic, they are used frequently. You should include them in your common DTD.

You can see that you can reuse a substantial amount of the information in the DTD in figure 11.1. Remove it from the DTD. Figure 11.2 shows what the revised DTD looks like.

```
<!-- ********************************************** -->
<!-- AnyCorp, USA                                  -->
<!--                                               -->
<!-- Product Advisory DTD version 1.5, 21 Sep 95   -->
<!-- ********************************************** -->
<!DOCTYPE advisory [
<!--   Entity Definitions    -->
<!ENTITY % common PUBLIC "-//ANYC//DTD Common Elems//EN">
%common;
<!--   Product Advisory Structure    -->
<!ELEMENT advisory - - (idinfo,subject,subsec+)>
<!ELEMENT idinfo    - - advnbr,type,dateiss,daterev,product)>
<!ELEMENT subject   - - (#PCDATA)>
<!ATTLIST subject       safety (y|n) "n">
<!ELEMENT advnbr    - - (#PCDATA)>
<!ELEMENT type      - - (#PCDATA)>
<!ELEMENT dateiss   - - (#PCDATA)>
<!ELEMENT daterev   - - (#PCDATA)>
<!ELEMENT product   - - (#PCDATA)>
                  ]>
```

Fig. 11.2

In this DTD, the common elements have been removed.

The product advisory now looks a little different. The structural components that are specific to this document type remain, but the objects common to this and other DTDs are no longer in residence. In their place is a PUBLIC parameter entity reference to the common entity.

Simplifying DTD Maintenance

By making this change, you give the DTD a simpler look. If you come back to it in a year, it will be easier to understand and modify. But what about the elements that you removed from the advisory DTD? You might have to modify them next year, as well. Figure 11.3 shows the new common DTD, which contains the reusable document components.

Although this common DTD is simpler than most, its format is similar. It is logically organized, and groups of related objects are located together. When you return to this DTD to add and modify document objects, you will appreciate the fact that you have to make changes in only one area.

The changes to a common DTD often involve making reusable objects broader in scope as you add documents to your SGML universe. In the common DTD in figure 11.3, for example, you might want to add table definitions to the content model. You could add the necessary definitions to define the table components, along with references to tables in elements in which they might occur, such as in the parael paragraph element entity and the item list element.

III

Content Modeling

Fig. 11.3

This common DTD defines reusable document components.

```
<!-- ********************************************** -->
<!-- AnyCorp, USA                                   -->
<!--                                                -->
<!-- Name:       common.dtd                         -->
<!-- Purpose:    Define common elements shared by   -->
<!--            SGML collection                     -->
<!-- Project:    Nimbus 95                           -->
<!-- Version:    2.3                                 -->
<!-- Date:       April 5, 1995                       -->
<!-- Public Identifier:                              -->
<!-- "-//ANYC//DTD Common Elems//EN"                -->
<!-- ********************************************** -->
<!--           Revision History                     -->
<!--                                                -->
<!-- Author    Date     Reason                       -->
<!-- ======    ======   ==========================   -->
<!-- WNH       8/09/95  Add <list> element           -->
<!-- ********************************************** -->
<!DOCTYPE common [
<!-- Content Model Modules -->
<!ENTITY % parael "para¦blist¦list¦nlist¦graphic">
<!-- Subsections, Titles Paragraphs, Lists -->
<!ELEMENT subsec   - - (title,(%parael;)?)>
<!ELEMENT title    - - (#PCDATA)>
<!ELEMENT para     - - (#PCDATA)>
<!ELEMENT blist    - - (item+) -(nlist)>
<!ELEMENT nlist    - - (item+)>
<!ELEMENT list     - - (item+)>
<!ELEMENT item     - - (para¦blist¦nlist¦graphic)+>
<!ELEMENT graphic  - o EMPTY>
<!ATTLIST graphic        filename CDATA #REQUIRED
                         artno    CDATA #IMPLIED>
                    ]>
```

Note

Although you can include a number of reusable document objects in your common DTD, you don't have to use all of them in each DTD that references them. Think of a common DTD more as a tool box with a lot of useful items, only some of which you might use in each case.

Making Your DTDs More Consistent

Now that you have separated the common, reusable objects from the document-specific DTD, you can easily reuse them across various document types.

Suppose, for example, you have been assigned to develop a DTD for an instruction manual for a product line. As you consider what you need to include, you should examine the common DTD. It already contains the standard elements that you need. Thus, you can create a new DTD in record time. (Sometimes things do get easier!) Figure 11.4 shows the new DTD for instruction manuals.

Note

If the common DTD does not contain all of the standard elements, you need to decide whether new/additional standard elements should be shared in current and future DTDs. If they are to be shared, they should probably be included in the common DTD.

```
<!-- ********************************************* -->
<!-- AnyCorp, USA                                  -->
<!--                                               -->
<!-- Instruction Manual DTD version 2.0, 1 Sept 95 -->
<!-- ********************************************* -->
<!DOCTYPE instruct [
<!--   Standard Module Entity Definitions    -->
<!ENTITY % common PUBLIC "-//ANYC//DTD Common Elems//EN">
%common;
<!--   Instruction Manual Structure    -->
<!ELEMENT instruct   - - (tpage,contents,intro,assem,
                          install,oper,maint,errors,index) >
<!-- Major Document Sections   -->
<!ELEMENT tpage       - - (title , pub-info) >
<!ELEMENT contents    - - (subsec+) >
<!ELEMENT intro       - - (subsec+) >
<!ELEMENT assem       - - (subsec+) >
<!ELEMENT install     - - (subsec+) >
<!ELEMENT oper        - - (subsec+) >
<!ELEMENT maint       - - (subsec+) >
<!ELEMENT errors      - - (subsec+) >
<!ELEMENT index       - - (list+) >
<!-- Section Components   -->
<!ELEMENT pub-info    - - (#PCDATA) >
]>
```

Fig. 11.4

When you reuse common elements, developing new DTDs can be simplified.

In creating this DTD, you examine your existing collection of reusable elements. Reusing common document objects promotes consistency and commonality among document types. In this way, modular document components further enable you to make your DTDs and the documents that they model more consistent.

How To Make Components

Now that you are convinced of the benefits of modular DTDs, you are faced with the choice of which method to use. Three methods that you can use include:

- Fragment assembly
- DTD redefinition
- Element definition via parameter entities

III

Content Modeling

Fragment Assembly

The previous example showed how to make components through fragment assembly. You define a DTD (or document) fragment and give it a PUBLIC name. You reference this public entity in your DTD and include the objects—elements, attributes, and so on—that are defined in the fragment.

Document fragments typically are not full-blown DTDs on their own. They normally consist of object definitions through elements, attributes, and entities. They can be referenced by other objects within the fragment DTD. Think of them as toolboxes, full of bits and pieces that come in handy from time to time.

You can take several approaches with the fragment assembly method. You can include all the reusable document objects in one fragment or many. If your document universe is complex, you can have a correspondingly complex collection of reusable document DTD fragments.

Table 11.2 describes some of the purposes for which fragment libraries are used.

Table 11.2 Uses of DTD Fragment Libraries	
Fragment Type	**Usage**
Standard document structures	Define standard and generic objects commonly used in documents, such as subsections, tables, and lists.
Special procedures	Define special document sections that occur across multiple types of documents, such as assembly procedures and safety instructions.
Special characters or symbols	Define non-standard characters that are commonly used across documents, such as mathematical symbols and foreign language character sets.
Graphics or illustration structures	Define a standard set of graphics definitions, such as separate definitions for raster and vector graphics data references.

Tip

When you use fragment libraries, be sure to define the appropriate parameter entity in your DTD before you reference the document objects contained within it. If you don't, you won't be able to find the referenced object.

DTD Redefinition

DTD redefinition enables you to override an original object definition. Consider figure 11.5. This DTD contains the definition of a procedure.

```
<!  --  First DTD  -->
<!ENTITY  %      idinfo     "(advnbr,type,product)">
<!ENTITY  %      docpart    " %idinfo,subject,subsec+)">
```

Fig. 11.5

In this example, objects are defined through the use of entities.

The element `advisory` definition includes the entity reference `%idinfo`. Note that `idinfo`, as defined, contains the elements `advnbr`, `type`, and `product`.

Tip

Remember: You must reference entities before you can use them.

Now suppose that you want to use these same objects in a new DTD, but with a twist. You want to include the same information, but you want to have an expanded definition for what is in the entity `idinfo`. You want to define `idinfo` so that it contains `advnbr`, `type`, `product`, and `date`. Because the SGML syntax ignores attempts to redefine an entity, you can create a new definition of `idinfo` before you call the old one by means of an entity reference to `docpart`. Figure 11.6 shows you how to do this.

```
<!  --  'Redefining' DTD  -->
<!ENTITY  %      idinfo     "(advnbr,type,product,date-iss)">
<!ENTITY  %      first      SYSTEM "r:/reuse/dtd/first.dtd">
<!ELEMENT  newdoc     - -   (%docpart,subject,subsec+)>
```

Fig. 11.6

By 'redefining' an entity before its reference, you can override its original definition.

In this example, because the entity `idinfo` is defined so that it contains `date`, this definition holds even after you call the subsequent definition of `idinfo` contained in the entity `docpart`. In other words, because you defined the entity before the call in a different definition of the same entity, the first definition remains current.

Note

If entities are redefined, the new definition is ignored.

Defining Parameter Entities as Elements

This approach to modularization is the most powerful—and most complex. With it, you can define a SYSTEM entity, which might contain a database query or check an online news feed, for example. The entity could contain the results of the query or check. It could also contain the result of specific processing on the values obtained from the query or check. You can use the entity to define an element dynamically, as shown in figure 11.7.

III

Content Modeling

Fig. 11.7

By defining DTD elements through parameter entities, the results of complex external processing can be used.

```
<!  --  'Redefining' DTD  -->
<!ENTITY  %       datafeed    SYSTEM "Read Online Feed X6a">
<!ELEMENT  chgdoc      - -    (intro,part1,part2)>
<!ELEMENT  intro       - -    (stdstuff) >
<!ELEMENT  part1       - -    (othrstuf) +(%datafeed)>
```

The results of the datafeed entity could result in the dynamic construction of the document definition, or content model, itself. (Remember: The entity is composed of a processing command.) Through this mechanism, you can conceivably construct documents on the fly. You can choose key components of the document model depending on user queries and the like.

 ▶▶ See "Object-Oriented Technology and the Future of SGML Development," p. 550

From Here...

In this chapter, you examined how to use modular DTD components. You saw that a modular approach can often simplify both your DTDs and the effort required to maintain, modify, and enhance them. You saw various ways to make your DTDs more modular.

When you find yourself in a dynamic SGML environment, the modular approach can speed the DTD development cycle and help ensure a common look across your various document types.

In the following chapters, you will examine ways to make your DTDs more intelligible. You will find out what makes a DTD good and how parsers can help you in the process.

For more information, refer to the following:

- Chapter 12, "Formatting the DTD for Humans," covers tips to make your DTD more understandable to humans.
- Chapter 13, "Evaluating DTDs and Using Parsers," discusses how to ensure your DTDs meet your needs, and how to use parsers in the process.
- Chapter 14, "Following Good SGML Practice," examines recommended approaches and practices in using SGML.

Formatting the DTD for Humans

This chapter is short—but important. Formatting DTDs is something that you do every time you write one. It is a simple practice, but very necessary.

You can look at a DTD in two ways: the whole DTD at once and the single line declaration. To format a DTD correctly, you need to consider both.

In this chapter, you learn:

- Why formatting DTDs is important
- How to make comments in a DTD
- How to separate a DTD into logical groups of elements
- How to group tags with their first model instance
- How to list attributes
- How to align individual declarations

Why Formatting DTDs Is Important

By now you have seen different ways of looking at an SGML DTD. You have learned how to make declarations in SGML. When you designed the SGML environment and related elements together in Chapter 8, "Relating Elements to Each Other," you did so at a distance.

The immediate problem is that new people eventually will have to work with your DTDs. Even if your documents and all your SGML code get thrown into the garbage, someone might resurrect them later. Your documents and DTDs might be around for a long time in this electronic age.

Old Documents and New People

Bad things happen when people who need to understand your intentions cannot do so because you did not leave a trail for them to follow. All documents become old. Right now, it's tempting to believe that no one but you needs to understand your documents—or perhaps the people who have been a part of your SGML design team. It's tempting to think in terms of only the people who are working on a project today. Many more people, though, will be affected in the future by the decisions that you make today.

Consultants are likely to use your DTDs over the lifetime of your documents. They might add capabilities to your documents that you did not think useful—or possible. You prevent them from doing this if you do not format your DTDs adequately. Don't put future users in the position of having to improvise because you failed to make allowances for them. Consultants are not the only ones to consider. There are also all of the readers and document users whose names you will never know.

Documents—especially electronic ones—are more likely than ever to outlive their creators. As archival capacities become more intelligent and efficient, the documents that you create today can remain online and accessible for years. Indeed, it is often more cost-efficient for system administrators to add storage capacity than to spend the time deleting old documents. The longevity of your documents increases the need for your DTDs to be understandable, efficient, and easy to follow.

> **Note**
>
> When consultants cannot immediately understand your DTDs, they must make assumptions—sometimes inaccurate—about what you intended. Save them that trouble by making your DTDs clear.

Consider the DTD in listing 12.1. It looks busy and obscure. Elements are not grouped together, and there are no comments. Different components of the declarations are not aligned.

Listing 12.1   A Poorly Formatted but Parsable DTD

Notice, there are no historical comments about what the DTD is for, when it was revised, or whom to contact with questions.

```
<!DOCTYPE general PUBLIC "ISO 8879:1986//DTD General Document//EN" [
  <!ENTITY % ISOnum PUBLIC
    "ISO 8879:1986//ENTITIES Numeric and Special Graphic//EN">
  <!ENTITY % ISOpub PUBLIC
    "ISO 8879:1986//ENTITIES Publishing//EN">
  %ISOnum; %ISOpub;]>
```

Notice, there are no comments about what any of these entities are used for.

```
<!ENTITY % doctype "general" >
<!ENTITY % p.em.ph "hp1¦hp2¦hp3¦hp0¦cit">
<!ENTITY % p.rf.ph "hdref¦figref" >
<!ENTITY % p.rf.d  "fnref¦liref" >
<!ENTITY % p.zz.ph "q¦(%p.em.ph;)¦(%p.rf.ph;)¦(%p.rf.d;)" >
<!ENTITY % ps.ul.d "ol¦sl¦ul¦nl" >
<!ENTITY % ps.list "%ps.ul.d;¦dl¦gl">
```

```
<!ENTITY % ps.elem "xmp¦lq¦lines¦tbl¦address¦artwork" >
<!ENTITY % ps.zz   "(%ps.elem;)¦(%ps.list;)" >
<!ENTITY % s.p.d   "p¦note" >
<!ENTITY % s.top   "top1¦top2¦top3¦top4" >
<!ENTITY % s.zz            "(%s.p.d;)¦(%ps.zz;)¦(%s.top;)" >
<!ENTITY % i.float "fig¦fn" >
<!ENTITY % fm.d                    "abstract¦preface" >
<!ENTITY % bm.d   "glossary¦bibliog" >
<!ENTITY % m.ph       "(#PCDATA¦(%p.zz.ph;))*" >
<!ENTITY % m.p       "(#PCDATA¦(%p.zz.ph;)¦(%ps.zz;))*" >
<!ENTITY % m.pseq  "(p, ((%s.p.d;)¦(%ps.zz;))*)" >
<!ENTITY % m.top   "(th?, p, (%s.zz;)*)" >
<!ELEMENT %doctype;   - -  (frontm?, body, appendix?, backm?)
                                +(ix¦%i.float;)>
```

Notice, there is nothing telling you that the entity declarations have ended and the
element declarations have started.

```
<!ELEMENT frontm    - O  (titlep, (%fm.d;¦h1)*, toc?, figlist?)>
<!ELEMENT body      - O  (h0+¦h1+)>
<!ELEMENT appendix  - O  (h1+)>
<!ELEMENT backm     - O  ((%bm.d;¦h1)*, index?)>
<!ELEMENT (toc¦figlist¦index)  - O  EMPTY >
<!ELEMENT titlep    - O  (title & docnum? & date? & abstract? &
(author¦address¦%s.zz;)*)>
<!ELEMENT (docnum¦date¦author)
        - O  (#PCDATA) >
<!ELEMENT title     - O  (tline+) >
<!ELEMENT tline     O O  %m.ph; >
<!ELEMENT h0      - O  (h0t, (%s.zz;)*, h1+) >
<!ELEMENT (h1¦%bm.d;¦%fm.d;)
                    - O  (h1t, (%s.zz;)*, h2*) >
<!ELEMENT h2        - O  (h2t, (%s.zz;)*, h3*) >
<!ELEMENT h3        - O  (h3t, (%s.zz;)*, h4*) >
<!ELEMENT h4        - O  (h4t, (%s.zz;)*) >
<!ELEMENT (h0t¦h1t¦h2t¦h3t¦h4t)
                    O O  %m.ph;     >
```

Again, there are no comments for how to use any of these elements.

```
<!ELEMENT top1      - O  %m.top; -(top1)>
<!ELEMENT top2      - O  %m.top; -(top2) >
<!ELEMENT top3      - O  %m.top; -(top3) >
<!ELEMENT top4      - O  %m.top; -(top4) >
<!ELEMENT th              - O  %m.ph; >
<!ELEMENT address   - -  (aline+)>
<!ELEMENT aline     O O  %m.ph; >
<!ELEMENT artwork   - O  EMPTY>
<!ELEMENT dl          - -  ((dthd+, ddhd)?, (dt+, dd)*)>
<!ELEMENT dt        - O  %m.ph; >
<!ELEMENT (dthd¦ddhd)- O  (#PCDATA) >
```

Notice that alignment of declarations is hardly existent.

```
<!ELEMENT dd          - O  %m.pseq; >
<!ELEMENT gl          - -  (gt, (gd¦gdg))* >
<!ELEMENT gt        - O  (#PCDATA) >
```

(continues)

Listing 12.1   Continued

```
<!ELEMENT  gdg           - O  (gd+) >
<!ELEMENT  gd            - O  %m.pseq; >
<!ELEMENT  (%ps.ul.d;) - -  (li*) >
<!ELEMENT  li                - O  %m.pseq; >
<!ELEMENT  lines          O O  %m.pseq; >
<!ELEMENT  (lq¦xmp)      - -  %m.pseq; -(%i.float;) >
<!ELEMENT  (%s.p.d;)      O O  %m.p; >
<!ELEMENT  tbl           - -  (hr*, fr*, r+)>
<!ELEMENT  hr            - O  (h+) >
<!ELEMENT  fr             - O  (f+) >
<!ELEMENT  r             O O  (c+) >
<!ELEMENT   c            O O  %m.pseq; >
<!ELEMENT   (f¦h)        O O  (#PCDATA) >
<!ELEMENT  (%p.em.ph;)  - -  %m.ph; >
<!ELEMENT  q             - -  %m.ph; >
<!ELEMENT  (%p.rf.ph;)  - -  %m.ph;  >
<!ELEMENT  (%p.rf.d;)    - O  EMPTY  >
```

Notice that these figure-related elements could easily be identified as a group of related elements, but still there is no comment.

```
<!ELEMENT  fig           - -  (figbody, (figcap, figdesc?)?) -(%i.float;)>
<!ELEMENT  figbody      O O  %m.pseq; >
<!ELEMENT  figcap        - O  %m.ph; >
<!ELEMENT  figdesc       - O  %m.pseq; >
<!ELEMENT  fn            - -  %m.pseq; -(%i.float;) >
<!ELEMENT  ix            - O  (#PCDATA) >
```

Notice these attributes are all grouped together instead of next to their respective element declarations.

```
<!ATTLIST %doctype;     security CDATA  #IMPLIED
                        status   CDATA   " "
                        version  CDATA  #IMPLIED>
<!ATTLIST title    stitle   CDATA  #IMPLIED>
<!ATTLIST (h0¦h1¦h2¦%bm.d;¦%fm.d;)
                  id       ID     #IMPLIED
                  stitle   CDATA  #IMPLIED>
<!ATTLIST (h3¦h4)    id        ID  #IMPLIED>
<!ATTLIST artwork     sizex    NMTOKEN  textsize
                  sizey    NUTOKEN  #REQUIRED>
<!ATTLIST gl         compact  (compact) #IMPLIED
                  termhi   NUMBER  2>
<!ATTLIST dl         compact  (compact) #IMPLIED
                  headhi   NUMBER  2
                  termhi   NUMBER  2
                  tsize    NUMBERS  9>
<!ATTLIST gd         source   CDATA  #IMPLIED>
<!ATTLIST (%ps.ul.d;) compact  (compact) #IMPLIED>
<!ATTLIST li         id       ID     #IMPLIED>
<!ATTLIST xmp        depth    NUTOKEN  #IMPLIED
                  keep     NMTOKEN  all
                  lines    (flow¦lines) lines>
<!ATTLIST tbl        cols     NUMBERS  #REQUIRED>
```

```
<!ATTLIST c          heading   (h)   #IMPLIED>
<!ATTLIST (%p.rf.ph;) refid     IDREF  #CONREF
                     page     (yes¦no)  yes>
<!ATTLIST fnref        refid     IDREF  #REQUIRED>
<!ATTLIST liref        refid     IDREF  #REQUIRED
             page     (yes¦no)   yes>
<!ATTLIST fig         id      ID   #IMPLIED
               frame   (box¦rule¦none)    none
           place   (top¦fixed¦bottom)  top
           width   (column¦page)    page
           align   (left¦center¦right) center
           lines   (flow¦lines)   lines>
<!ATTLIST ix         id      ID   #IMPLIED
           print    CDATA  #IMPLIED
           see     CDATA  #IMPLIED
           seeid   IDREF  #IMPLIED>
<!ATTLIST fn        id      ID   #IMPLIED>
<!ENTITY    ptag    STARTTAG  "p"   >
<!ENTITY    qtag    STARTTAG  "q"   >
<!ENTITY    qetag   ENDTAG   "q"   >
<!ENTITY    endtag  ENDTAG    ""    >
<!SHORTREF docmap   "&#RS;&#RE;" ptag
                 '"'      qtag  >
<!USEMAP    docmap  %doctype;>
<!SHORTREF qmap     '"'       qetag  >
<!USEMAP    qmap  q>
<!SHORTREF ixmap   "&#RE;"      endtag >
<!USEMAP    ixmap  ix>
```

To improve this DTD, you might:

- Add comments
- Call elements in order after their first model
- Separate logical groups of elements
- Align declarations

These changes make the difference between a confusing DTD and one that can be followed easily.

The Friendly DTD

Listing 12.2 shows a revision of the DTD from listing 12.1.

Listing 12.2   The Revised, Easy-to-Follow DTD

Notice the introductory and copyright information. Private DTDs could have company contacts and revision information.

```
<!-- (C) International Organization for Standardization 1986
     Permission to copy in any form is granted for use with
     conforming SGML systems and applications as defined in
     ISO 8879, provided this notice is included in all copies.
-->
```

(continues)

Content Modeling

III

Listing 12.2   Continued

```
<!-- Public document type definition.  Typical invocation:
<!DOCTYPE general PUBLIC "ISO 8879:1986//DTD General Document//EN" [
  <!ENTITY % ISOnum PUBLIC
    "ISO 8879:1986//ENTITIES Numeric and Special Graphic//EN">
  <!ENTITY % ISOpub PUBLIC
    "ISO 8879:1986//ENTITIES Publishing//EN">
  %ISOnum; %ISOpub;
      (Parameter entities and additional elements can be defined here.)
  ]>
```

Good comment sections describe uses of document type. Note above describes additional extension that can be added.

```
-->
<!ENTITY % doctype "general" -- Document type generic identifier -->
<!-- This is a document type definition for a "general" document.
It contains the necessary elements for use in many applications, and is
organized so that other elements can be added in the document type
declaration subset. -->

                  <!-- Entity Naming Conventions -->
<!--
              Prefix = where used:
     p.      = in paragraphs (also in phrases if .ph suffix)
     s.      = in sections (i.e., among paragraphs)
     ps. = in paragraphs and sections
     i.      = where allowed by inclusion exceptions
     m.      = content model or declared content
     a.      = attribute definition
     NONE= specific use defined in models
              Suffix = allowed content:
     .ph = elements whose content is %m.ph;
     .d      = elements whose content has same definition
     NONE= elements with unique definitions
-->
```

Notice like declarations are grouped together, explained, and aligned.

```
                       <!-- Element Tokens -->
     <!ENTITY % p.em.ph   "hp1¦hp2¦hp3¦hp0¦cit"       -- Emphasized phrases -->
     <!ENTITY % p.rf.ph   "hdref¦figref"              -- Reference phrases -->
     <!ENTITY % p.rf.d    "fnref¦liref"               -- References (empty) -->
     <!ENTITY % p.zz.ph   "q¦(%p.em.ph;)¦(%p.rf.ph;)¦(%p.rf.d;)"
                                                      -- All phrases -->
     <!ENTITY % ps.ul.d   "ol¦sl¦ul¦nl"               -- Unit-item lists -->
     <!ENTITY % ps.list   "%ps.ul.d;¦dl¦gl"               -- All lists -->
     <!ENTITY % ps.elem   "xmp¦lq¦lines¦tbl¦address¦artwork"
                                                      -- Other elements -->
     <!ENTITY % ps.zz     "(%ps.elem;)¦(%ps.list;)"
                                                      -- Para/sect subelements -->
     <!ENTITY % s.p.d     "p¦note"                    -- Simple paragraphs -->
     <!ENTITY % s.top     "top1¦top2¦top3¦top4"            -- Topics -->
     <!ENTITY % s.zz      "(%s.p.d;)¦(%ps.zz;)¦(%s.top;)"
                                                      -- Section subelements -->
     <!ENTITY % i.float   "fig¦fn"                    -- Floating elements -->
```

```
<!ENTITY % fm.d       "abstract¦preface"                   -- Front matter -->
<!ENTITY % bm.d       "glossary¦bibliog"                   -- Back matter -->

                      <!-- Model Groups -->
<!ENTITY % m.ph       "(#PCDATA¦(%p.zz.ph;))*"             -- Phrase model -->
<!ENTITY % m.p        "(#PCDATA¦(%p.zz.ph;)¦(%ps.zz;))*"
                                                  -- Paragraph model -->
<!ENTITY % m.pseq     "(p, ((%s.p.d;)¦(%ps.zz;))*)"
                                                  -- Paragraph sequence -->
<!ENTITY % m.top      "(th?, p, (%s.zz;)*)"                -- Topic model -->

                      <!-- Document Structure -->
<!--      ELEMENTS    MIN  CONTENT (EXCEPTIONS) -->
<!ELEMENT %doctype;   - -  (frontm?, body, appendix?, backm?)
                                                  +(ix¦%i.float;)>
<!ELEMENT frontm      - O  (titlep, (%fm.d;¦h1)*, toc?, figlist?)>
<!ELEMENT body        - O  (h0+¦h1+)>
<!ELEMENT appendix    - O  (h1+)>
<!ELEMENT backm       - O  ((%bm.d;¦h1)*, index?)>
<!ELEMENT (toc¦figlist¦index)          -- Table of contents, figure list, --
                      - O  EMPTY  -- and index have generated content -->

                      <!-- Title Page Elements -->
<!--      ELEMENTS    MIN  CONTENT (EXCEPTIONS) -->
<!ELEMENT titlep      - O  (title & docnum? & date? & abstract? &
                           (author¦address¦%s.zz;)*)>
<!ELEMENT (docnum¦date¦author)
                      - O  (#PCDATA)    -- Document number, etc. -->
<!ELEMENT title       - O  (tline+)              -- Document title -->
<!ELEMENT tline       O O  %m.ph;                    -- Title line -->

                      <!-- Headed Sections -->
<!--      ELEMENTS    MIN  CONTENT (EXCEPTIONS) -->
<!ELEMENT h0          - O  (h0t, (%s.zz;)*, h1+)          -- Part -->
<!ELEMENT (h1¦%bm.d;¦%fm.d;)
                      - O  (h1t, (%s.zz;)*, h2*)          -- Chapter -->
<!ELEMENT h2          - O  (h2t, (%s.zz;)*, h3*)          -- Section -->
<!ELEMENT h3          - O  (h3t, (%s.zz;)*, h4*)          -- Subsection -->
<!ELEMENT h4          - O  (h4t, (%s.zz;)*)            -- Sub-subsection -->
<!ELEMENT (h0t¦h1t¦h2t¦h3t¦h4t)
                      O O  %m.ph;                 -- Headed section titles -->

                 <!-- Topics (Captioned Subsections) -->
<!--      ELEMENTS    MIN  CONTENT (EXCEPTIONS) -->
<!ELEMENT top1        - O  %m.top; -(top1)                -- Topic 1 -->
<!ELEMENT top2        - O  %m.top; -(top2)                -- Topic 2 -->
<!ELEMENT top3        - O  %m.top; -(top3)                -- Topic 3 -->
<!ELEMENT top4        - O  %m.top; -(top4)                -- Topic 4 -->
<!ELEMENT th          - O  %m.ph;                    -- Topic heading -->

                 <!-- Elements in Sections or Paragraphs -->
<!--      ELEMENTS    MIN  CONTENT (EXCEPTIONS) -->
<!ELEMENT address     - -  (aline+)>
<!ELEMENT aline       O O  %m.ph;                    -- Address line -->
<!ELEMENT artwork     - O  EMPTY>
<!ELEMENT dl          - -  ((dthd+, ddhd)?, (dt+, dd)*)>
```

(continues)

Listing 12.2 Continued

```
<!ELEMENT dt          - O  %m.ph;                    -- Definition term -->
<!ELEMENT (dthd¦ddhd)
                      - O  (#PCDATA)        -- Headings for dt and dd -->
<!ELEMENT dd          - O  %m.pseq;          -- Definition description -->
<!ELEMENT gl          - -  (gt, (gd¦gdg))*             -- Glossary list -->
<!ELEMENT gt          - O  (#PCDATA)                  -- Glossary term -->
<!ELEMENT gdg         - O  (gd+)           -- Glossary definition group -->
<!ELEMENT gd          - O  %m.pseq;              -- Glossary definition -->
<!ELEMENT (%ps.ul.d;)
                      - -  (li*)                   -- Unit item lists -->
<!ELEMENT li          - O  %m.pseq;                       -- List item -->
<!ELEMENT lines       O O  %m.pseq;                  -- Line elements -->
<!ELEMENT (lq¦xmp)    - -  %m.pseq; -(%i.float;)       -- Long quote -->
<!ELEMENT (%s.p.d;)   O O  %m.p;                       -- Paragraphs -->

                      <!-- Table -->
<!--      ELEMENTS   MIN  CONTENT (EXCEPTIONS) -->
<!ELEMENT tbl         - -  (hr*, fr*, r+)>
<!ELEMENT hr          - O  (h+)                         -- Heading row -->
<!ELEMENT fr          - O  (f+)                         -- Footing row -->
<!ELEMENT r           O O  (c+)               -- Row (body of table) -->
<!ELEMENT c           O O  %m.pseq;             -- Cell in body row -->
<!ELEMENT (f¦h)       O O  (#PCDATA)           -- Cell in fr or hr -->

                      <!-- Phrases -->
<!--      ELEMENTS   MIN  CONTENT (EXCEPTIONS) -->
<!ELEMENT (%p.em.ph;)
                      - -  %m.ph;              -- Emphasized phrases -->
<!ELEMENT q           - -  %m.ph;                       -- Quotation -->
<!ELEMENT (%p.rf.ph;)
                      - -  %m.ph;              -- Reference phrases -->
<!ELEMENT (%p.rf.d;)
                      - O  EMPTY             -- Generated references -->

                      <!-- Includable Subelements -->
<!--      ELEMENTS   MIN  CONTENT (EXCEPTIONS) -->
<!ELEMENT fig         - -  (figbody, (figcap, figdesc?)?) -(%i.float;)>
<!ELEMENT figbody     O O  %m.pseq;                   -- Figure body -->
<!ELEMENT figcap      - O  %m.ph;                  -- Figure caption -->
<!ELEMENT figdesc     - O  %m.pseq;           -- Figure description -->
<!ELEMENT fn          - -  %m.pseq; -(%i.float;)          -- Footnote -->
<!ELEMENT ix          - O  (#PCDATA)                   -- Index entry -->
```

Notice the explanatory comments below about specific features.

```
                    <!-- Attribute Definition Lists -->
<!-- As this document type definition is intended for basic SGML
     documents, in which the LINK features are not supported, it was
     necessary to include link attributes in the definitions.
-->
<!--          ELEMENTS    NAME     VALUE   DEFAULT -->
<!ATTLIST %doctype;   security CDATA   #IMPLIED
                      status   CDATA   ""
                      version  CDATA   #IMPLIED>
```

```
<!ATTLIST title          stitle   CDATA    #IMPLIED>
<!ATTLIST (h0¦h1¦h2¦%bm.d;¦%fm.d;)
                         id       ID       #IMPLIED
                         stitle   CDATA    #IMPLIED>
<!ATTLIST (h3¦h4)        id       ID       #IMPLIED>
<!ATTLIST artwork        sizex    NMTOKEN  textsize
            -- Default is current text width in column. --
                         sizey    NUTOKEN  #REQUIRED
            -- (Sizes are specified in the units supported by the
               application in which this declaration appears;
               for sizex, the keyword "textsize" can be used
               to mean "the width at which previous text was set").
            -->
<!ATTLIST gl             compact  (compact) #IMPLIED
                         termhi   NUMBER    2>
<!ATTLIST dl             compact  (compact) #IMPLIED
                         headhi   NUMBER    2
                         termhi   NUMBER    2
                         tsize    NUMBERS   9
            -- The number of dt elements per dd must equal the
               number of numbers specified for tsize (here 1).
               The number of dthd elements must be the same.
            -->
<!ATTLIST gd             source   CDATA     #IMPLIED>
<!ATTLIST (%ps.ul.d;)    compact  (compact) #IMPLIED>
<!ATTLIST li             id       ID        #IMPLIED>
<!ATTLIST xmp            depth    NUTOKEN   #IMPLIED
                         keep     NMTOKEN   all
                         lines    (flow¦lines) lines>
<!ATTLIST tbl            cols     NUMBERS   #REQUIRED
            -- The number of c elements per r must equal
               the number of numbers specified for cols
               (similarly, the number of h per hr and f per fr).
            -->
<!ATTLIST c              heading  (h)       #IMPLIED
            -- If h is specified, cell is row heading.
            -->
<!ATTLIST (%p.rf.ph;)
                         refid    IDREF     #CONREF
                         page     (yes¦no) yes>
<!ATTLIST fnref          refid    IDREF     #REQUIRED>
<!ATTLIST liref          refid    IDREF     #REQUIRED
                         page     (yes¦no) yes>
<!ATTLIST fig            id       ID        #IMPLIED
                         frame    (box¦rule¦none)    none
                         place    (top¦fixed¦bottom) top
                         width    (column¦page)      page
                         align    (left¦center¦right) center
                         lines    (flow¦lines)       lines>
<!ATTLIST ix             id       ID        #IMPLIED
                         print    CDATA     #IMPLIED
                         see      CDATA     #IMPLIED
                         seeid    IDREF     #IMPLIED>
<!ATTLIST fn             id       ID        #IMPLIED>
```

(continues)

III

Content Modeling

Listing 12.2   Continued

Notice explanatory comments about short reference structures.

```
                     <!-- Entities for Short References -->
   <!ENTITY            ptag    STARTTAG "p"       -- Paragraph start-tag --
>
   <!ENTITY            qtag    STARTTAG "q"     -- Quoted phrase start-tag --
>
   <!ENTITY            qetag   ENDTAG   "q"     -- Quoted phrase end-tag --
>
   <!ENTITY            endtag  ENDTAG    ""  -- Empty end-tag for any element -->
   <!SHORTREF docmap                                    -- Map for general use --
                     "&#RS;&#RE;" ptag                  -- Blank line is <p> --
                     '"'         qtag                     -- " is <q> -->
   <!USEMAP   docmap   %doctype;>
   <!SHORTREF qmap                                     -- Map for quoted phrases --
                     '"'          qetag  -- " is </q> -->
   <!USEMAP   qmap q>
   <!SHORTREF ixmap                                     -- Map for index entries --
                     "&#RE;"      endtag                 -- Record end is </> -->
   <!USEMAP   ixmap ix>
```

Chapter 9, "Extending Document Architecture," discussed extensions that you should include in your DTDs. You should consider adding the following to your DTDs:

- Hypertext extensions
- Multimedia extensions
- Indexing and cataloguing capabilities
- Revision and configuration management information
- Security classification information

Documents without these extensions will eventually be as uncommon as a new personal computer without speakers is now. Anticipate improvements and prepare for them now. If you group elements, group tags by type, and align declarations, users will thank you when they want to modify your DTDs.

▶▶ See "Separating the DTD into Logical Groups of Elements," p. 217
▶▶ See "Aligning Declarations," p. 224

The Common DTD

Another reason to keep your DTDs easy to follow is because of the common DTD. SGML installations usually share DTDs. Element modules make it possible to fix or change DTDs in one place and have those improvements ripple throughout the entire installation.

Listing 12.3 shows what a common DTD looks like. Elements are organized by logical group, and tags are grouped by type. Comments guide users easily through the DTD. All the declarations are aligned.

Listing 12.3   A Common DTD

Notice revision tracking and background info for future users of in-house DTD.

```
<!--****************************************************************-->
<!--    AnyCorp, a BIG Corp company                                -->
<!--                                                               -->
<!--    Name:    Common DTD                                        -->
<!--    Purpose:   Define common elements shared by documents      -->
<!--    Project:   Electronic Document Project                     -->
<!--               AnyCorp electronic document project             -->
<!--    Version:   1.25                                            -->
<!--    Date:      Today's Date, 199?                              -->
<!--    Public Identifier:                                         -->
<!--    "-//ANYCORP//DTD Common Shared Elements//EN"               -->
<!--                                                               -->
<!--****************************************************************-->
<!--****************************************************************-->
<!--                   Revision History                            -->
<!--                                                               -->
<!--    Author        Date           Reason                        -->
<!--    ======        ====           ============================  -->
<!--                                                               -->
<!--    ABC           Today, 199?    Needed to add <eqnnew> element -->
<!--                                                               -->
<!--****************************************************************-->
```

These content modules are shared as entities among several DTDs. This avoids tedious duplication of identical content models.

```
<!--          Content Model Modules   -->
<!ENTITY % parent          "para¦texeqn¦eqnsec¦stdeqn¦blist¦
                            nlist¦dlist¦table¦illus¦note¦caut¦warn">
<!ENTITY % miscstr         "(((%parent;)+, SubSec*)¦SubSec+)">
<!ENTITY % minmum          "#PCDATA¦emph¦rdi¦partno¦
                            partname¦manufact¦product">
<!ENTITY % data            "(%minmum;¦xref¦eref¦appref)+">

<!--          Attribute Modules   -->
```

These attribute models can now be shared by several DTDs without having to declare the same attributes again and again.

```
<!ENTITY % mattrib         "id          CDATA            #IMPLIED
                            addinfo      CDATA            #IMPLIED
                            securOwn     CDATA            #IMPLIED
                            securLvl  (public¦iuo¦coconf¦critical) #IMPLIED
                            %mattrib;">
```

(continues)

III

Content Modeling

Listing 12.3   Continued

```
<!ENTITY % stanat       "Custno      NUMBER              #IMPLIED
                         customer    CDATA               #IMPLIED
                         pubdate     cdata               #IMPLIED
                         %mattrib;">

<!ENTITY % sattrib      "">

<!--   Subsections, Title Paragraphs, Equations, Lists          -->

<!ELEMENT SubSec  - -  (title, (%miscstr;)?)>
<!ATTLIST              %sattrib;
                       %stanat;>
<!ELEMENT title   - -  (%minmum;¦xref)+>

<!ELEMENT para    - -  %data;>
<!ATTLIST para         wrap        (n)   #IMPLIED
                       indent      (y)   #IMPLIED
                       %stanat;>
<!ELEMENT eqnsec  - -  (para¦txteqn¦stdeqn)+>
<!ELEMENT txteqn  - -  (#PCDATA¦emph)+>
<!ATTLIST txteqn       %stanat;>
<!ELEMENT stdeqn  - -  CDATA        -- Pull ISO DTD here -->
<!ATTLIST stdeqn       %stanat;>
<!ELEMENT blist   - -  (item+)      -(nlist)>
<!ATTLIST blist        %stanat;>
<!ELEMENT nlist   - -  (item+)>
<!ATTLIST nlist        %stanat;>
<!ELEMENT dlist   - -  (def+)>
<!ATTLIST dlist        %stanat;>
<!ELEMENT def     - -  (term,item)>
<!ATTLIST def          %stanat;>
<!ELEMENT term    - -  %data;>
<!ATTLIST def          %stanat;>
<!ELEMENT item    - -  (para¦blist¦nlist¦dlist¦
                       note¦caut¦warn¦table¦illus)+>
<!ATTLIST item         %stanat;>
```

Notice now all elements are grouped by function and usage. Attribute models come right after the applicable element declaration.

```
<!--        Table Elements                        -->

<!ELEMENT table    - -  (title,((tgroup+,tnote?)¦graphic))>
<!ATTLIST table         %stanat;
          label         CDATA         #IMPLIED>
<!ELEMENT tgroup   - -  (colspec*,spanspec*,thead?,tobody)>
<!ATTLIST tgroup        cols    NUMBER              #REQUIRED>
<!ELEMENT colspec  - -  EMPTY>
<!ATTLIST colspec       colnum   NUMBER             #REQUIRED
                        colname  NMTOKEN            #IMPLIED
                        align    (left¦right¦center))#IMPLIED
                        colwidth CDATA              #IMPLIED>
```

```
<!ELEMENT spanspec - - EMPTY>
<!ATTLIST spanspec namest      NMTOKEN            #REQUIRED
                   nameend     NMTOKEN            #REQUIRED
                   spanname    CDATA              #REQUIRED
                   align       (left¦right¦center)) "center">
<!ELEMENT thead      - - (row+)>
<!ELEMENT tbody      - - (row+)>
<!ELEMENT row        - - (entry+)>
<!ATTLIST row           %stanat;>
<!ELEMENT entry      - - (txtentry¦strentry)>
<!ATTLIST entry      colname     NMTOKEN            #IMPLIED
                     spanname    CDATA              #IMPLIED
                     wrap        (n)                #IMPLIED
                     align       (left¦right¦center) #IMPLIED
                     %stanat;>
<!ELEMENT txtentry o o %data;>
<!ELEMENT strentry o o (para¦nlist¦blist¦note¦caut¦warn¦txteqn¦stdeqn)+>
<!ELEMENT tnote      - - (para+)>
<!ATTLIST tnote      %stanat;>

<!ELEMENT illus      - - (title?,graphic,keylst?)>
<!ATTLIST illus      %stanat;
                     label       CDATA              #REQUIRED>
<!ELEMENT graphic    - o EMPTY>
<!ATTLIST graphic filename       CDATA              #REQUIRED
                  artno          CDATA              #IMPLIED>
<!ELEMENT keylst     - - (title,tgroup)>
<!ATTLIST keylst  %stanat;>
<!ELEMENT scand      - o EMPTY>
<!ATTLIST scand filename         CDATA              #REQUIRED>
<!ELEMENT note       - - (para+)>
<!ATTLIST note    %stanat;>
<!ELEMENT caut       - - (para+)>
<!ELEMENT caut    %stanat;>
<!ELEMENT warn       - - (para+)>
<!ATTLIST warn    %stanat;>

<!--     Data Elements             -->

<!ELEMENT  emph       - - (#PCDATA¦xref¦emph)+>
<!ATTLIIST emph       type (sup¦sub¦ul¦bold¦supul¦supbold¦supboul
                      ¦subul¦subbold¦subboul¦boldul) #REQUIRED>
<!ELEMENT  rdi      - - (#PCDATA)>
<!ATTLIST  rdi    %stanat;>
<!ELEMENT  partno   - - (#PCDATA)>
<!ATTLIST  partno   %stanat;>
<!ELEMENT  partname - - (#PCDATA)>
<!ATTLIST  partname %stanat;>
<!ELEMENT  manufact - - (#PCDATA)>
<!ATTLIST  manufact %stanat;>
<!ELEMENT  product  - - (#PCDATA)>
<!ATTLIST  product  %stanat;>

<!--   References  -->
```

III

Content Modeling

(continues)

Listing 12.3 Continued

```
<!ELEMENT  xref      - - (%minmum;)+>
<!ATTLIST  xref   idref  CDATA    #REQUIRED>
<!ELEMENT  eref      - - (%minmum;)+>
<!ATTLIST  eref   book   CDATA    #REQUIRED
                  idref  CDATA    #REQUIRED>
<!ELEMENT  appref    - - (%minmum;)+>
<!ATTLIST  appref applic CDATA    #REQUIRED
                  args   CDATA    #REQUIRED>

<!--     Character Entities        -->

<!ENTITY % ISOpub
         PUBLIC "ISO 8879-1986//ENTITIES Publishing//EN">
<!ENTITY % ISOnum
         PUBLIC "ISO 8879-1986//ENTITIES Numeric and Special Graphics//EN">
<!ENTITY % ISOgrk3
         PUBLIC "ISO 8879-1986//ENTITIES Greek Symbols//EN">

%ISOpub;%ISOnum;%ISOgrk3;
```

Notice several things about this common DTD:

- It has an abundance of comments, including a revision history, authors, and a change history.
- Clearly divided partitions describe the elements that they contain.
- The order of the list of elements parallels the order of the content model. For example, if the content model includes (para¦txteqn¦stdeqn)+, the elements para, txteqn, and stdeqn are defined in the same order—unless they have already been defined.

Since the common DTD makes references to and from other DTDs, you need to format your DTD so those references appear clearly.

Making Comments in DTDs

You have seen this before, but it bears repeating. The first thing that you see in a good DTD is a list of comment lines. Look at listing 12.3. You can learn much about the document just from the first few lines of comments. Comments throughout the document help, too. Comments are the lines that resemble the one below:

```
<!--       Table Elements                        -->
```

Notice the `<!--` at the beginning of the line and the `-->` at the end of the line. These are opening and closing delimiters for comments.

Make comments whenever you want to:

- Identify groups of elements
- Make the order of the DTD more obvious
- Describe anything out of the ordinary
- Explain the history behind an unusual decision

You can make two types of comments in a DTD: full comment declarations and inline comments.

Full Comment Declarations

The comments that you see at the beginning of easy-to-read DTDs are full comment declarations. They start with <-- and end with -->.

Tip

Don't confuse -- (used in comment declarations) with - - (used to indicate minimization of open or close delimiters).

In the following full comment declaration, the delimiters do not appear on the same line:

```
<!--This is a comment. You can put any sort of symbol you like in here,
within reason, because the parser ignores everything between the first
comment symbol and
-->
```

The style of comment above, where the delimiters do not appear on the same line, works best in the middle of a DTD between groups of declarations, or in the middle of a declaration that requires special explanation. This example comes from listing 12.2:

```
                <!-- Attribute Definition Lists -->
<!-- As this document type definition is intended for basic SGML
        documents, in which the LINK features are not supported, it was
        necessary to include link attributes in the definitions.
-->
```

Although full comment declarations like this one certainly are acceptable, they some-times are not as striking as they need to be, as at the beginning of a DTD, for example. The following comment is better when you need to grab the reader's attention:

```
<!--**************************************************-->
<!--   Here's another example of a comment line.       -->
<!--   Each line begins and ends with a                -->
<!--   delimiter; there is little chance of mistaking   -->
<!--   this text. You can also add more formatting by   -->
<!--   using white space and headings, such as         -->
<!--                                                   -->
```

```
<!--                                                  -->
<!--  Heading here:                                   -->
<!--                                                  -->
<!--              Heading info here                   -->
<!--                 (more heading info)              -->
<!--                                                  -->
<!--                                                  -->
<!--                      And then,                   -->
<!--                      when you're finally ready,  -->
<!--                                                  -->
<!--                                                  -->
<!--                                                  -->
<!--  You can come back to your original format       -->
<!--  as though nothing different happened            -->
<!--  because as far as the parser is concerned,      -->
<!--  nothing did happen.                             -->
<!--***************************************************-->
<!--***************************************************-->
```

As far as SGML is concerned, you may use whatever special symbols you like—asterisks, pound signs, and equal signs—between comment delimiters as long as they are part of the ASCII character set.

Tip

You can combine both ways of making full comment declarations in one DTD. For single-line comments, use delimiters at the end of each line. When you need to write a quick paragraph of explanation, use one <-- on the top line and one --> at the end of the bottom line.

Stay away from an accidental close delimiter that SGML might react to in your comments. For example, if you write:

```
<!--  Don't say --> inside a comment line, 'cause    -->
<!--  that could get SGML all confused and bothered  -->
```

the result might be an error message. Be careful about what you place between comment delimiters.

Inline Comments

Use inline comments when you need to say something within another declaration. They come in handy when you want to leave a hint about a content model. For example:

```
<!ELEMENT  book    - -  (chapter¦frontmtr) -- no bakmtr -->
```

This comment refers the user to another DTD or a DTD fragment:

```
<!ELEMENT comment - -  (%stuff;)     -- see common DTD ref-->
```

An inline comment is a quick note—sometimes a reference to another source of information. If it's more than a quick note, you should make a full comment declaration instead.

Separating the DTD into Logical Groups of Elements

Elements are declared in logical groups. Put elements in the groups where you best can maintain them and most easily keep track of them. A DTD typically has:

- Groups of elements that belong to the same type of document structure (such as paragraph elements, table elements, art elements, and embedded object elements).

- Groups of elements that are used in only one place (such as indexing elements, table of contents elements, bibliography elements, and equation elements).

- Groups of elements that are used in any place or every place (such as footnote elements, special symbol or character elements, and special entity declarations).

- Special processing elements that vary according to the circumstance (such as a call to a formatting DTD or a source that contains shared elements).

In most DTDs, the groups of elements follow these guidelines. If a DTD does not obey these guidelines exactly, it usually follows some of them and uses whatever organization is best for the application. In a mathematics application, for example, you might group elements according to the different types of equations or according to the different types of calculations involved.

Listing 12.4 shows another type of element group: processing instructions.

Caution

Processing instructions are normally machine-specific, so avoid putting them in your DTDs. They limit the usefulness of a DTD, but sometimes they are necessary.

Listing 12.4   A DTD with Logically Grouped Elements

```
<!-- This is a Document Type Definition for newspapers
     with special consideration  of requirements for Persons
     with special needs to be presented in Braille,
     as large print editions or by artificial speakers -->

<!-- This DTD was written by Manfred Kruger (MID Logistics
     Heidelberg, Germany) on the base of a paper written
     by Uli Strempel (SBA), entitled 'Pre-final verbal
     description of the HAN-DTD-NP (EIF VER. 0.9)', dated
     July 24, 1992, and on the DTD called BRL-2, written
     by Yuri Rubinsky (ICADD); not all concepts contained in this
     paper and the DTD are taken into consideration. It was
     furthermore discussed and elaborated by some members
     of the CAPS Consortium:
```

(continues)

III

Content Modeling

Listing 12.4   Continued

```
- Uli Strempel (Stiftung Blindenanstalt, Germany)
- Rolf Schmidt (Stiftung Blindenanstalt, Germany)
- Pierre Bazex (Universit&eacute; Paul Sabatier, France)
- Keith Gladstone (RNIB, Great Britain)
- Henryk Rubinstein (Textalk, Sweden)
- Bart Bauwens (Katholieke Universiteit Leuven, Belgium) -->

<!-- Version 1.0
Author: Manfred Kruger
Started: October 17, 1992 (MK)
Last Changes: May 18, 1993 (BB)

Logfile of changes:
* October 20, 1992: parameter entity %spndata; added (BB)
* October 21, 1992: minimization type of end-tags of several
  elements were changed to 'O'; further study of the
  minimization types may be necessary.
* February 27, 1993:  first update; changed pictures
  and figures concept (BB)
* May 18, 1993: added ICADD table (BB)
-->

<!-- Special needs data -->
<!ENTITY % spndata      "(#PCDATA ¦ abbr ¦ unct ¦number)+"
-- special needs data containing a mixture of abbreviations,
uncontractable elements, numbers and PCDATA -->

<!-- Parameter entities; following AAP -->
<!ENTITY % i.float    "fig¦picture¦ipp"    -- floating elements -->
<!ENTITY % p.em.ph    "it ¦ b ¦ bi ¦ e1 ¦ e2 ¦ e3" -- emphasis -->
<!ENTITY % p.rf.ph    "xref"            -- internal crossrefs -->
<!ENTITY % p.zz.ph    "q ¦ emq ¦ lang ¦ (%p.em.ph;) ¦ (%p.rf.ph;) ¦
                      sup ¦ inf"
                      -- phrases -- >
<!ENTITY % p.el       "ul"          -- unordered lists -->
<!ENTITY % p.tbl      "table"           -- table matter -->
<!ENTITY % p.zz       "%p.el; %p.tbl;" -- paragraph subelements -->
<!ENTITY % m.p        "(%spndata; ¦ (%p.zz.ph;) ¦ (%p.zz;))*"
                      -- paragraph text -->
<!ENTITY % m.ph       "(%spndata; ¦ (%p.zz.ph;))*" >
<!ENTITY % para       "(p ¦ cap ¦ (continrf,continpt))+">

<!-- Main structure for a newspaper -->

<!ELEMENT capsnews - - (issue, (group¦advert¦newssect¦newstbl¦
                      picture¦fig)+)

-- It is assumed that a document instance of capsnews represents one
edition of one newspaper. The newspaper may consist of a collection of
article groups, advertisements, (short)news and pictures.
They may occur in any order. M.K. -->

<!-- Issue related information -->
```

```
<!ELEMENT issue    - - (pinfo, npinfo, edinfo)

-- The issue elements are taken from the MAJOUR-application
   as far as applicable for newspapers M.K. -->

<!-- Publisher Information -->

<!ELEMENT pinfo    - O  (pnm, loc*)+  >
<!ELEMENT pnm      - O  %spndata; -- name of the publisher-->
<!ELEMENT loc      - O  (#PCDATA) -- location -->

<!-- Newspaper information -->

<!ELEMENT npinfo   - O  (npid, nptl, npsbt?)>
<!ELEMENT npid     - O  %spndata; -- newspaper identifier -->
<!ELEMENT nptl     - O  %spndata; -- newspaper title -->
<!ELEMENT npsbt    - O  %spndata; -- newspaper subtitle -->

<!-- Edition information -->

<!ELEMENT edinfo   - O  (loc, yid, iid, cd)>
<!ELEMENT yid      - O  (#PCDATA) -- year identifier -->
<!ELEMENT iid      - O  (#PCDATA) -- issue identifier -->
<!ELEMENT cd       - O  (#PCDATA) -- cover date -->

<!-- Group structure -->

<!ELEMENT group    - - (grtitle, (group ¦ article)+)>

<!-- Article structure -->

<!ELEMENT article - - (kwd*, hdline?, atl, sbt?,  edloc?, artdate?,
                       source?, abs-p?,  au?, %para;, au?, source?)
                       +(%i.float;)>

<!ELEMENT grtitle - O %spndata;  -- group title -->
<!ELEMENT hdline  - O %m.ph; +(lb) -- this headline should be
                                      considered as a supertitle -->
<!ELEMENT atl     - - %m.ph;  +(lb) -- article title -->
<!ELEMENT sbt     - O %m.ph; +(lb) -- article subtitle -->
<!ELEMENT au      - O %spndata; -- can include the text around
                                    the author's name  M.K. -->
<!ELEMENT edloc   - O %spndata;  -- editing location -->

<!ELEMENT artdate - O (#PCDATA) -- article date -->

<!ELEMENT source  - O %spndata; -- source (a news agency or
                                    the newspaper itself) -->
<!ELEMENT abs-p   - O (%m.p;) -- highlighted paragraph,
                                 often used for summarizing or
                                 abstracting purposes -->
<!ELEMENT p       - O (%m.p;) -- normal paragraph -->
<!ELEMENT cap     - O %spndata; +(lb)
-- caption; used simply as some highlighted text between paragraphs-->
```

(continues)

```
Listing 12.4   Continued

<!ELEMENT continrf - O (#PCDATA) -- continuation reference;
only necessary where the continuation of the article is separated -->

<!ELEMENT continpt - O %spndata; -- continuation point;
                                  often repeating the article title
                                  in abbreviated form -->


<!-- Following first level elements in capsnews are not
     yet examined. M.K.
  -->

<!ELEMENT (advert|newssect|newstbl)
                       - - CDATA -- has to be defined. M.K. -->

<!-- Paragraph subelements; following AAP -->
<!-- Phrases -->

<!ELEMENT q        - - %m.ph;   -- (inline) quotation -->
<!ELEMENT emq      - - %m.ph;  -- embedded quotation -->
<!ELEMENT lang     - - (pht?,npht) -- foreign language text -->
<!ELEMENT pht      - O (#PCDATA) -- phonetic transcription -->
<!ELEMENT npht     - O %spndata; --nonphonetic part-->
<!ELEMENT (%p.em.ph;) - - %m.ph;   -- all emphasizes -->
<!ELEMENT (%p.rf.ph;) - - %m.ph; -- all crossrefs -->
<!ELEMENT abbr     - - (#PCDATA) -- abbreviated term,
                                 to be spoken as letters -->
<!ELEMENT unct     - - (#PCDATA) -- not contractable in Braille -->
<!ELEMENT number   - - (#PCDATA) -- number which requires
                                   special formatting in Braille -->
<!ELEMENT ipp      - - (#PCDATA) -- ink print page number -->
<!ELEMENT (sup | inf) - - (#PCDATA) -- superscript and subscript -->


<!-- Paragraph subelements -->
<!ELEMENT ul       - - (lh?, li)* -- unordered list -->
<!ELEMENT li       - - (p+) -- list item; simplified content model;
                             may be sufficient for newspaper articles.
                             M.K. -->
<!ELEMENT lh       - - %m.ph; -- list header -->
<!ELEMENT kwd      - O %spndata; -- keyword -->

<!-- Tables : we refer to the ICADD table DTD:
     this DTD has also some provisions for the print disabled -->

<!ENTITY % tables PUBLIC "-//EC-USA-CDA/ICADD
                         //DTD ICADD-4//EN" "ICADD.Tables">
%tables;

<!-- Figures: see declarations in DTP DTD -->

<!ELEMENT fig      - - (gfc, fignum?, ti?, figdesc?, sfigdesc?) >

<!ELEMENT (fignum |figdesc | sfigdesc)
                   - O %spndata;
                   -- figdesc gives a description of the figure,
                      sfigdesc gives a shorter description   -- >
```

```
<!-- Pictures: similar to figures -->

<!ELEMENT picture - - (gfc, ti?, figdesc?, by?)>
<!ELEMENT by       - O %spndata; -- contains the source -->
<!ELEMENT ti       - - %m.ph;     -- title -->

<!ELEMENT gfc      - O EMPTY  -- notation attributes may be added -->
<!ELEMENT lb       - O EMPTY>

<!ENTITY invblk    "[invblk]" -- invisible blank -->

<!-- public entities as per ISO/IEC TR 9573 -->

<!ENTITY % ISOLAT1  PUBLIC "ISO 8879-1986//ENTITIES Added Latin 1//EN">
%ISOLAT1;
<!ENTITY % ISOLAT2  PUBLIC "ISO 8879-1986//ENTITIES Added Latin 2//EN">
%ISOLAT2;
<!ENTITY % ISOPUB   PUBLIC "ISO 8879-1986//ENTITIES Publishing//EN">
%ISOPUB;

<!-- Attribute definition lists -->

<!ATTLIST capsnews language  NAME       #REQUIRED
                   -- The name has to be given according to ISO 639 --
                   topics    NMTOKENS   #IMPLIED>

<!ATTLIST  cd      year      NUMBER     #REQUIRED
                   month     NUMBER     #REQUIRED
                   day       NUMBER     #REQUIRED>

<!ATTLIST edinfo   topics   NMTOKENS   #REQUIRED
                   -- The topics (sections) making up the edition
                      are listed here as attribute values.
                      Each article will have the theme name it
                      is belonging to.-->

<!ATTLIST group    level   (1¦2¦3¦4¦5¦6¦7) #REQUIRED
                   grtitle CDATA          #IMPLIED>

<!ATTLIST article  language NAME          #IMPLIED -- only necessary
                      to be specified where the language of the article
                      differs from the language attribute value given
                      in capsnews --
                   topic    NMTOKEN        #IMPLIED
                   id       ID             #IMPLIED
                   page     NUTOKEN        #REQUIRED
                   pagepos  NUTOKEN        #IMPLIED
                   pgspused NUMBER         #IMPLIED
                   sizewrds NUMBER         #IMPLIED
                   noarch   (yes¦no)       yes
                   boxed    (true¦false)   false >

<!ATTLIST hdline   pointsz NUMBER         #REQUIRED >

<!ATTLIST atl      pointsz NUMBER         #REQUIRED
                   font    NMTOKEN        #REQUIRED
```

III

Content Modeling

(continues)

Listing 12.4   Continued

```
                        fstyle (regular¦bold¦italic¦boldital)
                                            #REQUIRED>

<!ATTLIST source    source (newsagcy ¦ own) #IMPLIED >

<!ATTLIST artdate   year    NUMBER          #IMPLIED
                    month   NUMBER          #IMPLIED
                    day     NUMBER          #IMPLIED>

<!ATTLIST cap       pointsz NUMBER          #REQUIRED
                    emph    (reg ¦ it ¦ b ¦ bi ¦ other)   reg
                    struct  (section ¦ inbetw) inbetw
      --may express sectioning or simply in-between titleing -->

<!ATTLIST continrf  rid     IDREF           #REQUIRED
                    page    NUTOKEN         #REQUIRED
                    pagepos NUTOKEN         #REQUIRED>

<!ATTLIST continpt  id      ID              #REQUIRED>

<!ATTLIST lang      lang    NAME            #REQUIRED >

<!ATTLIST number kind (normal¦tele¦other) #IMPLIED >

<!ATTLIST fig       id      ID              #IMPLIED
                    page    NUTOKEN         #REQUIRED
                    pagepos NUTOKEN         #REQUIRED
                    pgspused NUMBER         #REQUIRED >

<!ATTLIST (%p.rf.ph;) rid   IDREF           #IMPLIED>

<!ATTLIST picture   id      ID              #IMPLIED
                    page    NUTOKEN         #REQUIRED
                    pagepos NUTOKEN         #REQUIRED
                    pgspused NUMBER         #REQUIRED>

<!ATTLIST gfc       id      ID              #IMPLIED
                    sizex   NUTOKEN         #IMPLIED
                    sizey   NUTOKEN         #IMPLIED
                    unit    CDATA           #IMPLIED>
```

Notice that the DTD above follows the four groupings mentioned earlier: elements of the same document structure, elements used only in one place, elements used anywhere, and any special processing elements. Each of the groups above has a comment explaining what elements are in the group and how they are used.

When you must deal with an odd element, put it in the most logical place in your DTD—which might even be by itself.

Declaring Elements After Their First Content Model

Grouping element declarations by type is important for formatting your DTDs properly. Within groups, it makes sense to declare elements the first time they are modeled. That way, whenever you see elements as part of a model group, you know that they are already defined or the current model group is the first model group. For example:

```
<!ELEMENT stuff      O O (bigstuff¦littlestuf) --gag me-->
<!--           STUFF ELEMENTS                      -->
<!ELEMENT bigstuff   O O (tinystuff?, morestuff+)       >
<!ELEMENT littlestuf O O (%stuffies;)                   >
```

In this example, `tinystuff` and `morestuff` have already been defined. Otherwise, you would define them immediately after the `bigstuff` element. `%stuffies;` was also defined previously—probably with the parameter entities at the beginning of the DTD.

Note the comment line immediately after the `stuff` element declaration. It helps you understand the elements when their names do not make sense. Names are often cryptic, so comments really help. For example:

```
<!--*********************************************-->
<!--              IPL ELEMENTS                  -->
<!--            (Illustrated Parts List)        -->
<!--*********************************************-->
<!--                                            -->
<!--         INTERLEAF 5.3.1 STYLE COMPONENT    -->
<!ELEMENT    line10   - - (inum, partn, pardes, qty)  >
<!--                  INDEX NUMBER              -->
<!ELEMENT    inum     - - (#PCDATA)                   >
<!--                  PART NUMBER               -->
<!ELEMENT    partn    - - (#PCDATA)                   >
<!--                  PART DESCRIPTION          -->
<!ELEMENT    pardes   - - (#PCDATA)                   >
<!--                  QUANTITY PER ASSEMBLY     -->
<!ELEMENT    qty      - - (#PCDATA)                   >
<!--*********************************************-->
```

Sometimes you must provide extra comments just to make sense of the element names, especially with specialized document types. For instance, the illustrated parts list in the previous example is a highly defined document type, but it can be confusing to someone who has not worked with it before. Many such document types exist, and they need extra comments to describe their elements.

In the previous example, the elements are declared in the same order as they were first modeled, which makes each grouping of elements more coherent and easier to follow. For instance, because the sequence is `line10`, `inum`, `partn`, `pardes`, and `qty`, that is the order in which the elements are declared.

Where To Define Attributes

Machines don't care how attributes and their elements look. A machine doesn't care whether you place the ATTLIST declaration a page away from its element. Doing so, however, makes it harder for you—and others—to understand the DTD. It's far better to make attribute declarations either immediately after the elements to which the attributes apply or in their own group in the DTD.

In the following example, artfig is defined for the first time, and all its attributes are defined as well. You could put the ATTLIST elsewhere in the DTD after you have declared more elements, but that makes it difficult to find. It's much better to declare attributes directly after the elements to which they apply.

```
<!ELEMENT  artfig    - O EMPTY                         >
<!ATTLIST  artfig
        artno        ID      #IMPLIED  -- art file number--
        artsz        NUTOKEN #IMPLIED  -- size of frame   --
        artrv        CDATA   #IMPLIED  -- art revision     --
        stdart       (y¦n)   #IMPLIED  -- standard art    -->
```

In this excerpt from listing 12.2, the attributes are grouped separately in the DTD:

```
<!--        ELEMENTS    NAME     VALUE   DEFAULT -->
<!ATTLIST   %doctype;   security CDATA   #IMPLIED
                        status   CDATA   ""
                        version  CDATA   #IMPLIED>
<!ATTLIST title         stitle   CDATA   #IMPLIED>
<!ATTLIST (h0¦h1¦h2¦%bm.d;¦%fm.d;)
                        id       ID      #IMPLIED
                        stitle   CDATA   #IMPLIED>
<!ATTLIST (h3¦h4)       id       ID      #IMPLIED>
<!ATTLIST artwork       sizex    NMTOKEN textsize
            -- Default is current text width in column. --
                        sizey    NUTOKEN #REQUIRED
            -- (Sizes are specified in the units supported by the
               application in which this declaration appears;
               for sizex, the keyword "textsize" can be used
               to mean "the width at which previous text was set").
            -->
```

Aligning Declarations

The key to making your DTDs clear is aligning all the element declarations and model groups. Even if you get everything else right, improperly aligned declarations make it difficult to find components. Aligning similar components is at the heart of a visually pleasing DTD. Listing 12.5 shows a DTD that is properly grouped and that has attributes called separately and clearly. Its first part is difficult to follow because the entity declarations, models, and comments are not aligned. The last part of the DTD is easy to follow because it *is* aligned.

Listing 12.5   DTD with Partly Aligned Declarations, Partly Not

```
<!-- Public document type declaration subset. Typical invocation:
<!DOCTYPE book PUBLIC "-//USA/AAP//DTD BK-1//EN"
 [<!ENTITY % ISOnum PUBLIC "ISO 8879-1986//ENTITIES Numeric and
          Special Graphic//EN" >
  <!ENTITY % ISOpub PUBLIC "ISO 8879-1986//ENTITITES
          Publishing//EN" >
  %ISOnum;   %ISOpub;
  <!ENTITY % srmaps PUBLIC "-//USA/AAP//SHORTREF SR-1//EN" >
  %srmaps;
]>
-->
<!--This is the AAP's document type declaration for a book/monograph.
It contains the necessary elements for use as a technical report,
conference proceedings, or a thesis or dissertation.  It is also suitable
for textbooks. -->


             <!-- Entity Naming Conventions -->
<!--
                Prefix = where used:
     p.  = in paragraphs (also in phrases if .ph suffix)
     s.  = in sections (i.e., among paragraphs)
     i.  = where allowed by inclusion exceptions
     m.  = content model or declared content
     a.  = attribute definition
     NONE= specific use defined in models
              Suffix = allowed content:
     .ph = elements whose content is %m.ph;
     .d  = elements whose content has same model as defaults
     NONE= individually defined elements
-->
<!ENTITY % book   "book" -- default document type generic identifier -->

            <!-- Specialized Elements -->
```

Notice that the content models for these entity declarations are not aligned, and it does make them harder to read.

```
<!ENTITY % ade.ph "str¦cty¦sbd¦cny¦pc¦san¦ead" -- address elements -->
<!ENTITY % bib "au¦cau¦msn¦srt¦loc¦pdt¦pp¦atl¦sct¦obi" -- bibliographic-->
<!ENTITY % bmcps.d "vt" -- back matter cps elements -->
<!ENTITY % bmsec.d "awd¦bib¦notes" -- back matter sections -->
<!ENTITY % bmsec.i "gl¦idx" -- indexes and glossary -->
<!ENTITY % fmcps.d "ack¦ded¦abs¦smtl" -- front matter cps elements -->
<!ENTITY % fmsec.d "fwd¦pf" -- front matter sections -->
<!ENTITY % pub   "cgs¦cgn¦rps¦crt¦pdt¦pnm¦loc¦cng¦avl" -- pubfm -->
<!ENTITY % pub.ph  "cdn¦aon¦isbn¦lcn¦rid¦ed¦vid¦cip¦phi¦prc¦ext¦pkg¦pid" >

            <!-- Basic Document Elements -->
<!ENTITY % i.float "fig¦fn¦nit" -- floating elements -->
<!ENTITY % p.e1 "dl¦oad¦iad¦art¦bq¦lit¦pdt¦bb¦bibl¦itml¦au¦cau"
                                              -- general -->
<!ENTITY % p.em.ph "it¦b¦bi¦rm¦scp¦e1¦e2¦e3" -- emphasis -->
<!ENTITY % p.lst.d "l¦l1¦l2¦l3¦l4¦l5" -- list, types 1 thru 5 -->
<!ENTITY % p.rf.ph "ntr¦fnr¦fgr¦tbr¦artr¦apr¦srr¦rb" -- references -->
```

(continues)

Listing 12.5 Continued

```
<!ENTITY % p.tbl "tbl" -- table matter -- >
<!ENTITY % p.zz "(%p.e1;)¦(%p.tbl;)¦(%p.lst.d;)"
                                     -- paragraph subelements -->
<!ENTITY % p.zz.ph "q ¦pp¦(%p.em.ph;)¦(%p.rf.ph;)¦gk¦cyr¦emq"
                                     -- phrases -->
<!ENTITY % s.h.ph "h¦h1¦h2¦h3¦h4" -- headings -->
<!ENTITY % s.top.d "top1¦top2¦top3¦top4" -- topics -->
<!ENTITY % s.zz "p¦(%p.zz;)¦(%s.h.ph;)¦(%s.top.d;)"
                                     -- section subelements -->

                 <!-- Models -->
<!ENTITY % m.addr  "(%ade.ph;)*" -- address (no name) -->
<!ENTITY % m.bib "(no?, ti, (%bib;)*)" -- bibliographic entry -->
<!ENTITY % m.copy  "(crd¦crn¦cci)+" -- copyright notice data -->
<!ENTITY % m.cps "(h?, p, (%s.zz;)*)" -- captioned par seq -->
<!ENTITY % m.date "(mo?, day?, yr)" -- date components -->
<!ENTITY % m.fig "EMPTY" -- default FIG content -->
<!ENTITY % m.name"(fnm?, snm, (deg¦sch)*, role*, (%ade.ph;)*, aff?)" >
<!ENTITY % m.org  "(onm, odv*, %m.addr;)" -- organization name -->
<!ENTITY % m.p "(#PCDATA¦(%p.zz.ph;)¦(%p.zz;))*" -- paragraph text -->
<!ENTITY % m.ph "(#PCDATA¦(%p.zz.ph;))*" -- phrase model -->
<!ENTITY % m.pseq  "(p, (p¦(%p.zz;))*)" -- P with sequence -->
<!ENTITY % m.rep "(rep1, (rep2, rep3?)?)?" -- repeating information -->
<!ENTITY % m.rep1  "(ti)" -- repeating identifier 1 -->
<!ENTITY % m.rep2  "(pdt)" -- repeating identifier 2 -->
<!ENTITY % m.rep3  "(vid)" -- repeating identifier 3 -->
<!ENTITY % m.sec "(st, (%s.zz;)*, ss1*)" -- section -->
<!ENTITY % m.tcchp "(no?, ct, pp*, tcsec*)" -- TOC chp model -->
<!ENTITY % m.tcpt  "(no?, pp*, tcchp*)" -- TOC part model -->
<!ENTITY % m.tcsec "(no?, st, pp*, tcss1*)" -- TOC sec model -->
<!ENTITY % m.tcss1 "(no?, st, pp*, tcss2*)" -- TOC ss1 model -->
<!ENTITY % m.tcss2 "(no?, st, pp*, tcss3*)" -- TOC ss2 model -->
<!ENTITY % m.tcss3 "(no?, st, pp*)"         -- TOC ss3 model -->
<!ENTITY % m.toc "(tcpt+¦tcchp+)?"       -- TOC elements -->
<!ENTITY % m.idx "(%m.sec;¦itml¦((idxn¦idxs)*,pp*))" --model for
                        indexes and glossary -->

            <!-- Attribute Definitions -->
<!ENTITY % a.id  "id ID #IMPLIED" -- ID attribute definition -->
<!ENTITY % a.rid   "rid IDREF #IMPLIED" -- IDREF attribute definition:
                        content must be empty if IDREF is specified. -->
<!ENTITY % a.sizes "sizex NUTOKEN #IMPLIED sizey NUTOKEN #IMPLIED
                                             unit CDATA #IMPLIED"
                   -- unit must be specified if sizex or sizey are. -->
```

Notice that these declarations are nearly all aligned, and they are much easier to read.

```
            <!-- Data Content Notations -->
<!NOTATION cyrillic PUBLIC "-//USA/AAP//NOTATION CYRIL-1//EN">
<!NOTATION greek PUBLIC "-//USA/AAP//NOTATION GREEK-1//EN">

<!--        ELEMENT        MIN  CONTENT            (EXCEPTIONS) -->
<!ELEMENT (%book;)         - -  (fm, bdy, appm?, bm?)  +(%i.float;)>
```

```
<!--                    FRONT MATTER ELEMENTS -->

<!ELEMENT fm                  O O  (tig, (au¦cau)*, %m.rep, pubfm?,
                                    (%fmsec.d; ¦ %fmcps.d;)*, toc?)>
<!ELEMENT (%fmsec.d;)         - O  %m.sec;>
<!ELEMENT (%fmcps.d;)         - O  %m.cps;>


<!--                  Title Group -->
<!ELEMENT tig                 O O  (msn?, srt?, no?, ti, sbt?)>
<!ELEMENT (ti¦sbt)            O O  %m.ph;>


<!--                  Author Group -->
<!ELEMENT au                  - O  %m.name;>
<!ELEMENT (onm¦snm)           O O  %m.ph;>
<!ELEMENT (fnm¦role¦deg¦odv)  - O  %m.ph;>
<!ELEMENT (aff¦cau¦sch)       - O  %m.org;>
<!ELEMENT (%ade.ph;)          - O  %m.ph;>


<!--                  Repeating Elements -->
<!ELEMENT rep1                - O  %m.rep1;>
<!ELEMENT rep2                - O  %m.rep2;>
<!ELEMENT rep3                - O  %m.rep3;>


<!--              Publisher's Front Matter -->
<!ELEMENT pubfm               - O  ((%pub;) ¦ (%pub.ph;))*>
<!ELEMENT (%pub.ph;¦cgn)      - O  %m.ph;>
<!ELEMENT (pnm¦avl¦cgs)       - O  %m.org;>
<!ELEMENT rps                 - O  (%m.org;¦%m.name;)>


<!--                    Copyright -->
<!ELEMENT crt                 - -  %m.copy;>
<!ELEMENT cci                 - -  %m.org;>
<!ELEMENT crn                 - -  (%m.org;¦%m.name;)>
<!ELEMENT crd                 - O  %m.date;>


<!--                  Conference Group -->
<!ELEMENT cng                 - -  (cnn?, cnm, cnd?, cnp?, cns?)>
<!ELEMENT cnd                 - O  %m.date;>
<!ELEMENT (cnm¦cnn)           - O  %m.ph;>
<!ELEMENT cnp                 - O  %m.addr;>
<!ELEMENT cns                 - O  %m.org;>


<!--                Table of Contents -->
<!ELEMENT toc                 - O  %m.toc;>
<!ELEMENT tcpt                - O  %m.tcpt;>
<!ELEMENT tcchp               - O  %m.tcchp;>
<!ELEMENT tcsec               - O  %m.tcsec;>
<!ELEMENT tcss1               - O  %m.tcss1;>
<!ELEMENT tcss2               - O  %m.tcss2;>
<!ELEMENT tcss3               - O  %m.tcss3;>


<!--                    BODY ELEMENTS -->
<!--        ELEMENT         MIN  CONTENT                 (EXCEPTIONS) -->
```

(continues)

III

Content Modeling

Listing 12.5 Continued

```
<!--                     Body Structure  -->
<!ELEMENT bdy                    0 0  (part+¦chp+)>
<!ELEMENT part                   - 0  (no?, pt, (%s.zz;)*, chp+)>
<!ELEMENT chp                    - 0  (no?, ct, (%s.zz;)*, sec*)>
<!ELEMENT sec                    - 0  (no?, %m.sec;)>
<!ELEMENT ss1                    - 0  (no?, st, (%s.zz;)*, ss2*)>
<!ELEMENT ss2                    - 0  (no?, st, (%s.zz;)*, ss3*)>
<!ELEMENT ss3                    - 0  (no?, st, (%s.zz;)*)>
<!ELEMENT no                     - 0  (#PCDATA)>
<!ELEMENT (pt¦ct¦st)             0 0  %m.ph;>


<!--                 Section Subelements  -->
<!ELEMENT p                      0 0  %m.p;>
<!--      Null or blank paragraphs should be ignored.  -->
<!ELEMENT (%s.h.ph;)             - 0  %m.ph;    -- headings  -->
<!ELEMENT (%s.top.d;)            - 0  %m.cps;   -- topics  -->


<!--                Paragraph Subelements  -->
<!ELEMENT bq                     - -  %m.pseq;>
<!ELEMENT oad                    - 0  %m.org;  -- organization address  -->
<!ELEMENT iad                    - 0  %m.name; -- individual address  -->
<!ELEMENT art                    - 0  EMPTY>

<!ELEMENT lit                    - -  CDATA>

<!ELEMENT (%p.lst.d;)            - -  (lh?, li)*>
<!ELEMENT li                     - 0  %m.pseq;>
<!ELEMENT lh                     - 0  %m.ph;>

<!ELEMENT dl                     - -  ((dthd, ddhd)?, dt, dd)*>
<!ELEMENT (dt¦dthd¦ddhd)         - 0  %m.ph;>
<!ELEMENT dd                     0 0  %m.pseq;>

<!ELEMENT bibl                   - 0  (lh?, bb)*>
<!ELEMENT bb                     - 0  %m.bib;>
<!ELEMENT (atl¦obi¦sct¦srt¦pp)   0 0  %m.ph;>
<!ELEMENT loc                    - 0  %m.addr;>
<!ELEMENT msn                    - 0  (#PCDATA)>

<!ELEMENT itml                   - 0  (lh?, itm)*>
<!ELEMENT itm                    - 0  (sit1, (sit2, sit3*)*, pp*)>
<!ELEMENT (sit1¦sit2¦sit3)       0 0  %m.ph;>


<!--                     Phrases  -->
<!ELEMENT q                      - -  %m.ph;>
<!ELEMENT emq                    - -  %m.ph;>
<!ELEMENT (%p.em.ph;)            - -  %m.ph;>
<!ELEMENT (%p.rf.ph;)            - 0  %m.ph;>
<!ELEMENT gk                     - -  %m.ph;>
<!ELEMENT cyr                    - -  %m.ph;>
<!ELEMENT pdt                    0 0  %m.date;>
<!ELEMENT (mo¦day¦yr)            - 0  %m.ph;>
```

```
<!--                    Floating Elements -->
<!ELEMENT fig            - O  %m.fig;>

<!ELEMENT fn             - -  (no?, %m.pseq;) -(%i.float;)>

<!ELEMENT nit            - -  (no?, %m.pseq;)>
<!--                    Tables -->
<!ELEMENT tbl            - -  (no?, tt, tby, src?)
                                  -(%i.float;|%p.tbl;)>
<!ELEMENT tt             - O  %m.ph;>
<!ELEMENT tby            - O  (th*, tsh*, row*)>
<!ELEMENT row            - O  (tsb?, c*)>
<!ELEMENT (th|tsh)       - O  %m.ph;>
<!ELEMENT (tsb|c)        - O  %m.pseq;>
<!ELEMENT src            - O  %m.bib;>


<!--             APPENDIX ELEMENTS                     -->
<!--     ELEMENT         MIN  CONTENT        (EXCEPTIONS) -->
<!ELEMENT appm           - O  (app+)>
<!ELEMENT app            - O  (no?, apt, (%s.zz;)*, sec*)>
<!ELEMENT apt            O O  %m.ph;>


<!--             BACK MATTER ELEMENTS                  -->
<!--     ELEMENT         MIN  CONTENT        (EXCEPTIONS) -->

<!ELEMENT bm             - O  ((%bmcps.d;)|(%bmsec.d;)|(%bmsec.i;))*>
<!ELEMENT (%bmcps.d;)    - O  %m.cps;>
<!ELEMENT (%bmsec.d;)    - O  %m.sec;>
<!ELEMENT (%bmsec.i;)    - O  %m.idx;>
<!ELEMENT (idxn|idxs)    O O  %m.ph;>


<!--         Attribute Definition Lists   -->
<!--   ELEMENT    ATTRIB DEF   -->
<!ATTLIST src     %a.id;>
<!ATTLIST fn      %a.id;>
<!ATTLIST nit     %a.id;>
<!ATTLIST tbl     %a.id;>
<!ATTLIST gk      lang NOTATION (greek) greek>
<!ATTLIST cyr     lang NOTATION (cyrillic) cyrillic>
<!ATTLIST fig

                  %a.id;
                  %a.sizes;>
<!ATTLIST bb      %a.id;>
<!ATTLIST (%p.rf.ph;) %a.rid;>
<!ATTLIST art

                  %a.id;
                  %a.sizes;>


<!--             Short References -->

<!USEMAP bkmap %book;>
<!USEMAP listmap (%p.lst.d;)>
<!USEMAP dlmap dl>
<!USEMAP qmap q>
<!USEMAP tblmap tby>
```

> **Note**
>
> You can see how much more difficult the first part is to follow when you compare it to the carefully aligned second part.

In the following example, one model group has a long name. The name of the last element group is too long to enable the minimization delimiters to be aligned on the same line. To keep the delimiters aligned, the declaration is continued on the next line.

```
<!ELEMENT  firstelm        - - (alpha, bet+)                        >
<!ELEMENT  alpha           - - (CDATA)                              >
<!ELEMENT  bet             - - (CDATA)                                >
<!ELEMENT  (a¦bc¦cd¦ef¦gh¦hi¦lm¦no¦pq¦rs)
                           - - (#PCDATA)  --this stays aligned-->
```

It is not always necessary to align all parts of declarations with such fastidiousness, particularly when you're simply trying to get it to parse. But as you refine the DTD, and as it becomes more of a tool for your daily work, you'll find it easiest to keep it aligned thoroughly, much as a good mechanic keeps his or her toolbox tidy and organized.

You should try to keep the following items aligned in a declaration:

- Opening delimiters of the declaration
- Element and attribute names
- Minimization delimiters
- Content model or content value declarations
- Any relevant comments or types of comments (aligning inline comments is optional but preferred)
- Closing delimiters for declarations

In other words, you should align everything in a declaration or comment that can be reasonably aligned. It's pleasing to the eye and it makes a DTD easier to use.

Consider the comments in listing 12.2. The comments for each group of elements are aligned on the same column. Furthermore, the comments within each group are aligned. Even the line comments are aligned more or less at the end of the declaration lines.

From Here...

You have made it through the essential principles of content modeling and document analysis. You are nearly through developing the DTD.

For more information, refer to the following:

- Chapter 13, "Evaluating DTDs and Using Parsers," tells you how to parse DTDs.
- Chapter 14, "Following Good SGML Practice," helps you avoid some common pitfalls in an SGML installation.
- Part IV, "Markup Strategies," helps you through more challenges, including output specifications and specialized content.

III

Content Modeling

Evaluating DTDs and Using Parsers

As you've seen in previous chapters, the process of developing your own DTD can involve a number of factors. So far, you've looked at the SGML declaration syntax that you use to define your DTD, how to create modular DTDs, and how to make your DTD readable.

In Part II, "Document Analysis," you examined a variety of topics relating to document analysis. These included issues relating to environment, element definition, and extending document structure. Chapters 10-12 introduced you to SGML syntax and the construction of DTDs. Now you'll take a look at some factors relating to your DTD from a different perspective: ensuring that they fit your environment and your documents.

In this chapter, you learn how to:

- Evaluate DTDs, along with the related issues that ensure your DTDs meet your needs
- Use parsers on both DTDs and SGML document instances

When you're done, you will have a better idea of what makes a "good" DTD, what issues should be considered when developing your own DTDs, and how DTDs can be used as a tool to gain greater consistency in your SGML documents.

After your examination of parsers is complete, you will have an understanding of what they do (and don't do) and what you might do if you run into parsing problems.

Evaluating Your DTD

DTD evaluation should be thought of as an iterative process. That is to say, it is a process that you'll want to do from time to time over the course of a DTD's lifetime. In the early phases of your SGML project, you'll want to consider a host of issues before you even begin DTD development. Evaluating existing DTDs before you develop new ones can often be a useful exercise.

> **Tip**
>
> Even if you plan to use an existing DTD (such as one that is publicly available), you should still perform DTD evaluation and analysis. Doing this will help you maintain a balance between your documents and your DTD.

While you are developing your DTD, you should continually evaluate it to make sure that what you are creating is best suited for your needs.

After you have developed your DTD and put it into production in your SGML system, you might want to re-examine it after a period of time. When you do so, you may find yourself looking at a DTD after six months, thinking "Hmmm, I think I would have done it a little differently if I were writing it today."

This is normal. For one thing, there's a learning curve associated with developing DTDs; you get better at it over time as you gain experience with what works and what doesn't. Additionally, your needs, which determine how you define your document, can change over time. For example, if you create a DTD initially to handle printed documents and you later want to also support electronic delivery, you will face a number of issues in providing support to both. In other cases, there might be issues related to the particular software that you use in your SGML environment.

Writing DTDs can be thought of as a mixture of art and science. Bear in mind that there is no "perfect" DTD. Rather there are DTDs that do a very good job of modeling documents in certain situations and those that are less effective. In your examination of DTD development issues , you will take a look at some of the necessary factors to consider when developing DTDs. In this way, you'll be able to develop the DTD that takes into consideration the environment and special needs of you and your organization.

As you examine the factors that affect what you want your DTD to do, consider the following:

- Document scope (Who will use the document and why?)
- Document lifespan (How long will it be used?)
- Sanity checking (Does it fit your needs?)
- Balancing between standards enforcement and flexibility (How much structure should be required versus how much flexibility?)
- Maintaining your DTD
- Parsing your DTD (What you're actually doing, why, and how)

Document Scope

As you consider how to model your documents in a DTD, there are various factors that will influence your decision. Foremost among these are issues related to the scope (or environment) of the document. Who uses it and how do they use it? What's the place like where it's built? How many flavors does it come in? All of these issues should play a role in how your DTD is constructed.

How Will Your Document Be Used? Consider how your document will be used. Will readers read it from front to back, or will they skip around between various chapters and sections? For example, suppose that your document is a repair manual for a car. Readers might use the manual in a variety of ways.

Some readers (such as new owners) might concentrate on introductory sections of each chapter to understand the high level topics of how their car is constructed. Others might skip around various chapters as they attempt to troubleshoot problems in their car. Still others might go step-by-step through detailed procedures to rebuild a transmission or replace valves.

As a result, certain features gain importance over others depending on the reader navigating your document. Table 13.1 illustrates how some of these features might apply to your car repair manual.

Table 13.1 Desirable Document Features: Car Repair Manual	
Reader Type	**Important Features**
New owner	Overall features list, General tips, Descriptive introductory sections in chapters, Maintenance information, Spare parts lists
Troubleshooters	Diagnostic fault tables, Cross references to related sections, Detailed indexes
Rebuilders	Step-by-step procedures, Detailed parts lists, Assembly illustrations

By looking at your classes of readers, you can see that different readers have different approaches to a document, resulting in a different set of important features.

In What Environment Will It Be Used? With the growth of the Internet, many organizations are rushing to provide an electronic delivery of information to their customers, members, supporters, and so on. As they go through the process of preparing information for electronic delivery, providers are discovering that many of their existing notions (derived from their experience with hardcopy document preparation) need to be rethought.

Even if you are preparing a class of documents for hardcopy delivery only, you might want to stop and reflect, "Might I want to someday use this document in a different environment?" Chances are, if you will be using these documents for several years, the answer just might be yes.

Planning for electronic delivery (either now or in the future) can impact some important facets of your DTD (and document) design.

Electronic delivery systems, such as the Internet and electronic books on CD-ROM, have brought a new emphasis to non-linear navigation approaches. Through the use of hyperlinked references, for example, readers can take a path through a document (or collection) that was completely unanticipated by the document authors.

This method of traversing related data can greatly emphasize the importance of indexing links in documents and collections.

Document Lifespan

How long you will use and maintain your SGML documents (or the information within them) plays an important role in your DTD-based document model. Earlier in this book, you learned that a long-lived document might start in a hardcopy format and change to an electronic one later.

The DTDs that you use and maintain for a long period of time might go through a long series of modifications, enhancements, and additions. In those circumstances, a highly flexible arrangement in your DTD will likely become a high priority.

Sanity Checking Your DTD

No matter how good your DTD looks, it always helps to perform sanity checking before you put it into production. By doing this, you confirm that your assumptions within the DTD are correct and in line with the concepts of others involved in the documents and the steps in their production.

Sanity checking can take two forms:

- Validating the DTD concept (the document model) with people familiar with what the document is supposed to do
- Comparing the DTD document model against various versions of the document type

Does the DTD Content Model Match Other People's Expectations? In many situations, it can be helpful to validate your DTD by comparing its concept of the document model with the concept of others. For example, if you are going to convert an existing class of operations manuals to SGML, you might want to meet with a number of people throughout your organization who are familiar with these documents.

When you compare the concept of the document (as modeled in the DTD) with others, it really doesn't matter if they are not familiar with SGML. What *does* matter is that they are familiar with the document that you're modeling. When that is the case, these individuals can often provide invaluable insights on a type of document that might vary quite a bit across its various examples.

Take a look at a specific example. Imagine that you're in the process of writing a DTD for an installation and operation manual for your company. In it, you will have a standard approach for handling both types of actions (installation and operation) of various products that your company produces. Although your company produces a variety of products, the operations manuals are pretty similar across product lines. In the process of document analysis, you determine that these manuals contain the specific sections in the following order:

I.   Introduction

II. Safety Notes

III. Installation

    A. Component Assembly

    B. Component Installation

    C. Component Checkout

    D. Package Checkout

IV. Operation

    A. Overview

    B. Controls

    C. Operation

    D. Shutdown

    E. Maintenance

After developing a DTD that reflects this structure, you proceed to your validation and meet with people to confirm your document model. When doing so, you might want to confirm that your DTD passes the following tests.

Does your DTD work for:

- A simple version of the document?
- A complex version of the document?
- An oddball version of the document?

As you work with your group, you might run across some variance in the range of possible ingredients in your "standard" document type. Your DTD might work well for simple versions of the document, for example. Users might suggest a simple version: "Check the Lemur 100, it has all of the basic parts but no options." However, complicated examples might not fit into your document model: "...But the Okapi 9750 has 26 options to be covered."

In other cases, oddball versions of your document might not fit. As you explore various types of installation and operation manuals, you might encounter observations like "It's always in that order, except for the Wombat 2000 model. In that case, we make 'package checkout' a major section and put it last."

The question of detail in your document model is often worth exploring at this point. Compare your range of document samples with your DTD and ask some questions: Does your DTD include the right amount of detail in its document model? In some cases, you might want to model generic sections in your document. In others, you might want to require specific named document sections in a specific order to enforce a standard document format.

III

Content Modeling

Standards Enforcement versus Flexibility

If you are creating your documents in a structured SGML authoring environment, you might choose to use your DTD to enforce a standard structure. One way to do this is by associating specific types of document sections with specific elements.

In the previous example, you were developing a DTD for an installation and operation manual. If you want to have an enforcing DTD for this document, you might develop a DTD that requires your specific objects (or sections) to appear in a specific order (see fig. 13.1).

Fig. 13.1

An enforcing DTD.

```
<!-- ********************************************** -->
<!-- AnyCorp, USA                                   -->
<!--                                                -->
<!-- Installation and Operation Manual DTD          -->
<!--     version 2.0, 1 Sept 95                     -->
<!-- ********************************************** -->
<!DOCTYPE inst-ops [
<!-- Standard Module Entity Definitions   -->
<!ENTITY % common PUBLIC "-//ANYC//DTD Common Elems//EN">
%common;
<!-- Installation and Operation Manual Structure   -->
<!ELEMENT inst-ops  - - (intro,safety,install,oper) >
<!-- Major Document Sections   -->
<!ELEMENT intro        - - (subsec+) >
<!ELEMENT safety       - - (subsec+) >
<!ELEMENT install      - - (assem,cinstal,ccheck,pcheck) >
<!ELEMENT oper         - - (oview,contrl,ops,sdown,maint) >
<!-- Section Components   -->
   <!-- install   -->
<!ELEMENT assem        - - (subsec+) >
<!ELEMENT cinstal      - - (subsec+) >
<!ELEMENT ccheck       - - (subsec+) >
<!ELEMENT pcheck       - - (subsec+) >
   <!-- oper   -->
<!ELEMENT oview        - - (subsec+) >
<!ELEMENT contrl       - - (subsec+) >
<!ELEMENT ops          - - (subsec+) >
<!ELEMENT sdown        - - (subsec+) >
<!ELEMENT maint        - - (subsec+) >
]>
```

In this example, an author using this DTD is required to include elements corresponding to each document section in the defined order. This structure can be defined down to as many levels as is required.

But suppose that you don't want to enforce such a structure, preferring instead to allow flexibility in the content and order of the sections of a document. In that case, you might define the document model in a different way so that flexibility is permitted (see fig. 13.2).

```
<!-- ********************************************* -->
<!-- AnyCorp, USA                                  -->
<!--                                               -->
<!-- Installation and Operation Manual DTD         -->
<!--     version 3.0, 1 Oct 95                     -->
<!-- ********************************************* -->
<!DOCTYPE inst-ops [
<!-- Standard Module Entity Definitions    -->
<!ENTITY % common PUBLIC "-//ANYC//DTD Common Elems//EN">
%common;
<!-- Installation and Operation Manual Structure    -->
<!ELEMENT inst-ops   - - (section+) >
<!-- Major Document Sections    -->
<!ELEMENT section    - - (chapter+) >
<!ATTLIST section          sname (intro¦safety¦install¦
                                 oper)    #REQUIRED >
<!-- Section Components   -->
<!ELEMENT chapter    - - (subsec+)
<!ATTLIST chapter          cname (assem¦cinstal¦ccheck¦
                                 pcheck¦oview¦contrl¦
                                 ops¦sdown¦maint)  #REQUIRED

]>
```

Fig. 13.2

A flexible DTD.

In this approach, you use generic element definitions for the major document sections and the chapters within them (the elements section and chapter). You can still identify which section and chapter you're in through the use of attributes for section and chapter names. (In fact, they're required in this example.)

Notice that in this example, you can have sections and chapters in any order and in any combination from the choices identified in your attributes.

Maintaining Your DTD

Although this was discussed in earlier chapters, it's necessary to stress the importance of structuring your DTD to be readable. The samples that follow illustrate this importance.

The following DTD is of the quick and dirty, unformatted school (see fig. 13.3). No extra time has been wasted on unnecessary comments, extra formatting, or organization.

III

Content Modeling

Fig. 13.3

*A sample DTD
(unformatted).*

```
<!DOCTYPE instruct [
<!ELEMENT instruct   - - (tpage,contents,intro,assem,
install,operation,maint,errors,index)  >
<!ELEMENT title   - - (#PCDATA) >
<!ELEMENT nlist   - - (item+)  >
<!ELEMENT graphic  - O  EMPTY   >
<!ELEMENT item       - - (para¦blist¦nlist¦graphic)+>
<!ELEMENT errors  - - (subsec+)  >
<!ELEMENT maint  - - (subsec+)  >
<!ELEMENT operation  - - (subsec+)  >
<!ELEMENT para  - - (#PCDATA)  >
<!ELEMENT blist   - - (item+) -(nlist)  >
<!ELEMENT install   - - (subsec+)  >
<!ELEMENT subsec  - -
(title,(para¦blist¦nlist¦list*¦graphic)?)  >
<!ELEMENT assem   - - (subsec+)  >
<!ELEMENT intro   - - (subsec+)  >
<!ELEMENT contents  - - (subsec+)  >
<!ELEMENT tpage   - - (title,pub-info)  >
<!ELEMENT list   - - (item+)  >
<!ELEMENT index   - - (list+)  >
<!ELEMENT pub-info   - - (#PCDATA)  >
<!ATTLIST graphic    filename  CDATA    #REQUIRED
  artno  CDATA    #IMPLIED >
]>
```

As you glance at the preceding figure, try to relate the document elements, attributes, and so on to each other. (Then imagine that this DTD is much longer, more complex, and you haven't looked at it in a year!)

In contrast, look at the following formatted version and see if it's any easier to understand (see fig. 13.4).

Notice that the formatted version is easier to read and understand. As you can see, a little formatting and alignment, coupled with descriptive comments and some white space to break things up, can make life a lot more bearable when it comes to reading and understanding DTDs.

Here's a quick refresher course of helpful formatting tips for maintaining your DTDs:

- Use comments generously
- Align DTD declarations for readability
- Use comments for section delineators
- Group the logical sections within DTD
- Use standard locations for entities, DTD fragments
- Follow element definitions with related attribute lists
- Group common model components together logically

```
<!-- ************************************************ -->
<!-- AnyCorp, USA                                     -->
<!--                                                  -->
<!-- Instruction Manual DTD version 1.5, 15 Aug 95 -->
<!-- ************************************************ -->
<!--   History:                                       -->
<!--   1.0  7/1/95    Initial Version                 -->
<!--   1.5  8/15/95   Added 'blist' component         -->
<!--                                                  -->
<!-- ************************************************ -->
<!DOCTYPE instruct [
<!ELEMENT instruct   - - (tpage,contents,intro,assem,
                         install,oper,maint,errors,index)
>
<!-- Major Document Sections   -->
<!ELEMENT tpage      - - (title , pub-info) >
<!ELEMENT contents   - - (subsec+) >
<!ELEMENT intro      - - (subsec+) >
<!ELEMENT assem      - - (subsec+) >
<!ELEMENT install    - - (subsec+) >
<!ELEMENT oper       - - (subsec+) >
<!ELEMENT maint      - - (subsec+) >
<!ELEMENT errors     - - (subsec+) >
<!ELEMENT index      - - (list+) >
<!-- Section Components   -->
<!ELEMENT subsec     - - (title,(para¦blist¦nlist¦list*¦
                         graphic)?)>
<!ELEMENT title      - - (#PCDATA) >
<!ELEMENT para       - - (#PCDATA) >
<!ELEMENT blist      - - (item+) -(nlist)   >
<!ELEMENT nlist      - - (item+)   >
<!ELEMENT list       - - (item+) >
<!ELEMENT graphic    - O  EMPTY   >
<!ATTLIST graphic
          filename        CDATA    #REQUIRED
          artno           CDATA    #IMPLIED  >
<!ELEMENT item       - - (para¦blist¦nlist¦graphic)+>
<!ELEMENT pub-info   - - (#PCDATA) >
]>
```

Fig. 13.4

A sample DTD (formatted).

Parsing the DTD

When you parse your DTD, you are running it by a "review committee" of sorts. The parser evaluates your DTD and gives you its verdict on whether or not the DTD is ready for production.

Similar to software compilers, parsers evaluate your DTD (and SGML document instances), ensuring that you haven't missed any of the fundamental components.

III

Content Modeling

Typical simple errors uncovered by parsing include:

- Missing start and end tags
- References to undefined elements
- Invalid SGML syntax

The next section covers the role of parsers in more detail, examining their use in both the validation of DTDs and their corresponding SGML documents (i.e., specific document instances).

Parsers

In order to have an SGML document system, you must have a parser. The parser ensures that your DTD is legal according to the rules of SGML. In addition, it ensures that your SGML document instances are in conformance to the document model defined by the corresponding DTD.

Without a parser, all you really have are documents with a lot of tags. In a sense, you can think of the parser as your auditor in that it verifies that all of your SGML system components (your DTDs and SGML documents) are in accordance to the requirements specified.

Parsers can come in two forms: a limited version that does only limited checking of tags, and the more full-featured variety, called a *validating* parser. It's important to understand this distinction because only a validating parser confirms that your DTDs and SGML documents are in conformance.

Note

A copy of the validating SP parser is on the CD-ROM included with this book.

▶▶ See "SP/NSGMLS Parser," p. 490

What Validating Parsers Do

As previously noted, parsers are used to validate both DTDs and specific document instances. When a DTD is parsed, it is checked for conformance to the rules of SGML and "completeness." This includes ensuring the correct use of the proper syntax (as specified in the SGML standard). It also includes a verification that elements included as content in another element's definition are defined themselves.

The range of tasks performed by a validating parser includes a number of items. Table 13.2 lists the tasks performed by a parser when it is used to validate documents and DTDs.

Task Performed	SGML Document Check	DTD Check
Validate for conformity to SGML syntax	X	X
Validate content with document models		X
Identify ambiguous data structures		X
Enforce structure standards	X	X
Expand entity references	X	X
Validate attributes of elements	X	

Table 13.2   What Parsers Do (When Validating Documents and DTDs)

Validation of document content with the document structure defined in the document's DTD serves to ensure logical consistency.

When parsing a DTD, entity reference expansion brings in that part of the document model that was previously defined via an entity (either internal or external to the DTD). In order to do this, the parser must be able to locate the source of all entities defined in the DTD. For entities defined externally, the parser must be able to locate (or *resolve*) the external reference.

When parsing a document, entity reference expansion locates (and "brings in") such objects as special characters or notation (such as mathematical symbols), standard text sections (boilerplate), or graphical data (such as company logos).

Attribute validation ensures that the attributes found in an element are within the rules defined for that attribute in the attribute list. For example, if the attribute is required, its presence is confirmed (its absence triggers a parsing error). Similarly, if an attribute must be one of several choices, its content is validated against the legal possibilities.

What Parsers Don't Do

Within the SGML syntax, you can define very complex document structures. As a result, the capabilities in the validating parser necessary to validate this structure can be very complex.

However, parsers can't perform magic. There are certain tasks that a parser *doesn't* perform:

- Doesn't ensure content
- Doesn't validate element content
- Doesn't distinguish between valid markup and correct markup

If the content of a document instance is legal according to your DTD, it will almost parse correctly. However, the content can still be incorrect in other ways. For example, if you have an element defined for troubleshooting and it contains information on spare parts instead, the parser can't point this out. The parser has no way of knowing what the correct content should be.

III

Content Modeling

In this sense, the parser should be thought of as a tool to verify *valid* document markup rather than *correct* markup.

What To Look for in a Parser

Parsers come in many shapes and sizes. When looking for a parser, there are features to look for. As a minimum, ensure that your parser is a *validating* parser. If it's not, you can't be sure what you're really getting. Other optional features of parsers that can be nice to have are listed in table 13.3.

Table 13.3 Optional Features of Parsers	
Feature	**Description**
Add Omitted Tags	When tag minimization is used, this feature resolves and inserts tags that were omitted in the document markup. This feature can be present as an option.
Suggest Error Corrections	Upon encountering an error condition, the parser may suggest ways to correct the error.
Warn of Potential Problems	In some cases, it is possible to have conditions that are legal but frowned upon in SGML syntax. This parser feature warns you of such conditions.

Evaluating Parser Output Messages

At first, the output of a parsing session might look rather strange and mysterious—something like the utterances of the Oracle of Delphi. The messages might use SGML terminology that you're not familiar with. In this event, you should check your parser documentation for the terms that are unfamiliar.

When you receive an error message, the parser normally gives you a line number to identify the location of the error. In some cases, you might look at the line and not see an error condition. If this is the case, start looking at lines in your source document (DTD or instance) prior to the identified error location.

If you still can't locate the source of the error, look at the next higher object in the structure. For example, if you encounter an error dealing with the element `title` but can't locate the cause, look at the next higher level element that contains that occurrence of `title`.

SGML parsers are not "lookahead" in their operation. That is, they stop upon encountering an error. Therefore, your early attempts at parsing might seem somewhat time-consuming as the parser stops at each error, you correct it, rerun the parser, and it stops at the next error.

In some cases, you might encounter errors that seem to contradict the rules of the SGML standard (ISO 8879). When this happens, you might want to double-check the rules. Still can't find the source of your parsing error? Check your SGML declaration closely for subtle errors. If you still encounter errors, you might want to use a different parser.

From Here...

This concludes your look at the evaluation of DTDs and the issues involved in ensuring that your DTD meets your needs. In doing so, you examined the differences between an enforcing (or "strict") DTD and a flexible DTD. You also examined what tasks a parser performs (and which ones it doesn't).

For more information, refer to the following:

- Chapter 14, "Following Good SGML Practice," looks at the techniques and approaches that ensure your approach to SGML is practical and maintainable.
- Part IV, "Markup Strategies," examines the issues, challenges, and strategies involved in converting your documents into SGML.
- Part V, "SGML and the World Wide Web," examines how SGML relates to the Internet and the related issues and implications.

III

Content Modeling

Following Good SGML Practice

You know how to do some SGML now, but there is much more to SGML than just writing a DTD or marking up a document instance. There is the issue of good judgment when it comes to design. Design issues quickly become maintenance issues. If you inherit someone's DTD that was not designed well, then you have a maintenance problem.

In this chapter, you learn:

- How to choose whether to use an element or an attribute
- How to handle inclusions and exclusions
- What to do about mixed content models
- How to avoid ambiguous content models
- How flexible a DTD should be
- How to avoid other problems

These questions are important because SGML does not always alert you when you do something wrong—at least not right away. It lets you get away with many mistakes. Parsing errors mainly deal with syntax, not overall design. In this chapter, you learn how to avoid the major pitfalls.

Choosing Elements or Attributes

Deciding whether to make a tag an element or attribute is difficult when you can't decide what the object you're working on really does and how it does it. Suppose, for example, that you want to describe where a graphic object is located. Call it `fileloc` for *file location*. The object is visible in the document. You could tag it every time it appears. Do you call it an element or an attribute?

> **Note**
>
> When you think you understand the difference between elements and attributes, look at the structural objects in a magazine article. Pretend that you're the production editor and the SGML analyst. See whether you can figure out what the elements are for the document—the article—and its attributes. Whether you are right or wrong is not so important. The exercise in thinking about elements and attributes will be worth far more to you in the long run than getting it right.

The following note about elements being the object and attributes defining an aspect of the object helps, but sometimes there's more to it. Remember when you were in a class, and there was someone who just did not get it? Or maybe the someone was you when your dad was explaining something about cars or refrigerators. You felt like the odd person out. Everyone else in the class seemed to understand. What everyone else had was the "feel" of the subject matter. SGML is like that when it comes to attributes and elements.

> **Note**
>
> The element is the structural object, and the attribute defines an aspect of it. If the element were <GRAPHIC>, the attribute could be `location` and the values could be `local` and `remote`. If the element were <ATTENDANCE>, the attribute could be `status` and the values could be `present` and `absent`.

Types of Attributes

The question becomes, "Is it an attribute or not?" It is probably an element if it is not an attribute. The other choice is an entity, which is discussed in Chapter 10. There are four main types of attributes:

- Attributes that define aspects about the element; if the element is `block`, its attributes might be `size`, `color`, `weight`, and `shape`

- Attributes that contain formatting information or other information that affects the appearance of the element; if the element is a `paragraph`, it might be `indented`, `justified`, `columns`, and so on

- Attributes that locate an internal object, such as a cross reference, a footnote, or a graphics file name

- Attributes that locate an external object, such as a link to a different document or another file on a related network

◀◀ See "Entities: Their Use and The ENTITY Markup Declaration," p. 184

There are other types of attributes; not all attributes fall into these categories. You can call your objects whatever you want, as long as you follow SGML syntax.

Attributes as Aspects of an Element. The first example of how attributes appear is as descriptive aspects of an element. Attributes tell you something more that you need to know about the object. The element is, after all, an information object. For example, your DTD might specify whether a <DOCUMENT> element has a security status of internal or public. You might also specify whether the legal department has approved it, which comes in handy if the document type is a contract. You might add an attribute for the sales order number so that you can track the document type by project (see fig. 14.1).

```
<!ELEMENT document  - - (A¦B¦C¦D) >
<!ATTLIST document
  securitystatus    (internal¦public)       "public"
  legalapprove      (yes¦no)                 "no"
  salesorder        CDATA                    #REQUIRED
  revisiondate      CDATA                    #IMPLIED
  productline       (centaur¦saturn¦other)   "other" >
```

Fig. 14.1

Attributes can explain different aspects of an element.

These attributes are a little long if you have to type them each time, but you get the point. The <DOCUMENT> element now has a useful way of tracking important information, and there is a convenient place to keep recurring information uniform and tidy.

Tip

If you need a pigeonhole for information about an element that will pertain to every instance of it, use an attribute for it. In figure 14.1 for example, the attributes productline, revisiondate and the rest apply to every instance of the <DOCUMENT> element. There will always be some value each attribute will have at all times.

Information about How an Element Looks. Often, you want to express something about an element that has nothing to do with its content, but that has everything to do with how the content looks. You probably would not want to create an element for this information because there are a few standard alternatives, and the information you're interested in pertains to an element rather than to the whole document. This is formatting information. Consider figure 14.2.

```
<!ELEMENT  graphic   - - (X¦Y¦Z) >
<!ATTLIST  graphic
  sizeframe    (qtrpage¦halfpage¦fullpage)   "fullpage"
  artfilenum   CDATA                          #IMPLIED
  turnpage     (yes¦no)                       "no"
  location     (inline¦float¦anchor)          "float"
  filetype     (CADDS¦TIF¦PCX¦RASTER)         #REQUIRED >
```

Fig. 14.2

Attributes can provide formatting and layout information.

III

Content Modeling

Appearance sometimes overlaps with the informational aspects of the element. For example, the sizeframe attribute affects the appearance of the <GRAPHIC> element, but the artfilenum attribute does not. Obviously, if you have the wrong art file number, it drastically affects the appearance of the figure. Assuming you have the right file number in your document, the attribute does not affect the appearance otherwise. Neither does the filetype attribute. The turnpage attribute, however, definitely does affect the appearance. So does the location attribute; it directly affects where the graphic appears on the page.

Identifying an External Object. The artfilenum attribute shown in figure 14.2 identifies a discrete graphic object. Many large publication houses use a numeric tracking number system for their massive inventory of art files. This art file number is vital. Without it, you can't find the right piece of art when you need it.

Identifying an object as a graphic or another kind of file or object is a constant task. You do it in all kinds of documents, and it's a perfect way to use an attribute. Here's an example of how a document instance might appear:

```
<P>Meteors look impressive when seen flying through space with telescopic
photography. <graphic artfilenum=12c4567 filetype=PCX>
Figure 14-30</graphic> shows one such photograph taken from
Mount Palomar's observatory.</P>
```

Figure 14.3 shows how the DTD declares the attributes used for the <graphic> element.

Fig. 14.3

Attributes can identify an external object.

```
<!ELEMENT  graphic   - - (X¦Y¦Z) >
<!ATTLIST  graphic
    sizeframe    (qtrpage¦halfpage¦fullpage)   "fullpage"
    artfilenum   CDATA                         #REQUIRED
    turnpage     (yes¦no)                      "no"
    location     (inline¦float¦anchor)         "float"
    filetype     (CADDS¦TIF¦PCX¦RASTER)        #REQUIRED >
```

Note

There is a mistake in the previous DTD and document examples. Now is a good time to point it out.

Figure 14.3 uses a content model of (X¦Y¦Z). This assumes that the graphic is made up of elements (X¦Y¦Z) that are all parsed character data (PCDATA). Most likely, your graphics are a special kind of file, such as targa (TGA) or bitmapped (BMP). They are not PCDATA.

The way you deal with this in SGML is to give <GRAPHIC> an EMPTY content model. If you declare the content value EMPTY, the parser doesn't try to make sense of the graphic object, which is probably UUEncoded or adheres to another encoding scheme. This tactic works for all encoded objects that are not PCDATA, including sound files, film files, and film clips.

Whenever you declare the content of an attribute value to be EMPTY, you must set the end tag delimiter to 0—instead of -—to allow for not having to specify the location of the end tag delimiter. Because the graphics object—or whatever kind of file it is—is encoded, you would not know where to put the end tag anyway. That's why you have to do this.

To do this right, you should change the <graphic> element's content value to EMPTY. When you do this, you must take out the end tag from the document instance. Figure 14.4 shows what the DTD would look like.

```
<!ELEMENT  graphic  - 0 EMPTY >
<!ATTLIST  graphic
   sizeframe    (qtrpage¦halfpage¦fullpage)   "fullpage"
   artfilenum   CDATA                         #REQUIRED
   turnpage     (yes¦no)                      "no"
   location     (inline¦float¦anchor)         "float"
   filetype     (CADDS¦TIF¦PCX¦RASTER)        #REQUIRED >
```

Fig. 14.4

The correct way to use an attribute to bring in a graphics file.

Because you have minimized the close tag for <GRAPHIC>, you must adjust the markup in the document instance. For example:

```
<P>Meteors look impressive when seen flying through space with telescopic
photography. <graphic artfilenum=12c4567 filetype=PCX> Figure 14-30 shows
one such photograph taken from Mount Palomar's observatory.</P>
```

The close delimiter tag no longer appears.

◀◀ See "Parsing the DTD," p. 241

Identifying Internal and External Objects (ID and IDREF). When you link back and forth between cross references or even hypertext links between different elements, you can refer to specific and unique IDs by using ID and IDREF pairs together. Parsers check these pairs together to make sure that they link up properly, so that you can get some extra validation of your links. You can also reference external files by using ID and IDREF pairs.

Consider figure 14.5. It assumes that you have a <P> element and a <GRAPHIC> element. You must also have a <GRAPHICREF> element. You need one element to make the reference and one element to be referred. You also need an element for the graphics object itself, <OBJECT>. Here is how the DTD would look. It's simplified a little so that you can see the ID and IDREF features more clearly.

III

Content Modeling

Fig. 14.5

An example of using attributes with ID *and* IDREF.

```
<!ELEMENT P              - - (a,b*)+  +(graphicref)      >

<!ELEMENT graphicref - o   EMPTY
<!ATTLIST graphicref idref  IDREF     #REQUIRED         >

<!ELEMENT graphic    - - (caption,object)               >
<!ATTLIST graphic    id     ID        #IMPLIED          >
<!ELEMENT caption    - o (% text;)
<!ELEMENT object     - o   EMPTY
<!ATTLIST object
              artfilenum       CDATA   #REQUIRED         >
```

The document instance might look like:

```
<P>When looking at meteors through a telescope, you should know how to
calibrate the instrument. See <GRAPHICREF idref="fig59-3">Figure 59-3 for
the location of the calibration tuner widget.</P>
```

In Chapter 59, you could locate the part of the document that talks about calibrating a telescope and has a picture that locates the tuner widget. The markup for that graphic might be:

```
<GRAPHIC id="fig59-3"><CAPTION>Here's the telescope's calibration tuner
widget</CAPTION><OBJECT artfilenum="12a345"></GRAPHIC>
```

The object can reside in the file called Chapter 59, or you can use a macro to find fig59-3 and load it into the document on demand.

Tip

If an object has:

■ Descriptive information about its element

■ Formatting information

■ Pointers and links

■ Nontext data, such as encoded graphics or compressed film clips

use an attribute instead of creating a new element. It will keep your SGML installation simpler—and keep you out of trouble.

Common Mistakes with Attributes

There are several ways to misuse attributes. Here are some of the more common ones.

Attributes as Documentation. Do not use attributes for documentation in your DTD. Do not try to use an attribute for what should be a comment. For example, if you want to make a note about an element's structure with an attribute, don't. Figure 14.6 shows an example of what is not good.

```
<!ELEMENT table  - -  ((P¦NT¦TC¦HT),X,Y,Z)  >
<!ATTLIST table
    colspec        CDATA #IMPLIED
    onepage        (yes¦no)  "yes"
    tabletype      (a¦b¦c¦d)   "a"          >
```

Fig. 14.6

It is a poor idea to use attributes as documentation inside elements.

The `tabletype` attribute expresses a different type of structural element. Presumably, table type a would be different structurally from table types b, c, and d. The type of table is so different structurally that it should be a different element. Do not stress a single structural element just because you think attributes can save you. If the table type is that different, it deserves its own element. Don't try to make an attribute serve as a structural comment. If you need to make a comment, do what is done in figure 14.7.

```
<!— ===============Table Elements====================== —>
<!—                         —>
<!— Note: Elements tablea, tableb, tablec, tabled differ
        fundamentally in structural ways. A separate for
        each table type was created instead of trying to
        use attributes to distinguish this difference.

        tablea is used for Volume 1 & 2 of 5 volume set.
    —>
<!ELEMENT tablea - - ((P¦NT¦TC¦HT),X,Y,Z)              >
<!ATTLIST tablea
    anocolumns   NUMBER    "1"
    anorows      NUTOKEN   #IMPLIED
    anutherattr  CDATA     #REQUIRED
>
<!—   tableb is used for volume 3 only of volume set.
        Do not use for any other volume in the set.
    —>
<!ELEMENT tableb - - ((P¦NB¦TB¦A),X,Y,Z)   >
<!ATTLIST tableb
    bnocolumns  NUMBER    "1"
    bnorows     NUTOKEN   #IMPLIED
    bnutherattr CDATA     #REQUIRED
>
```

Fig. 14.7

It's a good idea to document information about elements and their content models, but do it this way rather than using attributes.

Notice how the comments introduce each element as a separate structure with a separate content model. The attribute names are unique to each element. This is a much better way to do tables rather than to use attributes to distinguish between different types of tables.

Identical Attribute Names in the Same Element. No two attributes in one element can have the same attribute name in their declared value lists. This is particularly dangerous when you use entities. It's easy to lose track of what all those entities do inside your DTDs. Figure 14.8 shows an example of what you should not do.

III

Content Modeling

Fig. 14.8

Identical attribute names in the same element are a mistake.

```
<!ENTITY % chessent
       team      (red¦gold¦blue)      "red"
       noplayr   NUMBER    #REQUIRED
>
<!ELEMENT chessgam     - - (content model)           >
<!ATTLIST chessgam
       team      (home¦visitors)      "home"
       %chessent;
>
```

In effect, the attribute `team` is used twice in the same element. When the parser resolves the content for the `%chessent` entity, it will stumble on the `team` attribute again. This is a mistake.

Identical Attribute Values in the Same Element. Sometimes two attributes listed in the same element have an identical value in their respective content models. This creates a problem. Consider figure 14.9.

Fig. 14.9

Don't use identical attribute values in the same element.

```
<!ELEMENT chessgam     - - (content model)       >
<!ATTLIST chessgam
       noteams    (2¦4¦6¦8)            "2"
       colors     (white¦black)        "white"
       time2mov   (1¦2¦3¦4¦5)          "1"
>
```

SGML parsers will have a problem keeping the value straight for the `noteams` and `time2mov` attributes because attribute values may be encountered in any order in a document, not just the order in the DTD. If there are two or more attributes for which the value "2" may apply, the parser will not be able to resolve which attribute receives the value. This is called *attribute name omission* because the parser cannot connect the attribute value with the correct attribute name. For this reason, don't use overlapping content models in attribute declarations.

To fix this problem, you must use a token. In this case, you might use the NUTOKEN value in the value list, as shown in figure 14.10.

Fig. 14.10

Use NUTOKEN declared content to overcome this problem.

```
<!ELEMENT chessgam     - - (content model)       >
<!ATTLIST chessgam
       noteams    (2¦4¦6¦8)                    "2"
       colors     (white¦black)                "white"
       time2mov   NUTOKEN         #IMPLIED
>
```

Number tokens and other tokens are handy and effective in attribute value lists. Use them for just such occasions.

◄◄   See "Types of Data for Attributes," p. 136

◄◄   See "Attributes: Their Use and the ATTRIBUTE Declaration," p. 182

If you steer clear of these name collisions, you will be much closer to clearing your DTDs—and especially your attribute lists—of parser problems. Even if you find a parser that somehow does not catch these errors, your attributes will be much clearer and more meaningful by following the conventions covered here.

Staying out of mischief by correctly choosing whether to use an element or an attribute helps a lot.

Handling Inclusions and Exclusions

Inclusions and exclusions are both examples of *exceptions* in SGML. Including and excluding elements from content models is a powerful feature in SGML. It is also one of the easiest aspects of DTD development to abuse.

> **Note**
>
> Inclusions and exclusions are exceptions to a specific content model. An exception refers to something added to or removed from a content model. For example:
>
> ```
> <!ELEMENT friedchk - - (KFC¦homemade¦other) +(fatfree) >
> ```
>
> The fatfree value is being added to the normal content value, so it is an exception to the normal content. It is an *inclusion*. In:
>
> ```
> <!ELEMENT friedchk - - (KFC¦homemade¦other) -(KFC)   >
> ```
>
> the exception is KFC, which is being removed from the content model. It is an *exclusion*.

Exception Reminders

You need to remember several things about all exceptions to content models:

- Exceptions apply to all parts of the element's content model; for example, if you add a locator to an endnote element's content model, each of the elements in the model can now have a locator

- Exceptions are not just simple additions for the sake of convenience; they apply pervasively throughout the document

- You can avoid many of these problems by using simple data models and good DTD design principles

- Exclusions appear before inclusions when they both appear after the same content model

III

Content Modeling

Common Mistakes

You can abuse the use of exceptions if you are not careful. In fact, there are several common ways mistakes can be made with exceptions.

Inclusion at Too High of a Level. Sometimes you can include content values in such high-level elements that you must exclude them later in the smaller submodels of content. It's easy to get confused with long attribute lists and long content models for entities. Don't make inclusion statements on content models that are top-level and are the larger DTD elements. When you make inclusions at such a high level of structural order, you will likely have to make an exclusion statement later just to compensate. It is much better to simply modify the content model itself without an exclusion statement. Consider figure 14.11.

Fig. 14.11

Don't make inclusions at too high of a document level.

```
<!ELEMENT chapter   - - (para¦section)*  +(table¦graphic)*         >

<!ELEMENT para      - - (equation¦graphic¦para¦footnote)*          >

<!ELEMENT section   - - (heading,para)*                            >

<!ELEMENT equation  - - (%mdata,frame,%stuff)* -(table¦graphic) >
```

This shows that the inclusion added to the <CHAPTER> element had to be removed from the <EQUATION> element later on.

Excluding Explicitly Declared Content. Sometimes people exclude content that was explicitly declared in the content model. For whatever reason, they choose not to update the content model itself, but to declare the exception to the content model anyway. This is not always a good practice. You should probably just update the content model. If you're not updating the content model, it probably means that you have not defined the structure of the document very thoroughly. If you're trying to patch together the content model with exception statements, you are glossing over a deeper structural problem with your DTD. If you run across something that looks like the following, there is a deeper problem in your document design that you should be looking at:

```
<!ELEMENT chapter - - (body, heading)          >

<!ELEMENT body    - o (P¦A¦MA¦W¦CAU¦subsec)  -(subsec) >
```

If <BODY> doesn't need the <SUBSEC> element, the content model itself should be updated. Don't try to remove the <SUBSEC> element with an exclusion. Make the fix at the structural level, not at a superficial level.

Inclusion at Too Low of a Level. This is just the opposite of including at too high of a level. This accident usually happens when a vital element has been accidentally excluded at a higher level of DTD structure. It then must be included in a content model at a lower level. The moral of the story is to not exclude it in the first place—

create another element with a different content model. You can also create an entity to serve the type of special need that you were trying to fix with the inclusion. Figure 14.12 shows an example of the problem.

```
<!ELEMENT big       - - (medium¦A¦B¦C¦D)    -(E)      >

<!ELEMENT medium  - - (little¦C¦D)                     >

<!ELEMENT little  - - (F¦G)      +(E)                  >
```

Fig. 14.12

Don't use inclusion at too low of a level in the document type.

For whatever reason, at the higher level it looked like a good idea to exclude <E>. When you got down to the element <LITTLE>, you needed to put the content back in. Figure 14.13 shows a fix.

```
<!ENTITY %extra "(E)"   --especially for "little" element-- >

<!ELEMENT big       - -  (medium¦A¦B¦C¦D)                  >

<!ELEMENT medium  - -  (little¦C¦D)                        >

<!ELEMENT little  - -  ((F¦G)¦%extra;)                     >
```

Fig. 14.13

You can use entities to overcome the problem illustrated in figure 14.12.

Now the <E> element can remain apart from the higher element's content while still being allowed within the <LITTLE> element. This is a handy use for entities, and one reason why you run into them so often.

A more concrete example will further explain this problem. Suppose you want to enforce the exclusion of footnotes at the <BIG> level of a document type, but you want to allow authors to include footnotes (the <E> element) inside the <LITTLE> element. By using <E> as the content model for the %extra; entity, you can enforce the exclusion of footnotes at the higher level, but permit including it at the lower level. The parser will return an error to authors who include footnotes any higher than the <LITTLE> element.

Inclusion Instead of OR Connectors. Sometimes people want to use inclusion instead of adding another OR connector to the content model. This might be faster, but it's much more dangerous. This is a good example of a structure that would satisfy the parser quickly, but it's dangerous in that you leave a half-completed content model for someone else to clean up later. Here's an example:

```
<!ELEMENT chapter   - - (heading,section)          >
<!ELEMENT section   - o (para*) +(note¦%text;¦ref¦list¦%P;) >
```

Don't ever do anything like this. Restructure your content model instead, or use a parameter entity to alter the content model.

◄◄ See "Entities," p. 58

◄◄ See "Entities: Their Use and the ENTITY Markup Declaration," p. 184

This scenario probably happened because several people worked on content models for elements, and they did not agree on the values beforehand. One person thought he would make a quick fix. It parsed the DTD, but it's a dangerous design. He should have made the fix properly by correcting the content model together with his partners.

Dealing with Mixed-Content Models

A mixed-content model contains character data mixed with elements or entities. Mixed-content models can parse cleanly, but you should attempt them only under safe circumstances. The best advice is just to avoid them altogether, because they can lead to unpredictable parsing errors that are difficult to track down. Here is an example of mixed content:

```
<!ELEMENT para - - (#PCDATA, textstuf)          >
```

Mixed-content models are a bad practice because the parser makes a bigger deal out of different characters of the text string than it should when it encounters them. Consider carriage returns, for example. When the parser runs into carriage returns in a <PARA> element, it executes them instantly, whether you want them there or not.

> **Note**
>
> The tricky part about these bad models is that the DTD parses. You might parse a hundred documents that have a DTD with a faulty content model. Sooner or later, if you don't eliminate these practices from your DTDs, you'll run across a document instance that will give you a problem. If you run into some oddball parsing errors that you don't recognize, consider whether a bad content model might be the cause.
>
> Mixed-content models cause parsing errors because the parser interprets carriage returns, tabs, and space characters as data. The DTD might pass the parser test, but when you come to some specific document instances, you will have problems. The parsing results can vary among parsers, but mixed content nearly always causes you headaches.

Figure 14.14 and figure 14.15 show a DTD declaration and document instance of mixed content.

Fig. 14.14

This is an example of a mixed-content model.

```
<!ELEMENT article - - (para)+                   >
<!ELEMENT para    - - (#PCDATA,ulist*)          >
<!ELEMENT ulist   - - (#PCDATA)                 >
```

```
<ARTICLE><PARA>The quick brown fox jumped over the log for which
of the following reasons?</PARA><PARA>Here's some #PCDATA
<ULIST>Because he saw a hare</ULIST>
<ULIST>Because he felt like just doing it</ULIST>
<ULIST>Because the hounds were hot on his trail and they
couldn't do logs</ULIST>
</PARA></ARTICLE>
```

Fig. 14.15

Here is the problem text from the mixed-content model shown in figure 14.14.

This markup shown in figure 14.15 above does not parse because the parser interprets the spaces after the </ULIST> elements as a carriage return and gives you an error. However, the markup above makes logical sense and should pass parsing. That's the problem with using mixed-content models.

If you change your document instance to the markup in figure 14.16, it passes parsing.

```
<ARTICLE><PARA>The quick brown fox jumped over the log for which
of the following reasons?</PARA><PARA>Here's some #PCDATA<ULIST>
Because he saw a hare</ULIST><ULIST>Because he felt like just
doing it</ULIST> <ULIST>Because the hounds were hot on his trail
and they couldn't do logs</ULIST></PARA></ARTICLE>
```

Fig. 14.16

This is one way to fix the parsing problem shown in figure 14.15.

I recommend that you do not fiddle with where you place your tags. That is not the real problem. Even though the second markup instance above would pass parsing, just fix the content model instead. The best policy here is to just avoid mixed-content models altogether. If you want to use a mixed-content model, make an entity declaration and make it #PCDATA. You can also add a proxy for the data that you want to the content model. You'll be much better off in the long run.

> **Note**
>
> If you decide that you must use mixed content, remember these two rules: Put everything inside one group, and make the entire group repeatable. For example:
>
> ```
> <!ELEMENT article - - (para)+              >
> <!ELEMENT para    - - (#PCDATA,ulist)*     >
> <!ELEMENT ulist   - - (#PCDATA)            >
> ```
>
> parses cleanly because the * occurrence indicator moved from (#PCDATA,ulist*) to (#PCDATA,ulist)*, which is acceptable. If you must use mixed content, use it this way.

Dealing with Ambiguous Content Models

Ambiguous content models cause more parsing errors. This happens when the parser cannot decide whether an element that it encounters belongs to the content model of one structure or to the content model of another structure. This happens because the structures were not defined clearly in the first place.

Your parser must be clear about which content model the element it encounters belongs to. If it comes across an <a> element and both <X> and <Y> contain an <a> element, the parser must not have any confusion about which <a> element is in question.

Consider the following DTD:

```
<!ELEMENT article - - (title, (note,caution)?,(note¦figure¦list¦p)+)>
```

If you have dealt with these ambiguous models before, you can recognize this from 100 yards away. When the parser gets to the <note> element, does it belong to the second or third part of the model? You can't tell from the way this content model currently exists. The second part of the group is optional. The parser has no way of knowing whether to require a caution when it sees the first note.

Figure 14.17 is a document instance that illustrates the confusion caused by an ambiguous content model.

Fig. 14.17

This is an example of a document marked up according to an ambiguous content model.

```
<TITLE>The Curious Mating Habits of the Aardvark</TITLE>
<NOTE>This section contains graphic sexual discussion of an
adult nature. Please do not continue if you are under seventeen
years of age.</NOTE> <P>Here goes the first paragraph of a graphic
sexual nature concerning the mating habits of the Aardvark.</P>
```

This is an ambiguous content model. The parser does not know whether to look for a caution following the note.

There are other possible ambiguous content models. Imagine the situation in which the content of one element resembles the content of the second sequential element, but the first sequential element has a minimized end tag notation, and the second element has a minimized start tag. What do you do when the first element is followed by the second element? For example:

```
<!ELEMENT A - O ((H1¦H2),(P¦L¦G)+)*>
<!ELEMENT B O - (H1,(P¦L¦G)*)>
```

Figure 14.18 shows the document instance.

Fig. 14.18

This is another example of a document marked up according to an ambiguous content model.

```
<A><H1>Here's some good heading stuff from the first element.</H1>
<P>Here's some good content from the first element</P>
<H1>Here's the second heading</H1>
<P>Here's the second paragraph.</P>
<H1>Here's a third heading.</H1>
<P>Here's a third paragraph.</P>
```

If you were the parser, you would not know whether the third paragraph is part of the first element or the second element. You would return an error.

How Flexible Should DTDs Be?

The nice thing about DTDs is that they can keep a group of writers from being too creative. However, DTDs are flexible enough to allow for creative change and innovation. You select the range of flexibility that you want your DTD(s) to permit.

 ◀◀ See "Decide What Standards and Policies You Must Obey," p. 112

In the environment definition part, you determine whether any standards need to be followed. If there are standards, such as ATA 100, you should incorporate that much rigidity into your DTDs. That way, your writers will not get so creative that they neglect conforming to the standards.

> **Tip**
>
> The main question to ask is what can change more easily in your situation—the document structure or the DTD?

Before you can answer whether the document or the DTD is easier to change, you must have as large a sample of documents as you can manage. You must be sure that the structure for your document type is consistently represented in your DTD. Then, if you need to keep a fairly loose structure, you can build that flexibility into the DTD. Or, if you must follow a strict structure, as in a military technical manual, you can build rigidity into the DTD. In either case, you must have a clear picture of the document's structure from a large sample of documents of that type.

Then, as for determining whether to change the document or the DTD, it depends on which can be more flexible. After looking at a large sample of documents, you might decide that your technical manuals do have various structures. For example, you might observe that some technical manuals have complicated tables and equations while others have none. Build the flexibility into your DTD and allow your writers to be more creative.

On the other hand, if your technical manuals must follow a rigid form, build that strictness into your DTD. The basic questions you should ask are:

- Should the DTD enforce rules?
- Can document structures still be changed for the sake of SGML rules without compromising other rules that must be followed?
- Can SGML rules be adapted to accommodate your unique application?
- Do you know enough about your document instances to accurately specify content models?

III

Content Modeling

The question of how rigid to make your DTDs is a highly individual one. The answer depends on many factors specific to you and your installation. Here are some examples:

```
<!ELEMENT strict      - - (a,b,c,d)            >
<!ELEMENT medium      - - (a¦b¦c)+,(d¦e)+      >
<!ELEMENT wildthing   - - (a¦b¦c¦d¦e¦f)*       >
```

Most likely, SGML can accommodate your most constrictive scenario or your most indulgent scenario—possibly even both. That's the advantage of using an international standard. It has already done a lot of adapting.

Miscellaneous Reminders

If you observe the precautions discussed in this chapter in your DTD design, you go a long way toward writing clean and workable applications. Here are a few more rules you should try to follow. They are mostly common sense.

Processing Instructions

This is one practice that you should try to avoid, but that you will probably find irresistible. The problem with processing instructions is that they are different for each system that must do the processing. Therefore, whenever you include these instructions, you must make them fit the machine that executes them. But, whenever you do that, you make your document less transportable. The idea behind SGML is to make your document more standardized with generic markup. If you include processing instructions, your document is no longer generic.

In SGML, marked sections are a convenient place to use processing instructions, when you must use them. Within the marked sections, you can include the specific instructions within parameter entities. That way, when you must change the processing instructions to fit another system, you can change the values of the parameter entities to do so. For example:

```
<![ IGNORE [<?.cc 10>]]>
```

shows the marked section and the processing instruction for TeX. You can make an entity declaration in the DTD that can define a processing system, such as TeX. For example:

```
<!ENTITY % tex "IGNORE">
```

For the TeX processing system, you can use something like the following in your document for TeX commands:

```
<![ %tex; [
<!ENTITY newpage "<?\newpage>">
]]>
```

You can include as many TeX commands as necessary and make each one an entity. If you need another processing system, use it within another marked section and declare another entity for that particular processing system. Instead of changing each processing system command, change the values of the entities. That saves a lot of work.

▶▶ See "External Processing of Equations," p. 425

Note

You'll notice another way of invoking the TeX equation editor system in "The NOTATION Declaration" section in Chapter 16. The procedure above using parameter entities is simply one more approach to using processing instructions with TeX as an example.

Remember: The more you use processing instructions, the more you compromise your generic markup. It's far better if you stick to the output specification and stylesheet scenario for designing the final product output.

User Involvement

The more you involve your users, the more useful your SGML installation will be for them. In many corners, SGML still has an esoteric aura that scares away many users. This can be a problem when they are your employees and are getting scared away from one of the fundamental tools that they need to do their jobs. The more you encourage them to involve themselves in the overall process, the more quickly they will become accustomed to using SGML.

Moreover, your employees are in the best position to recognize what works. By involving them in creating and maintaining the SGML installation, you get their input. Even if their input is not overly technical, they can discuss nuances of documents and their structures that you could never know.

Frequent Validation and Model Testing

It's worth repeating that you should use a big document sample to define your document types. As you develop your DTD, you should test as many document instances against the DTD as you have time for. This is where you can have users to help you, too. Have them bring their most obscure and difficult document instances to you. Challenge them to find the most unusual instance of the document type that you are currently working on. Mark up the document instances and parse. That will test your DTD.

You should do this frequently as you develop and add features to your DTD. It's best to parse as you add features. That way, when you run into errors, you can track them more easily. If you parse after incorporating many changes, you won't know which change caused the error.

III

Content Modeling

◀◀ See "Parsers," p. 242

Use several parsers in the parsing process. Use a nonvalidating parser to get the most gentle parse. When you are more confident that you have a solid structure and good content models, use a validating parser. It works your DTDs and documents more carefully and precisely. As you change and mold your DTD, make sure that you keep your original purpose for the document type in mind. Make sure that each test and its results bring you closer to the original purpose for which you defined the document type. Don't get distracted from what you originally intended just for the sake of parsing convenience.

Consistent Documentation

You should maintain three types of documentation for your DTDs:

- Pre-design documentation from your workshops
- Documentation inside the DTD itself in the form of comments
- Documentation outside the DTD itself, including the element dictionary

Don't skimp on any type of documentation. Get into the habit of maintaining documentation together with the DTDs. When you change a content model because of a parsing error on a particular document instance, put a record of that change into each type of documentation. Do this religiously. That means that you should have these documents in a particular place and in a specific format. Stick to that format. Don't let these volumes be borrowed by people who promise to bring them back someday. Keep control over these documents so that they are not lost. At the same time, make them accessible so that they can be useful to users and updated as needed.

You should also keep a record of your decisions on document design. People often forget what they agreed upon concerning the purpose of a document design. If you keep a record of what everyone has agreed upon, you maintain control of the situation. Surprises will not occur so often.

◀◀ See "Making Comments in DTDs," p. 214

From Here...

This chapter covered DTD design issues. These are issues that affect you severely if you ignore them. The problems that these design issues cause are sometimes small, but other times they are severe. This chapter also marks the end of Part III, "Content Modeling: Developing the DTD."

For more information, refer to the following:

- Part IV, "Markup Strategies," offers tips and covers the pitfalls of incorporating markup into documents.

■ Chapter 15, "Automatic versus Manual Tagging" covers different approaches to getting tags into documents, and talks about autotaggers, transformers, editors, and hybrid tools.

■ Chapter 16, "Markup Challenges and Specialized Content" talks about notation, short references, marked sections, include and exclude tagging, and equations.

■ Part V, "SGML and the World Wide Web," covers design issues that affect SGML and the Internet.

■ Chapter 24, "Understanding and Using Output Specifications" talks about the different environments for which you might have to develop SGML. It provides a good explanation of output specifications.

■ Chapter 25, "Handling Specialized Content and Delivery," talks about SGML tables, graphics, multimedia extensions, and linking.

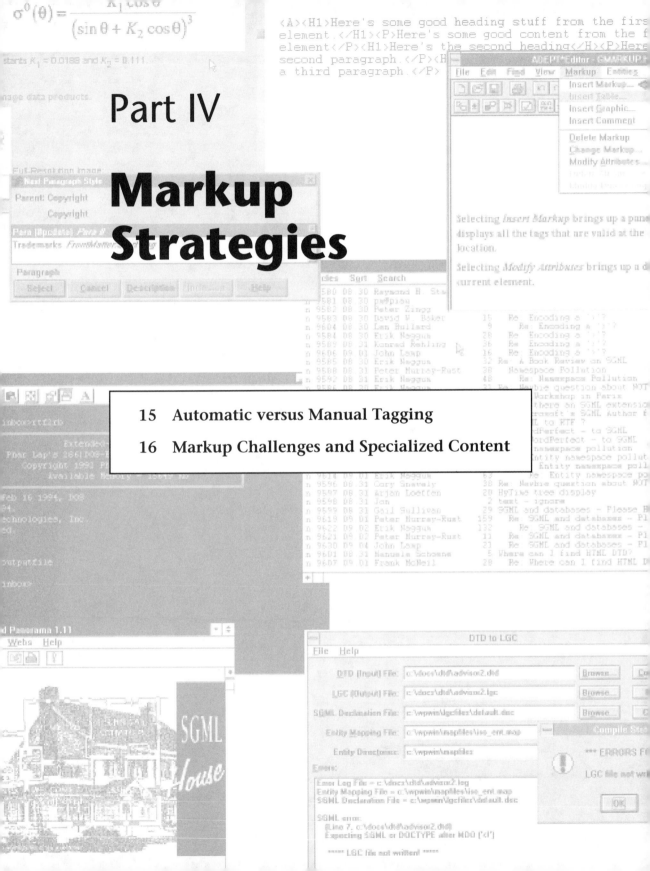

Part IV

Markup Strategies

15   Automatic versus Manual Tagging

16   Markup Challenges and Specialized Content

CHAPTER 15

Automatic versus Manual Tagging

This chapter talks about getting SGML markup into documents. Chapter 5, "Two Scenarios," discussed how you build an SGML installation. You either create an SGML environment from scratch or filter a legacy of existing documents. Often, though, you need to do both operations. This chapter discusses the tools required for each approach.

In this chapter, you learn:

- The best way to get tags into documents
- What types of conversion tools you can use to get documents marked up with SGML
- What types of structured authoring tools you can use to get documents marked up with SGML

Deciding which Markup Method Is for You

It all comes down to your document collection. If you have a backlog of diverse documents, you need document conversion. If you're starting with a clean slate, you emphasize structured authoring. To decide where you fall between these extremes, consider these questions:

- How big will the SGML installation be? How many documents will it have?
- How complex are the document types?
- Are there many legacy documents that must be converted?
- Are you committed to software or hardware platforms that dictate how you create or process documents?
- Can the people in your group learn to author or edit documents differently?

- Are you constrained by the types of file formats that you receive from information providers or provide to clients?

- What sort of turn-around times must you adhere to in processing your documents? What are your time constraints?

How you answer these questions determines which markup method you should choose.

Big Installation versus One-Person Hobbyist

The large installation will most likely need much more document conversion than a one-person hobbyist. The hobbyist will primarily be a structured SGML author. Also, the hobbyist has fewer time restrictions than the large installation, which is most likely a commercial enterprise. So, the hobbyist can afford to experiment and search for the most cost-effective ways of doing things. The large enterprise will likely need to just get the job done—downtime costs more money for them. The one-person installation, however, will probably be using less expensive tools, and will use as many public domain programs as possible, whereas the large enterprise will buy expensive suites of software from commercial SGML software vendors.

Complex versus Simple Hardware and Software

Large corporations sometimes have a substantial commitment to a specific hardware and software platform that can dictate their requirements, whereas smaller companies or hobbyists have much more flexibility. If the hardware and software requirements are too unusual and no SGML support exists for that platform, the SGML enterprise is forced to insert tags manually, or they must hire someone to build an SGML processing system for their platform. The SGML standard was designed so that tags could be inserted using simple text editors, but it is very laborious. Also, public domain parsers exist for many different platforms, even many unusual ones. Still, building validating parser—as well as authoring and document conversion—tools is sometimes necessary for unusual platforms.

Simple Documents or Complex Document Collection

Collections of simple documents are easier to manage than collections of complex documents. Simple requirements can be met with fewer and less expensive tools for document conversion and structured authoring. A hobbyist can spend $400 on an MS Word add-on program, and he will have filled his entire requirement because of a simple document collection. A corporation could easily spend 100 times that amount on a team of analysts working full-time to build DTDs for all their documents to be authored, buying industrial strength tools from the finest SGML firms, and further handling the many exceptional legacy data challenges during document conversion.

Short or Long Timeline

Large companies spend large amounts of money for being late with documentation to customers, whereas if a hobbyist doesn't get his SGML Web site operational until next month, there is no harm done. If you have time to experiment, you will iron out many potential problems before they happen and you will have time to educate yourself about the various conversion and authoring tools, as well as get your system up and working without having to learn as you go. Sometimes large companies must be in such a hurry that they don't have time to test their authoring and conversion solutions before they use them, and this causes problems. The longer your timeline, the better your authoring and document conversion solutions will be.

There are essentially three approaches for marking up documents. You must choose an approach or combine them when you incorporate document markup. You can:

- Insert tags manually with a simple text editor
- Do structured authoring by using an SGML authoring and editing tool
- Convert existing electronic or paper documents into SGML documents

Manual Markup

Manual markup is fine if you don't have many documents or suffer from time constraints and boredom. It can get tedious manually inserting tags into a long document with a complex document structure. This approach, however, offers the greatest flexibility for markup.

SGML files are simple ASCII text files with an *.SGML or *.SGM file extension. You can view them with any text viewer, but an SGML processing system is required to interpret the tags and build the document those tags define.

Tip

Use a simple text editor that saves the file without formatting. If you save the file in a proprietary format, such as a WordPerfect or Word file, you limit yourself. Eventually, you will have to resave the file as an SGML file anyway. In other words, don't use a tool that embeds special codes.

If flexibility is a high priority for you and you don't have many complex documents, manual markup is an option. The useful thing about inserting tags manually is you can put them anywhere. That does not mean that your document instance will parse, however, but you can parse separately. You also do not have to buy expensive SGML software.

There are trade-offs, of course. Because you can put tags wherever you want, you can make more errors than you would had you used an SGML structured authoring tool. For example, if your DTD calls for a <FIGURE> element to be used only within a <PARA> element, the structured authoring tool will not let you stick it in a <HEAD1> element. A manual text editor doesn't care where you put any tags. Although the structured authoring tool can be frustrating when you author a document, it ensures that it will parse according to your DTD. A manual text editor gives no such assurance.

The flexibility that comes from manual markup is not always good. Because it's easy to manually markup small HTML documents with non-SGML element structures, you can run into a variety of problems. Certain browsers, for example, support non-standard extensions to the HTML DTD. These extensions cause problems on the World Wide Web, such as:

- They make the document an invalid HTML document
- They make the document somewhat less transportable and accessible from other browsers
- They emphasize appearance and formatting over content and structure
- They short-circuit the process of information sharing

> **Note**
>
> The short-circuit referred to above happens because some browser developers want their product to be the most popular, so they make theirs "better" than the standard browser by anticipating improvements to the HTML DTD. But by supporting non-standard extensions, they encourage their customers to develop Web pages that not everyone can read. Their customers are sharing attractive graphics, but those graphics can be viewed by fewer people because they're non-standard. A better approach is to extend the standard, even though this does take time.

When you use a text editor to insert tags manually, you open the door to this haphazard approach to document creation. You should always remember to validate your documents.

SGML, as the international standard, enables you to load DTDs as needed without violating the HTML 2.0 standard. Therefore, you can use the Netscape extensions—as well as many others—without compromising the HTML DTD. Until Panorama is as popular as Netscape, however, you must be disciplined when you manually markup an HTML document. Figure 15.1 shows a non-standard <BLINK> element.

Fig. 15.1

You can create this
<BLINK> element using a
text editor, even though it
does not parse.

```
Benjerry - Notepad                                                _ 8 X
File  Edit  Search  Help
<IMG SRC="library/images/holiday/turkey.gif" WIDTH=89 HEIGHT=110
ALIGN=RIGHT ALT="[A turkey]">
<A NAME="turkey-hunt">                           I
<BLINK><H1>Thanksgiving Contest!<BR>
Turkey Hunt</H1></BLINK></A>
<BR>
<H1>How To Play Ben & Jerry's Thanksgiving Turkey Hunt</H1>
<P>To enter our Turkey Hunt contest, you have to find the five turkeys
that we've placed on our pages. The turkeys look like the turkey above this
paragraph except that they all have names. Once you've found
ALL FIVE, go to the <A HREF="turkey-hunt.html">Turkey Hunt entry form</A>
and send us your name and address
(the usual stuff) and the names of the turkeys.</P>
<H2>Some General Guidelines For Hunting Turkeys</H2>
<UL>
<LI>No guessing, find the turkeys and write down the names so you don't
forget them.<BR>
<BR>
<LI>Once you have found all FIVE (5) of the turkeys, go to the <A HREF="turkey
form</A> and then tell us the names.<BR>
<BR>
<LI> Partial or multiple entries will be disqualified. Don't fill out the
form until you have all five turkeys.<BR>
<BR>
<LI> All the turkeys are on <EM> our </EM> pages, they're all in our domain
(www.benjerry.com) we didn't hide them anywhere else.<BR>
<BR>
<LI> Have fun, relax. Turkeys can sense hostility and frustration.<BR>
```

Document Conversion

There are many kinds of document conversion tools. This approach to creating SGML documents is useful when you want to upgrade HTML documents to other types of DTDs. Automatic tagging approaches such as this one enable you to convert documents to a neutral file type first, and then to SGML.

 ▶▶ See "Avalanche/Interleaf: FastTAG," p. 495

Suppose, for example, that you have many documents in a proprietary word processing format called WordWiz. No SGML conversion tool exists for that file format. You must first convert the documents to a neutral markup scheme, such as RTF, and then convert them to SGML. Figure 15.2 shows an example of this chapter converted into RTF and then into HTML.

Before you seriously consider automated document conversion, you must have a consistent document structure. You'll need to have a specific translation scheme for each type of document. To create any SGML document type, you need document analysis. Suppose, for example, that some of your memos have a return address paragraph; other ones do not. Your DTD for the memo document type calls for a return address. To convert your memos into SGML, you must first add a return address to every instance that does not already have one. This is because when the SGML parser goes to each instance of a memo, it expects to see the return address as specified in the DTD. If it does not find one, the document fails to parse.

Fig. 15.2

The program RTF2HTML converts RTF documents into HTML documents.

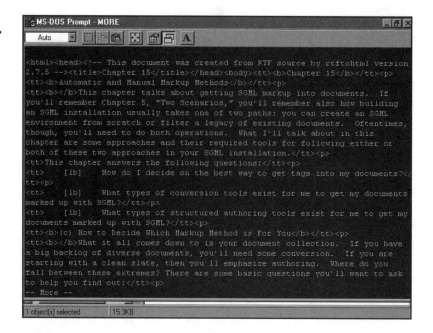

In short, document analysis is crucial, even when documents are already created. You must look at your legacy documents and go through the document analysis steps discussed in Part II, "Document Analysis." These steps are:

- Define the environment
- Define the elements
- Relate the elements to one another
- Extend the document architecture

◀◀ See "Document Analysis," p. 97

You must review these steps for document conversion to SGML. You probably need to convert documents gathered from elsewhere in your SGML environment as well.

Structured Authoring

Structured authoring in SGML normally requires an SGML authoring tool. Using such a tool helps you avoid the inconsistency of document structure that makes document conversion a challenge. In SGML, you must design the structure of a document type before you can create an instance of that document type. Whether you create an instance of a document type by conversion or with an authoring tool, you're basically filling in structural pigeonholes with specific document content.

When you use an SGML authoring tool, it's impossible to create document content that falls outside the structural pigeonholes. Before you can enter content, you must select the correct pigeonhole from the elements specified in the DTD for that document type. This guarantees that the SGML documents you create with the tool parse properly. Figure 15.3 shows an example of a powerful SGML structured authoring tool.

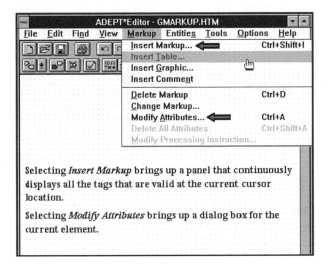

Fig. 15.3

With ArborText's ADEPT*Editor, you can insert different types of document content only at specific locations.

Fortunately, some tools with which you can do structured authoring have become affordable for the individual author creating documents outside of an industrial orga-nization. In the past, it was common to pay $3000 or more for such an authoring tool. Now, there are alternatives for well under $1000. While still expensive for the home user, it is attainable. And there are still more cost-effective alternatives to authoring for home users. One class of tools are extensions to existing word proces-sors that, in effect, turn them into SGML authoring tools. This type of tool has gained favor in HTML authoring, but SGML extensions to MS Word, for example, have been around for only a few years. Other programs convert Word or other word processing files into SGML documents. Strictly speaking, they are conversion tools, but they simulate the structured authoring found in dedicated SGML authoring tools.

▶▶ See "SGML Authoring Tools," p. 434
▶▶ See "SoftQuad Author/Editor 3.1," p. 469
▶▶ See "The World of Perl," p. 491

These add-on tools make Word, and other word processors, an effective SGML authoring tool. They force you to create only documents with highly defined stylesheets, which become the basis for converting the documents into document instances of an SGML DTD. You must create the stylesheets and templates according to the DTD for the document that you create. Then, you must map the DTD and the stylesheet template together so that the document conversion utility can easily con-vert the word processor output into an SGML document instance.

Document Conversion and Its Tools

Suppose you find something that you just have to have in SGML. Especially with the Internet being so convenient, you can find public domain documents at an FTP site that might be great to have in an SGML Web site. Likewise, you might find an article in the newspaper that you want to scan and put on your Web site. In cases like these, you must convert the documents from one document file type into SGML.

> **Caution**
>
> Before you publish copyrighted material on your Web site, be sure that you are not illegally using that material. Newspaper articles may only be used according to the limitations specified in their copyright statement.

There are three types of conversion tools:

- Tools that convert word processing formats into SGML
- Tools that convert a common intermediate file type into SGML
- Tools that convert specialized file types into SGML

Word Processing Conversion Tools

Most of these tools require you to author in a word processor, such as Word, and to save the file with an SGM extension. These add-on tools are not true structured SGML authoring tools, such as Near & Far Author. Essentially, you create a Word file and then make it into an SGML file.

 ▶▶ See "WordPerfect SGML Edition," "SGML Author for Word," and "Near & Far Author," pp. 434, 440, 445

One popular tool is Microsoft's SGML Author, which is reviewed in Chapter 26, "Tools for the PC: Authoring, Viewing, and Utilities." Essentially, you first create a DTD. Then you create a Word file template with a consistent style and relate the styles in the template to the elements in your DTD. SGML Author creates a marked-up SGML file that passes muster with most parsers.

The steps are:

1. Do the document analysis, and create the DTD in a text editor or use an existing DTD.
2. Create the stylesheet template in the word processing program according to the elements in the DTD.
3. Use SGML Author to map the styles in the template to the elements in the DTD.
4. Create your document strictly according to the stylesheet template that you just created.
5. Save your document as an SGML document.

You now have one or more DTDs, one or more stylesheet templates, and one or more document instances that are all SGML documents. This is the basic scenario for hybrid converters using popular word processing programs.

These tools usually meet the basic needs of home users or builders of small installations. By extending this scenario, you can even have many people all creating SGML documents according to accepted stylesheet templates. If you can enforce the discipline of those stylesheets, you can make this process work for a larger SGML installation.

Converting documents in this way involves risks:

- Even when you use stylesheets, it's possible to introduce structure to the document that will not be accepted or recognized when the document is parsed

- You might not understand the whole process of creating SGML documents without additional help

- It's sometimes awkward to introduce substructures—such as attribute entities—into the document from within the authoring environment itself

- Authors do not have to remain focused on document structure, as with a structured authoring program; they can tinker with formatting instead of with stylesheets and output specifications

- These tools are sometimes weak when it comes to handling output specifications and SGML stylesheets

Specific conversion programs have different trade-offs. Some don't really suffer much from these weaknesses. Keep them in mind when you consider how to convert word processing files to SGML.

Note

The key to making this approach work is to create *consistently* structured documents from within the word processor. That way, when you use a utility, such as *FastTAG* from Avalanche, to convert them, you will not have as many parsing errors. The danger with structured authoring in a word processing environment is that it enables you to do things that you should not. A true SGML structured authoring tool never lets you get close to mischief—or, at least, makes it very difficult.

Suppose, for example, that according to your DTD the <NOTE> element can occur only within a <PARA> element. A word processor does not know the difference, and it lets you put it anywhere. A good SGML structured authoring tool, on the other hand, won't let you put the <NOTE> element where it doesn't belong.

Conversion Tools for Intermediate File Types

These tools convert an intermediate file type, such as Rich Text Format (RTF), into an SGML document instance for a particular DTD. This approach succeeds where word processing file conversion fails because not everyone uses a popular word processing program that has extensive SGML support.

What if your platform does not support WordPerfect, Word, or Interleaf? What if you have to do a project on an old mainframe or minicomputer that supports only a limited range of text editors and file formats? You can probably create a file type for which a conversion utility already exists. Because you can do this, you have a solution.

There are many intermediate file types. In fact, there are transformer utilities that enable you to convert from various SGML DTDs to other SGML DTDs. There are tools that convert a document and automatically generate a DTD. These include:

- Tools that convert from RTF, TeX, or a generic file type to a document type instance for a single DTD
- Tools that convert a document instance of one DTD into a document instance of another DTD, such as AAP2ISO and DTD2HTML
- Tools that convert highly individualized file formats into a highly individualized document instance for a DTD, such as i2c for ISO/CALS table conversions and SGML Exportfilter for FrameBuilder
- Hybrid tools, such as SGML Hammer and DynaTag

Some tools have been used extensively, and you can rely on them. No matter what platform you're used to working on, you can find a conversion utility for it. A good place to start looking is Robin Cover's SGML repository of tools on the sil.org SGML home page:

http://www.sil.org/sgml/sgml.html

You should also check out his public domain tools link at:

http://www.sil.org/sgml/publicSW.html

Steve Pepper's Whirlwind Guide to SGML tools is another good source of SGML conversion tools:

http://www.falch.no/~pepper/sgmltool/

The following FTP repository has SGML conversion tools as well:

http://www.w3.org/hypertext/WWW/Tools/
Word_proc_filters.html

One popular converter is RTF2RB, shown in figure 15.4. The only requirement is that you can convert your file types into RTF. If you can, you can convert the file into the Rainbow DTD in SGML. The Rainbow DTD is highly flexible and is designed to accommodate many file types. Once you translate a file into this DTD, you can convert it into another document instance for another DTD.

You still have to pay attention to document analysis with this approach, of course. A wide variety of utilities convert first to an intermediate file type, so it is impossible to specify the requirements for each one. In general:

- Have a specific DTD in mind when you convert to SGML.

- Be aware of the differences between strains of intermediate file types; for example, ASCII and RTF can exist in several strains that might affect the conversion

- When you convert from HTML to another DTD, make sure that the HTML document parses completely; many non-standard HTML documents take advantage of browsers that support non-HTML elements.

Fig. 15.4

RTF2RB is a popular document converter utility that exists in the public domain.

IV

Markup Strategies

Conversion Between SGML Document Types

As you have seen, it's possible to convert first to HTML and then to another DTD application in SGML. When you can't find an intermediate file type into which you can translate your target document, you might be able to translate it into an SGML document type instance—such as HTML—and then transform it into a document instance of another SGML application file type.

Although HTML is a popular DTD, others exist that you can try. Before HTML became a favorite, The Text Encoding Initiative (TEI) had—and still does have—some very successful DTDs. Some nice publishing DTDs exist from the AAP, and there is a conversion tool called AAP2ISO that will convert instances of their document type to other document type instances.

To convert between SGML document types, you can use:

- Tools that convert HTML files to other SGML application instances

■ Tools that transform one document type instance into an instance for another DTD

The first category exists only because HTML is so popular. The second category is one to pay attention to. Those tools require that you have DTDs handy for the target and source document types; the source document instance must be handy, too. The source file needs to be valid SGML; it has to parse.

Several popular conversion tools exist in the public domain. These include:

■ CoST (Copenhagen SGML Tool)

■ qwertz

■ Rainbow

■ SGML2TeX (which converts only to TeX)

■ SGMLS.pm

The SGML archive at **ftp://ftp.ifi.uio.no/pub/SGML** contains the latest versions of all these tools. If you don't find them there, do a Lycos or WebCrawler search for them.

Structured Authoring and Its Tools

Genuine structured authoring tools have a reputation for being expensive. With few exceptions, that reputation is well deserved. The best known and most widely used tools are Author/Editor by SoftQuad, DynaText by EBT, and ADEPT*Editor by ArborText. They make it difficult for you to create a document that does not structurally follow your DTD. Once you have mapped in your DTD, these tools do not allow you to create a component outside of its parent element. When you author inside a particular element, you can create only the subelements specified in the content model for it.

 ▶▶ See "SGML Authoring Tools," p. 434

Newer tools are being developed all the time to bridge the gap between word processor add-ons and true structured authoring tools. This is the latest trend in structured authoring. Because HTML plug-in authoring tools have become so amazingly popular, everyone is sure to appreciate easy-to-use SGML authoring tools that you can plug in to Word or WordPerfect.

Hybrid tools combine the best features of dedicated SGML authoring tools with the convenience of word processors. They make word processors even more powerful and useful. Figure 15.5 shows Near & Far Author. Its document structuring capability keeps you honest when you create SGML documents.

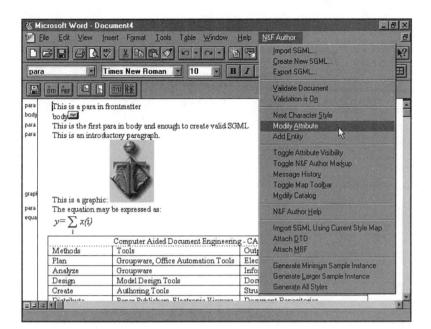

IV

Fig. 15.5

Near & Far Author keeps you honest when you author highly structured SGML documents from within Word.

Markup Strategies

From Here...

You have seen how to create SGML documents from scratch and convert non-SGML documents into SGML documents. Public domain and commercial applications can help you transform document type instances for one DTD into document instances for another—one reason why you put all those tags in your documents.

For more information, refer to the following:

- Chapter 16, "Markup Challenges and Specialized Content," covers specialized markup situations.

- Part V, "SGML and the World Wide Web," discusses how SGML and the Web have changed each other forever.

- Part VII, "SGML Tools and Their Uses," goes into more detail about the tools mentioned in this chapter. Tools for the PC, the Mac, and UNIX machines are discussed.

Markup Challenges and Specialized Content

As you go through the process of converting documents into SGML markup, you may encounter a number of situations that call for special treatment. For example, you might wish to build a document that is different depending upon the user and his or her needs or situation. Other situations may arise where you want to include specialized content, such as scientific notation, graphics, or multimedia files, such as video or sound clips.

In other situations, you may find yourself putting tags into a document by hand. Fortunately, this is less common today, but far from unusual in the not too distant past.

Until very recently, the process of getting to actual SGML output was often a painful one. Getting authors in the SGML "frame of mind" was difficult. Finding the right tools to use in producing SGML was even harder.

Fortunately, SGML provides a rich feature set to handle these challenges of tagging and special content. In this chapter, you will examine some of the practical ways in which SGML deals with such special situations. The methods discussed are by no means the only ways available of handling some of these needs. As your SGML experience grows, you will often find several ways to accommodate a specific requirement or situation.

In this chapter, you will examine a number of SGML options for:

- Recreating standard data or boilerplate
- Building conditional documents
- Including specialized content (e.g., graphics, equations, multimedia clips)
- Simplifying the tagging process for manually generated tags

Using Standard Data in Documents

In many standard document types, there is data—called *standard text* or *boilerplate*—that is repeated in the same fashion in each document instance.

For some documents, this may be as simple as the To: and From: in a standard interoffice memorandum. Other instances might include quite lengthy bits of verbiage, such as legal disclaimers or government mandated statements. A simplified example is shown in figure 16.1.

Fig. 16.1

As in this example, standard reusable text (boilerplate) can be rather lengthy in some instances.

> FCC Statement: This equipment has been tested and found to comply with the limits for a Class B digital device, pursuant to Part 15 of the FCC Rules. These limits are designed to provide reasonable protection against harmful interference in a residential installation. This equipment generates, uses, and can radiate radio frequency energy and, if not installed and used in accordance with the instructions, may cause harmful interference in radio communications.

Whether you wish for legal reasons to use the same standard text, you want to minimize reentry of standard text, or you just want a "standard look" to your documents, entity references can provide a solution to your boilerplate blues.

> **Tip**
>
> Some packages allow you to use entity references in your output specification (or stylesheet). In this case, their usage can also serve to greatly reduce the length of your actual SGML document instances. Imagine a collection of product advisories in which each individual advisory contains standard text (such as an FCC warning). By placing it in the stylesheet once, you can avoid unnecessary replication of the information in each advisory.

Using Entity References for Boilerplate

Using entity references to repeat standard text in document instances is pretty straightforward (recall that you looked at entities in Chapter 10). A noticeable difference from most entities might be the length of the declaration.

The previously examined FCC warning can be done as illustrated in figure 16.2.

Fig. 16.2

Through the use of an entity declaration, boilerplate text can be standardized and easily reused.

```
<!ENTITY    fccnote      CDATA    "FCC Statement: This equip-
ment has been tested and found to comply with the limits for a
Class B digital device, pursuant to Part 15 of the FCC Rules.
These limits are designed to provide reasonable protection
against harmful interference in a residential installation.
This equipment generates, uses, and can radiate radio frequency
energy and, if not installed and used in accordance with
the instructions, may cause harmful interference in radio
communications."  >
```

Although the specifics of using such an entity in the output specification of your program are subject to some variance (check the specific documentation for your software), a typical example of its usage is illustrated in figure 16.3.

```
<style name="STD_ADVISOR">
    <left-indent>    +=40         </>
    <first-indent>   -40          </>
    <text-before>    &fccnote     </>
    <hrule>          after        </>
</style>
```

Fig. 16.3

Boilerplate text often can be included through the use of entities in an SGML application's output specification.

Notice, in this example, that the entity fccnote is specified as a text-before. This will cause it to occur prior to the element being output.

Building Conditional Documents

In some cases, you might want to construct documents that contain sections that vary according to circumstances. These circumstances can include multi-level service manuals, instructions in various languages, or common instruction manuals to be used across a family of related products.

Imagine a comprehensive repair manual for a large ship engine. Depending on the level of service to be performed, you might want to show different levels of detail. The levels can be defined as shown in table 16.1.

Table 16.1 Ship Engine Maintenance Levels

Level	Maintenance Type	Servicer
1	Preventive Maintenance	User
2	Assembly Replacement	Field Representative
3	Assembly Repair	Depot
4	Engine Overhaul	Overhaul Facility

If you're responsible for the repair manual documentation for this engine, you might want to construct it so that you could have all of the maintenance and repair information in one manual. But, you would print out multiple versions of the manual that include levels of detail according to which maintenance level the user is qualified to perform. (Or, if you want to display the manual electronically, you might want to only show those types of maintenance that the reader is trained for.)

To build your conditional document, use the following SGML features:

- Declaring marked sections
- INCLUDE and IGNORE processing

Examine each feature in turn, and then see how you can use them for your conditional document.

Declaring Marked Sections

To indicate a marked section, you must use the `marked section` declaration in your SGML document instance (rather than in your DTD). By using this declaration, you indicate the section's status (such as `INCLUDE` or `IGNORE`), followed by the actual content within the section.

Fig. 16.4

The marked section declaration.

```
<![ status keyword    [ marked section content ]]>
```

The status keyword can be one of the types illustrated in table 16.2. Notice that you can nest some types of marked sections.

Table 16.2 Marked Section Status Keywords

Keyword	Usage	Nested Marked Sections Allowed
INCLUDE	Section is included in processing and is parsed.	Yes
IGNORE	Section is not included in processing. Parsing of the section is limited to the recognition of any 'begin marked section' and 'end marked section' nested within this section.	Yes
CDATA	Section is included. Contents are not parsed.	No
RCDATA	Section is included. Entity references and character references are resolved by parser.	No
TEMP	Used mainly for easy identification of section that can later be removed. Similar to INCLUDE.	Yes

Where nested marked sections are allowed, those sections nested within another marked section will be processed according to the processing of the parent. That is, a nested `IGNORE` section within an `INCLUDE` section, will be ignored (based on its own keyword value). However, an `INCLUDE` section within an `IGNORE` section will also be ignored (based upon its parent section keyword value).

The `CDATA` type of marked section is useful when the marked section includes content that may otherwise be (incorrectly) interpreted as SGML content by the parser. Through the `CDATA` keyword, the parser knows to ignore any markup within this section.

Include and Ignore Processing

Used by itself, the marked section is of limited value in building conditional documents. After all, if you have a document with a number of sections that looks like figure 16.5, making any conditional changes can be both tedious and cumbersome.

```
<![ IGNORE    [<note>Engine removal shortcut tips (to be performed
only by personnel trained in these procedures), are discussed in
the Advanced Procedures section. Use of these procedures by
untrained personnel may risk serious damage to expensive engine
components.</note>]]>
```

Fig. 16.5

When used by itself, a marked section can be difficult to maintain.

Fortunately, there is an easy solution to this dilemma; use entities to define your marked sections. The following section shows you how to accomplish this.

Using Entities with Marked Sections

As you recall the example of the ship engine maintenance manual earlier in the chapter, remember that there are four levels of engine maintenance:

- Level 1   User Maintenance
- Level 2   Field Representative Maintenance
- Level 3   Depot Level Maintenance
- Level 4   Overhaul Facility

As the levels increase, the technical information included in your manual becomes increasingly complex. Because repair personnel familiar with higher levels of maintenance are also familiar with the lower levels, you want to include all lower levels of maintenance up to the level that a person is qualified for.

Suppose you want to deliver a manual that includes those sections up to a Level 3. How would you do this with entities and marked sections in your document instance? Figure 16.6 illustrates how you might go about building your conditional document.

Notice, in this example, that you have defined several entities that correspond to the maintenance level to be addressed (Level 1, Level 2, etc.). Because you want to include all levels up to the level a person is qualified for (Level 3 for this example), you have set Levels 1, 2, and 3 as INCLUDE in your entities. Level 4 is set to IGNORE because you do not wish to have it processed in your document.

In this example, you wanted to make a document that included progressively more detailed information. In other cases, you might have either/or situations where the document conditionally includes one set of information or another (such as with different language versions of the same document). To achieve this, you can simply set one marked section entity at a time.

Fig. 16.6

When used in combination with entities, marked sections can be both easy to maintain and a powerful mechanism for making conditional documents.

```
<!DOCTYPE MAINT  SYSTEM "maint.dtd" [
<!— Complexity level entities definition —>
<!ENTITY % LEVEL1 "INCLUDE">
<!ENTITY % LEVEL2 "INCLUDE">
<!ENTITY % LEVEL3 "INCLUDE">
<!ENTITY % LEVEL4 "IGNORE">
]>
<maint>
<intro>Ongoing maintenance consists of a number of operations
which can be performed....</intro>
<sect>
<title>Inlet Filters</title>
<para>Inlet filters should be replaced on an ongoing basis
according to the schedule outlined in maintenance inter-
vals.....</para>
<![ %LEVEL2 [<para>When performing 2000 hour maintenance, ensure
that the inlet filter housing is correctly sealed using the
clearance tool X-359 included within the standard maintenance
kit.....]]>
<![ %LEVEL3 [<para>In the case of inadequate sealing of the inlet
filter assembly housing, the housing cover can be machined up to
.5 mm to compensate for warpage. This machining should only be
performed on equipment which can ensure these tolerance lev-
els....]]>
<![ %LEVEL4 [<para>During overhaul, the inlet filter housing
should be removed and discarded. Upon reassembly following
overhaul, it should be replaced with revised filter housing Z-
1934. This revised filter housing has been redesigned to correct
a warpage problem which has been observed in field use....]]>
```

Tip

This sample document fragment is constructed for a conditional hardcopy document. If you want to deliver a conditional document electronically, you can set the appropriate entities earlier, external to this document section. (Recall, from Chapter 10, that only the *first* declaration of an entity is processed.)

Including Specialized Content

Because SGML is a markup language for text, it does not directly support other forms of data content. In many documents, you might want to include other data objects, such as graphical figures or equations. For electronic documents, you might want to include multimedia content, such as sound or video clips.

One mechanism provided in SGML to handle non-textual content is the NOTATION declaration. Through it, you can include data that can be "excused" from evaluation by the SGML parser.

The *NOTATION* Declaration

This declaration is constructed according to the syntax illustrated in figure 16.7. In this example, the SGML keyword NOTATION identifies the declaration type. The name of the notation being declared is listed following the keyword (indicated by not-type). The notation identifier can be either SYSTEM or PUBLIC.

Note

SYSTEM identifiers are used to specify system-specific data objects (commonly through the use of a system-specific identifier such as 'c;\caution2a.dat').

PUBLIC identifiers are used to specify data objects with a mechanism that is usable across various computer systems or software environments. A PUBLIC identifier can be identified in a way that has a registered owner associated with it. Through the use of such 'formal' PUBLIC identifiers, the uniqueness of a data object can be preserved.

```
<!NOTATION 'not-type'      SYSTEM "external identifier">
```

Fig. 16.7

The NOTATION declaration.

To use a declared NOTATION in an element, link it to the element in an attribute list. For example, to use it for equations, you might use the commonly available TeX equation editor in the following way:

```
<!NOTATION TeX            SYSTEM >
<!ELEMENT  Pcurve    - -   CDATA>
<!ATTLIST  Pcurve    form  NOTATION  TeX>
```

Tagging Shorthand

In the past, people working in SGML often found themselves in the position of putting tags into documents by hand. In a lot of cases, it was the "path of least resistance" for getting many documents converted into SGML.

Fortunately, the SGML world has changed a great deal in just a few short years. Today, a great many tools are becoming available to help automate the process. However, the situation may still arise where you find yourself faced with the need to pound out some tags manually.

The short reference (or *shortref*) provides you with the capability of using shorthand to reference longer, or more complex, text strings. If you're inputting your SGML text by hand (a not so common experience these days), you might use the shortref to aid you in defining such things as tags for tables (columns, rows, cells, and so on). It is most commonly used to map SGML tagging sequences to easily accessible keys on standard typewriter/computer style keyboards.

Be aware that the use of the shortref can be complex.

Because the shortref was more commonly used in the days before the existence of sophisticated SGML authoring tools, this chapter will not examine it in detail. Instead, you'll get a brief overview of some of the issues involved with its use.

Shortref Usage

Through character set mapping, you can use the shortref to map standard, easily typed key patterns to specified SGML tags or tag fragments. Behind the curtains, this is accomplished through a linkage of entity references that are resolved during the parsing stage.

You can define your own mapping schemes or use those in the standard reference concrete syntax of SGML. Those included in the standard set are listed in table 16.3.

Table 16.3 Short References: Reference Delimiter Set	
String	**Usage**
&#TAB;	Horizontal Tab
&#RE;	Record End
&#RS;	Record Start
&#RS;B	Leading Blanks
&#RS;&#RE;	Empty Record
&#RS;B&#RE;	Blank Record
B&#RE;	Trailing Blanks
&#SPACE;	Space
BB	Two or More Blanks
"	Quotation Mark
#	Number Sign
%	Percent Sign
'	Apostrophe
(	Left Parenthesis
)	Right Parenthesis
*	Asterisk
+	Plus Sign
,	Comma
-	Hyphen
- -	Two Hyphens

IV

Markup Strategies

String	Usage
:	Colon
;	Semicolon
=	Equal Sign
@	Commercial At
[	Left Square Bracket
]	Right Square Bracket
^	Circumflex Accent
_	Low Line
{	Left Curly Bracket
}	Right Curly Bracket
|	Vertical Line
~	Tilde

To use the shortref, you must include three components in the form of SGML markup declarations:

- A general entity declaration that defines what the reference is mapped into
- A shortref mapping declaration that defines a map name and lists the character string associated with it
- A shortref usage declaration that maps a particular shortref to an element where it can be used

> **Note**
>
> As previously mentioned, this look at shortref usage includes only a brief overview. For further information on shortrefs, the reader should reference the SGML standard, ISO 8879.

From Here...

This concludes your look at tagging challenges and specialized content. Through the use of entities, you saw that you could easily reproduce standard text. You also saw how to produce "conditional" documents through the application of marked sections.

For more information, refer to the following:

- Chapter 25, "Handling Specialized Content and Delivery," examines the use of specialized content in SGML documents.

- Part V, "SGML and the World Wide Web," examines the use of SGML on the World Wide Web.

- Part VI, "Learning from the Pros," examines specific topics relating to special areas of SGML implementation.

- Part VII, "SGML Tools and Their Uses," examines a variety of useful tools now available to help you use SGML.

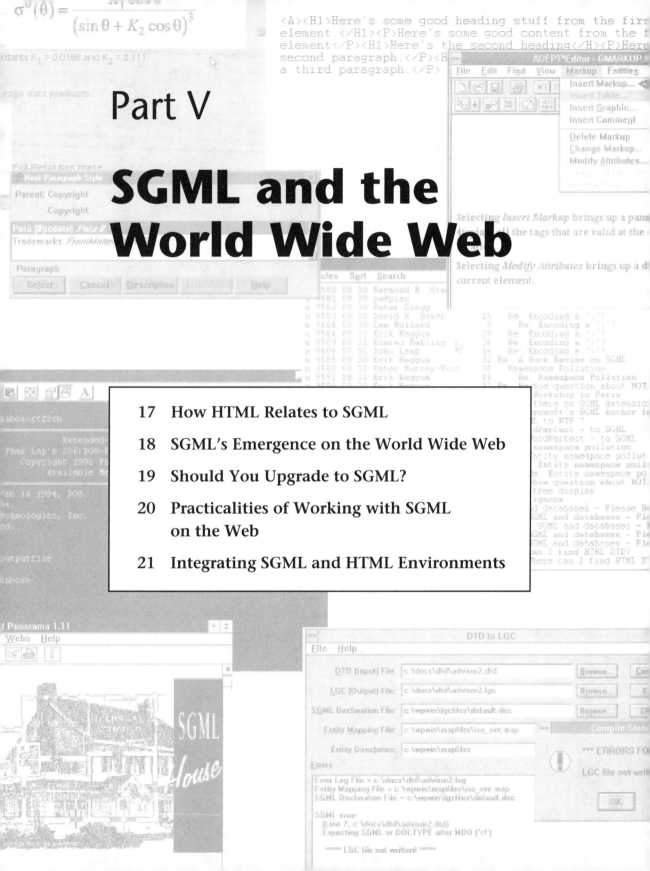

Part V

SGML and the World Wide Web

17   How HTML Relates to SGML

18   SGML's Emergence on the World Wide Web

19   Should You Upgrade to SGML?

20   Practicalities of Working with SGML
     on the Web

21   Integrating SGML and HTML Environments

CHAPTER 17

How HTML Relates to SGML

If you have read straight through from the beginning of the book, you can probably write this chapter yourself. It answers some basic questions, just in case you skipped a few chapters.

In this chapter, you learn:

- How HTML is related to SGML
- What SGML includes that HTML does not
- How SGML can make Web sites more flexible
- Whether SGML will make HTML obsolete

How SGML and HTML Are Related

As you have probably gathered by now, HTML is one SGML application. It is a single DTD. SGML is the parent of HTML, and they relate as parent and child.

When the founding fathers of the World Wide Web wanted to create a markup language implementation, they chose SGML for a number of reasons. The most important was that they needed a reliable standard file type that could be compatible with most of the existing applications and protocols of the Internet, such as SMTP mail, FTP, Gopher, WAIS, and UseNet news. SGML offered the potential to build such a Web application.

Why SGML?

HTML is a chip off the old block, so it helps to understand why SGML fit the bill in the first place. That way, you can see what HTML inherited from SGML.

The World Wide Web is only a few years old. The European Laboratory for Particle Physics (CERN) introduced a new set of protocols in 1989. Although they were originally designed to help physics research groups share their data more easily, the protocols had far-reaching implications. Other organizations adopted the CERN protocols, including a new group called the W3 Consortium. They still pool resources to keep improving the World Wide Web standards.

They originally required a proven standard that:

- Was compatible with existing Internet applications and protocols
- Could apply an object-oriented approach to handling binary files that external applications could deal with
- Could be modified easily and grow as technology improved
- Was independent of hardware, software, or any specific environment
- Offered universal access

SGML fulfills every requirement, so SGML was chosen to build the application that solved each problem that the people at CERN were having.

 ◀◀ See "SGML and the ISO and CALS Standards for Data," p. 10

SGML has a long history, so it is a proven standard. It handles diverse and challenging types of documents. Many huge corporations have selected it for their applications, and it serves them well. Governments have used SGML under challenging conditions, and it has met their needs. CALS is one prominent example.

The capability to encompass existing applications meant that a new protocol was required. It had to be a hypertext protocol because the CERN physicists knew that many kinds of data and documents would be needed. Their documents had to be highly modular. The new protocol would have to absorb SMTP, FTP, and NNTP, as well as other protocols. This is the type of application building that SGML supports. Nothing does hypertext as well as SGML.

 ▶▶ See "The Ways of Organizing Knowledge," p. 500
▶▶ See "How Modular Information Drives the Information Revolution," p. 513
▶▶ See "Object-Oriented Technology and the Future of SGML Development," p. 550

Object-oriented is a buzzword today, but it is actually part of the information revolution. Older Internet applications, such as Telnet, NNTP, and FTP, are not object-oriented enough to be compatible with one another. They can't deal with enough instances of different documents in a coherent way. SGML's beauty is that it's generalized and standardized, and it's completely transportable. It does not depend on any one environment. It does not get in the way of a document, no matter how odd that document is. HTML inherited part of this capability from SGML. As HTML matures, it will probably become more flexible so that it can deal with even more types of documents.

 ◀◀ See "Simplifying DTD Maintenance," p. 195

HTML, as the new markup tool, needed easy maintenance. SGML provides many easy ways to keep documents and document exchange tidy. As you learned in Chapter 11,

"Using DTD Components," there are many ways to get fancy with DTDs to help simplify maintenance. DTDs are powerful, and the applications that you build with them can be comprehensive and powerful. HTML is just such a DTD. Version 3.0 of that DTD is under review, and new extensions and features are being suggested all the time. The DTD was the perfect solution to maintaining the new Internet tool.

With so many computers hooking up to the Internet and so many organizations involved in projects about how to communicate over the Internet, the new tool needed to be independent. It needed to be free from any one type of software, hardware, language, culture, or discipline. It needed to be universal in the computer user sense. Nothing is as broad-based and portable as SGML. HTML pages appear in many different languages, run on all kinds of hardware, and are available through any type of HTML browsing software. When full-blown SGML browsing tools become as widespread as HTML browsing tools, you will be able to view even more types of files and applications.

HTML keeps borrowing capabilities from SGML to add to its own capabilities. People offer support for the HTML extensions that are not even officially released yet.

On the CD

> **Note**
>
> Several browser companies add support to their browsers for features that are not officially a part of HTML yet. One example is Microsoft's Internet Explorer, which adds some SGML capabilities to its browser. When the new HTML version 3.0 is accepted, Microsoft's Internet Explorer will already support many of those features.
>
> It also helps the people who design the standard. They receive some real-life input on what works well. It shows them what the market likes. Most browsers experienced success in the shareware market before they were offered commercially.

V

SGML and the WWW

What SGML Includes That HTML Does Not

SGML probably has many capabilities from which HTML could benefit. At the same time, some proponents of HTML want to keep many of SGML's features out because they fear that HTML will become too complicated and cluttered. Table 17.1 describes the versions of HTML.

Table 17.1 Versions of the HTML DTD	
Version	**Features**
HTML 1.0	Simple file structures for maximum transportability
HTML 2.0	Deprecates older entity structures; adds forms capability; adds more flexible linking than version 1.0
HTML 3.0	Tables; figures and math support; client-side event handling; some presentation support with linked stylesheets

What HTML 3.0 Adds

Version 3.0 of the HTML DTD adds the following features. Some are not terribly significant, but others are important.

- Easier hot zone shaping

> **Tip**
>
> A *hot zone* is a vectored portion of an image that is mapped with a specific hyperlink. Your mouse cursor changes shape while over the hot zone to indicate to you that it is linked to another resource. When you click on the hot zone, your browser jumps to the URL associated with that hot zone.

▶▶ See "DSSSL," p. 419
▶▶ See "Panorama Pro," p. 453

- The CLASS attribute for easier use with Stylesheets or DSSSL Lite
- The ALIGN attribute for mathematical equations
- The CLEAR attribute for directing text flow
- Entities for standard icons (%HTMLicons) and math symbols (%HTMLmath)
- Math and equation structures to facilitate external equation macro languages like TeX
- Entities for special symbols other than math symbols
- Powerful table support
- More extensions, including FILE (for uploading files to a server) and AUDIO (for playing and recording audio samples)

Likewise:

- The <BASE> element lets you de-reference URIs that get in your way
- The <STYLE> element lets you override stylesheets and have more flexibility
- The <RANGE> element lets you address marked ranges more easily
- The SRC attribute has been added to the <SELECT> element for support with graphical selection menus
- More flexibility is available for linking with the %linkType, %linkName, and %ToolBar entities; you can have links that are almost two-way
- More Web pages can take advantage of the %heading entity and the <TITLE> element
- The new <BANNER> element for banners at the top of the window does not scroll with the rest of the page; this helps when you are working with corporate logos and disclaimers

- Tighter SGML declarations appear throughout; older and more dangerous structures are marked `deprecated`

In the pipeline for the next revisions are:

- Support for client-side scripts that work with programming objects
- Table entry capabilities, so that visitors to a Web site can enter tables
- More flexible formatting options for TEXTAREA fields

Table Support. Tables are one of the most difficult challenges in SGML. That is because they demand a balance between format and content. If you markup the information just to satisfy the formatting requirement, you lose track of the meaning of the content. If you markup the information strictly according to content to facilitate database searches and manipulation, then you must redesign the table structures each time the meaning of the content changes. It is very difficult to strike the balance between the formatting and content requirements of tables in SGML.

▶▶ See "Handling Tables," p. 421

However, the recent CALS table model attempts to strike such a balance by giving the SGML processing system—and external search engines as well—a way of locating information in SGML tables. The key to the solution lies in relating the cells of a table to columns, and the columns to values in table headings. By assigning attributes to table formatting elements that correspond with the meaning of the content, SGML markup structures can help search mechanisms locate information in variable content tables. This powerful type of table model is included in HTML 3.0.

Equation Support. Because HTML was originally developed for science researchers, you would think it should already contain support for equations. But the fact is, equations are difficult. Not only do you require numerous public entity sets with special symbols, but you must also have an automated way of displaying them in the proper relation to each other. Nowadays, there are many public entity sets with math and equation symbols, but displaying them in the proper format still requires either extensive DTD structures, an external equation editor, or both.

▶▶ See "Handling Math and Equations," p. 424

The proposed HTML 3.0 revision adds still more math symbols and equation entities, but it also accommodates arrays for storing macros that can execute formatting tasks. This way an external language like TeX could be used to format complex equations for Web pages instead of displaying equations as graphic images, or not at all, which is so common today.

Client/Server Document Structures. The File and Audio extensions, as well as the table entry capabilities, suggest more interchange of individual document structures between server and Web client. As the difficulties of this process become resolved, paradigms for server-side SGML document validation can possibly emerge and be tested. This means that when you are using your SGML browser to research documents, servers can validate their local SGML documents and resolve conflicts—like missing DTDs, entity sets, and public declaration files—before your SGML browser returns an error to you.

Because SGML documents can be more demanding than HTML documents, they often require more external public resources for an SGML viewer to display those documents. But network connections sometimes break and make those resources unavailable, which causes your SGML browser to return an error. One solution to this problem is server-side validation, where the server can identify missing resources during its "off hours" and prevent your browser from returning errors when you need a file. The experience gained from the File and Audio extensions can be a beginning to this type of client/server interchange.

More for SGML To Add to HTML

The biggest thing SGML can add to HTML is nearly unlimited document diversity. There is no type of document that SGML cannot handle, and SGML specialists are trying to write DTDs for every type of document imaginable. The Text Encoding Initiative (TEI) and the Davenport Project are two such projects.

> ▶▶ See "SGML Requires More Thinking Up Front," p. 356
> ▶▶ See "SGML's Future on the Web," p. 379
> ▶▶ See "Current Collaborative Projects on the Web," p. 519

The trade-off is simplicity. To handle all these types of documents, you must handle all the different types of DTDs. That gets complicated. Therefore, many people don't want to add too much to the HTML standard. They do not expect that others will learn much more about SGML.

Perhaps those same people are actually surprised by how enthusiastic everyone has been about HTML. If users are that excited by one DTD, they will appreciate the flexibility to handle multiple DTDs and applications.

> **Note**
>
> The goal is to expand the HTML DTD with features from SGML. The next section of this chapter talks about SGML on the Web so that you can access the documents in SGML that HTML browsers cannot. Keep in mind the distinction between upgrading the single DTD and adding the capability to handle all DTDs.

Future upgrades to the HTML DTD might include the following SGML features:

- Elements that support real-time conversion of existing SGML documents into HTML documents. (This would actually be an application like SGM2HTML.exe, but the HTML DTD could be augmented to better host this kind of translation. Perhaps a special declaration that would locate this sort of utility on the Web could be added.)

- More HyTime functionality to facilitate interfacing with multimedia applications such as video-conferencing, interactive game playing, and cable-service features over the Internet

- Implementation features that are kept as notes in a non-local document whose location is referenced in the DTD

- Special extensions that would allow tags for different levels of security

What SGML Can Add to Web Sites

Just think of adding the capability to use more DTDs to Web sites. If one application, HTML, has become so popular so quickly, imagine how many new applications might appear—not just extensions to existing applications. Even now, you can't walk into the computer book section of a bookstore without being buried in books about HTML and the World Wide Web.

Part of the flexibility of SGML is that it can accommodate different applications and extensions. Virtual Reality Modeling Language (VRML), which describes three-dimensional geometry, makes virtual worlds easy to create and access, for example. Another application is Standard Music Description Language (SMDL), which was created to handle the time-sequencing information necessary to play audio files in real-time during Web sessions. Java is yet another application.

The Case for the Web to Upgrade to SGML

This question becomes whether the World Wide Web should upgrade the current standard from the HTML DTD to the entire superset of SGML capabilities.

If the World Wide Web is upgraded to SGML, you will be able to access all SGML documents, not just HTML documents, which make up only a small percentage of all the SGML documents available. The goal is not just to extend the HTML DTD with different features, but rather to be able to display any valid SGML document or its DTD.

Web browsers today follow a simple schedule. They perform a series of tasks. They scan the HTML document for tags, read the generic identifier (the tag), process the tag, and then look for the next tag.

The current Web browsing software processes the generic identifiers as the program code according to how the browser says it should. A <P> gets translated into a new paragraph because that is written into the program code. The programmer essentially decides how to process the tag. The current HTML DTD determines the list of tags—plus whatever the programmer throws in.

The proposal to expand SGML capability throughout the Web implies that the browser loads the DTDs and processing rules separately for each document. The DTD and stylesheets are loaded dynamically as the browser fetches the document from the server. The browser follows a new sequence of steps. It:

1. Scans the document's SGML declaration for DTD and stylesheet information and external viewer requirements.

2. Fetches and loads the DTD and stylesheet information if they are not already resident from the remote server.

3. Checks the local system for required external applications, notifies of a shortfall of resources, and initializes required programs.

4. Scans and processes each document tag by tag according to the applicable DTD and stylesheet information.

Each server on the Net is responsible for identifying a document as a valid SGML document.

This is just one possible scenario for a new generation of full SGML Web browsers. These browsers might be extensions or add-ons to existing HTML browsers—just as Panorama is now—or next generation browsers, such as Netscape and Mosaic, with SGML-aware coding built into them.

The advantage of this sort of capability is that each author can write his own DTD and stylesheet. The author—not a remote standards committee—has control over his document. If he needs tags that are not in the HTML feature set, he can create them. Moreover, if he wants to create a different document structural relationship between tags, he can. He does not have to follow the structural rulebook of a single DTD. He can create as unique a tag set as he needs. The document author—not the browser client programmer—controls the document.

This is the best way to go. Instead of trying to incorporate the ever-growing backlog of features into the existing HTML DTD, simply add the capability to process DTDs and stylesheets on-the-fly. The SGML standards exist. That is, most types of documents can be handled by existing DTDs, and new DTDs can be built for the exceptions. No one DTD can ever absorb all the possible features that will ever be required by any document.

What Is Needed

What is needed are SGML browsers or SGML add-ons to the existing HTML browsers. Add-on browsers, such as Panorama, are the obvious choice in the short term. Eventually, SGML-capable browsers will probably evolve. The requirements for this approach include:

- Creating a common way of defining stylesheets so that all stylesheets can be read by the same kind of mechanism

- Making each HTTP server responsible for having DTD and stylesheet information available for each document

- Making each HTTP server responsible for validating its SGML documents with complete tagging

- Standardizing HTTP header markup to facilitate the extra information

- Making all browsers "parser smart" so that they do not duplicate what the HTTP server already should have done, or what they should not attempt to parse

- Making all browsers support full SGML two-way links—the SGML browser must talk back to the HTML browser (under the external browser scenario)

Note

A complete proposal resides on the Internet. Check out the essay by C. M. Sperberg-McQueen and Robert F. Goldstein, "HTML to the Max." It's available at:

> **http://www.ncsa.uiuc.edu/SDG/IT94/Proceedings/Autools/
> sperberg-mcqueen/sperberg.html**

With the introduction of Panorama, the SGML browsing add-on capability exists today. Other issues will take time to resolve. Some servers will get smart sooner than others, which has always been the case with servers connected to the Internet. The richer range of SGML document interchange can provide the profit incentive for all servers to catch up.

What SGML Flexibility Can Do for Web Sites

The payoff is more document diversity and function. Likewise, SGML capability in Web sites might spawn a whole new generation of clients for document browsing. New external object-oriented applications for viewing multimedia files and programs will appear even faster. Java is one example, but the specification must be configured to be SGML-friendly. In other words, the language—or future interpreted languages like Java—must conform to the requirements of SGML-friendly servers. Developers who resist SGML will have to be compatible with SGML or find another place to play.

With an SGML Web site, you can handle multiple document types—whole new applications. That is flexibility. You can use Panorama to visit some of the Web sites listed in the SoftQuad SGML tour of the World Wide Web. Pay a visit to the site shown in figure 17.1. It's a good example. Point your Web browser (with Panorama installed) to:

http://www.oclc.org:5046/oclc/research/panorama/panorama.html

SGML adds many literary and mathematical possibilities. You rarely see footnotes in HTML documents. That is because two-way links are so difficult in HTML. Some good books already exist in SGML on the Web, as shown in figure 17.2.

Fig. 17.1

The astronomy Web site shows the same sort of eye-dazzling graphics as HTML pages, as well as all the functionality of full-blown SGML.

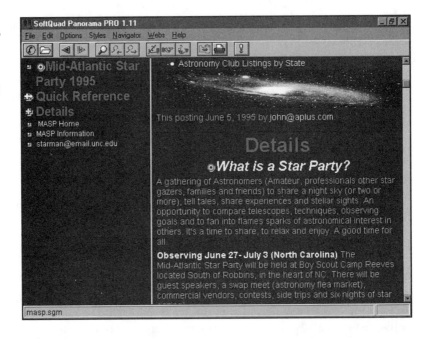

Fig. 17.2

This Web site shows how easy footnotes can work in an SGML Web document.

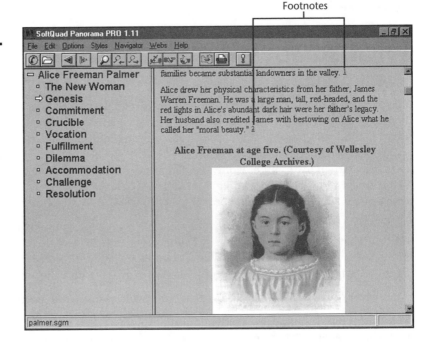

Notice the footnotes. This type of loopback is challenging in HTML. It requires a two-way link. With SGML, this isn't difficult because you can define both ends of the link and access it from either the jump point or the target point. Both windows of the corridor open equally well. With HTML, you need the Forward and Back buttons on the browser because links are not so robust or two-way as with a full-blown foot-note structure in SGML.

◀◀ See "Adding Hypertext Links to a Document," p. 160
▶▶ See "Footnotes and Endnotes," p. 427

The mathematical possibilities are also useful in SGML. The following SGML Web page, shown in figure 17.3, includes NASA research data.

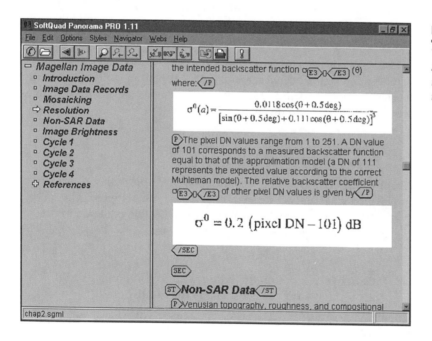

Fig. 17.3

The math capabilities of SGML Web pages appear in this NASA research report.

V

SGML and the WWW

SGML and HTML Obsolescence

If there is one truth about computers, it is this: It is only a matter of time before anything becomes obsolete. The same applies to SGML and HTML. Someone will someday create another super application that will make SGML obsolete.

HTML has already become "obsolete" twice, and the third time is in the works with the third revision to the HTML DTD. Instead of obsolescence, a better term is evolution. It is the process of outgrowing one paradigm and moving on to another one.

The next five years will probably see full SGML interchange in place on the World Wide Web. It is inevitable. Too many people are working with too many diverse types of documents to be satisfied with a single DTD. The short-term issue is how to handle the transition to full SGML implementation—either with external SGML add-ons to existing browsers, or with a new browser that is fully SGML aware.

▶▶ See "SGML's Future on the Web," p. 379

▶▶ See "Current Collaborative Projects on the Web," and "Collaboration on SGML Standards," pp. 519, 523

▶▶ See "What Can a DTD Do for Object-Oriented Development?" p. 537

Add-ons—such as Panorama, and even VRML browser add-ons and further plug-ins to existing HTML browsers—will most likely continue being popular on the Net. New SGML-aware browsers will find their way into the shareware market. This will be a test bed for new applications.

HTML will never become obsolete, but your needs will outgrow it. HTML will probably become a smaller part of the overall markup language picture. Today's tools will outgrow their current paradigms. Full SGML is the next step because it can accommodate so many other applications and diversity.

From Here...

You are just starting on the World Wide Web and SGML. It's an exciting subject. In this chapter, you learned where HTML came from and how it's related to SGML. SGML is its parent. SGML can add flexibility. You saw what SGML could do for the World Wide Web if it were incorporated as the Web's standard.

For more information, refer to the following:

- Chapter 18, "SGML's Emergence on the World Wide Web," contains a brief history of SGML on the Web and discusses what the future holds.
- Chapter 19, "Should You Upgrade to SGML?" discusses whether to upgrade your Web site to SGML.
- Chapter 20, "Practicalities of Working with SGML on the Web," discusses where to find tools and how to change your thinking.
- Chapter 21, "Integrating SGML and HTML Environments," compares the compromises and complications involved in doing SGML in an HTML world; it covers the tools that will help you the most.
- Chapter 22, "Developing for the World Wide Web," discusses what is already happening on the Web and how to make an innovative SGML Web page.

CHAPTER 18

SGML's Emergence on the World Wide Web

It's odd to talk about SGML's emergence on the World Wide Web because HTML—the document type used for the Web—is itself an SGML application. SGML is such a well kept secret that people forget where HTML comes from. That is changing rapidly as interest in SGML increases.

In this chapter, you learn:

- Why SGML is such a well kept secret
- What SGML's role on the Web is
- What SGML resources are available on the World Wide Web today
- What SGML resources will be available on the Web in the future

Why the Secret about SGML?

Although the Department of Defense uses SGML routinely, there is nothing secret about SGML. SGML, unfortunately, has a reputation as being arcane and obscure. That's only because most people haven't needed to know it. Reasons why SGML has a reputation for being inaccessible include:

- Only scholars and experts have published books about it
- There are extremely few books for newcomers to SGML
- Teachers of SGML are usually highly-paid consultants whom only large companies can afford to hire
- SGML has a confusing vocabulary; common-sounding words have specialized meanings
- Before the advent of the World Wide Web, most SGML novices had no idea what to use SGML for
- Before the advent of the World Wide Web, major corporations and institutions had used SGML for diverse applications, but most HTML users have not yet discovered related applications spawned by SGML

■ Most of the software for developing SGML documents has been expensive for users of home computers

Scholarly and Expert Clientele

It's no secret that when people are left alone to do a unique task, they develop a shorthand language to make their work easier. Consequently, SGML professionals talk about DSSSLs and FOSIs just as sailors talk about port and starboard. Likewise, SGML people talk about elements and attributes in terms of their specific meanings in the context of SGML. When you try to find sources for learning SGML, you might have trouble finding adequate material that you can understand.

Because colleges and universities have been SGML clients, publishing about the subject has often been formal. Scholarly journals have treated SGML with much interest. SGML has a certain snob appeal, which makes it difficult for novices. Even though these articles are extremely helpful once you have had SGML 101, you still need the prerequisites.

▶▶ See "Books on SGML," p. 565

These challenges—the lack of beginner-level material and the scholarly tone of SGML articles—are disappearing. More materials are appearing, and many informal sources are becoming available. As you search the World Wide Web for new information about SGML, you will find new documents in plain English every day that help you understand the intricacies of SGML. To access these resources, you need to go no further than your Internet service provider and your favorite Web browser.

> **Tip**
>
> Robin Cover's SGML home page is still the best starting point for finding information on SGML. It has terrific links to introductions to SGML, as well as links to more specific, even arcane, aspects of SGML. The home page is at:
>
> **http://www.sil.org/sgml/sgml.html**
>
> Take a look at "The Gentle Introduction to SGML" for a light but effective example of how SGML can be taught to novices.

SGML's high-level clientele has created materials primarily for other scholars and publication specialists. Now that anyone with a personal computer and Microsoft Word can become a global publisher via the World Wide Web, however, publication specialists are popping up all over the planet. Global publishing is now a popular hobby. Web pages have been appearing as often as daisies in backyard gardens during springtime. You don't have to be an expert to publish, any more than a gardener needs a Ph.D in botany to grow flowers.

It helps to have some expertise, though—especially if you're designing a large SGML installation. If you're building a small suite of HTML pages, you can learn as you go. Because you need to educate yourself in SGML—there are few courses in the subject— you need books—usable and accessible books.

The Dearth of Easy-to-Use Books on SGML

For many years, *The SGML Handbook* by Charles Goldfarb was the only source for authoritative self-study. It's still an excellent reference book. But, using it is rather like using the Oxford English Dictionary to learn English as a second language. It works better as a handy reference than as something you should read from cover to cover.

Several books have emerged to help beginning SGML students. They are listed in more detail in Appendix B, "Finding Sources for SGML Know-How." *The ABCD...SGML,* by Liora Alschuler, takes SGML out of the ivory towers and introduces it to beginners (see fig. 18.1). It's not a guide to syntax, but it does introduce theory.

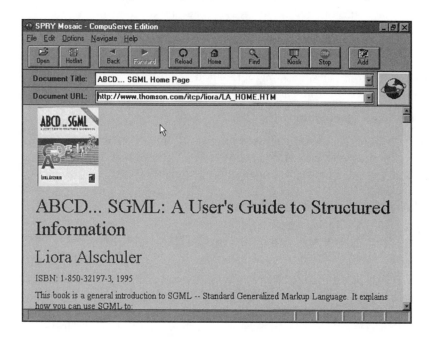

Fig. 18.1

The ABCD...SGML is one example of a new type of beginner's guide to SGML.

People from nearly every background are trying to find out more about SGML. A new book market is emerging. Just walk into any bookstore and notice how many books there are about HTML. The chances are that SGML books will become just as popular.

Expensive SGML Software

Until very recently, finding SGML software that was inexpensive and easy to use was a pipe dream. Even Microsoft's own SGML Author for Word retails for several times the cost of Word, for which the SGML client was built. This is starting to change.

The expensive SGML software is dedicated to SGML. It includes tools such as ArborText's ADEPT*Editor, SoftQuad's Author/Editor, and Electronic Book Technologies' DynaText. These software programs are at the top of their field. If there is a bell or whistle that can be rung or blown, these programs have it. You pay for that capability, of course. To buy all of the software for an SGML installation can cost thousands of dollars—far more than the average home user is willing to spend. These programs are designed for commercial customers. Just as a new UNIX workstation costs many thousands of dollars more than a new PC with a Pentium microprocessor, dedicated SGML software costs much more than an add-on program to a word processor.

Add-on SGML programs to word processors are becoming popular. They are also effective. The basic trade-off is that you need to exercise discipline in creating your SGML documents because you can introduce non-SGML characteristics into your documents more easily than with a dedicated tool.

Many add-on tools now have built-in parsing capabilities. The likelihood of creating a document that is non-conforming SGML decreases as add-on tools become smarter. One impressive tool is Near & Far Author. It closely approximates a dedicated SGML authoring tool. It is commercially available. Other tools, including Tag Wizard, are publicly available and downloadable from FTP sites. This add-on for Word is widely available as shareware from FTP sites. A registered, non-expiring version is available for a fee. You can download it from Nice Technologies page at:

http://www.nicetech.com

Expensive tools are no longer the only options for creating and maintaining an SGML installation. You can find terrific tools for about what word processors cost a few years ago. They're still not cheap, but they are much more affordable.

HTML's Many Sister Applications

SGML is a prolific parent. HTML is its most famous child. HTML is like a celebrity whom everyone knows. Now that people know what HTML can do, they want to find out what SGML's other offspring can do.

Major corporations use private SGML applications all the time, and numerous public projects use SGML applications to meet their objectives. The International Committee on Accessible Document Design (ICADD) project promises to help many visually challenged people gain access to information by automatically outputting SGML documents in Braille format. Whereas it is normally a laborious project to translate a document into Braille, SGML technology can do it automatically.

Many other public SGML projects will offer people access to the world's great sources of electronic information, such as current scientific research data, the world's finest literature, important historical texts, as well as a host of creative projects currently in progress. They include:

▶▶ See "Current Collaborative Projects on the Web" and "Collaboration on SGML Standards," pp. 519, 523

- TEI P3
- The Rainbow DTD
- The University of Michigan Modern and Middle English Collections
- Center for Electronic Texts in the Humanities (CETH)
- NASA's Magellan SGML documents from the Jet Propulsion Laboratories
- Intel's component technical documentation

More information about these projects can be learned from the following Web sites:

TEI P3: **http://www.sil.org/sgml/p3.html**

Rainbow DTD: **ftp://ftp.ifi.uio.no/pub/SGML/Rainbow/Rainbow 2.2.dtd**

Umich: **http://www.hti.umich.edu/english/**

CETH: **http://cethmac.princeton.edu/CETH/ceth.html**

NASA: **http://nssdc.gsfc.nasa.gov/planetary/products.html**

Intel: **http://techdoc.wais.net:2160/default.html**

These sister applications to HTML show you what you can do with SGML technology. Just as HTML enables a world of Web clients to share hypertext information effortlessly, other SGML applications offer their clients easy access to information in many flexible output formats.

SGML on the Web

Because HTML is an SGML application, it's impossible to discuss the history of the World Wide Web without talking about SGML. This section refers to SGML applications other than HTML. Increasingly, you can access resources on the World Wide Web that are not written in HTML.

Many of these materials were recently translated from native environments into SGML; they have resided in SGML for years. They have only recently become available to HTML Web browsers. SGML resources on the World Wide Web fall under three categories:

- Resources that reside as SGML document types other than HTML, but which can be translated into HTML on demand
- Native HTML documents already accessible through Web client software
- Documents other than HTML instances that are accessible through an SGML browser, such as SoftQuad's Panorama

SGML Resources That Translate to HTML

There is software that translates SGML document type instances into HTML instances. More often, an HTML version of a page exists alongside other document type instances. For example, both an SGML and an HTML version of the SGML Open House home page exist. The address is:

http://www.sgmlopen.org/

There's also the case in which an SGML document type instance is translated to an HTML Web page document instance on demand, the moment you access it. Common Web browser software can then view it easily. This capability is like a word processor being able to create electronic ASCII or text documents. If the only type of electronic file a word processor could create was its own proprietary format, it probably would not sell well, because only people with the same word processor could electronically share files. The capability to create an HTML file is pretty convenient because the HTML DTD is so popular and widely used. Creating an HTML document on demand is not too different from saving a word processing document as an electronic ASCII or text file.

Note

It's common among SGML people to say that saving a document as HTML is like saving a word processing document in its proprietary format rather than as a text or ASCII document. The idea behind SGML is to enhance document sharing irrespective of software or hardware.

This is a limited analogy. Nearly as many people can view an HTML document now as could view a text or ASCII document in years past. HTML browsers are nearly as commonplace as text editors nowadays. So if you save a document as an HTML document, lots of people can view it using their favorite Web clients. That's why allowing SGML document instances for various DTDs to translate on the fly into HTML is like saving a word processing document as an ASCII or text document.

 ◀◀ See "Conversion Between SGML Document Types," p. 279

Chapter 15, "Automatic versus Manual Tagging," talks about tools that translate document instances from one DTD into instances of another DTD. That's essentially what happens with these Web pages.

As with all document conversions, the trick is to maintain the original flavor of the document as it gets squeezed into the HTML mold. Some documents have many features that are not supported as well in HTML as they are in their native DTD. Documents with tables and equations, for example, frequently suffer when they are translated.

Note

Document conversion can be a challenging task since some document types require structures that cannot be supported in other DTDs. Scientific papers with extensive tables, equations, and special types of footnotes, for example, would be difficult to translate into HTML because these features are not fully supported under the HTML DTD. It is possible to translate some or many structures into comparable structures, but what is often lost is the "flavor" of the original document, or the subtle ways of presenting the data that the author originally created, even though the raw data remains intact.

To see an example of documents that are translated on demand, check out the Electronic Text Center at the University of Virginia. The address is:

http://etext.virginia.edu/modeng.browse.html

This is a wonderful resource of literature. To have full access to this electronic library, you must make special arrangements with the university, but you can read the public domain classics that are online. The texts were originally marked up according to the TEI DTD, but they translate to HTML on demand (see fig. 18.2).

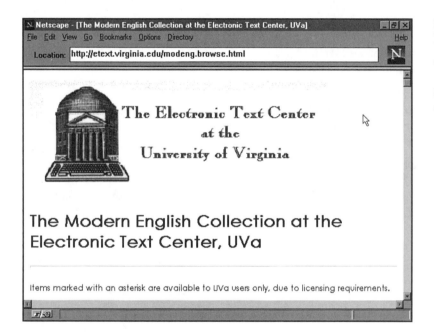

Fig. 18.2

The Electronic Text Center at the University of Virginia translates titles from TEI instances into HTML.

The advantage of translating into HTML on demand might be short-lived. In the long run, many of these documents will outlive their original medium, just as the works of Shakespeare have outlived their original published volumes. By then, SGML will be more common than HTML.

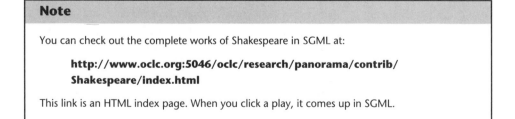

Note

You can check out the complete works of Shakespeare in SGML at:

**http://www.oclc.org:5046/oclc/research/panorama/contrib/
Shakespeare/index.html**

This link is an HTML index page. When you click a play, it comes up in SGML.

Converting to HTML is popular now, primarily because of the dearth of native SGML Web browsers. Panorama enables your Web browser to read and parse SGML document instances under their native DTDs. This is useful because you are not confined to a single DTD. You can handle tables and equations—or any other challenge—with all the flexibility of SGML.

Native HTML Documents as SGML Resources

Even though HTML is not full-featured enough to satisfy everyone, it is still a powerful markup language. It's more than adequate for the vast majority of Web authors. The World Wide Web owes its success, in large measure, to the simplicity of HTML. HTML was never intended to be the be-all and end-all. The founders of the Web knew that there would be trade-offs under HTML.

The Bandwidth Dilemma. An important controversy concerning HTML has to do with the original purpose of HTML and its current adaptations.

When the Web became popular in 1993, the bandwidth available over the Internet appeared to be a limitation. The people who started the Web understood the demands placed on the Internet's resources. Their documents, therefore, didn't occupy great amounts of bandwidth.

The old saying that one picture is worth a thousand words has received a new twist on the Internet: "One picture may be worth a thousand words, but it's also worth 100 times the bandwidth." The point is that pictures take vastly more resources to transmit than text. In the time that it takes a Web server to transmit a one megabyte picture, it can transmit 100 times as much content in textual form (assuming that picture were worth 1000 words). That's why some Web "purists" complain about the heavy graphics on so many Web pages. Although the speed of a typical modem has improved since 1993, the relative speed of the actual server may have declined. Much more is demanded of Web servers and hardware today because of the heavy graphics and multimedia resources being transferred over networks.

Note

Bandwidth refers to the amount of space and time that a file takes up in a network's connection lines. A bigger file takes up more space and time when it's transferred, whereas a smaller file takes up less space and time. Hence, smaller files require less bandwidth than bigger files. They also require less attention from the network's servers than do bigger files.

Bandwidth becomes a measurement of bytes or kilobytes per second or minutes. The longer a server must take on a single file, the fewer files it can deal with from other network clients. Higher average bandwidth makes a network relatively less efficient than networks with lower average bandwidth, as measured by the number of network clients served.

Loading up documents with multimedia content in proprietary and specialized formats defeats the purpose of SGML, whose goal is to enable document interchange among people irrespective of their software or hardware. It's not that SGML doesn't want to do the job. The problem is that people have not agreed on a single common standard for handling graphics. In fact, there are too many standards, most of which are not readily available on all hardware platforms. For example, the GIF—the proprietary Graphical Interchange Format popularized by CompuServe—works well as a standard graphics file format for PC users, but it isn't good for someone on a Sparc station who doesn't have a UNIX-compatible viewer that handles GIF. Incompatibility is a bigger problem on the Web than many people imagine.

Standardization versus Innovation. Another hotbed of controversy is the trade-off between standardization and innovation. The idea is that if everyone follows standards religiously, how could you ever introduce anything new and wonderful into the mix by way of innovation and experimentation?

Consider Netscape, for example. This powerful Web browser supports extensions that are not a legal part of HTML, which enables creators of Web documents to add special features that Netscape can exploit. This strategy has made Netscape an extremely successful provider of Web software and server resources. Many Web pages now have a statement at the bottom that reads "Powered by Netscape." The special non-HTML features—such as the `<BLINK>` element—usually don't bother non-Netscape browsers, but only Netscape can interpret the tag. When you use Netscape, the documents look attractive. Other browsers ignore the special features.

> **Tip**
>
> Even though adding special non-HTML enhancements to your documents invalidates them as HTML document instances or valid SGML, you can sometimes still get them to parse. People often go to great lengths to parse semi-HTML documents as valid SGML document instances. The best policy is to stick with valid HTML. It's a habit that will keep you safe and on good terms with Web masters and Web clients.

Because these documents are customized for Netscape, they are no longer valid SGML document instances. They do not parse as instances of the HTML DTD. So now you have all these documents in Web space that are not valid SGML documents. They sacrifice transportability and universality for innovative features.

No one has the best answer to the dilemma of balancing innovation and standardization. Throughout the history of the computer age, sharing has been sacrificed when the marketplace has been flooded with proprietary technology. People and companies that can't upgrade to that technology are left out in the cold because now their hardware or software is no longer compatible. This approach promises profits to the innovators of new technology, but it causes incompatibility problems for people unwilling or unable to purchase the latest technology. Standardization and cooperative innovation are necessary for technology to advance. Competition must be ameliorated by cooperation.

Keep in mind that your creative decisions affect not only yourself, but also every Web server that must transmit your documents and every Web client whose users click the appropriate link. The world is interconnected. When you make a document public, you must keep it standardized and accessible. If you customize a document to make it more innovative and creative, it's no longer fully public.

SGML Resources as Non-HTML Document Instances

The advent of SGML browsers for the World Wide Web has introduced a wealth of native SGML documents that can now be viewed in their intended format and structure. Although HTML is useful and workable, you can use other SGML DTDs just as easily with an SGML-capable browser.

 ▶▶ See "Collaboration on SGML Standards," p. 523

SGML-capable browsers open the door to a wealth of document content. You don't have to settle for HTML's limited support for tables or equations for your Web documents; you can write your own customized DTDs to support whatever document features you need. The same goes for other special features—graphics, music, Braille translation, newspaper columns, and so on. Simply make sure that your DTDs and documents are valid SGML by parsing them completely and by making them public so that the SGML browser can locate them and process them. If there are any applicable output specifications or stylesheets, they must be made publicly available as well. Also make public any additional processing software (on all possible platforms) for handling special file types, such as music or Braille.

This type of SGML document is new on the Web. SGML documents have been available via FTP for some time, but you had to browse them offline. Only now is it becoming possible to easily browse them online as if they were HTML documents. The next section discusses the variety of SGML documents available.

SGML Resources Available on the Web

After you obtain an SGML browser, take a tour of SGML documents in their native DTDs. Native DTDs mean non-HTML DTDs, and non-HTML document instances on the Web are rather new. This tour starts at:

http://www.ncsa.uiuc.edu/SDG/Software/Mosaic/WebSGML.sgml

Figure 18.3 shows what this home page looks like. It has links to a variety of document instances for SGML DTDs.

By following these links, you can see that when you break the mold for HTML, different types of document features become easier and more feasible. Figure 18.4 shows you how well tables can be handled by using a DTD other than HTML.

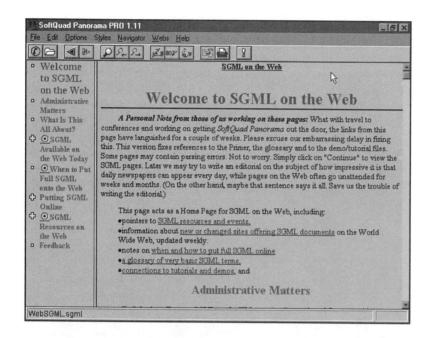

Fig. 18.3

The SGML Tour of the Web is a starting point for a tour of different SGML document types—not just HTML.

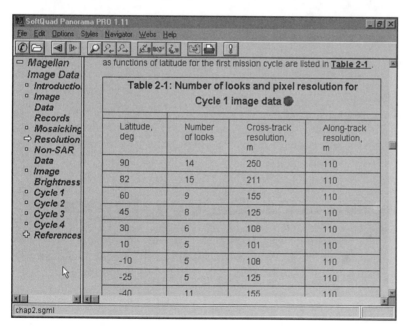

Fig. 18.4

This SGML Web page illustrates the advantages of not being limited to one SGML document type. The tables here are done according to the AAP DTD.

V

SGML and the WWW

Figure 18.5 shows a document that HTML could not handle as well as another SGML DTD. The equations would challenge an HTML author.

Fig. 18.5

HTML could not handle this SGML document type well. The equations are from the AAP DTD.

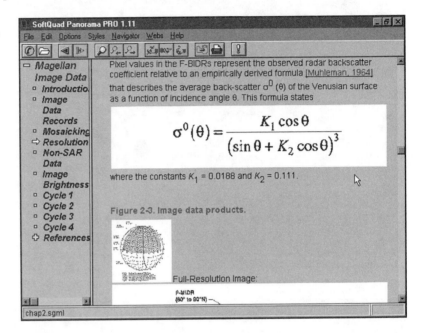

Publishing on the World Wide Web is still a new phenomenon, and much experimentation is going on. Only in the last several months have people been customizing the backgrounds of home pages with different wallpapers. This feature is not strictly SGML, and it is not supported by all browsers. However, it shows that authors want to experiment. As more SGML browsers appear on the market, more authors of HTML Web pages are becoming interested in authoring more than one type of SGML document.

SGML Resources Available on the Web in the Future

The creativity evident on the World Wide Web leads to valuable resources. Judging by some of today's projects, the SGML resources of the future will be abundant.

▶▶ See "Current Collaborative Projects on the Web," p. 519

Too many projects are in progress to discuss in detail, but some of the most down-to-earth ones have been the most helpful. TEI, for example, has provided useful DTDs that are currently in use. The Modern English Electronic Library at the University of Michigan uses the TEI P3 DTD, and all those wonderful classics are now available as SGML documents.

Scientific and Technical Data

Scientific literature will become more accessible. These documents can be more challenging to make accessible than straight text. DTDs have been made and are continuously being upgraded. TEI is again an example of this. Novell and Intel have made numerous technical documents accessible to the Web; they are both part of the SGML Tour that Panorama starts you off on (refer to fig. 18.3.) These documents require full SGML—even more so than literary documents—because of their intense use of tables, equations, and graphics.

SGML will enable even more scientific and technically oriented graphics than HTML currently does. The trouble with graphics is that there are so few formats that translate easily for all platforms, including PC, Mac, and UNIX. With SGML's use of stylesheet and resource grabbing from locations around the Web, these compatibility issues might be minimized.

Stylesheets

Another bright prospect for the future of SGML has to do with alternative stylesheets for home pages. There is a large appetite for graphics on Web pages. A Web user today has little choice in how to view Web pages that are full of graphics. He can turn off inline graphics and see no graphics, or he can leave it on and wait while his browser loads enormous quantities of graphics on some pages. Web authors under SGML can configure multiple stylesheets for the same page, each offering the Web client a different viewing alternative. The same page can be configured with heavy graphics, medium graphics, or few graphics, depending on the Web client's preference and the connection speed. Every Web page then becomes several pages; each page has its own stylesheet. Both the client and the author are happy.

The debate between standardization and innovation will continue to escalate, but SGML's use of multiple DTDs and stylesheets may help. Because SGML allows more flexibility than HTML, ambitious Web authors can attempt more daring feats that do not defy standards. Netscape, for example, does not adhere to the HTML standard—and it is wildly successful. Stylesheets and flexibilities with DTDs would seem to answer many of the demands for further creativity. The special Netscape-enhanced tags, like <BLINK> and others, could be supported under full SGML without invalidating the HTML standard, and various stylesheets could support many of the other graphic-oriented Netscape innovations, all without violating the international standard. As full SGML becomes more popular, the flexibility that SGML offers can only be exploited by following standards carefully. Otherwise, accessibility is compromised.

Multimedia and Hyper-G

Hyper-G is an exciting new technology being developed in Graz, Austria, at Graz University of Technology and the Institute for HyperMedia Systems of Joanneum Research, with aid from many other organizations all over the world. It's called a second-generation networked hypermedia information system that is compatible with other network protocols, such as http. It offers highly robust hyperlink consistency, especially with multimedia documents, with a UNIX-like security system and gateways to the World Wide Web. It's possible in the future that Hyper-G and HyTime technologies will operate together cooperatively on the Web through a single browser. Right now, Amadeus and Harmony (the Hyper-G browsers for the Windows and UNIX platforms, respectively) do not support full-blown SGML or HyTime, but they do provide access to HTML resources on the Web.

Multimedia content will become even more important as SGML becomes more popular and as bandwidth increases on the Net. HyTime will become less private, and the price of HyTime applications will drop as demand for them encourages more developers to add to the supply of HyTime applications. Maybe HyTime and Java will even cooperate. Innovation in this area could be fruitful. The standardization that HyTime offers might add more universality to Java applications.

From Here...

You have learned about the history of SGML on the World Wide Web and why SGML has a reputation as being inaccessible and arcane. You saw some of the newly available SGML sources. You also have an idea what the future of the Web holds for SGML.

For more information, refer to the following:

- Chapter 19, "Should You Upgrade to SGML?" discusses the pros and cons of developing documents under other DTDs.

- Chapter 20, "Practicalities of Working with SGML on the Web," talks about what you have to do when you become part of the dedicated SGML frontier; it covers tools, planning, and the flexibility necessary for maintaining an SGML Web site.

- Chapter 21, "Integrating SGML and HTML Environments," discusses compromises and complications involved in creating SGML documents for the World Wide Web; it talks about tools for authoring SGML Web pages.

- Chapter 22, "Developing for the World Wide Web," talks at length about the origins and the destiny of SGML on the World Wide Web; it offers advice on how to add real value to the Web by creating SGML pages.

- Part VII, "SGML Tools and Their Uses," discusses the software and hardware necessary to author SGML documents for your enterprise.

- Part VIII, "Becoming an Electronic Publisher," explains some of the mysteries of the information revolution.

CHAPTER 19

Should You Upgrade To SGML?

The World Wide Web has brought more attention to SGML than anything else. Most WWW documents (other than bit-mapped graphics) are SGML documents that use the HTML DTD. If you're using HTML, you're using SGML, although there's much more to SGML. On the other hand, most Web browsers don't support any other DTDs besides HTML. This means that all the other SGML data in the world can't be browsed easily on the Web. (But take heart! You'll learn about several solutions in this chapter.)

This chapter begins by telling you how SGML relates to HTML and what's happening with SGML on the Web already. Then you learn about the practical issues: how to decide whether to go with HTML or SGML for your Web data, and how you can take advantage of each one's strengths and avoid their weaknesses:

In this chapter, you will learn how to:

- Describe the relationship between HTML and SGML
- Understand what data is already in SGML
- Understand why this data is in SGML, not HTML
- Decide whether your data belongs in SGML
- Overcome the challenges of upgrading
- Benefit the most from upgrading

How HTML and SGML Relate

People often say that HTML is a subset of SGML. This is nearly right, but it's a bit more complicated. Technically, HTML is an *application* of SGML. This means that it's really a DTD, a set of tags and rules for where the tags can go. SGML is a language for composing DTDs that fit various kinds of documents. There are many applications, and therefore many DTDs (HTML, the DTD for the World Wide Web, is probably the best known one).

You already know that a DTD is always designed for some particular type of document: business letters, aircraft manuals, poetry, and so on. An important question when deciding whether to put some data in HTML or another SGML DTD is "What kind of documents is the HTML DTD meant for?"

Here is a sample of the kinds of tags that exist in HTML (the new version 2.1 of HTML is being finalized even as I write, and further improvements are still coming, so this list will improve a bit very soon). First, HTML has a lot of tags for marking up common kinds of structures (all of which are not listed here):

- Headings: H1, H2...
- Divisions (the actual big containers like chapters and sections, that *contain* headings and other data): DIV
- Basic document blocks (paragraphs, block quotations, footnotes, various kinds of lists): P, BQ, FN, OL, UL, DL
- Tables and equations (only in newer browsers): these involve many different element types
- Text emphasis: EMPH, STRONG
- Hypermedia links: A, IMG
- Interactive forms: INPUT, TEXTAREA

HTML also includes several element types that express formatting rather than structure. These pose some portability problems, but they can be useful in cases where you simply *must* have a certain layout:

- Font changing, such as for getting bold and italic type: B, I
- Various extensions that work only with certain browsers: BLINK, FONT, etc.
- Forced line breaks (most used in code samples, "pre-formatted text," and similar examples): BR, PRE
- Drawing rules, boxes, and so on: HR

From the selection of element types, you can easily see the kinds of documents HTML is best for: fairly simple documents with sections, paragraphs, lists, and the like. In fact, most of the HTML element types are pretty generic; nearly every DTD has paragraphs and lists in it. One place where HTML excels, however, is in linking. Although it only has a couple of element types for links, they can use URLs to point to any data anywhere in the world. For more details on HTML, you may want to read Que's *Special Edition Using HTML*.

So, why use other SGML DTDs? The main reason is that not all documents consist of only these basic kinds of elements. Whenever you run across some other kind of element, you have to "cheat" to express it in HTML. A very common example is the level-6 heading element in HTML (H6). Because the first browsers formatted H6 headings in small caps and there was no text emphasis tag that would give the same effect, people got in the habit of using H6 to mean "small caps." Of course, some people also use H6 as a heading, and many people use it both ways.

This works fine—until something changes. Suppose that a browser comes along that lets users adjust the text styles for different tags, for example. Someone changes H6 to look like something besides small caps, and everyone who was counting on small caps is surprised. Sometimes this won't matter, but it might; what if the user wants all the headings big and all the text emphasis small? Or what if the user is blind? When his browser runs across an H6 element, it wouldn't do any good for his browser to put it in large type, so instead maybe its computer-generated voice says "section" and reads the heading loudly; in the same way, maybe such a browser is not supposed to do anything special for small caps.

The most important problem, though, is that you might want to use the tags for something completely different than formatting later. What if a browser is really friendly and makes automatic outlines by grabbing all the headings? Or what if you want to do a search, but only for text in headings (you might want to do that because if a word occurs in a heading, it's probably more important than if it just occurs in the main text)?

Using a tag because it gets the right formatting effect is always a problem, usually a delayed one; it works fine when you do it, but the "gotcha" comes later. People working with the distant ancestors of SGML made up a name for this: "tag abuse syndrome."

The only thing to do about tag abuse syndrome is to make sure you have the right types of tags available. Few people would use H6 for small caps if there were a more appropriate emphasis element available. That is exactly why SGML is important for the Web; a lot of documents contain elements that don't fit into the HTML set. Here are some kinds of tags that aren't available in HTML:

- Poetry and drama: STANZA, VERSE, SPEECH, ROLES
- Computer manual-speak: COMMAND, RESPONSE, MENUNAME
- Bibliographies, card catalogs, and the like: AUTHOR, TITLE, PUBLISHER, EDITION, SUBJECT-CODE, DATE
- Back-of-book indexes: ENTRY, SUBENTRY, PAGEREF
- Dictionaries: ENTRY (of many levels), PRONUNCIATION, ETYMOLOGY, DEFINITION, SAMPLE-QUOTATION

This problem will continue to exist even though later versions of HTML add many useful new tags—no one can predict all the kinds of documents that people will invent. SGML provides the solution, because when you need a new kind of element, you can create it. You can avoid problems by trying not to force every kind of document into a single mold (just as you don't try to make a single vehicle do the work of a bicycle, car, and Mack truck).

From time to time as you tag a document, you might feel as if the right tag just isn't available. How often this happens is a good way to tell how well the DTD you're using fits the document you're working with. If the fit is too poor, the time may come to extend the DTD, or switch to an entirely different one—though this shouldn't happen very often. It's better to use the right DTD for each job than to force-fit; to be able to do this, users must have software that handles SGML generically rather than forcing data into any one mold.

> **Tip**
>
> Moving data from one DTD to another can sometimes be easy. It helps to have at least a little skill with some programming tool like Perl, as well as SGML. Even so, the job is not always easy. If the two DTDs use similar structures and mostly differ in tag names, it may be as easy as running some global changes to rename tags. If you aren't using much SGML minimization, non-SGML tools like Perl or even a word processor's "Search and Replace" command may be enough, because all the tags are right there: you can search for a string like <P> and change it to <PARA> (but remember to allow for tags with attributes!). On the other hand, if you're using a log of omitted tags or changing to a very different DTD where you have to add or subtract containers, re-order things, and so on, it can be a lot more work.
>
> There are also special tools available to help transform SGML documents in this way. Among them are OmniMark from Software Exoterica, the SGML Hammer from SoftQuad, and Balise from AIS.

What Data Is Already in SGML?

A lot of data is already available in SGML, and a lot of that has already gone onto the Web. Because SGML was adopted first by large organizations (after all, they had the biggest document problems to solve), those organizations have been able to make a lot of data available.

From Commercial Publishers

Many publishers are moving to SGML for all their documents. Some want to preserve their investment so they can reproduce books even after the latest wiz-bang word processor is history. Some want to simplify the data-conversion they do when authors send in their drafts. Some want to support new forms of multimedia delivery, information retrieval, and so on.

One of the earliest success stories for SGML in publishing is the many-volume Oxford English Dictionary (OED). For many decades, the entire OED used rooms full of 3x5 cards. But in the early 1980s, the publishers decided to go electronic. They worked with Waterloo University and developed sophisticated conversion programs to get the whole dictionary into SGML. One of the hardest tasks was teasing apart 25 or so different uses for italics in the scanned text: book titles, foreign words, emphasis, word origins, and so on. This is just a severe case of tag-abuse syndrome (one they couldn't avoid, since they had to work from scanned text, and scanners can't tell you much about distinctions other than font choice). Success in this conversion made it much easier to keep the dictionary up to date; it's also resulted in a great electronic edition that can be searched in very sophisticated ways. Because of the up-front tagging work, if you ask for all the words with Latin origins, you don't also get all the places where "Latin" happens to show up as an emphatic word or in a book title.

Another major SGML publishing project is the Chadwyck-Healey *English Poetry Database*. This project is collecting all English poetry from the earliest stages of English up to 1900 and publishing it on a series of CD-ROMs with sophisticated search software. Some of it everyone has read, some of it only an English professor could love—but it's all going to be there, in SGML.

Journal publishers have recently started using SGML to speed up the review and publishing cycle (see fig. 19.1). Platform and format independence make it easier to ship files to the many people involved. The fact that all kinds of software—from authoring to online and paper delivery systems—can now deal with SGML also makes it a good common format for them.

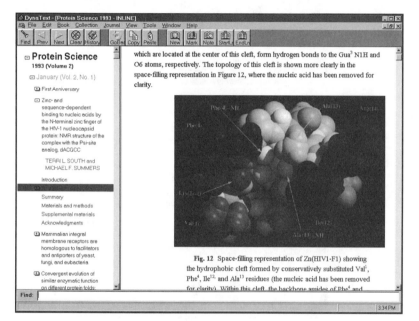

Fig. 19.1

SGML is being used for a variety of sophisticated documents, including technical and scientific journals. Screen shot courtesy of Lightbinders, San Francisco (http://lbin.com).

From Computer Vendors

When computer companies started using SGML, SGML won the battle. Now that the publications and documentation departments right inside computer companies are demanding good SGML tools, the need is obvious to those companies. When software companies notice a problem, there's a nice side benefit: they not only notice, but can do something about it, and so new tools are beginning to appear.

Silicon Graphics, Inc. was one of the first companies to move its documentation to SGML, calling its system "IRIS InSight" (see fig. 19.2). SGI makes the high-end graphics workstations that bring us a lot of special effects. Novell moved too, and reportedly saves millions of dollars (and trees) per year by shipping NetWare documentation on CD-ROM rather than paper. Novell used SGML to its advantage in moving to the Web; in only a few days, a single person set up over 110,000 pages of NetWare documentation for Web delivery, using a Web server that can convert SGML portions to

HTML on demand. The data is still stored and maintained in generic SGML using its original DTDs, and so is always up-to-date without a complicated conversion and update process.

Sun Microsystems, AutoDesk, Phoenix (of BIOS fame), and many others also use SGML heavily, and there are reports that Microsoft does the same in-house. As one SGML Web publisher put it, a lot of the information you *have to* have is going onto the Web in SGML. IBM started using a predecessor of SGML, called GML, long ago, and may have more data in SGML-like forms than anyone.

Fig. 19.2

SGI customers access documentation using the IRIS InSight system.

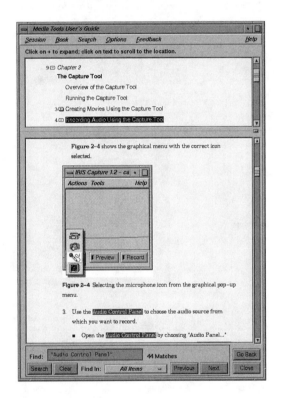

From Libraries and Universities

Libraries already use a standard computer form for card-catalog information, called MARC (MAchine-Readable Catalog). This is not SGML, but the DTD for an SGML equivalent is being worked out right now. SGML is also being used for *finding aids*, which are the equivalent of catalogs for unique items like special collections of archives, personal papers, and manuscripts. The University of California at Berkeley's library is spearheading this work, quietly converting huge numbers of finding aids into SGML and working with many other libraries to refine a DTD. They can (and do) deliver this information easily on any medium from CD-ROMs to the Web (see fig. 19.3).

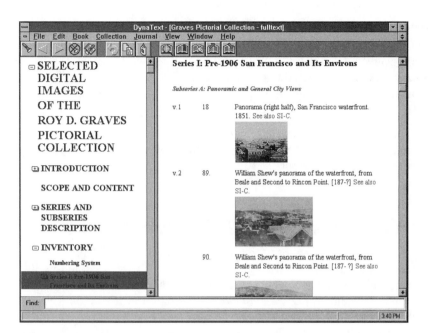

Fig. 19.3

Berkeley and many other libraries have cooperated to develop the "Encoded Archival Description" DTD to help give easy access to a wide variety of manuscript and other collections.

Scholars and teachers also have put a lot of information into SGML and are starting to move it to the Web. The Brown University Women Writers' Project is collecting and coding as many English documents as possible from female authors prior to 1950. Several theological tools, such as CDWord, provide access to sacred texts, commentaries, and the like. And the complete works of philosophers as varied as Nietzsche, Wittgenstein, Pierce, and Augustine are in various stages of conversion to SGML.

The Oxford Text Archive and the Rutgers/Princeton Center for Electronic Texts in the Humanities are developing large literary collections in SGML; some parts are already available on the Web. Many individuals also encode and contribute their favorite literature, as part of research or teaching.

From Industry

High-tech industries moved to SGML very early because of its power for managing large documents. Aircraft and similar industries use many subcontractors; assembling complete manuals using parts from a variety of sources is hard unless you set up some standards. So the aircraft manufacturers and the airlines got together and set up a DTD. The companies that make central-office telephone equipment have done the same.

Not long after these industries went to SGML, the automobile and truck industries did also; companies like Ryder and FreightLiner have improved their speed of repairs and overall reliability using SGML. Other success stories abound in power companies, copier and other office machine companies, and many others.

V

SGML and the WWW

From Government and the International Community

They say the U.S. government is the world's biggest publisher, and it's probably true. The Patent Office puts out about 109M of new patent text per week (not counting figures); the Congressional Record adds a lot too. Both of these are moving to SGML, though it's a challenge because they must be very careful not to disrupt current practices or delay delivery during the transition.

Internationally, there is much interest in SGML in Europe, and increasing interest in Asia. The International Organization for Standardization (ISO, despite the English word-order), which put SGML together in the first place, uses it for publishing some of its standards.

Why Is This Data in SGML, Not HTML?

Because of all these users, there is a lot of SGML data out there. Why did all these companies choose SGML instead of HTML? Mostly because it's a generic solution; it lets them use tags appropriate to the kinds of documents each one cares about. This means describing the document parts themselves rather than how they should appear on today's output device. This generic approach is why SGML data outlasts the programs that process it, and that can mean huge long-term savings. HTML can do this for a limited number of cases, but not in general. There are other reasons for using SGML:

- *Scalability*. SGML has features, such as entity management, that make it easier to work with large documents. A printed airplane manual often outweighs the plane itself, and the documentation system better not choke.

- *Validation*. SGML's ability to check whether documents really conform to the publisher's rules is important in industry, especially in the current world of liability lawsuits. However, validating a document doesn't ensure it makes sense, any more than spelling correctly ensures it makes sense.

- *Information retrieval*. Big documents are hard to work with, and SGML tagging puts in the "hooks" you need to make search and retrieval software work much better. True containers for big organizing units are especially helpful here, like CHAPTER and SECTION instead of just H1 and H2.

- *Version management*. High-tech manuals and ancient literature share a common problem because they come in many versions; it can make a big difference which one you get. Although not a true version-management system by itself, SGML has features that form a good foundation for one (such as marked sections, attributes, modularity, boilerplating, and so on).

- *Customizable presentations*. This relates to version management, too. Because SGML doesn't predefine formatting and layout, delivery tools can customize the display for each user as needed—show extra hints for novices, hide secret information, and so on. This is what Ted Nelson (he invented the term *hypertext*) calls *stretchtext*: the document should smoothly expand and contract to match the user's interests.

■ *Access for print disabled.* Again because SGML gets away from formatting details, it is easy to convert SGML documents for delivery in Braille, via text-to-speech converters, and so on. Several books have been converted this way in record time.

All these advantages apply to paper production, online delivery, and information retrieval. But once you lay out pages for print, most of these advantages disappear; once all the lines and page breaks are set, the page representation takes over and getting back to the structure is very difficult.

Five Questions To Ask about My Data

Given all the advantages of generic SGML for big projects, yet all the simplicity of HTML for simple ones, how do you decide which way to go? There are five questions you can ask that will help you choose.

What Functionality Do I Need?

If your documents fit the HTML model and consist mostly of the kinds of elements HTML provides, HTML is probably a good choice. This is especially true if the documents are also small (tens of pages, not thousands). But if you have big documents or documents with special structures or elements, SGML will take you a lot farther.

If you need to do information retrieval, SGML is also better. You can search HTML, but you can't easily pin down just *where* hits are. This is because the HTML tags don't divide data up as finely as you can with full SGML, and HTML doesn't typically tag large units such as sections (the tags have only been added in the latest revision, and they're still optional).

Finally, if you need to deliver in more forms than just the Web, you should consider SGML. Tools are available to turn SGML not only into Web pages, but into paper pages, most kinds of word processor files, CD-ROM publications, Braille, and many other forms. This can all be done with HTML in theory, but it's harder in practice.

Do I Need Flexible Data Interchange?

SGML eases data interchange in several ways. Because it helps you avoid using tags for things they don't quite fit, your data is easier to move to other systems, especially if the tags can take advantage of finer distinctions. For example, if you tag book titles, emphasized words, and foreign words as <I> in HTML, you have a problem when you move to something that can distinguish book titles and emphasis, such as a program to extract and index bibliographies. If you make the finer distinctions, you have a choice later whether to treat the items the same or differently.

Computers are pretty bad at sorting things into meaningful categories when they look the same. You almost need artificial intelligence to decide which italic text is a book title and which is something else. The good news is that computers are really good at the opposite task; if you've already marked up book titles and emphasized words as different things (say, <TI> and <EMPH>), it's no problem at all for a computer to show them both as italic.

Because of this, down the road interchange is much easier if you break things up early and make as many distinctions as practical. On the other hand, each distinction may be a little extra work, so you need to balance long-term flexibility versus how much time and effort you can put in up front. To figure out this balance, be sure to consider just how long you think your data will last (you're safest to at least double your first guess) and how important your data is.

Importance and lifespan don't always go together. Stock quotes are pretty important when they're current, but after a year, only a few specialists ever look at them. At the other extreme, some literature that started out on stone tablets thousands of years is still important. Where does your data fit?

How Complex Are my References and Links?

HTML has great strength as a linking system. This is mostly because URLs can point to any data in any format, and browsers provide a very convenient way to get any of that data. *URLs* (the most commonly available way of identifying information on the Net, though more advanced ways are coming) can get data via all these protocols (Web-speak for "methods") and others:

Protocol	Description
ftp	The data is copied down to your local machine.
http	The data is formatted and shown in the browser itself (or by a helper application for graphics, sound, video, and so on).
e-mail	Communication works like electronic mail.
news	Postings from network newsgroups are retrieved and presented.

HTML does all of this with only a few tags, mainly <A> and <IMG>. This means that the linking *itself* is not very complex or sophisticated, even though the data that the links point to is. For example, both <A> and <IMG> are *one-way links*; they live somewhere in document A and point to document B, as shown in figure 19.4. But if you're in document B, you don't know that document A exists or that it points to you.

If you click a link and travel from document A to document B, most browsers will remember where you were and provide you with a Back button to return to the same document (though perhaps not to the same *place* in that document). That's an important feature, but not at all the same as also being able to get from document B to document A in the first place—with true *two-way links* you know while in document B that there's a link from document A.

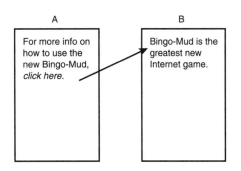

Fig. 19.4

The HTML <A> tag makes one-way links.

> **Note**
>
> It's also hard with HTML links to go from document A to a specific place inside document B because URLs normally point to whole files. HTML does give rudimentary support for getting a whole file *and then* scrolling it to some element with a given "name" (like an SGML ID). This is useful, but doesn't help much with larger SGML documents. With large documents, the problem of having to wait for the whole thing to download (even though you only need a small portion of it) becomes very important.
>
> Link precision will probably improve in the future with conventions for a URL to give not only a file, but an ID or other location within a file, and to use this information to optimize downloading, not just scrolling. In fact, some servers already let you add a suffix to a URL to pick out a certain portion. For example, a server could let you put an SGML ID on as if it were a query, and then just serve up the element with that ID (including all its subelements, of course):
>
> ```
> <a href="http://xyz.org/docs/book.sgm?id=chap4">
> ```

Though you can simulate a *bi-directional* (or two-way) link in HTML, you have to do it by creating two links (one in document A and one in document B). This poses a couple of problems; the most important one is that you have to actually go in and change both document A and document B, so you can't just do this between any two documents you choose. Even if you can get at both documents to insert the links in the first place, it's easy to forget to update one "half" of the link when you update the other. Such links gradually tend to break.

What do other hypermedia systems do about this? The best ones, SGML-based or not, provide a way to create links that live completely outside of documents, in a special area called a *web* (that name may change now that it's popular as a shorthand for the World Wide Web). In that case, the picture looks more like figure 19.5. Many systems provide both methods, not just one or the other.

Fig. 19.5

An external web lets you create two-way links.

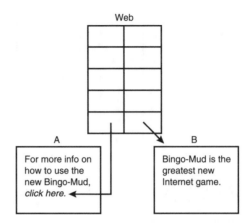

This is a much more powerful system, and you can do it with a number of SGML linking methods, such as HyTime and the TEI guidelines, and some recent systems like Hyper-G. It seems to have originated with the Brown University InterMedia system. Doing links this way has these benefits:

- Because links live outside the documents, anyone can create them without needing permission to change the documents themselves. You can even link in and out of documents on CD-ROM or other unchangeable media. This is especially important for big data like video, because it's still much more effective to keep local copies on CD-ROM or similar media than to download huge files every time they need to be viewed.

- Because documents aren't touched every time a link is attached, they can't be accidentally trashed. Most HTML links have this advantage at one end since the destination document needn't be touched. But the only way for HTML to point to a particular place *inside* a destination document is via an ID; so to do that you may have add one, and in that case HTML loses even this one-ended advantage.

- Because a set of links is a separate thing, you can collect links into useful groups and ship them, turn them off or on, etc. Siskel's and Ebert's links to movie-makers' home pages can be in two separate webs, so you can choose to see either or both.

If you don't need this more sophisticated linking, HTML's links may be just fine. Otherwise, you need to go beyond HTML and beyond what current HTML browsers can do. The good news is that such a web can still use URLs and related methods to do the actual references, so you can keep the power HTML gets from them. You can add URL support (or even the `<A>` and `<IMG>` tags themselves) to another DTD that packages them up to provide greater capabilities.

> **Note**
>
> TEI and HyTime links provide a very good way to express this kind of linking. We talk about them quite a bit more in Chapter 21.

What Kind of Maintenance Is Needed?

There are two areas where HTML files run into maintenance problems that SGML can help with:

- Links tend to break over time.
- HTML itself changes through improvements such as new tags.

While the URLs and other identifiers that HTML uses for links are very powerful, the most common kind right now, the URL itself, is also fragile. A *URL* names a specific machine on the Internet, and a specific directory and file name on that machine (technically, this doesn't have to be true, but in practice it almost always is). This method has an obvious maintenance problem: what if the file moves? A URL-based link can break in all these ways:

- The owner moves or renames the file, or any of its containing directories (say, to install a bigger disk with a different name).
- The owner creates a new version of the file in the same place and moves the old one elsewhere (there's an interesting question about which version old links *should* take you to, but you needn't get into that here).
- The owner's machine gets a new domain name on the Internet (for example if someone else trademarks the name the owner had).
- The owner moves to a new company or school and takes all of his data with him.

The Internet Engineering Task Force (IETF) is working hard on *Uniform Resource Names* or *URNs*, which let links specify names instead of specific locations. This is like specifying a paper book by author and title, as opposed to "the fifth book on the third shelf in the living room at 153 Main Street." URNs will make links a lot safer against simple changes like the ones just mentioned.

SGML provides a similar solution for part of the problem already, through names called *Formal Public Identifiers* or *FPIs* for entire documents or other data objects. SGML IDs for particular places *within* documents can be used both in general SGML and in HTML. By using FPIs or URNs to identify documents, you can ignore where documents live. When a document is really needed (such as when the reader clicks a link to it), the name is sent off to a "name server" that looks it up and tells where the nearest copy is. This works a lot like library catalogs and like the Internet routing system used for e-mail and other communications.

V

SGML and the WWW

> **Note**
>
> You can make HTML links a little safer against change by using the new BASE feature. Very often, a document will have many links that go to nearly the same place as the document itself, such as to several different files living in the same directory on the same network server, or in neighboring directories. When this happens, the beginning of the URLs on those links are all the same, such as:
>
> **http://www.abc.com/u/xyz/docs/aug95/review.htm**
> **http://www.abc.com/u/xyz/docs/aug95/recipe.htm**
>
> Instead of putting the full URL on every link, you can "factor out" the common part and put it on the BASE element in the header. The links all get much shorter, but the bigger plus is that you can update them all in one step if the server or a directory moves:
>
> ```
> <BASE ID=b1 HREF="http://www.abc.com/u/xyz/docs/aug95/">
> ..
> <A BASE=b1 HREF="review.htm">
> ...
> <A BASE=b1 HREF="recipe.htm">
> ```

HTML is constantly being improved. While this is a good thing, it also poses compatibility problems. In HTML 1.0, <P> was not so much the start of an SGML element as a substitute for the Return key. It was an EMPTY element, so the content of the paragraph was never actually part of the P element, and there was normally no <P> tag before the first paragraph in any section. This has been fixed in HTML 2.0, but funny things can happen if you view an old document in a new browser or vice-versa (for example, you might not get a new line for the first paragraph after a heading).

A newer issue is tables: HTML 2.1 adds a way to mark up tables and get good formatting for them; they can even adjust automatically when the reader changes the window-width. But what about tables in earlier documents? Authors often deleted their tables entirely, but when they couldn't, they had to type tables up e-mail style, using HTML's preformatted-text tag (<PRE>) and putting in lots of spaces:

```
<PRE>
....China....1400.million
....India.....800.million
....USA.......250.million
....France.....50.million
....Canada.....25.million
</PRE>
```

These will still work in a new browser (because the <PRE> tag is still around), but they don't get the advantages or capabilities that the new tables support. They won't re-wrap to different window widths, you can't wrap text within a single cell, and so on. So you can end up with awful effects like this:

```
    China    1400
million
    India     800
million
```

```
      USA       250
million
     France     50
million
     Canada     25
million
```

To get the new capabilities, you have to go in and actually change the documents. This is one reason it's considered bad form in SGML to use spaces for formatting. SGML helps you avoid this painful updating because you can represent your documents in whatever form makes sense for the documents themselves. That form is much less likely to change than the way you have to express it in one fixed DTD or system.

With SGML, if you need to accommodate software that doesn't handle your markup structures, you can use a "down-translation"—that is, a process that throws away anything in your markup that a certain HTML version can't handle. For tables, you can mark them up in any table DTD you want (CALS is the most popular) and use a program as needed to translate them to a simpler form, even the HTML 1.0 formatted kind. Then when table support is common in browsers, you just throw the down-translation program away and deliver the same data without conversion.

This works where "up-translation" won't because computers are so much better at throwing information away than creating it. Tables are a lot like the earlier example with italics: if your DTD distinguishes book titles and a few (or a thousand!) other kinds of italics, it's easy to write a program to turn all of them into just <I> for HTML-only browsers. The reverse is much harder.

Can I Make Do with HTML?

Given all these tradeoffs, here are the main things to think about when making the HTML versus full SGML decision for Web delivery:

The form the data is already in. If your data is already in SGML (or in something conceptually similar, like LaTeX), it's much easier to stick with full SGML and have tags that fit your data naturally. This way you don't have to design a complicated set of correspondences, and whatever data conversion you do will be simpler.

The document size and number of authors. If your documents are small, don't have a lot of internal structure, and don't need to be shared among multiple authors or editors, HTML may be all you need. But a little Web-browsing easily shows the bad things that can happen when people try to break big documents into little pieces: the forest can be lost by dividing it into separate trees.

The structures needed for searching. If you need to do searches that target specific data in your documents, you'll probably need SGML to label that data. Doing without it is like doing a personnel database without having names for the fields; if you searched for people with salaries less than $30,000, you'd get not only that, but all the people who are less than 30,000 years old!

The frequency of changes. If your data is going to change frequently, you're better off in SGML, where you can modularize your documents using marked sections (see Chapter 16), entities (Chapters 3, 10, and 16), and other features.

All these things relate to each other, so you often can't answer one question without thinking about the others. One example is that frequent changes to a document matter a lot less if the document is really small and you have complete unshared control over it. But if a document is big and several authors have to cooperate to maintain it, frequency of changes matters a lot.

How to Use HTML Safely

If you choose to put your data in HTML rather than another SGML DTD, there are several things you can do to make a later transition easier. These things are also helpful in the short term because they make your HTML more consistent, portable, and reliable.

- Make sure your HTML is really valid. Run it through an SGML parser—such as sgmls, yasp, or sp—or use one of the HTML "lint" programs (they're called that because they go looking around for unwanted dirt that accumulates in dark pockets of HTML documents). Weblint is one such program (you can find it at **http://www.unipress.com/weblint**).

- Be very careful about quoting attributes. Any attribute value that contains any characters other than letters, digits, periods, and hyphens needs to be quoted (either single or double quotes are fine, but not distinct open/close curly quotes).

> ### Tip
>
> There are a couple very common HTML errors that you can get away with in some browsers, but that will break others, and will prevent you from using generic SGML tools. The biggest one is failing to quote attributes, as just described. Probably the next biggest is getting comments wrong. These are right:
>
> ```
> <!-- some text of a comment -->
> <!-- another comment, with two text parts -
>      -- of which this is the second -->
> ```
>
> But these are wrong (that is, they're not comments):
>
> ```
> <!-- this comment never ends --!>
> <! This is an SGML syntax error !>
> <-- This is just data to SGML -->
> <!-- This one -- really -- is not a comment -->
> ```

- Avoid any part of HTML that is labeled "deprecated" in the HTML DTD or its documentation. Deprecated is a polite term standards use to say, "Don't use this, it's dangerous, not recommended for the future, and not even universally supported at present."

- Be sure to use the HTML "DIV" containers, not just free-standing headings—especially in larger documents. This makes the structure of your document easier for programs to find and process, and it can also help you find tagging errors.

- Avoid colliding with SGML constructs, even if some HTML parsers ignore them. For example, don't depend on an HTML parser failing to know that the string <![starts a marked section, that <? starts a processing instruction, or that <!-- starts a comment; always escape such strings, for example, by changing the < to <.

Challenges of Upgrading

If you decide to put your data in an SGML DTD other than HTML, there are a few "gotchas" to watch out for. None are fatal, but you'll want to start out knowing the rules of the game. The issues are briefly summarized here. The next chapter, "Practicalities of Working with SGML on the Web," discusses a lot more specifics.

Fewer Browsers To Choose from

At this time, only a few networked information browsers can receive and format SGML regardless of the DTD. Most Web browsers have the HTML tag names built right into the program, and require a new release to add new ones. This is true even if the new ones don't require any new formatting capabilities; adding a BOOK-TITLE element type won't work, even though you may only want it to mean "show in italics."

The main exception that is already released is a viewer called Panorama, developed by Synex and marketed by SoftQuad. Panorama is an add-on "helper" to existing browsers, like various graphics viewers. This means it does not talk to the network by itself; instead, when a Web browser follows a link and notices that the data coming back claims to be "SGML," it can forward the data to Panorama for display.

On the CD

If there are Internet-based links in the SGML, Panorama calls the browser back to retrieve them. If the destination is HTML or GIF, it shows up directly in the Web browser. If it's SGML, the browser calls Panorama again.

Another SGML-capable Web browser was shown at the last Web conference and is being released right around the time this book appears. It's a new version of the DynaText SGML delivery system that can view SGML or HTML off a hard disk or CD-ROM, across the Net, out of a database, or from a compiled/indexed form used for big documents. It provides a unified environment for viewing all these data types, as well as graphic and multimedia formats.

Although there aren't many SGML-capable Web browsers, these two are very flexible and give you a lot of control over formatting, style, and other capabilities. Hopefully, more browsers will start to support generic SGML over time.

In the meantime, there are several server-end options available, too. You can always create and maintain documents using full SGML, and then run a conversion program to create HTML from it and put that on the Web. This is especially useful if you have an SGML-based authoring system in use for general publishing or other applications.

There are also Web servers available that can store SGML directly and then translate it to HTML on demand (for example, DynaWeb from Electronic Book Technologies— you can try it out at **http://www.ebt.com**). This method has the advantage that you can adjust the translation rules any time without re-running a big conversion process over all your data. It also means the translation can be customized as needed, for example, to adjust to whichever browser is calling in, or even to modify the document by inserting real-time information during translation.

A DTD To Choose or Design

Even if you have all the software you need, with full SGML you'll need to answer a question that never arises with HTML: What DTD should I use? Very good DTDs are already available for a wide range of document types, and you can probably put off DTD-building for as long as you want by using them. This makes the task a lot easier. But even so, you have to think about your documents and then learn at least enough about a few DTDs to make a choice. You may also want to tweak an existing DTD— this is easier than starting from scratch, but still takes skills beyond those needed for tagging.

More Syntax To Learn

If you want to make up your own DTDs, you need to deal with all kinds of declarations, parameter entities, content models, and so on; there's a lot of syntax to learn (tools like Near & Far help a lot). If you use an existing DTD, there is less syntax to worry about, but there's still a little more than with HTML.

SGML provides many ways of saving keystrokes in markup, and many special-purpose constructs you never see used in HTML (as you learned about in chapters 3 and 16). Using these constructs in an HTML document will result in errors of one kind or another. For example, if you try to "comment out" a block of HTML with a marked section, its content is still there because typical HTML parsers don't recognize marked sections. In fact, for them the characters <![IGNORE [and]]> all count as text content!

```
<P>
<![ IGNORE [ This text is not part of the document, really.
    In fact, it's <EMPH>really </EMPH> not there. ]]>
    And the paragraph goes on right here.
</P>
```

In an HTML application that isn't quite following the rules, this might be taken as just a paragraph that starts with some funny punctuation marks (a really bad HTML implementation might instead complain that you used a tag named ![). If you got used to this, you might be surprised when you go to a more generic SGML system and discover that the <![in your document causes some very different effects—this is something you just have to memorize and know. In this case, the first two lines within the paragraph are not part of the content at all, and a browser shouldn't show them to you.

Using a WYSIWYG SGML editor helps a lot, for the same reasons that using MS Word is a lot easier than typing Microsoft's RTF interchange format directly. But even with the best tools, you can be surprised if you're not aware of such restrictions (for example, you might get a "beep" whenever you try to type <![in a paragraph, and not know why).

Benefits of Upgrading

If there's less delivery software to choose from and more to learn, why bother? The reasons are mostly the same ones that influenced big publishers to go with SGML, although which reasons are most important varies from project to project.

Platform Independence

Other SGML DTDs are even better at abstracting formatting than HTML. SGML can be re-targeted to anything from a top-line photocomposition system down to text-only browsers like Lynx, Braille composers, and anything in between. SGML itself greatly benefits flexibility. HTML accomplishes this to some extent, but less so because a small and fixed tag set can force authors to think more about display effects and less about describing structure.

Browser Independence

Because generic SGML software (by definition) handles many DTDs, using a new or modified DTD won't faze it. If it works for CALS and TEI, it'll almost certainly work for whatever DTD you choose.

SGML vendors spend a lot of time testing interoperability. A standard demo at trade shows used to be to pass a tape or disk of SGML files from booth to booth throughout the show. Each product had to read the data, do whatever it did with the data (like let you edit or format it), and then write it out to pass on—without trashing it.

The "SGML Open" vendor group gets together regularly online, at shows, and at special meetings to work out agreements on details and make sure SGML documents can move around easily. For example, a popular DTD for tables has a "rotate" attribute to let you lay out tables in either portrait or landscape mode, but doesn't say whether rotation is clockwise or counterclockwise. The vendors sat down and decided, so now they all do it the same way. Simple agreements like this can save a lot of pain for end users.

> **Note**
>
> The central point for finding out about SGML Open activities is **http://www.sgmlopen.org**. Most companies that support SGML are involved in SGML Open, and you can find links to their home pages from the SGML Open Web site, along with links to much other useful SGML information.

V

SGML and the WWW

If you use an SGML-aware server, you can benefit from greater browser independence—even on the Web. Each Web browser has its own strengths and weaknesses. If you can ship slightly different HTML to each one, you can capitalize on the strengths and avoid the weaknesses. This is easier if your data uses a more precise DTD; clients tell servers who they are, so a server that has enough information can down-translate appropriately for each one.

HTML Revision Independence

Keeping your data in SGML also lets you avoid re-coding it each time a new HTML feature arrives. You learned earlier about tables—how you'd have to completely re-work them if you started by assuming the browser can't support table markup, and then had to change your data when browsers caught up. The same problem came up when Netscape introduced their FRAME element and a lot of re-authoring had to happen. The same problems can happen with any kind of markup. By keeping your documents in DTDs designed to fit, you can leave them untouched and merely adjust a conversion filter.

Appropriate Tag Usage

The biggest fundamental benefit of going to SGML is that your markup can tell the truth about what components are in your document, even if the document doesn't fit into any pre-existing scheme. If the tags you need are there (or, at worst, you can add them yourself), you avoid having to "pun" and use a single tag for a bunch of purposes it may not have been meant for.

Note

The question of having the right tag available for the job is very important, so here are a few examples. We've already talked about how sixth-level HTML headings (H6) get used to mean small caps, and how italics (I) get used to mark many things like emphasis, foreign words, book titles, and so on.

Sometimes preformatted text (PRE) gets used for quick-and-dirty tables. Line-break (BR) gets used heavily for forcing particular browsers to lay things out a certain way (and usually that way only works well for certain browsers, certain window widths, and so on).

Another big example is equations; since there are not yet HTML elements for doing math, journal publishers and others are stuck turning equations into graphics for Web delivery. This sort of works, but the fine print tends to disappear, and zooming in doesn't help. This is a case where there's dire need for a more adequate set of tags. And there are already some very good equation DTDs in wide use outside the Web.

Large Document Management

SGML helps you manage the conflict between big documents and slow modems. You can't very well ship a whole manual or a lengthy paper of any kind every time a user wants to see the *nth* paragraph (even if browsers could handle documents that big, which many can't)—no user would wait for the download to finish. Novell certainly couldn't ship tens of thousand of pages of NetWare manuals every time a user wanted a summary of some installation detail.

The only viable option with documents bigger than several tens to hundreds of pages is to break them up; you can make many smaller documents, say one for each subsection, and a bunch of overview documents that give you access similar to the table of contents in a paper book. This is usually done manually for HTML because HTML documents don't usually contain explicit markup for their larger components (some do now that HTML has added the DIV element). This method works except for these problems:

- If you are also publishing a paper document, you have to maintain two quite different forms.

- The document ends up in many pieces that aren't visibly related; only a person can tell whether some link between HTML files A and B means they're part of the same document, or two somehow-related documents. This makes it hard to maintain consistency between all the parts of your original document.

- If users want to download the whole document for some reason, it's very hard to do. First, they have to find all the pieces, distinguishing "is-part-of" links from "is-related-to" links; then they have to assemble all the parts in the right order and put the larger containing structures in. It's not enough to just pack them end-to-end because some of the connections between lower sections appear only in "header" or "table of contents" documents.

- Users can't scroll smoothly through the complete document; at best, you can carefully provide Next Portion and Previous Portion buttons on every piece.

Internationalization

A final benefit of other SGML DTDs over HTML is that they have more provisions for international and multilingual documents. HTML prescribes the "Latin 1" character set. Latin 1 includes the characters for most Western European languages, but not Eastern European, Asian, or many other languages. Future revisions will probably support "Unicode," a new standard that includes characters for nearly all modern languages. SGML itself lets each document specify a character set, and doesn't particularly care whether characters are one, two, or more bytes wide.

Many DTDs also provide a way to mark that individual elements are in different languages. This can have a big effect on display and searching. For example, it helps a lot if you're searching for the English word "die," to not get the German word "die," which means roughly "the," and so is very common.

DTDs that specifically mark language are also very helpful when you want to create multilingual documents or documents that can customize to the reader's language. You can create documents where every paragraph has a subelement for each language, and then set up your software to show only the type the user wants; this automatically customizes the document for the reader's own language:

```
<P>
   <ENGLISH>...</>
   <FRENCH>...</>
   <ITALIAN>...</>
   <GERMAN>...</>
   <SPANISH>...</>
   ...
</P>
```

Better Support for Large Documents

SGML is especially strong for large or structured documents, documents where several authors share writing and editing, and documents that have components HTML doesn't provide. A single DTD such as HTML may not provide the types of elements your documents need, in which case you end up using some other type because it gets the desired appearance in the authoring software. This leads to problems down the line. HTML also has only limited support for expressing larger units such as sections, and that makes document management a bit harder.

From Here...

This chapter has discussed the pros and cons of upgrading from HTML to generic SGML, and given some examples of who is already using SGML and how and why they do. It has given some questions you should consider in deciding whether to upgrade, and what costs and benefits you're likely to encounter if you do.

For more information, refer to the following chapters:

- Chapter 20, "Practicalities of Working with SGML on the Web," more specifically talks about how to manage SGML data on the Web and what tools are available to help.
- Chapter 3, "SGML Terminology," covers various SGML methods and structures in general terms.
- Chapter 10, "Following General SGML Declaration Syntax," covers how to declare and use those structures.
- Chapter 16, "Markup Challenges and Specialized Content," covers some special SGML methods, such as marked sections, that are also useful even though they may be less common than others.

CHAPTER 20

Practicalities of Working with SGML on the Web

This chapter covers some of the tools and techniques for managing SGML data on the World Wide Web. It is an overview of tools rather than a guide to using any particular tool. The following general information is covered first:

- Tactics for using SGML on the Web
- Tools

The chapter then moves on to more specific issues that you will encounter as you plan a Web SGML strategy:

- Planning
- Consistency and flexibility
- Allowances for HTML
- The danger of overusing optional SGML features

Chapter 26, "Tools for the PC: Authoring, Viewing and Utilities," and Chapter 27, "Tools for the Mac: Authoring, Viewing, and Utilities," have more detailed information about selected SGML tools available on the Mac and PC.

Tactics for Using SGML on the Web

The Web defines how to use text data in one SGML DTD, namely HTML. Because of this, most Web-specific tools support only HTML. This leads to a problem if you have (or want) generic SGML. You can't ship SGML files in any other DTD to typical browsers, such as Mosaic and Netscape Navigator. Or rather, you *can* ship files around, but HTML browsers won't know what to do with them when they get there.

When data moves around in the Web, it carries a *MIME (Multi-purpose Internet Mail Extensions) type* that says whether it's a GIF file, a sound file, HTML, or something else. Browsers use this information to decide whether they can show the data by themselves, or through some external helper application. Suppose you click a link like this one, which points to a source for information about Internet Draft standards-in-progress:

```
<a href="http://ds.internic.net/ds/dspg0intdoc.html">Internet Drafts</a>
```

The server knows this is an HTML file, and says so when it sends it back to the client that requested it, by labeling it with MIME type "Text/HTML."

If a file is in some other SGML DTD, the server would have to say something else, not "Text/HTML." A working group in the Internet Engineering Task Force (IETF) is finalizing the exact definition of MIME types for SGML. There will probably be two types: "Text/SGML" and "Application/SGML." The main differences between them are:

- Systems are free to convert line-ends between Mac/DOS/UNIX conventions in "Text/" files, but not in "Application/" files.

- Any "Text/" file should be human-readable—which is very subjective. For HTML and SGML, most files are human-readable, but ones with really dense tagging may not be.

The IETF is also working on a standard method for accessing DTDs, SGML declarations, stylesheets, and other related data given an SGML document file.

If you have software that can interpret SGML, you should be fine whether the server sends MIME type Application/SGML or Text/SGML; if not, "Text/SGML" tells your browser that it's okay to bring the file up in a plain-text editor, such as emacs, MS Write, or SimpleText, and "Application/SGML" says that it isn't, in which case you'll probably get a dialog box that says the file can't be displayed.

There is a third option. The server can lie and say a file is HTML even when it's in some other DTD. If the SGML is very simple and shares its most commonly used tag names with HTML, the result is probably usable. Many DTDs use obvious names, such as P for paragraph, H1...Hn for headings, LI for list items, and I for italics or emphasis. If the SGML file uses common tags, a sufficient number of elements may turn out fine and make the file readable. Most HTML parsers are not picky. However, the other tags will be ignored, and that will make many SGML files look very poor. Depending on the particular browser, "ignored" may mean the non-HTML tags get discarded, they get discarded along with all their content, or they get displayed as if they were just text, or possibly something else.

Another problem is that lots of SGML constructs aren't noticed at all by most HTML parsers. Marked sections are a good example. Most browsers will get the interpretation wrong if your documents contain anything like this (whether or not they conform to the HTML DTD!):

```
<p>By providing a common public vocabulary for text markup, texts
as  important  and  useful  as  they  ought  to  be,  <![  IGNORE
[ and achieved lasting world peace. ]]> <![ INCLUDE [ but only
one step.]]></p> <author>C.M. Sperberg-McQueen</author>
```

Because most HTML parsers don't support marked sections, the display would include them literally and the reader would see confusing and misleading formatted text like this:

> By providing a common public vocabulary for text markup, you will have taken one major step toward making electronic texts as important and useful as they ought to be, <![IGNORE [and achieved lasting world peace.]]>
> <![INCLUDE [but only one step.]]>
>
> (C.M. Sperberg-McQueen)

Of course, what the reader should have seen is this:

> By providing a common public vocabulary for text markup, you will have taken one major step toward making electronic texts as important and useful as they ought to be, but only one step.
>
> (C.M. Sperberg-McQueen)

Trying to pass a document in another SGML DTD off as HTML causes problems. If all the circumstances are exactly right (a very big "if"), it might be workable. But it's like trying to finish the last 100-mile leg of a car trip on a spare tire that says "Good for 50 miles."

Fortunately, there are two much better, more realistic ways to use SGML on the Web despite the limitations of many browsers. First, you can use client-end software that *can* read generic SGML. Second, publishers can use special servers (or server add-ons) that accept full SGML, but translate it to HTML before sending it to clients so that even HTML-only clients can see it.

Tools

The two methods just described each require quite different tools. For client SGML software, the key question is "How fully is the SGML-aware viewer integrated with the HTML viewer?" Products vary in how they answer this question. In this case, servers don't really need to know that they're dealing with SGML—they just ship the bits. Therefore, the only options to figure out are at the client end. The section "SGML-aware Viewers (for CD, LAN, and Mostly WAN)" covers these options.

When the server manages SGML and converts it to HTML, many more tools come into play and you can provide a wide variety of "value-added" capabilities. The tools discussed in this chapter fall under these categories:

- *Integrated SGML converters.* These sit in or immediately behind the Web server, and convert other SGML documents to HTML on the fly whenever a client requests one. Using one of these converters is the most sophisticated and feature-complete solution, but it requires more sophisticated programs at the server end.

- *Generic conversion tools.* You can use these tools as "batch" converters to translate the SGML to HTML offline—you can then treat what you translated just like any other HTML. Because the SGML is gone before delivery, this solution provides less high-end functionality, but may, in some cases, be easier to manage (for example, if you have separate people responsible for data conversion and Web site management).

- *Retrieval engines*. These tools keep the SGML in a relational or object-oriented database, and pull parts out as needed. They are typically closely tied to one of the other categories for batch or on-the-fly HTML conversion, but add sophisticated information retrieval and searching features. These vary greatly in ease of use.

- *The big document problem*. No matter what tool you use, you'll find that big documents pose special problems. Some tools help keep Web browsing responsive by minimizing the number of bytes that have to go across the Net at any given time.

SGML-aware Viewers (for CD, LAN, and Mostly WAN)

If the client who receives SGML data through the Web has some kind of SGML-aware viewer, he can view it. This process is straightforward, except for a couple of steps:

- Somehow, the SGML data has to get from the program that talks to the network to the program that actually views it.

- Somehow, the DTD, the SGML declaration, and any needed external entities need to get to the client (that is, the main SGML file [the "document entity"] itself isn't enough).

The first problem has several solutions. The cleanest is to use a single full-function program to view HTML, SGML, graphics, and so on all in one environment (see fig. 20.1). This solution is especially easy because HTML is a special case of SGML—a generic SGML viewer should have little trouble managing HTML data.

Fig. 20.1

An integrated data viewer gives a unified interface to all the data types it supports.

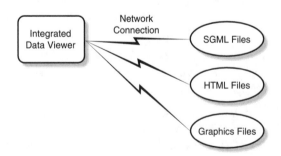

You don't have to bounce back and forth between the "HTML application" and the "SGML application" because they're the same. You save time and screen space, and other SGML documents can appear in exactly the same window as the HTML that linked to them (and vice versa). The interface for links in all documents can work the same way as the interface for links in HTML documents, which greatly improves usability. Because the SGML viewer can talk directly to the network, it can fetch DTDs, SGML declarations, stylesheets, and external entities whenever it needs to.

> **Note**
>
> An SGML viewer that can talk to the network as needed has a big responsiveness advantage as well. Documents often have many, many links to other documents, references to graphics, and so on. If a viewer can't get to those things on demand (when the user clicks on a link), the server may have to send all possible linked data ahead of time—for example, it might have to bundle up 100 graphic entities along with the document, just in case the user wants to see one. That wastes a lot of network speed and leaves the user waiting, too.

The problem with this approach right now is that no integrated data viewer exists. None of the Web browsers speak SGML other than HTML, and none of the SGML viewers speak to the Web. One Net-aware SGML viewer product is in beta-testing and will probably be available around the time this book appears: The DynaText SGML delivery system is adding built-in support for communication via HTTP and built-in support for HTML viewing. You can get information about it on the Net at **http://www.ebt.com/**.

At the other extreme, SGML can be handled by a completely separate helper application, just like unusual graphics or sound file types. When the HTML browser sees a file come in with MIME type "Text/SGML," it simply looks up what application can handle it and forwards the data (see fig. 20.2).

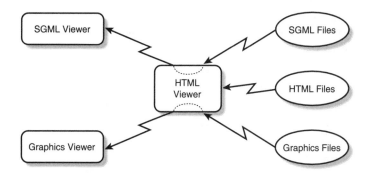

Fig. 20.2

An SGML viewer can also be a helper application, called as needed by an HTML viewer.

You don't have to wait for existing HTML viewers to add SGML support, and you don't have to add network capabilities to SGML viewers. You just get the helper application and tell the HTML viewer that it's there. On the other hand, you have two viewers to manage that are doing almost the same thing. The formatting capabilities of your HTML and generic SGML viewers may differ; their interfaces certainly will. You might have to click a different mouse button to follow links depending on whether you're viewing a document in HTML or in a different DTD, and use different menus for all the functions.

This problem would be minor if HTML and generic SGML document viewers "felt" different to the user. However, the differences between HTML and other SGML documents are often not evident just from formatting. They both typically end up as wrapped text with various fonts, colors, indents, and so on (although SGML viewers tend to provide a wider variety of extra navigational tools, such as tables of contents). Given the similarity, users will probably wonder why they have a different interface for what looks like pretty much the same thing.

On the other hand, the differences between a viewer for JPEG graphics and an HTML viewer are obvious to users; they know right away that those two viewers are different, and probably won't be surprised at a slightly different set of menu items, cursors, and so on. Because the two applications are different, they operate differently.

A similar problem with the "helper application" approach is that the HTML viewer and the generic SGML viewer have separate history lists of places you've been. So when you click the Back button, you won't get the same results from each application. This difference in operation may be confusing, since when you follow a link, you never know if the result will appear in the same window with the same interface, or will be somewhere completely different.

The problem is complex. With a helper application like a JPEG viewer, all the HTML client has to do is forward the JPEG data to it. But an SGML file may refer to other data that is still living somewhere else on the network. For example, the SGML viewer may need to get the DTD or a bunch of entities that are included by reference from the initial SGML file. Because the SGML viewer in this approach can't go out to the network to fetch data, it has to be able to send a signal back to the HTML client, which gets the data and then sends it back to the SGML viewer. This kind of two-way communication between separate programs is a little tricky on current systems, though it can definitely be done.

There is a product that serves as an SGML helper application in much this way. Panorama is available from SoftQuad for MS Windows. A free version is available from **http://www.oclc.org:5046/oclc/research/panorama/panorama.html**.

▶▶ See "Other SGML Tools," p. 453

Panorama Pro is a commercial version of the same system. Both can read SGML regardless of the DTD used, and you can set up most HTML-based Web clients to send SGML data to them.

Although the solutions already described (SGML clients and SGML helper applications) are much better solutions because the advantages of SGML survive at the client end, there are also advantages to just sending HTML across the Net.

- Readers can use any client that supports HTML (although they can get only the client formatting and search functions that HTML can support).

- Publishers can avoid sending their "real" data across the Net, thus making copies distinct from originals. Users can download and save the HTML, but the publisher can still have added value in the original data, which they don't have to give away.

- Because the data at the client end *is* HTML, the problem of having a different interface in a helper application disappears.

- Because translation is going on, publishers can choose to do multiple translations and turn their original SGML data into HTML 2.0 for some clients, HTML 3.0 for others, HTML "à la company X" for browsers that have nonstandard features, text-only for Lynx, and so on.

- For the same reason, servers can customize the data (sort lists, hide overviews or excessive detail, and so on). They just need to leave some of the SGML out entirely, or use different HTML tags for it to create very different views.

Integrated SGML Converters

The first group of SGML to HTML tools converts data on the fly, as part of the file-serving process. So publishers author their data in any SGML DTD using whatever tools they normally use and simply install the SGML on the server. Then they set up a conversion filter that maps their SGML data from its original DTDs into HTML. They don't run that filter program ahead of time (except to test it!). Instead, whenever the server gets a request and sees that the data is in SGML, it fires up the converter and ships out the filtered result. Figure 20.3 illustrates the process.

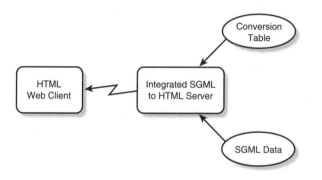

Fig. 20.3

An integrated server (or server add-on) converts SGML to HTML on the fly.

Suppose a software company wants to put its documentation on the Web. A lot of software companies use the "DocBook" standard DTD for their manuals; to use an integrated SGML conversion server, they would specify one conversion table that the server would apply to any of the data. Then, when a request comes in, the server parses or retrieves the document and converts the elements it finds according to the table.

Note

Information about the DocBook DTD is available on the Internet from **http://jasper.ora.com/DocBook**.

An HTML conversion table for DocBook might look something like this (only one table is needed for each DTD—not one for each document):

```
# DocBook tag          HTML tag
para                   p
orderedlist            OL
listitem               LI
chapter                [untag]
section                [untag]
chapter/title          H2
section/title          H3
```

Many common element types map one-for-one, such as PARA to P. Some other elements in DocBook don't have an HTML equivalent, so this conversion table says "untag," meaning that the convertor shouldn't give them any start or end tags at all, but just send their content through untagged.

The last two cases are more interesting. In HTML, headings of different levels have different names: H1, H2, and so on. These elements just contain titles, not whole sections. But DocBook has containers, such as CHAPTER and SECTION, that really are the entire units. CHAPTER and SECTION elements both have titles that appear in sub-elements. The titles are tagged TITLE regardless of whether they're titles of CHAPTERs or of SECTIONs. Programs can tell from context which are chapter titles and which are section titles. This kind of difference in tag usage arises all the time when you convert data from one SGML DTD to another.

Because of this difference, it wouldn't be accurate to just convert all DocBook TITLE elements into the same HTML element (such as H1). If you did, chapter titles and section titles would end up looking exactly the same. Instead, you would convert titles within CHAPTER elements to H2, but titles within SECTION elements to H3 (of course, any title within a SECTION is also inside a larger CHAPTER, but for converting, you care only about what the title is *directly* within). The last lines of the example above are there to cover these cases. They state that certain TITLE elements qualify to turn into H2, and certain others into H3.

Putting a container name in front of a tag name (with some character like a slash to separate them) is one way to state such a restriction. Many conversion programs provide a method like this, and you can get far better results using it.

Remember, though, that a string such as chapter/title or list/item/p isn't really a tag name—you won't see <chapter/title> in a valid SGML file. Most people call these *qualified tag names* or *qualified GIs*. These are used in various programs that process SGML, not in SGML itself.

Note

To see how well you remember all the SGML minimization rules, try answering this question: "If <chapter/title> did show up in an SGML file, would it necessarily be a syntax error, or would it mean something valid to the SGML parser (and if it's valid, what would it mean)?"

Two products are already available that translate SGML documents to HTML on the fly and serve it to the Web. One is from Open Text. It uses script programs to do the conversion and works with standard Web servers to ship out data from an indexed SGML form. The other is DynaWeb from Electronic Book Technologies, which does much the same thing except that the translation is done within the program based on the same stylesheet tools used for formatting SGML for CD-ROM delivery, print, and other uses. Both of these tools are highly effective for delivering SGML on the Web, can handle very large and complex documents, and include fast search and retrieval features.

Generic Conversion Tools

The second major category of "SGML to HTML" Web solutions is pretty similar to the first, except that conversion is done ahead of time in a *batch process*. That is, authors or publishers prepare their data in SGML as usual, but rather than install the SGML on the server (to be converted on the fly), they convert the SGML to HTML and put the HTML on the server. Figure 20.4 illustrates the process. The SGML to HTML converter does not have to run on the same system as the HTML server.

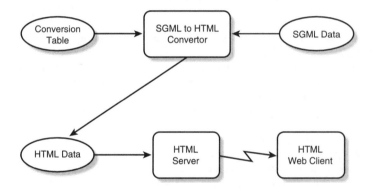

Fig. 20.4

You can also convert SGML documents to HTML ahead of time using any generic conversion tool, and then install the HTML on a Web server.

Even though the processes are fairly similar, there are a lot of consequences depending on which you choose. The plusses for the batch-conversion approach are:

■ You save a lot of processor time in the long run, because the data is only processed once (or at least, only once per revision or modification).

■ You can use any conversion tool you want; it doesn't have to have the capability to be hooked up to a Web server. UNIX gurus can use sed, awk, and similar tools; programmers can use C or Icon or any other programming language; and lots of people can use Perl.

On the other hand, there are some minuses:

■ You have to maintain two copies of all the data, one in HTML and one in SGML.

■ If you want to take advantage of a newer version of HTML, you have to reconvert all your data, not just change the conversion filters.

■ You have to ship the *same* HTML to all clients. You miss a big advantage of the integrated conversion approach; you can't customize what you send.

This last point is a big one. Current Web clients have a tendency to add proprietary extensions to HTML. Using the ones for client X provides nice additions *for users of client X,* but means no other users see the right thing. With integrated conversion, you can check what client is calling in, look up a different conversion filter for each one, and send data that's optimized for just that client. This allows publishers to present their material in the best possible way for each reader without forcing them all to buy and use the same Web client—that, after all, is one of the advantages HTML is supposed to provide in the first place.

The same argument applies as new versions of the HTML standard come out. Some clients will support HTML 2.1 earlier than others. With integrated conversion, you not only can customize for client extensions, but you can customize for client versions and what level of HTML they support.

Note

Customization is a nice feature for everyone, but it's especially important for visually impaired users. They have good reasons to prefer special Web clients that are compatible with text-to-speech systems and provide usable presentations of documents. They may prefer to get a textual description of each graphic rather than the image itself (they shouldn't have to waste the bandwidth to get both if they aren't going to use the image anyway). Integrated conversion permits you to tailor the data for many different users.

Theoretically, you can get the same advantage by running many different batch conversions and saving a separate variation of the HTML files for each client: mybook.lynx, mybook.mosaic, mybook.netscape, and so on. Practically, this costs an enormous amount of space and raises huge data management problems (the chance of remembering to update every variant document every time something changes is pretty small). Each variant of each HTML file also needs a separate URL, so you have to make each conversion filter find all the links and change them during conversion. For example, a link from mybook.lynx should point to yourbook.lynx, not yourbook.mosaic.

Even worse, any documents elsewhere that point to yours can only point to specific URLs (and, of course, you can't fix other people's documents). If someone has a URL that points to the "regular" HTML version of a document and mails it to a visually impaired friend, it does little good. The recipient may not know that other more appropriate versions of the document exist, or how to get to them. You could make all the filters put "see also" links at the top of every document, but that gets cluttered and painful compared to having customization just work automatically.

Retrieval Engines

Retrieval engines work in combination with integrated or batch conversion solutions. With a batch solution, you would index the HTML version(s); with an integrated solution, you index the SGML. Both work fine for simple text searches. The difference comes if you want to search the SGML structure.

For example, suppose your SGML documents distinguish emphasis from foreign phrases from book titles, even though all will be tagged just `<I>` (italic) in HTML. If your retrieval engine is working from the SGML, clients can request searches that distinguish these types even though what they get back doesn't distinguish them. Because searching on the Web is mainly done at the server end, this can be a big advantage, and with HTML forms you can make very nice interfaces for doing structured searches.

Although there isn't space to talk in detail about the features and limitations of various search engines, it's worth noting that "SGML support" can cover a wide range. At the weakest extreme, some tools simply index SGML files without knowing SGML. In that case, searching for "section" would return three hits for this piece of the file:

```
<section><title>This section discusses dogs.</section>
```

That's not likely to be what you want—two of the hits are tags, not content. Also, if you try to use such an engine to limit hits to words occurring in certain contexts, it gets messy. To find "dog" in `<section>`, you have to use a regular expression or "wildcard" searching something like:

```
<section>.*dog.*</section>
```

This search may be slower than a plain string search, but a more important problem is that getting the query just right takes a lot of work. Here are some cases the query above will miss:

- What if there are attributes on the section start-tag?
- What if the start or end tags are short or omitted?
- What if the wildcard match includes more tags (for example, the expression just shown would match "`<section>Hi</section> <p>dog</p> <section>bye</section>`").

Some other tools deal with SGML by turning indexing off when they see < and back on when they see >—this, of course, rules out any structure searching, as well as gets things wrong in many cases like marked sections, minimization, and so on. One good test for any search engine that claims to support SGML is to see what it does for an ignored marked section (for details on marked sections, see Chapter 16):

```
<p>The most important thing is
<![ IGNORE [ tissue paper <!-- the text up to the next ">" isn't really
content --> ]]>
friends.</p>
```

An engine with *really* poor SGML support may decide to ignore half the marked section, and re-start indexing after the "`>`" in the middle, or may count the comment's content as part of the document content. An engine with *pretty* poor SGML support may get those cases right, but still happily find `tissue paper` and maybe even `IGNORE`, even though they're not part of the document's content. A good SGML engine will exclude all these non-content things from content searches. A remarkably good engine will give you the choice, and even let you specifically ask for searches in marked sections or comments (though that isn't a real common thing to want).

Other tools may parse correctly and be able to tell tags apart from content, but still not index tags, or index tags but not attributes, or index only a few specially chosen elements such as `AUTHOR` and `TITLE`. A few let you index as many element types as you want, but impose a space or speed penalty for each one or for indexing larger container elements.

If you want to do SGML searching, you need a retrieval engine that knows about the SGML syntax and structure. The more it knows, the better, at least about structure—it's less likely you'll need to do searches that worry about how the markup was typed. For example, it's very likely someone will want to retrieve just those cross-references that are inside footnotes; but unlikely that they'll want to retrieve all lists where there are two spaces between the tag name and the `TYPE` attribute (`<LIST  TYPE=NUMBERED>`), as opposed to one space (`<LIST TYPE=NUMBERED>`). Be sure you know exactly what level of SGML support you want from your retrieval engine, and whether you can get it.

The Big Document Problem

Conversion-based products address one more big issue not yet mentioned. Many SGML files are *big*. Because of network speed limitations, it isn't easy to put documents much over a few hundred kilobytes (say, about 50-100 page) on the Web. Because the Web method is normally to fetch a whole file at a time, putting a whole manual or book in one file imposes a burden on the network itself and on the end user who has to wait for it. It has these problems:

- Downloading takes a long time before you can see the whole document, which is annoying for the end user.
- While the long download is happening, part of your processing power and network capacity is used up. If you share your network connection with others, all those extra bytes slow them down, too.
- Most HTML browsers crash or get confused on big files because they try to load them entirely into memory at once (try creating a really big HTML file and feeding it to your favorite browser to see what happens).
- Big files are hard to navigate with just a scroll bar.

Because of such problems, you don't see a lot of whole books on the Web. Many books are available for downloading from the Internet, but few show up in HTML for easy interactive reading. It just would take too long. A 400-page book is about 800K of text (not counting any graphics)—here's how long that takes with different speed connections:

Speed	Time
9600 baud modem	14 minutes
28800 baud modem	5 minutes
ISDN connection	2 minutes
256K Internet line	30 seconds
T1 Internet line	5 seconds

These figures don't count processor time to parse all of that file, load it into memory, and format it. Netscape 1.1 takes 2 1/2 minutes to load an 800K HTML file from the local hard disk on my Mac Duo 210 and needs 5M of RAM. If I then resize the window, it needs 9M and another 2 1/2 minutes.

The figures also don't count sharing network connections among users. If each of your readers has a private top-notch Internet connection, this may work fine—but how many do? Few of us can afford a private T1 line; it takes a lot of users to justify the expense. But, on a shared line, no one gets the full bandwidth for very long.

When you open a book you should be able to start seeing it within a second, and if you immediately drag the scroll bar to the bottom, you shouldn't have to twiddle your thumbs or go for coffee. That's fine for downloading, but not good enough for browsing.

To put a book on the Web with reasonable performance, you pretty much have to break it up into small pieces. That brings us back to the servers that convert SGML to HTML; they can be set up to notice if you ask for something huge, and they can send a subset instead of sending everything. So if you ask for "hamlet.sgm," instead of the entire play, you can get the first scene and be there in a fraction of the time. DynaWeb is an example of a server that does just that.

You also can set up a server to always tack on an HTML link button called Next, so when someone reads to the end of Act I Scene 1, a single click takes them further.

Better yet, a server can extract any subset of the SGML document, not just a single block. For example, it can spot the difference between a request for "Hamlet" and a request for "Hamlet Act I Scene 1". For the first, it can send a table of contents or other navigation aid—maybe a list of the acts and scenes with their first lines or titles. Since the server determines what HTML really gets sent, it can tag each line as an HTML link that takes you to the right act or scene—instant Web navigation. For the second case, where the user makes a specific request for a manageable chunk of data, the server can just convert to HTML and send it.

V

SGML and the WWW

This kind of filtering can happen either on the fly or in batch. Doing it on the fly greatly eases document management for whoever owns the data. They can keep things in natural units that are dictated by the material, rather than in artificial units dictated by the speed of the Internet. And if they publish or revise a book, they don't have to re-break it up every time it changes.

SGML Requires More Thinking Up Front

SGML has many advantages for managing documents on the Web, providing more features and greater flexibility for your readers. However, this does not come for free. Authoring SGML in general takes more work than authoring HTML, and fewer tools are available. Two key areas require more work. First, you have to choose a DTD and (depending on that DTD choice) perhaps do more detailed tagging than would be needed in HTML; and second, you probably have to deal with more hierarchical structures instead of a pretty flat "list of paragraphs" model.

DTD Choice, Design, and Modification

If you're using HTML, you've already chosen a DTD, and the only details are deciding which proprietary extensions to permit (if any), and which revision of the standard DTD to choose. With generic SGML, you have many more options, and you need to see if there is a DTD already available for the kind of data you're dealing with. If not, and if no other one seems similar enough to use (as-is or after minor tweaking), you may end up creating a whole new DTD, and maintaining it as time goes on. For all the details on creating and maintaining DTDs, see Part III, "Content Modeling: Developing the DTD."

A related decision is just how to use the tags available. You can distinguish fine levels of detail, or you can throw many things into each of a few big buckets, or most likely of all, you can do some of each. The finer the distinctions you make, the more accurately you can search and the more refined you can make your formatting. On the other hand, each distinction you make implies a certain commitment; if you're tagging book titles as separate from italic for emphasis, the user may be surprised if you mis-tag one as the other.

Whenever you make tagging distinctions that go beyond marking up fonts, indents, and other obvious physical features, you're making human decisions. A scanner and good OCR software can flag every place where the text turns italic, bold, and back again—but it can't tell you why. For that, you need human intervention. Most of the time, the decisions are pretty easy for people. It's seldom hard to distinguish a title from a foreign phrase. But to do it really well on complicated texts with fine-grained markup is a lot more difficult: telling an etymology from a field-of-study marker in a dictionary entry is a lot more difficult; marking up the syllable structures in poetry and telling a theme from an allusion in literature are more difficult still, though literary scholars may do exactly that for the texts they study.

Decide up front how much tagging you need for your purposes; think about how much effort you can apply, and then find a sensible balance. It may be helpful to write down the decisions somewhere. After tagging a lot of text, the goals may get fuzzy. The goals are also useful information for end users of the text: They help specify what people can expect to do with the text. Because of this, it is often useful to include a summary of such decisions somewhere in the text, for example in a special element put in just for that reason.

Need To Think More Hierarchically

Hierarchies buy a lot of power over flatter, one- or two-level structures. At the same time, they can make for extra data preparation work, because most word processors have very little hierarchy. For example, most word processors have no notion of a "list," only list items—that's why they can't automatically keep list items numbered as you insert and delete them while editing. The same problem comes up with large containers, such as chapters and sections, and with blocks embedded in the middle of paragraphs. Moving data from such word processors to SGML requires some extra work, such as setting up the converter to group adjacent list items into a list, and to notice that the unindented "paragraph" following something is really a continuation of the paragraph element that was before it, and so on.

SGML Assures More Consistency and Flexibility

Maybe it's a payoff for all that extra up-front thinking. Once you have your data in SGML using an appropriate DTD, you can depend on it for a wider range of processing. Since SGML lets you validate certain structures, you can ensure that certain things are possible. For example, knowing that every section has a title means you have less to worry about when setting up a table of contents. Knowing that chapters can't show up inside of footnotes lets you optimize queries, simplify formatting specifications, and so on.

At the same time, SGML is more flexible than just HTML. If you need a new kind of element, you can create it. Since it's very hard to think of everything in advance, this kind of extensibility pays off in the long run.

SGML Helps Make Allowances for HTML

As important as consistency and flexibility, however, is the added power you get for Web delivery. Having your data in SGML lets you express a lot of information that helps you deliver better HTML.

If the data "knows" the difference between conceptual classes of elements (because the tagging distinguishes them), you can choose at any moment whether to collapse them into a single HTML (or other) element, or to keep them distinct. This is most effective under the integrated conversion model discussed earlier, but it also helps in batch models.

Because you can keep more distinctions than HTML provides, you can have more information. If you have more information, you can do more with your data. You've already seen how you can customize HTML data for different clients, different versions of each client, different users, and different views.

Another useful technique is to filter views down to show only the information that's relevant to the current user and his current needs. For example, a user can do a query and the server can pick out just the few pieces of the SGML document(s) that are relevant. Those then get tagged in HTML and sent back as a valid document. It may be that the pieces wouldn't be valid if they were just pulled out and stuck end-to-end (for example, the result might be missing required elements, such as front matter, titles, and so on). But the conversion tool can map them into a structure that conforms to HTML or some other specific DTD.

> **Note**
>
> In publishing (especially legal publishing), this is called *boilerplating*—you grab pieces of documents from a collection of useful bits and assemble the document you need from the pieces. SGML gives you the information *about* your information that makes this practical.

Overusing Optional SGML Features Is Dangerous

Another question is what to do with the many optional features in the SGML standard. Many of these have to do with minimizing tags—saving you from typing and making raw SGML easier to read (in case you ever have to!). But SGML minimization provides synonyms for things SGML can already express, so you can always do without it. Unlike synonyms in human languages, which always have subtle differences, a minimized SGML tag expresses *exactly* the same element structure as if it were unminimized, so using it doesn't add any subtle special meanings to your documents. It may make typing or reading the tag easier, but who wants to literally type tags anyway? Better interfaces are available. For instance, you can pick element types from menus and display them as icons, in the margins, or on request.

There are some good reasons to avoid using much minimization in your SGML data (perhaps this should be called *minimizing minimization*?). This is especially true on the Web, for a couple reasons.

First, systems vary in which optional features they support. Although most general SGML tools support the SHORTTAG and OMITTAG features, right now Web clients have much more limited, HTML-specific parsers. Even if they are extended to support DTDs other than HTML, they may not learn to handle marked sections, omitted start tags, and other capabilities (or they may not get the harder features exactly correct). By keeping your SGML as simple as possible, you can choose from a wider variety of tools to work with it.

If you avoid minimization, you can even use completely SGML-ignorant tools effectively. A global change from `<LI>` to `<ITEM>` is a fine way to change all instances of one kind of element into another (but don't forget `</LI>` to `</ITEM>`!). That is, it's fine unless you happened to just use `<>` or omit some start or end tags entirely. The same snags come up with the `Find` command in a generic editor if you minimize: Searching for `<P>` doesn't do much good if you left the tag out, to be implied via SGML's minimization features. If you plan to convert your SGML to HTML for Web delivery, this may be important to think about.

Another reason to avoid minimization is that you may want to be able to ship small pieces of an SGML document around. There's no guarantee that a piece of SGML can be interpreted right if it's taken out of context (the same thing is true in most languages, even English). An SGML document that doesn't use much minimization has a much better chance of being interpreted than one that does minimize. Think about what an SGML parser would have to do if it got an SGML portion like this:

```
<p>This is a sample/short paragraph</p>
```

You can probably interpret it right; it sure *looks* like a paragraph element with a few words in it. And it is, so long as a few things are assumed (besides that delimiters like < haven't been redefined in the SGML declaration):

- The piece didn't come out of someplace buried deep down, like inside a quoted attribute value (the SGML technical term is that the piece should start in CON mode).
- There are no marked sections left open, except maybe ones with the INCLUDE keyword.
- The piece didn't come out of the middle of a CDATA element, a CDATA entity, and so on.
- The piece didn't come out of the middle of a comment, processing instruction, or something else.
- There are no NET-enabling start tags hanging around. Those are a minimization capability in SGML, where if you code a start tag as `<X/` rather than `<X>`, the next / in text content counts as if it were the end tag `</X>`—so if one of those is pending, the slash in "sample/short" changes meaning, and serves as an end tag, not as text content).

> **Caution**
>
> Here are SGML examples to show the context problems described. In each case, the <p> isn't really a start tag. In the last example, the final </P> would probably be reported as an SGML syntax error (because the earlier slash ended the paragraph already). You should avoid cases like these in your SGML if you anticipate having servers ship out pieces of it on demand.
>
> ```
> <revision original="<p>This is a sample/short paragraph</p>">
>
>
> <![ IGNORE [ <p>This is a sample/short paragraph</p> ]]>
>
>
> <!ENTITY notags CDATA "<p>This is a sample/short paragraph</p>">
> ...
> <EXAMPLE>&notags;</EXAMPLE>
>
>
> <!-- deleted 4/2/95: <p>This is a sample/short paragraph</P> -->
>
>
> <SEC/ ...<p>This is a sample/short paragraph</P>...
> ```

There are not very many possible problems, and you can completely avoid most of them by deciding only to ship pieces that amount to whole elements, and to skip using a few SGML constructs that can have long-distance effects. The ones that pose the most problems for shipping pieces of an SGML file around in isolation are these:

■ Omitted or empty start tags

■ #CURRENT attributes

■ NET-enabling start tags

■ Marked sections (you can also solve this problem if your server or conversion process can be set up to resolve marked sections before shipping data; it can literally delete the IGNORE marked sections, and so on)

■ Declared content (RCDATA, CDATA, or EMPTY)

All these structures can have long-lasting effects that change how an SGML parser must interpret the incoming characters. If you avoid them, you can just ship any element out of the SGML stream and it is possible to parse it and get the start tags and end tags right (you do still have to include the DTD and declaration subset, or a way to get them, such as via a URL).

Remember that none of these structures are errors. They are all legal, valid SGML capabilities. If you're working in a generic SGML environment, they should all work just fine (unless the software has a bug, or the author creating the SGML misuses something). The precautions mentioned here are merely guidelines to help make the SGML easier to transport in Web-like environments where you simply can't afford to send entire documents in one fell swoop. Since these particular SGML capabilities are not commonly used anyway, you probably won't have to worry about them.

From Here...

This chapter covered the basic options for delivering SGML data over the Web regardless of its DTD. The biggest decision is whether to really ship SGML to client programs, or to translate to HTML at the server end.

For more information, refer to the following:

- Chapter 19, "Should You Upgrade to SGML?," covers the trade-offs involved in deciding how to prepare your data in the first place.
- Chapter 21, "Integrating SGML and HTML Environments," surveys a variety of successful uses of SGML on the Web, and covers the kinds of tools typically involved in building a complete system.

V

SGML and the WWW

Integrating SGML and HTML Environments

This chapter discusses what is happening with SGML on the Web and how you can get to that information, as well as what you need to get going with SGML on the Web. It doesn't cover all the details, but it gives an overview of several tools. You then can decide which tools fit your needs for Internet delivery of SGML information. This chapter also points you to many URLs that provide examples.

The discussion is divided into parts that cover:

- Some successful uses of SGML on the Web
- Current solutions and tradeoffs
- Tools and how to combine them

Can It Be Done?

Many people and companies have SGML data on the Web and several companies have introduced helpful products. So here are a few of their success stories, along with URLs so you can check them out directly.

> **Note**
>
> See Appendix B for a longer list of Internet sites that have SGML tools, information, and data content. This section focuses on locations that deliver SGML through the World Wide Web itself.

 ▶▶ See "Internet Resources," p. 569

Novell
www.novell.com

Novell delivers its NetWare documentation in multiple languages on CD-ROM using SGML. Novell has made this documentation available on the Web. The documents are over 100,000 pages in five languages and are marked up using the DocBook DTD (popular in the computer industry). Various other materials on Novell's site are in HTML, but the manuals are kept in SGML (using the DocBook DTD), and converted on the fly to HTML using EBT's DynaWeb system (see fig. 21.1).

Fig. 21.1

Novell delivers NetWare documentation to the Web directly from SGML.

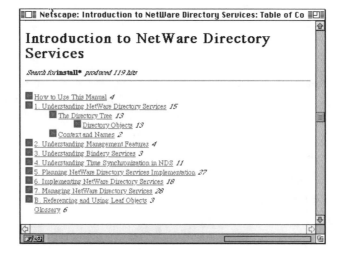

Text Encoding Initiative (TEI)
www.ebt.com/usrbooks/teip3 and etext.virginia.edu/TEI

Several universities are leaders in creating interesting and useful SGML data. Some of them have large literary SGML collections and make them available in various forms on the Web. The most easily available materials are significant works of English literature. Poetry, literature of other languages, and less-famous works of all kinds are also going online very quickly.

Many of the projects working with literature, poetry, drama, and other related areas use the TEI "Guidelines for Encoding Machine Readable Texts." You might wonder whether those guidelines are themselves available in SGML. They are: You can get them through the Open Text server running at the University of Virginia, or through EBT. If you're thinking of preparing any type of literary work in SGML, you can't do without these guidelines.

CD-ROM and paper versions also are available and are produced from the same SGML source files. The project maintains FTP archives at:

ftp-tei.uic.edu/pub/tei   (for users in North America)
ftp.ifi.uio.no/pub/SGML/TEI   (for users in Europe)
TEI.IPC.Chiba-u.ac.jp/TEI/P3   (for users in Asia)

The Oxford University Text Archive (OTA)
ftp.ota.ox.ac.uk

The Oxford Text Archive collects and distributes electronic texts as well as helps develop the TEI guidelines. Among the authors included in this archive are Charles Dickens, Mark Twain, H.G. Wells, and E.R. Burroughs. You can access many of these books, which are marked up (with the TEI DTD) and ready to drop into an electronic document system. You can use applications such as Fetch or Telnet to access the texts, or a Web client that supports the FTP protocol. You can also browse and search many of these texts by pointing your Web browser to **www.ebt.com/literature** (see fig. 21.2).

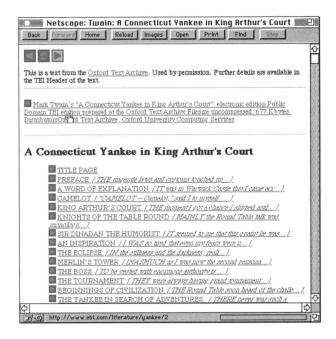

Fig. 21.2

The Oxford Text Archive has marked up many texts using the TEI DTD. This view shows one by Mark Twain, accessed via the DynaWeb SGML Web server.

V

SGML and the WWW

University of Virginia
www.lib.virginia.edu/etext/ETC.html

The University of Virginia has a major electronic text center that works with a wide variety of literature and mirrors a lot of information from other sites. Much of the information is in SGML and available on the Web. Start at the URL shown above to explore this collection (see fig. 21.3).

Fig. 21.3

A sample of Doyle's "The Red-Headed League" from the University of Virginia collection of SGML documents.

Center for Electronic Texts in the Humanities (CETH)
cethmac.princeton.edu

Rutgers and Princeton Universities together sponsor the Center for Electronic Texts in the Humanities, or CETH. CETH focuses on providing information on how to catalog, maintain, and distribute electronic documents; it also provides courses and periodicals to help in this effort.

Summer Institute of Linguistics (SIL)
www.sil.org

SIL has been working with highly structured electronic documents in many languages for many years, even before SGML was the way to do it. Through its Web site you can get a great deal of information about SGML, including a bibliography by Robin Cover that points to almost everything ever published on SGML (though not all of the more recent stuff—for the last couple years, there's been so much activity that no one can keep up with it all). You can find the *SGML Bibliography* at **www.sil.org/sgml/biblio.html**.

University of California at Berkeley
www.lib.berkeley.edu/AboutLibrary/Projects/BFAP

Through the Berkeley Finding Aids Project (BFAP), the UC Berkeley Library and others have developed a DTD for managing information about archives, personal papers, manuscripts, and other kinds of information found in libraries, special collections, and archives. Some of this information is becoming available on the Web. For more information, see the URL above (there are some especially nice pictures of San

Francisco from before the 1906 earthquake and fires). Duke University also participates actively in this project. Go to **odyssey.lib.duke.edu/findaid/** (this site has the nice feature of providing a choice of whether to see the data using the BFAP DTD or HTML).

Fig. 21.4

Thumbnails of photos from UCB special collections accessible on the Web. You can click the thumbnails to download higher-resolution versions.

SGML Open
www.sgmlopen.org/index.sgml

The companies that develop SGML products have a cooperative organization called SGML Open. On the SGML Open Web site, you can find a wealth of information about all aspects of SGML, and pointers to many companies with SGML products. Many of those companies have an interest in HTML as well, and provide products that apply in both worlds.

The Online Computer Library Center (OCLC)
http://www.oclc.org:5046

The Online Computer Library Center (OCLC) has put a lot of searchable data on the Web, and also provides a place to get Panorama, which is a product that can serve as a helper application to enable you to read SGML documents across the Web. You can find SoftQuad's Panorama at **www.sq.com/htmlsgml/htmlsgml.htm**, as well as on the CD-ROM included with this book.

On the CD

OCLC also provides a useful tool called Fred, which does two main things. First, you can send it an SGML document without a DTD, and it will send you back a DTD that matches. This won't be an ideal DTD, but it will at least get your document to parse, which opens the door to using SGML software to go farther. Second, Fred can do certain kinds of translation on SGML data, so it can help you move data from one DTD to another (even to HTML, or to non-SGML formats like TeX). You can reach Fred at **www.oclc.org/fred/**.

The big advantages these sites make use of are: 1) SGML's capability to adjust to whatever structure is appropriate for given document; 2) its capability to handle very large applications when needed; and 3) its capability to serve as an information-rich source from which you can generate many other formats at will (such as HTML).

Compromises To Be Made

Given these strengths and successes, you might wonder about the associated costs: how much extra time and effort are required to get the benefits. The biggest factor is that using SGML is an investment; you have to put in more up front to get even more return down the road. Here are some ways that shows up:

Conversion Can Be Expensive

Getting your data into a more effective SGML DTD will probably cost more than just getting it into HTML (this might mean time or money or both, depending on what you're doing and how you're doing it). Any off-the-shelf scanner with good OCR software can get you a text with the font changes and paragraph breaks marked. From there, it's pretty easy to get to HTML tags, such as <P>, <H1>, <I>, and <B>.

Tables, figures, equations, multi-column text, and footnotes are harder because scanners can't do as much to identify them for you. But if you have simple documents, a little scanning, a few global changes, and some proofreading can get them to be at least readable on the Web.

With more general SGML DTDs, you *could* just pretend most of the element types weren't there, and mark everything up using only a few types of tags. This can be useful as a starting point, especially if you're working from scanned documents or other unstructured data. But when you have a more powerful DTD, it's a shame not to make more use of it. In many DTDs, you have the possibility of making more useful distinctions, and using them lets you provide more features and flexibility to your readers.

For example, you could create a software manual using either HTML or DocBook. DocBook gives you many more choices of element types, such as for all the kinds of special "names" you run into in a software manual. For example, there are tags you can use to mark whether "Open" is being used as a menu item name, a button name, a command to type, and much more. In HTML, there aren't enough tags to go around, so you can't separate those types—you have to lump things into more general categories, like italic or bold.

Why does this matter? Not so much because of formatting, though that's a factor. The more important reasons have to do with flexibility. For example, if there's no distinction in the tagging, you can't provide readers with a reliable way to search for the word "Open" where it's mentioned as a menu item without getting all the other

"Opens" that are around. If they're in a hurry to look up how to use the "Open" menu item, they may not be happy about this. In the same way, if there's no distinction, you can't provide readers with formatting options, such as a way for them to ask to see all descriptions of error messages displayed in red today. That too can be a very handy option.

People may not expect this kind of sophisticated searching or flexible formatting from an HTML file, but they probably will expect it if you use DocBook, since DocBook provides these capabilities and most DocBook users make use of them.

On the other hand, to use that available power you have to do more detailed tagging, and that takes some work. If there are only a dozen distinct tags actually used, it doesn't matter much whether they're selected out of HTML or DocBook.

It's much less work if authors put in such distinctions when they write than it is to add them later. To continue the last example, documentation authors ought to know at the moment they write the word "Open" whether they mean a menu item name or something else. They probably have to do some action in their word processor to mark it (such as underline it or put it in quotes). Because of this, it isn't much extra work to pick "Mark as Menu Name" rather than "Mark as Underlined"—and if they have to do more than just one thing (like make it italic *and* put it in quotes), they should be ahead of the game by using a descriptive SGML tag rather than a bunch of specific formatting commands.

On the other hand, it can be a big pain to go through and add tags later. To do it, someone has to go through and read the whole document and decide which format changes were done for which reasons, or which entirely unmarked parts of the document should be identified in some new way. This may not cost a lot, but it certainly costs something.

The important questions are, "How much can you afford to mark up?" and "Which things are the most important?" Factors in deciding which things are important include: how the document will be formatted, how users can search it, how servers can process it for other uses (like converting it to HTML versions, to various output forms, and so on), and how users can refer to it.

Non-conversion Can Cost More Later

Have you ever gone through your old floppy disks and run across a file you wanted to look at again? Perhaps you're copying all your old 400K Mac disks to newer disks and you find that they seem to copy without a problem. However, you can't open the old documents on the new version of your word processor. The word processor is made by the same company and is the same product, but it's a couple versions later than the version with which you created the document. Nobody said your old files couldn't be read anymore; it just happened, and you only found out by chance.

HTML is changing in the same way. Like software products, it's getting better with each revision (well, at least that's how software is *supposed* to be!). But, because it is only one DTD, it can never contain everything everyone wants, and new versions will continue to appear. As new element types are defined and browsers start supporting them, you run into the same maintenance problem as with software upgrades.

You can already find pages all over the Web that use outmoded HTML tagging, or that have features that only work in some particular version of some particular browser. The problem will likely get worse. When browser makers create proprietary tags, they create incompatibility. This is especially true if those tags represent some formatting effect rather than some meaningful unit. But even in the best circumstances (namely, if everyone participates in the HTML revision process and every version of HTML manages to maintain backward compatibility), old files won't be able to take advantage of whatever new capabilities come from the new tags.

Note

One good example of a new HTML capability is the DIV element added in HTML 2.1. It works like the chapter and section elements in many other DTDs. That is, it's a container for *whole* units (in contrast, H1, H2, and so on are *titles of* containers). Using containers makes it much easier for software to manipulate them. A browser or server can generate an outline view, an editor can provide a "move section" command, and so on.

To use DIVs in HTML 2.1 or later, open a <DIV> right before each heading element (i.e., H1, H2) and close it right before the next heading of the *same or lower* level number (you really need to include the end tags for these). To be extra clear, you can also add a TYPE attribute with a value such as CHAPTER, SECTION, LEVEL1, LEVEL2, or whatever.

Flat HTML like this:

```
<h1>How to use the Web</h1>
<h2>Reading WWW pages</h2>
<p>Fire up a browser and click</p>
<h2>Creating your own WWW pages</h2>
<p>Type lots of pointy brackets</p>
<h1>How to use other Internet services</h1>
```

becomes hierarchical (there's added indentation here to make the structure stand out, but there's no reason you have to do this):

```
<DIV><h1>How to use the Web</h1>
 <DIV><h2>Reading WWW pages</h2>
  <p>Fire up a browser and click</p>
 </DIV>
 <DIV><h2>Creating your own WWW pages</h2>
  <p>Type lots of pointy brackets</p>
 </DIV>
</DIV>
<DIV><h1>How to use other Internet services</h1>
```

By setting up your data in an SGML DTD that fits it, changes only have to happen when you really want them to rather than because you need to accommodate a change to one particular DTD that isn't designed for your kind of data. Because you are not tied to a single DTD that may not be designed with your application in mind, you can stick with the one you have regardless of how HTML does or doesn't change.

You still may want to re-tag eventually; for example, you might discover some completely new kind of processing you want to do with the data for which your tagging isn't enough. The point is that *you* control the process. You can define the new element type, add it to the DTD, define it through stylesheets or a similar mechanism, and use it. And as browsers appear that aren't limited to the HTML DTD, you'll be able to use them.

Poor DTD Design Is Very Costly

Having your documents in a DTD of your choice preserves your freedom and control over your data. But as always, freedom has its own responsibilities and risks. HTML has a lot of design effort in it, and problems in its early versions were flushed out by a huge number of people using it and reporting whatever problems they ran into. This is also true for many other established DTDs, but it won't be true for one you write from scratch, or for any modifications you make to a standard DTD.

When you start making your own DTDs, be very careful, and think far ahead about the consequences for your data. Chapters 4 through 10 in this book show you how to go about designing a good DTD. Books and courses in DTD design are also helpful (Appendix B, "Finding Sources for SGML Know-How," lists some useful books). Another source of help is Internet discussion groups such as **comp.text.sgml**, where many experts participate and help others solve problems ranging from the simple to the very complex.

Tools Required and How To Combine Them

Putting SGML data onto the Web works best if you coordinate several steps. The first is to get the data into SGML somehow. Once it's there, you may need a way to get it into some final form, either by converting to HTML, printing it, or feeding it to something that can process it directly (like an SGML-aware Web browser). Finally, you'll likely need some tools for managing the data: tools that notice when documents change, check for broken links, and so on. This is doubly important on the Web, because a document may be linked to from many places that the document's owner doesn't even know about.

A lot of the tools center on the server—what your server stores and what it must send to clients. If the server stores SGML, you need to create the SGML somehow, and either use some protocol for sending it to SGML-aware clients or convert it to something your clients can handle. If the server only stores HTML, conversion moves back earlier in the process. In that case, you can use entirely offline processes (that is, create the HTML any way you can and just dump it on any Web server).

There is one other complication if you choose the offline conversion process: all of a sudden, you have to maintain two separate versions of the same document. Because of this, managing updates gets harder. For example, you may write an SGML document using your favorite DTD, then convert it to HTML and put the HTML form on your Web site. This immediately raises a question: which form is the "real" document? If the document never changes this may not be a big problem, but most documents do get changed or updated sooner or later. When that happens, you have to decide whether to update the original SGML and re-create new HTML from that, change the HTML and throw the original SGML away, or to try to separately edit both the original SGML and the HTML and keep them in sync. If you're using the SGML form for other purposes too, like print or CD-ROM publishing, the only practical choice may be to edit the SGML and re-generate the HTML (which is probably the best choice anyway). However you organize the process, it still involves extra work, and it's very easy to get files that don't quite match anymore.

Getting into SGML

Getting into SGML is something this book has talked about a lot; you can author in SGML or convert data from something else. Authoring systems give you a straightforward interface where you can create, move, edit, and delete elements and text intuitively. Many also validate your documents so you can always be sure there are no SGML syntax errors (SoftQuad Author/Editor, ArborText Adept, and Grif). SGML authoring systems have another advantage: They typically write out the documents without a lot of minimization, so you automatically avoid more difficult SGML details that not all software may fully support.

▶▶ For more information on SGML converters and other utilities, see Chapter 28, "Other Tools and Environments," p. 489

Converters come in two flavors—either built-in (like MS Word's and WordPerfect's SGML import/export features), or as standalone programs (like DynaTag, FastTAG, the SGML Hammer, OmniMark, Perl, and so on). The built-in kind have recently added validation features, and so are getting much more like native SGML authoring systems. Standalone programs have some tradeoffs. They can handle a wider range of input, even raw scanned OCR files, but they usually don't guarantee the result will be valid.

Caution

It's nearly impossible to guarantee producing valid SGML output when you have no control of the input (for example, if your data is coming from a scanner and OCR). Think about what would happen if someone tried to take a poem and "convert" it to SGML using a DTD meant for software manuals? Many of the required elements just wouldn't be there—like version numbers, an index of commands, and so on. You could set up a converter to create those elements, but there wouldn't be useful data to put into them. In the end, a converter can only do so much.

Getting Back Out to HTML

Once you have SGML, you're in good shape to convert to almost anything else, and HTML is an easy target. In the simplest case, you just do a bunch of global changes to rename tags from the names in your DTD to the names in HTML; for elements that occur in all kinds of documents this works just fine: lists, paragraphs, headings, and so on.

Caution

The first time people do this, they usually miss a few cases. Here are a few to watch out for if you're using software that doesn't really know SGML:

- Remember to allow for attributes in start-tags—you can't count on the ">" being right after the tag name.

- Be very careful if you use minimization. A tag could have either pointy-bracket missing, the element type missing, or the tag might be completely missing if you use OMITTAG (in that case, it might be a little hard to write a global change to catch it!).

- If you're changing between two different DTDs, be careful that the element types you change to are allowed in all the places they're used. Otherwise, the parser will either report an error (which makes the problem easy to find) or quietly recover by closing elements until it finds one where the new element is allowed (which can make it a lot more difficult to find).

- If you're converting HTML that you haven't run through an SGML parser, watch out for URLs that aren't quoted.

Usually when you convert from SGML to HTML, you end up throwing distinctions away, such as converting three different element types to just be tagged as italics (<I>) instead. This makes it very important to think of the SGML form as the "real" document, and keep it around for later when you may want to do a slightly different conversion on it.

See the previous chapter, "Practicalities of Working with SGML on the Web," for more details on tools for converting SGML to HTML. In particular, some Web servers do it on the fly, which is a big advantage for data management and overall flexibility. There are too many standalone tools to mention (Perl is one of the most popular and portable)—many useful tools are discussed at **www.undergrad.math. uwaterloo.ca**, for example /~papresco/private/calibre/sgml/tools/sgml2html.html).

As time goes on, the need to translate will shrink (it might eventually go away completely). It's not that much more difficult to program a browser that can accept any tags at all than one that can accept only HTML. The main addition is the need to access and read some kind of stylesheet that says what to do with each given tag. Panorama and DynaText have already proven that this approach works, and further solutions will continue to appear.

> **Note**
>
> C. M. Sperberg-McQueen and Robert F. Goldstein wrote a wonderful paper on the potential for extending Web clients this way, with the imposing title "HTML to the Max: A Manifesto for Adding SGML Intelligence to the World-Wide Web." You can get it from **www.ncsa.uiuc.edu** in the file SDG/IT94/Proceedings/Autools/sperberg-mcqueen/sperberg.html.

Getting Back Out to Print

In addition to Web delivery, you may want to provide printed output. Web browsers can do some level of draft printing on demand, but most are quite limited. For example, most, if not all, HTML-based Web browsers will not number your printed pages well, much less give you flexible control over page headers and footers, newspaper-style multi-column layouts, complicated tables, footnotes, and so on. Because of this, going through HTML as a way to print SGML isn't very effective.

SGML authoring systems can do quite nice printing, so if you have your data in one of them, you may be in fine shape. However, right now the most sophisticated print formatting tools don't directly accept SGML (some, like PageMaker, can read some limited SGML-like tagging). If you need high-end printing and typesetting capabilities, you will need to move the SGML data into a special paper-production system.

Remember that it's much easier to convert SGML to other forms, than other forms to SGML. That puts you in a strong position if you have SGML. You can probably get to any typesetting system you want without too much pain. Once you do that, your data will be in a system that book production specialists already know. They don't have to adopt or learn something new, and they can focus all their attention on getting you the best-looking result (of course, "they" might be "you" in many cases).

Here are some of the formatting capabilities that (if you need them) could force you to move to a specialized solution:

- Sophisticated footnote management (say, where footnotes might break across two pages, or require unusual numbering)
- Widow control (preventing the first or last lines of paragraphs from getting left on a separate page)
- Hyphenation (especially sticky cases like long, unusual, or foreign words)
- Special layouts such as tables, equations, text flowing around odd-shaped graphics
- Floating graphics (that automatically shift up or down relative to the text, to make for the best page layout)
- Book-level tools to build tables of contents, indexes, fancy title pages, and so on

For this level of features, you're best off moving your SGML into typesetting software such as QuarkXPress, PageMaker, TeX, or something similar. These tools are focused on doing one specific thing well, and so will do a better job at it than more general tools (which also have to devote effort to intuitive editing, search and retrieval, and so on).

Document Management

Most documents any longer than a business letter don't exist in only one form. They get re-edited, expanded, or even chopped up and included in other documents. As this happens, many problems arise. On any system that supports cross-references or hyperlinks to documents, a big problem comes up right away: What should the reference point to after the original document changes?

Let's say Mr. Smith writes an article and publishes it. A few months later, Ms. Jones reads it, finds a big flaw, and publishes a review criticizing it. Mr. Smith reads the review, realizes Ms. Jones is right, and re-writes his article fixing the problem. So far, nothing special; this happens all the time.

But what happens when some third person comes along later, and the first thing he runs into is the review? If this is all online, he'll probably follow a link that Ms. Jones made, that pointed to the worst part of Mr. Smith's article. Should he see the old version, or the new?

If he sees the old version, he gets the correct impression that Ms. Jones found a real problem, but Mr. Smith may be upset because even though he really did fix the problem since then, the later reader doesn't find that out. On the other hand, if the reader sees only the new version, it's a bit unfair to Ms. Jones, since it will look like her review was making up errors to complain about.

Doug Engelbart's "Augment" system dealt with this as far back as the mid-60s (he invented the computer mouse, multi-window displays, the outline processor, video-teleconferencing, and a few other things). In Augment, any time you made a document public a copy of that version was locked and kept around permanently. So links would always point to the same thing. The really nice touch, though, was that the system carefully kept track of which document and version was which, so when you followed such a link it could tell you immediately that a newer version(s) of the document was also around.

This seems fair to all concerned, and a system like that would help us a lot today. On the Web, documents change all the time and sometimes just disappear, all with no notice. Several companies are working to solve this problem by introducing Web site management tools. Object-oriented databases are being used very effectively in building this kind of tool.

Such tools keep track of versions of documents, and you can ask them what happened to a given version. The better ones will let you recover a version by date or name, and may even be able to say how it differs from some other version that was published at another time. These tools can also look around whenever you change a document, and warn you about particular links that are affected (either ones that break outright, or ones that might not be meaningful anymore, as in Mr. Smith's case).

No high-end Web-specific management tools are available yet. However, a couple have been announced, and a few sites are experimenting with similar tools that have been around for other purposes, such as RCS for managing computer program source

V

SGML and the WWW

code files. This area is expected to become very hot in the next several months. A good solution to the problems that arise when documents change and links break would be a huge step forward.

From Here...

There are many issues to consider as you prepare to supply SGML data via the Internet. What DTD to use; how, when, and whether to convert your documents to HTML; and what servers and data management tools to use. This chapter covered those issues and tradeoffs, and provided some key points to ask about when planning a Web-based SGML delivery system. One big plus for using SGML is the potential to use the same documents for a variety of purposes: Web delivery, CD-ROM or local-area network delivery, print production, information retrieval, and more. Many sites have done this successfully already.

For more information, refer to the following:

- Chapter 20, "Practicalities of Working with SGML on the Web," covers some of the tools you might need in more detail.

- Chapter 22, "Developing for the World Wide Web," covers several hot current topics, such as how the MIME standards are being enhanced to support SGML, some important related standards such as HyTime, and some tips to help you get professional-looking results.

- Appendix B, "Finding Sources for SGML Know-How," provides a variety of useful resources, such as books and Web sites.

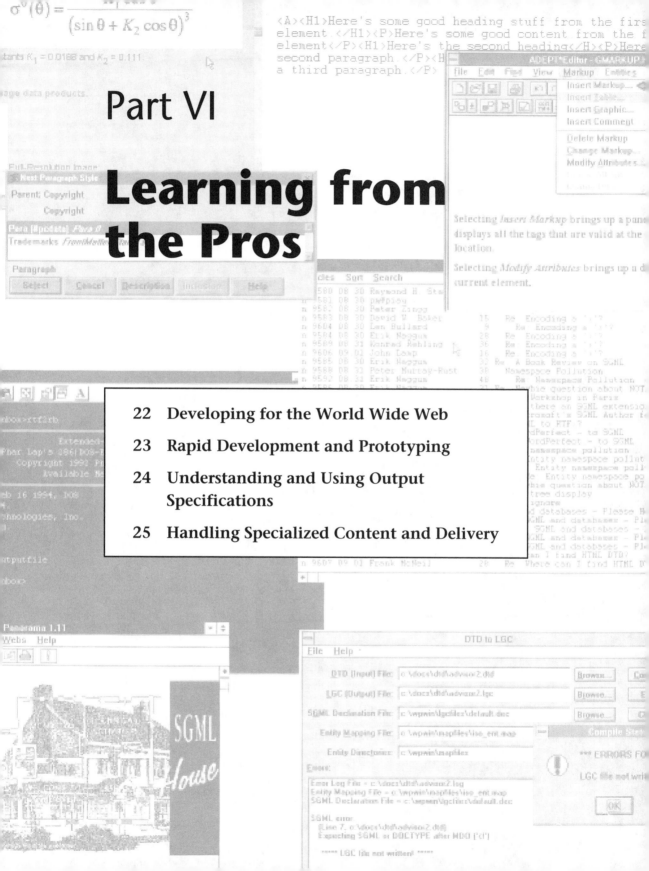

Part VI

Learning from the Pros

22   Developing for the World Wide Web

23   Rapid Development and Prototyping

24   Understanding and Using Output Specifications

25   Handling Specialized Content and Delivery

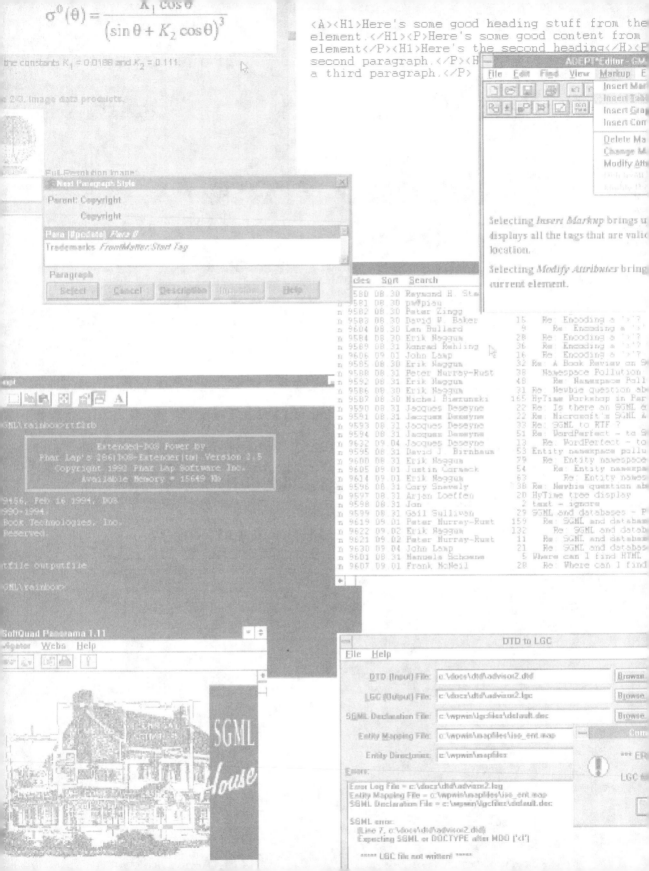

CHAPTER 22

Developing for the World Wide Web

To develop SGML data for the Web, you need to be familiar with the last few chapters. They discuss some of the tools and techniques available, and a lot of the costs, benefits, and design trade-offs you will be facing. This chapter talks about what really distinguishes effective use of SGML from boring use, or how to get the most out of your markup effort.

In this chapter, you learn about:

- How SGML and the Web are converging
- The HyTime standard, which builds on SGML to provide many hypermedia capabilities, and so relates closely to the Web
- Some practical ways to make your SGML data on the Web provide real value for your readers

SGML's Future on the Web

There are a few key problems people often run into on the Web which, as you've seen, even basic use of generic SGML can help solve. Some of these problems include:

- Having to convert data into one particular DTD (HTML)
- Sometimes having to use HTML tags in unconventional ways to get just the right formatting (that is, tags are too closely tied to particular formatting)
- Managing several flavors of HTML; a document that looks good in one browser may look horrible in a browser that supports a slightly different version or that has different proprietary extensions
- Breaking up big documents

Another problem is that links using URLs break easily (for example, if the destination file is merely moved or renamed) and are hard to fix, but that's not exactly an "HTML" problem (URLs are defined by another standard to which the HTML standard refers). HTML is gradually working to address many other problems, but no matter what happens with those, the problems above will still be with you—they're pretty much built in.

The only direction HTML can go without "trading up" to generic SGML, is to continually add more particular tags (well, it could discard structure entirely and say everyone has to send PostScript or bitmap pictures of pages—but that wouldn't really be HTML anymore, and it would be a big step backwards!).

Adding more tags to HTML means HTML has to go through a repeated standardization process, create a new (maybe incompatible) version, create incompatibilities in browsers, and so on. No matter how much you add, you'll never finish (it's like trying to finalize the English dictionary; people always spoil it by coming up with brand-new ideas and wanting words for them).

The fundamental direction of SGML for the Web is different. SGML just says, "Why fight? Let everybody create the tags they need." The DTD lets people *say* what tags they created. A good DTD will come with documentation and at least a sample stylesheet to explain what the tags mean. A client just reads the DTD, the document, and the stylesheet, and it works.

This is probably inevitable on the Web. In the long run, people won't accept a limited set of tags any more than they'd accept a fixed set of style names in a word processor or a fixed vocabulary for English.

To be completely fair, let's look at the other side of the coin too: how might HTML influence SGML? There are some traditional snags people run into with SGML—most of them have to do with having so many optional features available. When you first approach SGML, it can look a little like a new car with a 20-page list of options from which to choose; a lot of them look tempting and are useful for some people, but if you try to take too many, you can have problems. What if you ask for the CD *and* the DAT player for your car, and they don't both fit? Or four wheel drive *and* front wheel drive—do you get six wheels?

Every feature costs something, so think about what you need, want, and can afford, and pick just those features (and hope someone checks whether they go together, too!). With a car, the cost of each feature is hard cash. With computer systems, the cost may not be so obvious, but it's still there. Here are some of the costs of over-using features:

- Different programs may support different SGML options, so a document that uses them might not work everywhere. For example, only a minority of parsers and SGML systems understand SGML features like CONCUR, DATATAG, EXPLICIT, and so on—that's one reason we haven't focused on them here.

- Even with programs that support them, less-used options get less testing and less attention, and might, therefore, be less reliable.

- There's that much more to learn, and that many more controls to keep straight.

- Different options can bump into each other in surprising ways (if you order air conditioning for your car, you may get a slightly larger engine, too; if you use SHORTREFs in SGML, it might suddenly matter a lot more just where you put line breaks).

- Even without using the fancier SGML options, you can run into snags if you make up a DTD with very specialized semantics. For example, tables and equations are very complicated to format, and so SGML systems often build in special formatting features for the tags most commonly used for them (probably CALS for tables, and ISO 12083 for equations). If you make up your own DTD for tables or equations, you may have to set up all that complex formatting yourself. Usually, it's better to just go with what's widely supported.

- You might look a little silly if you load up on many options you don't really need. For example, if you use DATATAG and send your file to another SGML user, he'll probably think it's a bit odd, since DATATAG is so uncommonly used and so rarely supported.

HTML's huge success, despite ignoring almost every SGML option, says something: there's a lot you can do with "no-frills" SGML. You've seen there are important things you can't do, too, so maybe the real lesson is to make sure you get the options you need, but pick just what you need; don't waste much money or effort on other capabilities. With SGML, this usually means not bothering about fancy minimization controls like DATATAG and RANK, and not using regular features in really subtle ways, such as marked sections that cut sideways across entity or element boundaries.

Some users really need a dragster, not a road car. For them, the feature and option list is very short, but every one that remains is critical. A "dragster" version of SGML might optimize parsing speed, networkability, and other needs by using no minimization at all. It would also avoid some tricky constructs like #CONREF, #CURRENT, and declared content. Even drag racers, however, want to be able to choose their own color scheme, tread style, and the like. Likewise, even the most stripped-down SGML subset needs the capability to define new tags (essentially, this means keeping a DTD).

Batch versus On-Demand Models

Once you have SGML data, delivering it raises issues. There aren't a lot of tools that can view SGML directly over the Net; DynaText and Panorama are currently the main tools, although that is changing. If you use them, the advantage is that all of the information expressible in SGML can move across the Net; that means the client can search, format, navigate, and filter the document in any way the original markup makes possible, rather than only in the ways HTML provides. The DynaText network client is to be released about the time this book reaches the shelves, but figure 22.1 gives a preview of it, viewing a manual natively in SGML across the Internet.

The alternative is to use an HTML-only client, but then something is lost in transmission. For example, you can't search or edit as flexibly if all you get is the HTML form. So you have a choice to make with your Web data:

- Use Panorama or DynaText
- Wait for other tools to become available
- Batch-convert your data to HTML
- Use a server that can convert data on-demand

Fig. 22.1

The DynaText Web client can view and navigate SGML locally or across the Net, regardless of what DTD is used (even HTML).

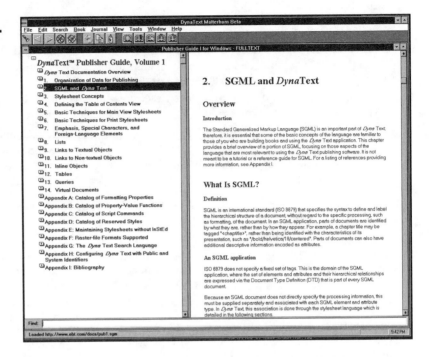

When it's possible, the last choice gives you the most flexibility because it lets you provide the data in the original or any derived form (or forms), any time you want. Ideally, such a server should not only support SGML-to-HTML conversions, but similar features for graphics. It should be able to send hi-res color images to people who have the bandwidth, hardware, and desire, but low-res versions of the same images to people who want to save time or have cheaper displays. This flexibility is also important to the visually impaired; such a server can send them text descriptions of graphics, which readers' terminals then read to them or display in Braille.

Some SGML Web sites let you choose the form you want—they have documents in many representations besides HTML, and can convert and serve them up in the best form for each individual client calling in. This is a lot like sites that let you choose between English, Spanish, French, and German when you enter the site. It gives a friendly feel, like the Web publisher is going out of his way to accommodate users.

Note

Here are some ways a server can customize for you. It's easy to see how each would be important for some users:

■ Pick out certain elements for certain users, such as <P LANGUAGE=GERMAN> for a German user.

- Suppress graphics and send their accompanying IMAGE-DESCRIPTION elements instead, when sending to blind users, users with non-graphical browsers, or users who just want to save bandwidth.

- Shorten the text by leaving out parts with certain PRIORITY attributes. For example, you could tag documents to respond cleverly depending on the reader's bandwidth, interest level, or expertise level.

- Check what client program is calling in, and optimize the formatting for it; use FRAME for Netscape, use Microsoft extensions for Explorer, full SGML for clients that support it, and so on.

If you're surfing the Web and you see documents optimized for your connection speed, your particular Web client, and version, the first thing you'll be asking is how it's done, and the second is how you can do it, too.

SGML makes it easy. You still have to set things up, say by noticing that Netscape has a format-oriented <BLINK> or <FRAME> tag that others don't, so your converter can put that tag in for Netscape and put in something else for others. But you only have to do that once, and you don't have to manage 20 slightly different versions of every page you have.

MIME Issues

The Internet standards groups are just now finalizing a MIME type for SGML (agreed-upon types are already there for HTML [TEXT/HTML], GIF [IMAGE/GIF], and so on). Until that's done, programs set up to receive SGML over the Net can't count on servers labeling the SGML documents with a certain known MIME type. In the meantime, systems tend to use "X-SGML" as their MIME type; the "X-" is reserved for trying a new MIME type out before it is standardized.

This is not a big problem. There are only so many different kinds of servers out there, so there won't be 20 different MIME types showing up anyway. But this is worth keeping an eye on, so as soon as a standard is final, you can look for servers that make use of it. Information about MIME standards can be found (among other places) at **http://ds.internic.net/rfc1521.txt**.

When the MIME standard arrives, some servers may need a slight tweak in order to label SGML correctly for MIME when they're sending it. The other case where servers need special attention is if you want them to be able to serve the same source SGML data in a variety of custom forms, such as HTML version X.Y, or various SGML DTDs.

High-End Search/Retrieval

You've probably used searching services on the Web. Some only index URLs, so you have to guess at least part of the file name to find something. Some index just the beginning of HTML files, extracting the content from a few special elements like TITLE. Some index just the titles, and a few index the entire text content.

VI

Learning from the Pros

A problem with most search tools is that they don't index the content in relation to the tagging. So even though you can search for "John" and "Smith," you can't insist that they show up in the same paragraph. You can't search for "Save" only where it's mentioned in a FORM element, or "Picture" only within an A (link) element. You especially can't search for "Save" where it's in the documentation of menu items for a software package (since HTML has no tag for that).

SGML-aware servers usually can do all these types of searches, and enable you to be much more precise in your queries. Even if your client is getting only HTML, it should still be possible for the server to search the original SGML for you. If it can't, you might want to look for a better server rather than changing your data.

> **Note**
>
> *Precise searching* is really a technical term for information retrieval nerds; it means that you don't get a lot of irrelevant information *in addition to* what you want. Watch out for the opposite problem too, even though it doesn't happen as much with most Web search tools; if you don't get enough of the information you *do* want, that's called a *recall* problem.

Link Persistence

URLs are notorious for failing when people get a new computer, a new disk, or even a new job. This is because the data moves. SGML's support for Formal Public Identifiers (FPIs) helps you get away from this. FPIs are expected to be generic, permanent identifiers for data, instead of today's location of the data.

Public Identifiers can sit around until needed, and only *then* get converted into a physical location. That way if the data's location changes, you can fix the problem by updating one table instead of every link everywhere in the world. The Internet standards groups are working on "URNs," which are a lot like FPIs and help in the same way.

> **Note**
>
> FPIs and URNs work a lot like a cellular phone. Behind the scenes a lot has to happen: as you move around and get "out of range" for one cell, you get switched to the next one. When that happens, you don't have to give everybody a new phone number to reach you—you don't even notice that anything happened at all. That's because your cell phone isn't identified by location (like a URL) but by a special, unique serial number that always stays the same for your individual phone, wherever you carry it (this is a lot like an FPI or URN).
>
> When someone calls you, the phone company looks up the serial number, and then uses it to look up your current location in a table somewhere and send the call to where you really are. When your phone switches to a new "cell," because the old one is too far away, your phone sends a little message to the new cell saying "I'm here." The new cell tells the phone company to update the table. Files on the Web will be able to move around just as freely once they're identified by names instead of locations.

In the meantime, you can make your links a little safer in two ways. First, use HTML's new BASE feature so that all your URLs are relative to a place you specify up front—then you only have to change that one place when something happens. Second, use SGML linking capabilities and leave it to your server to translate more generic pointers, such as FPIs, into URLs when it sends out your data. The next section goes into a lot more detail about some of the linking capabilities that have been built on top of SGML using the HyTime standard.

HyTime: SGML and Hypermedia

SGML provides a lot of tools for representing different kinds of documents, with the most important one being the ability to make up new tag-sets whenever you need to. But it only provides limited capabilities for creating links—SGML doesn't provide a standard way to mark up links between separate documents, for example.

ISO noticed this, and recently put out a standard that specifically extends SGML to deal with hypertext and multimedia. It's called HyTime.

Note

HyTime is built on top of SGML. After reading this book, you'll be ready to find out about HyTime. You can learn about it in Steve DeRose's and David Durand's book called *Making Hypermedia Work*. Your bookstore may have it already, or they can order it from the publisher.

HyTime specifies ways of using SGML to represent the things needed for hypermedia. These include references to documents, graphics, video, sound, and other media, as well as particular places in them; links to connect pairs or groups of such references; and ways to schedule presentations out of referenced pieces. Obviously, this is a whole lot more than <A>. HyTime, therefore, is a pretty big standard. The good news is that, like SGML, you can do a great deal even if you only learn a little bit of HyTime—you can always learn more as you need it.

HyTime support can be added on top of any system that supports SGML. Like SGML, HyTime has some very complex features, but you can accomplish a lot even by using only a few of the most basic features. Several SGML products have already added support for those more basic features already, and more are on the way.

Ultra-Basics of HyTime Links

HyTime links have three important parts:

- An *anchor* is the data that actually is at some end of the link. This can be anywhere, and you don't have to mark it in any special way for HyTime. Sometimes an anchor is loosely called an "end," since it's where you get to when you follow a link.

- A *location address* points to an anchor. There are many types of these: some refer to names, some let you count things, some let you do searches. You can even combine these, such as to ask for the third subelement of the element with ID=chap4 in such-and-such a document, or the upper-left quarter of the picture from minutes 2 through 12 of a video.

- A *link* puts together a bunch of location addresses to say they're related. Typically this ends up meaning that users are able to get from one to another with a single mouse click, but any other relationship is fine, too.

The A element in HTML is like a link with the location address included (on the HREF attribute). Whatever the HREF points to is one anchor; the other anchor is the contents of the A element.

How to Make HyTime Links

The most important step in making HyTime links is remembering to declare the object to which you're linking. You do this with a normal SGML ENTITY declaration that gives an appropriate public or system identifier, and the particular notation the object's data is in.

◄◄ For information about how to create ENTITY declarations, see "Specific Declarations," p. 176

```
<!ENTITY graphic12 SYSTEM "C:\artwork\original\chair.gif" NDATA GIF>
<!ENTITY mysound SYSTEM "http://xyz.com/sounds/python.wav" NDATA WAV>
```

Once you've declared the external objects to which you want to refer, you can make any number of pointers to each one, or to various parts of them. The main way to do this is with what HyTime calls a *nameloc*, used for locations, like entities, that have specific names:

```
<nameloc id=nl1><nmlist nametype=entity>graphic12</></>
```

This might look like a lot of markup, but it has a big advantage. It separates out that object's location or system id, and gives the object its own name (like "graphic12") in your document. Then you can refer to it as much as you want, and only have to fix the one declaration if the object moves. This is a lot like HTML's new BASE feature (HyTime and HTML developers do talk to each other).

Note

There is an update to the HyTime standard that's currently being finished. ISO calls it a *technical corrigendum* (or TC). It makes a number of fixes and changes, one of which is especially important here. It introduces a notion called *structured system identifiers*.

SGML and initial HyTime didn't say much about the "insides" of system identifiers. Most systems only let them be paths and file names, even though that's a restriction SGML has never required. The HyTime TC makes them a lot like URLs; they can start with a scheme name that

---

> says what follows, and then have whatever data is needed for that scheme. The TC also defines a bunch of useful schemes that you can use, much as the IETF has defined a bunch of useful schemes for URLs, like "http:" and "local:".
>
> The TC also adds an important link type called *nlink* that supports a wide range of existing linking conventions, such as the inter-book links in most industry-standard DTDs and links that work like HTML's A element.

Finally, you make an actual link in HyTime by referring to one or more of those pointers (using an IDREF). Links can live anywhere, but the simplest case is a one-way *clink* that contains its own caption and points to one other place. This is like A in HTML, except that instead of an attribute with a URL, it takes an attribute with an SGML IDREF:

```
<clink linkend="nl1">Click here to see Figure 12.</clink>
```

The link itself has to name an IDREF as its *linkend*. That means it can point to another element in the same document directly, but it can also point indirectly to anything else (like an element without an ID or a graphic). To do this, it uses an IDREF to point to any HyTime "location address" element (like the nameloc elements above). Then that element points somewhere else using whatever method is needed. You can make very long chains this way if needed, but you'll usually need only one or two steps, unless you're managing a lot of very sophisticated interacting links.

As mentioned, the HyTime TC adds a new link type, expected to be called *nlink*, that lets you point directly to destinations, even if they don't have IDs. This is how you can use HyTime to support HTML A elements directly. HREF works without changing any of what's there already—you just add two more attributes:

- HyTime=nlink tells HyTime that the element is an nlink as HyTime understands it, even though it's called "A."

- notation=HTML-LINK names an SGML NOTATION, declared in the DTD. The NOTATION refers to the HTML and WWW definitions for how HTML links work. That is, they point to the documents that say things like "put a URL on the HREF attribute" and "URLs look like..."

Given that, an A that's been modified for HyTime compatibility looks like this:

```
<a href="http://xyz.org/mydocs/homepage.htm" HyTime=nlink notation=HTML-
LINK>…
```

The problem with this is that it looks like you have to re-write all your HTML files to add the attributes. But that's not really true. You can leave the HTML files unchanged, and just tweak the DTD to set those attributes as defaults:

```
<!ATTLIST A HyTime NAME "NLINK"
  notation NOTATION (HTML-LINK) HTML-LINK>
```

You can even use SGML's #FIXED option to guarantee that no one sets those particular attributes to any value other than the one you specify. Having done this, you can leave the documents alone and just let the SGML parser fill in the right values as needed.

The final type of HyTime link is the most powerful. Clink and nlink both point in one direction, from a place in SGML to some other place. That is, the link must "live" right at one of its anchors. The third type, called an ilink, doesn't have those restrictions; it lists the location addresses that lead to *all* of its anchors, so its own location doesn't matter at all.

You can use ilinks to gather all your links together in one place. You can have a LINKS element at the end of your document, and collect all the links there. Better yet, you can move the links all the way out into a separate document that *only* has links. This can make it easier to manage the links, especially if there are a lot of them, or they connect many different documents. It also permits you to load different sets of links at different times, rather than having all links relevant to a document together even if half of them are only of interest to a few people.

 ◄◄ For a discussion of how links work when they are completely outside of the documents they link to, see "How Complex Are My References and Links?" p. 330

see "How Complex Are My References and Links?" p. 330

An ilink can also be two-way; it doesn't matter which end you start at, you can get from either end to the other. True two-way links also stay that way—in a system without them, you have to simulate them with two one-way links, and someday when one end moves or is updated, *half* of a link will break.

Since an ilink doesn't live at one end, there's no particular reason you can only have a total of two ends. You can have as many as you want. Most people find it a little hard to imagine, at first, just why you would want more than two ends to a link, but there are a lot of useful cases. Suppose you're writing a comparison between two earlier documents: you might want a link that points to part of one document, to a related part of the other, and to your comment about how they're related. That's three ends; to create a link connecting all of them, you'd use an ilink.

An ilink looks a lot like a clink, but doesn't need any content inside it to have a source anchor. Depending on how you set up your ilinks in the DTD, they can contain content, but, even so, the content isn't necessarily an anchor of the link. Like clink, ilink specifies its linkends with IDREFs, but on an attribute called "linkends" instead of just "linkend" (not very surprising, right?). The IDREFs can point either directly to anchors (for anchors that are elements in the same document, and that have IDs to point to), or indirectly, by pointing to location address elements that eventually lead to the anchors.

Here's an example of an ilink with three ends:

```
<p id=p1>The telephone was invented by Bell</p>
<p id=p2>The telephone was invented by Ring</p>
<p id=p3>"Bell" is the correct answer.</p>
<ilink linkends="p1 p2 p3">
```

The ilink just says that p1, p2, and p3 are related. There are some other constraints that you don't need much detail about. For example, you must declare a different SGML element type for ilinks with two ends, ilinks with three ends, and so on, as far as needed (you give them all attribute "HyTime=ilink" so a HyTime program can find them even though they have different names). Each kind of ilink also specifies a fixed set of *anchor roles*, a name for each anchor that (hopefully) describes its purpose. In this example, appropriate anchor roles might be "Quote Quote Comment" (to apply to the three ends in order—here p1, p2, and p3). Figure 22.2 is a diagram of such a link.

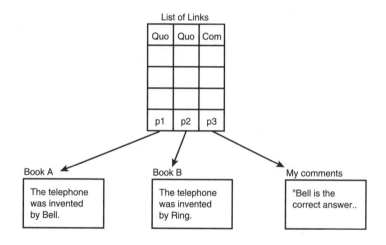

Fig. 22.2

HyTime "ilinks" don't live at any of their actual ends, but can go anywhere—so they can have any number of ends.

There's lots more to HyTime than this chapter can even begin to talk about, including many features for dealing with graphic, video, and other multimedia data. But this should give you a flavor for the kinds of powerful linking it provides.

How To Make Effective SGML Web Pages

Making a splash on the Web is a combination of many things. A lot of them have nothing to do with markup or even functionality. Probably the most important of all is that the information itself be interesting. You've probably sat through someone's pictures from a family vacation, and unless there's something more to it than that, it can be pretty boring. On the other hand, every now and then someone can do an amazing presentation of something that simple, and it will be remembered fondly for a long time. It probably has a lot to do with showmanship, photographic skills, and even tone of voice.

VI

Learning from the Pros

SGML won't buy you any of those things. Neither will HTML, JPEG, the latest hi-res color screen, or the fastest Internet connection in the world. Your information has to be interesting before you can really get off the ground. But suppose you get that far; you decided what you want to say, it's really interesting, and you even know how to say it in words and pictures. Once you have that, presentation skills and technology start to come into play: How well can your medium communicate your message? Can it at all? How do you organize your presentation? How do you make it flow? You can make a huge difference by using the best tools for the job.

Support for More Kinds of Documents

With HTML, you must fit all the parts of your information into one of a few catego-ries; there only *are* so many categories to go around. If you want subtle distinctions, you can't have elements for them, whether or not you want them to affect formatting.

One solution in HTML is to move some of your information into other media alto-gether—changing document portions into graphics or sound. It's very important to be able to do this when you want to—the problem is when you have to do it even if you don't want to. The most common case of that is equations. If you want to put infor-mation on the Web that has even simple math in it, like a Web site designed to help junior high students with math, or a guide to home mortgages or other things that involve financial calculations, there isn't a lot of help from the technology. Usually, you can do one of three things:

- Wait for HTML to add direct support for displaying equations. People are work-ing on this, but it's not there yet, and it may be a while before a really complete solution arrives because formatting math is complicated.

- Do your equations in something else (often TeX) and then save the output as a bitmap graphic, like a GIF file. This lets Web browsers display them inline, but they usually look pretty ugly, especially if you try to scale them up or down. Also, small characters, such as superscripts, can become small enough to drop out.

- Use a "helper application" to display equations stored in some other format, like TeX, DVI, or PostScript. This will look a lot better, but requires special plug-ins if the equations are to appear inline as if they were really part of the HTML (and at least right now, those plug-ins don't work across different browsers).

Equations in math and accounting documents are just one example. Lots of docu-ments need their own kinds of elements. SGML, of course, lets you support new kinds of objects as needed. SGML programs still need to support the concept of "equations" in their stylesheets—it wouldn't do much good to recognize a "superscript" tag if all you could do with it was to make it bold or italic! But the most basic assumption in an SGML system is that you'll be seeing new tags often, which you better be able to sup-port, so the chance of being able to rig up an SGML system to render even a very bi-zarre new tag is pretty good.

Support for Big Documents

The second area where SGML can help you make more Web impact is with big documents. HTML tends to assume your documents will be small (or that you'll make them small somehow before putting them on the Web). This means a lot of work as you try to manage lots of parts that are conceptually related, but physically separate. In contrast, because SGML came out of the commercial and in-house publishing industries, it's used to the idea of big documents with hundreds to tens of thousands of pages. SGML systems on the Web specifically deal with this, and take away the burden of creating and managing many little pieces of information when what you really had in mind was providing access to a few large ones.

We've talked earlier about how Web servers can be set up either to convert generic SGML to HTML on demand, or to send the SGML out directly to clients that understand it. For really big documents, you can still do it either way, but time becomes a big factor in both. Because of this, a good SGML server can also break documents down and send overviews, outlines, or successive pieces. That way you can get the part you want, without waiting to download the entire big document, or forcing the author to break it up into many little documents.

Focus on Your Data

The issue of large versus small documents brings you right back to the first focus: your own data. It's very important to develop a vision for what your Web site is all about, and make your data communicate that vision. Suppose you're doing a Web site about figure skating. You'll make a stronger impact if you do a few things:

- Don't limit yourself to your own information on the subject; actively go out and find more. Go to the library and get some out-of-copyright, but classic books on the subject, some relevant pictures, and so on. For skating, you might find interesting materials on its origins, early Olympic skaters, and so on. If you can get rights to newer materials, that's even better, but a lot of the best material is under copyright (you'd need to get clearance from the author or publisher to use it).

- Find out what else is on the Web, and make sure you link to it. But don't *just* link to it; add some commentary that will help people know what the information is about, and why they might want to follow one or another of your links. Help them save wasted trips, and help them be sure to make the trips they should. For the skating example, it would look bad if someone forgot to mention **www.cs.yale.edu/homes/sjl/skate.html**.

- Get others involved. If you're interested in some subject, you probably have friends who are, too. Get them to help out by adding their own perspectives. They don't even have to be on the Net! Maybe one of those friends is someone well-known. If they'll contribute, it can be a real draw for your site.

- Think about different ways people may want to get at your data. What kinds of searches should your data show up with? Should parts be organized chronologically, alphabetically, and other ways? Giving people many ways to get in makes for a strong site. A skating page might want chronological lists of upcoming competitions and telecasts, but should also give a way to get at the same information by skaters' names, locations, and so on.

- Think about subjects that are related, even indirectly. For our example, you might want to hook up to information about Eastern Europe and the Soviet Union, since political changes there heavily impacted world skating competitions.

- Reference material is something that is often forgotten. It doesn't seem flashy at all, and it can be a pain to deal with sometimes. But reference material is what people refer to again and again: information they *need*. One skating page has a really useful map of the stadium where this year's Nationals was held and information on rinks and schedules for many places. Travelers really appreciate it when they find that page.

Link to Important Related Data

Although this was mentioned, it's worth saying again. There's so much data out there that someone somewhere has data that relates to yours. Someone may even have the very same data already on the Web. It can look pretty silly if you put out a new site and a lot of it is redundant, unless you manage to develop a brand-new spin on it that really makes a difference. Short of hiring spin doctors, a good way to do this is to study what's there already; do a bunch of Web searches and jot down some notes on what you find. Go look at the pages and think of ways you can do it better. Make friends with the other people working on related data, and join forces if you can. Of course, be sure to avoid online comments like "This is the first Web site to do X," unless you're really, really, really sure it is.

Avoid "Only Works in Client X"

A final bit of advice is this: Don't lock yourself into a single browser, either by accident or on purpose. There are a lot of browsers out there. Probably neither Netscape nor Microsoft will wipe the other one completely off the face of the earth. And humble Lynx, the text-only browser used on a lot of non-graphical systems, will probably remain the browser of choice for the visually impaired, people with very low-bandwidth connections, and other special applications.

New browsers will be showing up, too. *PC Week* recently said "Look out, Netscape: Tests of a beta version of Oracle Corp.'s PowerBrowser show the company is taking dead aim at the dominant World-Wide Web browser with a free offering loaded with features that are unavailable or cost more from Netscape Communications Corp." No one knows yet how that product will do, but the point is that new browsers will come out all the time. If you lock your data into one, you'll just have to re-author it again and again.

How do you avoid locking in? In the HTML-only world, the only way is to always know what elements are really "in" the official DTD versus what ones are somebody's extensions. For the extensions, you need to know exactly who supports them (and if more than one browser supports tag X, you also need to figure out whether they all support it the same way!).

With generic SGML, you're a bit safer; creating new element types is a normal, every-day event that all generic SGML products expect and support. Maybe something really unusual will come in once in a while that requires everyone to add a new gadget to support it. But this is a rare event compared to adding a new tag that has behavior somewhat similar to others.

If you want your data to last, think hard before giving in to the temptation to be the first one to use the latest HTML extension. If some browser vendor introduces a new tag in a beta, you can find yourself having to re-author all your data when they drop or change it in the real released version. Of course, everybody who's using another browser will have problems when they try to read your data. On the other hand, you sure don't want to be the last to adopt a new thing either.

The trick is all in the timing, just like when you're signing up for a mortgage or play-ing the stock market. If you dive in too early, you're taking a risk on ideas that may not pan out (they may even be great ideas that just don't happen to catch on, or aren't profitable enough to hang on). But if you wait too long, you miss the chance to be on the cutting edge and do the most interesting things.

Too much hurry to adopt the very latest new feature may end up making you do more work. Next month, someone may look at the idea and find an easier way to do the same thing. One recent example was with Netscape Frames. When they first came out, the only way to take advantage of them was to laboriously re-mark-up all your data to do so. That is, you had to go around and insert <FRAME> everywhere (this usually meant a lot of rewriting, too, since people hadn't divided their files up to accommo-date multiple frames in the first place). Then, within a few weeks, one company came out with a server that could take SGML files and generate multi-frame views of them on demand, just by setting up a few options—without touching the data at all.

With stories like that, the win really lies in carefully balancing, and learning enough to guess, a good percentage of the time, where things will go. Here again, SGML helps since it destroys the limiting idea that there's "the" single set of tags. If you set up your data at this more abstract level, you partly insulate yourself from short-term variations, and your data can quickly adjust to make use of all the latest new tech-nologies as they appear.

From Here...

This chapter has covered several issues involved in using SGML effectively on the Web. These include the different standards involved, from MIME types to HyTime. They also include techniques you can use to make your data more interesting, better presented, and more useful to networked readers.

For more information, refer to the following:

- Chapter 17, "How HTML Relates to SGML," covers some basic related topics.
- Chapter 21, "Integrating SGML and HTML Environments," gives many examples of how SGML is being used on the Internet already.

CHAPTER 23

Rapid Development and Prototyping

Getting SGML implemented in an organization can be a complicated undertaking. Many issues must be addressed in order to successfully build and implement an SGML production system.

It's not uncommon to feel intimidated when you start out in your SGML project. As you consider all of the issues, challenges, questions, and topics up ahead, implementing an SGML system might seem like an overwhelming proposition.

Many people implementing SGML for the first time will feel the need to dive into document analysis, so that they can rapidly get to the goal of producing SGML documents. But before you dive in, you might want to perform some analysis up front. By performing this analysis, you might avoid a few mistakes later.

This chapter explores the issues and approaches that can aid you in successfully bringing this about. As with many things, there is no absolute correct way to go about this. Your individual circumstances may well dictate some deviations from the approach that this chapter takes. However, in this chapter, you will explore some ways and techniques to successfully complete an SGML project. As you do so, a framework will emerge.

To do this, you will examine the phases of SGML projects in the following sequence:

- Scoping (or bounding) the process
- Building your team
- Gathering your data
- Performing document analysis and design
- Designing your system
- Going into production
- Iterating the process

As you examine the issues involved in constructing your SGML environment, you should periodically ask yourself, "How does this issue affect me and my organization?" Although many of the same issues may be relevant to various organizations implementing SGML for the first time, the particular "mix" and importance of issues are likely to vary considerably depending on your own particular circumstances.

Scoping/Bounding the Process

In this phase, you should define just what you want to accomplish in your project: where you want to go, what you want to achieve, and in what timeframe. In other words, just what are you intending to accomplish by bringing SGML into your organization?

For example, do you intend to maintain a set of documents for a long time, say 10 years or more? If so, having a portable document repository maintainable across several generations of document processing systems may be very important to you.

Do you currently produce a variety of hardcopy documents, but want to position your organization to deliver information electronically, such as on CD-ROM or via the Internet? In this case, having a document production system and document architectures that facilitate both types of delivery may be a major goal.

In still other situations, you might want to build a repository of information "objects," organized so that you can build documents on the fly, maintaining reusable portions centrally. That way, you know that these objects are both consistent and accurate.

All of this and more can be facilitated through a thoughtful and focused use of SGML in your organization.

Defining Your Scope

To define the scope of your project, you should ask yourself a number of questions. Among these are the following:

- What do you want to achieve?
- What is your mandate?
- Who is your sponsor?
- Where do you want to be in the future?

As you look at what you want to achieve, talk to people. Ask them for their perspective on the project. Examine the mandate that you received when the project was first initiated. Talk to the sponsor of the project. Find out what their expectations are for success.

Examine your goals as they relate to the future. Do they relate to where your organization wants to be in two years? In five years? In 10 years?

After you have gathered all of this information, write it down and examine your findings. As you examine the list, ask yourself, "Is what I want to achieve realistic?"

Although there are many variables at play, it is not unreasonable to expect a significantly sized SGML project to take 2-3 years to bring into production. When you are going to spend that much time on a project, the up-front planning and analysis can be pivotal to success.

Defining the Document Set

As you lay out the scope of your project, you need to develop a list of the document types that you'll include. In looking at document types, you should consider "families" of documents. These may include such classes as Operations and Maintenance Manuals, User Manuals, Parts Lists, Product Data Sheets, Service Bulletins, and so on.

Document *families* should consist of documents that are related in structure, content, function, and appearance. For example, if your company produces both jet engines and toasters, it is a good bet that the User Manual for these two products would differ considerably and, therefore, not be in the same document family.

If your organization is new to SGML and your project is considered to be a pilot, you might want to define a limited document set for your initial efforts. Chances are that you will want to repeat the whole process later with the benefit of your experience from your initial efforts.

Defining Your Goals

When approaching your project, you should have a clear set of goals in mind. These goals might range from reducing documentation production costs to delivering your organization's information on the Internet. Some common goals of an SGML implementation project are:

- Document delivery across multiple mediums (hardcopy and electronic)
- Reduced document production time
- Increased document consistency
- Ease of conversion to new document preparation systems
- Increased document accuracy
- Electronic information delivery (Internet, CD-ROM, and so on)
- Reuse of document objects across multiple document types
- Reduced document production costs
- Reduced document shipping costs

The important part is that you have a set of goals that can be clearly communicated and understood by your project team. By clearly defining your goals, all of your project participants can share a common understanding of where you are headed.

Defining Your Timeframe

Just as you should clearly define where you are headed, you should also define your timeframe. Some SGML projects can be planned, designed, and put into full production in two or three years. Others, more broad in scope, can span 10 or 15 years and be an integral part of an organization's central strategic direction.

Your timeframe can have a central bearing on some of the decisions that you make in implementing your SGML system. For a larger, more ambitious development project, you might want to consider rapid prototyping across a range of document types or with several SGML implementation teams.

Defining Your Environment

Your document production environment and related organizational factors can have key impacts on how you implement your SGML system. Oftentimes, a combination of your environmental factors will work together to necessitate a specific approach in how you implement SGML into your organization.

For example, suppose that your company has a dedicated publications department that produces a range of technical publications. You are using an older publishing package with which the staff is quite comfortable. The personnel in the publications department are quite accomplished writers, but generally are not highly sophisticated computer users.

In this case, you might want to stay with your existing production systems and opt to convert the document output to SGML after the actual production phase. Using this approach, you could minimize the impact of change on the organization compared to the introduction of new software systems for producing documents via structured SGML authoring.

In another circumstance, you might actually be seeking radical changes in the way that you do business. In this situation, you might include a major work process redefinition as part of your SGML initiative. Some common environmental factors that can come into play when introducing SGML are:

- Multiple document production software packages versus a single software package
- Dedicated technical publications personnel versus documents produced by generalists
- State-of-the-art software versus older legacy software
- High computer skill level versus novice computer skill level
- Sophisticated information systems SGML experience versus no information systems SGML experience
- Organization open to change/high change environment versus traditional organization/change-resistant environment
- High production volumes versus low production volumes

Assemble Your Team

The team that you assemble to implement your SGML project is the single most important ingredient for your project's success. How you put it together is, therefore, a critical element to the process.

In short, diversity in your team is very important. A broadly based team can give you a wide perspective on the role of the documents that you will be converting into SGML, the factors that come into play when they are produced, and the environment in which they are used. All of these issues can be important to you as you go about designing, constructing, and implementing your SGML system.

Team Members

As you put your team together, strive to include all the players. Include the writers of the documents that your SGML system will process. If there are other departments "upstream" that produce the content with which your writers create these documents, include them.

Whenever possible, include representatives of the "end user" community, those who read (and use) the documents. "Not so easy," you say. "I can't involve outside customers in this project." Well, maybe not, but there are other alternatives. In the case of operations and maintenance manuals, your company might have field personnel who also use them. Individuals in your spare parts organization might use your illustrated parts lists on a daily basis. In short, you can often find "customers" much closer at hand than you first realize. Table 23.1 lists some of the knowledge that your team can gain from individual members.

Table 23.1   SGML Team Member Experience Factors

Team Member(s)	Knowledge They Bring
Content "Owner"	Accuracy of data sources and schedule of data availability
Writers	Production schedule and volume, current tools and methods, authoring process, and document structure
Readers	Document usage(s), desired changes to documents
Computer Personnel	Existing computer infrastructure, current computer-based authoring tools
Marketing Personnel	Customer desires and preferences

Involving a wide variety of players on your team need not mean having a cast of thousands. In fact, you will want to balance a variety of perspectives with a manageable team size. But the benefits of having diversity on your team usually include the chance to gain a rich understanding of the roles that your documents play in your organization.

On the computer side, the question comes up as to whether you use in-house personnel or outside consultants. You might think that the question is easily answered if your in-house information systems staff does not have SGML experience. As with many things, however, the answer is usually not decided so easily.

As is illustrated in table 23.2, there are pros and cons to using both in-house staff and outside consultants in your SGML projects. While the in-house staff might lack SGML experience, they are committed to making it work over the life of the project. The consultants' experience in a range of SGML projects will bring a valuable perspective to your team, but they may also bring in biases from previous experience (which may or may not be applicable to your situation).

Similarly, the consultants' lack of knowledge of an organization's culture can be both positive and negative. On the positive side, they may be unencumbered by the organization's traditional mind set, willing to propose and examine radically new ways of doing business. On the negative side, they may be unfamiliar with organizational issues that are critical to the successful implementation of new systems.

Table 23.2 SGML Information Systems Staff Issues: In-House vs. Consultant	
In-House Information Systems Staff	**Outside Consultant**
Lacks SGML experience	Experienced in SGML systems
Unencumbered by previous SGML experience	Subject to bias based on previous SGML experience
Will be around for the "long haul"	Short involvement cycle
Understands the dynamics and workings of organization	Lacks in-depth organizational knowledge
Familiar with organization's computing environment	Unfamiliar with organization's computing environment

Even though information systems or computing staff involving in-house resources or outside consultants is often looked at as an either/or issue, it really shouldn't be. When starting an SGML project from the ground up, you normally can benefit from having both on your team. In many respects, they can be used in different (and complementary) ways, with the consultant serving as an outside tutor and facilitator and the in-house staff being the team nucleus responsible for bringing about the implementation of your SGML system.

Team Member Personalities

As with most human endeavors, the personal quirks of your team members will add to the richness of your experience. But when talking about the personalities of team members, I don't mean to delve into issues of Freudian psychology. The issue is more a focus of an individual team member's attitude toward technology.

In some projects that I have worked on, team members were selected (at least in part) on the basis of their enthusiasm for new technology. In these cases, it was felt that the "skeptics" would only slow a project down because of their resistance to new technologies and methods.

To put it simply, this philosophy should be avoided whenever possible! Just as you want balance in your team from all the areas involved with your documents, you also should seek a balance between the technology enthusiasts and the skeptics. They both have a contribution to make.

In most organizations that I have seen, there is a fairly wide range of attitudes toward technology. Because they will all be living with the system that you develop, they should all participate in its development. The skeptics, in particular, often provide a useful function in pointing out flaws in your approach that might otherwise be overlooked by the more enthusiastic participants.

Conversely, the most skeptical participants in your project can often become the biggest proponents of your system once they are convinced. As a result, the extra time that it might take to win over the skeptical members of your team can be time extremely well spent. Their skepticism will often serve as a useful sanity check on the practicality of your SGML system design and implementation.

The Dynamics of Participation

To gain the maximum benefit from the combined talents of your SGML team, it is helpful to remember a few central concepts. By following them, you will encourage enthusiastic participation by all the members.

- Concept #1 is that you should arrive at decisions by consensus whenever possible. In the early stages of your team's work, it might seem to take forever to reach decisions. Persevere! This extra time spent up front can pay great dividends if it convinces the team of the importance of each member's contribution. Often, in long involved discussions of particular issues, a resolution might, at last, seem to be at hand. Just as a decision seems to be reached, however, a quieter (and perhaps more thoughtful) participant might make a seemingly small comment or observation that throws the whole decision into doubt. This is a common part of the consensus-based decision-making process. Using this approach, you have the best chance of covering all of the significant issues involved in developing the optimum SGML solution for your organization.

- Concept #2 is that you must strive to maintain the pace. (Although it may sound somewhat at odds with concept #1, it really isn't.) This concept really means that each working session of your team should be focused on reaching specific objectives. While the consensus-based approach might result in an unpredictable schedule for reaching individual objectives as you examine all the intricacies, details, and nuances involved with a particular issue, this second concept ensures that you accomplish the objectives that you set for each team meeting.

- Concept #3 is that you empower your group to make decisions and judgment calls. If you have put your team together to benefit from its collective knowledge, wisdom, perspective, and experience, make sure that you use it. If your team is not empowered to make decisions, it will probably quickly tire of the process, deciding that it is a waste of time.

An SGML consultant with good skills as a facilitator will pay dividends in the teaming process. By emphasizing these concepts, you will be able to aid your team in designing the optimal SGML solution for your organization.

Data Gathering

As you gather sample data for each document type to be incorporated into your SGML system, a few issues should be considered. The types of data to be gathered should span the range of what you will encounter in your typical document production environment. Table 23.3 lists a range of samples to gather for use in your document analysis process.

Table 23.3 Data Gathering: Document Samples To Look For	
Type	**Characteristics**
Typical	Average sample of the document type. Representative of document class.
Simple	Simple version of the document type. Complete, yet uncomplicated sample of document class.
"Sample from Hell"	Horrendously complex permutation of the document type. Uses many, if not most, of variations and complexities of document class.
Update Portions	Representative "chunks" of the document (or source data) at the level at which the document is updated or maintained.

The typical document should be used as your baseline. It represents the normal version of the document class that will be encountered in everyday production.

The simple document example can serve as a good sanity check on your document design (through your DTD), ensuring that your document model is not too complex to work well with simple versions of the class. When you are happy with how your document model works with typical and simple versions of the document, you're ready for the stress test: the sample from Hell.

The sample from Hell is the document sample that many people dread. It is often full of exceptions to the rule. Often it doesn't fit the model for various and sundry reasons: "We just put *Not Applicable* in the section for control systems for the X-95 because it's the only model that doesn't have one," or "All of our Part Breakdown documents have 12 standard sections except for the Loxomatic model, which has 238." In short, this type of sample is the one with the black motorcycle jacket; it breaks all the rules!

The samples with the exceptions will allow you to make decisions on what to do with your document model: Should you make it generic enough so that the sample from Hell fits in or do you require changes in the document that breaks the rules? (No easy answer here; your decision will depend on your particular situation.)

Tip

If you find yourself with a lot of samples that break the rules, you might be in a situation where two (or more) distinct classes of documents are being forced into one document model. If this is the case, you might consider breaking them down into separate document classes.

For documents that undergo frequent updates, a look at typical chunks that are updated will prove to be very useful. Because these portions often will be the most dynamic parts of a document class, analysis of these might result in them receiving special treatment in your document model (to make them more accessible, amenable to database manipulation, and so on).

Document Analysis

Because you examined document analysis in some detail previously in Part II, you don't need to examine all of the details here. Instead, take a look at some of the fundamentals of good document analysis:

- Use a top-down approach
- Work from the outside in
- Develop your document model
- Validate your design
- Iterate, iterate, iterate

When performing your document analysis, start from the beginning (or top) of your document and work your way down. Before you begin, you should review your goals.

As you examine your sample documents, work your way through the document sections. Working from the outside in, concentrate on the borders or boundaries *between* the high level sections before you look at their contents.

For example, in working through a structure for a book, your initial pass of high level objects could result in a document model that looks like figure 23.1. Note that only the high level objects have been identified at this point (TitlePg, TableContents, Foreword, and so on).

As you step through the process, you will work your way into the high level objects, defining the objects contained within them. You will continue iterating this approach until you have defined all of the objects (or elements) within your document model (see fig. 23.2).

Fig. 23.1

Document model with high level objects only.

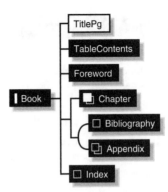

Fig. 23.2

Document model with low level objects included.

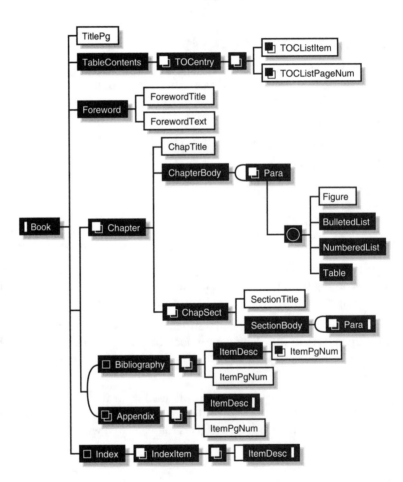

When you are satisfied with your document model, it's time to test it against your sample documents. In this process, you check to see that it works well with your samples (including the sample from Hell). It's quite possible that you will find some problems in a few places that will require another iterative pass through the process.

Repeating (or iterating) the steps in the process is a standard part of developing SGML document models. In fact, it's a common facet of many of the processes in SGML projects.

When performing document analysis, it's common to develop the document model for one type of document class and then perform the whole process all over again with the next document class. All of this iteration might seem unusual at first, but eventually it will feel routine and natural.

System Design

In a lot of ways, the design of your SGML system will parallel the design of your SGML document architectures. Just as you must consider your existing documents when designing your SGML document models, you must consider your current system as you plan your target system.

There is quite a bit of variance in SGML capabilities among the current generation of word processing and technical publishing systems. Although your current authoring program might offer SGML authoring features, you must ensure that the features offered fit your needs.

In many cases, organizations that want to make the transition to SGML authoring plan to use upgraded or enhanced versions of their current authoring package. However, upon examination of the specific SGML features offered in the enhancement, it is determined that the SGML support offered is not sufficient to their needs. In other cases, the current authoring package might offer no SGML support at all.

Thus, you are often at a crossroad as you plan your entry into the world of SGML. The question will arise, "Should I make the jump to a completely new authoring system to gain my SGML capabilities?" If this approach is the practical way to go, great. However, it often is a process that cannot be rushed, due to considerations relating to legacy data, staff training, investment in current systems, and so on.

When this is the case, you should consider the possibility of migrating to a "Transition" environment to bridge the gap between old and new (see fig. 23.3).

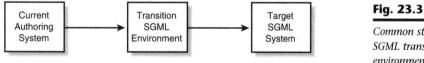

Fig. 23.3

Common steps in an SGML transition environment.

The transition environment can take a number of forms, depending on your needs. Commonly, it can include authoring in your current environment with a subsequent step of running conversion processing programs to convert the output documents into SGML.

Because the conversion processing is highly dependent on your document data formats, data structures, and related issues, it cannot be covered in detail here.

> **Tip**
>
> *Perl*, a text processing language, can be a very useful tool for performing SGML document conversion processing. It is examined in Chapter 28, "Other Tools and Environments." Perl is also included on the SGML CD-ROM. Instructions for installing it are included in Appendix A.

▶▶ See "The World of Perl," p. 491

▶▶ See "Perl," p. 559

From Here...

This concludes your look at development and prototyping. As you examined the issues involved, you saw the important roles played by the definition of goals, team building, data gathering, and planning the transition from old to new systems.

For more information, refer to the following:

- Chapter 24, "Understanding and Using Output Specifications," examines issues relating to stylesheets and output specifications.

- Part VII, "SGML Tools and Their Uses," examines a variety of useful tools now available to help you use SGML.

- Part VIII, "Becoming an Electronic Publisher," examines the issues involved in moving into electronic publishing.

Understanding and Using Output Specifications

Chapter 2, "SGML View of the World: Structure, Content, and Format," examined a central concept of SGML: documents consist of structure, content, and format. As you explored this view of documents, you could see the value of separating these three components to enhance a document's usability and portability.

You saw how the SGML world defines a document's *structure* with a DTD. After extracting the formatting component, the document *content* is contained in an SGML document instance, which consists of the text of the document surrounded by the document's SGML tag set.

But what about the document's *format*? As you saw in Chapter 2, processing instructions for a document's format is a major portion of word processors' proprietary document formats. In a similar vein, a document's format is often highly specific to the medium of the document's delivery. That is, formatting for a printed version of a document can vary quite a bit from the formatting of the same document to be delivered across the World Wide Web.

A major rationale for adopting SGML is output flexibility. This can range from flexibility in document authoring systems to that of document delivery methods.

This chapter examines the ways and mechanisms for specifying the output formatting of your SGML documents. To do this, you will look at the following items:

- A view of a document from an output perspective
- Issues involved with output specifications
- Handling hardcopy/printed output
- Handling electronic output
- Handling dynamic documents
- Difficulties with output specifications
- Output specification standards

The View of a Document from an Output Perspective

To understand the role of output specifications, think for a moment of a specific document instance in SGML. It consists of textual information structured via tags that relate document content back to the structure defined in its controlling DTD.

Put another way, the document instance can be thought of as a hierarchy of elements, with each occurrence of an element having a specific relationship to its parent, child, and sibling elements.

Let's take a look at an example. In Chapter 8, you examined a DTD for a book. Let's take a look at a revised version of that DTD (see fig. 24.1).

Note that the element Title is included as a subelement in four element declarations: Foreword, Chapter, CSect, and Table.

It is often important to treat the formatting of an element differently according to where it occurs within the document hierarchy. For example, you might want to format the element Title one way when it occurs within a Chapter, and another way when it occurs within a chapter section (CSect). To do this, think of the SGML document instance as a hierarchy.

Let's take a look at a specific example where you want to format elements differently and see how to go about it.

Formatting Elements Through Their Structural Occurrence

In the book DTD, the Title element occurs within the declaration of several parent elements. As you are laying out the output specification for a book, consider how you'll format this element when it occurs within a Chapter element and a chapter section (CSect) element. The formatting that you'll want to have is shown in figure 24.2.

Notice that the *chapter* title, "Back To the Future," has significantly different formatting than the title for the chapter *section* ("Case Study: International Food Franchising").

Table 24.1 lists the format properties of the two occurrences of the Title element.

```
<!DOCTYPE Book2 [
<!--Book Structure Model -- >

<!ELEMENT Book              - - (TitlePg,TblCon,Foreword,(Chapter+,
                                (Biblgrph?&Appendix*)),Index?) >

<!--Major Sub Elements -- >
<!ELEMENT TitlePg           - - (#PCDATA)  >
<!ELEMENT TblCon            - - (TOCentry+)  >
<!ELEMENT Foreword          - - (Title,FText)  >——— Foreword
<!ELEMENT Chapter           - - (Title,CBody,CSect+)  >—— Chapter
<!ELEMENT Biblgrph          - - (ItemDesc,ItemPNum)+  >
<!ELEMENT Appendix          - - (ItemDesc,ItemPNum)+  >
<!ELEMENT Index             - - (IdxItem+)  >

<!--TOC elements -- >
<!ELEMENT TOCentry          - - (TOCItem+,TOCpnum+)+>
<!ELEMENT TOCItem           - - (#PCDATA)  >
<!ELEMENT TOCpnum           - - (#PCDATA)  >

<!--Content elements -- >
<!ELEMENT Title             - - (#PCDATA)  >
<!ELEMENT FText             - - (#PCDATA)  >
<!ELEMENT CBody             - - (Para+&Figure*&BList*&
                                  NList*&Table*)
                                +(FigRef,ListRef,TblRef)  >

 <!ELEMENT CSect            - - (Title,SectBody)  >——— CSect
 <!ELEMENT SectBody         - - (Para+&Figure*&BList*&
                                  NList*&Table*)
                                +(FigRef,ListRef,TblRef) >
 <!ELEMENT Para             - - (#PCDATA)  >
 <!ELEMENT Figure           - - (#PCDATA)  >
 <!ELEMENT Table            - - (Title,TblBody)  >———————Table

 <!ELEMENT TblBody          - - (#PCDATA)  >

<!--Index elements -- >
<!ELEMENT IdxItem           - - (ItemDesc)  >
<!ELEMENT ItemDesc          - - (ItemPNum+)  >
<!ELEMENT ItemPNum          - - (#PCDATA)  >

<!--List elements -- >
<!ELEMENT NList             - - (ListItem+)  >
<!ELEMENT BList             - - (ListItem+)  >
<!ELEMENT ListItem          - - (#PCDATA)  >

<!--Reference elements -- >
<!ELEMENT ListRef           - - (#PCDATA)  >
<!ELEMENT TblRef            - - (#PCDATA)  >
<!ELEMENT FigRef            - - (#PCDATA)  >
]>
```

Title ——

Fig. 24.1

A DTD defines a specific document structure or hierarchy of elements. Each occurrence of an element has a specific relationship to its parent, child, and sibling elements.

VI

Learning from the Pros

Fig. 24.2

Desired output formatting sample.

Chapter: **Back To the Future**

The rapid pace of change that was to occur within the industry in the coming decade was foretold by Erwin Noche in his 1968 book, "The Future of Franchises." In this book, Noche accurately predicted the globalization of franchised businesses, from fast food to personal & home care products.
This chapter will examine the remarkable prescience that Noche displayed in his book when analyzing how the industry would develop in the next 10 years. Through a series of examples, presented as case studies, he presented a case for each trend that he predicted would soon sweep through the franchising world. In this chapter we will examine various case studies presented in his book, contrasting them will actual industry developments.

Case Study: International Food Franchising
In his examination of food franchising, Noche predicted the globalization of the business. In examining the various competitors from around the world, he noted the strengths, weaknesses, and key differentiating features of each.

Table 24.1   Sample Element Formatting Properties

Element	Context	Description
Title	child of: Chapter element	Precede with New Page, and text "Chapter: " 19 Point Bold Font Follow with: New Line Horizontal Line Revert to Former Font
Title	child of: Chapter Section element (CSect)	Precede with New Line 13 Point Times Bold Italic Font Follow with: New Line Revert to Former Font

Because you can specify each occurrence of the Title element in the document hierarchy, it is relatively simple to differentiate the formatting by situation (or context).

Let's take a look at how you can go about doing this.

Note

The actual syntax for defining the output format will differ depending on the type of output specification used. The examples illustrated here were prepared using the Layout Designer provided with WordPerfect SGML Edition.

Let's start with a look at the output format for the Title element when it occurs as a child of Chapter (see fig. 24.3).

Notice that the definition of the element begins with notation that indicates its context: the <Title> element as a child of the <Chapter> element.

```
<Title> in:
<Chapter>

[ Start Tag Layout ]
FONT SIZE = 19p
NEW PAGE
TEXT = Chapter:
FONT APPEARANCE = Bold

[ End Layout ]
NEW LINE
HORIZONTAL LINE
[ After-Revert Section ]
FONT SIZE = Revert Group
FONT APPEARANCE OFF = Revert Group
NEW LINE
NEW LINE

<\Title>
```

Fig. 24.3

Output specification formatting: Title *element as a child of* Chapter.

In this context, you specify the formatting characteristics that you want for this element. These include:

- A specific font size
- Beginning this element on a new page
- Inclusion of standard text preceding the Chapter element
- A specific font appearance (Bold)

The processing instruction delimiter [Start Tag Layout] indicates the start of format instructions to be applied to this data object. The format properties that are defined will be applied when the processing system encounters the start tag indicating the Title element as a child of the Chapter element.

Following this processing instruction group are two additional delimiters: [End Layout] and [After-Revert Section].

The [End Layout] processing instruction group contains those instructions to be processed upon reaching the close tag of your element in the hierarchy (Title within Chapter). Note that they will be applied *before* output formatting returns to those instructions in effect prior to this element.

Tip

These formatting instructions can modify previous instructions. In this case, the instructions that they modify will include any that are in effect from the [Start Tag Layout] for this element.

The instructions that you have specified to process upon reaching the end of your close `Title` element (`<\Title>`) include:

- A new line
- A horizontal line

The [`After-Revert Section`] contains directives for specifying those formatting instructions to be processed *after* you have returned to the instructions in effect prior to encountering this element. In this case, you have specified the following instructions:

- Font size: Revert back to what it was previously (prior to element)
- Font appearance: Revert back to previous
- Two new lines

You might be wondering about the difference between the [`End Layout`] and [After-Revert Section] processing sections. If you are, a simple illustration may be in order. Notice that you have included instructions for two new lines in the [`After-Revert Section`]. These new lines, because they are included here, will have a height of the font that you are reverting to (in this case, it's 12 point). If you had included these new lines in the [`End Layout`] section, they would have had a height of the font in effect in that section—19 point, in this example.

The output format for the `Title` element occurring within the chapter section element (`<CSect>`) is illustrated in figure 24.4. Note that because you specify a specific font, font size, and font appearance for this element context, you also want to revert all of these characteristics upon exiting from the element context.

Fig. 24.4

Output specification formatting: `Title` *element as a child of Chapter Section (*`CSect`*).*

```
<Title> in:
   <CSect>

[ Start Tag Layout ]
NEW LINE
FONT = Times
FONT SIZE = 13p
FONT APPEARANCE = Bold Italic

[ End Layout ]
NEW LINE
[ After-Revert Section ]
FONT = Revert Group
FONT SIZE = Revert Group
FONT APPEARANCE OFF = Revert Group

<\Title>
```

In this example, you looked at portions of an output specification used in WordPerfect SGML Edition. Defining output specifications in other programs will differ in various ways. You will examine output specifications of various types later in this chapter.

> **Note**
>
> As an example of the differences in the formatting instruction approach between various programs, note the mechanism for indicating the end of a specific data element. In the example from WordPerfect above, the end tag is shown as <\Title>. If this formatting was performed using a DynaText stylesheet, the end tag would be indicated as </Title>.

Issues Involved with Output Specifications

Because output specifications specify the output formatting of a document, they have tended to be somewhat proprietary. That is, each SGML software package has its own way of defining output formatting. Stylesheets are a simple form of specifying output formats.

Nonetheless, certain aspects of output formatting are often common across the stylesheet syntaxes. Among these common aspects are the following:

- SGML syntax
- Group styles
- Entity usage
- Inheritance

SGML Syntax

In various degrees, most SGML software packages use some form of SGML syntax to define stylesheets. In the previous example, element formatting was indicated within SGML tags for the element concerned.

The stylesheet syntax for the DynaText SGML viewer, produced by Electronic Book Technologies, defines style properties as SGML elements. The property value is defined as the element's contents. (A sample portion of a DynaText stylesheet is shown in figure 24.5.)

Group Styles

The use of groups within stylesheets is often supported. Group styles can simplify the stylesheet development process tremendously. Through group membership, an element can "inherit" the group formatting instructions.

Through the use of group styles, you can minimize the amount of formatting that you must define for a DTD, with only exceptions to the group format requiring specific definition.

Fig. 24.5

Sample DynaText stylesheet formatting.

```
<style name="TYPE" group="mainitem">
        <left-indent>    +=95    </>
        <first-indent>   -=95    </>
        <text-before>&it-type    </>
</style>

<style name="REVNOTE" group="mainitem">
        <left-indent>    +=40    </>
        <right-indent>   +=40    </>
        <space-before>   14      </>
        <space-after>    16      </>
</style>

<style name="BULLETIN">
        <break-before>   Line              </>
        <space-before>   20                </>
        <text-before>    &doctitle         </>
</style>

<style name="BULLETIN,#TEXT-BEFORE">
        <font-size>      24                </>
        <font-weight>    Bold              </>
        <foreground>     Blue              </>
        <justification>  Center            </>
        <line-spacing>   26                </>
        <space-after>    12                </>
</style>
```

Entity and Attribute Usage

Many SGML software packages support the use of entities and attributes within a stylesheet or output specification. Such support is desirable, for it can provide an added degree of formatting flexibility.

When supported, entity usage can provide the same type of flexibility that it does within DTDs and SGML document instances. That is to say, entities can be used to provide the definition of such things as standard fonts and font sizes, boilerplate text, and other reusable values or data. When defined at the beginning of a stylesheet through entities, standard stylesheet characteristics (such as font types) can easily be revised.

Support for attribute recognition within the stylesheet can add a degree of intelligence to the output format processing. Depending on the value of an element attribute, different format processing can be enabled.

As an example, let's look at a portion of an SGML document instance for a product advisory (see fig. 24.6). Notice that the element <subject> has an attribute named safety and that, in this case, the attribute is set to "y".

In this product advisory document model, you use a "y" safety attribute value on the subject element to indicate safety related advisories.

```
<advisory>
<idinfo><advnbr>150</advnbr>
<type>Parts</type>
<dateiss>8/15/95</dateiss>
<daterev>8/25/95</daterev>
<product>Dizno 100</product></idinfo>
<subject safety="y">Defective Nebulizer Assembly</subject>
<subsec><title>Model D-100 Nebulizer</title><para>The Nebulizer
Assembly (part # 73490-A2) identified in the AnyCorp Model D-100
User's Maintenance Guide has been superseded, effective
immediately. Contact your AnyCorp Technical Support
Representative for a replacement part
```

Fig. 24.6

Product advisory SGML document instance.

Through conditional processing of the attribute value in the stylesheet, you can include additional information in your document output formatting. For this example, suppose you want to include a special warning in all safety related advisories (see fig. 24.7). This warning will display only when the safety attribute of the subject element indicates that it is safety related.

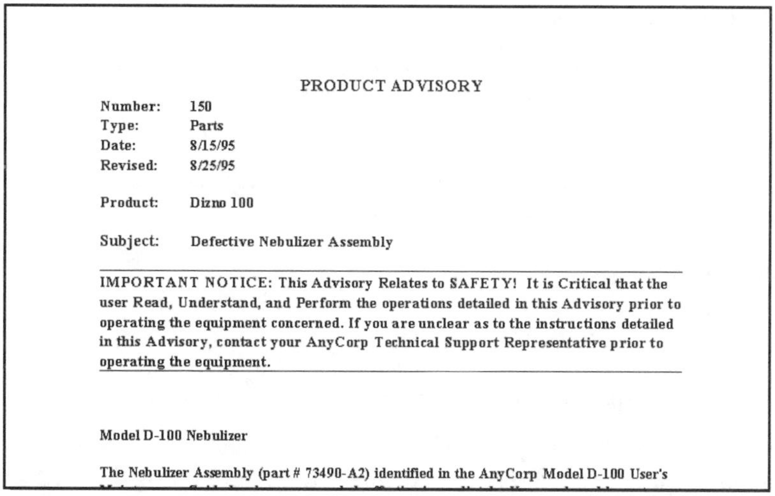

Fig. 24.7

Product advisory formatted output (with safety warning).

To accomplish this in your stylesheet, you can specify specific conditional output processing to be performed on the subject element only when the value of the safety attribute is true (i.e., equal to y). Figure 24.8 illustrates an example of this type of stylesheet processing using the Layout Designer of WordPerfect SGML Edition.

Tip

You may notice that the preceding text in the example above has been truncated. It is because WordPerfect/SGML Edition indicates only the initial portion of such lengthy text objects.

Fig. 24.8

Attribute-based conditional stylesheet processing.

```
<subject>
[ Attributes ]
safety = y

[ Start Tag Layout ]
FONT SIZE = 14p
FONT APPEARANCE = Bold
TEXT = Subject:
FONT SIZE = 13p
TAB = Soft Tab

[ End Layout ]
NEW LINE
NEW LINE
HORIZONTAL LINE
NEW LINE
TEXT = IMPORTANT NOTICE: This Advisory Relates to SAFETY!
It is Critical that the use
NEW LINE
HORIZONTAL LINE
NEW LINE
[ After-Revert Section ]
FONT SIZE = Revert Group
FONT SIZE = Revert Group
FONT APPEARANCE OFF = Revert Group
NEW LINE
NEW LINE

<\subject>
```

Style Inheritance

Through the use of specific formatting instructions for individual elements, you are able to get rather specific in defining the look of a document. Since you can go even further and actually specify specific formats for each element in each of the contexts that it occurs, the ability to specify formats is actually almost endless.

"But wait a minute," you say. "Is this powerful tool actually an ability or a requirement?" Good question! After all, if you have to define detailed formatting instructions for every element in every context that it occurs, you could easily devote the rest of your life to developing a stylesheet for one complex document.

Fortunately, there is an alternative. Suppose that you want to keep most of the formatting that you were using before you encounter a specific situation in which you have to apply a few changes? Through the use of *inheritance*, you can do just that.

Because you can often use most of the format properties in effect at the time of an element's occurrence, you can "inherit" them. Through inheritance, you only need to define those properties which differ from your inheritance. In many cases, the change is minimal.

For example, suppose that you wish to emphasize specific text within a passage. You can do this by defining this text through a special SGML element designed for this (Let's call it an "emph," or emphasis element.) A specific example might look like the following in an SGML document instance:

```
<para>The use of the <emph>element</emph> is a central feature in
defining document structure within SGML.</para>
```

In this case, the format changes required are very small. In fact, you may wish to have the only change be a font style change to italics. (Because you have chosen to have all emphasis elements formatted as italics, you don't have to specify specific element context.)

```
<emph>
[ Start Tag Layout ]
FONT APPEARANCE = Italic
<\emph>
```

> **Tip**
>
> Through a bit of planning, the use of inheritance can greatly minimize your use of redundant stylesheet formatting.

Issues in Specialized Output

As noted earlier, the specific features and syntax of output specifications vary between SGML software packages. Historically, the functionality provided in a particular vendor's package has tended to be oriented to the proprietary processing of that vendor's software. This is changing through the trend toward increasing communality in output specifications through a common standard. (The move to standards is discussed in "Output Specification Standards" later in this chapter.)

Your needs in output formatting will vary depending upon your mode of output. If your output is printed pages, it will differ from your needs for handling output via electronic display. In the electronic display environment, your output may even differ conditionally, depending upon a number of factors (such as the context of how the reader reached the document section, specific fonts, and the color of the fonts).

Handling Hardcopy/Printed Output

Output formatting for printed documents often focuses upon those issues related to specialized page-based composition. (In general, hardcopy document output places a much higher emphasis upon composition and layout support than that of electronic output.) Such issues may include special support for the following:

- Page numbering
- Header/footer processing

- Loose-leaf change page support
- Advanced composition support
- Wide range of font support
- Special formatting features (kerning, orphan/widow control, and so on)
- Vendor-specific support for specialized composition hardware/software systems

Because in many instances, the output equipment is predetermined, the output specification parameters (and support) may be tailored to a narrow range of devices. For example, book publishers preparing output to be printed on a Romulus 9000 high-speed printer might include commands that would only work when used with Romulus printers.

Handling Electronic Output

Options for the formatting of electronic output can vary significantly from those of hardcopy output. In many systems oriented to electronic output, extensive page-based composition features are omitted since the page-based composition approach is often not used in electronic delivery.

Since an electronic delivery system offers flexibility in user navigation, features which facilitate this are typically included. These features may include extensive support for hyperlinks to other parts of the document (or to other documents entirely) along with specialized search capabilities. Search support may include the capability for advanced features such as sophisticated context-sensitive searches.

Other capabilities important in an electronic environment include support for multimedia objects and the dynamic creation of tables of content based on stylesheet parameters. Sophisticated SGML viewers, such as EBT's DynaText, can support linkages to external applications to view external data objects, such as graphics and sound/video clips.

Handling Dynamic Documents

The increasing usage of electronic delivery for documents has led to increasing sophistication in their features and functionality. A major trend in this direction is a movement to tailor the document structure, content, and formatting according to the specific profile of the reader.

To support this, the SGML document may be tailored through a variety of techniques, including entity usage within an electronic document's stylesheet (as well as within the SGML document instance itself).

Dynamic documents can also be tailored to the user through the use of different stylesheets or the support of system variables in stylesheets.

 ▶▶ See "Using and Creating Output Specifications in Panorama Pro," p. 455 for an example of the use of different stylesheets on the same document.

Difficulties with Output Specifications

As you may have surmised, there have traditionally been problems in defining standards for output specifications. Although SGML has offered great flexibility in the use (and reuse) of structured information, the mechanisms for defining output formatting have tended toward the vendor-specific side.

The result has been that you could develop an SGML system for the reuse of transportable information, only to be stuck with spending a great deal of time and effort in the preparation of vendor-specific output specifications for your documents.

Output Specification Standards

Fortunately, the problem of vendor-specific output specifications is being addressed through the development of output specification standards. Beginning with the development of the FOSI and continuing with the advent of the DSSSL, the ability to support industry standard output specifications is starting to take shape.

The following sections examine several standards for common output specifications.

FOSI

The Format Output Specification Instance (or FOSI) was an early attempt at achieving a standard for an output specification. Developed early in the output standards process, it was an attempt to facilitate output formatting that was not vendor-specific.

As an early attempt at an output specification standard, it is limited in its functional capabilities. Perhaps its most important specific contribution is its ability to handle element formatting according to the element's specific context in the document structure hierarchy. As you saw earlier in the chapter, this capability facilitates flexibility in handling element formatting.

For example, context sensitivity allows you to format titles occurring within chapters differently from those occurring within appendixes.

DSSSL

Limitations in the FOSI led to an initiative for an approach offering greater flexibility in an output standard. A committee was formed to develop an ISO standard (ISO 10179) for a Document Style Semantics and Specification Language (DSSSL).

The desire to offer much greater flexibility and capability in the DSSSL (when compared with the FOSI) has resulted in a standard of considerable complexity. Thus its development has spanned a number of years since the establishment of the DSSSL committee in 1988.

DSSSL specification consists of two major parts:

- A specification for defining SGML structural transformation processing
- A specification for defining the SGML structural formatting process

The first part (for structural transformations) will serve to facilitate additional processing steps that traditionally have not been easy to accomplish with prior output specification standards. Prior to DSSSL, these steps may have required external processing by dedicated programs. These may include:

- Merging and splitting of documents
- Generation of indexes and tables of content
- Addition of structure to document instance
- Data extraction
- Additional validation

Formatting capabilities supported by DSSSL include the recognition of an object's context (as with the FOSI) but are much more comprehensive. Processing features supported include the capability to recognize specific content within the SGML document instance and structuring output formatting based upon that content.

Because of the complexities involved in the development of the DSSSL standard, an interim version (or subset) has been developed. Known as DSSSL Lite, it focuses on the structural formatting portion of DSSSL. By providing a subset of the structural formatting portion of DSSSL, DSSSL Lite is intended to be easy to include in current generation SGML software products. It supports both electronic and hardcopy formatting, although the composition capabilities of the latter are limited.

As the standard functionality defined in the DSSSL (and DSSSL Lite) standards are adopted by SGML vendors, the process of developing output specifications will become both easier and more standardized across SGML processing environments.

From Here...

In this look at output specifications, you have examined their relationship to the document content model. You also looked at issues involved in providing output formatting for SGML document instances, including those that apply to hardcopy and electronic versions of a document. The chapter closed with a look at the current state and future direction of output specification standards.

For more information, refer to the following:

- Chapter 25, "Handling Specialized Content and Delivery," examines issues and techniques for dealing with special data types such as tables, equations, graphics, multimedia objects, and hypertext links.
- Part VII, "SGML Tools and Their Uses," examines a variety of useful tools now available to aid you in your use of SGML.
- Part VIII, "Becoming an Electronic Publisher," examines the issues involved in moving into electronic publishing.

Handling Specialized Content and Delivery

As an international standard, SGML has an enormous job to do. You might say it carries the weight of the world on its electronic shoulders. If you measure weight in terms of bandwidth taken up by graphics and multimedia on the Internet, this is truer than ever nowadays, with HTML being an application of the standard. But as you've noticed if you've searched the Web or designed applications for local use, some content is just more challenging to manage than other content. Challenging content is the topic of this chapter.

In this chapter, you learn how to handle:

- Tables
- Math and equations
- Footnotes and endnotes
- Citations and bibliographies

Handling Tables

Tables can be one of the more challenging tasks in SGML. This is because they are heavily laden with formatting and can only appear in a certain way, predetermined by the author of the table. And, as any SGML purist will probably tell you, format is not something you should set your hopes on since structured content is what SGML is really all about anyway—except when it comes to tables.

When you think about it, the only difference between tables and text is the appearance of the data they present. The point of having a table is to make the data visually appealing and intuitively understandable. Consider the following paragraph:

> The average annual rainfall and tourist revenue, in cubic inches and in dollars, respectively, for the following cities is San Diego: 27 cubic inches and $5.7 million; San Francisco: 110 cubic inches and $10 million; and Indianapolis: 175 cubic inches and $1.9 million.

This information is understandable once you read it through a few times. If there were more cities or more years in the study, however, one would get lost even sooner than with this small example. But even with such a small sample of data, consider how much easier it is to follow when presented as a table.

City	Average Rainfall	Tourist Revenue
San Diego	27 cubic inches	$5.7 million
San Francisco	110 cubic inches	$10 million
Indianapolis	175 cubic inches	$1.9 million

The exact same data appears in the table that's in the paragraph of text. But it's so much easier to apprehend in a table that it nearly makes tabular presentation mandatory. Can you imagine how mandatory a table would be if you were presenting federal income tax tables for increments of $5000 to $250,000 plus? That would *have* to be presented in a table. Naturally, the IRS uses SGML to preserve the integrity of its data.

The Format versus Content Challenge

The problem with format-intensive SGML structures is that you lose the ability to track the *meaning* of the content or data. It's not that hard for the SGML processor to read tagged data and to build a table. The processor can reach into its electronic bag and pull out the right sequence of data blocks and lay them down one after the other, column after column, for as many rows as necessary. It can start with the table heading information—such as City, Average Rainfall, and Tourist Revenue—and lay this information like a mason builds a brick wall.

When the mason finishes the first row of bricks, he grabs the next brick and starts a new row on top of the first. The SGML processor does the same thing, cell after cell, row after row, until the </TABLE> tag turns off the table processing. The physical processing of the individual cell elements is relatively easy.

The problem is that the system now has no way of knowing what the meaning in those cells is. The system has no way of knowing whether <CELL>110 cubic inches </CELL> refers to a City, Tourist Revenue, or Average Rainfall. This causes difficulty when you want to perform a database query on SGML tables.

So another approach to handling tables is to make them content-driven. Instead of using <CELL>110 cubic inches</CELL> to mark the Average Rainfall for San Francisco, you could use a structure like:

```
<CITY><NAME>San Francisco</NAME><RAINFALL>110 cubic inches</RAINFALL>
<REVENUES>$10 million</REVENUES></CITY>
```

This approach lets you track the data. Now the system knows what it *means*. This approach works extremely well for database programmers who want to query the SGML table.

However, it presents a challenge to the SGML developer because he then has to create a DTD fragment for each and every single table based on table content. This can be extremely labor intensive. So the content-driven approach isn't very pragmatic for documents whose tables have many types of data.

You need to know whether your application must provide for *random* or *uniform content* in your tables. If your tables have aircraft parts one day and shoe prices the next, you need some other type of approach than the content-driven approach. If your tables deal only with one type of data, over and over again, like aircraft parts, the content-driven approach should work extremely well for you. But many applications must account for diverse types of content within their tables. They need a way to handle random content in tables.

Random content tables pose a challenge. The challenge is to present the information in a formatted table while retaining enough content-oriented information in the markup so that intelligent queries can be run without too much difficulty.

Hybrid Content-Format Table Structure

The more recent approach to solving the challenge of random content tables is to relate content to table position. In other words, you have to clearly specify the meaning of each cell by its position in the table so that it can be useful in a database query.

Consider the following DTD fragment structure:

```
<!ELEMENT table          - -      (colspec+, thead?, tbody)>
<!ELEMENT colspec        - 0      EMPTY                     >
<!ATTLIST colspec        width    NUMBER      #REQUIRED>
                         type     CDATA       #REQUIRED>
<!ELEMENT (thead¦tbody   - -      (row+)                    >
<!ELEMENT row            - 0      (cell+)                   >
<!ELEMENT cell           - 0      (#PCDATA)                 >
```

Following this structure enables the search engine to check the value of the <COLSPEC type=XXX> attribute and the values of the <THEAD> element. The database query can now locate a piece of information like you locate your position on a map. First you find the longitude and then you find the latitude. The query can proceed in much the same way.

Following the DTD fragment above, your table markup looks like this:

```
<TABLE><COLSPEC width="2" type="city"><COLSPEC width="3" type="rainfall">
<COLSPEC width="5" type="revenue"><THEAD><ROW><CELL>City<CELL>
Average Rainfall
<CELL>Tourist Revenue</THEAD><TBODY><ROW><CELL>San Diego<CELL>
San Francisco<CELL>Indianapolis
<ROW><CELL>27 cubic inches<CELL>100 cubic inches<CELL>175 cubic inches
<ROW><CELL>$5.7 million<CELL>$10 million<CELL>$1.9 million</TBODY></TABLE>
```

Suppose the query engine wants to know what the average rainfall was in San Diego. Now the engine has something to go on. It can first locate the <COLSPEC> element in which the attribute `TYPE="rainfall"` is true. In this case, that `<COLSPEC width="3" type="rainfall">` element is second in the sequence of three. That means there will be three columns in this table, and the Average Rainfall column will be the second. So now the processor knows where to look for rainfall numbers, but how does it know which number belongs to San Diego?

It has to go back to the `<COLSPEC>` element and look for the `type="city"` value. It turns out that the first `<COLSPEC>` element says `<COLSPEC width="2" type="city">`. Now it interrogates the `<TBODY>` element until it finds the `<CELL>` whose value is San Diego. That value turns out to be in the first row. Now the processor goes to the third column of the first row, whose value is located there. The processor finds the city name in the first column and the value for inches of annual rainfall in the second column. Because the processor had these two values, like the longitude and latitude coordinates of a map, it could find the value it was looking for in a database search.

Note

It's probably a good idea to consider external table processing. If you will be dealing with many tables in your documents, you might find it useful to process them outside of your SGML documents so that parsing problems with them will not necessarily mire the production process for the whole document.

You can bring the tables into the document via an entity reference, like &table1, for instance. This entity can be defined in the document prologue as:

```
<!ENTITY table1 SYSTEM "c:\SGML\ENTITY\table1.txt">
```

Whatever table processing system you decide upon can both read and write tables in SGML, or whatever other format with which you might be working.

Processing tables externally often makes sense because it simplifies document parsing.

Handling Math and Equations

Like tables, math equations are format-intensive. Some people get so frustrated dealing with these that they just make the equation into an image and load the equation into the document as a graphic. While this may work, it should only be used when all other alternatives have failed (for reasons explained in the next section).

There are really only three general ways to handle equations:

- Make the equation an image and load it as a graphic (even though it's discouraged against, it's still an option).
- Call on an external processor, such as a typesetting language or format processor (TeX or PostScript, for example).
- Build up the SGML structures in your DTD.

Equations as Graphics

This approach does work. However, it should be a last resort because graphic formats are not fully standardized and they take up more resources than text files with SGML or similar coding.

Web users seem to be resigned to waiting long periods of time for graphic files to load onto their Web pages. Perhaps this is just a phase; graphic-oriented pages may one day fall out of favor because of their bandwidth-hogging ways. Perhaps soon they'll pave the Information Superhighway with a fiber-optic cable for everyone and bandwidth will not be such a big issue. In any event, GIFs and JPEGs seem to be pretty common image formats at this point, so if you can screen capture your equation and make a graphic file out of it, you can make it accessible to an SGML or HTML processor to load into a document.

If your document deals with a lot of equations, however—as you do in scientific papers—this approach could cause problems. Because graphic files are so big compared to text files, you'd do better to code documents laden with equations using another approach.

External Processing of Equations

TeX and LaTex are popular typesetting languages to which math and scientific publishers frequently resort for handling equations. These languages require another application outside of your SGML application to process their code. An SGML document calls up the external application and makes a file or encoded symbols available for processing by that application.

This type of approach could be accomplished by using notation:

```
<!ELEMENT equation    - - RCDATA     --equation-->
<!ATTLIST equation   type NOTATION  (TeX|LaTeX|PS|mathcad) TeX >
```

The notation could be as follows:

```
<!NOTATION TeX LOCAL "c:\apps\tex\pctex.exe" >
<!NOTATION LaTeX LOCAL "c:\apps\latex\wtex.exe" >
<!NOTATION PS LOCAL "c:\apps\psview.exe" >
<!NOTATION mathcad LOCAL "c:\apps\mathcad\mc.exe" >
```

Of course, these notations won't work on anyone else's machine, so you probably want to make public notations where you can, or confine your external processors to publicly available software.

If you're doing heavy equation documents and you have a limited distribution for the documents, you might just pick a specific math program that's available to your audience. Mathcad has found some popularity among scientists, for example. Because you don't intend your documents to be widely distributed anyway, you won't miss the large audience who can't access your documents because they lack the special software/hardware they need. Anyone who wants to view your documents will be required to use Mathcad, or whatever software package you decide upon.

VI

Learning from the Pros

It's basically the same story with TeX. Your documents depend on your readers having the necessary external applications to view the equations. If they don't have the software, they don't get to use the equations. That's the big drawback of using external applications to view equations. The advantage is that they make equations look good on the display and paper.

Perhaps, one day, popular HTML browser developers will finally build in support for the math and equation features of the proposed HTML 3.0 revision. So far, the majority support flash over substance by supporting non-standard `<BLINK>` and `<BACKGROUND>` elements, but not supporting `<MATH>` elements.

Equation Structures in the DTD

Perhaps the most advantageous of these three approaches is to build the math structures up in your DTD. Not every machine has access to TeX and other typesetting languages. The whole point of SGML is to make a document transportable. Meeting that goal would presuppose the DTD route.

Many DTDs exist in the public domain for handling math. You can benefit by checking AAP, CALS, ISO12038, ISO/IEC TR 9573-11:1992E, and the Euromath DTD. Even the HTML 3.0 DTD has some math structures in it that might help. (Unfortunately, the latest browsers don't support HTML 3.0 math structures yet.)

> **Note**
>
> If you're publishing scientific documents that are filled with complex equations but have a very limited audience, you might consider using some proprietary processor system—as mentioned above—instead of SGML. One major reason for using SGML in the first place is to allow wide accessibility to your documents. If you don't need this advantage, and you're not deriving the benefit anyway, you might just consider sending Mathcad files back and forth.

The first general challenge you encounter with math DTDs is that they require lots of external parameter entities with symbols that you'll need. You'd better have all those entity sets locally on your system if you're in doubt as to which set contains which symbols. Check to see which public parameters came with your SGML application. Then check the SGML Archive for further math entities.

The second general challenge is that your math DTD must provide sufficient tags or substructures to break your equations into manageable chunks. Some complex equations might expand to 10 times their normal length when represented with SGML tags. It's easy to get lost in all those text strings unless you can include key "separating tags" to divide parts of the equation from each other. You might have an `<OVER>` element that separates the numerator from the denominator in an equation, or even a `<SDIFF>` element with substructures for simple differentiation. In other words, your DTD can contain an algebra section for algebraic equation structures, a calculus section for integration and differentiation equation structures, a symbolic logic section for symbolic logic structures, and so on. The point is to provide sufficient substructures in your DTD so that the parts of the equation are easy to follow.

Your formatting program also can take advantage of math substructures. Math substructures can tell your formatting program where to break two or more lines of the equation, to place one part of the equation over the other, or to place one equation segment in front of the equal sign and one after the equal sign.

Scientific documents can introduce you to another challenging type of content: footnotes and endnotes.

Linking Revisited

Chapter 9, "Extending Document Architecture," looked at one popular way of handling links—multimedia links—but SGML offers many different types of links. Sometimes, circumstances dictate that links be formatted a certain way, as in the case of footnotes and endnotes in a document. This chapter examines links of these types.

 ◄◄ See "Adding Hypertext Links to a Document," p. 160

Footnotes and Endnotes

In SGML, footnotes and endnotes can be treated as if they are the same. What you, as an SGML author, want to provide the readers with is some supplementary information—like a reference or citation, for example—without interrupting their flow of thought. This is not a formidable task in SGML. To avoid a parsing challenge, you need to look out for *recursion* in your DTD.

> **Note**
>
> Recursion is nesting elements inside each other in a type of loop. For example, suppose that your DTD states that A can contain B, B contains C, and C contains A. Therefore, C can contain A, B, or C.
>
> In the case of footnotes, this can be a little dangerous. Consider if <SECTION> contains <PARA>, which contains <FOOTNOTE>, which contains <PARA>. This is an example of recursion because this makes it possible to have a footnote within a footnote. This is probably not what you want in your document design.

With this type of structure in place, you will *not* get a parsing error when you should. You could actually have a footnote within a footnote within a footnote and not receive an error.

The most common way around this footnote challenge is to use inclusion at a high structural level and exclusion at a low structural level in the document. Here's an example of how it might appear in a DTD:

VI

Learning from the Pros

```
<!ELEMENT section      - -    (para+)         +(footnote)  >
<!ELEMENT para         - -    (#PCDATA)                     >
<!ELEMENT footnote     - -    (para+)         -(footnote)  >
```

This type of structure gives you the flexibility to put a footnote anywhere within a section, yet does not permit a footnote to occur within a footnote. It still allows paragraphs within footnotes, however. Just make sure that footnotes are included at a high enough level for you to use them as freely as you need to.

Citations and Bibliographies

The discussion of footnotes naturally leads into a related discussion about citations. How do you cite a work whose content is referenced in your writing? Much like a hard copy, you can put the citation in a footnote or endnote. However, because footnotes and endnotes are identical in SGML (the processing system determines where the notes are placed), they're much simpler to handle than on hard copy.

Suppose you're writing about a subject and want to make a citation to your source. Your markup might look like this:

```
We find that the latest research on the subject indicates no incidence of
side-effects on patients receiving 50mg per day of the drug whose medical
records showed no history of allergy. <cite>Hudson, B.W., <emph>Study for
Incidence of Side Effects with x-drug</emph>, BigCity [1996],
Big City Press; pp. 129&endash;175.</cite> The remaining research just
goes on and on about…
```

The nice thing about citation tags like this is that your processing system can use your <CITATION> tags to build a bibliography. This sort of structure lends itself to macro-oriented formatting by a processing system. Some formatter can extract all of the citations and alphabetically sort them, strip page numbers, and build a bibliography. That can be very useful.

Many times, you want to not only cite a source but make a reference to an endnote. This can be accomplished through markup similar to the following:

```
We find that the latest research on the subject indicates no incidence of
side-effects on patients receiving 50mg per day of the drug whose medical
records showed no history of allergy. <citref refid="Hudson1">The
remaining research just goes on and on about…
```

The citation collection could exist in a separate document or later in the same document:

```
<citation id="Hudson1">Hudson, B.W., <emph>Study for Incidence of Side
Effects with x-drug</emph>, BigCity [1996],
Big City Press; pp. 129&endash;175.</citation>
```

This is one effective way to handle citations. As you're authoring your document, you can place the <CITATION> information inline with the <CITREF> information. This leaves it to the text formatter to determine where to physically place the citations.

Multimedia Linking

◀◀ See "Adding a Graphic," p. 162

SGML offers many ways to link electronic documents to binary resources like video clips, graphics, and other multimedia resources. Making an EMPTY element point to an external resource with its attributes is only one possibility, as you saw in Chapter 9. There are others. For example, you can give names to multimedia files and declare them as entities, and then declare the name of the entity as a value for an attribute of the EMPTY element in your DTD:

```
<!ELEMENT multimed  - -      (multfil, title)           >
<!ELEMENT title     - o      (#PCDATA)                  >
<!ELEMENT multfil   - o      EMPTY                      >
<!ATTLIST multfil   - o      id      ID       #REQUIRED>
                             name    ENTITY   #REQUIRED>
```

Notice that the name attribute is required to be an entity. The declaration for that entity could lead the processing system to the file itself. Here's the declaration:

```
<!ENTITY mymovie  SDATA  "/usr/movies/home/mymovie.mov"    >
```

The markup is what unifies the name attribute with the entity itself in the following document instance excerpt:

```
My family and I are extremely happy, and you can see that in
<multimed><multfil id="0001" name="mymovie"> this home
movie</multfil></multimed>, and if you want a copy, just...
```

Now when the processing system sees that name="mymovie", it knows it is an entity because that is all the DTD allows it to be. The system will resolve the path to the file and link to it. In keeping with SGML's independence from specific hardware and software, this link processing is kept separate from the instance of the marked up file.

From Here...

This chapter covered a few special challenges that you're likely to encounter in your SGML endeavors. While it's by no means an exhaustive list, it will help you deal with content such as tables, equations, footnotes, and bibliographies.

For more information, refer to the following:

- Chapter 9, "Extending Document Architecture," covers ID and IDREF attributes that are helpful in linking information such as endnotes or footnotes.
- Chapter 16, "Markup Challenges and Specialized Content," covers some of the syntax with which you'll need to be familiar, such as NOTATION and marked sections.

- Chapter 24, "Understanding and Using Output Specifications," covers important considerations for handling heavily formatted document structures and making them look good.
- Appendix B, "Finding Sources for SGML Know-How," lists further sources to aid you in your research of difficult document structures.

Part VII

SGML Tools and Their Uses

26   Tools for the PC: Authoring, Viewing, and Utilities

27   Tools for the Mac: Authoring, Viewing, and Utilities

28   Other Tools and Environments

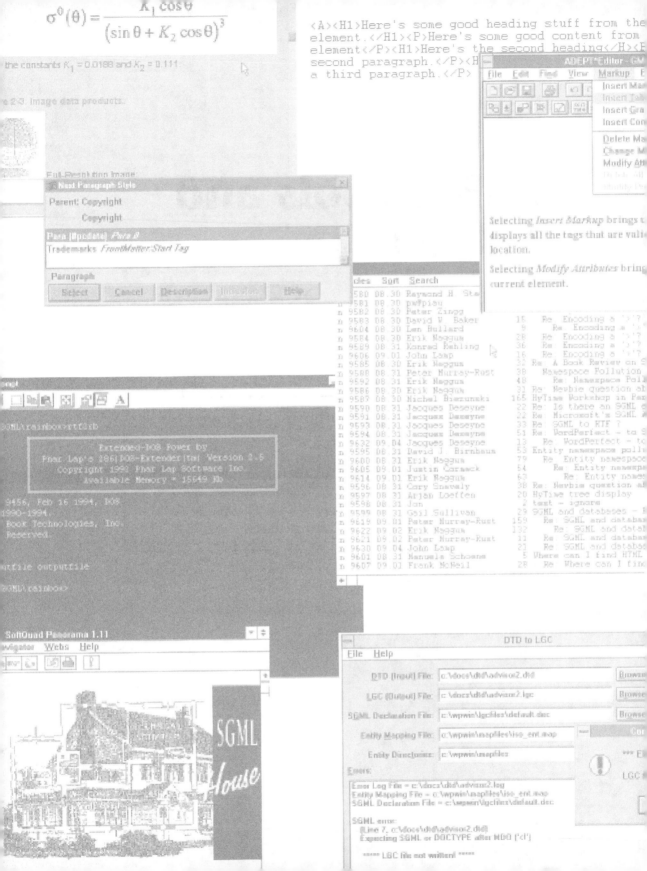

Tools for the PC: Authoring, Viewing, and Utilities

In the not-so-distant past, setting up SGML document systems involved a number of challenges. Foremost was a basic shortage of tools from which to choose. Compounding this problem was the fact that many of the available tools were quite costly to implement. This cost included both the initial purchase and the necessary system setup.

One reason why initial purchase costs were high was that many SGML authoring systems were based upon high-end publishing systems, often running on relatively expensive UNIX host computers. For the organization considering the move to SGML, an added significant cost was often that of training staff to use an entirely new authoring system—possibly on a new type of computer.

This chapter examines some of the best PC-based tools. The examination will include a look at the following:

- Authoring tools for SGML
- Other support tools for SGML, including document viewers and DTD design tools

A New Era in SGML Tools

The events of the last year have dramatically changed the picture for the individual or organization wanting to implement an SGML system. With the introduction of a powerful new set of inexpensive PC-based tools, the costs involved with implementing SGML in an organization have dropped dramatically. With a modest investment in time and money, you can now try out SGML. If you have been hampered by the limitations of HTML on the World Wide Web, you can upgrade to SGML.

Further brightening this picture is a key aspect of many of the new authoring tools. They are constructed as add-ons to standard Windows-based word processors. If your organization uses WordPerfect, for example, there is an SGML package for you.

Table 26.1 describes the software packages that are discussed.

Table 26.1 PC-based SGML Tools			
Name	**Type**	**Vendor**	**Description**
WordPerfect SGML Edition	SGML authoring	WordPerfect/ Novell	SGML authoring package compatible with WordPerfect
Near & Far Author	SGML authoring	Microstar	SGML authoring package compatible with Word
SGML Author	SGML authoring	Microsoft	SGML authoring package compatible with Word
Panorama Pro	SGML viewer and browser	SoftQuad	SGML browser for local and Internet and World Wide Web documents
Near & Far	DTD design tool	Microstar	Graphical document modeler and DTD creation, documentation, and maintenance tool

SGML Authoring Tools

The authoring tools are based on two standard Windows word processing packages—WordPerfect and Microsoft Word. Each program adds SGML capabilities to the word processing program. Learning the SGML authoring environment with these packages is much less difficult than it would be with an SGML-only package.

WordPerfect SGML Edition

This new SGML authoring tool from WordPerfect is built into the standard word processing package, version 6.1 of WordPerfect (and later versions) for Windows 3.1 and Windows 95. It includes full support for structured authoring with user-supplied DTDs. The interactive output specification designer enables you to generate specific output formatting based on the attribute values of specific elements.

Features. WordPerfect SGML Edition differs from its competitors in that the SGML features are integrated into the standard version of WordPerfect. The program is organized so that you can run either the standard version of WordPerfect or the SGML version. After installation, icons in the program group are available for the applications shown in table 26.2. They include programs to compile DTDs into the WordPerfect binary format, a program for designing output specifications, the SGML authoring version of WordPerfect, and other support programs.

VII

Table 26.2 WordPerfect SGML Edition Application Summary

Module	Description
DTD to LGC	Compiles DTDs to WordPerfect logic file format
Layout Designer	Output specification interactive design program
WordPerfect SGML Edition	Word processing application with SGML functions
WordPerfect	Standard word processing application
Learning SGML	SGML and program tutorial documentation in Envoy document format
SGML Setup	WordPerfect SGML Edition installation program

DTDs and Output Specifications. User-supplied DTDs must be compiled into the WordPerfect format to be used with WordPerfect SGML Edition. This compilation step produces a binary formatted logic file (LGC). The compilation process also parses the DTD. External entities are supported by means of an entity mapping file that associates entity names or system identifiers with the corresponding entity file.

The conversion of DTDs is a simple process. After you start the conversion program, an input form is displayed. You select the applicable input file (DTD), the output compiled DTD file (LGC), the SGML declaration file, and any applicable entity mapping files. A variety of standard SGML entity files and their corresponding mapping files are included with the program.

The process of compiling the DTD for use in WordPerfect includes a parsing step. The DTD must parse without errors for the process to generate compiled output. Parsing errors are clearly identified during the compilation step, as shown in figure 26.1.

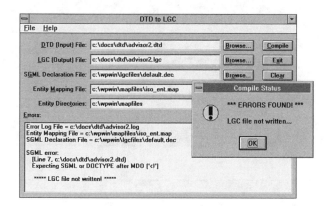

Fig. 26.1

DTDs must be compiled for use with WordPerfect SGML Edition. Parsing errors are identified in the DTD compilation process.

> **Note**
>
> A number of DTDs are included with WordPerfect SGML Edition, including those for HTML 2.0 and DOCBOOK.

You can create and modify output specifications, or stylesheets, for a specific DTD with the Layout Designer. When you create a new stylesheet, you import the appropriate compiled DTD—the LGC file. To modify an existing stylesheet, specify it instead.

After importing the DTD, you select individual elements and add the formatting values that you want. The available formatting includes standard formatting instructions such as font type, size, and style. Special text, new lines, a horizontal line, and other features can precede and follow the element. When you specify formatting to follow the occurrence of the element, you can locate the formatting before or after the element end tag, as shown in figure 26.2.

Fig. 26.2

You can set up stylesheet formatting to apply before or after the element. When it follows the element, it can occur either before or after the end tag.

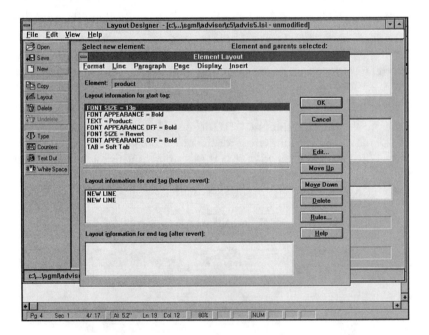

> **Note**
>
> Placing formatting instructions before the element end tag affects the subelements included within the element. Placing formatting instructions after the end tag does not.

You can set up element formatting to be conditional, depending on the element's parents or the value of its attributes. For example, if the subject of a bulletin is indicated to be safety-related by a safety attribute, special formatting might include a specific safety warning when the element is encountered with that attribute value. A second format for the element might be used for conditions when the safety attribute is not set. To set conditional format processing, you specify the conditions in the Element Rules dialog box (see fig. 26.3).

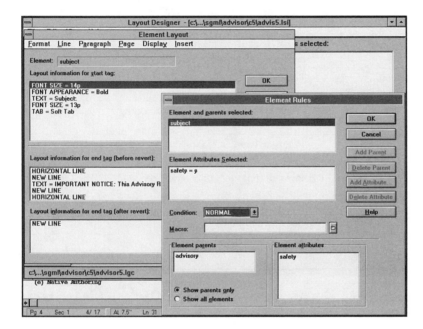

Fig. 26.3

Elements can be formatted conditionally, according to specific values of element attributes.

SGML Authoring. To perform SGML authoring in WordPerfect, you use the SGML features available in this version of the program. They are accessible through a special SGML toolbar. You author documents in WordPerfect SGML Edition according to the rules of a specific DTD. To do structured authoring, you first "check in" the DTD with or without an accompanying stylesheet. Do this with the Document Types tool on the toolbar. Table 26.3 describes all the SGML features.

Table 26.3 SGML Features in WordPerfect SGML Edition

Icon	Name	Description
	Document Types	Displays and installs available DTDs
	Open SGML File	Opens SGML document instance with applicable DTD and output specification (LSI file)
	SGML Preferences	Displays and sets SGML tag display options

(continues)

Table 26.3	Continued	
Icon	**Name**	**Description**
	Elements	Displays and selects elements allowed in current document location
	Edit Attributes	Displays or modifies attributes corresponding to the selected element
	Tag Tables	Performs automatic table tagging
	Logic Errors	Displays SGML logic errors
	Validation	Parses the SGML document
	ID/IDREF	Displays a list of ID and IDREF attributes
	File References	Inserts an entity reference
	Text References	Inserts a character entity reference
	Root Element	Specifies a new SGML root element for the current document instance
	SGML Ignore	Specifies text that parser should ignore

After you select a DTD, you can begin writing. To make the SGML tags visible in your document, use the SGML Preferences tool button.

You select an element with the Element pop-up window, which is invoked with the Element tool. Available elements are displayed in a context-sensitive manner. That is, only those elements, element closings, and element contents that the DTD allows in that location of the document are displayed on the element list. You can leave the Element window as you author your document.

If you select DTD and a corresponding stylesheet and layout file is available, your document is displayed according to the stylesheet formatting. This includes preceding text, spacing, and font layout instructions. Figure 26.4 shows a document that has a layout file being authored. The SGML options have been set to show tags. The text in bold—**PRODUCT ADVISORY**, `Number:`, `Date:`, `Revised:`, and `Number:`—is inserted automatically by the program because it is specified in the stylesheet as Text Before.

You can also select additional options with the Elements pop-up window, such as logic chaining. When selected, this feature takes you to the next required element in the structure. It automatically closes the current element and opens a new one according to the document model defined in DTD as you press Enter. If the next element allowed is actually a choice of elements, the Elements window pops up to show which elements are currently available.

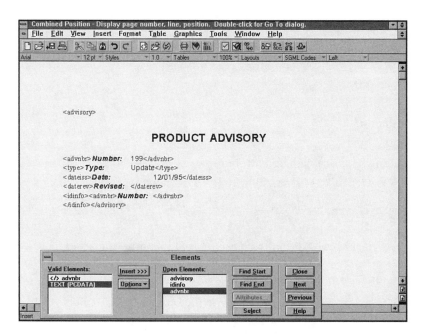

VII

SGML Tools and Their Uses

Fig. 26.4

The Elements pop-up window displays only those elements, element closings, and contents that are allowed at that position in the document.

Another option is a prompt for entering attributes. When you select this option, a pop-up window prompts you to enter values for the attributes associated with the current element.

Other authoring features include support for automatic table tagging, validation of ID and IDREF attributes, and insertion of external entity references. You can also specify a designated root element for use in a particular editing session, which is useful when you author a portion of a large document.

Conversion to and from SGML. To convert existing files in other formats to SGML, you can use several options, including:

■ Convert the document into ASCII text. Then cut and paste it into an empty SGML document template.

■ Use a WordPerfect macro file.

■ Use an outside package—for example, a Perl program or a commercial conversion program such as Avalanche's FastTAG.

▶▶ See "The World of Perl" and "Avalanche/Interleaf FastTAG," pp. 491, 495

Converting from SGML to other file formats is straightforward in WordPerfect SGML Edition. You simply perform a Save As operation and specify the format that you want to use.

Document Parsing and Validation. Document parsing occurs in two situations: when you save a document as an SGML document and at your request. You select the validation features. They include:

- Character mapping
- Entity validation
- Entity declaration
- ID and IDREF
- Logic, including tag placement and attribute values
- Text sequence, such as SGML markup with the document content

Because you can select each type of error checking, it is easy to author and convert a document in stages.

Highlights. WordPerfect SGML Edition is a powerful tool for authoring SGML documents. Its output formatting capabilities are noteworthy. Multiple stylesheets are available for the same DTD, and it has conditional formatting capabilities.

The integration of SGML authoring capabilities into the standard WordPerfect authoring package makes WordPerfect SGML Edition easy to use if you are already familiar with the standard WordPerfect word processing package.

WordPerfect Corp.,
1555 N. Technology Way
Orem, UT 84057

Web: **http://wp.novell.com/elecpub/sgmlweb.htm**

Near & Far Author

Perhaps one of the slickest products on the SGML Authoring list is Microstar's new Near & Far Author. This program operates alongside Microsoft Word. It customizes the Word interface to facilitate structured authoring. What makes the program so slick is its graphical mapping of document structure. It teaches authors intuitively about structure better than any SGML seminar ever could.

Features. Near & Far Author, shown in figure 26.5, is very forgiving. It is not just intended for use by SGML experts. A writer who is familiar with Word stylesheets can write structured documents and create SGML files. Instead of designing your own DTD, you can create a quick-and-dirty map by importing an existing document model and publishing a default map. The program designs its own map for you automatically from that imported model. This structure map becomes the foundation of your authoring template and the structure of your SGML instance. It is intuitive and friendly, enabling authors who do not know SGML to produce structured documents.

The product is simple to use. Select Create New SGML from the Near & Far Author menu, and choose a DTD. Near & Far Author creates and parses a default MAP file that enables you to create an SGML file immediately.

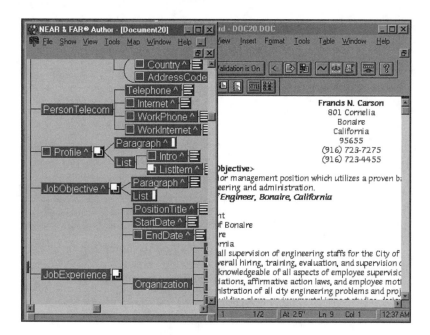

Fig. 26.5

Microstar's Near & Far Author is a smart authoring tool and a surprisingly good design tool.

DTDs and Output Specifications. No direct support for creating DTDs is provided with Near & Far Author. However, you can build document models that you can use to build structured documents for SGML authoring. Combined with Near & Far, this feature enables you to build terrific DTDs. As soon as you create a new SGML instance, the program asks you to select a DTD. When you do, it validates the DTD.

What is helpful is the product's capability to edit document maps. The interactive structure tree makes it easy to select an element and edit it for content.

Near & Far Author does not directly support output specification creation. It performs a similar function through the use of document maps for mapping to standard Word formatting functions.

Native SGML Authoring. Perhaps the greatest strength of Near & Far Author is its native authoring environment. When validation is turned on, your document is compared to the document model as you type. It is actually difficult to create an invalid document. The buttons and help menus are intuitive. Even writers with little SGML experience can create valid document instances.

Table 26.4 describes the Near & Far Author tool buttons.

Table 26.4 Near & Far Author Tool Buttons		
Icon	**Function**	**Description**
⊞	Import SGML	Imports an SGML document

(continues)

Table 26.4 Continued

Icon	Function	Description
	Export SGML	Exports an SGML document instance
	Validate Document	Validates the current SGML document instance
Validation is On	Validation Status	Toggles validation errors on and off
	Next Character Style	Toggles between legal character styles
	Modify Attribute	Brings up the Attribute Edit dialog box
	Add Entity	Displays the Add Entity dialog box
	Toggle Attributes Visibility	Makes attribute markers in a document visible or invisible
	Toggle NFAuthor Markup Visibility	Makes tags in text visible or invisible
	Message History	Displays error message history
	Toggle Map Toolbar	Makes the map toolbar visible or invisible
	NFAuthor Help	Activates the help utility
	Import SGML Using Current Style Map	Imports an SGML file by using the active style map
	Attach DTD	Attaches an external DTD
	Attach MBF (Microstar Binary File)	Used for creating authoring templates
	Generate Minimum Sample Instance	Creates a sample document instance from an active DTD
	Generate Larger Sample Instance	Creates an expanded sample document instance from an active DTD
	Generate All Styles	Generates styles in Word that are created from a MAP file
	Modify Catalog	Activates the Modify Catalog dialog box

As you create an SGML document instance, Near & Far Author forces you to choose legal styles for the next paragraph. The Next Paragraph Style dialog box, shown in figure 26.6, displays the options from which you can choose.

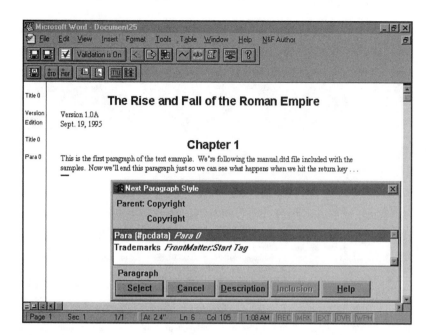

Fig. 26.6

Near & Far Author forces you to choose only legal styles.

With automatic validation turned on, you know immediately when you create an invalid document. A warning error signals you that a problem exists and suggests how to fix it.

Conversion to and from SGML. Conversion from SGML is pretty smooth, so long as the program can locate all the entities and external files. Otherwise, the error messages are collected in the Message History dialog box, which explains why the file loading process failed (see fig. 26.7).

It is easy to create a new SGML file according to your favorite DTD. Select Create New SGML from the N&F Author pull-down menu. The program asks you to select a DTD from the Open File dialog box. It parses the DTD and creates a structure tree and document model for you to follow. You can modify them easily. Simply point to the element on the graphical structure tree and select Element Map from the Map pull-down menu. The dialog box shown in figure 26.8 appears.

Document Parsing and Validation. Document parsing can take place as you author if you turn on the automatic validation device. It also occurs when you save a document as SGML. In each case, the program prompts you with clear error messages that collect in a dialog box.

Document model validation is easy, too. From the Map pull-down menu, select Publish Map; the active map is validated. This is a handy feature when you need to modify a map or when you want to adjust a DTD directly on the structure tree.

Highlights. The symbols on the structure tree show occurrence and value content by icons, so you can see at a glance how often an element appears. PCDATA appears as a small paragraph. When you expand the entire structure tree, you can see hierarchy, occurrence, and default value content (see fig. 26.9).

Fig. 26.7

As an SGML file loads, parsing errors collect in the Message History dialog box.

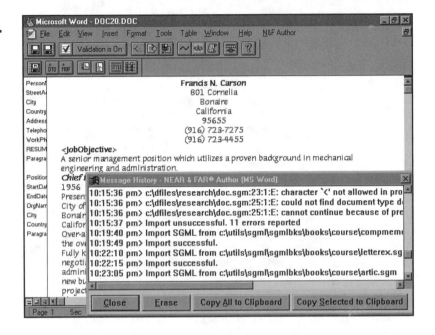

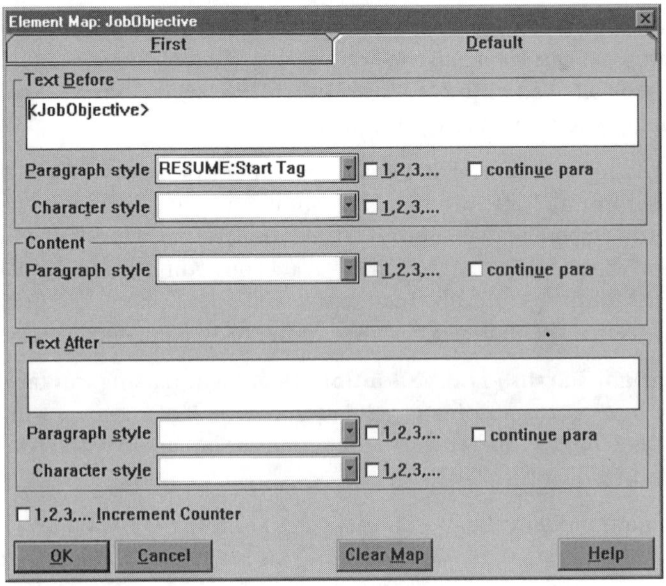

Fig. 26.8

The Element Map dialog box enables you to add before and after text and to adjust the properties of styles.

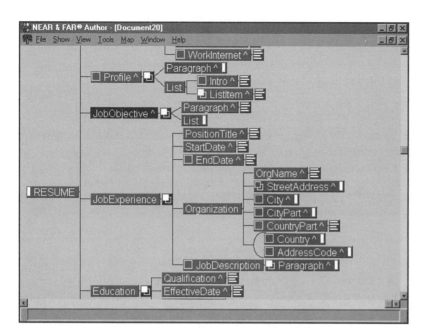

Fig. 26.9

The Near & Far Author structure tree shows the hierarchy of the elements, occurrence, and declared value content.

Near & Far Author is the most enjoyable and intuitive package to use. There is nothing daunting about it. It enables you to create SGML painlessly. Microstar includes many sample DTDs and test files, and you can modify and validate sample documents.

> Microstar Software, Ltd.
> 3775 Richmond Road
> Nepean, Ontario, Canada K2H 5B7

> Web: **http://www.microstar.com**

SGML Author for Word

Microsoft's SGML Author for Word is designed to convert between native SGML documents and Word. It uses specialized templates to enable structured authoring in SGML by creating a Word document that you can save as SGML. Version 1.0 was released in 1994.

Avalanche and SoftQuad offer companion products—Avalanche SureSTYLE and SoftQuad Enactor—that help you use this product. SureSTYLE applies consistent styles to Word documents so that they can be converted easily to structured SGML by SGML Author for Word. Enactor has an interface similar to Word's. It enables you to validate native SGML documents by using context-sensitive menus.

Features. SGML Author for Word is essentially a conversion filter that enables you to save Word files as SGML and to open SGML files in MS Word. After installation, you have your choice of where to put the program icons. Installation modifies the Word menus and creates new subdirectories under the winword directory. As with most

Word add-on tools, you use styles intensively and you must map your DTD to the styles on your Word template. You do this with an association file, which is what SGML Author actually creates. SGML Author comes with templates and ISO character sets that make this process easier, as well as sample files on which you can practice conversions.

The conversion process happens with the SGML converter program, which operates rather invisibly behind the Word interface. Whenever you save a document as SGML or open an SGML document instance in Word, the converter does its magic. Table 26.5 describes the basic components of SGML Author for Word.

Table 26.5 Components of SGML Author for Word	
Module	**Description**
SGML Author	This is the program in which you create the association (MAP) file that the converter uses to translate Word styles into SGML tags.
Converter program	This program operates transparently but does the real work for this application. It uses the MAP file intensively.
Word templates	These templates enable easier structured authoring within Word. You can create your own templates, too. For macros to be active in your SGML authoring templates, the template must have an associated INI file.
Sample conversion files	The sample documents come with applicable MAP, INI, DOT, DCL, and DTD files.
ISO character sets	Specialized character sets and an ISO equation set are included.
Help files	The help file and the system administrator's guide that come with the package are useful.

SGML Author for Word contains the essentials for creating valid SGML document instances. It was apparently designed for authors who must author documents but not design document types. To create DTDs, you need to create text files with Word or buy another tool specifically for that task. SGML Author for Word gives you everything that you need to map Word paragraph and character styles to a DTD of your choice. It enables authors to create Word documents according to that structure.

DTDs and Output Specifications. SGML Author for Word does not provide specialized tools for creating DTDs. You can design a structured authoring interface for authoring documents in Word. You must create the DTD with another tool. The program does a parsing check on the DTD when you associate the DCL file, however, and it shows you the parsing errors in a Notepad file.

SGML Author does not support external output specifications. It assumes that the document is presented only in Word. You can design several presentations in Word for a single DTD and document instance, however.

The closest to an output specification that you can come is to map a DTD to more than one Word template for conversion from SGML to Word. This gives you multiple appearances for the same SGML document. You can create several formats by adding the letters prn (for presentation) to Word templates for a single authoring template. For example, if you use the sample DTD, you can create SAMPRN1.DOT and SAMPRN2.DOT for different presentations of the same content and structure.

You can map a single DTD to multiple DOT files—but only one at a time. When you convert a single SGML document instance into a Word document, you are asked to select the declaration file (DCL), the association file (MAP), and the SGML authoring template (DOT or INI, which launches the DOT file). All these files must be ready before you convert the document.

> **Note**
>
> *Descriptors* in SGML Author for Word associate Word styles with the markup in the DTD. Simple descriptors map to discrete elements, and complex descriptors map to nested elements. MAP files are the association files that contain the descriptors and their default values.

When you author an SGML document, you can create multiple MAP files for different Word presentation formats. You control the default values of descriptors during conversion. Therefore, you can alter the appearance of a MAP file as you want.

Native Authoring. SGML Author for Word is designed for the structured authoring of Word documents that convert easily to SGML. By using custom authoring templates, you create Word documents that follow the structural model of the DTD on which the template is based. Specialized SGML buttons become part of the interface to help you follow the model (see fig. 26.10).

Before you author a document, however, you must have a valid DTD for which you can create a DCL file. You associate the DCL file with an INI file, which is the SGML Author for Word template file that actually creates the type of environment shown in figure 26.10. Before you author, you must:

1. Choose a DTD to work with.
2. Create a DCL file for the DTD.
3. Create an association file for the DCL file.
4. Create new or modify existing SGML authoring templates.

At this point, you are ready to start authoring. The documents that you create will most likely translate easily into valid SGML documents.

◀◀ See Chapter 10, "Following General SGML Declaration Syntax," p. 171, for information on the DOCTYPE statement and SGML declaration.

Fig. 26.10

Specialized authoring templates help you create structured Word documents that convert easily to SGML document instances.

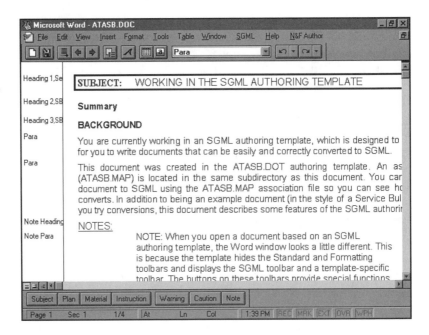

Creating the DCL file is simple. Edit a text file with a `DOCTYPE` statement that points to the location of your DTD. For example:

```
<!DOCTYPE example SYSTEM "example.dtd">
```

This statement assumes that `EXAMPLE.DTD` resides in the same directory as the file on which you are working. If your `DOCTYPE` declaration does not follow concrete reference syntax, you must add an SGML declaration to the DCL file.

After you create the DCL file and place it in the same directory as the file on which you are working, you must create the association (MAP) file. This is the file that SGML Author for Word lives and breathes by. It enables conversion between Word and SGML.

Creating the MAP file is the biggest part of this endeavor. It involves associating and setting conversion defaults for all the styles and attributes, creating and editing the descriptors, associating the descriptors, and testing the associations. You do this from within the SGML Author for Word program itself (see fig. 26.11).

The beauty of SGML Author for Word is the association interface. The right side is the SGML side, and the left side is the Word side. The buttons on the left modify Word construct options. The buttons on the right affect SGML structure display options. The buttons between them affect the conversion between document types. When the association is complete, you can author structured documents for conversion into SGML.

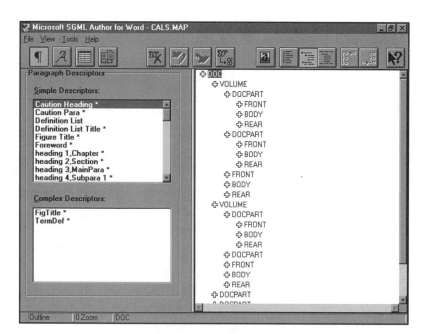

Fig. 26.11

You create the MAP file by associating the DTD elements with the Word constructs. The association values are stored in descriptors.

The authoring environment enables you to create valid SGML files easily by moving the toolbars away and adding buttons, such as the Next Legal Style button (see fig. 26.12).

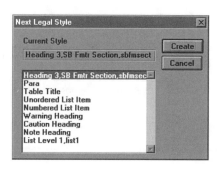

Fig. 26.12

The authoring environment enables you to create valid SGML files easily by moving toolbars away and adding buttons, such the Next Legal Style button.

Each authoring template has its own default toolbar layout. You can modify it by modifying the authoring template, just as you do with a standard Word template. The toolbar buttons for this ATA template (supplied with SGML Author) are described in table 26.6.

Table 26.6 The Toolbar Buttons for the ATA Authoring Template

Icon	Name	Description
	New Document	Opens a new document that is based on the SGML authoring template
	Save as SGML	Saves the document as an SGML instance, but displays a feedback file if parsing errors or warnings exists
	Next Legal Style	Shows a dialog box that lists the next legal styles, as defined in the INI file by association with the DTD
	Promote Heading	Moves the current heading up in the hierarchy to the next legal level permitted by the DTD, as specified in the INI file
	Demote Heading	Moves the current heading down in the hierarchy to the next legal level permitted by the DTD, as specified in the INI file
	Make Bold	Applies bold
	Make Italic	Applies italics
	Make Underline	Applies underlining
	Character Styles	Displays the Character Styles dialog box
	Attributes	Displays the Attribute dialog box for inserting attributes
Heading 1	Style Drop-down Menu	Displays the current style and shows the list of legal styles available
	Undo	Undoes the most recent change
	Redo	Redoes the most recent change

The authoring template supplies everything that you need to create valid SGML documents. Although the CALS and ATA templates that come with SGML Author are complete, you probably want to create your own template.

The authoring templates are designed to be modified from Word authoring templates that you are already using. If you use the NORMAL.DOT template, for example, you start by saving it under another name. Next you use Word's template organizer, under the File menu, to copy the macros, toolbars, and autotext entries from the SGML authoring templates, which are supplied with SGML Author, into the new authoring template. Finally, you save the new template.

> **Note**
>
> You must have created the association file for the new template before you customize. The INI file for the new template requires information about the associations. If they are not created yet, you cannot provide them. The initialization file launches the macros that go along with the new template.
>
> If you do not intend to use the macros in the supplied authoring template, however, you do not need an INI file. This is unlikely, because macros permit the buttons to behave as described. Consider the Next Legal Style button on the authoring template, for example. The INI file enables the template to find the legal styles according to the DTD and to display them.

To create an INI file for the new authoring template, copy the INI file for the supplied SGML authoring template to a new name. Modify it by adding a section for each template style, specifying hierarchical relationships among the styles, setting default styles, and configuring the Attribute dialog boxes. This is easier than it sounds, and it can be time-consuming. You can also add macros in Word Basic or C—the C macros must be converted to Word Basic. When you are done, you have a new SGML authoring template customized to your needs.

Conversion to and from SGML. Converting from Word to SGML is easy, provided that you have a DTD, a DCL file, and an association file created in SGML Author for Word. You must also have a document that conforms to your DTD. Conversion errors are reported in the SGMLTMP.ERR file.

There are a few caveats, however. Tables must follow the CALS model, and not all the attributes of all the elements of that model are supported during the conversion. Equations must follow the ISO equation tag set for proper conversion. As long as your documents are not heavily laden with complex tables and equations, you are in good shape.

Once you save the Word file, the SGML file appears in the window in the SGML Authoring view. Parsing errors are saved in a feedback file with a FBK extension (see fig. 26.13).

Once you solve these problems, you have a valid SGML file. To view it, open it as text only.

Converting an SGML file to Word is more challenging, depending on the SGML features that are in it. SGML Author for Word does not fully support many features. The ISO equation set and the CALS table model are supported. To venture beyond them is to invite trouble.

You must have in place the DCL file, the MAP file, the Word DOT file, and the DTD. The converter program must recognize all the descriptors and be able to associate all the SGML tags with them. If it does not recognize something, it tries to continue parsing and converting. When the converter encounters unrecognized tags with content, it either creates a new paragraph or appends the tagged characters to the previous paragraph. The converter applies the Normal style as the default.

Fig. 26.13

*The feedback file summa-
rizes the parsing errors
encountered when the
document is saved as an
SGML instance.*

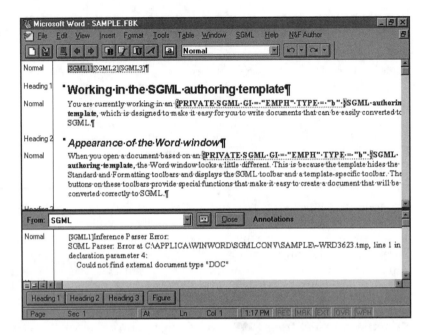

Round trip conversions—that is, conversions to SGML and back to Word—offer a few anomalies. They can change the document. The converter adds private fields that contain default attribute values to the document so that information is not lost when the document is converted back to SGML. For example:

```
<EMPH VAL="i">Italic text</EMPH>
```

gets converted to the following in Word:

```
{PRIVATE SGML GI="Emph" Val="i"}Italic text
```

Another anomaly is that the converter loses multiple styles associated with one element when it is translated back into Word. For example, list items often include a final item with white space that separates it from the next legal style. Because the other list styles normally do not have this separating space, there must be two list styles for each list—the regular list style and the last list style. For example:

```
Here's a first list item in Word. Normal spacing.
Here's a second list item in Word. Normal spacing.
Here's a last list item in Word, with extra space after it to set it
off from the next style.
```

The last list item adds white space to the end of the style before the next paragraph begins. The reason is because in Word it is a style different from the previous two list items. In Word, you can apply different, although similar, styles to the first two list items and the last list item. The anomaly is that when the document is converted to SGML, all the list items are tagged (such as with the tag <LITEM>). Later when you convert back to Word, the converter becomes confused when it finds two styles that apply to the <LITEM> element—unless you declare a different element for each style.

The converter knows only one element—one Word style—so it chooses the last style that you used between the two list styles. The way around this is to make sure that you declare one element for each style in Word.

Another anomaly is the bookmark feature in Word documents. The converter program has difficulty maintaining a two-way cross reference on a round trip conversion.

All in all, document conversion using SGML Author for Word is efficient and pain-free. When problems occur, they generally involve associating descriptors with Word styles.

Document Parsing and Validation. You cannot entirely parse as you go in SGML Author for Word. The parsing and validation takes place during the conversion process, and you cannot customize which document elements you will parse. For example, you cannot parse only ID and IDREF and entity declarations, as you can with WordPerfect SGML Edition. The SGML Author feedback file and the SGMLTMP.ERR file help resolve parsing errors that occur during conversion.

Highlights. Since its introduction over a year ago, SGML Author for Word has been one of the leading SGML authoring tools in its price range. It will probably be upgraded to remain competitive with the latest releases from Microstar and WordPerfect.

For creating SGML structured documents that transform easily into SGML, you might want to keep SGML Author for Word on your machine. It is a trusted, reliable, no-frills authoring tool. If you must work with several templates and keep multiple authors focused on a disciplined document structure, check out this product. It is designed especially for the system administrator who guides authors in creating valid SGML documents.

> Microsoft Corporation
> One Microsoft Way
> Redmond, WA 98052
>
> Web: **http://www.microsoft.com/Products/**

Other SGML Tools

In addition to authoring programs, other tools that support SGML-based document systems are available. They include tools for viewing SGML documents electronically and for maintaining an SGML document system. The rest of this chapter looks at two of these packages: Panorama Pro and Near & Far. Panorama Pro is a new package for browsing SGML documents electronically. Near & Far is a tool for designing and documenting DTDs.

Panorama Pro

The advent of the World Wide Web made HTML a popular way to present documents electronically. Its limitations, however, have led many people to explore the richer feature set possible with robust SGML implementation.

Until recently, the use of full SGML capabilities on the World Wide Web was limited by the lack of an SGML-browser compatible with Web viewing. This has changed with the availability of Panorama. Developed by SoftQuad, it uses a set of software routines from Synex Information AB. It serves as an electronic browser for SGML documents.

Panorama is available in two versions: Panorama Free and Panorama Pro. Both versions enable you to view complex SGML data structures, such as tables, and special data, such as equations and graphics. Panorama Pro adds capabilities, such as functions, for developing output specifications.

> **Note**
>
> A copy of Panorama Free is included on the CD-ROM that accompanies this book.

On the CD

Features. Panorama Pro supports the viewing of both remote SGML documents—such as those obtained over the World Wide Web—and local SGML documents. To view an SGML over the Web, you use Panorama Pro in combination with a standard HTML browser, such as Mosaic or Netscape. Panorama temporarily downloads the document's DTD and stylesheet. Table 26.7 describes features of Panorama Pro.

Table 26.7   Features of Panorama Pro

Feature	Description
Web browser compatibility	Views World Wide Web documents through links to common Web browsers
Stylesheet support	Uses SGML output specifications and can create and edit stylesheets interactively
Table of contents	Generates a table of contents for the document from SGML dynamically
Document searches	Enables the user to control content searches, including context-sensitive Searches
Bookmarks and annotations	Enables the user to define bookmarks and annotations in documents
Graphics support	Supports the BMP, GIF, and WMF graphics formats
Document publishing	Publishes documents for use on the World Wide Web
Hypertext dynamic linking	Links between documents, document sections, and other objects (such as graphics and multimedia)
Tables and equations	Supports tables and equations, including a subset of the CALS table model

When used with a Web browser, Panorama Pro is called automatically when SGML documents are encountered. Figure 26.14 shows Panorama Pro viewing a document on the World Wide Web. The document viewing window is configured to show the table of contents of the document.

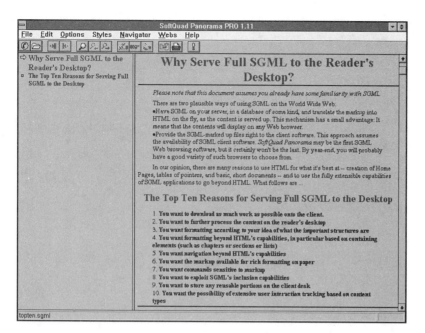

Fig. 26.14

You can use Panorama Pro to view documents on the World Wide Web.

Tip

If you have trouble getting Panorama Pro to operate with the Netscape browser, make sure that you start Netscape before you start Panorama.

Using and Creating Output Specifications in Panorama Pro. Panorama Pro supports output specifications—stylesheets—that can format elements. You can create multiple stylesheets for the same DTD. Consider the document in figure 26.15. It is presented as text with only a slight amount of format instructions. With a different stylesheet, the same document is formatted as a table, as shown in figure 26.16.

The flexibility of multiple stylesheets enables you to adjust the document presentation to suit different situations, environments, or circumstances. Figure 26.17, for example, shows how a large typeface document can be formatted for use by the visually impaired.

To create and modify stylesheets, you use an interactive stylesheet editor. The steps are:

1. Attach a stylesheet from the Styles menu.
2. Name the stylesheet.
3. Create the appropriate element properties.

Consider each step in detail. Start with an SGML document, such as a product advisory bulletin (see fig. 26.18).

Fig. 26.15

You can use multiple stylesheets for the same document.

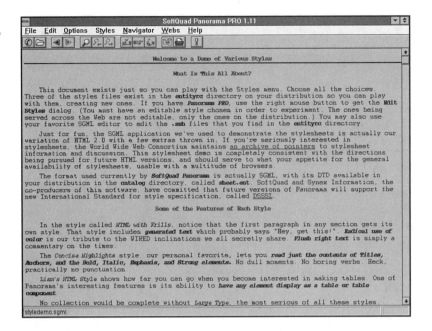

Fig. 26.16

Here is the same document formatted as a table.

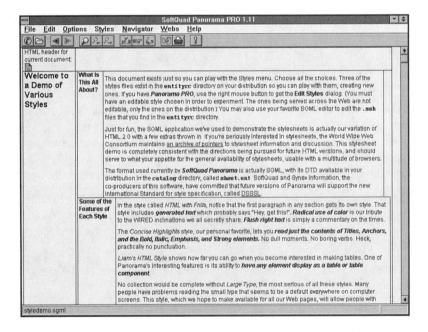

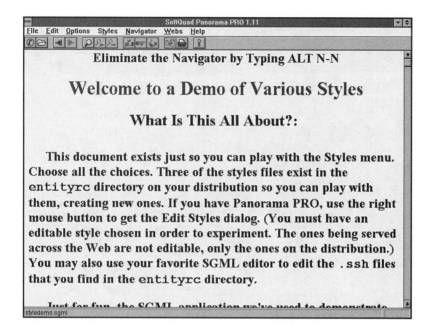

VII

SGML Tools and Their Uses

Fig. 26.17

Here is another view of the same document. It uses large type for use by the visually impaired.

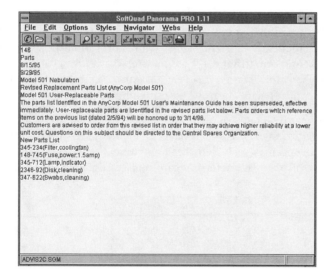

Fig. 26.18

Here is a view of an unformatted SGML document.

To format the individual elements, you must select them. You do this with the elements in the document or in an optional SGML element tree by clicking the right mouse button while moving the cursor over them. When you select a menu, the Style Sheet Editor is invoked.

Beginning with the major elements, you can select formatting. Formats are specified in the editor by selecting from a menu or by entering data (see fig. 26.19).

Fig. 26.19

Formatting is added interactively with the Panorama Pro Style Sheet Editor.

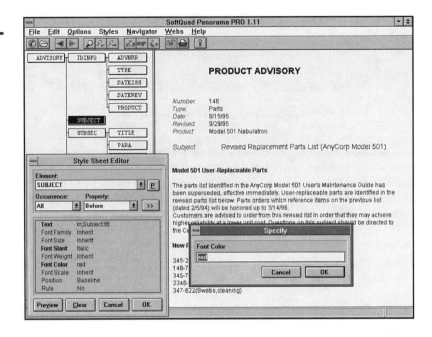

You can format elements according to specific qualifications, such as their location in the SGML structure, their position in a sequence, or the value of their attributes. You can apply properties to elements that cover content, paragraph formatting, "before element" and "after element" formatting, table formatting, math formatting, and link formatting. SoftQuad, the creator of Panorama Pro, has announced that it will support the DSSSL standard for output specifications when it is completed.

Creating Navigators. Creating a table of contents—called a *navigator* in Panorama Pro—is similar to creating stylesheets. You first select an element. With the Navigator Editor dialog box, you can specify which elements to include, the font sizes in the table of contents, and the display parameters for captions (see fig. 26.20).

Fig. 26.20

Creating a table of contents with the Navigator Editor dialog box is similar to creating stylesheets.

Performing Document Searches. You can search for specific text in Panorama Pro by:

- Searching the entire document
- Searching for the occurrence of the text within the context of specific elements

Both types of searches are performed in a similar manner. To search the whole document—a full text search—select the search choice in the Edit menu or click the Search icon on the toolbar. Enter the search term in the pop-up menu.

If items matching the search are found, you are taken to the first match. The number of matches is shown in a window in the lower-right corner. Their distribution and relative locations in the document are indicated by the lines on the display bar to the right of the document, as shown in figure 26.21. The number of bars indicates the number of hits in each area of the document.

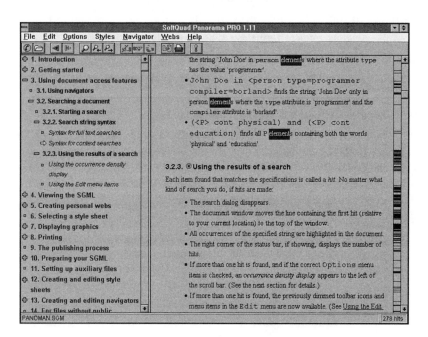

Fig. 26.21

The number of matches in a search is indicated by the frequency bar on the right edge of the document.

To perform a context search, you indicate the conditions under which you want to search. For example, to search for the term Troubleshooting in document sections pertaining to turbine engines, you would enter:

```
Troubleshooting in <section subject=turbine>
```

Supported Graphics Formats. Graphics included in an SGML document are typically handled by Panorama Pro through the use of external entities. The graphics viewer included in Panorama Pro supports the following formats:

- BMP (Microsoft Windows bitmap)

- GIF (Graphics Interchange Format)
- WMF (Microsoft Windows metafile)

With the NOTATION declaration, you can call viewers that support other graphics file formats.

Publishing Documents with Panorama Pro. You can use Panorama Pro to prepare SGML documents for electronic delivery, such as on the World Wide Web. Because HTML is an implementation of SGML, Panorama Pro can be used for both HTML and other implementations of SGML.

To publish documents on the World Wide Web, you must first check the public identifiers, validate the document instances, check the graphics, and build the directory trees. The specific steps are:

1. Add and validate public identifiers to the SGML document instances.
2. Validate—parse—the document instances and the DTDs.
3. Check and validate all the document links.
4. Check and validate the graphics file markup.
5. Validate that any external programs—such as graphics viewers—are operating correctly.
6. Validate the filename syntax and filename location.
7. Check the availability of applicable DTDs in the correct format.
8. Set up the directory structure for document and supporting files—DTDs, entities, graphics, and so on.

> **Note**
>
> The syntax checker in Panorama Pro is not a validating parser. All document instances and DTDs should be parsed by a validating parser such as SP, which is included on the CD-ROM that accompanies this book.

On the CD

▶▶ See "SP/NSGMLS Parser," p. 490

Highlights. Panorama Pro is a versatile product. It supports World Wide Web and local SGML documents. Its support for multiple stylesheets with a variety of formatting capabilities and its ease of use make it a useful tool for viewing electronic documents.

SoftQuad, Inc.
56 Aberfoyle Crescent
Toronto, Canada M8X 2W4

Web: **http://www.sq.com/products/panorama/panor-fe.htm**

Near & Far

Designing and developing SGML documents is labor-intensive. During document analysis, a project team analyzes the structure and usage of a document type and translates the document model into a DTD. Although this approach is useful, creating it is a manual process that requires you to translate the document model into a DTD. Near & Far, a companion product to Near & Far Author, is an automated tool for constructing DTDs. With its drag-and-drop interface, Near & Far enables you to construct a graphical model of your document, validate it, and output the corresponding DTD.

Features. Near & Far—part of Microstar's computer-aided document engineering (CADE) system—is a groupware application based on Lotus Notes. It facilitates the collaborative development of SGML document designs and architecture. The features provided in Near & Far include a useful tool set for creating, documenting, and maintaining DTDs. It is useful across the many phases of the DTD creation and maintenance cycle. Table 26.8 describes the features of Near & Far.

Table 26.8 Near & Far Features

Phase	Features
Creation	Graphical design of document models DTD generation
Documentation	Graphical view of document models Document model tabular reports Internal DTD documentation and comments
Validation	Content model parsing

Building a Document Model with Near & Far. Creating a document model with Near & Far is a straightforward process. After you start the program, the opening screen displays the menu and toolbar, which show the basic operations available.

You use the toolbar icons, which are described in table 26.9, when you graphically create a DTD model. They include functions to identify the occurrence of an object, an object's type, the ordering of subobjects contained within an object, inclusion and exclusion definitions, and single content type parsable character data (PCDATA).

Table 26.9 The Near & Far Toolbar Icons

Icon	Class	Type
	Occurrence indicators	One
	Occurrence indicators	None or one
	Occurrence indicators	One or more

(continues)

Table 26.9 Continued

Icon	Class	Type
	Occurrence indicators	None or more
	Object	Element
	Object	Named group
	Connectors	Ordered
	Connectors	Unordered
	Connectors	Selection
	Inclusion and exclusion	Inclusion
	Inclusion and exclusion	Exclusion
	Content type	PCDATA
	Other	Trashcan

To create a document model, pick New under the File menu. Near & Far creates a new model with a single element. It gives it a default name. To change the name, you select Element under the Edit menu, and modify the element.

After you create and name the root element, the process is simple. Working through the document model, you drag and drop connectors and elements. When you create an element, you can use a pop-up window to name it and to specify its occurrence. After you name an element, you can add a more descriptive title for use with the report generation functions.

Tip

If you have multiple document models open, you can cut and paste elements—or portions of content models—between models. This feature enables you to reuse portions of similar content models.

Near & Far presents information graphically, so the document content model is easy to understand. Color is used to indicate which object of the model is currently selected for an operation, which elements have no content, and the occurrence of content in the model. You can tailor the level of detail to fit your needs as you edit the model. Figure 26.22, for example, shows two levels of detail for the same model. In the first, only the top two levels of the model appear. In the second, all levels of the model appear.

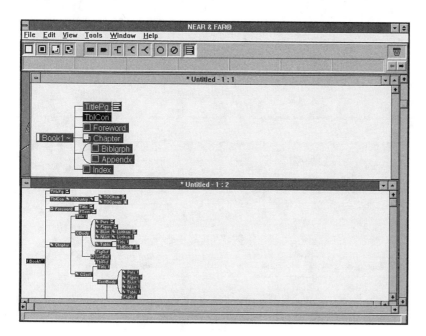

Fig. 26.22

Near & Far enables you to view different levels of detail in a document model.

Report Generation. System documentation helps you maintain an SGML system with multiple or complex DTDs. Depending on your needs, this documentation can include cross references to elements and attributes, a list of all the objects that occur within a DTD, and lists of elements in which actual data content occurs—that is, terminal data elements.

Preparing system documentation can be tedious if you have to gather the data manually. Near & Far's reporting capabilities simplify the process. With the report generation feature, you can generate descriptive DTD reports (see fig. 26.23). Table 26.10 describes all the reports that you can generate. You can print them or export them in electronic format for inclusion in your system documentation.

Table 26.10 Near & Far Reports	
Type of Report	**Description**
Element or group cross reference	Lists elements organized by parent element group where they occur
Attribute or element cross reference	Lists attributes with elements where they occur
Element or attribute cross reference	Lists elements with applicable attributes

(continues)

Table 26.10 Continued

Type of Report	Description
Supplemental objects	Lists additional SGML data objects, including data types, insertions, local substitutions, and external substitutions
Terminal data	Lists the actual data content occurrence by element
Object summary	Lists the objects that occur in the document model
Model summary	Lists elements and attributes with titles and descriptions

Fig. 26.23

You can generate useful reports automatically in Near & Far.

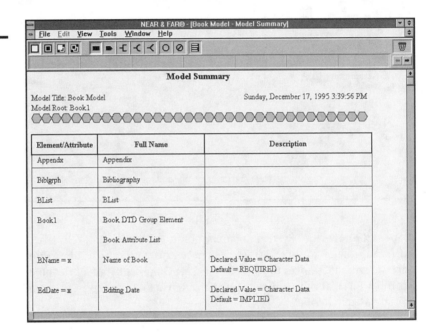

Highlights. Near & Far is a convenient tool for developing, modifying, and documenting DTDs. Its graphical interface enables you to manipulate document content models easily. Its reporting capabilities alone justify its purchase for projects that require extensive documentation. Although Near & Far does not eliminate the need to do rigorous document analysis, it makes you much more productive.

Microstar Software, Ltd.
3775 Richmond Road
Nepean, Ontario, Canada K2H 5B7

Web: **http://www.microstar.com**

From Here...

The products discussed in this chapter are some of the most practical yet powerful products available. They offer immediate and pragmatic solutions for SGML design and authoring. More expensive products are on the market, of course. If you are a high-end business user, look into purchasing those products.

For more information, refer to the following:

- Chapter 27, "Tools For the Mac: Authoring, Viewing, and Utilities," examines the various SGML tools available for the Apple Macintosh.

- Chapter 28, "Other Tools and Environments," surveys other SGML tools for performing data conversion, validation, transformation, and document viewing that are available on a number of computer platforms.

- Part VIII, "Becoming an Electronic Publisher," covers the issues involved in moving into electronic publishing.

VII

SGML Tools and Their Uses

Tools for the Mac: Authoring, Viewing, and Utilities

This chapter examines the SGML document preparation process using an Apple Macintosh computer. Although the Mac environment is ideal for text editing and writing, it's not as well supplied with specialized SGML tools as Windows and UNIX are. Don't despair, however. There are SGML document preparation tools for the Mac, and many of the same public domain and freeware tools that run on UNIX and DOS also run on the Mac.

In this chapter, you learn about:

- Mac-specific authoring and conversion tools and strategies
- SGML delivery tools for viewing and printing from SGML
- Public domain and network resources for SGML on the Mac

This chapter also includes examples of how to cope with common SGML tasks on the Mac, including:

- Document conversion from an RTF file
- Document conversion from plain text
- Document conversion from HTML to a more complex DTD

Planning an SGML Project on the Mac

When you set up an SGML project, you need to carefully plan the work environment, tools, and your goals. The basic process of any SGML project is the same:

1. Select, create, or customize a DTD.
2. Enter and mark up or convert the document.
3. Create the final product.

Not all these phases are essential—SGML might be your final product. However, you might need to process your SGML document in order to print, display, or index it, or you might need to convert it from SGML to HTML.

A little extra planning helps ensure a smooth work process and enables you to use your time sensibly. Much of the SGML software for the Mac is public domain code, which is freely available over the networks. Carefully selecting your tools in advance is especially important, given the smaller selection of tools for the Mac.

One way to deal with the limited software choices for the Mac is to extend the range of software by building a mixed-platform environment from the beginning. A UNIX workstation that the editorial staff shares can be very useful. It not only makes a good central file space, but it also provides the most flexible scripting environment if the production process involves complex file conversion steps. A workstation is the ideal environment for inexpensive batch-style processing because the public domain tools for the Mac do not support scripting. Good ways to integrate a workstation and Macs for SGML projects are:

- Use the workstation for initial and final document conversion. Use the Mac for editing and formatting final output.
- Use Macs for creating documents, and edit with a specialized SGML editor. Use the workstation for batch conversion and formatting.
- Use the workstation for capturing or creating documents and for post-processing the SGML. Use the Mac for formatting and layout.

The real strengths of the Mac in a mixed environment are an easier user interface, easier system and file management, and good mouse-based editing. A UNIX workstation provides superior batch processing facilities, easier programming for knocking out quick conversion or update scripts, and the greatest number of public domain tools—as long as you have the technical support to compile them. The drawback is the obvious need for technical support. Likewise, the powerful free software available for UNIX, such as the PSGML mode for emacs, tends to have cryptic interfaces.

Authoring and Conversion Tools for the Mac

Document conversion is a constant problem in text processing. SGML eases the task by providing a common language that can be easily processed and exchanged. Nonetheless, you often need to convert legacy documents or create non-SGML output formats for input to other tools. In these cases, the best approach depends on whether you are converting to or from SGML.

Converting to SGML is a task that depends greatly on the structure and regularity of the input files. You can often accomplish 90 percent of a simple conversion by using the global change facilities of a word-processor or ASCII editor. Complicated or irregular formats might be better converted by using a programming tool to match patterns and to reorder and format the output. Conversion from SGML is usually accomplished with an SGML parser coupled with a programming language. It is also done with the global changes or general-purpose scripting tools.

SoftQuad's Author/Editor is a popular commercial SGML authoring environment on the Mac. It's an editor for SGML that uses the structure of a particular DTD to prompt and control how documents are entered. A separate utility compiles the DTD into an internal form that controls how the SGML document is created, and ensures that the result matches the DTD. During editing, Author/Editor stores the document in an internal form for fast access. You must export the document to get a conforming ASCII SGML file.

Stilo is another structured editor for SGML. Its basic features are similar to those of Author/Editor, but DTD compilation is integrated into the basic editor. Stilo features an innovative graphical display of the structure of the DTD.

Another approach is simply to use an ASCII editor targeted to programmers. They are generally well suited to demanding editing tasks and support regular expressions, global changes, and keyboard and programmed macros for repetitive work. When you use an SGML-unaware editor, you need a separate validator for the resulting files to ensure that they actually follow the rules of SGML and your DTD.

If your DTD is not very complex, you might be able to take a low-tech approach and use popular HTML tools. You can customize many of them with new tags to accommodate the rapid changes in the HTML DTD. If the DTD is simple enough that the tagger needs little help other than a separate validation pass at the end, this is a plausible, low-budget solution.

SoftQuad Author/Editor 3.1

In addition to HotMetal Pro, its HTML editor, SoftQuad has a number of Mac SGML products. Author/Editor 3.1 is the first and most full-featured SGML editor for the Mac. Unlike many other SGML products, which reveal their Windows or UNIX origins by their non-standard interfaces, Author/Editor has a Mac-like feel that you can learn easily. Any complexities that you encounter are likely due to the program's full set of advanced SGML capabilities. If you're familiar with SGML, however, or are working with someone who is, Author/Editor is a good choice for data entry. It is best suited for entering a document from scratch, rather than fine-tuning a partially marked up document.

Author/Editor enables authors to submit manuscripts to their publishers in SGML. This enables authors to concentrate on authoring and publishers to concentrate on typesetting and publishing. This program shelters you from many of the difficulties of SGML, protects you from making SGML errors, and leads you through the process of creating a document. However, you are restricted to working with correct documents. This can make it difficult to work with partially correct SGML or to modify a DTD during the authoring process.

Author/Editor reads a compiled DTD. It helps you write correct SGML by permitting you to insert elements and attributes only in their correct contexts. Author/Editor has formatting, editing, and SGML capabilities. It comes with good documentation and a series of tutorials.

> **Note**
>
> Author/Editor is a *conforming* SGML system. This means that its SGML parser conforms to ISO 8879, the SGML standard, and that its output is acceptable to the Department of Defense and other contractors who require strict conformance. It can handle markup minimization, and it enables you to change many of the parameters in the SGML declaration.

Author/Editor 3.1 requires System 7 and a minimum of 6M of RAM. It is copy protected. After you install it, you must run a special program to activate it, which requires a serial number. Author/Editor files, like most word processing files, are not text files. They are binary files, which means that you can read them only with Author/Editor. To share your SGML files with people who use different SGML software, you must export the file from Author/Editor so that it becomes a standard, text-only SGML file. While it is an extra step, exporting is as simple as choosing the Export to SGML option from the File menu.

Formatting and Views. Author/Editor displays a text file either with or without tags. When tags are displayed, they appear as icons in the text, as shown in figure 27.1. You can apply formatting styles to each element, which makes it easier to read and edit the document, even when tags are not displayed. The Styles feature makes data entry easier by using colors or text styles to indicate different elements. Author/Editor also provides two other views of an SGML document: the structure view and the context view.

Fig. 27.1

Author/Editor shows tags as icons in a document.

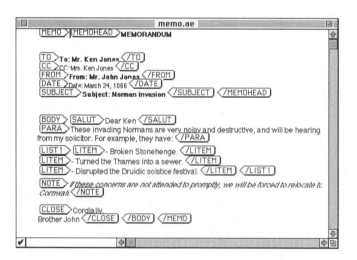

Author/Editor's structure view displays the document as an indented SGML tree, similar to the outliners in many word processors, as shown in figure 27.2. You use this display for navigation. It provides a useful structural overview of the text. As with an outliner, you can click elements to expand or hide their contents. You can use this feature to locate places in your document where the SGML is correct, but where the tagging is inappropriate. It can help you find missing tags that are required. This enables you, for example, to scan quickly to ensure that every chapter element has a title element.

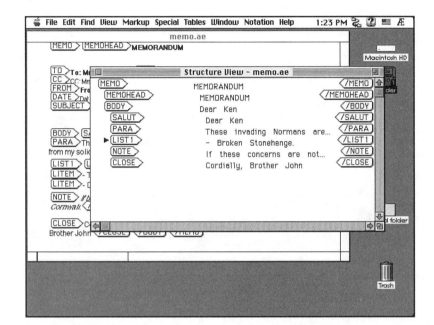

Fig. 27.2

You can navigate an Author/Editor document by using an outline view.

The context view shows all the elements that contain the current element (see fig. 27.3). If you move the cursor, the current element changes. You can get useful information for determining whether part of a document has been tagged correctly. This can be a lifesaver, especially when a document has a deeply-nested structure. For instance, the context view can help you determine quickly the nested list to which a particular list item belongs.

Editing. Editing an SGML document in Author/Editor is easy. You can import a text file and tag it. You can import partially tagged documents and complete their tagging using the program. Likewise, you can type a document in Author/Editor and tag as you write. Author/Editor has menu items and keyboard commands for a variety of SGML-based editing activities. You can:

- Insert the next allowable element
- Split an element into two
- Join adjacent elements with the same tags
- Surround text with a particular tag
- Edit attributes
- Insert entities

Fig. 27.3

Use the context window to determine the nesting of an element.

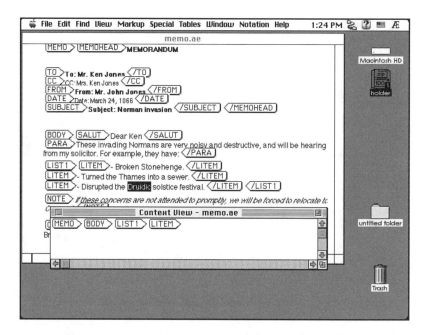

You can use each function by using either display. You also can control how strictly Author/Editor follows the DTD. In Rules Checking On mode, you cannot write SGML that does not match the DTD. In Rules Checking Off mode, you can break the structure defined in the DTD restrictions, which is useful for temporary work on documents in progress.

Whenever you are ready, but before you finish, you should validate your document. The validation process runs your document through the Author/Editor SGML parser. It finds and displays even the most minor SGML errors. In particular, it will detect missing elements that are required. This is a task that interactive rules checking cannot do and still allow a reasonable editing process. Verify periodically as you work to check the state of the document. Make sure to run it at least once at the end, of course, so that you can perform any needed final clean up. It helps you tie up all the loose ends and make the document completely legal. Author/Editor also has a graphical table editor, so you can edit tables easily.

SGML Features and Setup. Installing Author/Editor on a Macintosh is easy—simply run the installer. If you're using one of the common DTDs and ISO entity sets included in Author/Editor, you are ready to work in SGML.

If you want to use your own DTD, however, you must prepare it so that Author/Editor can read it. This step creates a binary file with the information from the DTD. It is equivalent to the process of importing an SGML file. Compile it with SoftQuad's RulesBuilder, a separate product. Put the resulting binary file in the Rules folder in the Author/Editor folder so that Author/Editor can find it. You do not insert DOCTYPE declarations at the top of your SGML files. When you open or import a new file, a dialog box asks you which DTD you want to use. Your new DTD appears as one of the choices.

Author/Editor comes with a variety of precompiled industry-standard DTDs, such as CALS (Department of Defense), ATA (Air Transport Association), docbook (documentation), HTML, helptag (help systems), ISO 12083 (books and articles), and j2008 (automotive manuals). Softquad plans to include other DTDs in future versions, including TEI (Text Encoding Initiative).

Author/Editor can handle advanced SGML features, such as marked sections. It can edit and display tables, and it can display external, non-SGML files using the NOTATION mechanism.

Trouble spots. Author/Editor is the first SGML product created specifically for the Mac, and it is easy to use. It does have some drawbacks, though. Some of its problems are a direct result of its strengths. For instance, some people find it difficult to work within its controlled and structured editing style.

Tip

Unless you have a top-of-the-line machine, Author/Editor runs slowly. This will remain a problem until the next update, because version 3.1 is not native to the PowerMac.

Changing a DTD. If you want to use a DTD not provided with Author/Editor, you must purchase a separate program called RulesBuilder. This is primarily because Author/Editor separates the roles of author and document designer in its work model. To make changes to a DTD, you must open RulesBuilder, make the changes, recompile the DTD, and reload the SGML document. This is time-consuming. On the other hand, you can download precompiled DTDs for common formats from many World Wide Web and FTP sites. Although the separate work steps are not a significant problem, the need to purchase two software licenses makes using custom DTDs or modifying standard ones expensive.

Importing. Author/Editor's import uses the validating SGML parser. It expects to see documents that do not contain fatal SGML errors. In fact, the best way to use Author/Editor as an SGML validator is to import a document. Because an import uses the validator, it's not always easy to import partially tagged documents, especially if they're tagged incorrectly. The biggest problems typically are elements not defined in the DTD, overlapping elements, and elements that are never closed. These problems cause Author/Editor to refuse to import your document. If they are bad enough, they can crash the system.

Which DTD? Another drawback of Author/Editor is that you cannot see which DTD a document is using unless you export the document as an ASCII SGML document, in which case, you get a `DOCTYPE` declaration at the top of the file. This is not a problem if you aren't developing DTDs. It is often important, however, to know which DTD a document is using.

Editing with Another Program. The final drawback—or advantage, depending on your point of view—is that Author/Editor files, because they are essentially WYSIWYG SGML files, are not stored as ASCII files in their native format. Therefore, you can read them only with Author/Editor. You can export them to a standard ASCII SGML format. That takes time, and it is inconvenient if you're using multiple tools to enter, tag, and clean up documents, or if you need to move documents between tools frequently. On the other hand, the WYSIWYG format makes it much easier to read and edit files.

SoftQuad, Inc
56 Aberfoyle Crescent
Toronto, CANADA M8X 2W4
(416) 239-4801 or (800) 387-2777
(416) 239-7105 FAX

http://www.sq.com

SoftQuad RulesBuilder 3.0

RulesBuilder is the companion program to Author/Editor. You use it to create, edit, and compile DTDs. It consists of a bare-bones ASCII editor with a regular expression find and change feature. The main purpose of RulesBuilder is to compile your DTD into a binary file that Author/Editor can read, as shown in figure 27.4. After you write a DTD, you build the rules file. You move this file into the Author/Editor Rules directory and select it when you edit or import a new document.

Unfortunately, RulesBuilder does not provide templates for the basic DTD formats, such as <!ELEMENT ... > and <!ATTLIST ...   >, to help you as you type your DTD. You have to remember all the SGML syntactic details on your own.

http://www.sq.com
For full contact information, see "SoftQuad Author/Editor 3.1."

SoftQuad Sculptor 1.0

Sculptor 1.0 is an application builder for Author/Editor based on the Scheme programming language. It's an expensive commercial version of the toolkit that SoftQuad uses to customize and enhance its products. You use Sculptor to customize Author/Editor. You can, for example, change the menus or menu items to add functionality, incorporate Author/Editor into another program, or make it communicate with the Mac operating system.

Sculptor is a powerful programming tool that requires technical knowledge, but it enables you to redefine almost every aspect of how the editor supports specialized interface needs or document preparation procedures. You are most likely to need it if you are setting up a long-term SGML project that uses uniform data and performs the same tasks repeatedly. In this case, customizing the environment cuts down on training time for staff and allows significant gains by automating repetitive tasks.

Customizing is less appropriate for one-time conversion or tagging projects because of the preparation required and the high price of the software.

http://www.sq.com

For full contact information, see "SoftQuad Author/Editor 3.1."

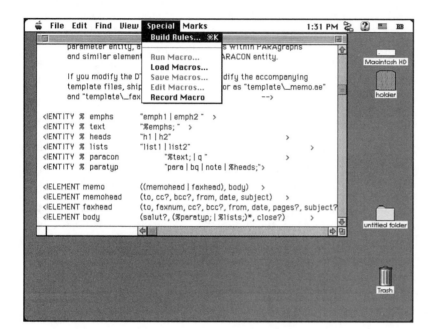

Fig. 27.4

Use RulesBuilder to edit and compile your DTDs.

Stilo

Stilo, a program being developed by Stilo Associates in the United Kingdom, provides another editing option for SGML on the Mac. It has some promising features. Like Author/Editor, Stilo is fundamentally oriented to structural editing—it rigorously enforces the DTD. It comes with many already compiled DTDs. It uses its own compiled document and DTD formats for editing; SGML export is the final stage of the editing process.

Unlike Author/Editor, however, the DTD compiler is built into the basic Stilo editor. This promises to make Stilo a more economical solution than Author/Editor, particularly for those who need to change or customize DTDs in their projects. Stilo's editing model is oriented to data entry, rather than document conversion. Stilo allows for a DTD to be saved by itself, or in conjunction with a *template* document containing text and markup to be automatically entered into new documents.

◀◀ See "Entities: Their Use and the ENTITY Markup Declaration," p. 184

Another feature of Stilo that is not in Author/Editor is support for SGML external entities. A single Stilo file can be split across multiple files. This feature enables you to split large documents for separate editing, which makes document management and collaboration in groups much easier. It also makes reusing common material much easier, by enabling it to be shared among documents. The export to SGML command preserves these entity divisions. It produces SGML in separate files that refer to one another by using SGML's standard entity declarations and references. A simple list dialog box enables you to define new external entities for a particular document or in a DTD file. That way, you can use entities for managing standard document types, as well as in individual documents.

Stilo also provides a graphical viewer on the Mac for the DTD itself, as shown in figure 27.5. This view represents the parts of the DTD as nested boxes; each box represents an element. Display this graphical view while you edit a document. By highlighting the current element, it provides visual information on the structure of the document. As you change position in the document, the relevant portion of the DTD is always displayed, indicating what options for data entry and structuring are available.

You can use this view to get an overview of the whole DTD. Because the key relationships among the elements of a DTD are not represented in the visual structure of its definition, graphical tools like this one are invaluable. They make the structure of complex DTDs much more accessible.

Stilo Associates
Empire House
Mount Stuart, Cardiff
CF1 6DN, UK
(44) 1222-483-530

info@stilo.demon.co.uk
http://www.demon.co.uk/stilo

Qued/M, Alpha, and BBEdit

If you do not have access to—or cannot afford—the commercial products for authoring SGML on the Mac, you might be able to use an ASCII programmer's editor to tag or convert your SGML. These editors do not offer special SGML support if you enter a document from scratch, but they speed up the process of converting OCR files and files that were saved in RTF or other word processor conversion formats.

These editors support powerful find and change commands that use text patterns called *regular expressions*. Qued/M, a commercial editor made by Nisus Software, enables you to save regular expressions as macros. You can build a library of simple conversion patterns that apply to the formats of your documents.

Alpha is a shareware programmer's editor. It handles standard regular expressions. It has a powerful HTML mode that you can—with perseverance—extend to handle simple SGML. In HTML mode, anything within angle brackets is highlighted in blue, which makes it easy to separate tags from text. You can automate sequences of change commands in Alpha, but you must be prepared to deal with its textual programming interface. Alpha has the most complete and easily programmable scripting facilities of these three products.

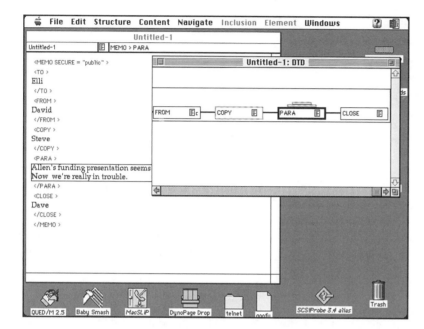

Fig. 27.5

A view of the pre-release Stilo editor and its DTD viewer.

BBEdit exists in both shareware and commercial forms. It is the most popular ASCII editor for the Mac. It has several HTML modes. They are not as easily extensible as Alpha's because they are implemented as binary plug-ins rather than as macros. BBEdit handles regular expressions. The HTML modes in both BBEdit and Alpha do not know how to validate tags, and they cannot prevent you from placing them incorrectly. All they do is automate the typing involved in tagging a document.

One of these editors, or something similar, is an essential tool if you're going to convert much existing electronic text. The more you work with one-of-a-kind formats—which make automatic conversions impossible—the more this is likely to be true. If you use an editor that is not SGML-aware—such as this one—you also need to run an SGML validator on your converted and tagged documents to make sure that your SGML has no errors.

Qued/M
Nisus Software Inc
PO Box 1300
Solana Beach, CA 92075
(800) 922-2993 or (619) 481-1477
(619) 481-6154 FAX

http://www.nisus-soft.com/product_info.html#QUEDM

BBEdit and BBEdit Lite (shareware)
Bare Bones Software

http://www.tiac.net/biz/bbsw
ftp://ftp.netcom.com/pub/bb/bbsw

Alpha (Shareware)
Pete Keleher
8006 Barron St.
Takoma Park, MD 20912

http://www.cs.umd.edu/~keleher/alpha.html
ftp://www.cs.umd.edu/pub/faculty/keleher/Alpha

SGMLS

SGMLS is the most commonly used public domain SGML validator available. It exists
for almost every platform and was the first free parser to run on the Mac. The best
place to get copies of SGMLS is the SGML FTP archives. The best place to learn more
about updates and upgrades is the SGML newsgroups. There are other public domain
parsers—some of which are newer and better than SGMLS—but none has been ported
to the Mac.

SGMLS is a stand-alone program. It reads a text file, a DTD, and (if necessary) an
SGML declaration, and then it parses the document. To report the SGML errors that it
finds, it uses error messages based directly on the ISO 8879 standard. Several versions
of SGMLS for the Mac are available at the FTP sites. The earlier version, compiled using Think C, was slower and had a more difficult interface. The new version, described
here, is compiled with Metrowerks and is available for PowerPC and 68K Macintoshes.
It has added interface features that make it easier to use.

Note

SGMLS is a program written for a command line interface, and it does not shake that paradigm, even though on the Mac it has dialog boxes and buttons. You actually have to type in
information that on a Mac you would usually select with menus and dialog boxes.

Running SGMLS. The interface to SGMLS is an unadorned dialog box divided into
three parts (see fig. 27.6). The top section contains a box where you type the name of
the file that you want to validate and any switches that you want SGMLS to use. The
lower-left section of the dialog box indicates input options, and the lower-right section indicates output options.

To validate a file using SGML:

1. Double-click the application.

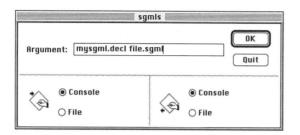

Fig. 27.6

SGMLS has a simple interface that mimics a command line.

2. Enter the name of your file in the dialog box. If you need to use a modified SGML declaration, enter the name of the SGML declaration before the file name. For example:

mysgml.decl alice.sgml

 ◄◄ See "DTDs and Declarations for Elements, Attributes, and Entities," p. 62

3. Don't change the radio buttons at the lower left, which indicate input. You want input to occur from the console.

4. Select the File radio button at the lower right if you want your error output to go to a file. This is generally easier if you expect to have many errors or if you are validating a long file. If you select the Console radio button, error messages appear on the scrollable Console window.

5. Choose OK to validate the file.

6. Correct the errors in your SGML file, and repeat steps 1 through 5.

Common Problems with SGMLS. SGMLS has little documentation beyond a lengthy UNIX man page. It contains a large amount of technical information, most of which you do not need. However, you can obtain the names of the basic switches and parameters from it, if you need them. All implementations of SGMLS work the same, so the documentation applies to all platforms.

Command Line Switches. SGMLS assumes that you are using SGML's standard defaults unless you specify otherwise. These defaults impose constraints that you might not like. Element names are restricted to eight characters, and literal values are restricted to 240 characters. If you want to change these values, you must edit the SGML declaration and then tell your SGML software which file contains the declaration. You can use a custom declaration by providing the name of the declaration file before the name of the SGML document.

 ◄◄ See "Attributes: Their Use and the ATTRIBUTE Declaration," p. 182

You can use other switches with SGMLS. For example, you can specify how you want error messages to be printed, which kinds of errors you want to know about, and how SGMLS should resolve Generic Public Identifiers.

Finding the Document's DTD and Other Referenced Files. Your document might give you an error message that sounds as though it does not recognize any elements or attributes. For example:

```
Error at file.sgm, line 11 accessing "file.dtd":
SGML error at file.sgm, line 12 at record start:
No definition for HELLO document type; "HELLO O O ANY" assumed
```

In this case, SGMLS cannot find the document's DTD. Check the DOCTYPE declaration at the top of the SGML file to make sure that you specified it correctly. The easiest way to do this is to use a SYSTEM identifier. Type the file name, enclosed in quotes. Remember that this requires you to specify the actual file path for the DTD file; the directory that contains SGMLS is assumed to be the root directory. Simply put SGMLS and your file in the same directory.

 ◀◀ See "The DOCTYPE Declaration," p. 177

You can also specify the DTD by putting it in a separate file and listing it on the command line between the SGML declaration and the file that contains the document.

The most complicated way to specify the DTD is in the document file with a PUBLIC identifier. You then must follow the instructions in the manual page to create a catalog file that resolves public identifiers into file names, and tells the program where to find the catalog file at runtime. This is the most foolproof way if you are modifying files and file names and using them in different directories.

SGMLS also has a facility for mapping public identifiers directly into file names. This method is complex. Because of its dependence on UNIX environment variables, it does not work on the Mac. Even on UNIX, users regularly experience problems when they use it for the first time.

Cryptic Error Messages. The error messages that you get from SGMLS and other validators use specialized SGML terminology defined in the SGML standard. They can be difficult to understand if you do not know SGML terminology. The most important thing to look for is the line number. The most important thing to remember is that SGML error messages often do not appear where an offending tag or missing quotation mark occurs. Instead, they occur at a later point, when the SGML parser finally sees something that makes the error clear. Look at that line in your document, and read backward to find the point that caused the error.

You can use the switches on the SGMLS command line to make error messages more or less wordy. For simple validation, the most useful switch is the suppress output switch, or -s. The text of the document is normally printed with open and close tag indicators as part of the error stream. This is because many people process this output, which is called the ESIS. If you want to see only the error messages, use the -s switch. For example:

```
-s mysgml.decl alice.sgml
```

SGMLS: **ftp://ftp.stg.brown.edu/pub/sgml**
This program can also be found at other SGML FTP sites.

▶▶ See Appendix B, "Sources for SGML Know-How," p. 565

Scripting Languages

Scripting languages are general programming languages with good support for string processing and pattern matching. They are tailored for writing file conversion programs and for automating system management tasks. Conversion to and from SGML is a typical file conversion task, so you might find these languages useful if you have some exposure to programming and are willing to learn a general tool. When a conversion is too complex for global changes in an editor, these languages are the next thing to try. They provide the full power of programming in a form that is easy to apply to conversion problems.

You should invest the effort of writing conversion scripts only if you have a very large document, many similar documents to convert, or a conversion that will be repeated many times—for example, a file that is converted whenever it is updated. Writing conversion scripts is often more enjoyable than making changes manually in an editor. However, it is usually not more productive unless you are dealing with a book-sized document or with extremely complex document structures.

You are likely to encounter and use two scripting languages in SGML conversion tasks: Perl and TCL.

▶▶ See "The World of Perl," p. 491

Perl is currently the most popular language for scripting and file conversion. Despite its obscure syntax, Perl's integrated pattern matching makes it easy to use for text transformations. It can take a while to learn because it has many built-in features for specific tasks.

TCL can be used for the same tasks as Perl. However, its syntax is much simpler, and it has fewer built-in features. Therefore, it's easier to learn, but it lacks many of the convenient features of Perl. You are more likely to encounter TCL in one of the specialized SGML tools that use it than you are to use it for writing conversion scripts from scratch.

There is a wide choice of free SGML-specific software packages available based on scripting tools. Several of them are mentioned briefly here. Because Perl and TCL run on the Mac, these packages also run on the Mac, even though many were designed for UNIX.

SGMLSPL is a Perl script shell that works with SGMLS. It parses the output of the SGMLS parser and separates its parts. That way, the script can easily process the output. On the Mac, this requires you first to run SGMLS and save the output in a file. Then you must run the Perl program on the resulting output file.

The SGMLPERL package contains an SGML parser written in Perl that calls user-specified scripts. This offers the advantage of an integrated, one-step conversion solution. Because of the difficulties in writing an SGML parser, input to the program must first be validated with a conforming SGML parser to ensure that the file is free of errors.

Another possibility is to use the free TCLYasp conversion tool. It's a general SGML parser, YASP, integrated with the TCL scripting language. You can use it to create one-step conversion scripts. TCLYasp is similar to a tool called CoST; both integrate an SGML parser with TCL (CoST uses sgmls, TCLYasp uses YASP). CoST has not been ported to the Mac yet, however. TCLYasp is designed around a simple sequential model of parsing. It is simple to learn, but it is better for straightforward conversions than for complicated structural transformations.

SGMLSPL: **http://aix1.uottawa.ca/~dmeggins/ sgmlspl/sgmlspl.html**

CoST: **http://www.art.com/cost ftp://ftp.crl.com/users/je/jenglish**

TCLYasp: **ftp://ftp.stg.brown.edu/pub/sgml**

 ▶▶ These programs can be found at other SGML FTP sites. For URLs, see Appendix B, "Sources for SGML Know-How," p. 565

Viewing and Printing Tools

Once you tag your document with SGML and verify that it's correct, you might want to do something with it. For example, you might want to display it on the screen or print out a formatted version of it. It is in this area that the Mac is weakest. There are no add-ons for common word processors as there are in Windows, which enable you to import text marked up in SGML and to apply formatting styles to it. SoftQuad's Panorama Pro, a helper application for World Wide Web browsers, can download and display text in SGML with styles and links. It is not yet available for the Mac, however.

Two publishing solutions available for the Mac are FrameMaker and QuarkXPress. They come from high-end desktop publishing environments and are intended for creating traditional paper products, not electronic editions. EBT's DynaText, which requires some preparatory steps on a UNIX or Windows computer, can create SGML-based interactive electronic books. Another low-budget, but powerful, solution is to take advantage of World Wide Web browser technology. Convert your SGML source into HTML documents for viewing with a Web browser program.

SGML Enabler

SGML Enabler, from SoftQuad, is a QuarkXPress extension that makes it easy to format and print SGML files. It is a useful tool if you are making SGML on the Mac and want to print it out with a sophisticated page layout program. It requires, however, that you know how to use QuarkXPress and configure its styles.

>**http://www.sq.com**
>For full contact information, see "SoftQuad Author/Editor 3.1."

FrameMaker+SGML

Framemaker, from Adobe Systems, is one of the most powerful page layout programs for publishing and editing book-length documents—especially long, structured documents such as technical documentation. It has its own markup language—MIF. FrameMaker+SGML is an option for FrameMaker version 5 that provides fully integrated SGML support. It enables structural editing of SGML documents similar to Author/Editor, and it also provides a high-quality page layout view.

FrameMaker+SGML does not have a graphical DTD browser, but it does provide a graphical context display that shows the elements in a document and can be expanded and contracted like an outline. Like Stilo and Author/Editor, it hides the details of SGML syntax, so structural errors are the only kind possible. Unlike Stilo and Author/Editor, FrameMaker does not prevent you from creating structurally invalid documents. It merely flags structural errors in the context display. This makes editing simple, even when it involves intermediate stages that do not match the DTD.

With its powerful typesetting features, FrameMaker+SGML is overkill for an SGML project that is producing high-quality printed output. It is ideal, though, when print production is the primary delivery medium for the data.

>**http://www.adobe.com/Frame**
>1-800-U-4-FRAME

DynaText

EBT's DynaText is the leading SGML electronic delivery platform. Although EBT does not support publishing on the Mac, its browser works on the Mac (see fig. 27.7), which makes the Mac a possible delivery platform for SGML data. EBT file formats are platform independent. Therefore, the same files can be delivered to Windows, UNIX, or Mac environments.

One disadvantage of DynaText is the use of a compilation process. Although this enables you to create full-text indexes for searching document text quickly, it creates a batch-style bottleneck when you publish data.

The latest UNIX and Windows versions of DynaText add the capability to deliver DynaText documents that use uncompiled SGML files. This feature is not suitable for large document applications because it stores the entire document in RAM, but it is ideal for publishing small single documents or collections of interlinked small documents. Unfortunately, a Mac version of the updated product is not available.

Electronic Book Technologies
1 Richmond Square
Providence, RI 02906
401-421-9550

http://www.ebt.com

Fig. 27.7

You can create electronic books that are easy to search and browse with DynaText.

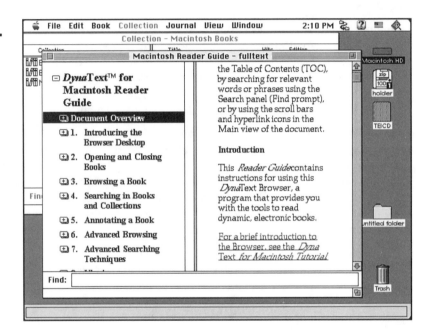

Document Conversions

Document conversion is a recurring—and often unpleasant—part of document processing. Fortunately, public domain scripting tools, such as Perl and TCL, are available for the Mac.

There are no commercial document conversion tools currently available for the Mac. You can use a variety of public domain tools, however. Some of these are general-purpose tools that can be adapted to the task of converting to or from SGML. Others are SGML-aware tools suitable for more complex conversions. Remember: When you convert from SGML to another format, even a complex SGML-aware tool might be easier to use than a simpler SGML-unaware tool.

The following sections discuss scenarios that you are likely to encounter when you convert documents. They describe some of the tools and approaches that you can use. Unfortunately, document conversion is a messy problem that varies from job to job.

VII

SGML Tools and Their Uses

It defies generalization—and accurate estimates of time and effort. The documentation available for many non-SGML data formats is poor.

Converting from Plain Text

If you have an SGML-aware editor, such as Author/Editor or Stilo, open the file and use the editing features to tag it as you go. Start with Rules Checking mode turned off.

If you do not have an SGML-aware editor, you can use an ASCII editor, such as Alpha, Qued/M, or BBEdit. The steps are:

1. Open the file with the editor. Make global changes, using the regular expression features when necessary.

2. Finish the tagging by hand. You can rarely perform a whole conversion automatically.

3. Use SGMLS to validate the file. Make any necessary corrections.

If you know how to use a scripting language and have multiple files to convert or will be converting the same file several times, it might be worthwhile to write a program to handle all the conversions that can be automated. The steps are:

1. Work over your file as though you were going to do the conversion by hand, so that you can see what types of changes are necessary.

2. Write a program in Perl or TCL to perform the changes as well as others that the programming language allows.

3. Convert the file.

4. Put in any final tagging by hand.

5. Use SGMLS to validate the file. Make any necessary corrections.

Converting from an RTF File

The best way to convert from RTF is to use an SGML converter that can read RTF files. There are several—including three Word for Windows add-ons, EBT's Dynatag, and WordPerfect's SGML module—but they all run under Windows. You can also try an RTF-to-HTML converter, such as the public domain rtf2html, SoftQuad's HoTMetaL Pro, or ClarisWorks. These programs start the process of tagging your document. You then must convert the HTML tags to their SGML equivalents and insert any other tags that do not have HTML equivalents.

If that is not possible, try to convert the RTF yourself, using the regular expression feature of an ASCII editor or a scripting language. In either case, it is important to have RTF that is as clean and consistent as possible. The document that is to be converted from RTF should be authored with consistent styles, which should be designed to handle interparagraph spacing, indentation, and other formatting features, so that extra returns and tabs are not inserted. You can also try inline text styles—such as bold, italic, and underline—to indicate phrase-level elements. For example, you might use italic to indicate only foreign words and underline to indicate technical terms.

If you do not have access to other software or are working with many authors, a word processing program provides a good way to get text into electronic form and on its way to being tagged in SGML.

> **Caution**
>
> All RTF is not created equal. Certain word processors that can output RTF do not preserve style information. Without styles, this system does not work.

Suppose, for example, that you are using Word. The steps are:

1. In the Word file, edit all the styles under the Styles menu item so that they have the same characteristics as the Normal style. In other words, the text remains assigned to a particular style, but when you look at it, it appears uniformly as Normal on the screen.

2. Save the document as RTF.

3. Open the RTF document with another editor, such as Qued/M, Alpha, or BBEdit. Look at the top of the file—where the RTF definition is—to see the style definitions. In the forest of curly braces, you will find a section labeled `stylesheet`. It contains style definitions, each of which is enclosed in curly braces. A style definition looks like this:

   ```
   {\s1 \f22 \sbasedon222\snext1 FT;}
   ```

   `\s1` is the number of the style, and `FT` is its name. The material in between is not important. You need to retain the paired names and numbers because that is what you will look for in the document.

4. Delete all the RTF information at the top of the file to the point where the text begins.

5. Look for RTF information inside the document that looks as though it is repeated everywhere. Use a global change command to delete it. It might look, for example, like `\pard\plain` and `\sa240\sl240`. You want to be left only with style numbers in the form `\sx`, where x is a number, and inline styles, such as bold and italic in the form `{\b ...}`. Note that paragraphs end with `\par`, which you also need to preserve.

6. Convert the styles to your element names. Use global changes and regular expressions. Check carefully that you are not losing information as you do this. You might be able to write a program that does this.

7. When you have converted all you can automatically, do the rest by hand. It's difficult to automate document conversion completely with this system because RTF does not map easily to SGML. It contains less information and does not apply it correctly in a uniform way across paragraph boundaries.

Converting from SGML to Another DTD or Data Format

This kind of conversion is generally much easier than converting from another format into SGML. Both data formats are defined, and the DTD documents maintain the structure of the source document. With a valid SGML document, you rarely have to guess what a document creator might have intended when he put a list item inside a chapter heading. The best way to take advantage of the regularity of structure in an SGML document is to use an SGML parser to process it. Perform the conversion based on the output.

You can often convert SGML by using an editor rather than a specialized tool. This technique is not generally suitable for complex DTDs with deeply-nested structures. In such DTDs, it is frequent for the output created by a tag to depend on the tags surrounding it. This kind of dependency is impossible to handle in an editor unless the relevant tags are adjacent in the file.

You can use a straight Perl or TCL script for simple DTDs when an editor cannot do the job. To handle simple context dependencies, keep track of a global state as the script processes the document. This approach is possible as long as the context is strictly limited. Attempting to track the interaction of many global states generally leads to a programming nightmare that will be hard to maintain and will likely have obscure failures.

From Here...

This chapter examined a variety of tools and strategies that you can use for editing, viewing, and converting SGML documents on a Macintosh. While commercial offerings exist for all tasks but conversion, they can be expensive for small projects. However, there is a lot of good public domain software to fill in the gaps. If you can take advantage of a mixed environment, it will be possible to use the Mac for editing and printing and do conversion on another platform, such as Windows or UNIX. If however, you intend to use only the Macintosh, with a little ingenuity, you can still put together a powerful suite of tools and complete your project successfully.

For more information, refer to the following:

- Chapter 26, "Tools for the PC: Authoring, Viewing, and Utilities," examines the various SGML tools available for the PC.

- Chapter 28, "Other Tools and Environments," surveys other SGML tools available on a number of computer platforms for performing data conversion, validation, transformation, and document viewing.

- Part VIII, "Becoming an Electronic Publisher," examines the issues involved in moving into electronic publishing.

Other Tools and Environments

The process of building an SGML document system can involve a large number of separate steps and processes. Depending on your specific situation, you might find yourself looking for ways to perform a number of steps involved with creating, managing, and validating SGML documents.

In many cases, you might need to bring non-SGML documents into your SGML system; data conversion tools are particularly useful for doing this. In this chapter, you'll look at the following:

- Legacy data conversion (into SGML)
- Data validation
- Data transformation
- Other data manipulation

Fortunately, there is a rich set of tools available. These tools range from commercial software products for performing specialized tasks to a complete programming language package that can be used for SGML data conversions, UNIX system administration, and much more.

Though this chapter covers some notably useful software tools, by no means is this summary considered to be a definitive list of SGML tools! The world of SGML software tools is growing rapidly, and many powerful new products are appearing all the time.

Many of these tools are available on a variety of computer platforms. In fact, those tools that are available in shareware or similar licensing agreements often include the actual source code so that they can be adapted for use on those computer systems for which they are not currently available.

The review of each tool includes a reference listing to the item that identifies its type, the computer platform that it runs on, the provider/author name, a source for obtaining it, and contact information (such as Internet address or company telephone number).

Specific Computer Platform Usage

When setting up an SGML document processing system, one consideration is the choice of computer platforms to use. Most organizations will have one or more types of computers in place prior to starting an SGML document system.

In authoring systems, the prospective SGML implementer has a range of choices. Several existing high-end publishing systems that support structured SGML authoring are available on a number of computer platforms, most notably DOS/MS Windows PCs and UNIX computers.

Electronic browsers for SGML documents are also available across a number of platforms, notably DOS/MS Windows PCs, and Macintosh and UNIX computers.

However, in the area of document conversions and parsing, the UNIX-based systems are usually predominant. This is due to the higher processing capabilities of reduced-instruction set (RISC) based UNIX computers. As a result, if you are anticipating a large volume of intensive document conversions, UNIX based systems will probably be your computer platform of choice for converting documents into SGML.

SP/NSGMLS Parser

On the CD

In selecting a parser for use in validating DTDs and document instances, the SGML user has a variety of choices. Fortunately, one of the best, the sp/nsgmls parser by James Clark, is publicly available.

> *Product:* nsgmls
>
> *Type:* SGML Parser
>
> *Platforms:* MS/DOS, Windows, UNIX
>
> *Provider:* James Clark
>
> *Contact Locations:* James Clark, Indiana University
> **http://www.jclark.com/sp.html**
> **http://www.cs.indiana.edu/hyplan/asengupt/**
> **sgmlsoft.html#sgmls**

The nsgmls parser is included in a package of SGML parsing tools and utilities called SP. Also included in the SP package are tools for performing normalization of SGML tags within a document instance.

This parser, a descendent of the earlier sgmls parser, is available in versions for various computer systems. These include MS/DOS, Windows/NT, and various flavors of UNIX (including LINUX). The source code is available for those wishing to port it to other platforms.

> **Tip**
>
> If you are considering installing nsgmls/SP on a different computer, you will probably want to review Nelson Beebe's notes on his experience with installing the package on various computers at: **http://www.math.utah.edu/~beebe/sp-notes.html**

While this parser is extremely useful, some people have noted that the documentation that accompanies it (in the form of UNIX-style manual or "man" pages) is rather obscure. As a result, a careful reading of the documentation will prove helpful.

> **Note**
>
> The following files are necessary to parse a document:
>
> - SGML document instance, containing the actual document markup
> - An SGML declaration, specifying character sets, features, and so on
> - The applicable DTD
> - An entity mapping file

The World of Perl

Perl (Practical Extraction and Report Language) is a computer language for text processing. Developed and maintained by Larry Wall, its origins are said to date back to when Larry needed utilities to aid in the administration of several UNIX computer systems.

On the CD

As a computer language, Perl can be said to share characteristics from C, c-shell, awk, and sed computer languages/programs. Perl really excels in its text recognition and pattern-matching capabilities. To put it in perspective, you can often perform tasks requiring these capabilities using, say, 100 lines of Perl code, that would require 1000 lines in another language.

Product: Perl

Type: Text Recognition and Manipulation Language

Platform: Many

Provider: Larry Wall

Contact Location: University of Florida Perl Archive
http://www1.cis.ufl.edu/perl/

From the SGML perspective, Perl is extremely useful in several respects. By itself, it can be used to write programs for data conversion and other tasks. Its usefulness in this regard cannot be overstated.

For example, in a rather complicated SGML production system that myself and others have developed, Perl programs are used in a variety of ways. These tasks include those listed in table 28.1.

Table 28.1 Perl Program Sample Tasks	
Task	**Description**
Document Conversion	Converts Interleaf source documents into SGML
File Rename	Renames large numbers of scanned art files into SGML system format
SGML Post Processing	Adds "floating" content tags into SGML document files
Graphics File Manager	Builds document association files that bind graphics files with associated hotspot layers
Document Conversion Error Scanning	Scans document conversion output files for error messages and reports to user
Source File Art Identification	Scans source document files and identifies names of all referenced art files
Document Comparison	Contents of a parts list document are compared with the corresponding bill of materials
Library Management	Intermediate art library collection processed periodically; when disk is full, those files not accessed for 30 days are deleted

As you can see, Perl programs are used to perform a number of tasks in this SGML system. Perl's flexibility in textual pattern recognition make it a valuable tool in SGML system conversions and data manipulation.

There are a number of sources for Perl on the Internet. Among these is the University of Florida Perl Archive (see fig. 28.1).

Perl's flexibility and utility are becoming increasingly recognized in the software development community. As a result, many users have built various tools and utilities with Perl that perform a number of functions, including those related to SGML processing.

SGML Utilities Using Perl

A number of useful tools for SGML processing based on Perl are available, usually through the Internet. In fact, it seems that as people appreciate the utility of Perl, the available number of tools will continue to grow.

On the CD

perlSGML. Written as a collection of Perl programs and utility libraries, perlSGML provides various support for SGML document processing. It provides a number of functions for manipulating SGML document instances and DTDs.

Product: perlSGML

Type: SGML Utilities

Platform: UNIX

Provider: Earl Hood

Contact Location: Earl Hood
http://www.oac.uci.edu/indiv/ehood/perlSGML.html

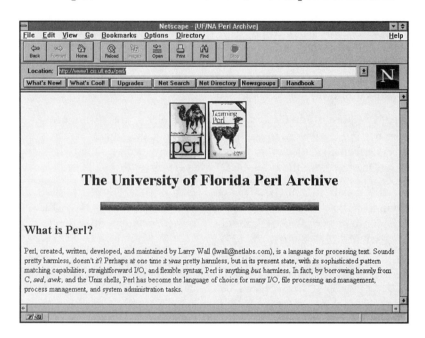

Fig. 28.1

The University of Florida Perl Archive contains a wide variety of Perl software versions and other related information.

The functions supported by perlSGML include:

- DTD parsing support libraries
- HTML document generator for documentation of SGML DTDs
- Tool for listing changes to a DTD
- DTD content hierarchy tree generator
- SGML document instance parser
- SGML document instance markup removal (removes SGML tags from tagged documents)

Electronic Book Technologies: DynaText

DynaText is a browser for viewing SGML documents electronically. Through a compilation process, DynaText indexes SGML documents into electronic book collections.

On the CD

Product: DynaText

Type: SGML Book Browser (Reader)

Platform: MS/Windows, Macintosh, UNIX

Provider: Electronic Book Technologies, Inc. (EBT)

Contact Location: Electronic Book Technologies, Inc. (EBT)
Telephone: (401) 421-9550
http://www.ebt.com/

The DynaText browser is particularly noteworthy for its ability to support any DTD (rather than a particular set of standard DTDs). It includes support for hypertext navigation, context-sensitive full text search. Native graphics support includes TIFF and CALS raster formats. CGM vector graphics support is available as an option. The display of complex tables is also supported.

DynaText is particularly powerful in its suitability to particularly large documents (see fig. 28.2). Unlike other SGML viewers, it can handle very large documents without a major downturn in performance. Its ability to perform reformatting on-the-fly on very large documents sets it apart from the other SGML viewers currently available.

The output formatting capabilities of DynaText are highly flexible. Similar to the FOSI output specification in its use of SGML syntax, DynaText's output formatting will shortly support the more powerful DSSSL Lite subset of the Document Style Semantic Specification Language (ISO/IEC standard 10179).

On the CD

Note
A sample version of the DynaText book browser is included along with sample books.

DynaText is part of a family of products from Electronic Book Technologies that supports SGML document systems. Their full range of SGML related products is shown in table 28.2.

Table 28.2 EBT's SGML Software Products

Product	Description
DynaText	SGML document viewer
DynaTag	Document conversion tool
DynaBase	SGML data repository and document management system
DynaWeb	SGML based World Wide Web server
CADLeaf Batch	Batch graphics extraction and conversion

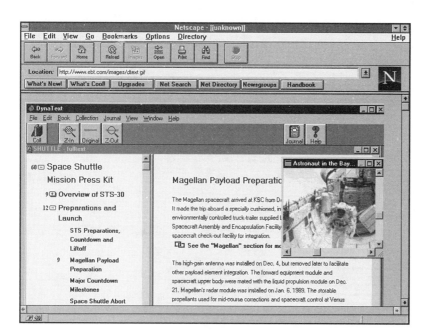

Fig. 28.2

DynaText electronic book browser is a powerful tool for viewing SGML documents. It is particularly noteworthy for its ability to handle very large documents.

Avalanche/Interleaf: FastTAG

FastTAG is a commercial package for adding structure to input documents as part of a conversion process. It is particularly useful for converting documents into SGML because of its visual recognition capabilities.

> *Product:* FastTAG
>
> *Type:* Pattern Recognition and Conversion Package
>
> *Platforms:* MS/DOS, Windows, UNIX
>
> *Provider:* Interleaf/Avalanche
>
> *Contact Location:* Interleaf/Avalanche
> Telephone: (303) 449-5032
> **http://www.ileaf.com/avhome/homepage.html**

SGML conversion processing often involves the input of documents produced in word processors without the benefits of structure (such as through the use of common styles). Such documents typically "suggest" structure through various types of formatting (font type and size, bold text, the use of white space/blank lines, and so on).

The process of translating such "suggested" structure into the formal structure that can be defined in a DTD can be difficult and time-consuming. Without specialized tools to aid in the process, such conversions can be highly manual activities.

FastTAG is a powerful tool for performing such conversions. Using a "visual recognition engine," FastTAG provides the capability of recognizing data objects in the context of the visual "look" within a document. (This capability is particularly useful in the conversion of tables that occur within a document.) After specific objects are recognized, they can be processed according to specific user-created processing instructions. The functional capabilities of FastTAG are illustrated in figure 28.3.

Fig. 28.3

The FastTAG pattern recognition/conversion package uses a "visual recognition engine" to recognize data objects within documents.

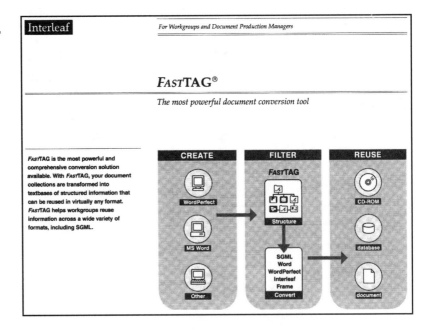

Avalanche's companion product, Hammer, provides the capability to translate SGML documents into other formats, including proprietary formats (such as Microsoft Word, WordPerfect, FrameMaker, and Interleaf) as well as other SGML document formats.

From Here...

This concludes our look at the range of tools available for creating and maintaining SGML documents. Because of the rapid pace of change in available programs that support SGML, you should expect more and more choices in this area as vendors enhance their current products and introduce even more new products.

From here, you should examine the following:

- Part VIII, "Becoming an Electronic Publisher," examines the area of electronic publishing. You'll take a look at the issues involved with electronic publishing and how they are changing. Among these issues is the mix of new technologies, such as the use of SGML with object-oriented technology.

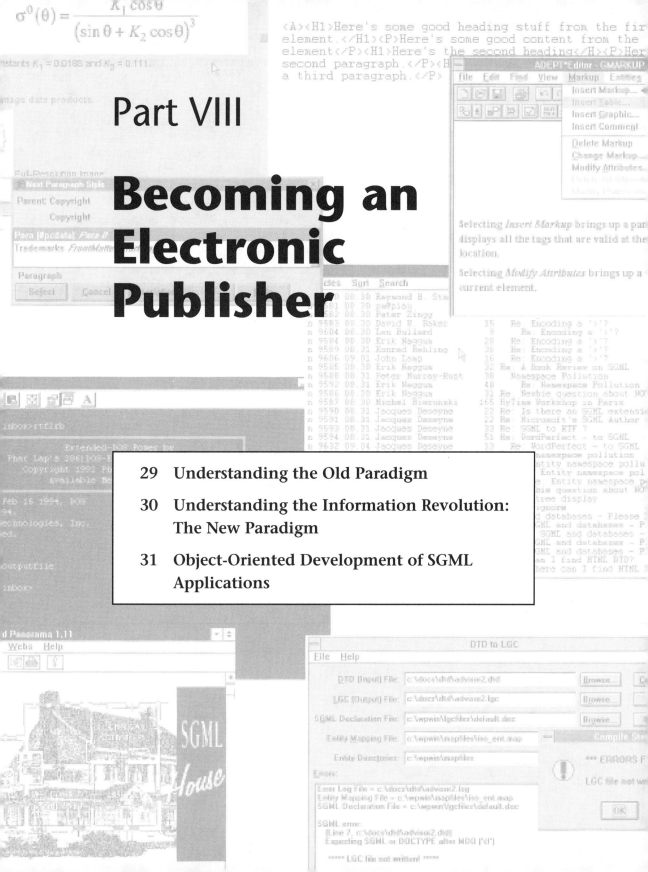

Part VIII

Becoming an Electronic Publisher

29 Understanding the Old Paradigm

30 Understanding the Information Revolution:
The New Paradigm

31 Object-Oriented Development of SGML
Applications

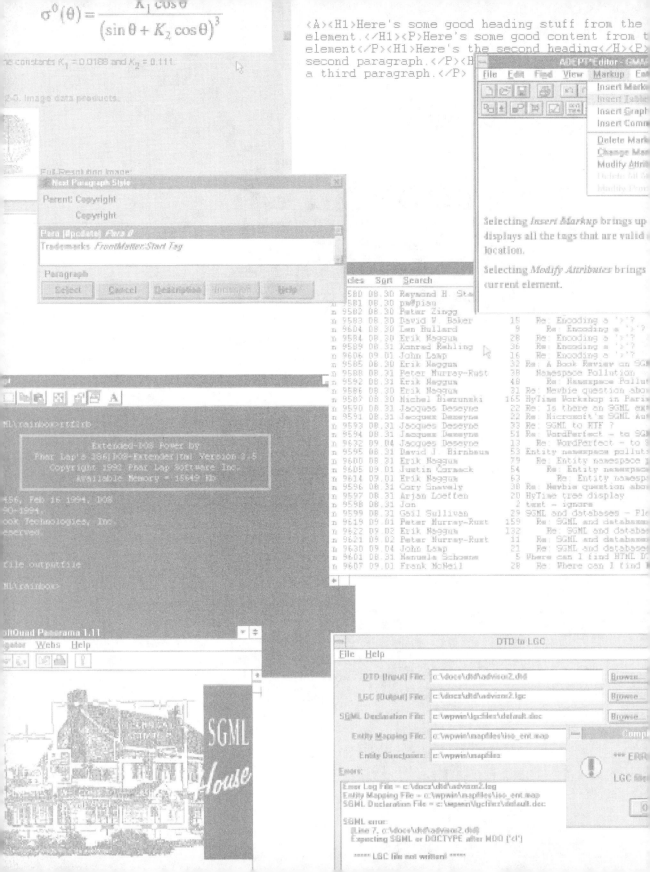

$$\sigma^0(\theta) = \frac{K_1 \cos\theta}{(\sin\theta + K_2 \cos\theta)^3}$$

the constants $K_1 = 0.0188$ and $K_2 = 0.111$.

2-0. Image data products.

Full Resolution Image

Next Paragraph Style

Parent: Copyright

Copyright

Para Update: Para 0

Trademarks *FrontMatter:Start Tag*

Paragraph

Select   Cancel   Description   Initialize   Help

<A><H1>Here's some good heading stuff from the
element.</H1><P>Here's some good content from t
element</P><H1>Here's the second heading</H><P>
second paragraph.</P><H
a third paragraph.</P>

ADEPT*Editor - GMA

File Edit Find View Markup En

Insert Mark
Insert Table
Insert Graph
Insert Comm

Delete Mark
Change Man
Modify Attri

Selecting *Insert Markup* brings up
displays all the tags that are valid
location.

Selecting *Modify Attributes* brings
current element.

dies Sort Search
9580 08.30 Raymond H. Sta
9581 08.30 pw@piso
9582 08.30 Peter Zingg
9583 08.30 David W. Baker   15   Re: Encoding a '>'?
9604 08.30 Len Bullard   9   Re: Encoding a '>'?
9584 08.30 Erik Naggum   28   Re: Encoding a '>'?
9589 08.31 Konrad Rehling   36   Re: Encoding a '>'?
9606 09.01 John Lamp   16   Re: Encoding a '>'?
9585 08.30 Erik Naggum   32 Re: A Book Review on SGM
9588 08.31 Peter Murray-Rust   38   Namespace Pollution
9542 08.31 Erik Naggum   40   Re: Namespace Pollut
9586 08.30 Erik Naggum   31 Re: Newbie question abou
9587 08.30 Michel Biezunski   165 HyTime Workshop in Paris
9590 08.31 Jacques Deseyne   22 Re: Is there an SGML ext
9591 08.31 Jacques Deseyne   22 Re: Microsoft's SGML Aut
9593 08.31 Jacques Deseyne   33 Re: SGML to RTF ?
9594 08.31 Jacques Deseyne   51 Re: WordPerfect - to SGM
9632 09.04 Jacques Deseyne   13   Re: WordPerfect - to S
9545 08.31 David J. Birnbaum   53 Entity namespace polluts
9600 08.31 Erik Naggum   79   Re: Entity namespace p
9605 09.01 Justin Cormack   54   Re: Entity namespace
9614 09.01 Erik Naggum   63   Re: Entity namesp
9596 08.31 Cory Snavely   30 Re: Newbie question abou
9597 08.31 Arjan Loeffen   20 HyTime tree display
9598 08.31 Jon   2 text - ignore
9599 08.31 Gail Sullivan   29 SGML and databases - Fi
9619 09.01 Peter Murray-Rust   159   Re: SGML and databases
9622 09.02 Erik Naggum   132   Re: SGML and databas
9621 09.02 Peter Murray-Rust   11   Re: SGML and databases
9630 09.04 John Lamp   21   Re: SGML and databases
9601 08.31 Manuela Schoenre   5 Where can I find HTML D
9607 09.01 Frank McNeil   28   Re: Where can I find H

ML\rainbow>rtfdir

```
        Extended-DOS Power by
Phar Lap's 286|DOS-Extender(tm) Version 2.5
    Copyright 1988 Phar Lap Software Inc.
        Available Memory = 15649 Kb
```

456, Feb 16 1994, DOS
90-1994.
ook Technologies, Inc
eserved.

file outputfile

ML\rainbow>

oftQuad Panorama 1.11

igator Webs Help

SGML
House

DTD to LGC

File Help

DTD (Input) File: c:\docs\dtd\advisor2.dtd   Browse
LGC (Output) File: c:\docs\dtd\advisor2.lgc   Browse
SGML Declaration File: c:\wpwin\lgcfiles\default.doc Browse
Entity Mapping File: c:\wpwin\mapfiles\iso_ent.map
Entity Directories: c:\wpwin\mapfiles

Errors:

Error Log File = c:\docs\dtd\advisor2.log
Entity Mapping File = c:\wpwin\mapfiles\iso_ent.map
SGML Declaration File = c:\wpwin\lgcfiles\default.doc

SGML error:
(Line 7, c:\docs\dtd\advisor2.dtd)
Expecting SGML or DOCTYPE after MDO ['<!']

***** LGC file not written! *****

*** ERR
LGC file

CHAPTER 29

Understanding the Old Paradigm

To appreciate the importance of SGML, you need to think about how information has been modeled until now. It all depended on how the information was delivered—through books. That has changed. Books are still important, but computers have created more possibilities. It is time to upgrade how information is organized.

In this chapter, you learn:

- The components of information delivery
- The ways of organizing knowledge
- The implications of the linear organization of knowledge
- The role of format
- The role of structure and the new paradigm

The Components of Information Delivery

The basic components of delivering information are structure, content, and format. They apply to the ways in which information has been gathered until now. They fit the old paradigm.

Components besides structure, content, and format exist. They include the media for delivering information, such as a sheet of paper, a book, or computer network. Spoken languages, tribal dances, and stone tablets engraved with symbols all convey information. Fortune cookies, chalkboards, traffic lights, roadside milestones, and calculators and abacuses convey information, too. The components of information delivery are innumerable, but structure, content, and format are always necessary.

Even with a fortune cookie, the boundary of the medium defines the structure. In this case, a small slip of paper that fits inside the cookie defines the boundary. With a calculator—or even a cave wall—physical boundaries define the limits of the structure. Content must fit the limits of structure. Format is applied on top of that.

Information can now be delivered by more abstract methods; many physical limitations no longer apply. To convey information by means of cave paintings, for example, you are limited by the space available on the cave wall. If you communicate by speech alone, you are limited by memory and time—sooner or later your voice goes out. When you store information on paper, you are limited by the size of the page.

The Ways of Organizing Knowledge

You can organize knowledge in many ways, two of which are *linear* and *modular*. Linear means from first to last, from front to back, and from start to end. You know what the beginning and the end are because you know where to look for them. Modular means there is not necessarily a beginning or an end by virtue of the structure of the information. For example, the whole contents of a library are modular; you don't go into a library and read the first book on the shelves and proceed systematically through to the last book. You read a book here and a book there—the modules are relevant to you. However, individual novels are intended to be read from beginning to end, in a linear fashion. Figure 29.1 illustrates the difference between these two approaches to organizing knowledge.

Fig. 29.1

The linear approach emphasizes the sequence of information, whereas modular approach emphasizes information modules.

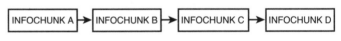

Linear approach to organization

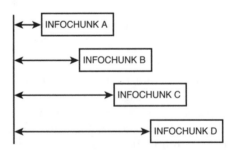

Modular approach to organization

As for an individual book, if you read the middle section first or the first chapter last, you are using modular information retrieval. It is modular because "first" and "last" do not apply to the way in which you deal with the information's structure. Many problems arise because books are often regarded as always being linear rather than modular.

Linear Books

How books and information have been organized indicates how people have looked at information. The sequential, step-by-step way of organizing knowledge implies that:

■ You must read and understand Chapter 1 before you can understand Chapter 2.

■ Everything in Chapter 4 builds on the material in Chapters 1, 2, and 3.

■ If you read chapters out of sequence, they will not make sense.

■ It is physically impossible to place Chapter 3 after Chapter 7.

■ All types of information should be organized from beginning to end.

■ No one wants information to be organized in a modular way.

Many of these conclusions are no longer true. When books existed only on paper, it was physically impossible to put Chapter 3 after Chapter 7—the physical position of the chapters dictated their names. In other words, if you placed Chapter 3 immediately after Chapter 7, it would be called Chapter 8. With the advent of hypertext and hypermedia, all this has changed. The electronic age enables you—even forces you—to rethink how you structure information. It is no longer physically impossible to place Chapter 3 after Chapter 7. This idea is the crux of the information revolution. It is the reason why SGML is so important. Even reference books like this one are organized into information modules to facilitate random retrieval of information. Many books have turned from presenting information linearly to modularly, as shown in figure 29.2.

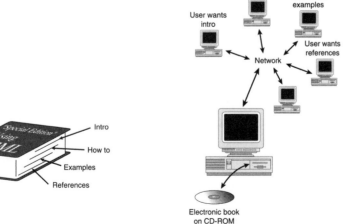

Fig. 29.2

Linear books and modular books structure information differently. Today, linear books are becoming like modular books.

SGML is the ultimate tool for making information modular. That's because modular books must be highly structured books, and structure is what SGML defines in documents.

Modular Books

When you organize knowledge, you often think of the book paradigm. Books will remain ultimately linear, but that is because of the physical limitations of the medium. You turn pages one by one, text flows in lines one word after another. You can still access a discrete part of the book any time you want, though. Highly structured reference books, like this book, make this possible.

Information Granularity. The more information you have, the more granular it becomes. Large stores of accumulated information, especially electronic and printed information, have made individual records of details and facts more granular, more fragmented, and more disconnected from bigger pieces of information. Finding the piece of information you want is like finding a particular grain of sand on the beach.

SGML enables these fragments of information to be associated with one another through electronic document structures. Paper documents and books also need to be accessed by information modules, and this need is the impetus for making modular books.

The Direction of Books. Paper-bound technical manuals are nearly modular. They are highly structured so that you can read information not just sequentially, but rather modularly, as you need it.

This book, for example, has a great deal of structure, which helps make it modular. You need to access the information here in pieces, which are as small and precise as possible. That is why headings are used so frequently. It's also why graphics and special formatting are used so often. Making information more modular costs less than making information monolithic and linear. See figure 29.3 for an example of a highly structured technical book.

The challenge arises from indexing all these smaller chunks or modules of information. How do you label all these bits of information so that people can find them? How do you mark all that information? SGML offers profound solutions to organizing the electronic information of the world. Since electronic authoring already accounts for much of what appears in print nowadays, electronic structured authoring is not too great an extension of how authoring already occurs.

HTML is only one application of SGML. It is just one DTD, and look what it has done. The information on the World Wide Web is not accessible linearly, but modularly. If you do a Web search on stock trading strategies, you will find more sources than you ever imagined—thanks to indexing and SGML. The ease of modular access has lead to the popularity of electronic books on CD-ROM, which often use SGML for indexing. As information becomes increasingly available in electronic and modular forms, you'll encounter difficulties from your habits of linear organization.

Contents

Introduction   **1**

   Is HTML Programming? 2
   HTML as Desktop Publishing 3
   HTML and SGML 4
   What to Do with HTML 5
   What This Book Is 7
   What This Book Is Not 9
   Conventions Used in This Book 9
   Taking the First Step 11

I The Internet and the World Wide Web   13

1 Overview of the Internet   15

   Growth of the Internet 16
   A Commercial Internet 17
   The Internet's Information Systems 19
      What Is UseNet? 20
      What Are Newsgroups? 20
   Who Is on the Net? 21
      Deciphering Internet Addresses 22
      "What's Your Domain?" 22
      Reach Out and Mail Someone 23
      Finding an Internet Address 24
   From Here... 27

2 Introduction to the World Wide Web   29

   Origins of the Web 30
   Mosaic Made It Simple 31
   What and Who Are on the Web? 33
   From Here... 35

3 The WWW and Other Internet Services   37

   The Internet's Information Services 38
   The World Wide Web as a "Super Service" 38
      WWW and Gopher 39
      WWW and FTP 41
      WWW and WAIS 44
   From Here... 45

Fig. 29.3

As you can see from the detailed table of contents, Que's *Special Edition Using HTML is highly structured in individual modules of information.*

VIII

Electronic Publishing

Implications of the Linear Way of Organizing Information

The linear approach to organizing knowledge can lead to bad habits. It causes you to think in outdated ways. These bad habits cause difficulties for you when you learn the SGML way of doing things. For example:

- You discount the importance of document structure.

■ You forget about how users use information.

■ You neglect more creative ways of structuring knowledge in favor of putting everything in one proper sequence.

For example, if you wrote about maintenance tasks for OS/2 Warp, you would typically focus on the sequential order of the tasks. If you think about the structure of the ideas, though, you can relate them to the same tasks in other operating systems, such as UNIX or Windows 95. The difference is that you are thinking about the ideas as building blocks in different houses that can be compared with one another, not just with other blocks in the same house.

Note

The ideas you write in a book are building blocks that fit into larger frameworks of ideas, which are themselves building blocks in larger structures. When you start relating structures of ideas by the structures of their electronic documents, you are beginning to think like an SGML developer. For example, if you wrote a DTD for Operation and Maintenance Instructions for operating systems, you might want to include a document structure that allowed you to relate similar tasks between different operating systems.

Under the linear approach to organization, OS/2 Warp and Windows 95 might never be compared by how they handle file defragmentation, for example; each system would have its own maintenance manual, but unless you had both books on your shelf, their respective procedures could not relate easily to each other.

Another bad habit is that you can forget how users use information. You become more concerned with the sequence of the steps than with how the ideas themselves relate to each other. In the real world, information often resembles a tool chest. You do not always reach for the same tool first whenever you change the spark plugs. One day, you might use the wrench to take the plugs out. Another day, you might need to replace the wires and use the pliers first.

Tip

The information you use today and the information you need tomorrow might be identical but in a different sequence. Don't commit yourself to organizing knowledge in a linear way. To be an SGML developer, you have to think about how your user can access it most easily. You have to understand that an OS/2 maintenance person might want to review the difference between HPFS and FAT disk formatting, and thus provide a document structure for making that comparison easy.

Another problem with linear structures of information is that you lose some of your creativity in how ideas relate to one another. Creativity enables you to see how the information you want today is meaningful to the information you acquired yesterday. When you are locked in the linear way of thinking, you lose touch with fresh ways of presenting related ideas in groups.

If you teach someone how to do basic commands in an operating system command line, he learns faster when you relate the command to a similar command he already knows. For example, you might compare the `dir` command in DOS to the `ls` command in UNIX. Because most people who want to know UNIX know how to list a directory in DOS, the comparison helps convey information.

Creativity in relating ideas and their documents is perhaps nowhere better evident than on the World Wide Web. The HTML DTD facilitates and encourages linking ideas together by means of relating their document structures together. Making relationships between ideas from different document structures requires creativity. You must go outside the standard parameters of linear thinking.

> **Tip**
>
> You can overemphasize order and sequence. Sometimes ideas have many different structures. Creativity also requires that you don't obscure the information that the user might really need.
>
> A lasagna recipe, for example, can contain many structures because the order of events is somewhat loose. Disarming a nuclear bomb, on the other hand, probably requires a precise, linear sequence. Likewise, the DTD for a government mil-spec manual will need to have more order and sequence than would a DTD for a newsletter.

◀◀   See "How Flexible Should DTDs Be?" p. 261

The Role of Format

Format is a holdover from linear thinking. Because it's difficult to present ideas in a nonlinear way, there must be a way of setting ideas apart. Italics and boldface are useful for this. In terms of structure, a chapter heading shows a single idea, and all the headings beneath it are part of the chapter heading's hierarchy. Format has been used to indicate structure—hierarchy, sequence, and occurrence. See figure 29.4 for an example of this.

VIII

Electronic Publishing

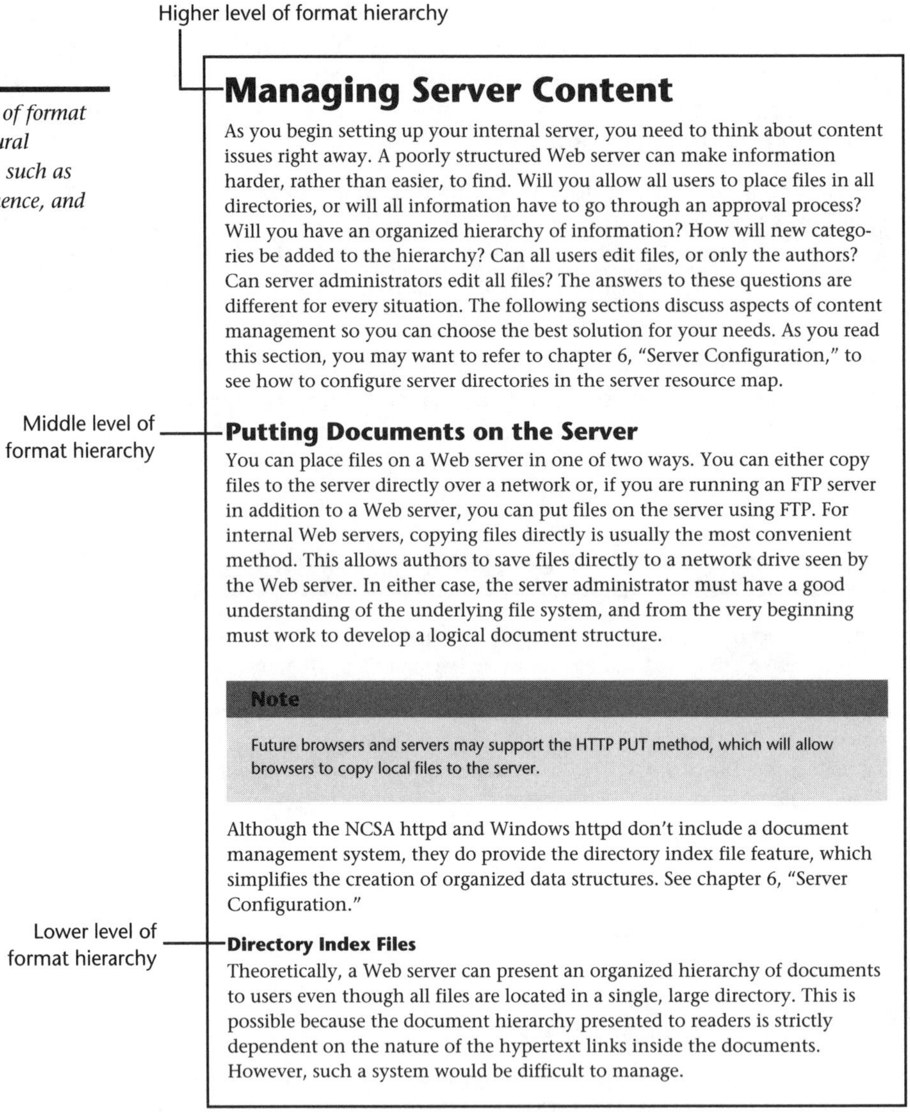

Higher level of format hierarchy

Fig. 29.4

Different types of format indicate structural considerations, such as hierarchy, sequence, and occurrence.

Managing Server Content

As you begin setting up your internal server, you need to think about content issues right away. A poorly structured Web server can make information harder, rather than easier, to find. Will you allow all users to place files in all directories, or will all information have to go through an approval process? Will you have an organized hierarchy of information? How will new categories be added to the hierarchy? Can all users edit files, or only the authors? Can server administrators edit all files? The answers to these questions are different for every situation. The following sections discuss aspects of content management so you can choose the best solution for your needs. As you read this section, you may want to refer to chapter 6, "Server Configuration," to see how to configure server directories in the server resource map.

Middle level of format hierarchy

Putting Documents on the Server

You can place files on a Web server in one of two ways. You can either copy files to the server directly over a network or, if you are running an FTP server in addition to a Web server, you can put files on the server using FTP. For internal Web servers, copying files directly is usually the most convenient method. This allows authors to save files directly to a network drive seen by the Web server. In either case, the server administrator must have a good understanding of the underlying file system, and from the very beginning must work to develop a logical document structure.

> **Note**
>
> Future browsers and servers may support the HTTP PUT method, which will allow browsers to copy local files to the server.

Although the NCSA httpd and Windows httpd don't include a document management system, they do provide the directory index file feature, which simplifies the creation of organized data structures. See chapter 6, "Server Configuration."

Lower level of format hierarchy

Directory Index Files

Theoretically, a Web server can present an organized hierarchy of documents to users even though all files are located in a single, large directory. This is possible because the document hierarchy presented to readers is strictly dependent on the nature of the hypertext links inside the documents. However, such a system would be difficult to manage.

Linear presentations of information depend highly on format. You can structure ideas in different ways, though. Suppose that you are discussing F. Scott Fitzgerald's drinking habits. If you write the article for a magazine, you need to use formatted headings to differentiate one idea from another—"How Fitzgerald's Drinking Affected His Fiction" and "How Fitzgerald's Fiction Affected His Drinking." If you write the same article for an online magazine or a Web page, you can show the same information in a completely different way. Format still exists, but not as much is required. Jump points replace headings. On an SGML Web page, you can turn off the highly formatted stylesheet and use a simple stylesheet with little formatting. See figure 29.5 as an example of these different types of stylesheets.

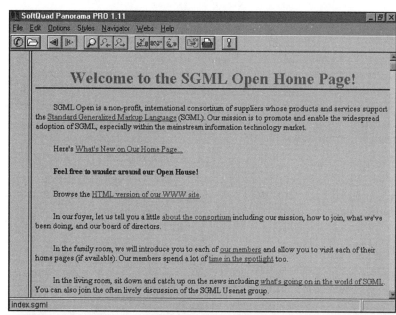

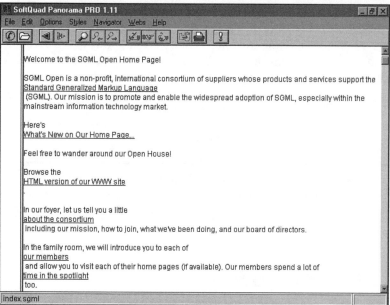

Fig. 29.5

Each window shows a different format and appearance of the same document. Structurally, the document has not changed.

VIII

Electronic Publishing

Information organized linearly is less flexible than modular information. Format tries to compensate for this weakness. If you can deliver information to a client according to a modular structure—instead of as a linear string of facts—you do not need to depend on format as much. Format becomes cosmetic. You can even let your client choose the format—playful, business-like, or generic. This idea of optional formats corresponds to templates or stylesheets in popular word processors.

An SGML stylesheet is a formatting choice. If you write a letter to your mother using SGML Author for Word, for example, you can create and choose the ask4mony.prn, iluvu2.prn, or thx4mony.prn printout format options, which correspond to SGML stylesheets. Each format is different, but they all enable the native structure of your letter home to remain the same. The format can change to suit your mother's moods and the size of your financial needs.

Formatting in this modular way becomes like a suit of clothes. You wear the ensemble appropriate to your needs. It does not change your identity. You are still your mother's son, so to speak. Unfortunately, under the linear model of information distribution, the clothes make the man. The man becomes Dr. Jekyll or Mr. Hyde, depending on what he wears, not who he is. Under SGML, the Jekyll/Hyde document could be designated as:

```
<!DOCTYPE freakdoc SYSTEM "c:\pervs\freakdoc.DTD">
```

But your processing system could provide alternate stylesheets called, say, `hyde.ssh` and `jekyll.ssh` as appropriate. Stylesheets become a document's suit of clothing that can change as appropriate to its audience.

The old linear paradigm relies heavily on format, whereas the new paradigm—discussed in Chapter 30, "Understanding the Information Revolution: The New Paradigm"—relies on document structure and uses format only as needed. Don't rely on format too much, and don't let it distract you from the content of what you want to say. Some people use format so much that it competes with the content. Their writing begins to resemble a cartoon. When you organize information modularly, you can remove either the cartoon text or the cartoon art. The meaning of the content is still apparent.

▶▶ See "How Modular Information Drives the Information Revolution," p. 513

The role of format differs dramatically in the old and new paradigms. It is less important in the new paradigm, and structure is more important.

The Role of Structure

Under the linear model of organizing information, structure pales in importance. Formatting tries to do all the work. Because everything is presented in a linear sequence, structure is arbitrary. You can structure a document according to its content or the intrinsic structure of the type of document. It doesn't make much difference. You still have to pick up the book and turn to the page where the information is. The information never comes to you, as it does when you browse a World Wide Web page.

With linearly organized information, you must follow the rules that the physical structure imposes on you. For example:

- *You have to access the whole book in order to access part of it.* You have to pick it up before you can find the page with the information that you want.

- *You must go to the information; it does not come to you.* You have to go to the library or borrow a book from someone.

- *You have limited opportunity to interact with the information.* You cannot make notes to the author. You have to take the information as is.

- *You cannot make your own book.* It costs too much. You do not know how to bind your own books, much less distribute them. You need a specialist.

The Whole Book or No Book Problem

Although books might appear to be modular, they cannot be easily broken down into smaller information chunks. You cannot rip out part of a book and take it home from the library with you. This whole book or no book problem can be a challenge. Under the new paradigm, it's not a problem.

The new paradigm, which includes SGML, is extraordinary. You no longer have to choose either the whole book or none of it. You can now make electronic links among books. Before, you could write a book and invite libraries to stock it. Now you can write a book and link it to every other relevant book electronically.

SGML allows electronic publishers and their readers a more collaborative relationship with their work. This "my book, our book" technique becomes possible as information becomes more granular. The modular approach to organizing knowledge makes this possible. Because you can easily add links to modules of information to any book, no book needs to be completely written.

How many times have you wished that you could have had another day, week, or month on a deadline for a book or a school paper? Deadlines will always exist, but you at least have the satisfaction of knowing your work does not have to stop. Through SGML, you can always add more information later, and everyone else can add links to further information if you want. Suppose that you have written the consummate work on the procreative habits of insects. Someone writing in the same area can add a link that relates directly to what you have done. Both works can be added to indefinitely by others.

The Stationary Information Problem

You can always take a book with you to the doctor's office or a ball game. Books are somewhat portable. The physical structure of a book, however, does not allow much flexibility in how you access information outside the book itself. For example, if the book was about baseball, and it referred to a statistic you'd like to double-check, you'd be out of luck. That information is portable unless it happens to be included in the book, and the factuality of the book is exactly what you're questioning. Also, you have the problem that the book must present its information in only one format. What if you and a friend both want to use the same baseball book, but the friend needs it in large print and you prefer small print? Then what do you do?

This is part of the stationary structure of information under the old paradigm. You can't always take it with you. When you reduce information to smaller streams of highly-portable electronic language marked up according to SGML, though, you can send it anywhere you want. Information under the new paradigm is completely portable. Not only will you be able to take it with you—as with a laptop computer with a cellular Internet connection—you one day might also take a smaller computer shaped as a paperback book in your back pocket while you are backpacking in the mountains.

> **Tip**
>
> Because you can make every character and symbol its own information module under the new paradigm, you can take *all* information with you wherever you go as long as you have a portable computing device. Information access devices under the new paradigm can become as commonplace as hand-held calculators, thanks to highly granular and standardized portable SGML information structures.

The Once and for All Information Problem

Discoveries that refute previously held ideas happen all the time. This is good, and as it should be, but it makes publishing a challenge under the old paradigm. Information retrieval evolves, and information delivery should as well. The linear model of information delivery makes this difficult, though. Once you have published your book and it has gone out to bookstores, you can't correct a mistake on page 275. However, information in standardized SGML structures that is online and accessible by means of a computer connected to a network can be updated at any time. The new paradigm overcomes the "once and for all" information problem.

> **Note**
>
> The old paradigm restricts thinking in terms of time and space. Once a book is distributed to bookstores, you have to wait until enough copies have been sold to justify another printing. If you made a mistake on page 275, you have to live with it—possibly for a long time.
>
> The time dimension is behind the once and for all problem. Once you accept that information delivery must evolve just as information itself does—that the information delivery process is ongoing—the problem begins to solve itself. The new paradigm makes the time dimension less important and allows information delivery to evolve alongside the information itself.

The Specialist Needed Problem

Not just anyone can make a book. You can write it, you can even write it electronically, but you can't do your own binding or sell it to bookstores nationwide. Every book is a collaboration of the talents and efforts of many people. Under the old paradigm, any quality book relies on the talents of many people, but much of that talent deals with improving the method of delivery rather than just presenting the information itself. Under this paradigm, you need a bookbinder, a printer, sales people, and literary agents. The electronic formats themselves don't need to be standardized. Under the new paradigm, not every book requires these specialists. The specialists can arrive on the scene after publication. Information can be shared because it's structured and standardized, thus accessible by all.

In the new paradigm, specialists can add their value after publication—if needed. Every potential author gets a chance to prove his or her worth. Professional publishers can support authors' efforts and improve the quality of a publication. Author, publisher, and public all benefit.

Because information is modular and standardized under the new paradigm, people share it easily. People can create many different works on the same subject. Each one adds something. Under the new paradigm, you become both an information shopper and an information provider. You can collaborate with authors if you want.

The specialist becomes a collaborator even more than under the old paradigm. Because information is distributed in modular structural units, and because these structural units follow the international standard of SGML, the specialist can add value to every module as it is created. The publishing timeline—from the manuscript creation to arrival at bookstores—has dropped dramatically as books are produced more and more electronically. As online books become just as profitable and convenient as hardcopy books, this timeline will decrease even more dramatically.

Structure Revisited

None of these problems could be solved without looking at structure creatively. The modular information model relies on being able to disassemble and reassemble documents easily. SGML requires documents to be completely defined and their individual structures to be declared and consistent. The old paradigm permits too much flexibility with document definition to allow widespread document interchange. You can violate your own rules with impunity; no one slaps your hand if you alter the structure of a chapter. If you try that trick in SGML, you're out of the information-sharing loop.

From Here...

In this chapter, you read about the old paradigm of information delivery. You saw how the linear way of organizing information is inferior to the modular way. You saw how format and structure of each paradigm differ. If you want to become an electronic publisher, you must understand the new paradigm.

VIII

Electronic Publishing

For more information, refer to the following:

- Chapter 26, "Tools for the PC: Authoring, Viewing, and Utilities," talks about tools for the PC that are used in electronic publishing.

- Chapter 27, "Tools for the Mac: Authoring, Viewing, and Utilities," talks about SGML tools for the Mac that are used in electronic publishing.

- Chapter 28, "Other Tools and Environments," talks about tools for other environments that are used in electronic publishing.

- Chapter 30, "Understanding the Information Revolution: The New Paradigm," discusses the new paradigm in detail.

- Part V, "SGML and the World Wide Web," covers what you need to know if you want to publish SGML on the Internet.

- Appendix A, "The SGML CD-ROM," discusses how to take advantage of the software on the CD that comes with this book so that you can begin publishing right away.

- Appendix B, "Finding Sources for SGML Know-How," helps you find others who can solve the problems that you run into.

Understanding the Information Revolution: The New Paradigm

The information revolution stems from the explosion of information that technology makes available and that modern society requires in order to function. Computers in the work place are nearly as ubiquitous as telephones. Until now, under the old paradigm, information has existed in separate computers that could communicate to some degree, but sharing documents has been limited. Under the new paradigm, information structure is standardized to facilitate widespread document sharing. All those computers are beginning to talk to each other, and the model of the isolated, unconnected computer is beginning to disappear. This chapter discusses what the information revolution really means and what the new paradigm has to do with it.

In this chapter, you learn:

- How modular information drives the information revolution
- What collaborative projects are currently happening on the Web
- What SGML standards are being developed and how they affect the Information Superhighway of the future
- How SGML promotes learning

How Modular Information Drives the Information Revolution

Chapter 29, "Understanding the Old Paradigm," discussed how old habits of organizing information linearly instead of modularly can complicate the process of information sharing. Under the old paradigm, computers—and the information on them—have only limited communications. Under the new paradigm, information is structured modularly in standardized ways according to SGML to facilitate document sharing by all computers. The Information Superhighway is really just in its infant stages. But its growth resembles the new America 400 years ago, as cyberspace today becomes colonized.

◀◀ See "Implications of the Linear Way of Organizing Information," p. 503

The information revolution results from the vast incentives to share information, profits, and technology that come when people pool their resources cooperatively. Since cooperative efforts are more efficient than competitive efforts, international standards can be agreed upon by many countries. This spirit of cooperation is why SGML has been so successful in unifying the efforts of both individuals and large organizations to change the way they think about structuring information.

The Reader Is a Collaborator

The information revolution consists of individual people who both provide and read information in standardized modular structures. The Information Superhighway consists of these individuals who are, at times, information providers and at other times information readers. Each individual helps to plan the architecture of the Information Superhighway by the resources he or she chooses. Web site patrons guide the decisions of Web site developers, for example, much as shoppers help the grocer decide what specials to feature in his or her store—by the decisions shoppers make about their purchases. In this way, information readers are collaborators with information providers.

◀◀ For more information on adding features like this to SGML documents, see "Adding Features to Documents," p. 155

Further, Web sites most often have mail forms built into their pages. This is no accident. The World Wide Web's popularity stems in large part from its interactive quality. You are involved in each online enterprise you take advantage of—you make a difference. Many enhancements to the World Wide Web resulted from suggestions that were sent via e-mail by readers of information who wanted to help out, to collaborate.

> **Note**
>
> Imagine how you feel when people read your published work on the Web. When they write and tell you what they think about your work, they are interacting with it. It feels good to have readers respond to your work. It's a way of saying that you have made a difference. That's why Web page authors include an E-mail Me icon at the bottom of their Web pages. Getting flamed is a risk, but being ignored is worse.

Likewise, readers appreciate knowing that their input is important. Until now, it has been difficult to contact an author and tell him how his work affected you.

It's different on the Web. Sending e-mail to someone is as easy as clicking a mouse button. You are involved. You can collaborate if you want. You can make suggestions about improving the Web site. F. Scott Fitzgerald and Ernest Hemingway cannot take your advice—they don't run Web sites (and they're no longer alive!)—but you can provide feedback to many Web authors. They will definitely consider your recommendations.

Information providers are interested in how you use their services, and which of their services you choose to patronize also is a form of collaboration. Web pages can measure the number of hits on their pages every day. You're helping to form the future of the Web by choosing which services to take advantage of. The Web is a free market, and it's still small enough where every hit makes a difference.

Many pages also keep usage statistics (see fig. 30.1). They tell you what other readers are interested in. You can find out what to include in your own Web site.

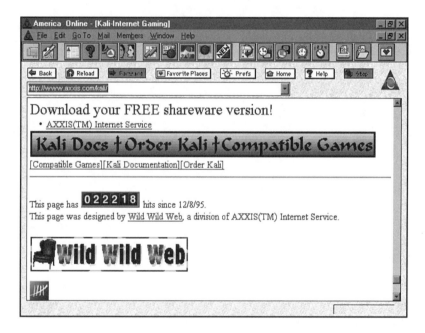

Fig. 30.1

Usage statistics are a form of collaboration. They tell users what's popular about a site.

VIII

Electronic Publishing

Collaboration is a type of document sharing that leads to more document sharing. Sharing documents on the Web, though, is just the tip of the iceberg of the information revolution.

Modular Document Sharing Is Only the Beginning

You have learned how to make documents available to anyone with a computer and a modem, including sound files, movies, and pictures. Most Web browsers can handle all these types of files. The excitement about sharing documents has led to new developments. Object-oriented programming applications can also interact with Web pages.

◄◄ See "How HTML and SGML Relate" p. 295

Java. The object-oriented programming language talked about the most today is Java. Java is an interpreted language that is multi-threaded and platform independent, developed from a team lead by Sun Microsystems. Check it out at **http:// java.sun.com** or a mirrored site. You need a java-compatible browser, such as Netscape 2.0 or HotJava, that will support the special DTD fragment that enables HTML pages to contain Java programs. The programs themselves, like graphics in Web pages, are ignored by the HTML parser but are recognized by the Java-compatible browser and are executed. These browsers support a non-standard HTML extension expressed by the following DTD fragment:

```
<!ELEMENT APPLET - - (PARAM*, (%text;)*)>

<!ATTLIST APPLET

        CODEBASE CDATA #IMPLIED   -- code base --

        CODE CDATA #REQUIRED      -- code file --

        NAME CDATA #IMPLIED       -- applet name --

        WIDTH NUMBER #REQUIRED

        HEIGHT NUMBER #REQUIRED

        ALIGN (left¦right¦top¦texttop¦middle¦

                absmiddle¦baseline¦bottom¦absbottom) baseline

        VSPACE NUMBER #IMPLIED

        HSPACE NUMBER #IMPLIED

>

<!ELEMENT PARAM - O EMPTY>

<!ATTLIST PARAM

        NAME NAME #REQUIRED    -- The name of the parameter --

        VALUE CDATA #IMPLIED   -- The value of the parameter --

>
```

The fact that HTML revisions come as slowly as they do is a disappointment for some because extensions like this <APPLET> tag seem to take forever to become implemented in the standard. This long lead time is perhaps another strong reason why the Web should adopt the full SGML standard, and so as not to encourage developers to violate the standard with extensions like these. Under full SGML, multiple DTDs and DTD fragments can be supported well within the accepted international standard.

The Web will change even more dramatically as more browsers support the <APPLET> element and Java. The implications for launching shared interactive applications over the Web are enormous. For example:

- People can watch a movie in real time, even if they're physically separated by many miles.

- People can carry on a video conference with sound and video support from a Web browser.

- People can access the same spreadsheet in real time without overwriting the work of others.

- People can play interactive virtual reality games over the Web and launch programs that interact with one another. This is somewhat possible today over TCP/IP with the Kali IPX emulator (see fig. 30.1), as well as other possibilities over the Internet Relay Chat channels.

- Programmers can work on the same project in real time over a network and add value as the application develops.

You can learn many things from programming applications that run from Web browsers. Figure 30.2 shows a Java page that executes a little multimedia program where the developer's smiling face bounces and revolves around in a little box. Other applications are more serious, of course, and the potential is enormous.

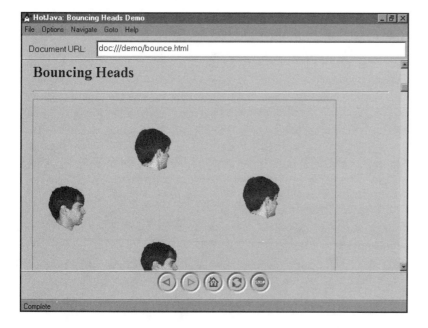

Fig. 30.2

Java is the first object-oriented program language designed to use the APP element.

VIII

Electronic Publishing

Virtual Reality Modeling Language. Virtual Reality Modeling Language (VRML) incorporates even more graphic capability into Web pages through access to three-dimensional graphic files that can constantly reorient themselves to give you the illusion that you are moving through a virtual world. Links to these *.wrl pages can be launched from an HTML page, but to interactively view the file, you need a VRML browser.

◀◀ See "Adding Multimedia Content," p. 161

VRML actually goes outside the boundaries of SGML. It depends on SGML inasmuch as the World Wide Web depends on SGML, to provide an overall connected resource in which to store three-dimensional files.

When SGML was devised, it was primarily concerned with two-dimensional graphics. It can handle three-dimensional graphics, but they must be delegated to another application to be viewed. In other words, SGML turns the tasks over to another application and concentrates on what it does best, which is structural document handling. VRML is one of the many additional types of resources that SGML can accommodate in its open design philosophy. SGML was designed to allow many different types of resources to interact without obstruction from the requirements of the international standard. The fact that VRML has become so popular on the Web demonstrates that it can work right alongside SGML documents without interfering with them.

The possibilities for VRML are magnificent. With VRML browsers, you can chase your friends through three-dimensional, interactive worlds. Recall figure 1.10, which shows a scene from the virtual reality game Descent. That could be you. Likewise, imagine walking down a virtual street in Hong Kong and opening a door that leads onto a street in Copenhagen. In a virtual world, you can do that.

Many developers are creating VRML browsers. Figure 30.3 shows one that works on PCs called WebSpace.

Fig. 30.3

VRML resources like this have mushroomed on the Web.

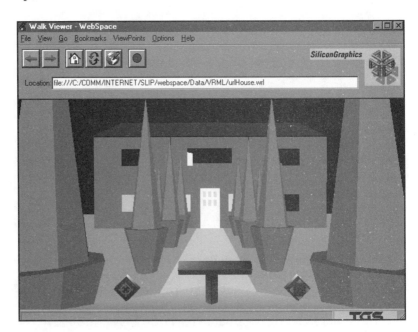

Modular Information and Collaboration

Document interchange and information sharing never happened before on the scale it currently is on the World Wide Web. Putting the information into information modules as SGML document structures is what's behind all the information now accessible on the World Wide Web. It's only been three years after the Web and the http protocol were started, and already we are talking about and interacting in three-dimensional cyberworlds. This is the power of the international collaboration that SGML has engendered.

◀◀ See "SGML on the Web," p. 311

◀◀ See "What Data Is Already in SGML," p. 324

SGML enjoys a unique position as the "father of the Web," for HTML is its offspring. With the success of the Web, SGML is no longer just for the erudite. It's a language that everyone can learn and use. If a single application can catch on so universally, just imagine what the parent application might do.

> **Note**
>
> The success of HTML on the World Wide Web proves that SGML is a language for everyone. If HTML can achieve celebrity status, so can SGML.

Current Collaborative Projects on the Web

Even though using information in the modular SGML way is new to many, the results have been exciting. Current projects are helping to establish the paths along which the industrial information vehicles of the future will travel. More is happening with SGML on the Web than can be summarized. The following sections briefly describe some of these projects, most of which are trying to build a body of standards that everyone can follow and that blend easily with existing projects.

> **Note**
>
> No matter how ambitious a project is, it isn't useful unless it can blend with everyone else's work. You'll notice that many of these projects deal with developing or extending current standards.

VIII

Electronic Publishing

TEI

The Text Encoding Initiative (TEI) is an international research project that is finding ways to translate existing texts into SGML so that they can be accessed worldwide. The goal is to be able to take any text from a library and convert it to an SGML document. The problem is that there is no easy way to handle the many document types that exist. You need a different application of SGML for each new document type. TEI works to simplify DTDs so as to avoid more DTDs than are needed, yet still be compatible with important existing DTDs.

One important source of information on TEI, and SGML generally, is the Electronic Text Center at the University of Virginia (see fig. 30.4). They have made the entire TEI Guidelines available.

Fig. 30.4

The Electronic Text Center at the University of Virginia (http:// www.lib.virginia.edu/etext/ ETC.html) is one definitive source for information on SGML topics, including TEI.

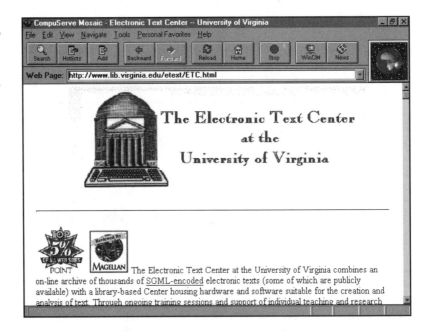

Another useful URL is **http://cethmac.princeton.edu/TEI2dtd/ DTD-HOME.html**, which has information on the TEI DTD.

The TEI project has special workgroups that develop approaches to developing SGML grammars (DTDs) for specific types of texts. The types of text include:

- General linguistics
- Spoken texts
- Machine-readable dictionaries
- Computational lexicons

- Character sets
- Hypertext and hypermedia
- Mathematical formulas and tables
- Verse
- Language corpora

The TEI project keeps two electronic mailing lists: TEI-L and SGML-L. It also maintains FTP archives with reports, DTDs, and entity sets. Do a Web search on TEI FTP for the latest locations. One URL is **http://wiretap.spies.com/ftp.items/alt.etext**.

Tip

Heavily-nested URLs tend to change more rapidly than short URLs. It's always a good idea to double-check an address.

TEI is full of material to explore. The diverse types of document structures required just by computational lexicons and machine-readable dictionaries alone would challenge many SGML developers. The TEI contributors include many of SGML's leading creators. The mathematical and tabular structures required by many of these types of texts are intricate. You'll recall a few challenges presented by math equations from Chapter 25, "Handling Specialized Content and Delivery."

 ◀◀ See "Handling Math and Equations," p. 424

AAP/EPSIG

The Association of American Publishers, Electronic Publishing Special Interest Group (AAP/EPSIG) maintains the AAP DTDs, which make up the AAP standard, whose official name is ANSI/NISO Z39.59-1988. It is currently in review. In coordination with TEI, AAP/EPSIG is working on tables and mathematics.

AAP/EPSIG focuses on electronic manuscript markup. It was transferred from the Online Computer Library Center (OCLC) to a group of three collaborating organizations. They are:

- The Association of American Publishers, which advise the SGML requirements for the AAP
- The Graphic Communications Association Research Institute, which provides organizational management
- McAffe & McAdam, a consulting firm that provides technical direction

> **Note**
>
> ISO 12083 is the successor to the AAP/EPSIG standard. Make sure that any DTD copies you get are the official DTDs and not any preliminary copies that EPSIG released earlier.

AAP differs from TEI in its focus on the electronic publishing process. Whereas TEI might invest much effort in determining the best ways to represent scientific or literary document structures efficiently, AAP concerns itself with how those structures can be streamlined industry-wide for publishers and their editorial and production functions.

Copies of these DTDs are available from the Exeter archive at:

ftp://info.ex.ac.uk/pub/SGML/AAP

More information about the AAP is available from the following URLs:

http://www.sil.org/sgml/gen-apps.html#aap

http://www.sil.org/sgml/bib-mn.html#nisoEPSIG

The Davenport Group

Without standards, the work of the few cannot be enjoyed by the many. The projects of the Davenport Group are aimed at unifying activity. They include:

- **DASH**: Short for Davenport Advisory Standard for Hypermedia. This project seeks to help systems vendors organize their documentation according to a single DTD, even when they have different document types.
- **DOCBOOK**: A DTD developed specifically for software documentation.
- **DECBOOK**: Digital Corporation's DTD. It's similar to DOCBOOK, but is more modular.

Check out **http://www.ora.com/davenport/README.html**. It gives a brief overview of what the Davenport project is all about.

SGML Open

This group of SGML developers came together in 1993. It is an industry consortium that wants to promote the interoperability of SGML applications and more widespread use of SGML.

SGML Open has a great Web site, shown in figure 30.5. Visit both the HTML version and the SGML version (via Panorama) of its home page.

SGML Open is in the business of developing and selling SGML products. If you want to know what's happening in the world of SGML products and applications, SGML Open can offer plenty of information.

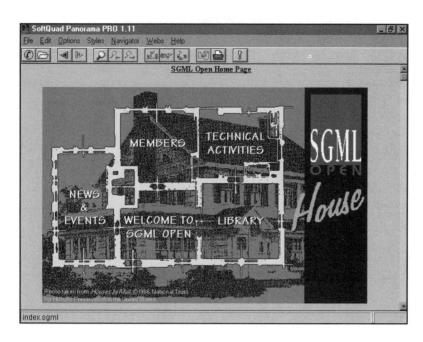

Fig. 30.5

The SGML Open home page (at http://www.sgmlopen.org) is one you should visit.

EWS

The European Workgroup on SGML (EWS) is a collection of European publishers, printers, and typesetters. It's responsible for a set of DTDs known as the *Majour DTD*. The DTDs are based on the AAP standard and cover scientific papers and journals. They are available through SGML browsers. For more information, see the following URL:

> **gopher://trick.ntp.springer.de/11/sgml**

Collaboration on SGML Standards

You can keep up on the ongoing standards development projects on the Web. One of the best sources of information is the SGML Web Page at **http://www.sil.org/ sgml/sgml.html** (see fig. 30.6). Robin Cover has done a marvelous job of organizing links to vital Web pages that you can use. You can spend months running down links on your favorite subjects.

You will find FAQs, tutorials, bibliographies, conference announcements, news, software reviews, information on current projects, and great miscellaneous links. The projects include:

- SGML Projects and applications—General projects and applications, academic projects and applications, and government and industry applications
- Special topics on SGML (ISO 8879)
- Standards related to SGML—document style semantics and specification language, standard page description language, open document architecture, and other standards

Fig. 30.6

The SGML Web Page helps you locate the information that you need on current SGML projects.

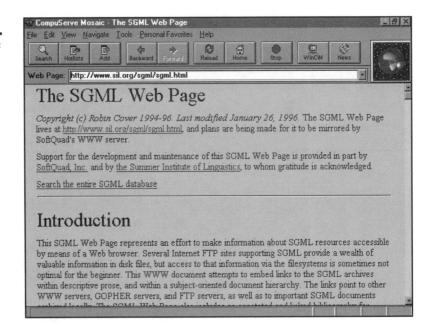

There is more here than you can imagine. The projects are important to keep an eye on.

HyTime

There is much to say about HyTime, short for Hypermedia/Time-based Structuring Language. The applicable standard is ISO 10744. As with most projects, HyTime deals with standards.

Do some reading on HyTime. Start with its Web pages at **http://techno.com/ TechnoTeacher/HyTime.html**, and chase down the links. This link should remain stable. When in doubt, go back to Robin Cover's page at **http://www.sil.org/ sgml/sgml.html**.

The official standard of HyTime is not in the public domain. A copy of it costs $98.

HyTime is an extension of SGML. It defines how SGML structures can be used to deal with individual document objects for use in hypermedia. HyTime engines, which are implementations of HyTime, enable development companies to build applications. Licenses are expensive, however.

Read *Making Hypermedia Work: A User's Guide to HyTime*, by Steve DeRose and David Durand. It costs approximately $70 and is worth it. You can obtain information on ordering a copy from **http://cs-pub.bu.edu/students/grads/ dgd/order.html**.

HyTime is one of the most important SGML projects today. It is another egg whose time to hatch has nearly come. It will attract much public attention in the next few years, so keep an eye on it.

SMDL

Standard Music Description Language (SMDL) is one of the HyTime applications. The applicable ISO standard is ISO 10743:1995. The architecture of applications built according to this standard supports music either alone or together with text and graphics. It handles the time sequencing information necessary for sound applications, so that you are not hung up by a network server wait signal in the middle of a waltz. The language can help build applications for business, publishing, or recreation.

ICADD

Not everyone who uses SGML has perfect sight. For those with visual disabilities, the International Committee on Accessible Document Design (ICADD) is a lifesaver. An ICADD DTD supports document definitions for Braille, large print, and voice synthesis. The applicable ISO standard is ISO 12083 ANNEX A.8. There's also an HTML-to-ICADD transformation service that translates HTML documents into Braille documents. Check the URL at:

http://www.ucla.edu/ICADD/html2icadd-form.html

UTF

News agencies have chosen SGML as their method for sending news around the globe. The DTD is still in development. Universal Text Format (UTF) will replace the current standards of the International Press Telecommunications Council and the Newspaper Association of America, IPTC 7901 and ANPA 1312.

Fred at OCLC

Fred at the Online Computer Library Center (OCLC) is not a standard, but it is an exciting project. It has real potential. It's still a private application, but portions of it are available on the World Wide Web. A list of related links can be found at the following URL:

http://www.sil.org/sgml/gen-apps.html#oclc

Suppose, for example, that you receive SGML tagged text without an associated DTD. That's a problem. Fred is designed to create a DTD from the document automatically by extracting its tags and building a grammar structure from the document instance.

How SGML's Modular Organization Promotes Worldwide Learning

SGML enables the World Wide Web to be the perfect teacher for the curious student. It tells you whatever you want to know. It doesn't reproach you for looking at subject matter for which you have no preparation. If you want to dive into quantum mechanics, you're free to click a URL that takes you into the thick of it.

You can take university courses over the Net or learn how to make a shepherd's pie. No matter how diverse your interests are, you can find something about them on the Net, which is really one big, informal classroom.

Pick one of your favorite subjects that is not computer-related. Suppose that you are into tennis. Use a search utility to do a Web search. Chances are that many of the sites you find did not exist a few months ago. That's how fast the Net is growing.

This explosive growth would not be possible without SGML's modular structuring of information. When you confine information to people who can access a linear source of information, you limit the amount of interaction and document sharing that's possible between users. SGML's use of structural modules of documents allows extremely flexible information interchange.

> **Note**
>
> Being able to ask obscure questions out of left field never was easy. There was the Eliza program of the late 1970s, but it was anybody's guess as to how meaningful its answer would be.
>
> With so many computers connected and sharing modular information databases, you can experience a modern Eliza. Any Web search utility can overload you with links to more sites than you ever wanted to know about anything. That's the power of modular information.

From Here...

This chapter has described the thinking behind the information revolution in terms of modular data organization. Because SGML forces documents to be structured into identifiable modules, computers can locate information quickly and promote global cooperation and collaboration on many different projects, such as Hyper-G, Java, VRML, and many others. As an international standard, SGML allows cooperation among different technologies that corporate competition often would otherwise preclude.

For more information, refer to the following:

- Chapter 31, "Oject-Oriented Development of SGML Applications," tells you about how to build an object-oriented database of SGML documents. It takes you deeper into the cooperation between object-oriented systems and SGML documents.

- Appendix A, "The SGML CD-ROM," introduces you to SGML software that's freely available in the public domain, as well as shareware demonstration versions of commercial software.

- Appendix B, "Finding Sources for SGML Know-How," suggests places from which to get answers to your questions. There are so many sources for SGML know-how; one of them is bound to have the answer.

CHAPTER 31

Object-Oriented Development of SGML Applications

SGML is about more than storing, formatting, and printing documents. As new kinds of media and software tools become available every month, an organization whose data is stored in SGML has a distinct advantage over the competition if it wants to take advantage of these new publishing opportunities—that is, if it can develop the applications that use this SGML data quickly enough.

Object-oriented technology has made great contributions to software development in the last 15 years. Its philosophy of treating program components and data structures as objects that send messages to each other has resulted in faster development, easier debugging, and more robust programs.

An SGML document has much in common with an object-oriented system. In addition to some key vocabulary, there are many parallels between the analysis and design processes used to develop SGML and object-oriented applications. By exploiting these common points, you can minimize the work necessary to turn an SGML system into a useful object-oriented application, which can greatly speed the work of the SGML developer. In the future, you'll see more and more SGML tools take advantage of this common ground and more object-oriented tools, such as object-oriented database managers, that offer immediate benefits to the SGML developer. A better understanding of this common ground makes it easier to fit these tools together into a complete system as they become available.

In this chapter, you learn:

- The basics of object-oriented development
- What object-oriented development techniques can offer the SGML developer
- What a DTD can do for an object-oriented system
- How an SGML-to-object-oriented system program can be automated
- How a sample Smalltalk system puts these ideas into practice
- The future of object-oriented development with SGML

Object-Oriented Technology: The Basics (and the Confusion)

You're probably tired of hearing people define object-oriented systems as systems in which everything is treated as an object. What is a software object, and why are the many explanations so confusing?

An *object* is a data structure with defined attributes and capabilities. Just as a database designer might decide on a table called Employees with columns in that table for First Name, Last Name, Hire Date, Employee ID Number, and Salary, an object-oriented developer can design a class of objects called "employee" that have attributes of first name, last name, hire date, employee ID number, and salary. When the object-oriented program creates a new employee object for Joe Smith, it's similar to the data-base designer's program adding a new row to the employee table for Joe Smith, except you're no longer thinking in terms of rows and columns; you're thinking of an em-ployee object named Joe Smith.

There's another key difference between this object and a row or record from a data-base: along with the data attributes, such as first and last name, it also has behavior or capabilities specified for it—in other words, what those objects can do. These capabili-ties may be as simple as the ability to tell you its attribute values when asked, or they may be complex operations that control other objects through the invocation of programs.

At this point, most explanations of object-oriented systems start throwing around terms like "inheritance," "polymorphism," and "overloading." These are not essential to understanding objects; object-oriented developers use them as convenience features to more easily create systems with many different classes of objects.

There are two other common sources of confusion in object-oriented technology. First, during a period somewhere after the reigning popularity of artificial intelligence as the Hot New Computer Technology That Would Change All of Our Lives and be-fore the current similar popularity of the World Wide Web, object-oriented technol-ogy held this title for several years. Because of this trendiness, software industry marketing people misuse much of the key vocabulary of object-oriented technology to make their products seem up-to-date. This misuse confuses people trying to learn about object-oriented development.

Another source of confusion is the common assertion that, in object-oriented systems, data and code are stored together. They're not stored together; they're defined to-gether. The code defining the capabilities of a given class' objects is stored with the code that defines the structure of those objects, not with the object's data. For ex-ample, the program that inserts new employees into the personnel system or prints out employee reports is not stored with the data "Joe Smith, 2/3/96, ID3543, $30,000"—it's stored with the code that says "an employee object consists of a first name, last name, hire date, employee number, and salary."

Why do you hear such great claims for object-oriented technology? How does it help software development, especially the development of applications that use SGML data? It's easier to understand if you first review the four stages of software development. These stages apply to all software development, object-oriented or not:

- *Analysis* answers several questions: What problem must the software solve? What work does it have to do? What data does it start with, and what output will the program's users expect?
- *Design* is the process of figuring out the data structures to represent the objects and processes identified in analysis.
- *Implementation* is the actual writing of the program code.
- *Compiling* turns the written code into a usable program. (Many include this step as part of implementation.)

All software development, whether object-oriented or not, starts off as a collection of objects in the developers' heads. Even NASA programmers working in FORTRAN thirty years ago thought about booster rocket objects with an attribute of potential thrust, or of earth and moon objects with gravitational pull as attributes. All software ends up as a series of tiny and tinier voltages that are represented with ones and zeros, which aren't very object-oriented.

Somewhere in these four steps, the application goes from an object-oriented representation to a non-object-oriented representation. In fact, it might even go back and forth between the two as it moves through these steps. The possibility of this back-and-forth transition adds a third reason for confusion about object-oriented technology: the possibility of hybrid development systems that are object-oriented for some steps, but not others.

Table 31.1 shows how step 3 alone can be object-oriented, traditional, or somewhere in between, based on the programming language one chooses for implementation. Any one of these could be used to develop an SGML application, although you'll soon see why the object-oriented ones are better fits. Advocates of languages designed from scratch as object-oriented consider them to be "purer" tools for object-oriented development, but the object-oriented extensions to more traditional languages have become more popular because they each build on a wider user base, creating a gray area that blurs and dilutes the object-oriented development process.

Table 31.1   Object-Oriented vs. Traditional Programming Languages Implementation

Object-Oriented	Traditional	Gray Area
Smalltalk	C	C++
Eiffel	Pascal	Object Pascal
CLOS	Perl 4	Perl 5
	Basic	Many others…
	Assembler	
	Many others…	

And that's just the implementation step! Much object-oriented literature goes on (and on and on) about the analysis and design phases, because more work devoted to these phases will make the pieces fall together more easily in the implementation phase. A traditional approach at these stages—for example, designing a database by worrying about how to fit all the data into table rows and columns with no data redundancy—makes it difficult to take advantage of a language like Smalltalk.

This brings us to the main advantage of object-oriented development: it provides a systematic way to put off the eventual, but necessary point where you can no longer think in terms of the objects that your application represents and manipulates. Eventually, your application ends up as ones and zeros on a disk, but object-oriented development lets you put off the stage where you can no longer think of it in terms of hammers, screwdrivers, and flashlights sitting in bins, or, for an SGML publishing application, of poems, titles, illustrations, and review questions. Instead, you let the computer worry about tables, pointers, and memory allocation. You can think more directly about solving the problem at hand.

> **Note**
>
> Object-oriented development means less worrying about low-level technical details and greater focus on the concepts represented in your program.

The object-oriented approach has other advantages, such as faster application development; you'll learn more about that shortly. First, let's look at an example of how object-oriented data structures make it easier to think about an application domain.

With an object-oriented approach to a hardware inventory system, you might define a bin class whose objects each had attributes of `BinID`, `ItemStored`, `ItemSupplier`, `AmountInStock`, and `DangerLevel`. (The bin's `ItemSupplier` would itself be an object with attributes such as `Address`, `PhoneNumber`, and `FaxNumber`.) The bin class's capabilities would include, along with setting and reporting object attribute values, the ability to increase and decrease `AmountInStock` based on appropriate stimuli. Because software objects can go beyond the capabilities of the real-world objects that they represent, the bin object could also send an e-mail warning message when the `AmountInStock` value decreases to equal the `DangerLevel` value.

Once such classes are defined, the process of creating a new object in memory (or, in object-oriented parlance, *instantiating* a member of this class of objects) is similar to creating a new variable—or better yet, a new record—of a previously defined type in a more traditional programming language. As with a record, you're saying "set aside some memory to store values for a specific instance of this thing that I defined over here in this record or class declaration, and give the new set of values such-and-such a name (for example, "bin 2A" or "Vulcan Tool Company") that I will use in the future to refer to it."

With a non-object-oriented system, such as a relational database, these bins and suppliers might be represented by tables. The Bin and ItemSupplier tables would have columns corresponding to the attributes listed for the Bin and ItemSupplier objects, plus an additional column to uniquely identify each row. A row of the Bin table doesn't have its supplier's entire address and phone numbers; it has the supplier code that identifies that supplier's entry in the Supplier table. If you stored the supplier's entire address in the Bin table, keeping data about multiple flashlight models from the same supplier would mean storing redundant copies of the supplier's address, which wastes disk space and is harder to update properly when the supplier moves to a new address.

You haven't yet learned the role of the capabilities, or the work expected of the traditional application that uses the data in these tables. The application can perform all the same tasks described in the object-oriented version, but it must also maintain and cross-reference these unique codes that identify each row to avoid the many potential problems.

In an object-oriented system, similar cross-referencing takes place, but you don't worry about it; it's the development software's job to see that it gets done. The developer can think in terms of flashlights and suppliers, without worrying about the creation, assignment, and maintenance of unique IDs that enable a report to find out a flashlight supplier's phone number or the type of battery needed for a given bin's contents.

To summarize, the object-oriented approach lets you deal with data at a higher level because it automates more of the low-level details.

Object-Oriented Development and SGML: Why?

What benefits can SGML provide to the object-oriented developer, and more importantly, what benefits can object-oriented technology provide to the SGML application developer?

If you take advantage of object-oriented techniques to develop SGML applications, don't give in to the temptation to coin some horrid new acronym like "OOSGML," because one key aspect of object-oriented systems is diametrically opposed to a key aspect of SGML.

An intrinsic part of an object-oriented system is the specification of object behavior. On the other hand, good SGML design specifies only object structure, intentionally excluding the behavior of "objects" (the document and its component elements) as much as possible to give the most flexibility to developers using that data.

> **Caution**
>
> Don't give in to the temptation to call SGML "naturally object-oriented." A lot of common ground between SGML and object-oriented systems can help the developer, but SGML objects need behavior defined for them before you can consider them object-oriented.

So if the key difference between SGML and object-oriented systems is that the former doesn't specify behavior for its "objects," then at the simplest level, defining some behavior for these objects should turn it into an object-oriented system. You can actually think of all SGML application development—the process of creating a useful application around a given DTD and its document instances—as adding behavior to SGML data, whether or not you take an object-oriented approach.

While examining the common ground between object-oriented systems and SGML, your two primary goals are:

- To take advantage of the similarities in the two development processes so that you can avoid redundant work
- To make up for the differences as painlessly as possible—that is, to figure out ways to automate this make-up work so that you end up doing as little work as possible

Common Vocabulary

Using the official ISO 8879 standard that defines SGML and Charles Goldfarb's commentary on it, along with the seminal works on object-oriented development by Grady Booch and James Rumbaugh, let's compare the definitions of key object-oriented and SGML terms to lay the groundwork for a discussion of what they have in common.

 ▶▶ See "Books on SGML," p. 565

The most important terms in object-oriented systems are *class*, *instance*, *attributes*, *state*, and *behavior*. The first three, in particular, will be familiar to SGML developers.

Class

In the object-oriented world, a *class* is a group of objects with similar properties, and an *instance* is a specific object, or member of a class. While the SGML use of these words is more limited, the terms *document type* and *element type* make up for this limitation. Comparing their definitions with the object-oriented concept of class shows how SGML documents and their components can be treated as objects, or, in object-oriented terms, as instantiations of predefined classes.

Section 4.102 of ISO 8879 defines a *document type* as "a class of documents having similar characteristics; for example, journal, article, technical manual, or memo." Later, it defines an *element type* as "a class of elements having similar characteristics." Neither definition mentions how a DTD, when specifying a document's elements and their legal arrangements, defines the structural relationships among a document's elements. This and SGML's use of the term "attributes" to identify element characteristics makes document and element types very close to the object-oriented concept of a "class" of objects. In the section "A Sample Smalltalk SGML System," later in this chapter, you'll see a Smalltalk application that does just that.

Remember, however, that SGML element classes still lack one key feature to make them proper object-oriented classes: definition of object (that is, element) behavior.

Instance

According to Rumbaugh, a class "describes a possibly infinite set of objects. Each object is said to be an *instance* of its class. Each instance of the class has its own value for each attribute, but shares the attribute names and operations with other objects of the class." A DTD's declaration of a chapter describes a possibly infinite number of chapters, which each have the same attribute names (for example, RevisionDate or an ID used for hypertext links to the chapter) but different values (or even the same values, as with two chapters that were revised the same day) for those attributes.

SGML uses the term *instance*, but only when referring to a document, not its component elements. There's nothing about the document's status as a special kind of element to prevent you from using the document term "instance" to apply to other SGML elements in addition to documents. Since documents are merely a special case of elements—in fact, an element like a chapter can be *the* document in one context, but a component of a larger document in another—you can treat specific examples of a particular element class as instances as well.

Attribute

The term *attributes* comes up often in both SGML and object-oriented discussions. Let's start with the SGML definition: ISO 8879 section 4.9 defines an attribute as "A characteristic quality, other than type or content." SGML recognizes two levels of attributes: primary and secondary. *Primary attributes* are the IDs unique to each declared element type that are sometimes called "generic identifiers" or just "GIs." These are used in the "tags" that identify the start and, if necessary, the end of elements. Generic identifiers usually do this by including this attribute in angle brackets and by preceding the closing tag's element name with a slash. For example, the second-level headers declared by many DTDs have a primary attribute of "h2" that is used in the <H2> and </H2> markup tags.

Additional attributes, such as the HTML anchor element's NAME attribute, which assigns a name to the anchor so that it can serve as a jump destination, or its attribute, which identifies a jump destination if the anchor is clicked, are considered to be *secondary attributes*. When SGML people talk about an element's attributes, they're usually talking about these secondary attributes.

An object-oriented system using SGML data would use each element's generic identifier to figure out which object class it belongs to and then use the secondary attributes as "attributes" in the object-oriented sense—as a set of values associated with each instance of that element type's "class." For example, the HTML A element's secondary attribute HREF, which identifies a location where the cursor should jump if the text tagged as an A element is clicked, is a value giving information about that tagged text.

State

An object's *state* is its current collection of attribute values. For an aggregate object (an object composed of a combination of other objects) such as an SGML document, this would include the values of its component objects' attributes—for example, a recipe's state would include the attribute values of its title, ingredients, and instructions' components. Determining possible object states and the role of state transitions plays a large role in many object-oriented analysis/object-oriented development systems (or, as they're more commonly known, "OOA/OOD methodologies"). The state transitions of a system are what make good analysis and design so important, because lack of control over these transitions, especially in a multi-user system, leads to the kind of concurrency problems that cause unpredictable behavior.

State transitions play a small role in an SGML system until you build an editor—especially a multi-user editor—on top of an object-oriented SGML system. Unlike, for example, a car undergoing assembly, there are few state transitions to plan around for an SGML object once its data and components are assigned at object creation time.

SGML data is typically used as a source format that makes it easy to create multiple different output formats, so transformation of the data is done to copied data being output, while the source is left alone. When writing code to define behavior in an SGML system that allows editing of the data, especially multi-user editing, keeping track of various states plays a more important role. The developer should be able to leave this work to an object-oriented database manager (OODBMS) that performs object locking and other database management functions that allow trouble-free multi-user access. (You'll learn about the tremendous benefits that an OODBMS can offer in the "Object-Oriented Technology and the Future of SGML Development" section.)

To keep this discussion simple, we'll only concern ourselves with static SGML data that does not change when a program is run. This doesn't sacrifice much, because of the number of SGML applications that make changes to a copy of the data in order to output data in some other format. So for now, don't worry about state changes.

Behavior

Booch defines *behavior* as "how an object acts and reacts, in terms of its state changes and message passing." Defining an object's behavior means writing code for each class to respond to messages sent to objects of that class. A block of code written to respond to a given message is analogous to a function or procedure written in a more traditional language; the "message" is equivalent to the function call.

As we saw, good DTD design deliberately avoids the definition of element behavior to allow the most flexibility possible to developers using that data, so defining behavior for SGML elements is the principle step toward treating SGML data as part of an object-oriented system. Because this assignment of behavior can be done by an external application that can leave the data and its structure alone, you can maintain the integrity of the SGML data, since you're only using the DTD as a starting point and then externally defining behavior to go with each of its elements.

Table 31.2 summarizes the correlations between object-oriented and SGML terms.

Table 31.2 Correlations between Key SGML and Object-Oriented Terms	
SGML Term	**Object-Oriented Term**
attribute	attribute
document instance	instance, object (Booch: interchangeable terms)
element	instance, object
element declaration	class
document class	class

What Can Object-Oriented Development Techniques Do for DTD Development?

An understanding of the parallels between object-oriented and SGML development lets SGML application developers take advantage of a great deal of existing research (and, in the future, development tools) that can speed their application development.

One important concept of object-oriented development, and another key to the object-oriented developers' claims of greater productivity, is the notion of design re-use in addition to code re-use. While traditional structured design encourages code reuse through the development of functions and procedures that can be called in a variety of situations, the object-oriented approach puts greater emphasis on the analysis and design stages so that the information gathered can be re-used in these crucial early stages of future application development. The analysis and design already done for the SGML developer result in the creation of a DTD, which specifies a large majority of the information an object-oriented developer needs to know to quickly create an application.

Most of the goals and even methods of DTD design have much in common with those of object-oriented analysis and design. For a developer using SGML data, the existence of a good DTD means that the majority of the analysis and design has already been done and stored in a clearly defined notation that a program can easily parse and use to declare classes in an object-oriented system. Analysis of typical SGML systems reveals more aspects that can be automated, reducing the developer's work even further.

VIII

Electronic Publishing

What if a DTD doesn't exist, and the SGML developer is working from the ground up? While current SGML literature offers little on DTD development, object-oriented literature has much to say about analysis and design that can benefit the DTD developer. The tasks described in this literature are the tasks that the DTD developer must take on; for example, Booch writes that "By studying the problem's requirements and/or by engaging in discussions with domain experts, the developer must learn the vocabulary of the problem domain. The tangible things in the problem domain, the roles they play, and the events that may occur form the candidate classes and objects of our design, at its highest level of abstraction."

DTD developers must become familiar with different roles of document elements in different output formats as well as the development and production process of publishing systems ranging from elementary school textbooks to nuclear reactor installation manuals. They also face problems similar to those of the object-oriented systems developer. For example, Rumbaugh writes that "In modeling an engineering problem, the object model should contain terms familiar to engineers; in modeling a business problem, terms from the business; in modeling a user interface, terms from the application domain." The DTD designer and the object-oriented system designer must both learn the language of their clients and the principles underlying the language so that they can understand exactly what the application needs.

Like Rumbaugh's designer, the DTD designer must work to get beyond the terminology, which can be misleading. Publishing professionals are worse than computing professionals in applying terms to concepts long after the concept has evolved to lose all relation to the term; perhaps the most well-known example is the still-common use of the term "leading" (pronounced "ledding") to describe the amount of space between printed lines because this was once done with the insertion of small pieces of lead between lines of type. A less picturesque example is the tendency by page layout people to think of the terms "emphasize" and "italicize" as synonymous, which causes problems in output media that allow emphasis but not italics. The SGML goal of separating structure from behavior (which, at the simplest level, means separating structure from appearance) is precisely what gives the object-oriented developer such a wide range of ways to use the data.

As an example of how the object-oriented emphasis on analysis could make for a better DTD, consider a multi-volume encyclopedia that has been published in hardcopy books and is being converted to SGML for easier production as an online hypertext version. Each volume has several chapters that contain the entries for a letter of the alphabet. Here is a simplified DTD:

```
<!DOCTYPE ency [
<!ELEMENT ency     o o (volume+)>
<!ELEMENT volume   o o (section+)>
<!ELEMENT chapter  - o (title,entry+)>
<!ELEMENT entry    - o (title,para+)>
<!ELEMENT title  o o (#PCDATA)>
<!ELEMENT para     - o (#PCDATA)>
]>
```

Following all the steps of a formal analysis might show that each volume had no spe-cial attributes to distinguish itself from other volumes. In fact, the only reason that the encyclopedia wasn't published as one big 8,000 page book is the impracticality of binding such a book. This analysis of the publication's information shows that the assumption that "volume" was an intrinsic part of the structure is unnecessary. We can then reduce a level of complexity in the encyclopedia's structure by removing that element and specifying that an encyclopedia is made of a collection of chapters, not volumes:

```
<!DOCTYPE ency [
<!ELEMENT ency     o o (chapter+)>
<!ELEMENT chapter - o (title,entry+)>
<!ELEMENT entry   - o (title,para+)>
<!ELEMENT title o o (#PCDATA)>
<!ELEMENT para    - o (#PCDATA)>
]>
```

There is nothing particularly object-oriented about this design decision (although it has even less relation to relational design, in which you have to figure out how to squeeze everything into tables). No DTD is more object-oriented than any other; the key is that the process of creating a DTD has enough in common with object-oriented analysis and design that the ample OOA/OOD literature available provides a great resource for a DTD designer looking for help in DTD creation—especially considering the current lack of material on DTD development in the SGML literature. The object-oriented belief that more attention to the OOA/OOD stages decreases the implemen-tation work leads to object-oriented methodologies with extensive, detailed advice on system analysis and design.

What Can a DTD Do for Object-Oriented Development?

Before identifying the specific work that a DTD has already done for the object-oriented developer, let's review the analysis and design work that an object-oriented developer needs done. This way, we can identify the work already done in DTD devel-opment that the developer can re-use and then identify the remaining tasks.

There are many, many books available on object-oriented development, but there are two in particular with the highest reputation. Grady Booch's *Object-Oriented Analysis and Design with Applications* is the most quoted, and by now considered the de facto most authoritative. His incorporation of concepts from many other popular object-oriented methodologies widens his perspective and lends weight to the book's author-ity. If you do any serious research into object-oriented development, you'll run across Booch's name repeatedly.

James Rumbaugh and several of his co-workers at General Electric developed another very important methodology, known as the Object Modeling Technique (OMT), that they describe in their book *Object-Oriented Modeling and Design*. Rumbaugh's name comes up nearly as often as Booch's in object-oriented literature. His recent acceptance of a position at Grady Booch's Rational Software corporation means a consolidation of the two most popular OOA/OOD methods into what many feel will be a default industry standard.

Booch's Object-Oriented Methodology

Booch recommends that you separate the logical and physical design of a system. This has particular relevance in SGML, in which good design means an awareness of the separation between logical structure and entity structure. Entity management is beyond the scope of this chapter, but as you'll see, a promising area for future research.

For object-oriented system development, Booch advocates something known as a spiral approach, in which the four basic steps of analysis and design are repeated at finer levels of abstraction:

1. *Domain analysis,* or the identification of the classes and objects necessary for the system. For an SGML system, this work is already done in the DTD design and creation. For example, the encyclopedia DTD we saw earlier tells us that the classes of objects in the encyclopedia are the encyclopedia itself, chapters, entries, paragraphs, and titles for the chapters and entries. So, Booch's first step is done for us.

   In a complete production system, a document would only be one component. You can think of the SGML document object's role as that of a server, providing information to other objects when they request it.

2. *Identification of the class and object semantics.* Because this part is deliberately left out of an SGML system, this seems to leave a lot of work for the developer. However, by analyzing currently typical SGML applications, you can identify enough semantics to automate the implementation of a useful core group.

3. *Identification of the relationship between the various classes and objects.* This, too, is already done for you in a DTD's explicit specification of the aggregation and ordering of each of a document's parts. The encyclopedia DTD defines a chapter as being made up of a title plus one or more entries, and an entry is a title plus one or more paragraphs.

4. *Implementation of these classes and objects.* This can be automated with a program that reads the DTD, creates classes for the declared document and element types, and implements the semantics identified for step two as the core behavior for these classes. In the section "A Sample Smalltalk SGML System," later in this chapter, you'll see an application that does just that.

So, for a simple enough application, a developer's task has been reduced from four steps to practically nothing. In more complex ones, the developer augments the work of step two and, to implement any newly identified features, the appropriate work on step four.

Rumbaugh's Object-Oriented Methodology

Rumbaugh's OMT approach concentrates on first building a model of the application domain and then working out implementation details during the design.

OMT has four basic stages (some summaries omit the fourth):

1. *Analysis* is the development of three related models of the problem domain: the object model describes the relevant objects; the dynamic model describes the behavior of each object by classifying its role in the various events that may happen within the system and the flow of data between objects; the functional model shows the steps necessary to perform any transformations of object data values.

2. *System design* breaks down a system into subsystems and allocates system resources to those systems.

3. *Object design* is the design of the objects that were identified and had their behavior classified in the first two steps.

4. *Implementation* is the actual coding of the working system. If the first three stages were done well, this is supposed to be a minor, mechanical part of development.

The second stage, system design, corresponds closely to the design of SGML entity structure, because it answers the questions "How do you break down your system into pieces?" and "How will you store these pieces?" Entity management is discussed more at the end of this chapter.

The fourth stage, implementation, corresponds to Booch's fourth stage and can be automated with a similar approach by a program that reads a DTD, creates classes for the declared document and element types, and implements the semantics identified in step one as the core behavior for these classes.

This leaves you with the analysis and object design stages. Here's a closer look at the three models created in the analysis stage:

- *Object Model.* Rumbaugh describes this as capturing "the static structure of a system by showing the objects in the system, relationships between the objects, and the attributes and operations that characterize each class of objects. The object model is the most important of the three models." It's the most important, and, for someone developing an application using SGML data, it's the one that's already done for you by the DTD, except for the specification of behavior, or "operations" that characterize each class of objects.

- *Dynamic Model.* According to Rumbaugh, this specifies "allowable sequences of changes to objects from the object model." How does this relate to SGML? Because the simplest level of useful SGML development takes static documents and manipulates copies to be output, you don't have to worry about changes once each object's values are assigned at creation time.

Dynamic behavior is described with state diagrams—to be honest, most object-oriented methodologies consist of the creation of lots and lots of diagrams—and Rumbaugh writes that you need "only construct state diagrams for object classes with meaningful dynamic behavior. Not all object classes require a state model." So you can forget about it in the single-state model of an SGML document that we're working with.

■ *Functional Model.* The third model specifies the algorithms necessary to transform data values, answering the question, "What do you need to do to the data?" If you view an SGML document as a database, it reduces your work if you heed the following advice from Rumbaugh: "By contrast [to interactive programs], databases often have a trivial functional model, since their purpose is to store and organize data, not to transform it." By "trivial," this means that you want to read data and insert new values, but you're not calculating the shape of a boat hull here—you can create a useful SGML application without worrying about complex mathematical operations.

How much of the work described by Rumbaugh to turn an existing SGML system into an object-oriented application is already done for you, and how much remains? Of the three models, you've seen that the dynamic model is irrelevant for static documents and the functional model is only necessary in highly complex systems. So of these three models, the object model, which identifies the objects and their attributes, relationships, and behavior, is the only one you need to worry about, and the DTD has done all but identify the object behavior. For example, the encyclopedia DTD explicitly described the breakdown of which components comprised each of the different parts of an encyclopedia.

Of the second through fourth stages, the system design stage has already been created in an SGML system's entity structure, the object design is done and stored in the DTD, and the implementation stage is mechanical enough to be automated. The DTD also takes care of much of the object design phase, in which you specify the structure of the individual objects identified in the analysis and the details of the behavior.

To summarize, what remains in the development of an object-oriented SGML application is the same thing that remains when you take the Booch approach; you look at the objects whose structure, relationships, and ordering are already specified for you in the DTD and assign behavior to them, and you'll have a document object that can easily be plugged into a complete object-oriented system.

Defining Object Relationships in an SGML System

We must consider one more key aspect of object-oriented design even though the SGML developer doesn't have to worry about it because, like so much else, a good DTD has already taken care of it. Object relationships must be carefully worked out in an object-oriented system, but the DTD has already done this for a document instance and its component "objects." When dealing with object structure, object-oriented methodologies such as Booch's and Rumbaugh's give you all kinds of object relationship options to consider, but one of these options covers just about everything that an SGML application developer needs to worry about: aggregation.

When you define the logical structure of a document in a DTD, you don't have to consider anything outside of the DTD. You have a document element, the pieces that comprise that document, and the pieces that make up those pieces. For example, the Bible is made up of testaments, which are divided into books, which are divided into chapters, which are divided into verses. A cookbook might be divided into chapters that are divided into recipes, which are divided into a title, optional illustration, optional attribution, introduction, ingredients, instructions, and suggestions for accompanying dishes.

In broader object-oriented development, aggregation is only one object relationship option, because some objects may be outside of other objects. If you're designing a bank simulation, with tellers, lines, and cash registers, none of these objects are parts of each other, and Booch, Rumbaugh, and others offer various categories in which to define the relationships between these objects. These options include the "using" relationship, in which an object of one class requires an object of another in order to perform some task (for example, a road crew worker can't dig a hole through the asphalt until a jackhammer is assigned for the task) and the "association" relationship, which identifies the relationship between objects of two classes, such as a cabdriver and that driver's assigned cab for the day. Other possible relationships, such as inheritance, instantiation, and metaclasses, have more bearing on object-oriented implementation issues than they do on the real world.

The aggregation category is all you need when dealing with SGML documents at the logical level—that is, when planning out the relationship of your document elements. (The SGML equivalent of the physical level, on the other hand, is the entity structure, which is not yet an issue when you're at the application analysis stage.)

Rumbaugh cautions against overuse of aggregation and says "when in doubt, use ordinary association." He includes several tests to consider if you're unsure whether aggregation is appropriate, and the relationship of an SGML document or element to its subelements passes all the tests:

- "Would you use the phrase *part of*?" Yes.
- "Are some operations on the whole automatically applied to its parts?" Yes; if you tell an application to print a book, you clearly mean to print the book's chapters.
- "Are some attribute values propagated from the whole to all or some parts?" Yes; if a legal code section has a status attribute with a value of "proposed" or "revoked," this applies to its subsections.
- "Is there an intrinsic asymmetry to the association, where one object class is subordinate to the other?" Yes; subordinate relationships are clear in hierarchies such as the Bible and cookbook structures described earlier.

Using the DTD To Automate Object-Oriented Development

We saw that the existence of a good DTD means that the majority of object-oriented system analysis and design has already been done and stored in a clearly defined notation that can be easily parsed and used to declare classes in an object-oriented system. The data structures have been defined the way an object-oriented developer needs them; all that's left for a proper object-oriented system is the specification of object behavior—in other words, what the document element objects will actually do.

An object-oriented SGML application can automate this process by:

1. Reading a DTD and declaring a class for each element type. Each class's attributes will be the attributes declared in the DTD for the corresponding element class and any PCDATA stored with that element.

2. After all the classes are declared, you can instantiate members of each class. A program can do this by reading a document instance and creating a new object for each document element that it reads.

In the section "A Sample Smalltalk SGML System," later in this chapter, you'll see a Smalltalk application that performs these two steps.

You'll then have a document object with component objects that fit nicely into a classic object-oriented system.

If good SGML design omits behavioral specification for document elements and object-oriented design requires it, what does a developer do about the behavior of these elements? Analysis of typical SGML systems reveals common services expected of many SGML elements; you can use this collection to define a core set of capabilities as a default starting point in an automated SGML-to-object-oriented application development system.

What services does a developer need from SGML objects?

- The simplest methods (blocks of code defining behavior in response to certain messages, analogous to functions or procedures in more traditional programming languages) would provide the ability to set and read each of an SGML element's attributes.

  At the simplest level, methods that set attribute values need only be invoked at object creation, but they can eventually prove useful for other application features.

- The ability to mix or replace attribute values in the output with arbitrary text. Most SGML development consists of conversion of the data to incorporate some other form of markup—for example, RTF, TeX, markup schemes used by online document viewers, or even a set of tags defined by another DTD—so the ability to freely mix new text with the output is essential. For example, the application should easily turn `<LI>New England` into `{\b 1.} New England\n`.

- The ability to query an object's state and act on the results. For example, the application should easily implement a query such as "output all the chapters that have the word 'prototype' in their summary." Being essentially a database format, an SGML system must allow applications to query various aspects of a document's state in order to enable the creation of different publications by extracting different subsets of information from the same SGML database.

How does an object-oriented system do this with SGML data?

Implementing the first category of methods would be trivial. For each of a given object's defined attributes, an object-oriented system that takes advantage of SGML data must also define a method to set that attribute's values and return that attribute's value when queried. To return the text contents of an element, the latter method must be recursive because many of a document's elements are made up of composite elements.

For mixing new text with object content in output, a convenient approach is one taken by the languages perl (a popular one among SGML developers), awk, and C: format strings. If specified symbols represent the contents of each of an element's attributes, they can be combined into a string that has other characters to be output at those positions relative to the attribute values. For example, if <> represents an element's text and <NAME> represents the value of its NAME attribute, then the string {\b <NAME>}: {\i <>} would format the element's output with the RTF codes necessary to print the NAME value, bolded, followed by a colon, a space, and the element's text in italics.

This string could be passed as a parameter to the object when requesting its contents, but the aggregate nature of the documents means that asking for a formatted version of a given element is also asking for all of its subelements, so it makes more sense to store a format string as a class variable (a single variable that can be referenced by all the objects of a particular class) for each element type. This way, you can specify all of the format strings before asking for the formatted aggregate version.

The third category of behavioral methods is the broadest. It's also the one on which developers moving beyond an automated SGML-to-object-oriented system will exert the most effort. Still, a core group of features can be observed in current typical systems and added as part of the automated system to provide much value to developers who take no trouble to extend this category.

The following shows several methods that would be useful in an SGML element to return information about that object. They're not based on any scientific study, but upon the kinds of values that I need to know about SGML elements in my day-to-day development of text conversion programs. I deliberately didn't mention any syntax for using these methods because this is still the design stage; we're making up for the object-oriented design steps not done for you by a DTD. Syntax is an implementation issue, and depends on what language you use to eventually implement an application.

VIII

Electronic Publishing

Method	Description
HasSubstring	A Boolean method that indicates whether the string passed as an argument is part of the object's content. A typical use would be an application that pulls out sections of a reference work with a given string in the section's title in order to create a more specialized document.
DocClass	A method returning the class of the root element in a document tree— that is, the class of document where the element resides. An application processing a chapter object could then treat it differently depending on whether it is a part of a software user's manual or a cookbook.
ClassOfParent	A method returning the class of an element's parent. A list item whose parent is another list item would be part of an embedded list, and require formatting different from a list item whose parent is a chapter or section.
IsFirst	A Boolean method that indicates whether a document element is the first of its kind sequentially—in other words, whether the sibling preceding it is an object of the same class. This is useful for formatting programs that want to, for example, put more space before the first item of a list than before the other items.

You could think of these as functions, but think of them as methods. You're not telling the application to return some value related to an object's state; you're executing a method defined as part of that object's capabilities, in which you ask that object to tell you some value related to that object's state.

Some of these methods are relevant to all SGML element objects, and some are not. For example, the last two; the root of a document tree has no parent or predecessors, so `ClassOfParent` and `IsFirst` are irrelevant to a document element.

These kinds of similarities and differences among element objects give you clues as to the classes you will need and, as Booch calls it, the "class structure," or hierarchical relationship created by the inheritance patterns of the different classes.

Inheritance? Didn't I say that you don't have to understand inheritance to understand the basics of objects? Well, you don't, but now it will be easier to see how it speeds application development.

When multiple classes have various methods or attributes in common, it would mean redundant work to specify the same things over and over for different classes. This is where the inheritance comes in; it allows you to define attributes and behavior for one class, and then to define another by saying, "this new one will have the same attributes and behavior as that one, but with these changes." Typically, this means defining a base class with all the attributes and behavior that the other classes have in common, and then basing the other ones on (or, in object-oriented technology, *deriving* from) that one. Figure 31.1 shows a diagram of the following classes, which would be used at the top of an SGML class hierarchy.

■ *SGMLObject.* It's often difficult to determine which classes have what in common and the most efficient inheritance structure, but for a system representing documents, it's not that bad. First, you define an *abstract class* (a class designed purely to provide a basis for descendant classes without itself ever having instantiations) called SGMLObject, from which you can derive all the other classes. This also makes it easier to add new methods that can be used by all the element classes, because you only need to add these methods to the SGMLObject class.

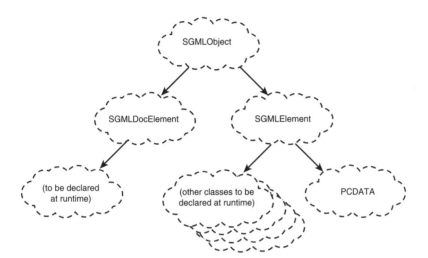

Fig. 31.1

Class structure of an SGML system (Booch-style diagram).

■ *SGMLDocElement, SGMLElement.* The root node of a document tree can have attributes (for example, the DTD) that its subelements do not, and the document's component objects can have attributes that the document object does not (for example, a parent attribute), so we derive two more classes from SGMLObject called SGMLDocElement and SGMLElement. Now, you can add new methods and attributes to all component objects without affecting the document object, and vice versa.

SGMLDocElement and SGMLElement are also abstract classes; you're not going to instantiate any objects to them. They only exist so that you can derive new classes from them. But why? Why not make each element that you read in from a document instance an object of one of these two classes, instead of deriving new classes based on the DTD declarations and making the elements objects of those new classes?

The answer highlights a principle advantage of using an SGML DTD for creating an object-oriented system: by treating SGML elements from different element types as members of different classes, you can assign specialized attributes and behavior to each element type. A DTD may have separate attributes defined for each element type, and you can use these element definitions to create attributes for the SGML element objects. This creates specialized classes for each SGML element, which is part of the point of inheritance—by allowing you to specify an ancestor and new attributes to set a class apart from its ancestor, you can easily re-use the code originally defined for the ancestor.

■ *PCDATA.* We also define one more descendant of this hierarchy: PCDATA, descended from the SGMLElement class. This is a *concrete* (that is, non-abstract) *class*; it will have instances. The instances of PCDATA, or *parsed character data*, make up the majority of the leaf nodes in a document tree. Internal nodes of the tree contain other nodes, but the leaves generally contain the character data that comprise a document. (I say "generally" because it doesn't have to; they may contain references to other entities as well, such as picture, sound, or video files, or PCDATA's cousins, CDATA and RCDATA.)

> **Caution**
>
> Don't confuse inheritance structure with object structure. Object structure defines an object's components and their ordering; inheritance structure is a convenient feature to reduce the developer's workload.

A Sample Smalltalk SGML System

Let's look at a Smalltalk program that I wrote to test all these ideas. The STSGML (for "Smalltalk SGML") application demonstrates how an SGML document instance, set up to be treated like other Smalltalk objects, can be plugged in and used in an object-oriented system. It reads a DTD, defines new classes for each element declaration, and then reads a document instance and instantiates its elements to the classes declared using the document's DTD.

This turns a DTD and document instance into an object-oriented system that allows the program's user to perform some simple, useful work—for example, conversion to TeX or RTF. It also proves that someone who didn't even know Smalltalk when he started thinking about the connections between SGML and object-oriented development can put all this theory into practice.

Why Smalltalk? There are two reasons:

■ We want our program to declare new classes at runtime. Being an interpreted object-oriented language, Smalltalk lets an application create and instantiate new classes each time the program is run. With a compiled object-oriented language such as C++, all classes must be declared before you compile and distribute your application, which contradicts the whole point of treating arbitrary SGML document instances with a pure object-oriented approach: you want to create a finished system that looks at a DTD and declares new classes based on the element types declared in that DTD.

■ Smalltalk is very object-oriented. I have heard of C++ programmers who learned Smalltalk and returned to C++ as better C++ programmers; Smalltalk treats *everything* as objects—even classes themselves. This forces you to model absolutely everything in terms of objects communicating via messages. In order to examine the potentially intrinsic object-oriented properties of SGML, I used Smalltalk because it forced me to think in object-oriented terms as much as possible. I didn't really know any Smalltalk when I started this, and thought it would be a good reason to learn.

STSGML has three key object classes that demonstrate the use of an SGML document and its components:

- An *SGMLObject* class is the base class from which you derive all document and document component elements, as you saw in figure 31.1.

- An object of the *STSGML* class is the engine that does all the work I've discussed. It reads a DTD, declares the element classes and their methods, and then reads in parsed SGML data, instantiating its elements to the appropriate declared classes. In a non-object-oriented application, this would be the program that you write that manipulates data. In an object-oriented application, where everything is an object with attributes and defined behavior, this too is an object for which you must define a class and then declare an instance in order to perform these functions.

- An object of the *STSGMLWindow* class provides a menu-driven interface to the use of the STSGML engine, allowing the user to save a document object in a plain text file or a formatted file, with sample formatting scripts provided to turn data conforming to two widely-used DTDs into RTF and TeX files. Any graphical user interface version of Smalltalk provides a way to take advantage of the Windows classes provided by Microsoft Windows, X Window, Macintosh interface windows, or whatever you use. My STSGMLWindow was a subclass of one of the basic Microsoft Windows classes, and I added behavior to it in the form of a menu and methods to be invoked by messages from other objects.

STSGML reads a document DTD for information about an SGML document's structure, but instead of reading the document instance directly, it passes the document data to SGMLS, a freely available validating SGML parser, and reads the SGMLS output. This frees STSGML to concentrate on manipulating a document's structure instead of worrying about whether the document conforms to the structure defined for it.

STSGML included several sample SGML files with which it was tested: several World Wide Web HTML files, the first book of John Milton's "Paradise Lost," and the first two chapters of Mark Twain's *Tom Sawyer*. The latter two used data from the Text Encoding Initiative, a project spread across several universities in the United States and Britain to create guidelines for the standard encoding of documents in the humanities. This work has resulted in a great deal of classic literature now being made publicly available in SGML format. Theoretically, the STSGML program could accept arbitrary DTDs, but I haven't tested it enough to stake my life on such a claim, because it may not handle every possible variation on how a DTD might declare an element or attribute.

I used Digitalk's Smalltalk/V Win32 2.0 because it was the most affordable Smalltalk system available in a windowing environment at the time. I also chose it because it could supposedly make stand-alone, executable Windows applications. Digitalk does this by letting you distribute your application with the subset of their classes that they judged to be necessary to run your application. They don't want your application's end-users designing their own applications with the subset that you give them, so the subset won't let you declare new classes. Unfortunately, the whole point of STSGML is to declare new classes (classes corresponding to a DTD's element declarations) at runtime, so STSGML doesn't work as a distributable stand-alone application.

To start it, execute the command that tells Smalltalk to create a new instance of the STSGMLWindow class and to open up that window:

```
(STSGMLWindow new) open
```

Smalltalk opens up the window, which has the pull-down menus specified in its class definition (see fig. 31.2).

Fig. 31.2

STSGML main window.

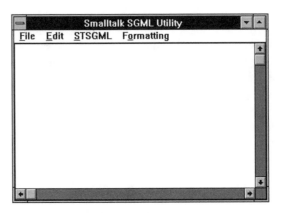

The File and Edit menus are standard, but the STSGML and Formatting menus were added in STSGMLWindow's class definition to provide the user with a way to tell the STSGML engine object what to do.

The STSGML menu (see fig. 31.3) makes it possible to read a document into a Smalltalk object and to output that object as either plain text, without tags, or mixed in with formatting tags specified using the Formatting menu.

If you select Read DTD and Document Instance, STSGML uses the standard Windows file selection dialog boxes to find out the names of the files where the DTD and document instance are stored. It then reads in the DTD, declaring a new Smalltalk class for each element type declared in the DTD using the following syntax:

```
newClass := SGMLDocElement subclass: (docElementName asSymbol)
instanceVariableNames: attributesString
        classVariableNames: ''          poolDictionaries: ''.
```

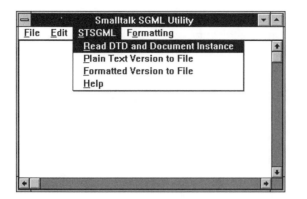

VIII

Electronic Publishing

Fig. 31.3

Choices on STSGML program's STSGML menu.

This is Smalltalk syntax. Other languages will have their own syntax to create a new class, but any object-oriented language will need the same information: the name of the new class (stored here in the variable docElementName), the existing class from which we're deriving the new class (in this case, we're deriving it from SGMLDocElement, the abstract class we saw in the Booch-style diagram), and the attribute values, or in Smalltalk vocabulary, the "instance variable names" that identify the particular pieces of information that we're keeping track of for this class. For the HTML A element that identifies the beginning and end of links, these would include the HREF and ID values—in other words, its attributes as declared in the DTD. (classVariableNames and poolDictionaries offer further options in new class creation, but they are being passed empty strings as parameters in the earlier example because they are not used here.)

As STSGML reads in the DTD and defines a new class for each of its element declarations, it displays its progress to the end user with the following two progress indicators shown in figures 31.4 and 31.5.

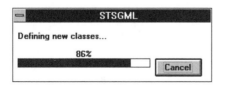

Fig. 31.4

STSGML reading in a DTD.

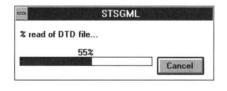

Fig. 31.5

STSGML defining new classes.

Once the new classes are defined, STSGML is ready to create objects of these new classes, and it reads in the specified document. It actually passes the document to the SGMLS parser, which checks for errors and stores the document in a format known as ESIS, which identifies element structure with nested parentheses. STSGML reads in the ESIS file and, for each document element it finds, declares a new object of that type using syntax similar to that shown above to declare a new object of the STSGMLWindow class. If the parentheses of the ESIS file show that one element is inside another, the outer one is defined as having the inner one as one of its components. For example, a chapter element within a book is identified as one of the parts making up that book element.

Once the new document object is defined with all of its component objects, it's sitting in memory waiting to be manipulated like any other Smalltalk object. The Plain Text Version to File and Formatted Version to File menu choices make it possible to save this document object as either a simple text file with no tags or as a file that has formatting codes (defined using the Format menu) embedded within it. The Format menu lets you define and edit format strings for each element on the fly as well as giving you the opportunity to read in a file of format strings; sample files make it possible to save TEI and HTML documents in RTF. Once the document exists as a Smalltalk object, this conversion to some other arbitrary format is possible with less than a page and a half of code, because Smalltalk makes manipulation of its objects so easy.

Object-Oriented Technology and the Future of SGML Development

To make things simpler for discussion, this chapter has been limited to object-oriented systems that process static SGML documents so that you didn't have to worry about state transitions and other issues raised by multi-user editing. Also, this chapter never mentioned a serious limitation of the STSGML program: its inability to use documents that can't fit into memory all at once. A serious SGML application should handle gigabytes of data.

What can current developments in object-oriented systems offer to these problems, and what other benefits might they provide?

Concurrency

Once you add the most basic features to an SGML system to make an object-oriented system, other properties of an object-oriented system can be added as needed. Candidates for these additional attributes are the kind of thing that separate one object-oriented methodology from another. For example, Booch describes a possible concurrency attribute for classes that allows simultaneous multi-user editing. Since many large SGML systems involve simultaneous authoring and editing by multiple users, features to allow proper concurrent use of data would clearly be useful.

SGML and Object-Oriented Databases

The way object-oriented developers describe it, you turn an object-oriented system into an object-oriented database by adding one feature, or rather, one attribute: persistence. Persistence makes it possible for created objects to exist after you've stopped using the program, so that they're available for you when you start up the program again.

This is another potential class property that would play an obvious role in an object-oriented SGML system, because documents and their elements clearly persist beyond the execution of the programs that create them. A lot of people use relational database managers as the engine behind SGML databases, but this isn't a very good fit. They're only doing it because of the current maturity of relational database management software compared with the current state of OODBMS software.

Several aspects of SGML make it hard to squeeze a typical document into tables:

- The variable size of text elements
- The sharing of subelements
- The frequent need to traverse hierarchical relationships
- The increasing use of SGML in multimedia applications

These make object-oriented database management systems a much better fit to SGML than relational systems.

The better fit of OODBMS systems to SGML, along with the lack of existing implementations, indicates an area with a lot of potential work to be done. An obvious extension of the STSGML system would be the use of a tool such as Gemstone or Versant to implement persistence with STSGML's Smalltalk objects.

SGML Entity Management

Section 4.123 of the ISO 8879 SGML standard defines an entity manager as "a program (or portion of a program or a combination of programs), such as a file system or symbol table, that can maintain and provide access to multiple entities."

Essentially, its job is to map logical references to entity references, so that an application dealing with a document in terms of its logical structure can still manipulate actual document instances. Goldfarb takes great pains to distinguish between the abstract, or logical structure of a document, and its entity structure, or the organization of its resource storage. He did this to maintain the system independence of logical document structure specification. (For example, a single document might be made of multiple files, and multiple documents can be stored in a single file, but this should be irrelevant to the DTD's specification of the document's logical structure—especially when you consider operating systems that don't store information in "files," such as MVS or OS/400.) The issue of entity management is, therefore, outside of a discussion of the use of a document's logical structure to automate the creation of an object-oriented system, yet still lurking close by.

A good place to start research on an object-oriented approach towards the organization of system resources would be the field of operating systems, where object-oriented technology has already played a role in the development of NextStep, OS/400, and other commercially available operating systems.

Entity managers are currently not that common because so many documents have an entity structure simple enough to require very little management. As more organizations use SGML for applications, such as multimedia that require more complicated entity structures, the need for powerful entity managers will increase, and it promises to be a growing area of SGML software.

The Future of SGML Application Developers

Whether using an object-oriented approach or not, it's exciting to think of the tremendous possibilities of SGML application development in the future. The vast majority of work in SGML up to this point has been the development of the most efficient possible data structures for terabytes of text and other data, and now you have all this data sitting in these efficient data structures waiting to be manipulated. Meanwhile, the possibilities of publishing with new kinds of media and interfaces continually expand.

You can complain about the lack of tools to manipulate them, or you can start creating these tools and manipulating that data. Much of the object-oriented philosophy, when put into practice, has resulted in tools that make tool development easier. Eventually, someone will come out with a self-contained, graphical user interface object-oriented database equivalent to something like Microsoft's Access or FoxPro or Borland's Paradox or dBase. An interface allowing such a product to read native SGML files will mean amazing opportunities for SGML application development. Developing this interface would mean working out and automating all the things that are discussed in this chapter. I've heard of people who are doing it, but in a very proprietary, in-house manner. I don't know when someone's going to do a more open systems, publicly available version, but it makes too much sense not to. When it happens, it's going to be great.

From Here...

This chapter demonstrated how the many concepts and key terms common to SGML and object-oriented development can help a developer take advantage of object-oriented technology when creating applications that use SGML data. This lets you take advantage of the many benefits that the object-oriented approach offers, such as faster development time and less worry about low-level technical details. As an example, the chapter described the creation and use of STSGML, a sample program for turning an SGML document into a Smalltalk object that could easily be output as plain text, RTF, or other formatted versions.

For more information, refer to the following:

- Part II, "Document Analysis," further describes the issues involved in document analysis.
- Chapter 28, "Other Tools and Environments," has more information about the SGMLS parser and its updated version, NSGMLS.
- Chapter 30, "Understanding the Information Revolution: The New Paradigm," gives further background on the Text Encoding Initiative.
- Appendix B, "Finding Sources for SGML Know-How," lists books where you can find out more about object-oriented technology.

VIII

Electronic Publishing

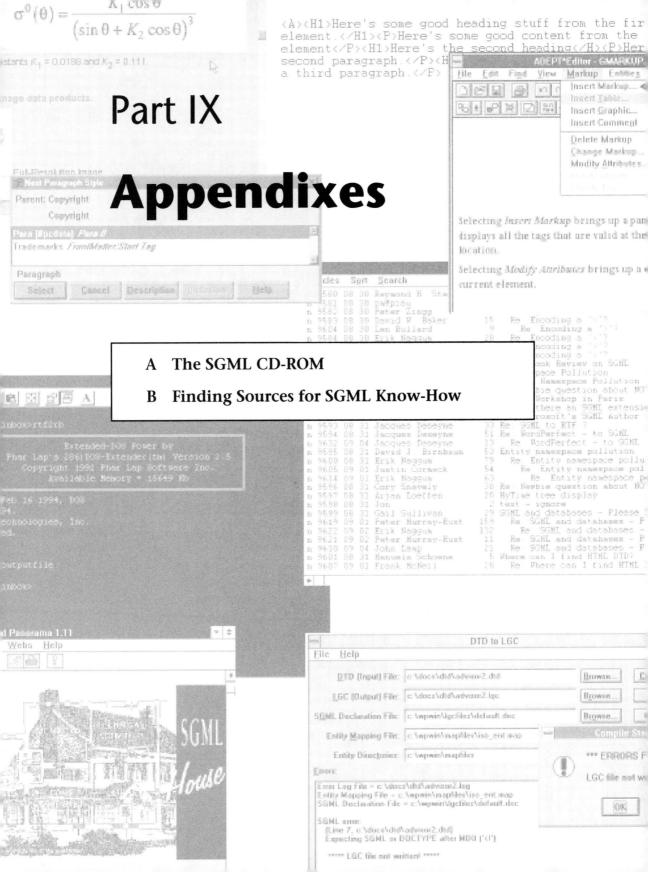

Part IX

Appendixes

A The SGML CD-ROM

B Finding Sources for SGML Know-How

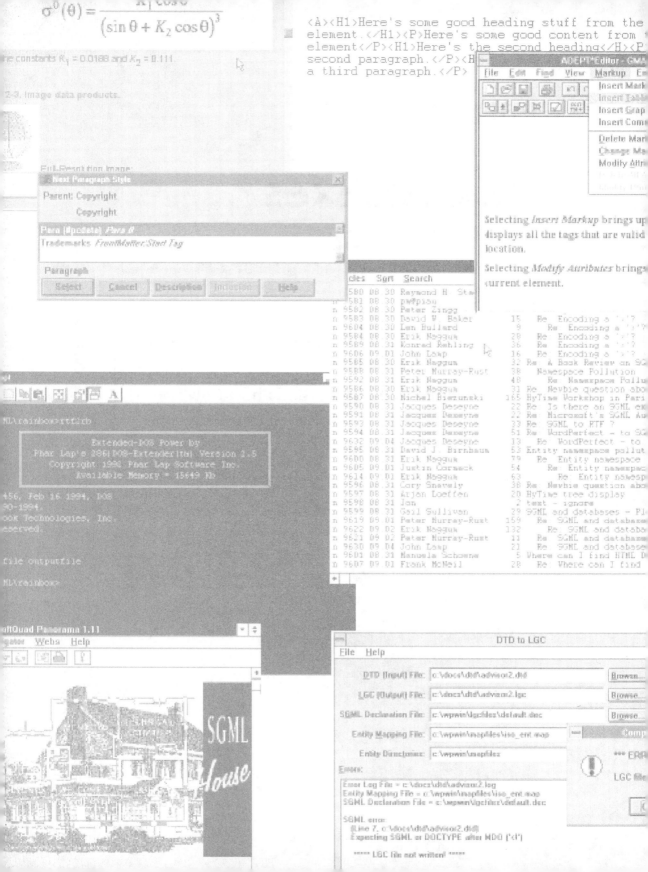

The SGML CD-ROM

As you read through this book, there have been numerous discussions on the availability of SGML tools. The last couple of years have witnessed the emergence of a number of exciting new tools in the SGML world. Some of the "tried-and-true" tools continue to evolve, adding more capabilities and "ease-of-use" features that enhance their value as well.

The tools included on the SGML CD-ROM span a variety of functions, from tools to aid in SGML authoring and data conversion, to DTD visualization and SGML document display.

Most of these tools are publicly available from various sources on the Internet. In general, these tools are made available to the public and subject to certain restrictions by their creators.

Note

Several of the authors and companies that provided software for the SGML CD-ROM have a notice of their copyright, shareware agreement, or license information included in their software files. The lack of such a statement printed in this book does not mean that the software is not copyrighted or does not have a license agreement. Please see the text or help files for any program for which you need copyright or licensing information. If this is not available or the terms are unclear, you should contact the software provider directly for information on their licensing arrangements.

Using the SGML CD

The CD can be browsed using any Web browser. Simply load the loadme.htm file from the root directory of the CD. If you don't have a Web browser, you'll find Microsoft's Internet Explorer in the MSIE 20 directory. You'll find a self-extracting file that will install the browser for you. If you wish, you can transfer the files using any file utility program. WINZIP is also on the disc to facilitate decompression of the "zipped" and "tarred" files.

Computer Platforms

The bulk of the software included on the CD-ROM is compatible with personal computers running Microsoft Windows (3.1 or higher). Because many SGML sites also use other computing platforms as well (particularly UNIX-based computers), an attempt has been made to include versions of the software that can be run on other machines as well.

When included, the software for other computer platforms has been stored on the CD-ROM in a compressed format to accommodate the filename length restrictions of MS-DOS and Microsoft Windows 3.1. (In some cases, the compressed version of a software distribution has been included along with the uncompressed version to facilitate data transfer between computers.)

File compression formats used include the ZIP format for PC-based applications and either the GZIP (or GNU compression) or the UNIX Compress format. GZIP compressed files can be identified by their .gz file extension and UNIX Compress files can be identified by a .z extension. Some files may also use the "tar" format in addition to the compression.

> **Note**
>
> If you use Windows 95, you can decompress your files using WinZip 6.0, included on the CD-ROM. This decompression software is located in the \winzip directory. For UNIX users, the UNIX Compress software is proprietary and should be available with your UNIX operating system.
>
> For other platforms, you can obtain the appropriate decompression software from publicly available archives on the Internet. Stroud's CWSApps List, at **http://cwsapps.texas.net/**, is a good place to start to find other software.

> **Tip**
>
> When using PKUNZIP decompression software, you should use the "-d" restore with subdirectories option.

What's Included on the CD-ROM

The software on the CD-ROM includes a number of tools that are useful in the SGML production process:

- SP/NSGMLS tools, including the NSGMLS parser and SPAM normalizer
- Perl, a text manipulation language
- perlSGML, a set of SGML and DTD development tools

- Near & Far Lite, a DTD visualization program
- DynaText, an electronic SGML book browser/reader
- Panorama, a World Wide Web SGML book browser

SP/NSGMLS Tools

SP consists of the NSGMLS parser and SPAM, an SGML normalizer. The programs both use dos4gw.exe, a royalty-free DOS/4GW 32-bit DOS extender that's provided with Watcom C++.

> *Name:* SP/NSGMLS
>
> *Category:* SGML Parser and Tools
>
> *Version:* 1.0.1
>
> *Platform(s):* MS-DOS, Solaris 2.3
>
> *Notes:* Source code included
>
> *Supplier:* James Clark
>
> *Contact:* **jjc@jclark.com**

Software Contents

The following table lists the contents of the SP software distribution.

Files	Version	Description
Programs		
nsgmls.exe	1.0.1	SGML parser
spam.exe	1.0.1	Lists changes in DTD
Libraries		
dos4gw.exe	1.97	DOS/4GW 32-bit DOS extender

An executable version for the Solaris operating system (version 2.3) and the source code (in the gz/tar format) are also included.

Installation

Refer to the readme.txt file in the docs subdirectory for information on installing SP.

Perl

The Perl language provides the capability to easily manipulate text and files. Originally available on UNIX machines, it has been converted to run on a wide variety of computer platforms.

Name: Perl

Category: Computer Language

Description: Text, file, and process manipulation language

Version: Perl 4

Platform(s): MS-DOS, MS Windows

Notes: Source code included (and other platform porting notes)

Supplier: Larry Wall, et al

Contact: University of Florida Perl Archives at
        http://www.cis.ufl.edu/perl/

Software Contents

The following table lists the contents of the Perl software.

Files	Version	Description
Programs		
perl.exe	4.036	Perl program
perlglob.exe	4.036	Perl glob program
wemu387.386	4.036	Coprocessor support
Libraries		
(numerous)	4.036	Various Perl support routines

Installation

Refer to the readme.dos and readme files for installation instructions.

perlSGML

perlSGML is a collection of Perl programs and libraries for processing SGML documents. These include programs for generating a content hierarchy (or structure) tree of SGML documents, an SGML DTD documentation/navigation tree, and a utility to remove SGML markup from documents. Also included are a number of Perl libraries to perform SGML-related functions.

Name: perlSGML

Category: SGML Tools

Description: A collection of SGML processing tools written in Perl

Version: 1995Dec08

Platform(s): Multiple (Must have Perl installed)

Notes: Runs under Perl 4 and 5

Supplier: Earl Hood

Contact: **ehood@convex.com**
       http://www.oac.uci.edu/indiv/ehood/perlSGML.html

Software Contents

The following table lists the contents of the perlSGML software distribution.

Files	Version	Description
Programs		
dtd2html	1.4.0	SGML DTD documentation/navigation tool
dtddiff	1.1.0	Lists changes in DTD
dtdtree	1.2.0	Generates hierarchy tree of SGML elements
stripsgml	0.1.1	Removes SGML markup from documents
Libraries		
dtd.pl	2.2.0	Perl library to parse SGML DTDs
sgml.pl	0.1.0	Perl library to parse SGML instances

Installation

Installation of perlSGML requires that you have Perl installed on your computer. After installation, refer to the readme.1st file for installation instructions.

The subdirectory compress in the perlsgml directory contains compressed collections of perlSGML in ZIP and gz formats.

> **Note**
>
> The documentation and Perl source files in perlSGML conform to the MS-DOS filename limitations (eight characters for the name and three characters for the extension). However, the example/sample files do not fit into the naming restrictions. Therefore, if your computer is not subject to these limitations, it is recommended that you use one of the compressed collections of perlSGML that is also included.

Near & Far Lite

Near & Far Lite is a demonstration version of the Near & Far program covered in Chapter 26, "Tools for the PC: Authoring, Viewing, and Utilities." It is similar in operation to Near & Far in its graphic visualization of DTDs, but it does not have the DTD creation and modification or reporting features of its commercial counterpart.

IX

Appendixes

Name: Near & Far Lite

Category: DTD Visualization Tool

Description: Provides visual diagram/representation of DTD

Version: 1.30

Platform(s): MS Windows (version 3.1+)

Notes: Source code included (and other platform porting notes)

Supplier: Microstar Software Ltd.

Contact: **http://www.microstar.com/**

Software Contents

The following table lists the contents of the Near & Far Lite software.

Files	Version	Description
Programs		
nflite.exe	1.30	Near & Far Lite program
clipwin.exe	1.30	Near & Far Lite support program
Libraries		
(numerous)	1.30	Various support files

Installation

From Windows Program Manager, run the setup.exe program in the nf-lite program directory.

Other Files

A demonstration version of Near & Far—showing the design features available with the full program—is also included on the CD-ROM.

DynaText

DynaText is a document viewer for SGML documents. It differs from Panorama in that documents must be compiled/indexed in order to view them. The compilation process results in higher performance when viewing large document sets.

> **Note**
>
> The next release of DynaText, currently in beta test, will support the viewing of uncompiled SGML documents.

Name: DynaText

Category: SGML Document Viewer/Browser

Description: Compiled SGML Document Viewer

Version: 2.3

Platform(s): MS Windows (version 3.1+)

Notes: Includes CIA World Fact Book in SGML

Supplier: Electronic Book Technologies

Contact: **http://www.ebt.com/**

Software Contents

The following table lists the contents of the DynaText browser software.

Files	Version	Description
Programs		
dtextrw.exe	2.3	DynaText browser program
dynatext.ini	2.3	DynaText ini (parameter) file
dtext.dll	2.3	DynaText dll support
Libraries		
dtext.dll	2.3	DynaText dll support library
(various)	2.3	Various support files

Installation

See the install.txt file in the EBT directory on the CD-ROM for installation instructions.

Other Files

Included with the EBT/DynaText software is a copy of the CIA World Fact Book in both compiled format and SGML. Also included are various files related to the Rainbow DTD.

Panorama Free

Panorama Free is the demonstration version of Panorama Pro covered in Chapter 26, "Tools for the PC: Authoring, Viewing, and Utilities." It differs from Panorama Pro in several significant respects:

- Panorama Free is restricted to viewing documents across the World Wide Web (compared to the local and Web capabilities of Panorama Pro)

■ Panorama Free does not include stylesheet creation and editing capabilities (Panorama Pro provides such capabilities)

Name: Panorama Free

Category: SGML Document Viewer/Browser

Description: Views SGML documents across the World Wide Web

Version: 1.11

Platform(s): MS Windows

Notes: Works in conjunction with a Web browser

Supplier: SoftQuad Inc.

Contact: **http://www.sq.com/**

Software Contents

The Panorama software is supplied in compressed format. When installed, it will include the following components:

Files	Version	Description
Programs		
panorama.exe	1.11	Panorama World Wide Web SGML browser program
Libraries		
(various)	1.11	Various support files

Installation

While in Microsoft Windows, start your Web browser program. Then run the program setup.exe from Program Manager or File Manager.

Finding Sources for SGML Know-How

Often, you'll run into some SGML task that is beyond your current abilities. At times like these, you need help. This appendix lists some resources that can answer your questions.

This appendix tells you:

- What books can help you
- What periodicals you can subscribe to that might help
- What groups meet regularly that you could join
- What Internet resources are available

Books on SGML

You'll be happy to learn that the SGML book market is becoming bigger and better. It wasn't long ago when you couldn't ask someone in a bookstore what HTML was, and now everyone knows. And they're learning about SGML, so the bookshelves are collecting more help from which to choose. Here's a list of books that you should consider:

- *ABCD...SGML: A User's Guide to Structured Information,* by Liora Alschuler.
- *A HyTime Application Development Guide*, by Ralph Ferris of Fujitsu Open System Solution, Inc. Freely available by anonymous FTP at **ftp.techno.com/pub/ HyTime/application_development_guide.**
- *Making Hypermedia Work*, by Steven J. DeRose and David Durand. Published by Kluwer Academic Publishers.
- *Object-Oriented Analysis and Design with Applications*, by Grady Booch. Redwood City, California: Benjamin/Cummings Publishing Co.
- *Object-Oriented Modeling and Design*, by James Rumbaugh and Michael Blaha, William Premerlani, Frederick Eddy, and William Lorensen. Englewood Cliffs, N.J.: Prentice Hall.

- *Practical Hypermedia,* by Eliot Kimber; edited by Dr. Charles F. Goldfarb. Published by Simon & Schuster.
- *Practical SGML,* by Eric van Herwijnen.
- *SGML: An Author's Guide to the Standard Generalized Markup Language,* by Mark Bryan.
- *The SGML Handbook: The Annotated Full Text of ISO 8879—Standard Generalized Markup Language,* by Dr. Charles F. Goldfarb.
- *The SGML Implementation Guide: A Blueprint for SGML Migration,* by Brian E. Travis and Dale C. Waldt.
- *The SGML Primer,* by SoftQuad Inc.
- *SGML Source Guide,* compiled by the Graphics Communications Association (GCA).
- *Standard Generalized Markup Language,* available through American National Standards Institute (ANSI) at 11 West 42nd Street, New York, NY 10036, (212) 642-4900.

While this is not a comprehensive list of books, these additions to your library will answer nearly any questions you might have. There are also many private sources for SGML publications. Robin Cover keeps a list of references and abstracts for over 1000 books that are updated regularly at the following Web page:

http://www.sil.org/sgml/biblio.html

SGML Periodicals

Periodicals on the subject of SGML have been notoriously academic and scholastic. But they still contain information that will help you through rough spots in your development. Here's a list of periodicals:

The Seybold Report on Publishing Systems
Seybold Publications, Inc.
428 East Baltimore Ave.
Media, PA 19063
USA

Telephone: (800) 325-3830 or (610) 565-6864
E-mail: **sedwards@sbexpos.com**

The SGML User's Group Newsletter
Database Publishing Systems, Ltd.
608 Delta Business Park, Great Western Way
Swindon Wiltshire SN5 7XF
UNITED KINGDOM

Telephone: +441 793 512 515
Fax: +44 793 512 516
E-mail: **kp@dpsl.co.uk**

<TAG>: The SGML Newsletter
Published by SGML Associates, INC.
6360 S. Gibraltar Circle
Aurora, CO 80016-1212
USA

Telephone: (303) 680-0875
Fax: (303) 680-4906
E-mail address: **tag@sgml.com**

Tip

Sometimes periodicals about SGML come and go, so you might keep an eye out on the Internet newsgroup **comp.txt.sgml**.

SGML User Groups

There are probably still more user groups for the Commodore C-64 personal computer than there are SGML user groups, but most likely that will change over time. These are the most widely known large user groups:

Electronic Publishing Special Interest Group (EPSIG)
EPSIG Membership Office
100 Daingerfield Rd., 4th floor
Alexandria, VA 22314-2888
USA

Telephone: (703) 519-8184
E-mail: **epsig@aol.com**

Graphic Communications Association (GCA)
(Printing Industries of America)
Graphic Communications Association
Attention: Marion Elledge (Director, Information Technologies)
100 Daingerfield Road, 4th Floor
Alexandria, VA 22314-2888
USA

Telephone: (703) 519-8160
E-mail: **sgml95@aol.com**

IX

Appendixes

International SGML Users' Group (SGMLUG)
SGML Users' Group,
Database Publishing Systems, Ltd.
608 Delta Business Park, Great Western Way
Swindon, Wiltshire SN5 7XF
UNITED KINGDOM

Telephone: +441 793 512 515
Fax: +44 793 512 516
E-mail: **kp@dpsl.co.uk**

SGML Hypertext and Multimedia SIG (SIGhyper)
Erik Naggum, Chairman
Naggum Software
Irisveien 12
POB 1570 Vika
0118 Oslo
NORWAY

Telephone: +47 2295 0313
Fax: +47 2216 2350
E-mail: **erik@naggum.no**
FTP: **ftp.ifi.vio.no/pub/sgml/SIGhyper**

SGML Open
SGML Open Headquarters
910 Beaver Grade Road, #3008
Coraopolis, PA 15108
USA

Telephone: (412) 264-4258
Internet: **laplante@sgmlopen.org**
(or) **sgmlopen@prep.net**

The SGML Project
c/o Univ. of Exeter IT Services, Laver Building
North Park Road, Exeter EX4 4QE
UNITED KINGDOM

Telephone: +441 0392-263-946
E-mail: **sgml@exeter.ac.uk**

These sources will certainly point you in the right direction for finding a user group that meets your needs. You might also check the local newspaper and computer magazines for user group advertisements.

Internet Resources

One nice benefit to using the Internet is that all the varied types of resources you have to deal with are connected in some way. If one Gopher site doesn't work out for you, then maybe it will at least point you to UseNet or FTP site.

New SGML resources appear on the Internet rather frequently, so this is by no means a complete list. These resources fall into four main categories:

- Internet mailing lists
- Internet newsgroups
- FTP archives
- Internet Web pages

Internet Mailing Lists

Mailing lists are mostly automated nowadays, so when you include a key phrase as indicated below, the mail server automatically strips out your e-mail address and adds it to the mailing list. Except for technical or network problems, you should receive an automated reply back within a day or two after subscribing to a LISTSERV. When in doubt whether to put the quoted key phrase in the body of the e-mail or in the subject line, put it in both locations. (Don't include quotation marks.) If you make a mistake, the listserver will usually notify you of the error and request you to resubscribe.

> SGML-AUSTIN
> Mail: "info sgml-austin" to **majordomo@hal.com**
>
> SGML-L: SGML-L mailing list
> Mail: "review SGML-L" to **listserv@vm.urz.uni-heidelberg.de**
>
> TEI-L: TEI-L mailing list
> Mail: "subscribe tei-l" in body of e-mail to **listserv@uicvm.uic.edu**
>
> SGMLBELU: Belgian-Luxembourgian SGML Users Group Reading List
> Mail: "review SGMLBELU" to **listserv@cc1.kuleuven.ac.be**
>
> The NEWSWIRE: An SGML Mailing List sponsored by Avalanche
> E-mail to: **sgmlinfo@avalanche.com** with a message requesting subscription
>
> DSSSL LITE: Discussion group on creating subset of DSSSL
> Mail "subscribe dsssl-lite *YOUR-USERID@YOUR-EMAIL-ADDRESS*" to
> **dsssl-lite@falch.no**
>
> COMP-STD-SGML: Erik Naggum's discussion list for SGML esoterica
> Mail: **comp-std-sgml-request@naggum.no** with the word "subscribe" somewhere in the message

SGML-INTERNET: EBT's mailing list for SGML Open
Mail: "subscribe sgml-internet *yourID@site.domain*" in body of e-mail to
sgml-internet-owner@ebt.com

RAINBOW: Rainbow Mailing List
For subscription information, send e-mail to: **rainbow@ebt.com**

SGMLBLGA: SGML Belux Users Group General Assembly Mail
Mail "review SGMLBLGA" to: **listserv@cc1.kuleuven.ac.be**

Internet Newsgroups (UseNet)

Currently, there is only one newsgroup, but it is an excellent one:

COMP.TEXT.SGML

There is also a topic-threaded digest of all the questions and comments posted to this group. To request a subscription, contact **comp-text-sgml-request@naggum.no**.

FTP Archive Sites for SGML

While there are many FTP sites with SGML information and resources, these are the most reliable (you can tell from the address if the resource is accessible through the World Wide Web):

- **ftp://ftp.ifi.uio.no/pub/SGML**
- **ftp://info.ex.ac.uk/pub/SGML**
- **ftp://ftp.th-darmstadt.de/pub/text/sgml**
- **gopher://ftp.sunet.se/11/pub/text-processing/sgml**
- **ftp://ftp.jclark.com/pub**
- **ftp.lysator.liu.se/pub/sgml**
- **ftp://ftp-tei.uic.edu/pub/tei**
- **ftp.ota.ox.ac.uk/TEI/**

SGML Web Pages

Some of these Web pages require an SGML-capable Web browser, such as Panorama. Others are accessible through any HTML Web browser. The extension on the Web page will tell you whether the following resources are HTML or SGML files.

Jump Pages to Other Collections of Links. Like so many subjects available for study on the World Wide Web, SGML has numerous resources that could quickly inundate you if you did a search for "SGML" from a popular search engine. These collections of links will direct you to some useful materials.

- **http://www.sil.org/sgml/archsite.html**
- **http://hike1.hike.te.chiba-u.ac.jp/ikeda/documentation/
  SGML-home.html**
- **http://www.sgmlopen.org/**

FAQs (Frequently Asked Questions). FAQs are useful especially to newer students of SGML, but they often contain some creative insights for everyone else, too. They are normally maintained by individuals who volunteer their time just because of their enthusiasm for SGML and their desire to help.

- **ftp://ftp.ifi.uio.no/pub/SGML/FAQ.0.0**
- **gopher://sil.org/11gopher_root%3a%5bsgml.sgml_faq%5d**
- **ftp://info.ex.ac.uk/pub/SGML/faq**
- **ftp://ftp.ifi.uio.no/pub/SGML/FAQ**

Summary

The resources mentioned in this appendix are just a start. SGML resources are cropping up all the time, so it's best just to keep track of the major indexes that track new resources; that's what these do. When something important happens in the SGML world, it usually appears in these pages pretty quickly.

Index

Symbols

% (parameter entities), 58
& (general entities), 58
+ notation, 149

A

AAP/EPSIG (Association of
American Publishers,
Electronic Publishing
Special Interest Group),
521-522
The ABCD...SGML (book),
309
abstract classes, 544
abstract names (tags), 52
add-on SGML tools, 309-310
addressing in HyTime,
164-165
aggregation
(defining object
relationships), 540-541
ALIGN attribute, 298
Alph authoring tool,
476-481
ambiguous content models,
259-261
<APPLET> element, 516

applications
HyTime, 385-389
components overview,
385-386
object-oriented
programming
applications, 515-518
WWW (World Wide Web)
DTD (document type
definition), 13
architecture
extending in documents,
76-77
templates in HyTime,
165-166
ATA authoring template
(SGML Author for Word),
450
ATTLIST declaration, 94
ATTRIBUTE declarations,
182-184
attributes
ALIGN, 298
CLASS, 298
CLEAR, 298
common mistakes with,
252-255
data types, 136-137
declarations, 136-137
defining, 224
definition, 533-534
as documents, 252-255

in elements, 55-58
entities, 58-61
format strings, 543
identical names in single
element, 253
identical values in single
element, 254
in elements, 249-254
NAME attribute, 533
in output specifications,
414-415
quotation mark usage
guidelines, 57-58, 336
selection suggestions,
247-255
SRC, 298
styles, 56
types, 248-252
Audio extension, 299-300
Augment system (document
management), 375
authoring tools, 372,
434-453
Alpha, 476-481
BBEdit, 476-481
SoftQuad Author/Editor
3.1, 469-481
Microsoft SGML Author,
445-453
ATA authoring template
toolbar buttons, 450
DCL file creation, 448

document conversion, 451

document parsing, 453

features, 445

MAP file creation, 448

native authoring, 447

Microstar Near & Far Author, 440-445, 461-464

document conversion, 443

document model creation, 461

document parsing, 443

features, 461

native SGML authoring, 441

output specifications, 441

report generation, 463

tool buttons, 441

Panorama Pro, 453-460

document searches, 459-460

features, 454

output specifications, 455-460

supported graphics formats, 459-460

WWW publishing, 460

Qued/M application, 476-481

SGMLS, 478-481

command line switches, 479-482

error messages, 480-482

SoftQuad Author/Editor 3.1

document formatting, 470

document imports, 473

DTD altering, 473

editing, 471

industry standard DTDs, 473

as an SGML validator, 473

SoftQuad RulesBuilder 3.0, 474

companion applications, 474-481

external entity support, 476

graphics support, 476

Sculptor 1.0, 474-475

Stilo companion application, 475-476

WordPerfect SGML Edition, 434-440

features, 437

B

backward compatibility (HTML documents), 369-371

bandwidth, 314-315

<BANNER> element, 298

<BASE> element, 298, 334

batch conversion tools (SGML to HTML), 351-352

behavior (objects)

automating via DTDs, 542-546

definition, 534-535

BFAP (Berkeley Finding Aids Project)

SGML usage on the World Wide Web, 366-367

bibliographies, 428-429

boilerplate, *see* standard data

Booch, Grady (object-oriented methodology), 537-538

books on SGML, 309, 565-566

Braille translations of SGML documents, 310

Brown University Women Writers' Project, 327

browsers, 297

displaying SGML documents, 343-345

DynaText, 493-496

Panorama (SoftQuad), 30

server-side validation, 299-300

SGML browser independence, 339-340

SGML-capable browsers, 301-303, 316, 337-338, 346-349

standardization versus innovation, 315-316

C

CALS (Continuous Acquisition and Lifecycle Support), 299, 11-12

CERN (European Laboratory for Particle Physics), 295

CETH (Center for Electronic Texts in the Humanities), 311, 366

Chadwyck-Healey English Poetry Database SGML publishing project, 325

character sets in multilingual documents, 341-342

citations, 428-429

CLASS attribute, 298

classes

definition, 532-533

inheritance, 544-546

STSGML sample application, 547-550

ClassOfParent method, 544

CLEAR attribute, 298

clink (HyTime application), 387

collaboration

World Wide Web, 514-515

SGML projects on the World Wide Web, 519-523

AAP/EPSIG, 521-522

Davenport Group, 522
EWS (European Workgroup on SGML), 523
SGML Open, 522
TEI (Text Encoding Initiative), 520-521
standards (SGML), 523-525
Fred (OCLC tool), 525
HyTime, 524
ICADD, 525
SMDL (Standard Music Description Language), 525
UTF (Universal Text Format), 525
COMMENT declaration, 178-179
commenting
marked sections in HTML, 338-339
coding in HTML documents, 336
commercial publishers (SGML document availability), 324-325
compatibility
parsing HTML for SGML compatibility, 336-337
SGML tools with computer platforms, 557-558
compiled object-oriented languages, 546
components
creating, 197-200
designing for DTDs, 79-80
document analysis, 91-92
in documents, 190-197
for HyTime, 166-167
fragment assembly, 198
compression formats, 558
computer companies (SGML document availability), 325-326
computer platforms compatible with SGML tools, 557-558

concrete classes, 546
conditional documents
creating, 285-288
marked section declaration, 286
Congressional Record, 328
connectors, 63-64
consistency of SGML, 357
consultants
preparation overview, 83-86
data issues, 84
document structure, 84
project definition, 84
content models, 54
ambiguous, 259-261
defining for ELEMENT declaration, 180
DTD usability tests, 77, 236-237
element declaration, 131-132, 223
exclusions, 255-258
for graphics, 250-252
inclusion compared to OR connector, 257-258
inclusions, 255-258
mixed, 258-259
DTD representation, 148
hierarchy, 132
sequence, 132
content standards (documents), 115-116
conversion tools
converting between SGML documents, 279-280
for documents, 273-274, 276-280
for intermediate file documents, 277-279
for word processing documents, 276-277
Robin Cover's SGML repository of tools, 278
Steve Pepper's Whirlwind Guide to SGML tools, 278

converting
SGML documents to HTML, 311-314, 372-374
generic conversion tools, 345-346, 351-352
integrated SGML converters, 345, 349-351
retrieval engines, 346, 353-354
customer tools, 120-122

D

DASH (Davenport Advisory Standard for Hypermedia), 522
data
for attributes, 136-137
CALS (Continuous Acquisition and Lifecycle Support), 11-12
developing for WWW, 379-385
effectiveness tips, 391-394
empty, 136
gathering tips, 402-403
ISO (International Standards Organization) 8879 document, 10-11
model sequencing symbols, 145
standard
entity references, 284-285
in documents, 283-285
data content in elements, 135-137
data interchange (selecting between SGML and HTML), 329-330
databases
compared to objects, 528, 530-531
object-oriented database management, 551

Davenport Group, 522
Davenport Project, 300
DCL files
    creating for SGML Author
      for Word, 448
    document conversion, 451
DECBook DTD, 522
declaration syntax, 172-173
    MDC (Markup Declaration
      Close), 173
    MDO (Markup Declaration
      Open), 173
declarations
    aligning, 224-230
    ATTLIST, 94
    ATTRIBUTE, 182-184
    Attribute List, 182-184
    COMMENT, 178-179
    components in DTD, 62
    data types in attributes,
      136-137
    DOCTYPE, 177-178
    DTD functions, 62
    ELEMENT, 179-182
    in elements, 63
    ENTITY, 184-188
    full comment, 215-216
    identifiers, 50-51
    in documents, 66
    in DTDs, 64-66
    inline comments, 216
    model groups, 65
    NOTATION, 289
    parameter entities, 60
    partially aligned (listing
      12.5), 225-229
    practice example, 187-188
    SGML, 176
    syntax, 176-186
    tag minimization (Omittag
      feature), 186-187
declarations (documents),
    48-51
dedicated SGML software,
    309-310
definitions
    process, 137-142

checking your
    work, 142
document type
    selection, 138
element comparison for
    relationships, 139-140
element dictionary
    assembly, 141
element list creation,
    138-139
element name, 138
missing elements
    check, 140
object relationships,
    540-541
structure tree
    construction, 140
designing
    DTDs, 371
    encyclopedia example,
      536-537
    object-oriented
      technology, 535-537
    object-oriented systems
      automating
        development via
        DTDs, 542-546
      Booch's methodology,
        538
      Rumbaugh's
        methodology, 539-540
diagrams, structure, 67-68
<DIV> element, 370
DocBook
    compared to HTML,
      368-369
    DTD, 349, 522
DocClass method, 544
DOCTYPE declaration,
    48-51, 177-178
document management,
    375-376
document structures (server-
    side validation), 299-300
document types, 532-533
documents
    advantages of SGML,
      357-358

analysis, 72, 91-92, 97-98
    element definition,
      73-76
    environment
      definition, 73
    expressing in SGML
      form, 77
analysis tips, 403-405
architecture extension,
    76-77, 155-157
attributes
    in elements, 249-252
    selection suggestions,
      247-255
    types, 248-252
authoring SGML
    documents for the World
      Wide Web, 371-372
authoring tools
    Microsoft SGML
      Author, 445-453
    Microstar Near & Far
      Author, 440-445,
      461-464
    Panorama Pro, 453-460
    WordPerfect SGML
      Edition, 434
backward compatibility,
    369-371
bibliographies, 428-429
citations, 428-429
commenting in DTDs,
    214-216
components, 190-197
    creating, 197-200
    fragment assembly, 198
computer platform usage,
    490-492
conditional
    creating, 285-288
    marked section
      declaration, 286
content
    overview, 37
content model
    DTD representation,
      148
conversion tools, 273-274,
    276-280

converting, 484-487
  compared to structured
    authoring, 103-105
  from plain text, 485
  from RTF file, 485-486
  scripting languages,
    481-482
  SGML to HTML,
    373-374
  to SGML, 82-83, 87,
    96-103
  WordPerfect SGML
    Edition, 439
damage assessment, 126
data-gathering tips,
  402-403
declarations list, 66
definition process, 137-142
  checking your work,
    142
  document type
    selection, 138
  element comparison for
    relationships, 139-140
  element dictionary
    assembly, 141
  element list creation,
    138-139
  element name, 138
  missing element
    check, 140
  structure tree
    construction, 140
developing for the
  future, 192
distinguishing between
  type and instance, 48
downloading large
  documents, 354-356
DSSSL (Document Style
  Semantics Specification
  Language), 82
DTDs
  consistency solutions,
    196-197
  development, 191
  evaluating, 233-239
  lifespan evaluation, 236

maintaining, 239-240
modules, 190
parsing, 241-242
project consultants, 191
redefining, 198-199
separating into logical
  element groups,
  217-222
standards enforcement,
  238-239
structure declaration, 78
user evaluation,
  234-236
dynamic (specialized
  output handling), 418
elements, 53-55
  + notation, 149
  appearance overview,
    249-252
  characteristics, 55
  content models,
    131-132
  data content, 135-137
  exclusion, 149-150
  formatting through
    structural occurrence,
    408-413
  groups, 150
  hierarchy, 132, 146-148
  inclusion, 149-150
  occurrence, 132,
    145-146
  paragraph, 94
  related to other
    elements, 76
  relationship
    definition, 72
  selection suggestions,
    247-255
  sequence, 132
  sequencing, 144-145
  sizing, 129-131
  subsec, 94
  top level, 93
endnotes, 428
entity additions, 156
environment definition,
  110, 125, 398

equation handling,
  424-427
feature additions, 155-157
footnotes, 428
format overview, 37-38
general entities (internal/
  external), 58-61
goal definitions, 90-91
hierarchies within SGML
  documents compared to
  word processing
  documents, 357
hypertext link additions
  (local/remote), 160-161
identifying user needs,
  117-122
  customer tools, 120-122
  input sources, 117-122
implementation tips,
  396-401
inclusion (model
  structure), 150-152
information delivery,
  component overview,
  499-500
linear books, 501
linear organization
  disadvantages, 503-505
link tips, 392
longevity overview, 193
maintenance, simplifying,
  195-196
maintenance
  considerations, 95-96
managing large
  documents, 340-342
marked section entities,
  287-288
markup
  declaration, 47-48
  tags, 47
markup methods, 269-275
  complexity suggestions,
    270
  installation suggestions,
    270
  manual, 271-272
  timeline suggestions,
    271

mathmatics handling, 424
model development with
   DTD design, 98
modeling, 92
modular books, 502
modular organization
   format, 505-508
multilingual documents,
   341-342
multimedia content
   additions, 161-164
      graphics, 162-163
      links, 427
      sounds, 163-164
      video files, 163-164
name selection, 123
organization, 500-502
output specifications,
   81-82, 408-413
Panorama Pro text
   locator, 459
parameter entities (as
   elements), 60, 199-200
parsing, 83, 102-103
      parser selection,
      490-492
      with WordPerfect SGML
      Edition, 440
planning SGML document
   markups, 356-357
printing SGML documents,
   374
PUBLIC identifiers, 50-51
revision tracking
   information additions,
   158-160
selecting SGML versus
   HTML, 329-337
      data interchange,
      329-330
      functionality needed,
      329
      hypertext links, 330-333
      maintaining links/
      elements, 333-335
set definition, 397
SGML
   advantages, 328-329

parts overview, 19
SGML documents available
   via World Wide Web,
   324-328
   from computer
      companies, 325-326
   from government, 328
   from industry, 327
   from libraries/
      universities, 326-327
   from publishers,
      324-325
simplifying, 193
specialized content,
   288-289
standard data usage,
   283-285
standardizing, 194-195
standards and policies,
   112-117
   content standards,
      115-116
   format standards,
      112-113
   structure standards,
      113-114
   types, 116-117
structure
   defining in SGML,
      42-44
   diagrams, 132, 150-152
   organization, 508-511
   overview, 36, 40
   section breakdown,
      40-42
   visual cues, 38
structured authoring,
   82-83
support tips, 390-391
SYSTEM identifiers, 50-51
tables
   format versus content,
      422-423
   handling, 421
tags, 51-53
   abstract names, 52
   components, 52

FastTAG application,
   495-496
selecting between SGML
   and HTML, 368-369
type inspection, 122-123
uprgrading, 123-125
usability testing, 236-237
usage decisions, 110
validating parsers, 242-243
downloading, 354-356
**DSSSL (Document Style
Semantics and
Specification Language),
82, 419**
DTD, 19, 338
flexibility of SGML for
   World Wide Web,
   301-305
HTML
   converting SGML
      documents to,
      311-314
   features of version 3.0,
      298-300
   future SGML upgrades
      to, 300-301
   obsolescence, 305-306
   relationship to SGML,
      295-297, 321-324
   SGML advantages over
      HTML, 369-371
   version descriptions,
      297
interoperability of SGML,
   339-340
planning SGML document
   markup, 356-357
**DTD (document type
definition), 13**
DTDs
advantages for object-
   oriented development,
   537-541
   Booch's methodology,
      538
   defining object
      relationships, 540-541
   Rumbaugh's
      methodology, 539-540

altering with SoftQuad
Author/Editor 3.1, 473
automating object-oriented
development, 542-546
BFAP (Berkeley Finding
Aids Project), 366
COMMENT declaration,
178-179
commenting in, 214-216
common, 210-214
common DTD example
(listing 12.3), 211-214
components
designing, 79-80
consistency solutions,
196-197
content modeling, 54, 77
DECBook, 522
declaration alignment,
224-230
declarations
groups, 64-65
lists, 66
components, 62-63
example, 187-188
designing, 371
encyclopedia example,
536-537
object-oriented
technology, 535-537
developing, 191
dividing into modules, 190
DocBook, 522
compared to HTML,
368-369, 522
DTD, 349
DOCTYPE declaration,
177-178
documents
components, 190-200
content models, 148
conversions from
SGML, 487
development, 192
dynamic (specialized
output handling), 418
fragment assembly, 198
lifespan evaluation, 236

longevity overview, 193
simplification, 193
structure declaration, 78
suggestions, 264-265
user evaluation,
234-236
ELEMENT declaration,
179-182
HTML, 29
industry standard
(SoftQuad Author/Editor
3.1), 473
inline comments, 216
logically grouped elements
(listing 12.4), 217-222
maintaining, 195-196,
239-240
model testing, 263-264
parameter entities (defined
as elements), 199-200
parsing, 95, 102-103,
241-242
partially aligned
declarations (listing 12.5),
225-229
poor format example
(listing 12.1), 202-205
project consultants, 191
redefining, 198-199
revised poor format
example (listing 12.2),
205-210
separating into logical
element groups, 217
Smalltalk sample SGML
application, 546-550
standards enforcement,
238-239
tag minimization (Omittag
feature), 186-187
usability testing, 236-237
validating parsers, 242-243
validation, 263-264
WordPerfect SGML Edition
output specifications, 435
**dynamic documents
(specialized output
handling), 418**

**dynamic model (OMT),
539-540**
DynaText, 562-563
browser, 493-496
SGML delivery system,
337, 347
DynaWeb, 338, 351

E

**e-mail reader collaboration
on Web sites, 514-515**
**electronic output
(specialized output
handling), 418**
**Electronic Text Center
(University of Virginia),
520**
**Electronic Text Center Web
site, 313**
**electronic-specific markup
language, 14**
**ELEMENT declaration,
179-182**
content model definition,
180
include/exclude
exceptions, 181
summaries, 182
tag minimization, 179
elements, 53-55, 322-324
+ notation, 149
appearance overview,
249-252
<APPLET>, 516
attributes, 55-58
entities, 58-61
quotation mark usage
guidelines, 57-58
styles, 56
attributes of, 249-252
<BANNER>, 298
<BASE>, 298, 334
characteristics, 55
connectors, 63-64
content models, 131-132
hierarchy, 132
sequence, 132

data content, 135-137
declarations
    after first content
        model, 223
    parts overview, 63
defining for documents,
    73-76
<DIV>, 370
empty data, 136
exclusion, 149-150
exclusions, 255-258
format strings, 543
formatting through
    structural occurrence,
    408-413
groups, 150
hierarchy, 146-148
identical attribute names/
    values, 253-254
inclusion, 149-150,
    255-258
marking text for data
    interchange, 329-330
methods, 543-544
minimized elements
    (optional SGML feature),
    358-360
misuse of tags, 340
mixed content models,
    258-259
model groups, 65
NOTATION declaration,
    289
occurrence, 63-64, 132,
    145-146
<P>, 334
paragraph, 94
as parameter entities,
    199-200
planning SGML document
    markups, 356-357
<RANGE>, 298
related to other
    elements, 76
relationship definition, 72
<SELECT>, 298
selecting between SGML
    and HTML, 368-369

selection suggestions,
    247-255
separating DTDs into
    logical groups, 217-222
sequencing, 144-145
sizing, 129-131
<STYLE>, 298
subsec, 94
too-high inclusion, 256
top level, 93
types, 532-533
**empty data (in
    elements), 136**
**encyclopedia example (DTD
    design), 536-537**
**[End Layout] processing
    instruction group, 411-413**
endnotes, 428
Engelbart, Doug, 375
entities
    adding to documents, 156
    external support with Stilo
        application, 476
    general (internal/external),
        59-60
    with marked sections,
        287-288
    mixed content models,
        258-259
    in output specifications,
        414-415
    parameter
        defining as elements,
            199-200
        internal/external, 60
    references, 284-285
    types, 58
**entities (markup
    component), 58-61**
ENTITY declarations
    General type, 185-186
    identifier, 51
    management, 551-552
    Parameter type, 185-186
    references, 184-188
entity parael, *see* paragraph
    element
environments

creating
    goal definitions, 89-96
    from scratch, 88-96
damage assessment, 126
defining for documents,
    73, 110
redefining, 125
standards and policies,
    112-117
    content standards,
        115-116
    format standards,
        112-113
    structure standards,
        113-114
    types, 116-117
upgrading, 123-125
equations
    as graphics, 425
    DTD structures, 426-427
    external processing,
        425-426
    handling in documents,
        424
    HTML 3.0 support for, 299
**European Laboratory for
    Particle Physics
    (CERN), 295**
**European Workgroup on
    SGML (EWS), 523**
**exceptions (too-high
    inclusions), 256-262**
**Exclude exception
    (ELEMENT declarations),
    181**
**exclusion (elements),
    149-150, 255-258**
**expert clientele
    (inaccessibility of SGML),
    308-309**
**external general entities,
    59-60**

F

**FAQs (Frequently Asked
    Questions), 571**

FastTAG application,
495-496

file compression
formats, 558

File extension, 299-300

filtering (document
conversion), 96-103

flexibility (SGML), World
Wide Web applications,
301-303, 357

footnotes, 303-305, 428

Formal Public Identifiers
(FPIs), 333

format standards
(documents), 112-113

format strings, 543

FOSI (Format Output
Specification Instance),
419

FPIs (Formal Public
Identifiers) support,
333, 384

fragments
assembling in documents,
198
libraries, 198

Fred (OCLC tool), 367-368,
525

Frequently Asked Questions
(FAQs), 571

FTP archives (SGML
resources), 570

functional model
(OMT), 540

functionality (selecting
between SGML and
HTML), 329

G

general entities (&), 58,
185-186

generalized markup
languages, 15-16

generic conversion tools,
345-346, 351-352

GML (Generalized Markup
Language), 15

Goldfarb, Charles F., 15

government SGML
document availability, 328

graphics
bandwidth problems,
314-315
format support in
Panorama Pro, 459
multimedia (adding to
documents), 162-163
Stilo application
support, 476
stylesheets, 319
VRML (Virtual Reality
Modeling Language),
517-518

group styles in output
specifications, 413

H

hardcopies
markup language, 14
specialized output
handling, 417-418

HasSubstring method, 544

helper applications (viewing
SGML documents), 347-349

hierarchies, 357

hot zones, 298

HTML (HyperText Markup
Language)
commenting out marked
sections, 338-339
compared to DocBook,
368-369
converting from SGML to
HTML, 373-374
converting SGML
documents to, 311-314
generic conversion
tools, 345-346,
351-352
integrated SGML
converters, 345,
349-351
retrieval engines, 346,
353-354

element types, 322
equations, 299
features, 298-300
future SGML upgrades to,
300-301
obsolescence, 305-306
parsing for SGML
compatibility, 336-337
relationship to SGML,
295-297, 321-324
selecting between SGML
and HTML, 329-337,
368-369
data interchange,
329-330
functionality needed,
329
hypertext links, 330-333
maintaining links/
elements, 333-335
SGML advantages over
HTML, 369-371
standardization
(relationship with
innovation), 315-316
tables, support for, 299
upgrading
features, 29
in SGML, 166
to SGML, 337-342
version descriptions, 297
see also World Wide Web

HTML to the Max, 303, 374

hybrid content format
structure (tables), 423-424

Hyper-G (multimedia
technology), 319-320

hypertext links
adding to documents,
160-161
hot zones, 298
selecting between SGML
and HTML, 330-333

HyTime (Hypermedia/Time-
based Structuring
Language), 164, 319-320,
385, 524
addressing, 164-165

architectural templates, 165-166
clink, 387
component requirements, 166-167
components overview, 385-386
goals, 164
ilink, 388-389
linkend (IDREF), 387
links, creating, 386-390
technical corrigendum, 386

I-J

ICADD (International Committee on Accessible Document Design), 310, 525
identifiers
    ENTITY, 51
    PUBLIC, 50-51
    SYSTEM, 50-51
IDREF linkend, 387
ilink (HyTime application), 388-389
images (hot zones), 298
inaccessibility of SGML, reasons for, 307-311
    expensive software, 309-310
    lack of books, 309
    scholarly/expert clientele, 308-309
Include exceptions (ELEMENT declarations), 181
inclusion
    in elements, 149-150, 255-258
    model structure, 150-152
industry SGML document availability, 327
information
    delivery (component overview), 499-500

modular organization, 513-519
    object-oriented programming applications, 515-518
    promoting learning, 525-526
    reader collaboration, 514-515
inheritance, 544-546
INI file creation for authoring template, 451
innovation (relationship with standardization), 315-316
instances definition, 533
integrated SGML converters, 345, 349-351
Intel technical documentation (Web site), 311
intermediate file conversion tools, 277-279
internal general entities, 59-60
International Committee on Accessible Documents Design (ICADD), 310
Internet
    HTML (HyperText Markup Language), 29-32
    IRC (Internet Relay Chat), 32-33
    multimedia extensions, 32-33
    SGML resources, 30-32, 569-571
Internet Explorer (browser), 297
interoperability of SGML, 339-340
interpreted object-oriented languages, 546
IRC (Internet Relay Chat), 32-33
IsFirst method, 544
ISO (International Standards Organization) 8879 document, 10-11

Java, 516-517

L

language (multilingual documents), 341-342
large documents
    downloading, 354-356
    management, 340-342
Latin 1 character set, 341
libraries/universities
    fragment, 198
    SGML document availability, 326-327
linear organization, 501-505
linkend (HyTime application), 387
links
    adding to document, 160-161
        local, 160-161
        remote, 160-161
    clink (HyTime application), 387
    document management, 375-376
    HyTime
        clink, 387
        components overview, 385-386
        creating, 386
        ilink application, 388-389
        linkend application, 387
    maintaining, 333-335
    managing large documents, 340-341
    multimedia, 427
    selecting between SGML and HTML, 330-333
    two-way links within SGML documents, 303-305
links (WWW), 384-385
listings
    1.1 Boeing ATA service bulletin DTD, 20-28

12.1 poorly formatted DTD example, 202-205

12.2 revised poorly formatted DTD example, 205-210

12.3 common DTDs, 211-214

12.4 DTD with logically grouped elements, 217-222

12.5 DTD with partially aligned declarations, 225-229

local hypertext links (adding to document), 160-161

M

Macintosh
  authoring tools, 468-481
    Alpha, 476-481
    BBEdit, 476-481
    Qued/M, 476-481
    SGMLS, 478-481
    SoftQuad Author/Editor 3.1, 469-481
    SoftQuad RulesBulider 3.0, 474
  SGML project planning, 467-487
mailing lists (SGML resources), 569-570
maintenance of links/ elements
  considerations, 95-96
  selecting between SGML and HTML, 333-335
Making Hypermedia Work: A User's Guide to HyTime, 524
MAP files (creating for SGML Author for Word), 448
marked sections
  commenting out in HTML, 338-339
  declaring in documents, 286

markup component entities, 58-61
markup languages
  electronic-specific, 14
  generalized, 15-16
  hardcopy, 14
  HTML (HyperText Markup Language)
    compared to DocBook, 368-369
    future SGML upgrades to, 300-301
    obsolescence, 305-306
    relationship to SGML, 295-297, 321-324
    selecting SGML versus HTML, 329-337
    SGML advantages over HTML, 369-371
    upgrade features, 29
    version descriptions, 297-300
  introduction, 9-10
  SMDL (Standard Music Description Language), 301
  standard generalized, 17-19
  types, 13-19
  upgrading to SGML, 166-167
  VRML (Virtual Reality Modeling Language), 301
markup methods
  complexity suggestions, 270
  installation suggestions, 270
  manual, 271-272
  suggestions on, 269-275
  timeline suggestions, 271
mathmatics
  handling in documents, 424
  HTML 3.0 support for, 299
MDC (Markup Declaration Close), 173
MDO (Markup Declaration Open), 173

menus (STSGML sample application), 548
methods
  ClassOfParent, 544
    for SGML elements, 543-544
Microsoft SGML Author, 445-453
  ATA authoring template toolbar buttons, 450
  DCL file creation, 448
  documents
    converting, 451
    parsing, 453
    validating, 453
  features, 445
  MAP file creation, 448
  native authoring, 447
Microstar Near & Far Author (authoring tool), 440-445, 461-464
  documents
    converting, 443
    model creation, 461
    parsing, 443
    validating, 443
  features, 461
  native SGML authoring, 441
  output specifications, 441
  report generation, 463
  tool buttons, 441
MIME (Multi-purpose Internet Mail Extensions), 343, 383
minimized elements (optional SGML feature), 358-360
mixed content models, 258-259
model/name groups, 65
model testing, 263-264
modeling (documents), 92
modular information, 513-519
  object-oriented programming applications, 515-518

promoting learning,
525-526
reader collaboration,
514-515
**modular book organization
format, 502-508**
modules (DTDs), 190
**Multi-purpose Internet Mail
Extensions (MIME), 343**
**multilingual documents,
341-342**
multimedia
adding content to
documents, 161-164
graphics, 162-163
sound, 163-164
video files, 163-164
document specialized
content overview,
288-289
Hyper-G technology,
319-320
HyTime application,
385-389
Internet extensions, 32-33
linking, 427

N

NAME attribute, 533
**name groups (declarations),
65**
**NASA Magellan SGML
documents, 311**
**Near & Far Author
(authoring tool), 310,
440-445, 461-464**
documents
converting, 443
model creation, 461
parsing, 443
validating, 443
features, 461
native SGML authoring,
441
output specifications, 441
report generation, 463
tool buttons, 441

Near & Far Lite, 561-562
**Netscape (standardization
versus innovation),
315-316**
**networks (large document
downloads), 354-356**
**newsgroups (SGML
resources), 30-32, 570**
**Nice Technologies Web
site, 310**
NOTATION declaration, 289
**Novell Web site (SGML
usage on the World Wide
Web), 364**

O

**Object Modeling Technique
(OMT), 537, 539-540**
object
object-oriented, 296
*Object-Oriented Analysis and
Design with Applications*,
537
**object-oriented database
management (future of
SGML development), 551**
**object-oriented
programming, 516-517**
**object-oriented
programming applications,
515-518**
object-oriented technology
advantages, 530-531
advantages of DTDs,
537-541
Booch's methodology,
538
defining object
relationships, 540-541
Rumbaugh's
methodology, 539-540
attribute definition,
533-534
automating development
via DTDs, 542-546
behavior definition,
534-535

class definition, 532-533
definition, 528-531
DTD development,
535-537
future of SGML
development, 550-552
concurrency, 550
entity management,
551-552
object-oriented database
management, 551
inheritance, 544-546
instance definition, 533
relationship to SGML,
531-532
Smalltalk (STSGML
application), 546-550
objects
compared to databases,
528, 530-531
content models, 250-252
definition, 528
identifying, 250-252
relationships, defining,
540-541
**obsolescence of HTML,
305-306**
occurrence indicators, 63-64
**OCLC (Online Computer
Library Center)**
Fred, 525
SGML usage on the World
Wide Web, 367-368
**OED (Oxford English
Dictionary) SGML
publishing project, 324**
Omittag feature, 186-187
**OMT (Object Modeling
Technique), 537, 539-540**
**OR connector (compared to
inclusion), 257-258**
**OTA (Oxford University
Text Archive), 365**
**output messages (parsers),
244-245**
output specifications, 81
attribute usage, 414-415
document view, 408

DSSSL (Document Style
Semantics Specification
Language), 419-420
entities, 414-415
for Panorama Pro
(authoring tool), 455
FOSI (Format Output
Specification Instance),
419
group styles, 413
SGML syntax, 413-417
standards, 419
style inheritance, 416-417
troubleshooting, 419
Oxford English Dictionary
(OED) SGML publishing
project, 324
Oxford University Text
Archive (OTA), 365

P-Q

<P> element, 334
Panorama, 303
browser, 337
helper application, 367
Panorama Free, 563-564
Panorama Pro (authoring
tool), 453-460
document searches,
459-460
features, 454
graphics format
support, 459-460
output specifications,
455-460
WWW publishing, 460
SGML helper application,
348
SoftQuad browsing
tool, 30
paragraph element, 94
parameter entities(%), 58-60,
185-186, 199-200
parsed character data
(PCDATA), 546
parsers
disadvantages, 243-244

introduction, 242-244
optional features
overview, 244
output message evaluation,
244-245
selecting, 490
validating, 242-243
parsing
ambiguous content
models, 259-261
documents, 83, 102-103
DTD evaluation, 81
DTDs, 95, 102-103,
241-242
HTML for SGML
compatibility, 336-337
Patent Office (SGML
document availability),
328
PCDATA (parsed character
data), 546
periodicals (SGML
resources), 566-567
Perl (Practical Extraction
and Report Language),
491-492, 559-560
perlSGML, 560-561
platform usage, 490
platforms
compatibility with SGML
tools, 557-558
SGML flexibility, 339
primary attributes, 533
printing
SGML documents, 374
tools, 482-484
DynaText, 483-484
FrameMaker+SGML,
483
SGML Enabler, 483
process instruction, 262-263
[After-Revert Section]
group, 412-413
[End Layout] group,
411-413
programming languages
Java, 516-517

object-oriented
technology, 529
Perl, 559-560
Smalltalk (STSGML
application), 546-550
VRML (Virtual Reality
Modeling Language),
517-518
PUBLIC identifiers, 50-51
public SGML projects,
310-311
publishers (SGML document
availability), 324-325

Qued/M authoring tool,
476-481
quoting (attributes), 336

R

Rainbow DTD Web site, 311
<RANGE> element, 298
reader collaboration (World
Wide Web), 514-515
regular expression syntax,
174-176
remote hypertext links,
160-161
resources (SGML)
books, 565-566
FTP archives, 570
mailing lists, 569-570
periodicals, 566-567
UseNet newsgroups, 570
user groups, 567-568
Web sites, 570-571
retrieval engines (document
conversion), 346, 353-354
revision tracking
information, 158-160
Robin Cover's SGML home
page, 308
Robin Cover's SGML
repository of tools, 278
RTF file document
conversion, 485
Rumbaugh, James, 537-540

S

scientific/technical
  documents availability via
  SGML, 319
scripting languages
  (SGMLSPL shell), 481-482
secondary attributes, 533
<SELECT> element, 298
sequencing
  data model symbols, 145
  elements, 144-145
server-side validation
  (browsers), 299-300
SGML (Standard Generalized
  Markup Language)
  advantages, 328-329,
    357-358
    for the World Wide
      Web, 295-297
    over HTML, 369-371
  authoring tools, 371-372,
    478-481
    command line switches,
      479-482
    error messages, 480-482
  books on, 309
  browsers, 301-303, 316,
    337-340, 346-349
  CALS (Continuous
    Acquisition and Lifecycle
    Support), 11-12
  collaborative projects on
    the World Wide Web,
    519-523
    AAP/EPSIG, 521-522
    Davenport Group, 522
    EWS (European
      Workgroup on SGML),
      523
    SGML Open, 522
    TEI (Text Encoding
      Initiative), 520-521
  converting documents to
    HTML, 311-314, 373-374
  declaration syntax,
    172-176

defining object
  relationships, 540-541
developing for World Wide
  Web, 379-385
displaying on World Wide
  Web, 343-345
document structure
  defining, 42-44
  overview, 36, 40
  section breakdown,
    40-42
  server-side validation,
    299-300
  visual cues, 38
documents
  content overview, 37
  conversion, 279-280
  format overview, 37-38
  implementation advice,
    396-398
  parts overview, 19
  printing, 374
documents available,
  324-328
  from computer
    companies, 325-326
  from government, 328
  from industry, 327
  from libraries/
    universities, 326-327
  from publishers,
    324-325
DTDs (document type
  definitions) intro-
  duction, 19
environments
  converting, 96-103
  creating from scratch,
    88-96
  goal definitions, 89-96
equation support, 299
flexibility/consistency,
  301-303, 357
FPIs (Formal Public
  Identifiers) support, 384
future upgrades to HTML,
  300-301

inaccessibility, reasons for,
  307-311
  expensive software,
    309-310
  lack of books, 309
  scholarly/expert
    clientele, 308-309
introduction, 17-19
ISO (International
  Standards Organization)
  8879 document, 10-11
markup types, 13-19
MIME data conversion,
  383
object-oriented technology
  terms
  attributes, 533-534
  behavior, 534-535
  classes, 532-533
  instances, 533
  states, 534
parsing HTML for SGML
  compatibility, 336-337
planning SGML document
  markups, 356-357
platform independence,
  339
project planning, 467-487
regular expression syntax,
  174-176
relationship to HTML,
  295-297, 321-324
relationship to object-
  oriented technology,
  531-532
resources
  books, 565-566
  FTP archives, 570
  mailing lists, 569-570
  periodicals, 566-567
  UseNet newsgroups,
    570
  user groups, 567-568
  Web sites and resources,
    316-320, 570-571
sample projects, 310-311

selecting between SGML and HTML (tagging documents), 368-369
selecting SGML versus HTML, 329-337
  data interchange, 329-330
  functionality needed, 329
  hypertext links, 330-333
  maintaining links/ elements, 333-335
standards, 523-525
  Fred (OCLC tool), 525
  HyTime, 524
  ICADD, 525
  SMDL (Standard Music Description Language), 525
  UTF (Universal Text Format), 525
tables, support for, 299
tools, 557-564
  computer platform compatibility, 557-558
  DynaText, 562-563
  Near & Far Lite, 561-562
  Panorama Free, 563-564
  Perl programming language, 559-560
  perlSGML, 560-561
  SP/NSGMLS tools, 559
upgrading to
  advantages, 339-342
  disadvantages, 337-339
  World Wide Web to, 301-302
user involvment, 263
World Wide Web sites, 363-368
  BFAP (Berkeley Finding Aids Project), 366-367
  CETH (Center for Electronic Texts in the Humanities), 366
  Novell, 364
  OCLC (Online Computer Library Center), 367-368
  Open House home page, 311
  Open Web site, 367
  Oxford University Text Archive (OTA), 365
  SGML Open, 367
  SIL (Summer Institute of Linguistics), 366
  TEI (Text Encoding Initiative), 364-365
  University of Virginia, 365
WWW page effectiveness tips, 389-393
see also DTDs
SGML Author for Word, 451
  ATA authoring template toolbar buttons, 450
  DCL file creation, 448
  document conversion, 451
  document parsing, 453
  document validation, 453
  features, 445
  INI file creation for authoring template, 451
  MAP file creation, 448
  native authoring, 447
***The SGML Handbook*, 309**
SGMLSPL shell, 482
Shakespeare (SGML publications of), 313
sharing information (modular information structure), 513-519
shortref tags, 289-291
SIL (Summer Institute of Linguistics), 366
sites
  AAP/EPSIG, 521-522
  BFAP (Berkeley Finding Aids Project), 366-367
  CETH (Center for Electronic Texts in the Humanities), 311
  Davenport Group, 522
  DocBook DTD, 349
  DynaWeb, 338
  Electronic Text Center, 313
  EWS (European Workgroup on SGML), 523
  HyTime, 524
  ICADD, 525
  Intel technical documentation, 311
  Java, 516
  NASA Magellan SGML documents, 311
  Nice Technologies, 310
  Novell Web site, 364
  OCLC (Online Computer Library Center), 367-368, 525
  Oxford University Text Archive (OTA), 365
  Panorama, 303
  Panorama (SGML helper application), 348
  Panorama helper application, 367
  Rainbow DTD, 311
  Robin Cover's SGML home page, 308
  SGML
    Open, 367
    Open House home page, 311
    Open vendor group, 339
    resources, 570-571
    Web Page, 523
  Shakespeare (SGML publications of), 313
  SIL (Summer Institute of Linguistics), 366
  TEI (Text Encoding Initiative), 364-365, 520-521
  TEI P3, 311
  University of Michigan Modern and Middle English Collections, 311
  University of Virginia, 365

upgrading to SGML,
166-167
Weblint, 336
**Smalltalk (STSGML
application), 546-550**
**SMDL (Standard Music
Description Language),
301, 525**
**SoftQuad Author/Editor 3.1
(authoring tool), 469-481**
documents
formatting, 470
importing, 473
sharing, 470-474
DTD altering, 473
editing, 471
industry standard
DTDs, 473
as an SGML validator, 473
**SoftQuad RulesBuilder
3.0, 474**
companion applications,
474-481
Sculptor 1.0, 474-475
Stilo, 475-476
**SoftQuad Sculptor 1.0
application, 474-475**
software
DynaText, 562-563
Near & Far Lite, 561-562
Panorama Free, 563-564
Perl programming
language, 559-560
perlSGML, 560-561
SGML add-ons, 309-310
SP/NSGMLS tools, 559
**software development
stages, 529**
**sounds, adding to
documents, 163-164**
SP/NSGMLS tools, 559
specialized output, 417-418
dynamic document
handling, 418
electronic output
handling, 418
hardcopy handling,
417-418

SRC attribute, 298
standard data, 283-285
**Standard Music Description
Language (SMDL), 301, 525**
**standardization
(relationship with
innovation), 315-316**
standards (SGML), 523-525
Fred (OCLC tool), 525
HyTime, 524
ICADD, 525
SMDL (Standard Music
Description Language),
525
UTF (Universal Text
Format), 525
state definition, 534
**Steve Pepper's Whirlwind
Guide to SGML tools, 278**
**Stilo (SoftQuad Author/
Editor companion
application), 475-476**
external entity
support, 476
graphics support, 476
**structure diagrams, 67-68,
132, 150-152**
**structure organization,
508-511**
**structure standards
(documents), 113-114**
**structure trees, constructing,
140**
structured authoring, 82-83
compared to document
conversion, 103-105
tools, 274-280
**structure declarations in
DTD, 78**
**STSGML application,
546-550**
<STYLE> element, 298
**style inheritance (in output
specifications), 416-417**
stylesheets, 319
subsec element, 94
**Summer Institute of
Linguistics (SIL), 366**

syntax
HTML compared to SGML,
338-339
in output specifications,
413
**syntax (SGML declaration),
172-173**
MDC (Markup Declaration
Close), 173
MDO (Markup Declaration
Open), 173
SYSTEM identifiers, 50-51
system design tips, 405-406

T

tables
format versus content,
422-423
handling, 421-424
HTML 3.0 support for, 299
selecting between SGML
and HTML, 334-335
structure (hybrid content
format), 423
Tag Wizard, 310
tags
abstract names, 52
abuse syndrome, 323
components, 52
FastTAG application,
495-496
introduction, 51-53
markup methods, 47,
269-275
complexity suggestions,
270
installation suggestions,
270
manual, 271-272
timeline suggestions,
271
minimizing in ELEMENT
declaration, 179
Omittag feature, 186-187
parser introduction,
242-244

shortref delimiter set, 289-291

technical corrigendum (HyTime update), 386

technical/scientific document availability via SGML, 319

TEI (Text Encoding Initiative), 300, 311, 364-365, 520-521

TEI P3 Web site, 311

tools

authoring, 434-453

Alpha, 476-481

BBEdit, 476-481

Macintosh based, 468-481

Microsoft SGML Author, 445-453

Microstar Near & Far Author, 440-445, 461-464

Panorama Pro, 453-460

Qued/M application, 476-481

SGMLS, 478-481

SoftQuad RulesBulider 3.0, 474

WordPerfect SGML Edition, 434-440

conversion between SGML documents, 276-280

intermediate document conversion, 277-279

PC based, 433-434

printing, 482-484

DynaText, 483-484

FrameMaker+SGML, 483

SGML Enabler, 483

structured authoring, 274-275, 280

viewing, 482-484

DynaText, 483-484

FramMaker+SGML, 483

SGML Enabler, 483

word processing document conversion, 276-277

tools (SGML), 557-564

computer platform compatibility, 557-558

DynaText, 562-563

Near & Far Lite, 561-562

Panorama Free, 563-564

Perl programming language, 559-560

perlSGML, 560-561

SP/NSGMLS tools, 559

top level elements (documents), 93

translating, *see* **converting**

troubleshooting output specifications, 419

two-way links

within SGML documents, 303-305

U-V

Unicode character set, 341

Uniform Resource Names (URNs), 333

Universal Text Format (UTF), 525

universities/libraries (SGML document availability), 326-327

University of California at Berkeley, 366-367

University of Michigan Modern and Middle English Collections, 311

University of Virginia, 365

upgrading

to SGML

advantages, 339-342

disadvantages, 337-339

World Wide Web to SGML, 301-302

URL links, 384-385

URNs (Uniform Resource Names), 333

user groups (SGML resources), 567-570

UTF (Universal Text Format), 525

validating parsers, 242-243

disadvantages, 243-244

optional features overview, 244

output messages evaluation, 244-245

parser selection, 490

video files (multimedia), adding to documents, 163-164

viewers, *see* **browsers**

VRML (Virtual Reality Modeling Language), 301, 517-518

W-Z

W3 Consortium, 295

Web sites, *see* **sites**

Weblint, 336

word processing

conversion tools, 276-277

moving documents to SGML, 357

WordPerfect SGML Edition (authoring tool), 434-440

documents

converting, 439

parsing, 440

validating, 440

features, 437

output specifications, 435

World Wide Web

advantages of SGML, 295-297

authoring SGML documents for, 371-372,

bandwidth, 314-315

browsers, 297, 301-303, 316, 337-338, 346-349

displaying SGML documents, 343-345

DTD (document type definition)

introduction, 13

flexibility of SGML,
301-305
FPIs (Formal Public
Identifiers) support, 384
high-end search/retrieval
tools, 383-384
HTML (relationship to
SGML), 295-297
Java, 516-517
links, 384-385
MIME data conversion,
383
modular information
promoting learning,
525-526
object-oriented
programming
applications, 515-518
Panorama (SoftQuad)
browsing tool, 30
publishing with Panorama
Pro, 460
reader collaboration,
514-515
SGML collaborative
projects, 519-523
AAP/EPSIG, 521-522
Davenport Group, 522
EWS (European
Workgroup on
SGML), 523
SGML Open, 522
TEI (Text Encoding
Initiative), 520-521
SGML data conversion
batch-conversion,
381-383
on-demand conversion
servers, 381-383
SGML documents
available, 324-328
from computer
companies, 325-326
from government, 328
from industry, 327

from libraries/
universities, 326-327
from publishers,
324-325
SGML pages
data tips, 391-392
document support tips,
390-391
effectiveness tips,
389-393
link tips, 392
SGML resources, 316-320
Hyper-G, 319-320
scientific/technical
documents, 319
stylesheets, 319
SGML sites, 363-368
BFAP (Berkeley Finding
Aids Project), 366-367
CETH (Center for
Electronic Texts in the
Humanities), 366
Novell, 364
OCLC (Online
Computer Library
Center), 367-368
Oxford University Text
Archive (OTA), 365
SGML Open, 367
SIL (Summer Institute of
Linguistics), 366
TEI (Text Encoding
Initiative), 364-365
University of Virginia,
365
sites for SGML resources,
570-571
upgrading to SGML,
301-302
VRML (Virtual Reality
Modeling Language),
517-518
see also HTML

A V I A C O M S E R V I C E

The Information SuperLibrary™

Bookstore

Search

What's New

Reference

Software

Newsletter

Company Overviews

Yellow Pages

Internet Starter Kit

HTML Workshop

Win a Free T-Shirt!

Macmillan Computer Publishing

Site Map

Talk to Us

CHECK OUT THE BOOKS IN THIS LIBRARY.

You'll find thousands of shareware files and over 1600 computer books designed for both technowizards and technophobes. You can browse through 700 sample chapters, get the latest news on the Net, and find just about anything using our massive search directories.

All Macmillan Computer Publishing books are available at your local bookstore.

We're open 24-hours a day, 365 days a year.

You don't need a card.

We don't charge fines.

And you can be as **LOUD** as you want.

The Information SuperLibrary

http://www.mcp.com/mcp/ ftp.mcp.com

Copyright © 1996, Macmillan Computer Publishing-USA, A Simon & Schuster Company

GET CONNECTED
to the ultimate source
of computer information!

The MCP Forum on CompuServe

Go online with the world's leading computer book publisher!
Macmillan Computer Publishing offers everything
you need for computer success!

Find the books that are right for you!
A complete online catalog, plus sample
chapters and tables of contents give
you an in-depth look at all our books.
The best way to shop or browse!

➤ Get fast answers and technical support for
MCP books and software

➤ Join discussion groups on major computer
subjects

➤ Interact with our expert authors via e-mail
and conferences

➤ Download software from our immense
library:

　▷　Source code from books
　▷　Demos of hot software
　▷　The best shareware and freeware
　▷　Graphics files

Join now and get a free
CompuServe Starter Kit!

To receive your free CompuServe Introductory Membership, call **1-800-848-
8199** and ask for representative #597.

The Starter Kit includes:
➤ Personal ID number and password
➤ $15 credit on the system
➤ Subscription to *CompuServe Magazine*

Once on the CompuServe System, type:

GO MACMILLAN

for the most computer information anywhere!

**MACMILLAN
COMPUTER
PUBLISHING**

CompuServe

Complete and Return this Card
for a *FREE* Computer Book Catalog

Thank you for purchasing this book! You have purchased a superior computer book written expressly for your needs. To continue to provide the kind of up-to-date, pertinent coverage you've come to expect from us, we need to hear from you. Please take a minute to complete and return this self-addressed, postage-paid form. In return, we'll send you a free catalog of all our computer books on topics ranging from word processing to programming and the internet.

Mr. ☐   Mrs. ☐   Ms. ☐   Dr. ☐

Name (first) ☐☐☐☐☐☐☐☐☐☐☐☐   (M.I.) ☐   (last) ☐☐☐☐☐☐☐☐☐☐☐☐☐☐☐☐☐☐

Address ☐☐☐☐☐☐☐☐☐☐☐☐☐☐☐☐☐☐☐☐☐☐☐☐☐☐☐☐☐☐☐☐☐☐

City ☐☐☐☐☐☐☐☐☐☐☐☐☐☐☐☐☐☐   State ☐☐   Zip ☐☐☐☐☐ ☐☐☐☐

Phone ☐☐☐ ☐☐☐ ☐☐☐☐   Fax ☐☐☐ ☐☐☐ ☐☐☐☐

Company Name ☐☐☐☐☐☐☐☐☐☐☐☐☐☐☐☐☐☐☐☐☐☐☐☐☐☐☐☐

E-mail address ☐☐☐☐☐☐☐☐☐☐☐☐☐☐☐☐☐☐☐☐☐☐☐☐☐☐☐☐

1. Please check at least (3) influencing factors for purchasing this book.

Front or back cover information on book .... ☐
Special approach to the content .... ☐
Completeness of content .... ☐
Author's reputation .... ☐
Publisher's reputation .... ☐
Book cover design or layout .... ☐
Index or table of contents of book .... ☐
Price of book .... ☐
Special effects, graphics, illustrations .... ☐
Other (Please specify): _____ ☐

2. How did you first learn about this book?

Saw in Macmillan Computer Publishing catalog .... ☐
Recommended by store personnel .... ☐
Saw the book on bookshelf at store .... ☐
Recommended by a friend .... ☐
Received advertisement in the mail .... ☐
Saw an advertisement in: _____ ☐
Read book review in: _____ ☐
Other (Please specify): _____ ☐

3. How many computer books have you purchased in the last six months?

This book only .... ☐   3 to 5 books .... ☐
2 books .... ☐   More than 5 .... ☐

4. Where did you purchase this book?

Bookstore .... ☐
Computer Store .... ☐
Consumer Electronics Store .... ☐
Department Store .... ☐
Office Club .... ☐
Warehouse Club .... ☐
Mail Order .... ☐
Direct from Publisher .... ☐
Internet site .... ☐
Other (Please specify): _____ ☐

5. How long have you been using a computer?

☐ Less than 6 months   ☐ 6 months to a year
☐ 1 to 3 years   ☐ More than 3 years

6. What is your level of experience with personal computers and with the subject of this book?

	With PCs	With subject of book
New	☐	☐
Casual	☐	☐
Accomplished	☐	☐
Expert	☐	☐

Source Code ISBN: 0-7897-0414-5

Which of the following best describes your job title?

Administrative Assistant .... ☐
Coordinator .... ☐
Manager/Supervisor .... ☐
Director .... ☐
Vice President .... ☐
President/CEO/COO .... ☐
Lawyer/Doctor/Medical Professional .... ☐
Teacher/Educator/Trainer .... ☐
Engineer/Technician .... ☐
Consultant .... ☐
Not employed/Student/Retired .... ☐
Other (Please specify): _____ ☐

Which of the following best describes the area of the company your job title falls under?

Accounting .... ☐
Engineering .... ☐
Manufacturing .... ☐
Operations .... ☐
Marketing .... ☐
Sales .... ☐
Other (Please specify): _____ ☐

9. What is your age?

Under 20 .... ☐
21-29 .... ☐
30-39 .... ☐
40-49 .... ☐
50-59 .... ☐
60-over .... ☐

10. Are you:

Male .... ☐
Female .... ☐

11. Which computer publications do you read regularly? (Please list)

_____
_____
_____
_____
_____
_____
_____
_____
_____
_____

Comments: _____
_____
_____

Fold here and scotch-tape to mail.

‖¹‖¹‖¹‖¹‖¹‖¹¹‖¹‖¹‖¹‖¹‖¹¹‖¹‖¹¹‖¹‖¹‖

FIRST-CLASS MAIL PERMIT NO. 9918 INDIANAPOLIS IN

POSTAGE WILL BE PAID BY THE ADDRESSEE

ATTN MARKETING
MACMILLAN COMPUTER PUBLISHING
MACMILLAN PUBLISHING USA
201 W 103RD ST
INDIANAPOLIS IN 46290-9042

NO POSTAGE
NECESSARY
IF MAILED
IN THE
UNITED STATES

Before using any of the software on this disc, you need to install the software you plan to use. See Appendix A, "The SGML CD-ROM," and use the HTML pages on the CD for the information you'll need.

If you have problems with the SGML CD-ROM, please contact Macmillan Technical Support at (317) 581-3833. We can be reached by e-mail at **support@mcp.com** or by CompuServe at GO QUEBOOKS.

Read This Before Opening Software

By opening this package, you are agreeing to be bound by the following:

This software is copyrighted and all rights are reserved by the publisher and its licensers. You are licensed to use this software on a single computer. You may copy the software for backup or archival purposes only. Making copies of the software for any other purpose is a violation of United States copyright laws. THIS SOFTWARE IS SOLD AS IS, WITHOUT WARRANTY OF ANY KIND, EITHER EXPRESS OR IMPLIED, INCLUDING BUT NOT LIMITED TO THE IMPLIED WARRANTIES OF MERCHANT-ABILITY AND FITNESS FOR A PARTICULAR PURPOSE. Neither the publisher nor its dealers and distributors nor its licensers assume any liability for any alleged or actual damages arising from the use of this software. (Some states do not allow exclusion of implied warranties, so the exclusion may not apply to you.)

The entire contents of this disc and the compilation of the software are copyrighted and protected by United States copyright laws. The individual programs on the disc are copyrighted by the authors or owners of each program. Each program has its own use permissions and limitations. To use each program, you must follow the individual requirements and restrictions detailed for each. Do not use a program if you do not agree to follow its licensing agreement.